1996/97 Florida Cruising Directory

NAVIGATING FLORIDA'S TELEPHONE SYSTEM

The telephone company has gerrymandered Florida's overloaded telephone system to add three new Area Codes, creating a new kind of navigational problem for cruising boatpeople. Both old and new Area Codes will work until the cutoff dates indicated, when the changes become permanent. It works most of the time...

Area Code 305 remains from North Miami Beach south through Miami to Key West.

New Area Code 954 takes over in Broward County (Hollywood to Deerfield Beach) after August 1st.

Area Code 813 remains in the Tampa/St. Petersburg area north to a pont above Tarpon Springs.

New Area Code 941 takes over the rest of Southwest Florida from Bradenton to Flamingo after March 1st.

Area Code 407 remains from Boca Raton to above Titusville.

Area Code 904 remains in the Panhandle and North Florida and southeast to below New Smyrna Beach.

New Area Code 352 takes over the Big Bend Coast from above Tarpon Springs to Steinhatchee after May 20th.

We have changed thousands of numbers in this issue, but if we missed updating the one number you wanted to call today, forgive us, then drop us a note so we can make it right next year.   *Dick Kirkpatrick*

CONTENTS

COVER PHOTOGRAPH
Andy Newman photographed this flybridge cruiser at Tavernier in the Keys. Courtesy Monroe County Tourist Development Council.

Founder — Pete Smyth

Editor .... Dick Kirkpatrick	**Publisher** .... Gina Smyth
Associate Editor .... John Yeager	**Business Manager** .... Ken Walker
Field Editor .... Doug Adams	**Advertising Sales Manager** .... Bill Tubby
Editorial Assistants .... Ben Hicks	**Advertising Sales** ...... Bill Walker and Celia Lester
and Inna Golovakha-Hicks	**Computer Consultant** ....Mike Higdon
Editorial Consultants: .... Patricia Thomas,	**Production Assistants** .... Philip Walker
Gloria Davidsaver, Ed. D. and Joyce Higdon	and Tim Walker

CHART

FEATURES

- **MONTY'S RESTAURANT** - World class dining and banquet facility

- **HOPKINS CARTER MARINE** - Full-service marine and bait store

- **DIVE CENTER** - Scuba/Dive facility

- **SUZANNE'S GOURMET MARKET** Deli, Grocery, Wines, Beers, Ice

- **MONTY'S RAW BAR** - Casual dining and drinks at poolside

- **SEAKRUZ** - Dining/Casino cruises

AT SOUTH BEACH
MIAMI BEACH MARINA
300 ALTON ROAD   MIAMI BEACH, FL 33139
PHONE (305) 673 - 6000
FAX (305) 538 - 1780

SERVICES:
- TEXACO STAR PORT & PUMP-OUT FACILITIES • BATHROOMS & SHOWERS
- DOCK ATTENDANTS • 24 HOUR SECURITY • LIGHTED PARKING • LAUNDRY
- HEATED SWIMMING POOL • ACCOMMODATIONS TO 240 FT. YACHTS
- 1000 FT. FLOATING DOCK • DOCKSIDE POWER; 30/50/100 AMPS
- FLOTILLA RATES • STATE-OF-THE-ART WEATHER EQUIPMENT
- FREE NEWSPAPER DELIVERY • CABLE TV • PHONES LINES • WATER
- GROCERY DELIVERY • CATERING • FULL SERVICE PRIVATE PARTIES

MIAMI BEACH
MARINA

MONITOR
CHANNEL 16 VHF

Managed by . . .
RCI Marine, Inc.

INDEX ——————————

THE YEAR OF THE

A one-two punch from Hurricanes Erin and Opal caused severe damage to the beautiful beaches and barrier islands of Florida's Panhandle in 1995, but...

In the cosmic crapshoot that is hurricane meteorology, famed forecaster William Gray at Colorado State led off six months in advance with the prediction that 1995 would be a big year for hurricanes. The Old Farmer's Almanac, which had predicted Hurricane Andrew on the nose in 1992, agreed. Gray raised the ante from 14 storms to 16 as the season neared, citing a lull in El Niño, the warm Pacific current which affects much of North American weather when it runs.

It had been twenty years since a major storm had struck the Panhandle, and in that time whole cities of people with little respect for hurricanes had sprung up on the available property along the beaches and barrier islands. Tourism, including cruising boats, had grown to seven million visitors a year, 17% of Florida's total. That those beaches and barrier islands were not a solid line of vulnerable structures like the Gold Coast is a tribute to the preservation of so much of the Panhandle gulfshore as parks and preserves.

The Panhandle had a rehearsal early in the season, when Hurricane Allison came northward out of the Gulf early in June, but the storm veered eastward at the last minute and blew ashore with 75mph winds and heavy rain on the sparsely inhabited Big Bend coast.

In late July Hurricane Erin formed over the Turks and Caicos, went straight through the Bahamas, came ashore at Vero Beach, moved across Central Florida, emerged into the Gulf by way of Tarpon Springs, and quickly regained its hurricane status. Erin was a "minor" hurricane, and its course seemed to be directly toward New Orleans. The Panhandle breathed a little easier on August 4th.

The next morning the Miami Herald reported: "Floridians went to sleep feeling sorry for Louisiana and awoke with Erin perched on their own bedsteads". Erin had veered northward overnight, swept ashore over the fragile sandbar of Santa Rosa Island and struck Pensacola head-on with 86mph winds and gusts over 100mph.

People who have never been through a hurricane tend to think of them as windstorms. People who have

been through one know better. Hurricanes are windstorms, rainstorms, and tidal phenomena combined, and of the three the wind is the least dangerous. Erin was a windstorm, and the damage she inflicted on the Pensacola area was mostly wind damage — trees and power lines down, roofs damaged and the like.

Unfortunately, marinas, boatyards and such are particularly vulnerable to wind. Many structures are little more than roofs on posts, and can fly away like kites when winds approach 100mph. Erin caused an

Pensacola photographer Bill Gonzales recorded the devastation on Perdido Key, where the tidal surge washed completely across at some points.

estimated $375 million in property damage. But with typical resilience, marina owners got most facilities back into at least limited service within a few days or weeks.

Then in late September Tropical Storm Opal formed in the western Caribbean, caused heavy damage and loss of life in the Yucatan Peninsula, then entered the Gulf and headed toward the Panhandle, building quickly into a potential killer storm. On October 4th the National Hurricane Center rated the storm Category 4, with winds near 150mph and gusts to 180, moving at 27mph with a tidal surge as high as 20-30 feet straight toward Navarre Beach, 20 miles east of Pensacola.

Emergency agencies issued evacuation orders for a 120-mile stretch of Panhandle coast from Pensacola to

HURRICANES

...the all-clear is up and there's no reason to put off cruising those wonderful waterways and visiting those historic and hospitable ports in 1996.

Panama City, and in an ominous note, ordered 300 body bags. The order sent 100,000 people inland toward shelters prepared for perhaps 20,000, on highways better suited to casual tourist traffic than mass evacuation. The fast-approaching hurricane outran many evacuees, who were forced to take shelter where they could find it.

Miraculously, Opal eased before coming ashore. Winds slacked to 135mph and the tidal surge eased to 15-18 feet. Still, it was the third most damaging storm in history after Andrew in 1992 and Hugo in 1989, causing

Shari Hauck of The Boat Marina at Fort Walton Beach sent this photograph of the damage inside the grounded 150-foot ship that houses their ship's store.

an estimated $3.75 billion in damage. Also miraculously, it only took two lives and none of the body bags were needed. The storm spent its fury on the beaches and barrier islands and did surprisingly little damage even a few blocks inland.

Erin was a windstorm, but Opal was a tidal storm that washed over the barrier islands, reducing them to moonscapes, sweeping stilt houses off their pilings, undermining structures on slabs, washing apartment buildings off their footings, and sweeping the sand out from under shore facilities. Hardly a structure on the barrier island or the beach was left undamaged. Docks and the fuel and electrical lines they support were particularly hard hit.

The dunes that are the area's main scenic attraction were damaged so badly that it will be years before they regain their former glory. Much of that sand was deposited in the waters inside the barrier islands, and new shallows may take years to mark . The surge took out whole sections of infrastructure, including roads, bridges, water and sewer lines, power and telephone systems, and some may not be restored for months.

Marine facilities are famous for their resilience, but their ability to rebound is often limited by their resources. A corporate facility may be back in service in days or weeks, but a struggling mom-and-pop operation may be put out of business entirely. In between, insurance coverage and claims service can make all the difference.

As they did in Miami after Andrew and earlier after Erin, the marinas and other facilities of the Panhandle proved tough enough for even the third-worst storm in history.

Directory correspondent Doug Adams in Pensacola summed up in December: **"The marina people here are a resilient lot. By and large most marinas, if not already operating, will be up and running in a month or two. Some few will be delayed until mid-spring, and a small number are unsure of the future. For the most part, nearly all will lick their wounds, repair their docks, and look to the future with hope, faith and hard work."**

As a result, boat people will find the Panhandle as cruisable as ever in 1996. The dunes are still beautiful, the water is still clear, and the people are as hospitable as ever. Marine sources warn only of occasional difficulty in fueling — fuel lines may not be restored to dockhead pumps at some locations — and in finding dock space — thousands of private docks were destroyed, and surviving boats still crowd some marinas.

The solution to both problems is simple — call ahead by radio or telephone well before running low on either fuel or daylight. You'll find the channels and telephone numbers on the charts in this Directory.

ADVERTISERS INDEX

BOAT RAMP INDEX

Launching ramps serving Directory waters

USEFUL NUMBERS

Emergencies 911

MEDICAL SERVICES

Duval County Medical Services 904-355-6561
Flagler County Medical Society 904-437-2044
Volusia County Medical Society 904-255-3321
Brevard County Medical Society 407-632-8481
Indian River County Medical Society 407-562-0123
St. Lucie Co - Lawnwood Medical Center... 407-461-4000
Martin County Medical Assn........................ 407-287-5200
Palm Beach County Medical Society 407-476-2636
Broward County Medical Assn 954-938-5006
Broward Cty. Osteopathic Assn. 954-792-6011
Dade County Medical Assn 305-324-8717
Dade County Osteopathic Assn 305-947-3200
Monroe County Medical Service 305-743-6619
Marathon 305-743-9089
Tavernier 305-852-9216
Collier County 941-261-6560
Lee County Medical Society 941-936-1645
Sarasota County 941-366-2700
Manatee County 941-541-1159
Hillsborough County 813-584-7860
Apalachicola (hospital) 904-653-8853
Port St. Joe (hospital) 904-227-1121
Bay County 904-769-1511
Panama City 904-769-8341
Fort Walton Beach (hospital) 904-244-0414

DENTAL SERVICES

East Coast Dental Society 305-944-5668
Jacksonville Dental Society 904-549-3222
Flagler County Dental Center 904-439-3142
Volusia County Dental Assn 904-257-4514
Brevard Dental Referral 407-269-3022
Indian River County Dental Assn. 407-567-8026
St. Lucie County Dental Assn. 407-464-8772
Palm Beach County Dental Assn 407-368-1949
Broward County Dental Assn 954-772-5461
Dade County Dental Assn 305-532-3300
Collier County 941-261-8455
Lee County Dental Referral Service.............. 800-243-4444
Manatee County 941-748-0666
Pinellas County 813-323-2992
Hillsborough County 813-238-7725
Bay County 904-763-8274
Pensacola 904-436-4942

UNITED STATES CUSTOMS

Jacksonville 904-356-4731
Port Canaveral 407-783-2066
West Palm Beach 407-844-4393
Miami 305-536-4423
Fort Myers 941-768-1000
Manatee County. 941-792-4457
Pinellas County. 813-461-5391
Tampa 813-228-2388
Panama City 904-763-8418
Pensacola 904-432-6811

LEGAL SERVICES

Jacksonville Area Legal Aid 904-356-8371
Brevard County Legal Aid 407-768-1105
Legal Aid Society of Indian River Cty 407-834-1660
St. Lucie County Bar Association.................. 407-461-2310
Legal Aid Society of Palm Beach 407-278-1944
Legal Aid Services of Broward Co. 954-765-8950
Legal Aid Society of Dade County 305-579-5733
Legal Services of the Florida Keys 305-743-0079
Collier County Bar 941-775-8566
Lee County Legal 941-334-6118
Sarasota County 941-366-1746
Manatee County 941-746-6151
Pinellas County Legal Aid 813-821-0726
Hillsborough Cty 813-272-5870
Pensacola 904-432-2336
Northwest Florida Legal 904-432-2336
Florida Bar 800-343-8011

FLORIDA MARINE PATROL

Jacksonville 904-359-6013
Titusville 407-383-2740
Jupiter 407-624-6935
Palm Beach 407-624-6935
Miami 305-467-4541
Marathon 305-289-2320
Fort Myers... 941-334-8963
Pinellas County 813-893-2221
Tampa 813-272-2516
Crystal River.. 352-628-6196
Carrabelle 904-697-3741
Panama City 904-233-5150
Pensacola 904-444-8978
Statewide, after hours: 800-432-3355

ALCOHOLICS ANONYMOUS

St. Augustine 904-824-4454
Daytona Area 904-756-2930
Brevard County 407-724-2247
Indian River County 407-562-1114
St. Lucie County 407-461-1799
Martin County 407-283-9337
Broward County 954-462-0265
Dade County 305-891-9239
Monroe County 305-743-3262
Jacksonville 904-399-8535
Collier County 941-262-6535
Lee County 941-275-5111
Sarasota County 941-951-6810
Bradenton 941-746-0999
St. Petersburg 813-530-0415
Tampa 813-879-1233
Panama City 904-784-7431
Fort Walton beach 904-244-2421
Pensacola 904-433-4191

USEFUL NUMBERS

NATIONAL WEATHER SERVICE

Jacksonville	904-741-4311
Daytona	904-252-5575
Orlando (recording)	407-851-7510
West Palm Beach (recording)	407-686-5650
Miami (recording)	305-661-5065
Key West (recording)	305-296-2011
Fort Myers	941-332-5595
Tampa (recording)	813-645-2506
St. Petersburg	813-287-0900
Apalachicola (recording)	904-653-9318
Pensacola(record)	904-453-2188
Pensacola	904-455-6211

VHF WEATHER BROADCASTS

Fort Myers	WX-3
Tampa	WX-1
Gainesville	WX-3
Panama City	WX-1
Pensacola	WX-2

U.S. COAST GUARD

National Response Center.	800-424-8802
Mayport	904-247-7301
New Smyrna Beach	904-428-9084
Station Port Canaveral	407-853-7601
Station Fort Pierce	407-464-6100
Palm Beach Base Lake Worth Inlet	407-844-5030
Documentation	407-833-7998
Boating Safety Detachment	407-833-6714
Fort Lauderdale Base	954-927-1611
Miami Base	305-535-4300
Seventh District Headquarters	305-536-4108
Bridge Information (day hours)	305-536-4108
Aids to Navigation	305-536-4108
Documentation	305-536-5651
Boating Safety	305-536-5184
Islamorada	305-664-8077
Marathon	305-743-6778
Key West	305-293-2256
Cortez	941-794-1261
Manatee Cty.	941-794-1607
St. Petersburg	800-732-6864
Panama City	904-234-2475
Destin	904-244-7146
Pensacola	904-455-2354

MARINE OPERATOR CHANNELS

AREA	CH	CALL SIGN	OP. ID
Fernandina Beach	25	KPB 689	Call sign only
Jacksonville	26	KFT 304	Call sign only
Marineland	27	WQZ 354	Call sign only
Daytona Beach	28	KWS 605	Call sign only
Cocoa	26	KTR 945	Call sign only
Vero Beach	27	KVY 628	Call sign only
Stuart	26	KYQ 841	St. Lucie
West Palm Beach	28 & 85	KGW 294	Palm Beach
Ft. Lauderdale	26 &84	KEW 823	Call sign only
Miami	24 & 25	KSK 279	Miami
Miami Beach	85	WHU 319	Miami Beach
Homestead	27 & 28	KLU 791	Homestead
Marathon	27	KSK 210	Call sign only
Key West	26 & 84	KQU 411	Key West
Isle of Capri	25	KQU 410	Call sign only
North Ft. Myers	26	KYH 550	Ft. Myers
Venice	28	KTD 563	Call sign only
Palmetto	85	WHU 763	Call sign only
Clearwater	24 & 26	KUZ 385	Call sign only
Crystal River	28	KWB 447	Call sign only
Apalachicola	28	KSK 339	Call sign only
Panama City	26	KLL 295	Panama City
Ft. Walton Beach	28	KWB 455	Call sign only
Pensacola	26	KLL 294	Pensacola

RADIO BEACONS

LOCATION	MORSE ID	kHz AM
Jacksonville	JA	344
St. Johns	R	306
Cape Canaveral	Z	313
Melbourne	SQT	257
Fort Pierce	FPR	275
Jupiter Inlet	J	294
Palm Beach	PB	356
Hillsboro Inlet	Q	299
Miami	U	322
Marathon	MTH	260
Fish Hook (Key West)	FIS	332
Tortugas	OE	286
Marco Island	MKY	375
Naples	APF	201
Egmont Key	H	310
Brooksville	BKV	278
Cape San Blas	W	320
Mobile Point	C	300
Marsh Harbor	ZMH	361
Walker's Cay	ZWC	280
Freeport	ZFP	209
West End	ZWE	317
Bimini	ZBB	396
Nassau	ZQA	251

PUMPOUT STATIONS
— Listed alphabetically by City within County —
This information furnished by Tallahassee's Office of Waterway Management in January '96

BAY COUNTY
Mexico Beach
Mexico Beach Canal Park
Panama City
Gulf Marina
Treasure Island Marina
Bay Point Marina
BREVARD COUNTY
Indian Harbour Beach
Indian Harbour Marina
Melbourne
Anchorage Yacht Basin
Eau Gallie Yacht Basin
Eau Gallie Harbor Club
Intracoastal Marina
Melbourne Yacht Club
F.I.T.
Merritt Island
Harbour Square Marina
Inland Marina
Port Canaveral
Cape Marina
Titusville
Titusville Municipal Marina
Kennedy Point Yacht Club
BROWARD COUNTY
Dania
Harbour Towne Marina
Fort Lauderdale
Lauderdale Marina
Bahia Mar Marina
Hall of Fame Marina
Pier 66 Resort & Marina
First Performance Marina
CHARLOTTE COUNTY
Englewood
Chadwick Cove Resort
Port Charlotte
Charlotte Harbor Yacht Club
Punta Gorda
Punta Gorda Marina
Riviera Marina
Fisherman's Village
CLAY COUNTY
Orange Park
Doctor's Lake Marina
Whitney Marine
COLLIER COUNTY
Naples
Naples City Docks
Wiggins Pass
Port of the Islands
Old Naples Seaport
  (frmr. Coconut Grove)
DADE COUNTY
Aventura
Turnberry Isle
Waterways Marina
Coconut Grove
Dinner Key Boatyard
Grove Isle Marina
Coral Gables
Cocoplum Yacht Club
Homestead
Elliot Key Harbor
South Dade Marina

Key Biscayne
Crandon Park Marina
Rickenbacker Marina
Miami
Matheson Hammock Marina
Pelican Harbor
Snapper Creek Marina
Four Ambassadors
Villa Regina Condominium
Fisher Island Club
Royale Harbour Yacht Club
DuPont Plaza Marina
Biscayne Bay Marina
Hardies Yacht Basin
Sunset Harbor Marina
Towers of Quayside
Black Point Marina
Biscayne Bay Marriott
Mystic Pointe Marina
Miami Beach
Morton Towers Apartments
Miami Beach Marina
Haulover Park Marina
North Bay Village
North Bay Landing Marina
North Miami
Williams Island Marina
North Miami Beach
Aventura Marina
Sunny Isles Marina
Maule Lake Marina
DIXIE COUNTY
Suwannee
Millers Marina
DUVAL COUNTY
Amelia Island
Amelia Island Yacht Club
Jacksonville
Edwards Marina
Sea Farer Marina
Mandarin Marine
Jacksonville Beach
Beach Marine
Mayport
Mayport Public Boat Ramp
ESCAMBIA COUNTY
Pensacola
Southwind Marina
Rod & Reel Marina
FLAGLER COUNTY
Palm Coast
Palm Coast Marina
FRANKLIN COUNTY
Carrabelle
Moorings at Carrabelle
**HILLSBOROUGH
COUNTY**
Ruskin
Bahia del Sol Marina
Shell Point Marina
Tampa
Harbour Island Marina
INDIAN RIVER COUNTY
Vero Beach
Sea Oaks Yacht Club
Vero Beach Municipal Marina
Grand Harbor Marina

LEE COUNTY
Boca Grande
Millers Marina
Uncle Henry's Marina Resort
Bokeelia
Bocilla Marina
Cape Coral
Tarpon Point Marina
Captiva
Tween Waters Inn & Marina
South Seas Plantation
Fort Myers
Fort Myers Yacht Basin
Jack's Marine South
Fort Myers Beach
Fort Myers Beach Marina
Palm Grove Marina
Moss Marine
Compass Rose
North Fort Myers
Marinatown Marina
Punta Gorda
Burnt Store Marina
Sanibel
Sanibel Marina
MANATEE COUNTY
Anna Maria
Galati's Marine
Longboat Key
Longboat Key Moorings
Palmetto
Regatta Point Marina
MARTIN COUNTY
Stuart
Mariner Cay Marina
Stuart Yacht Club & Marina
Indian River Plantation
MONROE COUNTY
Duck Key
Hawk's Cay Resort
Key West
Peninsular Marine Enterprises
Galleon Marina
Marathon
Faro Blanco Marine Resort
NASSAU COUNTY
Amelia Island
Amelia Island Yacht Basin
Fernandina Beach
Tiger Point Marina
OKALOOSA COUNTY
Destin
East Pass Towers
Waterview Towers
Dolphin Point Condominiums
Marina Cafe Yacht Club
Destin Yacht Club
Sun King Towers
Fort Walton Beach
Fort Walton Yacht Basin
Shalimar Yacht Basin
PALM BEACH COUNTY
Jupiter
Jonathan's Landing Marina
Admiral's Cove Marina

Palm Beach Gardens
Frenchman's Creek
Harbour Point Marina
Riviera Beach
Riviera Beach Marina
PINELLAS COUNTY
Clearwater
Clearwater Municipal Marina
Gulfport
Gulfport City Marina
Madeira Beach
Madeira Beach Municipal
  Marina
South Pasadena
Tracy's Cove
St. Petersburg
St. Petersburg Municipal
  Marina
The Harborage at Bayboro
Maximo Marina
Marina Point
Demens Landing South
St. Petersburg Beach
Blind Pass Marina
Tarpon Springs
Anclote Harbors Marina
Sail Harbor Marina
Tierra Verde
Tierra Verde Yacht Basin
Tierra Verde Marina
Island Marina
Tierra Verde Marine
SARASOTA COUNTY
Englewood
Stump Pass Marina
Longboat Key
Buccaneer Inn Marina
Sarasota
Marina Jack's
Gulfwind Marine of Sarasota
Holiday Inn Airport Marina
Venice
Gulfwind Marine of Venice
Venice Yacht Club
ST. JOHNS COUNTY
St. Augustine City Marina
ST. LUCIE COUNTY
Fort Pierce
Riverside Marina
Pelican Yacht Club
Fort Pierce Yachting Center
VOLUSIA COUNTY
Daytona Beach
Daytona Marina
Halifax Harbor Marina
DeLand
Hontoon Landing Marina
The Boat Show Marina
Sanford
Hidden Harbor Marina
Monroe Harbor Marina
Sanford Boat Works & Marina

Waterway Times Magazine

Waterway Times Magazine is South Florida's only local marine magazine. Each monthly issue features local, regional and national information and news, along with stories, both fact and fiction.

W h i l e visiting south e a s t e r n Florida, please pick up a free issue with our famous Local Tide Table Calender centerfold. It is calibrated for each of the four regional editions: Biscayne Bay, New River, Palm Beach, and Treasure Coast.

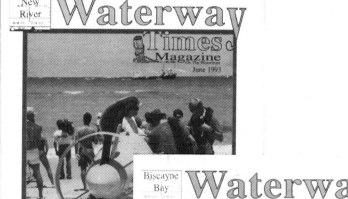

For a year's subscription, send $15.00 and indicate which edition desired, to:

WATERWAY TIMES
11 S.W. Tommie Terrace
Ft. Lauderdale, FL 33312
Tel: 954-761-1937   FAX 954-785-5228
or
WATERFRONT PUBLISHING, Inc.
429 Lamon Lane
Port St. Lucie, FL 34983
Tel. 407-871-1090   FAX 407-336-0755

On The Waterfront
in Dade, Broward, Palm Beach and Treasure Coast

LIVING ABOARD

The national bi-monthly magazine by, for and about those that live aboard or aspire to.

For a **FREE** sample copy call (504) 283-1312.

Name_____

Address_____

City_____State___ Zip_____

Phone (__)_____

Visa/MC#_____Exp_____

Name on card_____

1 year	$12
2 years	$20
3 years	$26

LIVING ABOARD

141 N. Roadway • New Orleans, LA 70124
or charge it to your Visa/Mastercard:
Call (504) 283-1312 • Fax (504) 283-1363

The Marine Web
Your On-line Marine Industries Resource

http://www.marineweb.com
marineweb@aksi.net

Look us up on the **Internet** for all your boating needs!

Go to **http://www.marineweb.com** to find:

- **New and Used Yachts for Sale** - Review detailed specifications of all types of yachts for sale.
- **Yacht Brokerages** - Read about each yacht brokerage and their special services.
- **New Yachts** - Page through colorful yacht brochures.
- **Charter & Management** - Select a yacht management company or make your own charter reservations.
- **Professional Services** - Select a yacht financier, USCG Documentor, electronics installer, yacht insurance, surveyor, maintenance company, and much more. . . .
- **Feature Articles** - Review the interesting monthly articles.
- **Destinations** - Select a cruising destination.
- **Useful Information** - Check out the current tides, weather and other boating needs!
- **Publications** - Select a magazine, cruising guide, video, and other publications.
- **Ships Store** - Order your boating supplies on-line.
- **Marinas & boatyards** - Select a marina or boat yard to berth, haul, store or fix your boat.
- **Associations & Organizations** - Find a member of the Florida Yacht Brokerage Association, read about Florida's new non-resident 90 day tax exemption. Look up a member of the Marine Industries Association of South Florida.

The most informative and interactive Marine Web Site on the Internet

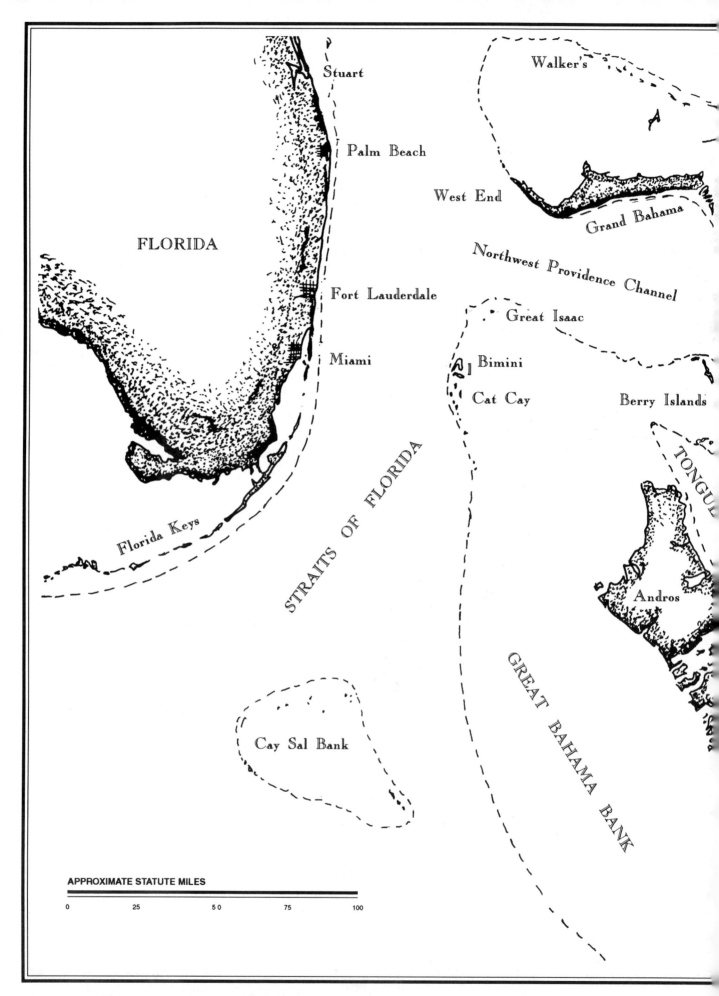

Stuart

Palm Beach

West End

Walker's

FLORIDA

Grand Bahama

Northwest Providence Channel

Fort Lauderdale

Great Isaac

Miami

Bimini

Cat Cay

Berry Islands

TONGU

STRAITS OF FLORIDA

Florida Keys

Andros

GREAT BAHAMA BANK

Cay Sal Bank

APPROXIMATE STATUTE MILES

0   25   5 0   75   100

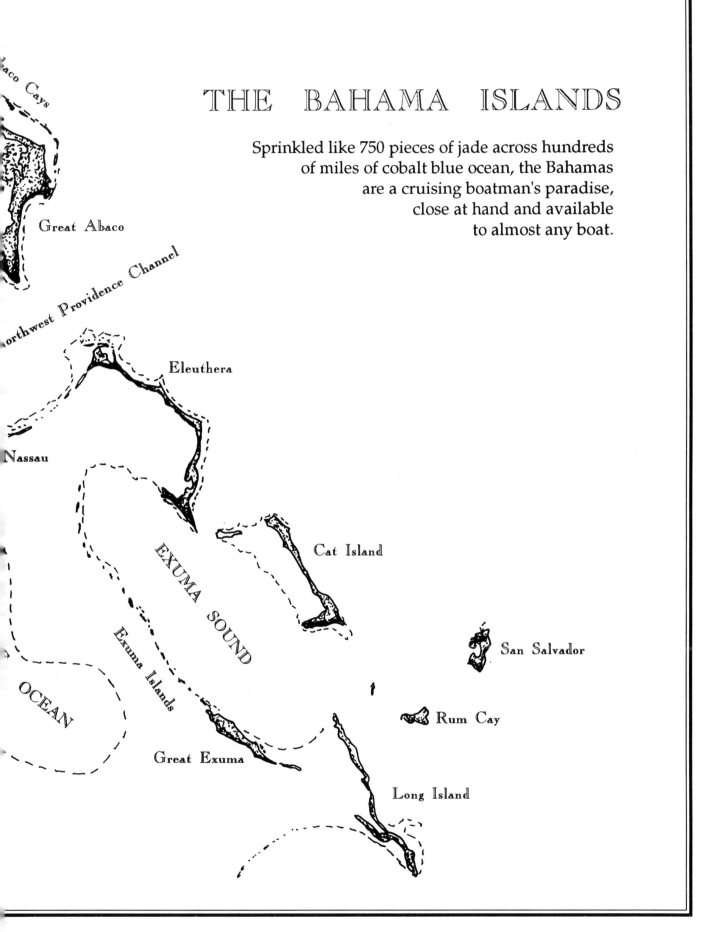

THE BAHAMA ISLANDS

Sprinkled like 750 pieces of jade across hundreds
of miles of cobalt blue ocean, the Bahamas
are a cruising boatman's paradise,
close at hand and available
to almost any boat.

Aco Cays

Great Abaco

Northwest Providence Channel

Eleuthera

Nassau

EXUMA SOUND

Cat Island

San Salvador

OCEAN

Exuma Islands

Rum Cay

Great Exuma

Long Island

Bahamas Marina Listings
Information Supplied by the Bahamas Ministry of Tourism - December 1995

Location/Marina Facilities   **Location/Marina Facilities**

NEW PROVIDENCE
NASSAU

Brown's Boat Basin
East Bay St.
PO Box N-7416
809-393-3331/3680
Fax: 809-393-1868

60 slips, but limited space available to transient vessels. Electricity. Fuel. Water. General boat and yacht engine repairs. Boat and bottom painting. Travel hoist facilities - 40 tons.

East Bay Yacht Basin
(formerly East Bay Marina)
East Bay Street
PO Box SS-6871
809-394-1816
Fax 809-394-1816

35 slips. Fuel. Water & Ice. Electricity. Showers. Washers. Dryers. Restaurants. Liquor Store. Dockage rates (daily): $0.70 per ft. for the one day. $0.60 per ft. for 2 or more days' stay. Dockage rates (monthly): $0.48 per ft. Electricity rates (daily): $12 - 110 V. $14 - 220 V. Electricity is optional. Water rates (daily): $3. Water is mandatory.

Lyford Cay Club
(private)
PO Box N-7776
809-362-4131
Fax 809-362-5062

74 slips. Depth channel: 10-12 ft. Can accomodate vessels with a max. draft of 8 1/2 - 9 ft. Cruising yachtsmen welcome up to four days. Fuel. Electricity. Water/ice. Complete shopping center at marina. Telephone, Cable TV hook-ups. Fishing charters half and full day. Bait. VHF 16. Dockage rates for transients: $2.10 per ft. per day. Utility rates (including water, Cable TV & telephone): $.25 per ft. per day. Electricity metered, $.26 per kw hour. Very limited space available.

Nassau Harbour Club
East Bay Street
PO Box SS-5755
809-393-0771-4
Fax 809-393-5393

65 slips with all concrete docks. T-head accomodates up to 200 ft. Fuel. Water. Ice. Electricity. Showers. Pool. Security. Laundry service. Shopping Center. Liquor store. Restaurant & bar. Satellite hook-up.

Nassau Yacht Haven
East Bay Street
PO Box SS-5693
809-393-8173/4

120 slips. Daily dockage rates: $0.90 per ft. Fuel. Water & Ice. Showers. Laundry Service. Liquor store. Electricity. Telephone hook-ups. 24-hour security. Satellite. Taxidermist agency. Charter fishing and charter boats available. VHF 16.

New Mermaid Marina
Deveaux Street
PO Box CB 12930
809-323-8426
Fax c/o 809-322-3018
Tel/Fax 809-327-7682

28 slips, 20' depth dockside. Water. Electricity, 30/50 amps. Restaurant/bar. Sailboat Charters. Charter fishing boats. Dockage rates (daily): $0.75 per ft. with a $25 minimum; (monthly): $0.40 per ft. Semi-submarine tours. Security.

PARADISE ISLAND

Hurricane Hole Marina
PO Box SS-6317
809-363-3600
Fax 809-363-3604

60 slips including T-Dock. Daily dockage rates: $1.15 and $1.25 per ft. Fuel. Water & Ice. Showers. Electricity. Sportfishing boats available. Can accommodate vessels up to 300 ft. Telephone and satellite hook-ups. Casino. Restaurants nearby. Security service. Laundry service. Golf course on island. VHF 16.

Paradise Harbour Club & Marina
PO Box SS-6317
809-363-2992
Fax 809-363-2840

20 slips. Water. Electricity. Telephone & TV hook-up. Accommodations. Dockage rates (daily): $0.90 per ft. Dockage rates (monthly): $0.80 per ft. Dockage rates (annually) $0.65 per ft. Electricity rates: $0.25 per kilowatt. Water rates: $32. per 1000 gallon.

GRAND BAHAMA

West End Marina
(formerly Jack Tar)
West End
809-346-6211
Fax 809-346-6546
N.B. Only the marina is operating. Hotel is closed.
Port of Entry

70 slips. Can accomodate vessels up to 80 ft. Fuel. Electricity (110/220 V). Water/ice. Showers. Laundry. VHF 16. Dockage rates (daily): 30 ft. - $20.00. Over 30 ft: $20.50 (standard rate). Electricity rates: $5.00 per day. $150 per month for live on guests. Water rates: $0.15 per gallon.

Ocean Reef Yacht Club
34 Bahama Reef Blvd.
PO Box F-2695
Freeport
809-373-4662
Fax: 809-373-8621

52 slips Can accomodate vessels up to 80 ft. Depth dockside: 6 ft. Electricity. Water/ice. Charter/boat rental. Accommodations. Tackle & Bait. VHF 16. Dockage rates: Up to 40 ft., $30.00 per day; 43 - 51 ft., $40; 52 - 61 ft., $50; 62 ft. plus, $60. $250. per month. No weekly rates. Dockage rates include water charges. Electricity rates: $0.16 per kilowatt.

Port Lucaya Marina
Port Lucaya
Marketplace
Seahorse Road
PO Box F-3233
Freeport
809-373-9090
Fax: 809-373-5884
Port of Entry

100 slips. Can accomodate vessels up to 130'. Daily dockage rate (In-season): $1.00 per ft., (Off-season) $0.75 per ft. Water/ice. Showers. Laundry. Marine/grocery supplies. Charter/boat rental. Accommodations. Telephone and cable TV hook-ups. Liveaboard welcome. Adjoins Port Lucaya Marketplace with shops, restaurants, bars and entertainment. Next door to Underwater Explorers Society (Unexso). Casino half block. Connected by waterwalk to the Dolphin Experience. Monitoring VHF 16/72.

Running Mon Marina & Resort
PO Box F-2663
Freeport
809-352-6834/5
Fax 809-352-6835
800-315-6054

60 slips. Daily dockage rates: up to 30 ft. $27.00, 31 - 40 ft., $36.00, 41 ft. - 50 ft., $45.00. Fuel. Electricity. Water/ice. Showers. Tami-lift to 40 tons. Complete marina service. Tackle shop plus bait. Taxidermist agency. Laundry. Cable TV. Accommodations. Charter fishing boats available. Snorkelling. Glassbottom boats. Courtesy bus.

Xanadu Beach & Marina Resort
PO Box F-2438
Freeport
809-352-6782
Fax 809-352-5799

77 slips. Can accomodate vessels 100 ft. plus. Daily dockage rates: up to 40 ft., $50; 41 - 50 ft., $60; 51 - 60 ft., $70; 61 - 70 ft., $80; 71 - 80 ft., $90. Depth dockside: 8 ft. Fuel. Water/ice. Laundry. Showers. Telephone. Cable TV. Restaurant/bar. Marine Tackle shop. Gift shop. Pharmacy. 38 ft. Sportfishing charter boat. Liquor store and casino nearby. Room service available to boats. Dive center. Monitoring VHF 26.

Lucayan Marina Village
PO Box F-42654
809-373-8888
Fax 809-373-7630
Port of Entry
See advertisement on page 27.

150 slips. Dockside depth 12 ft. (low tide), 15-18 ft. (high tide). Fuel. Water, Satellite TV, Telephone, Showers, Laundry, Ice, Bait & Pump-out station. Electricity: 25 / kw / hr. Dockage $1 per ft. per day; .70 per ft. per day. Long-term introductory rates available on request. 3 heated pools. Bars/restaurants. Free water shuttle to Port Lucaya's marketplace at visitors' convenience. Monitoring VHF 16.

ABACO
Marsh Harbour

Boat Harbour Marina
Marsh Harbour
PO Box 511
809-367-2858
809-367-2818

183 full service slips. Fuel. Electricity. Water & ice. Showers. Laundry. Restaurant/bar. Mechanical service on request. Ferry service to Hope Town and Man-O-War Cay. Fishing guides. Dive trips and rental boats can be arranged. Accomodations. Cable TV. Wet storage. Monitoring VHF 16.

Conch Inn Marina
PO Box AB 20464
Marsh Harbour
809-367-2319
Fax 809-367-2980

72 slips. Fuel. Electricity. Water & ice. Showers. Laundry service. Cable TV. Dive Shop. Guana Cay Ferry. Private beach. Hobie cats. Restaurant. Fresh water pool. Accommodations. Charters. VHF 16.

Harbour View Marina
PO Box 457
Marsh Harbour
809-367-2182

36 slips. Depth dockside at low tide: 6 ft. Can accomodate vessels up to 60 ft. Fuel. Electricity - 110/220 V. Water/ice. Showers. Laundry. Charter boat rental. VHF 16.

Marsh Harbour Marina
PO Box AB 20578
809-367-2700
809-367-2033

57 slips. Depth dockside: 7 ft. Fuel. Water/ice. Electricity. Showers. Laundry. Seafood restaurant/bar. Hobies and windsurfers can be arranged. Tour bus. Telephone. Mechanic available. Wet/dry storage. Monitoring VHF 16. Small coral reef 300 yards away.

Triple J Marina
PO Box AB 20512
Marsh Harbour
809-367-2163
Fax 809-367-3388

16 slips. Depth dockside: 5 ft. Fuel. Electricity (30/50 amps). Water/ice. Showers & Laundry. Accommodations. Wet storage. Tackle & Bait. Marine Store. VHF 16.

GREEN TURTLE CAY

Abaco Yacht Services
Green Turtle Cay
809-365-4033
Fax 809-365-4216

5 slips. Depth dockside; 6 ft. Electricity. Water. Ice. Showers. Laundry facilities. Boat reparis. Dry storage. 50-ton travel lift. Daily dockage rate: $0.60 per ft., including electricity. Water rate: $0.25 per gallon.

Bluff House Club & Marina
809-365-4241/4247
Fax 809-365-4248

25 slips. 5 moorings. Depth dockside:6 ft. Fuel. Electricity 30/50 amps. Water/ice. Showers. Laundry. Charter/boat rental. Accomodations. Wet/dry storage. Tackle & bait. Monitoring VHF 16.

Green Turtle Yacht Club Marina
809-365-4271
Fax 809-365-4272
See advertisement on page 26.

38 slips. T-dock. Depth dockside: 8 ft. Fuel. Electricity (30/50 amps). Showers. Laundry. Accommodations. Restaurant/bar. Gift shop. Self-drive rental boats 14-23 ft. available. Deep sea/reef fishing. Bone/deep-sea fishing guides. Weekly lobster buffet dinners with live bands. 36 moorings available. Diving facilities fully equipped with pontoon boat and compressor. Whalers available for rent, Snorkelling & scuba diving. Monitoring VHF 16, Unicom 122.8.

Other Shore Club
Black Sound
809-365-4195

20 slips (limited marine facilities). 6 ft. draft. Fuel. Electricity (30/50 amps). Water/ice. Showers. Marine & grocery supplies. Charter/boat rental. Accomodations. Swimming pool. Monitoring VHF 16.

GUANA CAY

Guana Beach Resort
Guana Cay
PO Box 474
Marsh Harbour
809-367-3590
Fax 809-367-3590

25 slips. Electricity. Water/ice. Restaurant/bar. Showers. Laundry. Marine & grocery supplies. Charter/boat rental. Accomodations. Monitoring VHF 16.

BERRY ISLANDS

Chub Cay Club & Marina
809-325-1490
809-322-5599
Fax 809-322-5199

80 slips. Daily dockage rate: $1.00 per ft. Fuel. Depth dockside: 9 ft. Electricity. Water/ice. Cable TV hook-up. Showers. Laundry facilities. Marine & grocery supplies. Restaurant & bar. Boat repairs. Accommodations. Monitors Channels 68 & 71.

HBL Marina/Great Harbor Cay Yacht Club & Marina
809-367-8114/8838
Fax 809-367-8115

80 slips. Depth dockside: 12 ft. Fuel. Electricity. Water/ice. Showers. Laundry. Marine/grocery supplies. Boat and electric repair. Accommodations. Wet storage. Daily dockage rates: $1.00 per ft. (March 15 - Sept. 15); $0.60 per ft. (Sept. - March). Daily electricity rates are $20/50 amps, $15/30 amps. There is a mandatory daily $10 charge for water. Monitoring channel 68.

ANDROS

Andros Beach Hotel & Villas
Nicholl's Town
PO Box 23050
809-329-2582

50 ft. long dock. Can accommodate six vessels between 40-60 ft. in length. Depth dockside: 5-8 ft. Fuel. Electricity. Water/ice. Charter/boat rental. Accommodations. Wet/dry storage. Tackle & bait. Showers. Laundry. Marine/grocery supplies. Boat/electrical repair available. Monitoring VHF 16. Electricity rates (daily): $0.25 per ft. Water rates: $0.25 per gallon.

Chickcharnie Hotel
Fresh Creek
809-366-2025/6

75 ft. dock can accommodate 2 vessels 32-36 ft. in length. Depth dockside: 8 ft. Fuel. Electricity (110/220 V). Water. Laundry. Grocery supplies. Charter boats, bonefishing, reef fishing. Accommodations.

Lighthouse Yacht Club & Marina
Andros Town
809-368-2305/7
Fax 809-368-2300

18 slips Depth dockside: 12 ft. Can accommodate vessels up to 100 ft. Fuel Electricity (30/50 amps). Fresh Creek. Water/ice. Showers. Laundry. Accommodations. Monitoring VHF 16. Dockage rates (monthly): $0.65 per ft.

BIMINI

Bimini Big Game Fishing Club
Alice Town
P.O. Box 699
809-347-3391/3/4
Fax 809-347-3392
P.O. Box 523238
Miami, FL 33152
800-737-1007

66 slips. 150 ft. long dock. Can accommodate vessels up to 130 ft. 6 ft. draft at low tide. Fuel. Electricity (30-50 amps). Water/ice. Showers and laundry service. Marine and grocery supplies. Accommodations. Tackle and bait. Monitoring VHF 16. Restaurant/bar. Tennis court. Liquor store. Freshwater pool/poolside bar. Dockage rates (daily): floating docks up to 30 ft. - $25. All other docks - $1.00 per ft./minimum $40 per day. Electricity rates (daily): up to 39 ft.- $15; 40-49 ft.- $20; 50-59 ft. -$30; 60-80 ft.- $37; 80 ft. and over - $50. Water rates (daily): $0.45 per gallon for non-members; $0.30 per gallon for members.

Bimini Blue Water Ltd.
Alice Town
P.O. Box 601
809-347-3166/3291
Fax 809-347-3293

32 slips. 2 docks, each 50 ft. in length. Can accommodate vessels up to 115 ft. Draft up to 15 ft. Fuel. Electricity (110-220 V) Water/ice. Showers. Charter boat rental. Accommodations. Wet/dry storage. Restaurant/bar. Monitoring channel 68.

Bimini Reef Club & Marina
South Bimini
904-255-9962 FL
800-329-1337 US

20 slips. 500 ft. dock. Can accommodate vessels up to 50 ft. 6 ft. draft. Fuel. Electricity (110-220 V). Water/ice. Showers. Laundry service. Scuba diving charters. Monitoring channel 68. Dockage rates: daily minimum - $30.00.

Brown's Dock
Alice Town
P.O. Box 601
809-347-3227

26 slips. Can accommodate vessels up to 110 ft. 15 ft. draft. Fuel. Water/ice. Electricity (110/220 V) Showers. Restaurant/bar. Marine and grocery supplies available. Gift shop. Boat and electrical repairs available. Charter boar rental. Accommodations. Wet/dry storage. Tackle and bait available. Monitoring channel 68. Dockage rates (daily): $5.00 - $20.00. Daily minimum - $15.00. Electricity rates (daily): $5.00 - $20.00. Water rates: $0.20 per gallon.

Cat Cay Yacht Club
809-359-4988
954-359-8272

80 slips. 12 ft. dockside. Can accommodate vessels up to 180 ft. Fuel. Water/ice. Electricity (30-50-100 amps). Grocery supplies. Showers/Washers/Dryers. Restaurant/Bar. Monitor Channel 16. Transient vessels are welcome up to 2 weeks. Daily dockage rates: $1.50 per ft. Water rates: $0.22 per gallon. Electricity: $0.25 per kilowatt hour.

Sea Crest Hotel & Marina
Alice Town
P.O. Box 654
809-347-3071

16 slips. 12 ft. draft. Can accommodate vessels up to 110 ft. Electricity (30/50 amps.) Water/ice. Showers. Boat and electrical repair available. Accommodations. Tackle and bait. Monitoring channel 16. Daily dockage rates: $30 minimum for boats up to 40 ft. Boats over 40 ft.: $0.75 per ft. per day. Daily electricity rates: $10 for boats up to 40 ft. Boats 41-50 ft.: $15. 51-60 ft.: $20. Boats 60 ft. and over: $25.

Weech's Dock
Alice Town
P.O. Box 613
809-347-3028

15 slips. 12 ft. draft. Can accommodate vessels up to 70 ft. Electricity (30-50 amps) Water/ice. Showers. Marine supplies. Accommodations. Charter boat rental. Channel 18. Dockage rates (daily): minimum $15.00. Electricity rates (daily): $7.50/110 V; $15.00/220V.

WALKER'S CAY

Walker's Cay Hotel & Marina
809-352-5252
Florida address:
Sea Lion Marina
700 SW 34th St.
Ft. Lauderdale 33315
954-359-1400
800-WALKERS

75 slips. Water/ice. Electricity (30/50 amps). Showers. Laundry. Ship's Store. Restaurant/bar. Sportfishing charter boats. Boat charters for reef and troll fishing. Accommodations. Tackle & bail. Marine supplies. Monitoring channel 68/16.

Bahamas Marinas continued . . . . .

Location/Marina   Facilities

HOPE TOWN
ELBOW CAY

Hope Town Marina
809-366-0003

14 slips. Moorings. Depth dockside: 7 ft. Water/ice. Electricity (30/50 amps). Showers. Laundry. Restaurant/bar. Boat/electrical repair. Charter/boat rental. Accommodations. Dry storage to 25 ft. Monitoring VHF 16, CB 11.

Lighthouse Marina
809-366-0154
Fax 809-366-0171

Limited transient slips. Fuel. Water/ice. Laundry. Marine hardware store. Sales and service of outboard engines. Monitoring VHF 16.

Sea Spray Resort Villas & Marina
Elbow Cay
809-366-0065
Fax 809-366-0383

20 slips. Depth dockside: 8'. Daily dockage rate: $0.50 per ft. Fuel. Electricity. Water. Ice. Showers. Laundry facilities. Boat repairs. Marine supplies. Accommodations. Tackle & bait. Monitors channel 16.

EXUMA

Exuma Docking Service
Kidd Cove
P.O. Box EX-29019
809-336-2578
Fax 809-336-2023

52 slips. 6 1/2 Ft. draft at low tide. Can accommodate vessels up to 140 ft. Fresh water. Fuel. Electricity (30/50 amps). Water/ice. Showers. Laundry. Marine accessories. Restaurant. Car rental. Liquor store. Monitoring VHF channel 16; call sign "Sugar One." Dockage rates: $0.60 per ft. per day, $0.50 per ft. monthly. Electricity rates: Yachts up to 40 ft.: 110 V/$8 - 220/$12; 41-50 ft.: 110V $12 - 220V/$17; 51 - 60 ft.: 100V/$20 - 220V/$22; 61 ft. +: 110V/$20 - 200V/$27.

Staniel Cay
Happy People Marina
809-355-2008
Fax 809-355-2063

7 slips. 8 ft. draft at low tide. Can accommodate vessels up to 140 ft. Electricity. Water/ice. Showers. Charter boat rental. Accommodations. Restaurant/bar. Wet storage. Monitoring VHG channel 16. Dockage rates (daily): $0.60 per ft. Electricity rates (daily): 110V - $15; 220V - $21.

Staniel Cay
Yacht Club
809-355-2024/2011
Fax 809-355-2044

3 docks: 40 ft., 140 ft. and 40 ft. 9 ft. draft. Can accommodate vessels up to 125 ft. Fuel. Electricity (50 amps). Water/ice. Showers. Charter boat rentals. Accommodations. Marine and grocery supplies. Straw craft shop. Fishing guides available. Air charter available. Dockage $0.75 per ft. per day. Electricity rates (daily): $13.00 minimum. 41-48 ft - $17.00; 49-55 ft. - $19.00; 56 ft. and over - $25.00. Water rates: $0.50 per gallon.

Highbourne Cay
c/o P.O. Box SS-6342
Nassau, Bahamas
809-355-1008
Ph/Fax 809-355-1003

6 slips with 1000 ft. of dock space can comfortably accommodate vessels between 40 ft. and 110 ft. 7 1/2 ft. draft at low tide. Fuel. Electricity. Water/ice. Marine and grocery supplies. Bait. Monitoring VHF 16. Accommodations. Dockage rates (daily): $1 & $1.15 per ft. Electricity rates (daily): $15/110V; $25/220V. Water rates: $0.30 per gallon.

Sampson Cay
Colony Ltd.
Sampson Cay
PO Box SS 6247
Nassau
809-355-2034

30 slips. 8 ft. draft. Can accomodate vessels up to 150 ft. Gas & diesel fuel available. Liimited marine repairs. Electricity (30 amps). Water/ice. Laundry. Grocery store. Limited marine supplies. Charter boat rental. Accommodations. Wet storage. Restaurant/bar. Scuba tank fills and rentals. Dockage rates (daily): $0.80 per ft. - (monthly): $10.50 & 13.50. The $13.50 includes electricity.

MAN-O-WAR

Man-O-War Marina
809-365-6008
Fax 809-363-6151

60 slips. Moorings. Depth dockside: 7 ft. Fuel. Water/ice. Electricity (30/50 amps). Showers. Laundry. Grocery/marine supplies. Restaurant/bar. Repairs and parts. Small boat and Windsurfer rentals and sales. Full service dive shop. Gift shop. Telephone. Excursions to neighboring cays. Fax service.

Edwin's Boatyard
809-365-6007
Fax 809-365-6233

10 slips + moorings. Haul to 65 ft. with 6.5 ft. draft. All general maintenance on boats. Dockage rates: (daily) $0.40 per ft.; (monthly) $250.

Location/Marina   Facilities

TREASURE CAY

Treasure Cay Beach Hotel & Villas
Treasure Cay Marina
Great Abaco Island
809-367-2577/2570
809-367-2847
Fax 809-367-3362

150 slips. Depth dockside:7 ft. Fuel. Electricity (30/50/100 amps). Water/ice. Showers. Laundry. Marine/grocery supplies. Restaurant/bar. Boat/electrical repair. Charter boat rental. Accommodations. Wet/dry storage. Monitoring VHF 16.

ELEUTHERA,
HARBOUR ISLAND,
SPANISH WELLS

Valentine's Yacht Club and Marina
P.O. Box EL 1
809-333-2142/2080
Fax 809-333-2135

38 slips. 10 ft. draft and low tide. Electricity. Water/ice. Restaurant/bar. Dockage rates (daily): $1.00 per ft. Electricity rates: $0.40 per kilowatt. Water rates (daily): $10.00.

Spanish Wells Yacht Haven & Marina
P.O. Box 27
809-333-4328/4255
Fax 809-333-4649

Dock; 30 slips. Fuel. Modern laundromat. Hot and cold showers. Electricity 110/220V Rental apartments. Restaurant/bar. Cable TV. Pool. Monitors VHF 16 and CB 9.

Harbour Island Club & Marina
Ph/Fax 809-333-2427

32 slips. Fuel. Electricity (30/50 amps) Water/ice. Showers/washers/dryers. Restaurant/Bar.

Harbour Island Town Dock

Limited facilities. Fuel available.

Spanish Wells Marina & Hardware
P.O. Box EL 27478
809-333-4122/39
Fax 809-333-4137

10 slips. 10 ft. draft at low tide. Electricity. Fuel. Water/ice. Boat repairs. Accommodations. Wet/dry storage. Tackle and bait. Dockage rates (daily): $0.30 per ft. Electricity rates (daily): $3.00/110V; $5.00/220 V.

Hatchet Bay Marina
Hatchet Bay
Ph/Fax 809-332-0186

12 slips. 10-12 ft. draft. Fuel. Electricity (30/50 amps) Water/ice. Boat/electrical repair. Wet storage. In immediate vicinity: marine supply and grocery stores; restaurant/bar and hotel. Monitoring VHF 16. Dockage rates (daily): $0.50 per ft. Electricity rates (daily): up to 30 ft. -$7.50, 30-40 ft.-$15.00, over 40 ft. according to consumption.

Cotton Bay Club
Davis Harbour
Rock Sound
809-334-6101-3

40 slips. 8 ft. draft. Fuel. Electricity (30/50/100 amps) Water/ice.. Showers. Laundry. Restaurant/bar. Fishing. Golf. Tennis. Diving. Monitors VHF 16.

INAGUA

Matthew Town Dock
Matthew Town

No dockage. Anchor in Bay. Water and fuel available upon request.

LONG ISLAND

Stella Maris Inn & Marina
Stella Maris
PO Box L.I. 30.150
809-336-2106
305-359-8236
Fax 305-359-8238
800-426-0466 US/Can

12 slips. 7 ft. draft at high tide. Can accommodate vessels up to 200 ft. Fuel. Electricity. Water/ice. Showers. Laundry. Grocery/marine supply stores nearby. Charter boats with captain. Accommodations. Wet/dry storage. Tackle & bait. Complete marine repair and maintenance services. Pool. VHF 16. Group fishing trips bottom/reef. Deep sea fishing. Dockage rates (daily): $0.50 ft. Discounts for longer periods. Electricity rates: $0.36 per kilowatt. Water rates: regular & drinking water free.

SAN SALVADOR

Riding Rock Inn & Marina
Cockburn Town
809-331-2631
Fax 809-331-2803

7 slips. Depth dockside 8 ft. Can accommodate vessels up to 100 ft. Fuel. Electricity (30/50 amps). Water/ice. Laundry. Restaurant/bar. Charter boats. Snorkelling & scuba diving. Showers. Dockage rates (daily): $0.80 per ft. Dockage rates (weekly): $4.80 per ft. Electricity rates: up to 40 ft. $15 per day. 41-50 ft: $18. per day. 51 ft. plus $20. per day or metered, whichever is greater.

CAT ISLAND

Hawk's Nest Resort & Marina
US Office: 407-597-3565

8 slips. Fuel. Water/ice. Showers. Laundry. Grocery. Deep sea fishing, bonefishing. Diving. Restaurant. Shopping. VHF 16/ Unicom 122.8.

CRUISING THE BAHAMAS

The Commonwealth of the Bahamas is a hospitable island nation only 42 miles from Florida's east coast, offering a cornucopia of cruising opportunities and a diminishing level of urbanization for 800 miles to the southeast and stretching 800 miles to within 250 miles of San Juan, Puerto Rico and halfway to Trinidad.

With 5,380 square miles of land area, the Bahamas are bigger than Connecticut, but that area is divided among more than 750 islands and countless islets and rocks spread over a region bigger than all of New England. If you superimposed a chart of the Bahamas over a map of the United States, West End on Grand Bahama would fall on Chicago and the easternmost island of Silver Bank on Norfolk.

As a result, the distances to be covered vary from a day trip for fishermen — who routinely run from Fort Lauderdale to West End or Bimini and back — to a major passage for those cruising to far islands like the Turks and Caicos. And destinations differ just as widely.

Sitting at one of the resort hotel marinas in Freeport, you could be in Miami. Swinging at anchor in Cat Island Sound, you could be in the Indian Ocean or a South Pacific atoll.

Only a handful of the Bahamian islands exceeds fifty miles in length, and only two measure over a hundred. A few have real heft to them but most are long and lean, and their total acreage would not make one good Texas ranch. Many of the others are in fact chains of very small islands like the Abacos, the Berrys and the Exumas, strung together like pearls on a necklace.

Although varying in size, the Bahamas are alike in that they are made of coral limestone and barely above sea level. Indeed, the highest point anywhere in the islands is 200 feet above sea level, on Cat Island, which is unique in that it stands alone on its own underwater plateau. All of the other islands are merely the above-water parts of two vast plateaus, the Great and Little Bahama Banks.

BAHAMAS TOURIST OFFICE

* Boating Flings

Let's Hip, Let's Hop, Let's Cruise to the Bahamas

* Boating Flings are escorted flotillas that leave points in Florida for destinations in The Bahamas, such as Freeport, Bimini, Great Harbour Cay, Treasure Cay and Green Turtle Cay. Besides having the comfort of companionship for crossing the Gulf Stream, boats joining the flotillas receive a YACHTSMAN'S GUIDE, two T-shirts, a cocktail party at the Captain's Briefing, participation in a fishing tournament and another cocktail party in The Bahamas, all for the small charge of $65 per boat.

The current schedule for 1996 Flings includes:

BIMINI FLINGS

July 11 - 14	Blue Water Resort
July 25 - 28	Blue Water Resort
Aug. 8 - 11	Bimini Big Game Club
Aug. 16 - 18	Bimini Big Game Club

FREEPORT FLINGS

| June 26 - 30 | Lucaya Marina |
| July 31 - Aug. 4 | Port Lucaya Marine |

GREAT ABACO/BERRY ISLANDS/ BIMINI via FREEPORT FLING

| July 31 - Aug. 11 | Abaco Beach/Great Harbour Cay/ Big Game Club/Port Lucaya |

This program is organized by The Bahamas Sports & Aviation Department, Miami.

Call 1-800-327-7678 for more information.

Come join us on our escorted flotillas to The Bahamas!

Separating the banks are channels of abyssal depths. Tongue of the Ocean, Northwest Providence Channel and Exuma Sound are all about a mile deep while Northeast Providence Channel has depths of over two miles. Yet on the banks themselves there is sometimes not enough water to get your pantlegs wet.

And therein lies the major difficulty in cruising the Bahamas: the water tends to be a bit thin in spots. Fortunately, given the crystal clear water typical of the islands, eyeball piloting is easy enough to learn with a little practice. And a system of channel and hazard markers is in the works. More about that later.

This sounds as though cruising in the Bahamas is an iffy sort of business. It isn't, although it does lack the buoy-defined exactitude of piloting Stateside. But, then again, the Bahamas, until rather recently, have always led an iffy sort of existence.

Prior to 1500, the islands were populated solely by Lucayan Indians. Columbus, of course, discovered America five hundred years ago by landing on San Salvador in the eastern Out Islands. Following closely behind him were Spanish explorers looking for gold and silver. They found neither; but they did find the Indians, who they promptly shipped off as slaves to the mines on Hispaniola. Very soon there were no Indians in the Bahamas — nor humans of any kind — until a band of English colonists calling themselves the Eleutheran Adventurers arrived from Bermuda and established themselves on the north end of that island in 1648.

Nassau was founded in 1670 and promptly attracted some of the worst pirates and scoundrels of the world, including Edward Teach, better known as Blackbeard, who came to prey on Spanish treasure ships and took lesser targets of opportunity as available. This lasted until Woodes Rogers, the first Royal Governor, arrived to hang a few, pardon some others, and chase the rest out of the colony.

The American Revolution brought prosperity to the Bahamas for the first time. Some 8,000 Tories — Colonists loyal to the British Crown including a number of wealthy southern plantation owners — came to the islands with all their worldly goods, including their slaves, seeking to recreate the gracious life they had known on the mainland.

Their hopes for a new life faded as their land proved increasingly unfertile. Slavery was abolished in 1838 and with it went any profit in plantation-style farming, and a series of hurricanes ended the dream.

The American Civil War provided the next injection of wealth. With England staunchly on the side of the Confederacy, Nassau was a natural base for running the Union blockade. While the war lasted, wealth in unbelievable amounts poured into the vaults of Nassau's Bay Street from a thousand Rhett Butlers.

Then the war ended and the Bahamas lapsed into a state of indigent sloth. It wasn't until Prohibition dried out the United States in 1922 that wealth returned again. Nassau, Bimini and West End were all perfect ports for rum runners, and running rum — actually Scotch whisky, gin and wines — was a natural for men whose grandaddies had run the Union blockade. But then, with Repeal in 1933, the carnival stopped again.

This time the financial drought was brief. World War II came along within a decade and marked the beginning of the islands' current prosperity. The Bahamas were strategically important, located as they are across the main ship lanes between Panama, the Gulf of Mexico and Europe and guarding the eastern approaches to the United States. As it did Florida, the war introduced the Bahamas to Americans. As American leisure and wealth increased, more and more of them flocked to the islands, and still do.

Since the 60s a new kind of smuggling, much deadlier than the Scotch and gin of the 30s, has appeared — the Bahamas are right on the path of seaborne drugs on their way from northern South America to the lucrative markets in Florida and up the Atlantic and Gulf Coasts. Bahamian authorities recognized that and adopted a zero-tolerance stance, a really tough attitude and really harsh penalties for trafficking of any kind. Some activity continues — drug money can buy its way anywhere — but smugglers have found easier and less costly ways to get to market and most avoid the islands.

Still more recently the contraband has been illegal immigrants headed for Florida, some from Haiti, Cuba, and other troubled Caribbean nations, others all the way from the Orient in search of a better life. They, too, are treated sternly by the Bahamian government, but desperation, like drug money, can find a way.

The bottom line is not to have anything whatever to do with anything that even smells of drugs or illegals, under penalties that your attorney can't plea-bargain.

Happily, the important trafficking is in the other direction. An amarda of private boats crosses the Gulf Stream every year to enjoy the peace and beauty of the Bahamas — more every year, but the thousands of miles of consummate cruising waters and beckoning beaches absorb them with equinamity, and the hospitable Bahamians look forward to more.

But first there are some things you need to know: When you arrive at your Bahamian port of entry, you have only to clear customs, fill out a few forms, pick up your Cruising Permit, and you're on your way. All you need are your ship's papers and proper identification for all aboard. Note that if your boat is documented, you (or your captain) must be an American citizen. Your driver's license is no longer valid identification, but your passport (even if it's expired), voter's registration or birth certificate will do. You will be expected to hoist the Q signal flag on entering harbor, and to leave it up until you've cleared customs, when it should be replaced by a Bahamian courtesy flag. Note that the Cruising Permit costs only a hospitable $15 and is good for a year, but extending it costs $500 a year. They want you to visit, but not to move in. U.S. Customs requires that you purchase a $25 user-fee decal before you leave the States; they'll ask for the number when you check in on return.

(Note that it is no longer necessary for pleasure vessels to stop at a specified marina and call customs on returning to the U.S. from foreign ports, including the Bahamas. You can now call them toll-free on 1-800-432-1216 from your first landfall, which can be any marina or even your home. Note also that only the master or owner may debark until clearance is granted.)

Pets can be taken to the Bahamas as long as they stay aboard the boat. Taking Rover ashore, even for a walk, requires compliance with stiff quarantine regulations and a special permit that must be applied for well in advance from the Bahamian Department of Agriculture in Nassau. It's seldom worth the trouble unless you're planning an extended stay.

Vehicles, including bicycles, aboard may be subject to relicensing and possible import duties if taken ashore. The combination of cost and bother can make it impractical to carry your own ground transportation. You can rent wheels of one kind or another almost everywhere, and your U.S. drivers license is valid.

Reasonable personal non-automatic firearms will be admitted as long as they are declared on entry and secured under lock and key while in the islands. Ammunition supplies may be inventoried both coming and going. Automatic firearms are banned, and violations of the strict Bahamian gun-control laws will get you into a Bahamian jail almost without exception.

Drugs, other than prescription drugs, are an absolute no-no. Prescription drugs must be in labeled containers. If your medicine is a controlled substance, you may be required to prove its legitimacy.

The Bahamas are increasingly environmentally sensitive. Diving and fishing are closely controlled and should not be attempted without getting the regulations and the necessary permits. Visitors are not permitted to hunt at all, and shooting of any kind is actively discouraged. Violation of fish, game and environmental regulations can result in severe penalties, including arrest and confiscation of boat and property.

Be aware that Bahamian laws, rules and regulations are different. You left the Constitution of the U.S. back at the dock in Fort Lauderdale along with the body of American law. For a serious offense you can be tried, convicted, and imprisoned in as little as three days.

Manners and customs are also different. Some places are quite laid back, but others are more formal than American boatpeople may expect. Some places like American tourists better than others, and some Bahami-

ans are more tolerant of American ways than others. Some islanders may take a little time to warm up, but it's just their naturally reserved manner, often justified by a couple of generations of Ugly Americans.

The best news in Bahamas cruising in years is that the Bahamas Marina Operators Association, in cooperation with the Bahamian government, has undertaken the enormous job of marking primary channels and hazards in the islands, starting in the popular cruising waters of the Little Bahamas Bank, Abaco Cays and the Abacos. One recent addition is a series of 16 (unlighted) markers that will lead cruising boats from West End on Grand Bahama Island across the Little Bahamas Bank to Marsh Harbour on Great Abaco. Red markers indicate the course; white markers mark shallows.

Another welcome group of markers has been placed at the southern approach to Spanish Wells on Eleuthera to lead boats between Russell and Charles Islands and into the harbor.

This sweeping and much-needed project will take a long time at best, and only partially funded by the Bahamian government. Private contributions and corporate sponsorships are welcome. For information, or to make a contribution or become a sponsor, contact BMOA at P.O. Box N4874, Nassau, Bahamas.

The worst news in a long time is that cellular telephone service, which many cruising Americans relied on in the islands, has been discontinued. Your cellphone will not "roam" in that part of Area Code 809 until further notice. Electronic thieves were picking up telephone numbers and serial number codes, brokering them around the world, and running up hundreds of millions of dollars in uncollectible bills. Cellular service will not be available until a secure system is installed.

PLAN AHEAD: To help you plan your Bahamian cruise, this directory lists marinas all over the islands. (And if you'd like to preview the islands before you go, try the two volumes of Waterways Videos that cover the Bahamas. See pages 25 and 28.)

One of the constants of Bahamian Cruising is inconstancy. Any chart or cruising guide must be constantly updated with local information and used with a combination of skepticism and common sense, and any such information learned in that school of hard knocks shoule be shared with other cruising skippers.

We recommend that when planning your Bahamian Cruise, you buy a current copy of the *Yachtsman's Guide to the Bahamas* before anything else, including the boat. It is the most up to date, most accurate, and most honest sourcebook available, and the best $25 you can possibly spend on planning. It's in marine bookstores or from the publisher, Tropic Isle Publishers, P.O. Box 610935, North Miami, Florida 33161. Don't head across the Stream without it.

DESTINATIONS IN THE BAHAMAS

BIMINI AND CAT CAY are the nearest landfall to South Florida ports, just 45 miles off Government Cut in Miami and right on the eastern edge of the Gulf Stream. North Bimini is a world-famous sportfishing base as a result, and offers a large sheltered harbor with five marinas, hotels, restaurants, supplies and amenities ashore. Facilities on North Bimini include Brown's Dock and Hotel, Sea Crest Marina and Hotel, Weech's Dock, Blue Water Resort, and the Big Game Fishing Club.

Ashore, Alice Town offers facilities and attractions which include Hemingway's hangout at the Compleat Angler Hotel, the popular Red Lion Pub and Restaurant, and a beautiful empty beach just across the narrow island. A ferry and taxi connects to South Bimini and the airstrip, Bimini Reef Club and a hotel and restaurant.

Cat Cay, south of Bimini, is a private club with beautiful facilities limited to members and guests but accepting transients as space permits for up to three days. A new clinic on the island is a welcome development should any medical emergency arise.

WEST END, logically enough at the west end of Grand Bahama Island, is 55 miles east of Palm Beach and both a sportfishing base and a port of entry for cruising boats enroute to Freeport and Lucaya and the out-island cruising grounds of the Abacos. Customs, fuel, ice, provisions and basic amenities are available at West End Marina, which once served the Jack Tar Hotel, still closed at last report. There are smaller hotels and restaurants ashore along the waterfront.

GRAND BAHAMA ISLAND literally offers something for everyone, from the Las Vegas-style pleasures of Freeport to the beach-resort lifestyle of Lucaya on the south shore to areas along the northern and eastern shores that are as remote as you can stand.

Freeport Harbour is primarily a commercial port although dockage is available for limited times and there is a good restaurant nearby.

The major yachting facilities are clustered further east along the Lucaya waterfront and include Xanadu Beach, Running Mon and Ocean Reef, with Port Lucaya and the newly reconstructed Lucayan Marina inside Bell Channel Bay still further east. Restaurants and shopping are in Port Lucaya Marketplace nearby; Freeport itself is a five-mile cab-ride inland.

The Grand Lucayan Waterway cuts across the island east of Bell Channel Bay, a shortcut to Little Bahama Bank and the Abacos for boats that can handle four or five feet of depth and a 27-foot fixed bridge.

On the east end of the island lies Deep Water Cay, a private fishing club that has moorings and limited facilities during its season from November through June. Once you get past the excellent fishing, the next important thing about the east end is that it's the jumping-off spot for cruising the Abacos.

WALKER'S CAY, the northernmost of the Bahamas, is at the west end of the arc-shaped chain of the Abacos, roughly 80 miles east of Stuart and Fort Pierce and is a resort, diving and sportfishing destination of such luxury and hospitality that many out-island-bound cruising boatmen have had second thoughts about continuing their float plans.

Visitors have the option of eating the lotus at Walker's Cay Hotel & Marina or using the marina as a base to explore the world-class fishing, diving and cruising from Walker's Cay eastward through the Abaco Cays to Little Abaco and Great Abaco.

THE ABACOS are a 130-mile archipelago curving eastward and southward from Walker's Cay and ending at the big island, Great Abaco. The chain creates 40 miles of unmatched cruising grounds of islands, bays, coves, flats, beaches and wetlands. Anchorages abound, and the fishing is rated among the best in the islands.

There are no facilities, and indeed, little habitation on the way; the first is at Fox Town on the west end of Little Abaco, where there is a gas dock, small hotel and two restaurants. The next facility, at Spanish Cay, was a resort but is now a very good marina.

From there, the southbound boat can island-hop down a chain of excellent resorts and marinas. Notable among them are the Green Turtle Club and Bluff House on Green Turtle Cay, Guana Beach Resort & Marina on Great Guana Cay, Man-O-War Marina on Man-O-War Cay, Treasure Cay Marina and Great Abaco Beach Resort, Conch Inn, Harbour View, Triple J, Marsh Harbour Marina and the new Admiral's Yacht Haven on Great Abaco, Lighthouse, Hope Town and Sea Spray marinas on Elbow Cay, and others spaced comfortably along Abaco Sound. Ashore, Marsh Harbour offers some of the most urban amenities in the Bahamas.

In the Bight of Abaco, west of the island chain, is the area known as The Marls — much shallower and hence less traveled, but offering more adventurous boats great cruising and fishing in relative solitude all the way south to the settlement at Sandy Point, where there is a gas dock with minimal facilities ashore.

THE BERRY ISLANDS lie south of Grand Bahama and west of the tip of Great Abaco on Great Bahama Bank, across the Northwest and Northeast Providence Channels and at the head of the Tongue of the Ocean. The 30-odd islands and countless little cays form a 40-mile arc with shallow flats on the west side but drop off to great depths on the east, creating great fishing and dozens of islands, coves and anchorages.

CRUISE THE BAHAMAS ON VIDEO!

Take your choice; The Bahamas in general or the Abacos in particular. Both tapes are about an hour long and feature extensive aerial video so that you can see all the islands as never before.

The Bahamas, the Available Paradise

This is billed as an introduction for flyers and boatmen and that is what it is; an overview of the most popular of the 700+ islands and cays that make up the Bahamas. Included are Bimini, Cat Cay, The Berrys, Grand Bahama, The Abacos, Nassau, The Exumas, Cat Island and Eleuthera. Includes full details for entering and leaving the islands for private yachts and aircraft and full information about marine and aviation facilities. 54 Minutes, $39.95

The Abacos

In contrast to **The Bahamas** tape, **The Abacos** is a detailed video cruising guide with extensive information about all the popular-and many of the less visited-ports of call along this chain of isolated cays. Included are Walker's, Grand, Double Breasted, Cay Sale, Strangers, Carter's, Allens-Pensacola, Manjack, Green Turtle, Man O' War, Treasure, Guana and Elbow Cays plus harbors like Marsh Harbour, Hope Town, New Plymouth and Little Harbour. 55 minutes, $39.95

**THESE TAPES, AND OTHER
WATERWAYS VIDEO CRUISING GUIDES,
ARE AVAILABLE AT DEALERS' THROUGHOUT THE STATE;
CALL 1-800-749-8151 FOR THE NAME OF THE ONE NEAREST YOU.**

Good facilities anchor the chain at Great Harbour Cay Marina on the north and at the Chub Cay Club on the south, Chub Cay is a popular stop on the way to Nassau and the club is a famous sportfishing center that's fast expanding into a first-class resort.

NASSAU, on New Providence Island, is the capital and commercial hub of the Bahamas, a world port with every marine and shore facility, and an international city that truly gives the look and feel of having cruised to another country, which of course you have. The attractions of Nassau and its environs are too numerous to mention here, but make it a port well deserving of its reputation as a superior cruise destination.

Facilities in Nassau Harbour are clustered around the bridge to sheltering Paradise Island, and include the famous Hurricane Hole Marina, East Bay Yacht Basin, Nassau Yacht Haven, and Brown's Boat Basin. Others include the Nassau Harbour Club and Claridge Marina. The harbor is a major port for cruise ships and commercial traffic, and must be negotiated with due care.

Everyone automatically thinks of New Providence as Nassau, but in fact the island itself offers roughly 50 miles of fine coastal cruising around its shorelines. East of Nassau on Paradise Island is a new resort and marina at Paradise Harbour Club. On the west end, Lyford Harbour on West Bay is a popular destination, with moorings, shore facilities and shopping available to transients at the Lyford Cay Club.

Further east on the south shore, the once-popular Coral Harbour Marina is now a Bahamas Defense Force base and closed to civilian craft except in emergencies or for shelter in a storm. The south shore of the island offers no facilities but many opportunities for cruising. Be aware, however, that some of the islands are private.

ANDROS ISLAND, only 15 miles south of Chub Cay and 20 miles west of New Providence Island, is the largest of the Bahamian islands and offers much to anglers and divers but little to cruising boatmen. Low, swampy and heavily forested, the island's interior and west shore are largely uninhabited, but its east shore provides out-island coastal cruising for shallow-draft boats and wonderful fishing for everything from bonefish on the extensive flats to blue-water billfish a short run offshore.

Limited facilities are in the small settlements down the east shore of the island, from Morgan's Bluff and Nicholl's Town on the north to Andros Town further south, where the happy exception is full service at the new Lighthouse Yacht Club and Marina. South of Andros Town, settlements are small and facilities are limited, but the people are hospitable and there are many anchorages in the bights and creek mouths. The three bights, cuts that bisect the island from east to west, offer ultimate gunkholing for shallow-draft boats, but local knowledge or a local guide is highly recommended.

Increased demand from fisherman is upgrading facilities on Andros rapidly, and it may one day become a more popular destination for cruising boatpeople. There is something to be said for enjoying its out-island charm while you can.

ELEUTHERA lies northeast of New Providence Island down a 30-mile chain of small cays from the justly popular winter resorts of Spanish Wells and Harbour Island on the north end, recently joined by the new Royal Island Yacht Club on Royal Island, Pool's Boatyard and Spanish Wells Yacht Haven on Spanish Wells, and Valentine's and the Harbour Island Club on Harbour Island further east.

Ninety miles long and often as little as half a mile wide, the island is beautiful, fertile and prosperous by Bahamian standards, and offers wonderful cruising down Eleuthera Bight and along the west shore, where the settlements and harbors are located. The east shore faces the open Atlantic.

Southward, settlements are spaced at Gregory Town, Hatchet Bay, Governor's Harbour and Rock Sound, with facilities at Marine Services of Eleuthera on the ocean side and at Cape Eleuthera and Davis Harbour Marinas at the south end.

THE EXUMAS are another crescent chain of more than 350 islands stretching 90 miles from Sail Rocks, midway between New Providence and Eleuthera, to the big island of Great Exuma. They are a paradise for cruising, fishing and diving, and good anchorages abound. There are few settlements and fewer marine facilities, but the people are friendly and helpful — no doubt a fuction of their distance away from Miami and off the more popular routes.

In A Class By Itself

Conner says: "Even I know quality!" *When you come to Grand Bahama Island, you have a choice. Lucayan Marina Village offers quality amenities expected by discerning yachtsman. Located in Port Lucaya- Make the right turn after entering Bell Channel.*

LUCAYAN MARINA VILLAGE
GRAND BAHAMA ISLAND

(809) 373-8888
Fax(809) 373-7630

The right choice!

On the way southward down the chain, there are facilities at Highburn Cay, at the Sampson Cay Club on Sampson Cay, at Happy People Marina and Staniel Cay Yacht Club on Staniel Cay, and at the Yacht Club on Little Farmer's Cay. On Great Exuma Island there are facilities at Exuma Docking Services in Elizabeth Harbour. Exuma Docking Services in George Town is near hotels, restaurants and shopping. Further east, Little Exuma and Hog Island offer great cruising and many anchorages but few settlements and no facilities.

LONG ISLAND lies 20 miles east of Little Exuma, 75 miles long and less than four miles wide, with a typical sheltered bight with shallows that force most cruising boats to use direct routes to destinations such as Galliot Cay and Stella Maris on the northwest end and Clarence Town on the southeast shore. There is a full-service marina at Stella Maris with hotel, restaurant and shopping ashore; dockage, service and shopping at Salt Pond further south, and Clarence Town has a town dock with a restaurant and shopping close by.

CAT ISLAND is yet another long, narrow island, 48 miles long and as narrow as one mile, and is the highest of the Bahamas with elevations over 200 feet. The island is roughly 20 miles from the southern tip of Eleuthera with a convenient steppingstone at Little San Salvador Island, which is known for its fine diving and bonefishing. Like Great Abaco and Eleuthera to the north, it offers great cruising in the bight of its sheltered west shore with superior diving and fishing on its coral reefs and flats, great gunkholing up several creeks, and interesting ruins of its plantation past.

There are limited facilities at Fernandez Bay on the bight, and marinas at Hawks Nest Resort and the Cutlass Bay Club on the south shore, but the only thing between are anchorages off small settlements or town docks that must be shared with commercial traffic.

SOUTH AND EAST from Long Island and Cat Island are what the Yachtsman's Guide to the Bahamas calls "The Far Out Islands", which are indeed far out.

Conception Island, San Salvador, Rum Cay, Ragged Island and the Jumentos Cays, Crooked and Acklins Islands, Mayaguana, Great Inagua and the Turks and Caicos Islands stretch like steppingstones for another 250 miles southeast from Long Island.

Note that the Turks and Caicos Islands are only a part of the Bahamas geographically. Politically they are still a British Crown Colony, with different customs, cruising permits, regulations and laws.

All of these are destinations demanding of boats and boatmen but rewarding in adventures that are more Caribbean than Bahamian. Only the well qualified cruise there, and they need no direction from island-hopping lotus eaters like the editors of this Directory.

BAHAMAS TIDE TABLES

Times & Heights of High and Low Waters, Hampton Roads (Sewells Pt.), Va. All times given are Eastern Standard Time; remember to add one hour if Daylight Time. Bahamas Tides are based on Hampton Roads, Virginia. To determine the tides at the following Bahamas locations and those on the opposite page, add or subtract the differences shown here. Note that these corrections are an average of high and low tide differences.

Nassau, New Providence Island,	-1:24
Eleuthera Island, West Coast,	+1:03
The Bight, Cat Island,	-1:50
San Salvador,	-1:25
Clarence Harbor, Long Island,	-0:32
Matthew Town, Great Inagua Island,	-1:05
Elbow Cay, Cay Sal Bank,	+0:05
Fresh Creek, Andros Island,	-0:12
North Cat Cay,	-0:51
North Bimini,	-1:05
Memory Rock,	-0:57
Abaco N. Bar Channel,	-0:55

For greater accuracy, consult the Federal Tide Tables.

[Monthly tide tables for Feb. 1996, March 1996, April 1996, May 1996, June 1996, July 1996, and Aug. 1996, each giving Time and Height (h m, ft, cm) of high and low waters for each day of the month.]

Time meridian 75° W. 0000 is midnight. 1200 is noon.
Heights are referred to mean lower low water which is the chart datum of soundings.

BAHAMAS TIDE TABLES

Times & Heights of High and Low Waters, Hampton Roads (Sewells Pt.), Va. All times given are Eastern Standard Time; remember to add one hour if Daylight Time.
Bahamas Tides are based on Hampton Roads, Virginia. To determine the tides at the following Bahamas locations and those on the opposite page, add or subtract the differences shown here.
Note that these corrections are an average of high and low tide differences. For greater accuracy, consult the Federal Tide Tables.

Nassau, New Providence Island, -1:24
Eleuthera Island, West Coast, +1:03
The Bight, Cat Island, -1:50
San Salvador, -1:25
Clarence Harbor, Long Island, -0:32
Mathew Town, Great Inagua Island, -1:05
Elbow Cay, Cay Sal Bank, +0:05
Fresh Creek, Andros Island, -0:12
North Cat Cay, -0:51
North Bimini, -1:05
Memory Rock, -0:57
Abaco N. Bar Channel, -0:55

Aug. 1996

Day	Time h m	Height ft	Height cm
16 F	0405 1012 1621 2222	0.2 2.8 0.4 2.8	6 85 12 85
17 Sa	0438 1047 1659 2258	0.3 2.8 0.4 2.8	9 85 12 85
18 Su	0511 1123 1740 2336	0.3 2.9 0.5 2.7	9 88 15 82
19 M	0547 1203 1825	0.3 2.9 0.6	9 88 18
20 Tu	0019 0628 1249 1916	2.6 0.4 2.9 0.6	79 12 88 18
21 W	0108 0716 1342 2015	2.5 0.4 2.9 0.6	76 12 88 18
22 Th	0206 0813 1442 2120	2.4 0.4 2.9 0.6	73 12 88 18
23 F	0311 0918 1548 2227	2.4 0.4 3.0 0.5	73 12 91 15
24 Sa	0420 1026 1655 2331	2.5 0.3 3.1 0.3	76 9 94 9
25 Su	0527 1133 1759	2.6 0.2 3.2	79 6 98
26 M	0030 0629 1237 1858	0.1 2.8 0.0 3.3	3 85 0 101
27 Tu	0123 0727 1336 1953	-0.1 3.0 -0.1 3.4	-3 91 -3 104
28 W	0214 0821 1432 2045	-0.2 3.2 -0.2 3.4	-6 98 -6 104
29 Th	0302 0912 1526 2135	-0.3 3.3 -0.3 3.3	-9 101 -9 101
30 F	0349 1002 1618 2223	-0.3 3.4 -0.2 3.2	-9 104 -6 98
31 Sa	0435 1052 1710 2312	-0.3 3.4 -0.1 3.0	-9 104 -3 91

September 1996

Day	Time h m	Height ft	Height cm
1 Su	0522 1141 1802	-0.1 3.3 0.1	-3 101 3
2 M	0001 0609 1232 1856	2.8 0.0 3.1 0.3	85 0 94 9
3 Tu	0051 0658 1324 1952	2.6 0.2 3.0 0.4	79 6 91 12
4 W	0145 0750 1420 2051	2.5 0.4 2.8 0.6	76 12 85 18
5 Th	0242 0846 1519 2151	2.4 0.5 2.7 0.7	73 15 82 21
6 F	0343 0946 1619 2249	2.3 0.6 2.7 0.7	70 18 82 21
7 Sa	0443 1045 1714 2341	2.3 0.7 2.7 0.7	70 21 82 21
8 Su	0538 1140 1804	2.4 0.6 2.8	73 18 85
9 M	0027 0627 1230 1848	0.6 2.6 0.6 2.9	18 79 18 88
10 Tu	0109 0712 1316 1929	0.5 2.7 0.5 2.9	15 82 15 88
11 W	0147 0752 1359 2006	0.4 2.9 0.5 3.0	12 88 15 91
12 Th	0222 0830 1439 2043	0.4 3.0 0.4 3.0	12 91 12 91
13 F	0257 0906 1518 2119	0.3 3.1 0.4 3.0	9 94 12 91
14 Sa	0330 0941 1557 2155	0.3 3.1 0.4 3.0	9 94 12 91
15 Su	0404 1017 1637 2233	0.3 3.2 0.5 2.9	9 98 15 88
16 M	0440 1055 1718 2313	0.4 3.2 0.5 2.8	12 98 15 85
17 Tu	0518 1137 1805 2358	0.4 3.2 0.6 2.7	12 98 18 82
18 W	0602 1224 1857	0.4 3.1 0.6	12 94 18
19 Th	0049 0654 1319 1956	2.6 0.5 3.1 0.6	79 15 94 18
20 F	0149 0754 1422 2102	2.6 0.5 3.0 0.6	79 15 91 18
21 Sa	0256 0903 1531 2208	2.5 0.5 3.0 0.5	76 15 91 15
22 Su	0407 1015 1639 2311	2.6 0.4 3.1 0.4	79 12 94 12
23 M	0514 1124 1743	2.8 0.3 3.2	85 9 98
24 Tu	0008 0615 1227 1842	0.2 3.0 0.1 3.2	6 91 3 98
25 W	0101 0712 1325 1935	0.0 3.2 0.0 3.3	0 98 0 101
26 Th	0150 0804 1419 2026	-0.1 3.4 -0.1 3.3	-3 104 -3 101
27 F	0237 0853 1510 2114	-0.2 3.5 -0.1 3.2	-6 107 -3 98
28 Sa	0323 0940 1600 2200	-0.2 3.5 -0.1 3.1	-6 107 -3 94
29 Su	0407 1027 1649 2246	-0.1 3.4 0.0 3.0	-3 104 0 91
30 M	0451 1113 1737 2333	0.0 3.3 0.2 2.8	0 101 6 85

October 1996

Day	Time h m	Height ft	Height cm
1 Tu	0536 1159 1827	0.2 3.2 0.4	6 98 12
2 W	0020 0623 1248 1918	2.6 0.4 3.0 0.6	79 12 91 18
3 Th	0110 0713 1339 2013	2.5 0.6 2.8 0.7	76 18 85 21
4 F	0205 0808 1435 2109	2.4 0.7 2.7 0.8	73 21 82 24
5 Sa	0304 0907 1532 2205	2.4 0.8 2.7 0.8	73 24 82 24
6 Su	0404 1008 1629 2257	2.4 0.8 2.7 0.7	73 24 82 21
7 M	0500 1106 1721 2343	2.5 0.8 2.7 0.7	76 24 82 21
8 Tu	0551 1159 1808	2.7 0.7 2.8	82 21 85
9 W	0026 0636 1246 1851	0.6 2.8 0.6 2.9	18 85 18 88
10 Th	0105 0717 1330 1931	0.5 3.0 0.5 2.9	15 91 15 88
11 F	0143 0756 1412 2011	0.4 3.1 0.4 3.0	12 94 12 91
12 Sa	0219 0834 1453 2050	0.3 3.2 0.4 3.0	9 98 12 91
13 Su	0256 0912 1534 2130	0.3 3.3 0.3 2.9	9 101 9 88
14 M	0334 0951 1617 2211	0.2 3.3 0.3 2.9	6 101 9 88
15 Tu	0413 1032 1701 2255	0.2 3.3 0.4 2.8	6 101 12 85
16 W	0457 1117 1749 2343	0.3 3.3 0.4 2.7	9 101 12 82
17 Th	0545 1208 1843	0.3 3.2 0.4	9 98 12
18 F	0037 0640 1304 1942	2.6 0.4 3.1 0.5	79 12 94 15
19 Sa	0139 0744 1407 2045	2.6 0.4 3.0 0.4	79 12 91 12
20 Su	0246 0854 1515 2148	2.6 0.5 2.9 0.4	79 15 88 12
21 M	0355 1006 1623 2249	2.7 0.4 2.9 0.2	82 12 88 6
22 Tu	0501 1115 1726 2346	2.9 0.3 2.9 0.1	88 9 88 3
23 W	0601 1217 1824	3.0 0.1 3.0	91 3 91
24 Th	0038 0656 1314 1917	0.0 3.2 0.0 3.0	0 98 0 91
25 F	0126 0746 1406 2006	-0.1 3.3 -0.1 3.0	-3 101 -3 91
26 Sa	0213 0833 1455 2053	-0.2 3.4 -0.1 2.9	-6 104 -3 88
27 Su	0257 0919 1542 2138	-0.1 3.4 -0.1 2.8	-3 104 -3 85
28 M	0340 1002 1627 2222	-0.1 3.3 0.0 2.7	-3 101 0 82
29 Tu	0423 1045 1712 2305	0.0 3.2 0.2 2.6	0 98 6 79
30 W	0506 1128 1757 2350	0.2 3.0 0.3 2.5	6 91 9 76
31 Th	0550 1212 1844	0.4 2.9 0.5	12 88 15

November 1996

Day	Time h m	Height ft	Height cm
1 F	0037 0637 1258 1932	2.4 0.5 2.7 0.6	73 15 82 18
2 Sa	0127 0728 1347 2022	2.3 0.7 2.6 0.6	70 21 79 18
3 Su	0222 0825 1440 2113	2.3 0.7 2.5 0.7	70 21 76 21
4 M	0319 0925 1535 2204	2.3 0.8 2.5 0.6	70 24 76 18
5 Tu	0415 1025 1629 2252	2.4 0.8 2.5 0.6	73 24 76 18
6 W	0507 1121 1720 2337	2.6 0.7 2.5 0.5	79 21 76 15
7 Th	0555 1212 1808	2.7 0.6 2.6	82 18 79
8 F	0021 0639 1259 1854	0.3 2.9 0.4 2.7	9 88 12 82
9 Sa	0102 0722 1345 1938	0.2 3.1 0.3 2.7	6 94 9 82
10 Su	0143 0804 1429 2022	0.1 3.2 0.2 2.8	3 98 6 85
11 M	0225 0846 1513 2106	0.0 3.3 0.1 2.8	0 101 3 85
12 Tu	0308 0929 1559 2152	0.0 3.3 0.1 2.7	0 101 3 82
13 W	0353 1015 1646 2240	0.0 3.3 0.0 2.7	0 101 0 82
14 Th	0441 1103 1736 2331	0.0 3.2 0.1 2.6	0 98 3 79
15 F	0534 1155 1829	0.0 3.1 0.1	0 94 3
16 Sa	0027 0632 1252 1925	2.6 0.1 3.0 0.1	79 3 91 3
17 Su	0129 0736 1353 2025	2.5 0.2 2.8 0.1	76 6 85 3
18 M	0234 0845 1458 2126	2.6 0.2 2.7 0.1	79 6 82 3
19 Tu	0341 0956 1604 2225	2.6 0.2 2.6 0.0	79 6 79 0
20 W	0445 1103 1706 2321	2.7 0.1 2.6 -0.1	82 3 79 -3
21 Th	0545 1205 1804	2.9 0.0 2.6	88 0 79
22 F	0014 0639 1301 1858	-0.2 3.0 -0.1 2.6	-6 91 -3 79
23 Sa	0103 0729 1352 1947	-0.2 3.1 -0.1 2.6	-6 94 -3 79
24 Su	0149 0815 1439 2033	-0.2 3.1 -0.1 2.5	-6 94 -3 76
25 M	0234 0859 1524 2116	-0.2 3.1 -0.1 2.5	-6 94 -3 76
26 Tu	0316 0940 1606 2158	-0.2 3.0 -0.1 2.4	-6 91 -3 73
27 W	0358 1020 1648 2240	-0.1 2.9 0.0 2.4	-3 88 0 73
28 Th	0439 1100 1728 2321	0.1 2.8 0.1 2.3	3 85 3 70
29 F	0520 1139 1809	0.2 2.7 0.2	6 82 6
30 Sa	0004 0604 1219 1851	2.2 0.3 2.6 0.3	67 9 79 9

December 1996

Day	Time h m	Height ft	Height cm
1 Su	0049 0651 1302 1934	2.2 0.4 2.4 0.4	67 12 73 12
2 M	0138 0742 1349 2019	2.2 0.5 2.3 0.4	67 15 70 12
3 Tu	0229 0839 1440 2107	2.2 0.6 2.3 0.4	67 18 70 12
4 W	0323 0938 1534 2157	2.3 0.6 2.2 0.3	70 18 67 9
5 Th	0417 1037 1630 2246	2.4 0.5 2.2 0.2	73 15 67 6
6 F	0510 1133 1724 2335	2.5 0.4 2.3 0.1	76 12 70 3
7 Sa	0600 1226 1816	2.7 0.2 2.3	82 6 70
8 Su	0023 0648 1317 1907	0.0 2.9 0.1 2.4	0 88 3 73
9 M	0111 0736 1405 1956	-0.1 3.0 -0.1 2.5	-3 91 -3 76
10 Tu	0159 0823 1453 2046	-0.3 3.1 -0.2 2.5	-9 94 -6 76
11 W	0248 0911 1541 2135	-0.4 3.2 -0.3 2.6	-12 98 -9 79
12 Th	0338 1000 1630 2226	-0.4 3.2 -0.3 2.6	-12 98 -9 79
13 F	0430 1050 1720 2319	-0.4 3.1 -0.4 2.6	-12 94 -12 79
14 Sa	0524 1143 1811	-0.3 3.0 -0.3	-9 91 -9
15 Su	0015 0623 1238 1905	2.5 -0.2 2.8 -0.3	76 -6 85 -9
16 M	0114 0725 1336 2001	2.5 -0.1 2.6 -0.3	76 -3 79 -9
17 Tu	0217 0832 1437 2059	2.5 -0.1 2.4 -0.2	76 -3 73 -6
18 W	0321 0940 1541 2158	2.5 0.0 2.3 -0.2	76 0 70 -6
19 Th	0425 1047 1644 2255	2.6 0.0 2.2 -0.2	79 0 67 -6
20 F	0526 1149 1743 2350	2.6 -0.1 2.2 -0.3	79 -3 67 -9
21 Sa	0621 1245 1837	2.7 -0.1 2.2	82 -3 67
22 Su	0041 0712 1335 1927	-0.3 2.7 -0.2 2.2	-9 82 -6 67
23 M	0128 0758 1422 2013	-0.3 2.8 -0.2 2.2	-9 85 -6 67
24 Tu	0213 0840 1504 2056	-0.3 2.8 -0.2 2.2	-9 85 -6 67
25 W	0255 0920 1544 2136	-0.3 2.7 -0.2 2.2	-9 82 -6 67
26 Th	0336 0957 1622 2216	-0.2 2.7 -0.1 2.2	-6 82 -3 67
27 F	0415 1033 1659 2254	-0.1 2.6 -0.1 2.2	-3 79 -3 67
28 Sa	0455 1109 1735 2333	0.0 2.5 0.0 2.2	0 76 0 67
29 Su	0535 1145 1811	0.1 2.4 0.0	3 73 0
30 M	0013 0617 1223 1848	2.1 0.2 2.3 0.1	64 6 70 3
31 Tu	0055 0703 1305 1929	2.1 0.3 2.2 0.1	64 9 67 3

January 1997

Day	Time h m	Height ft	Height cm
1 W	0144 0756 1355 2017	2.1 0.4 2.1 0.2	64 12 64 6
2 Th	0235 0853 1448 2107	2.2 0.4 2.1 0.1	67 12 64 3
3 F	0330 0954 1545 2200	2.2 0.4 2.0 0.1	67 12 61 3
4 Sa	0427 1056 1645 2256	2.4 0.3 2.1 0.0	73 9 64 0
5 Su	0524 1155 1744 2351	2.5 0.1 2.1 -0.2	76 3 64 -6
6 M	0620 1251 1841	2.7 -0.1 2.2	82 -3 67
7 Tu	0046 0713 1344 1935	-0.3 2.9 -0.3 2.3	-9 88 -9 70
8 W	0139 0805 1434 2028	-0.5 3.0 -0.4 2.5	-15 91 -12 76
9 Th	0232 0856 1524 2120	-0.6 3.1 -0.6 2.6	-18 94 -18 79
10 F	0325 0947 1613 2212	-0.7 3.1 -0.6 2.6	-21 94 -18 79
11 Sa	0419 1037 1702 2305	-0.7 3.0 -0.7 2.6	-21 91 -21 79
12 Su	0514 1129 1752 2359	-0.6 2.9 -0.6 2.6	-18 88 -18 79
13 M	0610 1221 1843	-0.5 2.7 -0.6	-15 82 -18
14 Tu	0056 0710 1317 1936	2.5 -0.4 2.5 -0.5	76 -12 76 -15
15 W	0155 0813 1415 2032	2.5 -0.2 2.3 -0.4	76 -6 70 -12
16 Th	0258 0918 1516 2130	2.4 -0.1 2.1 -0.3	73 -3 64 -9
17 F	0401 1025 1619 2229	2.4 0.0 2.0 -0.2	73 0 61 -6
18 Sa	0504 1128 1720 2326	2.4 0.0 1.9 -0.2	73 0 58 -6
19 Su	0602 1225 1816	2.4 -0.1 2.0	73 -3 61
20 M	0020 0653 1316 1907	-0.2 2.5 -0.1 2.0	-6 76 -3 61
21 Tu	0109 0739 1401 1953	-0.2 2.5 -0.1 2.1	-6 76 -3 64
22 W	0154 0821 1442 2035	-0.3 2.5 -0.2 2.1	-9 76 -6 64
23 Th	0236 0859 1520 2114	-0.2 2.6 -0.2 2.2	-6 79 -6 67
24 F	0316 0935 1556 2152	-0.2 2.6 -0.2 2.2	-6 79 -6 67
25 Sa	0354 1009 1630 2228	-0.2 2.5 -0.1 2.2	-6 76 -3 67
26 Su	0432 1043 1703 2304	-0.1 2.5 -0.1 2.2	-3 76 -3 67
27 M	0510 1117 1737 2340	0.0 2.4 0.0 2.2	0 73 0 67
28 Tu	0549 1153 1811	0.1 2.3 0.0	3 70 0
29 W	0018 0631 1232 1848	2.2 0.2 2.2 0.0	67 6 67 0
30 Th	0101 0718 1316 1931	2.2 0.3 2.1 0.1	67 9 64 3
31 F	0149 0812 1407 2021	2.2 0.3 2.0 0.1	67 9 61 3

Feb. 1997

Day	Time h m	Height ft	Height cm
1 Sa	0245 0914 1505 2118	2.3 0.3 2.0 0.0	70 9 61 0
2 Su	0346 1020 1609 2220	2.4 0.2 2.0 -0.1	73 6 61 -3
3 M	0450 1124 1714 2323	2.5 0.1 2.1 -0.2	76 3 64 -6
4 Tu	0553 1224 1816	2.7 -0.1 2.2	82 -3 67
5 W	0024 0652 1320 1915	-0.4 2.8 -0.3 2.4	-12 85 -9 73
6 Th	0122 0747 1412 2010	-0.5 3.0 -0.5 2.6	-15 91 -15 79
7 F	0218 0839 1502 2103	-0.7 3.1 -0.6 2.7	-21 94 -18 82
8 Sa	0313 0930 1550 2155	-0.8 3.1 -0.7 2.8	-24 94 -21 85
9 Su	0406 1020 1639 2247	-0.8 3.0 -0.8 2.8	-24 91 -24 85
10 M	0500 1110 1727 2339	-0.7 2.9 -0.7 2.8	-21 88 -21 85
11 Tu	0554 1201 1816	-0.6 2.7 -0.6	-18 82 -18
12 W	0032 0650 1253 1907	2.7 -0.4 2.4 -0.4	82 -12 73 -12
13 Th	0128 0750 1349 2001	2.6 -0.2 2.2 -0.3	79 -6 67 -9
14 F	0228 0852 1448 2059	2.4 0.0 2.1 -0.1	73 0 64 -3
15 Sa	0331 0957 1550 2159	2.3 0.1 2.0 -0.1	70 3 61 -3

Time meridian 75° W. 0000 is midnight. 1200 is noon.
Heights are referred to mean lower low water which is the chart datum of soundings.

CROSSING THE GULF STREAM

Getting There is Half the Fun

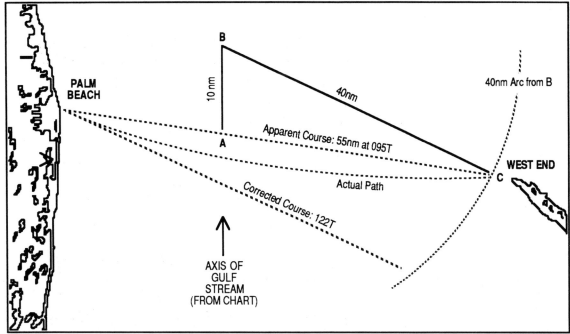

Whatever the destination, any Bahamas cruise involves a fifty-sixty-mile-or-more passage across the northward-flowing Gulf Stream. One of the wonders of the world, the Stream is by far the largest and strongest ocean current, carrying a volume 25 times the flow of all the rivers in the world at a speed averaging 2.5 knots.

When the wind is light and/or blowing with the current, passage to the Bahamas is a smooth and easy cruise. But when the wind opposes the current, it can be the longest sixty miles on earth. Whenever boatpeople play the game of "my water is rougher than your water", even nasties like the English Channel have to take second place to the Gulf Stream during a norther.

It goes without writing that the most important ingredient in any successful crossing is a good and accurate weather forecast. Your best friend is a weather forecaster with up-to-date information.

Be particularly alert for cold fronts moving southward and eastward down from the mainland in the winter months and for tropical storm formation the rest of the year. The "Hurricane Season" from June to November is a figure of speech; there have been hurricanes in every month on the calendar.

The next most important concern is navigating from the big solid mainland to a tiny island across a current that flows at near-right angles to your course at speeds that can vary from near-zip to over four knots but average two and a half knots from one side to the other.

Plotting a course across the Gulf Stream requires you to calculate how far the current will carry you to the north, then set a more southerly course to compensate for that drift. That's a function of how far the current will carry you compared to how far your boat will travel in the same time, and it's not all that difficult.

If you draw a triangle with its base along your apparent course, its height the speed and direction of the current, and its hypotenuse the speed of your boat, the angle of the hypotenuse will be your corrected course.

Let's assume you're on a ten-knot boat heading out of Palm Beach for West End on Grand Bahama. That's a distance of 55 nautical miles on an apparent course of 095 degrees true (the dotted line on the diagram above).

You first find the point where your course intersects the axis of the Gulf Stream (usually indicated on the chart) and mark it point A.

You then draw a line parallel to the axis that is equal to the amount of drift in any given period of time. (We chose four hours, but could just as well have used one hour or ten hours — the triangle would be the same except for its size.)

You draw a line 10 nautical miles long parallel to the axis, representing 2.5 knots of drift for four hours (2.5 X 4 = 10). Mark the end of the line Point B. Line AB is the distance your boat will drift in four hours.

From Point B, you draw an arc with its radius equal to the distance you will travel in the same arbitrary time (four hours at ten knots, or 40 nautical miles). Where the arc intersects the apparent course (the dotted line) you mark Point C. The angle of Line BC represents the corrected course to West End.

That's it. Transfer Line BC to a compass rose with parallel rules to find the bearing, in this case 122 degrees true (or 125 degrees magnetic).

In the calm knowledge that the Stream will not flow at the same rate all the way across, take position fixes with GPS or Loran or check with your radio direction finder as you go and adjust your course accordingly.

It's easy to depend on these conveniences, perhaps too easy. When something goes wrong with them, and it will, it's good to have the charts, equipment, and navigational know-how to get there the old way, and crossing the stream is a great way to keep in practice.

CRUISING FLORIDA'S

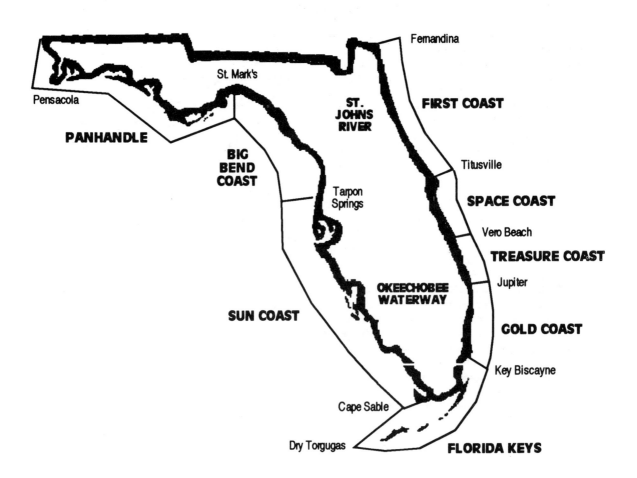

Fernandina

St. Mark's

FIRST COAST

Pensacola

ST. JOHNS RIVER

PANHANDLE

BIG BEND COAST

Titusville

SPACE COAST

Tarpon Springs

Vero Beach

TREASURE COAST

Jupiter

OKEECHOBEE WATERWAY

SUN COAST

GOLD COAST

Key Biscayne

Cape Sable

Dry Torgugas

FLORIDA KEYS

PANHANDLE COUNTIES
EAST FROM PENSACOLA
Escambia (Pensacola)
Santa Rosa (Gulf Breeze)
Okaloosa (Fort Walton Beach)
Walton (Sandestin)
Bay (Panama City)
Gulf (Port St. Joe)
Franklin (Apalachicola)
Wakulla (St. Marks)
Jefferson

GULF COAST COUNTIES
SOUTH FROM ST. MARKS
Taylor (Steinhatchee)
Dixie (Suwannee)
Levy (Cedar Key)
Citrus (Crystal River)
Hernando (Bayport)
Pasco (Hudson)
Pinellas (St. Petersburg)
Hillsborough (Tampa)
Manatee (Bradenton)
Sarasota (Sarasota)
Charlotte (Port Charlotte)
Lee (Cape Coral)
Collier (Naples)
Monroe (Flamingo)

EAST COAST COUNTIES
SOUTH FROM FERNANDINA
Nassau (Fernandina)
Duval (Jacksonville)
St. Johns (St. Augustine)
Flagler (Palm Coast)
Volusia (Daytona Beach)
Brevard (Titusville)
Indian River (Vero Beach)
St. Lucie (Fort Pierce)
Martin (Stuart)
Palm Beach (Palm Beach)
Broward (Fort Lauderdale)
Dade (Miami)
Monroe (The Keys)

COASTAL WATERWAYS

Nowhere on earth have geology and technology combined to present boatpeople with a finer cruising environment than the Intracoastal Waterways that circle the state of Florida, which welcome cruising boats from kayaks to megayachts with equanimity and hospitality.

The Atlantic Intracoastal Waterway is the great "ditch" that provides protected passage from Fernandina on the Georgia-Florida line to land's end at Key West, and the Gulf Intracoastal Waterway provides the same ease and safety up the Gulf Coast and across the Panhandle with gaps only past the western Everglades and up the Big Bend Coast.

Not really a ditch, but a series of natural rivers, bays, lakes, sounds and lagoons connected by canals, dredged to commercial depths, and marked better than most highways, the ICW is unique among the world's recreational waterways, yet recreation was the furthest thing from its builders' motives. In roadless pre-rail Florida, it was the main — and only — artery, plied by sail and steam boats carrying everything from southbound settlers to northbound pineapples.

The waterway was conceived in the mid-1500s by Spanish Colonial Governor Manuel de Montiado to move troops to defend his colony at St. Augustine.

Construction did not begin until 1853 when the Army Engineers dug through the Indian haulover between the Mosquito Lagoon and the Indian River to open a 150-mile stretch between New Smyrna Beach and Cocoa. The 1855 Florida Legislature offered land grants to developers to complete the waterway. In the post-hurricane bust of 1927 the legislature created the Florida Inland Navigation District to take over the project, and in 1935 the Army Engineers opened the last cut to complete the 525-mile Atlantic ICW as we know it.

Today the waterway has a project depth of 12 feet from the Georgia line to Fort Pierce, ten feet from there to Miami, and seven feet from Miami south, with a controlling height of 65 feet everywhere but under the 55-foot Julia Tuttle Causeway Bridge in Miami.

It is still owned by the F.I.N.D. and maintained by the Corps of Engineers, with its management shared between the U.S. Coast Guard and the Florida Department of Environmental Protection.

It remained for the Chambers of Commerce along the way to name their distinctive sections of coastline along the waterway — the First Coast, from the state line to Titusville; the Space Coast, from Titusville to south of Sebastian; the Treasure Coast, from Vero Beach to Jupiter; the Gold Coast, from Palm Beach to Key Biscayne, and the Florida Keys, which needed no Chamber of Commerce to provide a name that beckons cruising boatmen from everywhere in the world.

Not to be outpromoted, C-of-Cs on the Gulf Coast proclaimed the 175-odd miles from Marco Island to Tarpon Springs The Sun Coast. The Gulf Intracoastal Waterway through that area is largely natural, with the many barrier islands sheltering the route naturally and only a few short landcuts needed to connect them.

The Big Bend and Panhandle didn't need renaming, but the Panhandle did need a lot more work, to dig and dredge landcuts connecting Apalachicola Bay to Choctawhatchee Bay by way of St. Andrews Bay at Panama City Beach. The result is nearly 200 miles of protected cruising from Carrabelle to the Alabama border.

Inland, two unique freshwater waterways also beckon — the beautiful St. Johns River, winding deep inland for a third the length of the state, and the Okeechobee Waterway crossing the peninsula from Stuart to Fort Myers by way of Lake Okeechobee. These, too, offer sheltered cruising water and hospitable ports for cruising boatpeople to explore and enjoy.

Offshore, the Bahama Islands offer Caribbean cruising to exotic foreign ports as close as 42 miles from Florida's east coast and stretching 800 miles to the Turks and Caicos, halfway to Trinidad.

So much beautiful cruising water, so little space to describe it. Let's get to work:

CRUISING FLORIDA'S FIRST COAST

They call it the First Coast for two reasons: It was the first to be discovered — by French and Spanish explorers a hundred years before the Pilgrims landed at Plymouth Rock — and it is the first you come to as you enter Florida on the Intracoastal Waterway. Whichever, it's a wonderful introduction to Florida waters, with uncrowded cruising, anchoring and gunkholing, fishing and touristing and beaching opportunities everywhere, and served by excellent facilities.

The Georgia-Florida line runs through the middle of St. Mary's entrance at about Mile 712, with Georgia's Cumberland Island on the north and Florida's Amelia Island on the south. At this point the Intracoastal Waterway runs through a chain of rivers, creeks and sloughs that separate the mainland from the barrier islands. The area teems with fish and wildlife, and off-channel anchorages can be found almost everywhere.

Amelia Island is guarded by Fort Clinch, a pre-Civil War battlement that is now part of Fort Clinch State Park. The park welcomes visitors both by land and water, but seldom attracts enough to generate a crowd.

Further south lies the very old town of Fernandina Beach, which has the distinction of having existed under more flags than any other place in the country — eight: France, Spain, England, Mexico, the Republics of Georgia and Florida, the Confederate States and the United States.

Originally an important seaport and railhead, Fernandina gained popularity among early snowbirds who built wonderful Victorian houses there. The whole town has been restored, and is full of stores and shops from the familiar to the exotic. Tiger Point Marina is at the north end of the island right in Old Fernandina with a popular restaurant next door. Further south, the fuel dock at Florida Petroleum offers good prices to boats tall enough to reach its pumps.

Further downstream and right downtown in Fernandina Beach is popular Fernandina Harbor Marina, with an 800-foot floating breakwater and dock and a waterfront restaurant. If downtown docking isn't your style, Amelia Island Yacht Basin is further south on Kingsley Creek with its own entrance canal at Marker 13 just north of the bridge to the mainland. They welcome transients at floating docks in a sheltered basin and have complete boatyard facilities.

Cruising types who prefer isolation have a wide choice of anchorages among the many bayous, sloughs, meanders and rivers that adjoin the ICW proper. These include Nassau Sound, Fort George River, and the great St. John's River, which the ICW crosses just upstream

EDITOR's NOTE: This is based on the current list maintained by the Florida Department of Environmental Protection, and while it was updated shortly before press time, changes are constant and it's a good idea to check ramps in advance. Note that some ramps are in marinas, private clubs or condominiums where public access may be limited.

ST JOHNS COUNTY BOAT RAMPS

CRESCENT BEACH
Green Road County Boat Ramp — Green Rd. off SR 206 on Matanzas River
PALM VALLEY
Palm Valley Fish Camp — SR 210 on ICW
ST. AUGUSTINE
Boating Club Road Boat Ramp — 16th St. off US A1A on Tolomato River
Devil's Elbow Fish Camp — on Matanzas River
Faver-Dykes — US 1 on Pellicer Creek
Lighthouse Park — Off A1A on Anastasia Island on Salt Run off Matanzas River
North Beach Camp Resort — 2300 Coastal Hwy. on Tolamato River
Usina Fish Camp — 614 Euclid Ave., North Bch. on ICW
Viland Boat Basin — US A1A off Tolomato River
ST. AUGUSTINE BCH.
Palmetto Road County Boat Ramp — Palmetto Rd. on Matanzas River
Cooksey's Camping Resort — SR 53
Frank S. Butler Recreation Area — US A1A on ICW on Atlantic Ocean

VOLUSIA COUNTY BOAT RAMPS

DAYTONA BEACH
Halifax Harbor — 450 Basin St. *(Four ramps)*
Pelican Island Marina & Fish Camp — 3226 Riverview La. on Halifax River
Seabreeze Park & Boat Ramp — 100 Seabreeze Blvd. on Halifax River
South Peninsula Marina — 3348 S. Peninsula Dr. on ICW
DeLAND
Blue Lake Ramp — Blue Lake Ave.
Ed Stone Park — West SR 44
West SR 44 — At Boat Show Marina
EDGEWATER
Kennedy Park — Riverside Dr. on Indian River
Menard-Way Park — 400 S. Riverside Dr. on Atlantic Ocean
HOLLY HILL
Aloha Marina — 10 2nd St. on ICW
Sunrise Park — Riverside Dr. on Indian River
NEW SMYRNA BEACH
JB's Fish Camp — 859 Pompano St. on ICW
North Causeway Boat Ramp — SR 44 on Indian River
SOUTH OF NEW SMYRNA BEACH
Canaveral National Seashore — 7611 S. Atlantic Blvd., Mosquito Lagoon & Atlantic Ocean
OAK HILL
Bissett Bay Fish Camp — 251 Bissett Bay Rd. on ICW
Golden Bay Colony — on Indian River
LeFils Fish Camp — 1123 E. Halifax Ave. on Indian River
Lopez Fish Camp — on Mosquito Lagoon
Riverwood Park Campground — 398 HH Burch Rd. on ICW
ORMOND BEACH
High Bridge Park — US A1A on Halifax River (7 mi. n. of Ormond Bch.)
Ormond Marina — 1618 John Anderson Dr. on Halifax River
Tomoka State Park — SR 201, N. Beach St. on Tomoka River
PONCE INLET
Inlet Harbor Marina — 124 Inlet Harbor Rd. on Halifax River
Perry's South Peninsula Marina — 3948 S. Peninsula Dr. on ICW
PORT ORANGE
Port Orange Causeway — A1A & Dunlawton Ave. on Halifax River
Sailboat Headquarters — 914 Halifax Dr. on Halifax River
SOUTH DAYTONA
Riverfront Park — 1933 S. Palmetto Ave. on Halifax River

CLAY COUNTY BOAT RAMPS

GREEN COVE SPRINGS
Shands Bridge Pier & Ramp — SR 16 on St. Johns River

NASSAU COUNTY BOAT RAMPS

AMELIA ISLAND
Amelia Island Plantation — SR 108 on Amelia River
Nassau Sound County Boat Ramp — US A1A on Nassau Sound
FERNANDINA BEACH
Fort Clinch State Park — 2601 Atlantic Ave. on Amelia River & Atlantic Ocean
Fourteenth Street Marina — 1620 N. 14th St. on Egan Creek
Oceanfront Park — Centre St. on Amelia River
Oceanfront Park — Sadler Rd.
NASSAVILLE
Holly Point Community Park — on Nassau River

DUVAL COUNTY BOAT RAMPS

FORT GEORGE ISLAND
Oyster Shell Fish Camp — 9970 Heckscher Dr. on St. Johns River
Sisters Creek Boat Ramp — 8364 Heckscher Dr. on St. Johns River
JACKSONVILLE
Arlington Road Boat Ramp — West end of Arlington Rd., St. Johns River
Buddy's Fish Camp — 9023 Cedar Point Rd. on ICW
Clapboard Creek Fish Camp — 6233 Heckscher Dr. on St. Johns River
County Dock Road Boat Ramp — County Dock Rd. on St. Johns River
Fletcher Morgan Park — 6736 Beach Blvd.
Florida Yacht Club — 5210 Yacht Club Rd. on St. Johns River *(Private)*
Huguenot Memorial Park — 10980 Heckscher Dr., Ft. George Isl., St. Johns River
Lonnie Wurn Boat Ramp — 4131 Ferber Rd. on St. Johns River
New Berlin Road Boat Landing — Frederick Rd. on St. Johns River
Oak Harbor Boat Ramp — 2428 Seaway St. on Pablo Creek
Palms Fish Camp — 6259 Heckscher Dr. on Clapboard Creek
Pirates Cove Fish Camp — 8076 Heckscher Dr. on St. Johns River
Riverwalk Park — 901 Gulf Life Dr. on St. Johns River
T. K. Stokes Boat Landing — 2120 Riverview Ave. on Ribault River
JACKSONVILLE BEACH
Jacksonville Yacht Basin — 14603 Beach Blvd.
The Moorings — 14750 Beach Blvd. on ICW
MAYPORT
Mayport-Ocean Street Park — 4870 Ocean St. on St. Johns River

FLAGLER COUNTY BOAT RAMPS

FLAGLER BEACH
Launch Ramp Beach Access — At Moody Blvd. off A1A
Moody Boat Launch — SR 100 on ICW
MARINELAND
Marineland of Florida — 9507 Oceanshore Blvd.
PALM COAST
Palm Coast Marina — 200 Clubhouse Dr. on ICW
ST. AUGUSTINE
Bings Landing Park — on SR A1A, the Hammock, ICW 3 mi. s. of Marineland

MARION COUNTY BOAT RAMPS

FORT McCOY
Jano R. Recreational Development — On Lake George

Get it done RIGHT!

If your powerboat or sailboat needs work, St. Augustine Marine is a great choice. Friendly, knowledgeable people, quality service and the right equipment to make it happen. Want to do your own work? Help Yourself *PLUS* is a do-it-yourself yard program with expert advisors and service assistance available. Need parts? On-site supplies at catalog prices. So give us a call on your VHF, cellular or by land line. And enjoy all that St. Augustine has to offer while your boat is being repaired.

- **Long & short term dry storage**
- **Major do-it-yourself area with water & electric**
- **Advanced rigging service**
- **Repowering service, Yanmar & Marine Power warranty & service**
- **Inside painting facilities**
- **Carpentry, fiberglass, steel & aluminum fabrication**
- **On-site marine supplies at catalog prices**
- **75 Ton mobile boat hoist**
- **100 Ton railway**
- **Full service yacht brokerage on site**

ST. AUGUSTINE MARINE

404 South Riberia Street, St. Augustine, FL 32084
ICW Mile Marker 774 ■ VHF 16
Phone 904/824-4394
Fax 904/824-9755

from its mouth at Mayport. Be aware of the area's unusually wide tidal range — seven to ten feet — and the strong currents that result. A tide table is absolutely essential for everything from calculating bridge clearances to selecting an anchorage that won't be a mud flat in the morning. Note that the channel under the bridge at the mouth of the Nassau River has shoaled to impassibility.

Past Amelia Island the ICW follows a long cut down Sisters Creek. Past Jacksonville Marina and under the highway bridge at the mouth of Sisters Creek, you sail out into the broad St. Johns River with Mayport to the east and the river to Jacksonville to the west.

Here the cruising skipper faces one of the many win-win decisions typical in Florida cruising — whether to turn upstream to Jacksonville and the unequalled river cruising on the St. Johns, or to continue southward down the waterway toward the attractions that beckon every night with the glow they cast in the southern sky. Toss a coin; you can't make a bad decision. Better still, do both, as we will in the following pages.

The ICW crosses the St. Johns southward across Chicopit Bay and down Pablo Creek past Jacksonville Beach, then enters a long cut to the Tolomato River at Palm Valley, around Mile 750. Through that area, where the Engineers straightened rivers, they left oxbows such as the loop around Pine Island at Mile 765, which offer great anchorages and good fishing.

Marine facilities along this stretch tend to be clustered in groups. The most northerly group is at Atlantic Beach and Jacksonville Beach between Mile 745 and Mile 748, and includes Pablo Creek Marina. After that point there are some fishing camps and such along the way, but the next major facility is at Camachee Cove north of St. Augustine at Mile 775.7.

Camachee Cove is a very complete facility with dockage and restaurants and all the other features that make a great place to stop while you visit the nation's oldest town, St. Augustine. Other facilities include St. Augustine Marine, Sebastian Harbor, Conch House and Coquina Marina, which was formerly Oasis Marine. The city also offers room to moor or anchor right downtown at St. Augustine City Marina.

Heading south past Camachee Cove, the waterway passes under the old Vilano Beach lift bridge and boatpeople admire the new high bridge nearing completion. Below, just inside St. Augustine Inlet, strong tides, currents and winds combine with constant shoaling to test your ability to stay close to the center of the channel. The waterway turns west past St. Augustine, then south into the Matanzas River.

The Spanish settled St. Augustine in 1565, but it remained a remote and dangerous outpost until the 1880s, when it was discovered by Henry Flagler, who had made his first fortune as a partner of John D. Rockefeller in Standard Oil. He built a luxury hotel for snowbirds in St. Augustine and a railroad from Jacksonville to bring them in, and it was the beginning of his second fortune, as builder of the Florida East Coast Railroad. We run into his legacy time and time again as we move down the east coast.

South of St. Augustine at Mile 792 on the north shore of Rattlesnake Island lie the ruins of Fort Matanzas, built by the Spanish to guard the southern approach to St. Augustine. Matanzas means massacre, and the name commemorates the Spanish slaughter of the last of the French Huguenot colonists in Florida. Now part of the National Park System, the fort is open to visitors by boat or by ferry from the mainland. Matanzas Inlet rivals St. Augustine's for tides, currents and winds that make course-holding difficult, complicated by constant shoaling, especially along Rattlesnake Island. Its passing is best made on a highish tide.

Just down the coast from Matanzas Pass is the world's first oceanarium, Marineland of Florida, where a very popular marina offers full services including a hotel and restaurant on the beach and a great reputation for hospitality to transient boats.

South of Marineland the tide and current problems ease as you near the beautiful planned city of Palm Coast with Treworgy Yachts on the north and Palm Coast Marina, which has been described as "the nicest little marina on the east coast", on the south. Six miles further south inside Silver Lake, Flagler Marina and Boatyard also offers transient facilities.

On down the coast, the ICW alternates between narrow Smith Creek and even narrower land cuts past

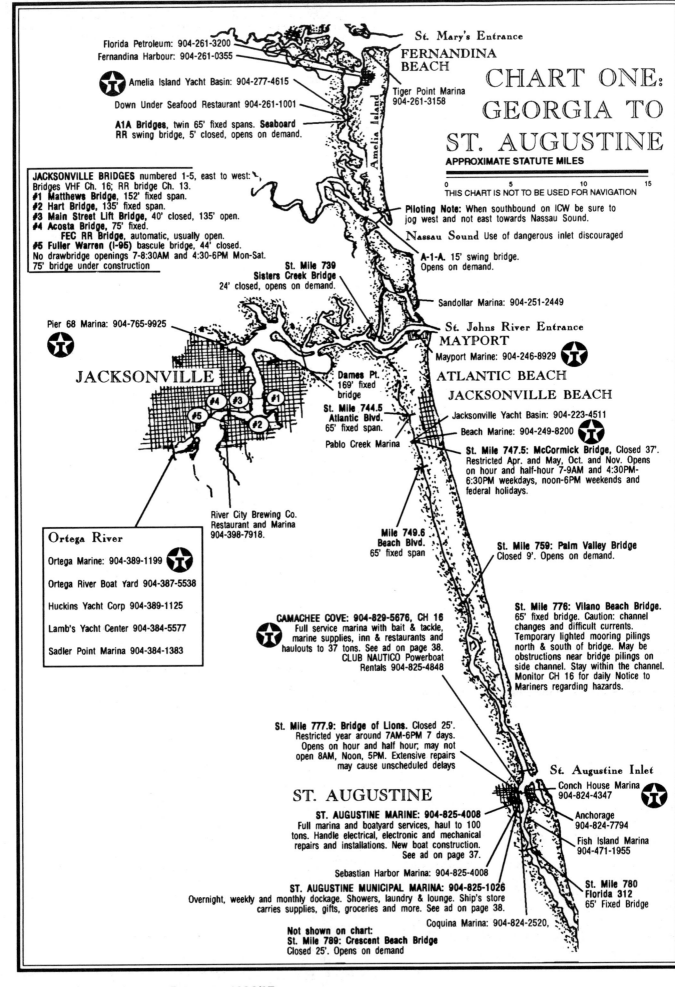

Florida Petroleum: 904-261-3200
Fernandina Harbour: 904-261-0355

Amelia Island Yacht Basin: 904-277-4615

Down Under Seafood Restaurant 904-261-1001

A1A Bridges, twin 65' fixed spans. **Seaboard**
RR swing bridge, 5' closed, opens on demand.

St. Mary's Entrance
**FERNANDINA
BEACH**

Tiger Point Marina
904-261-3158

CHART ONE:
GEORGIA TO
ST. AUGUSTINE

APPROXIMATE STATUTE MILES

0   5   10   15
THIS CHART IS NOT TO BE USED FOR NAVIGATION

JACKSONVILLE BRIDGES numbered 1-5, east to west:
Bridges VHF Ch. 16; RR bridge Ch. 13.
#1 Matthews Bridge, 152' fixed span.
#2 Hart Bridge, 135' fixed span.
#3 Main Street Lift Bridge, 40' closed, 135' open.
#4 Acosta Bridge, 75' fixed.
    FEC RR Bridge, automatic, usually open.
#5 Fuller Warren (I-95) bascule bridge, 44' closed.
No drawbridge openings 7-8:30AM and 4:30-6PM Mon-Sat.
75' bridge under construction

Piloting Note: When southbound on ICW be sure to
jog west and not east towards Nassau Sound.

Nassau Sound Use of dangerous inlet discouraged

A-1-A. 15' swing bridge.
Opens on demand.

St. Mile 739
Sisters Creek Bridge
24' closed, opens on demand.

Sandollar Marina: 904-251-2449

Pier 68 Marina: 904-765-9925

St. Johns River Entrance
MAYPORT
Mayport Marine: 904-246-8929

JACKSONVILLE

ATLANTIC BEACH
JACKSONVILLE BEACH

Dames Pt.
169' fixed
bridge

St. Mile 744.5
Atlantic Blvd.
65' fixed span.

Pablo Creek Marina

Jacksonville Yacht Basin: 904-223-4511

Beach Marine: 904-249-8200

St. Mile 747.5: McCormick Bridge, Closed 37'.
Restricted Apr. and May, Oct. and Nov. Opens
on hour and half-hour 7-9AM and 4:30PM-
6:30PM weekdays, noon-6PM weekends and
federal holidays.

River City Brewing Co.
Restaurant and Marina
904-398-7918.

Mile 749.6
Beach Blvd.
65' fixed span

St. Mile 759: Palm Valley Bridge
Closed 9'. Opens on demand.

Ortega River

Ortega Marine: 904-389-1199

Ortega River Boat Yard 904-387-5538

Huckins Yacht Corp 904-389-1125

Lamb's Yacht Center 904-384-5577

Sadler Point Marina 904-384-1383

St. Mile 776: Vilano Beach Bridge.
65' fixed bridge. Caution: channel
changes and difficult currents.
Temporary lighted mooring pilings
north & south of bridge. May be
obstructions near bridge pilings on
side channel. Stay within the channel.
Monitor CH 16 for daily Notice to
Mariners regarding hazards.

CAMACHEE COVE: 904-829-5676, CH 16
Full service marina with bait & tackle,
marine supplies, inn & restaurants and
haulouts to 37 tons. See ad on page 38.
CLUB NAUTICO Powerboat
Rentals 904-825-4848

St. Mile 777.9: Bridge of Lions. Closed 25'.
Restricted year around 7AM-6PM 7 days.
Opens on hour and half hour; may not
open 8AM, Noon, 5PM. Extensive repairs
may cause unscheduled delays

St. Augustine Inlet
Conch House Marina
904-824-4347

ST. AUGUSTINE

Anchorage
904-824-7794

ST. AUGUSTINE MARINE: 904-825-4008
Full marina and boatyard services, haul to 100
tons. Handle electrical, electronic and mechanical
repairs and installations. New boat construction.
See ad on page 37.

Fish Island Marina
904-471-1955

Sebastian Harbor Marina: 904-825-4008

St. Mile 780
Florida 312
65' Fixed Bridge

ST. AUGUSTINE MUNICIPAL MARINA: 904-825-1026
Overnight, weekly and monthly dockage. Showers, laundry & lounge. Ship's store
carries supplies, gifts, groceries and more. See ad on page 38.

Coquina Marina: 904-824-2520,

Not shown on chart:
St. Mile 789: Crescent Beach Bridge
Closed 25'. Opens on demand

Flagler Beach, finally entering the Halifax River at about Mile 818 and going through the city of Daytona Beach. The city is much better known for auto racing and spring break than for marine involvement, but there are half a dozen marine facilities spaced along the mainland side, including English Jim's right downtown and Halifax Harbor, which is the old Municipal Yacht Basin renovated into a first-class, state-of-the-art marina with facilities that include a clubhouse and a big launching ramp. Just south, above the Port Orange bridge on the mainland side, is Seven Seas Marina.

The Halifax River ends at Ponce de Leon Inlet, Mile 842. The lovely lighthouse that marks the inlet is back in operation, and includes a museum that you are welcome to visit. Facilities are on the barrier island and include Ponce Deepwater Landing, Lighthouse Boatyard and Sea Love Marina.

From the inlet the ICW follows the Indian River North southward to New Smyrna, another very old town. It was founded in 1763 by Andrew Turnbull, who indentured 1,500 Greeks to emigrate to the New World and work his indigo plantation. The Greeks named the new town for their old home, and the plantation flourished until Dr. Turnbull's heirs were forced to free the Greeks during the Revolution.

If you've always found New Smyrna Beach by using the water tower on your chart as a landmark, note that Commander H.C. Munns of the Coast Guard Auxiliary reports that it has been torn down.

Among the several marine facilities in New Smyrna is the Riverview Hotel at mile 845.3, now owned and operated by Jim and Christa Kelsey, who formerly operated the first-rate facility at Faro Blanco in Marathon. If anchoring out is more your style, the popular Sheephead Cut anchorage is on the south side of the island between the two bridges, half a mile by dinghy from downtown.

South of New Smyrna the Indian River North widens into Mosquito Lagoon, wide and beautiful but shallow, which extends 120 miles southward to St. Lucie Inlet and is home to everything from the spacecraft of Cape Kennedy to the alligators, eagles and pelicans of the two wildlife preserves it passes. There are hundreds of islands and plenty of places to anchor and dock, camp and beach. The lagoon is alive with dolphins, and the fishing is excellent.

For all of the natural beauty, most cruising types are happy to reach Mile 869, where the first land cut made for the ICW does a sharp turn to the west through the ancient Indian Haulover and into the deeper water of Indian River Lagoon.

The area is steeped in history, with its oldest settlements dating to the early 1800s – Titusville was the northern terminus of the steamboat line that once carried passengers south and fruit north to and from towns like Cocoa, Melbourne, Vero Beach and Fort Pierce to its southern terminus at Jupiter.

Then, in a cruising version of Future Shock, you find yourself suddenly out of the oldest of the "Coasts" and into the newest.

EDITOR's NOTE: This is based on the current list maintained by the Florida Department of Environmental Protection, and while it was updated shortly before press time, changes are constant and it's a good idea to check ramps in advance. Note that some ramps are in marinas, private clubs or condominiums where public access may be limited.

OKEECHOBEE WATERWAY

COUNTY/RAMP NAME	LOCATION
GLADES	
Alvin Ward, Sr. Memorial Park	US 27 at Daniels Rd., Moore Haven
Meadowlark Campground	On Caloosahatchee River, Moore Haven
Moore Haven Rec. Village	1st St. N.
Ortona Lock Public Use Area	Off SR 80 & 78 on Caloosahatchee River
Sportsman's Marina	Moore Haven, off SR 78 on Lake Okeechobee
Uncle Joe's Fish Camp	Canal off Lake Okeechobee, Moore Haven
HENDRY	
Belle-Hatchee Marina	121 River Bend Dr.
Clewiston Rec. Area	Lake Okeechobee
LaBelle	Hendry County Wayside Park off CR 78, 1 blk. w. of Hwy. 29 bridge.
LaBelle Lion's Club Park Bob Mason	Caloosahatchee River
LEE	
Alva Boat Ramp	17200 Josephine St. on Caloosahatchee River
Davis Blvd. Boat Ramp	2227 Davis Blvd. on Caloosahatchee River, Ft. Myers
Franklin Locks Rec. Area	SR 78 on Caloosahatchee River, 1 mi. e. of Olga
Island Club Marina	1687 Inlet Dr. on Caloosahatchee River, North Fort Myers
MARTIN	
Hosford Park	7474 SW Gaines Ave., S. Fork of St. Lucie River, Stuart
Indiantown Marina	16300 SW Famel Ave., Indiantown
Lare Okeechobee Boat Ramp & Pier	Wood St. off US 98 & 441 at
Chancey Bay	Lake Okeechobee, n. of Port Mayaca
Pendarvis Point Park	1100 SW Chapman Way on St. Lucie River, Palm City
Phipps Park	2175 SW Locks Rd. at Gregor Way (FL tpke to Stuart, W. on 714, 1 mi. to 76A, S. for 5 mi. Turns into S76A. Follow over Okeechobee, then 1.2 mi. to Locks Rd. Signs to Phipps Park [& St. Lucie Lock & Dam]. Take Locks rd. to Phipps Park, follow dirt rd. to tpke. overpass. Ramp is under tpke.)
Port Mayaca Public Use Area	SR 76 & US 441 on Lake Okeechobee
St. Lucie Lock Public Use Area	Off SR 76A on St. Lucie Canal, SW of Palm City
PALM BEACH	
Belle Glade Rec. Area	Off CR 717, Lake Okeechobee
Canal Point Public Use Area	N. of Pahokee
J-Mark Fish Camp	SR 717, Torry Island on Lake Okeechobee, Belle Glade
Pahokee Marina Ccmpground	190 Lower Lakeview Dr.
Slim's Fish Camp	Belle Glade
South Bay Access Area	US 27 & Rim Canal

ST. JOHNS RIVER BOAT RAMPS

COUNTY/RAMP NAME	LOCATION
BREVARD	
Camp Holley Fish Camp	US 192, Melbourne
Lake Poinsett Lodge & Marina	5665 Lake Poinsett Dr.
Lone Cabbage Fish Camp	1104 Lake Poinsett Dr., Cocoa
CLAY	
Black Creek Marina	1492 River La., Green Cove Springs
Governor's Creek Park	Green Cove Springs US Hwy. 17
Riverview Travel Trailer Town	Green Cove Springs, 2982 US 17 N.
Williams Park	US 17, 6 mi. s. of Green Cove Springs
DUVAL	
Fla. Community College	GETS Marine Ctr. 6935 Evergreen Ave.
Goodby's Lake Marina	8931 San Jose Blvd.
Jacksonville NAS	US 17
Old Buccaneer	9636 Heckscher Dr., Ft. George Island
Rudder Club of Jacksonville	8533 Malaga Ave., Orange Park
LAKE	
Astor-Butler St. & Pearl St.	Off SR 40, end of Butler St. & Pearl St.
Lake George Boat Ramp	Off SR 40, End of Lake George Rd., NW of Astor
Powell's Marina & Campground	Off SR 40, Moses Levy Grant, Astor
Palatka	US 17 in Palatka, s. on River St. to ramp
PUTNAM	
Brown's Landing	Lundy Rd. on St. Johns River, 2 mi. s. of Palatka
Elgen Grove Launch Area	SR 207A, East Palatka
J.C. Godwin Riverfront Park	River & Laurel Sts., Palatka
Merck's Landing	Off SR 309, Georgetown
Palatka River Boat Ramp	US 17 to Pico St., West to ramp, East Palatka
Palmetto Bluff Rd. Boat Ramp	Off SR 209 on St. John's River, Bridgeport
Shell Harbor	Off SR 309, 2 mi. n, of Welaka
St. Johns Dock & Ramp #33	N. 33rd & River St., Palatka
Sunset Landing	Front St. off CR 308B
Trail Boss Fish Camp	Front St. off CR 308B, Welaka
Welaka Boat Ramp	SR 309 & Front St.
SEMINOLE	
Lake Monroe Wayside Park	Off SR 600/US 17 on Lake Monroe, 3 mi. nw of Sanford
Monroe Harbor Marina	531 N. Palmetto Ave., Sanford
Osteen Bridge Fish Camp	SR 415 on St. Johns River
ST JOHNS	
Palmo Cove	SR 13 n. of SR 208, w. on Palmo Cove Rd. 1.75 mi. to ramp
Riverdale Park	CR 13 s. of CR 214
Tocoi Fish Camp	St. Augustine
VOLUSIA	
Ed Stone Park	SR 44 , 4 mi. w. of DeLand
High Banks Boat Ramp	High Banks Rd., DeBary
Lemon Bluff	SR 415, 4 mi. se of Osteen

CRUISING THE ST. JOHNS RIVER

One of the few north-flowing rivers on the continent, the St. Johns flows deep and smooth from the wetlands west of Vero Beach past Jacksonville to its mouth at Mayport. For the cruising boatman, it offers one of the finest river cruises in the country, in three markedly different sections:

From River Statute Mile One, at the junction of the ICW with the St. Johns at the mouth of Sisters Creek, the first is the five-mile side trip past Mayport and Mayport Naval Station to the Atlantic. It's a striking contrast between the busy fishing port and naval station on the south shore and beautiful windswept dunes on the north. The short cruise past Fort George and Huguenot Memorial Park and out to the river mouth is a pleasant one, and Mayport is famous for its seafood restaurants, although none are right on the waterfront.

Upstream from the ICW junction the busy deep-water channel winds 15 miles upstream to Jacksonville, where the redeveloped riverfront and Riverwalk are both beautiful and inviting and every urban attraction is immediately at hand. Dockage is available short-term at Jacksonville Landing right downtown, at River City Brewing Company Marina near the Riverwalk, and in several marinas in nearby Trout and Ortega Rivers. The latter offers half a dozen wall-to-wall facilities along its north shore which include Ortega River Boat Yard and Lambs Yacht Center.

Jacksonville's five bridges are clustered along the five-mile switchback the river makes through the center of the city, and if you can clear 40' you can pass through all five without concern except for the occasionally heavy commercial traffic. A low railroad bridge closes only when a train is coming, which unfortunately happens often and can take quite a while.

As you leave Jacksonville, the river changes character and the second section begins — a 40-odd mile stretch of broad, deep estuary with half a dozen marinas spaced comfortably along the shores, notably in Doctors Lake and at Julington Creek opposite. A 45-foot fixed bridge may stop some sailboats at Green Cove Springs. Doctors Lake is a popular anchorage for those who can clear its 37-foot fixed bridge.

Palatka, at Mile 83, is an old river town full of 1800s buildings that shouldn't be missed. It's also blessed with one of the friendliest and most helpful of facilities, Boathouse Marina.

South of Palatka the third phase begins as the river narrows and begins to twist and turn its way southward toward Sanford. Ten miles upriver from Palatka, Dunn's Creek makes off to port. After you turn off into Dunn's Creek, just before the new high bridge, Murphy's Creek makes off to starboard in one of the prettiest sections on the river.

Back on the main river, from Dunn's Creek southward the beauty continues, with dozens of excellent anchorages among the Seven Sisters Islands. The aborted Cross-Florida Barge Canal intersects below the islands but is best left to the many bass boats that run west in the old canal to the stump-and-bass-filled waters of Lake Rodman.

Mile 99 marks the town of Welaka, the last convenient place to stock up on supplies north of Sanford. Not too far above Welaka, at Mile 105, is the entrance to Lake George, a bass fisherman's paradise. Branching off from the black waters of the lake are two perfectly clear springs on the west side. The northern-most, Salt Spring Creek, has a bar across its entrance that limits exploration, but Silver Glen Spring to the south is more accessible and a very popular place among local boatmen on weekends.

The 35-odd miles from Lake George to Lake Monroe is the most beautiful and least developed stretch of the river. Four miles south of Lake George is the village of Astor with a number of waterside restaurants and fish camps. Seventeen miles south of Astor at Crow's Bluff, Boat Show Marina offers full services. At about Mile 151 is Hontoon Island and State Park and Hontoon Landing Resort and Marina, a full-service facility and home to a good many rental houseboats. Further upstream on the Beresford Cutoff is Hidden Harbor Marina.

A few miles south at Mile 161, the river enters Lake Monroe, and across the lake at Marker 143 is Sanford, an oasis of civilization and hospitality with Monroe Harbor Marina right downtown. For a break ashore you can dock at the Marina Hotel and enjoy their restaurant and lounge. The pleasant downtown area is within walking distance, and the many attractions of the Orlando area are only 20 miles away.

Less than two miles above Sanford, the Sanford Boat Works and Marina lies just below the 25' fixed bridge at Indian Mound Slough, and above the bridge the St. Johns reverts to the primitive state and becomes outboard-and-stern-drive country. But for the 160-plus miles from Mayport to Sanford, it offers unparalleled cruising, scenery, facilities, fishing and hospitality to all. To bypass the St. Johns is to miss the very essence of Florida's freshwater cruising.

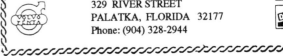

CHART TWO: ST. JOHNS RIVER

APPROXIMATE STATUTE MILES

0 5 10 15 20

THIS CHART IS NOT TO BE USED
FOR NAVIGATION

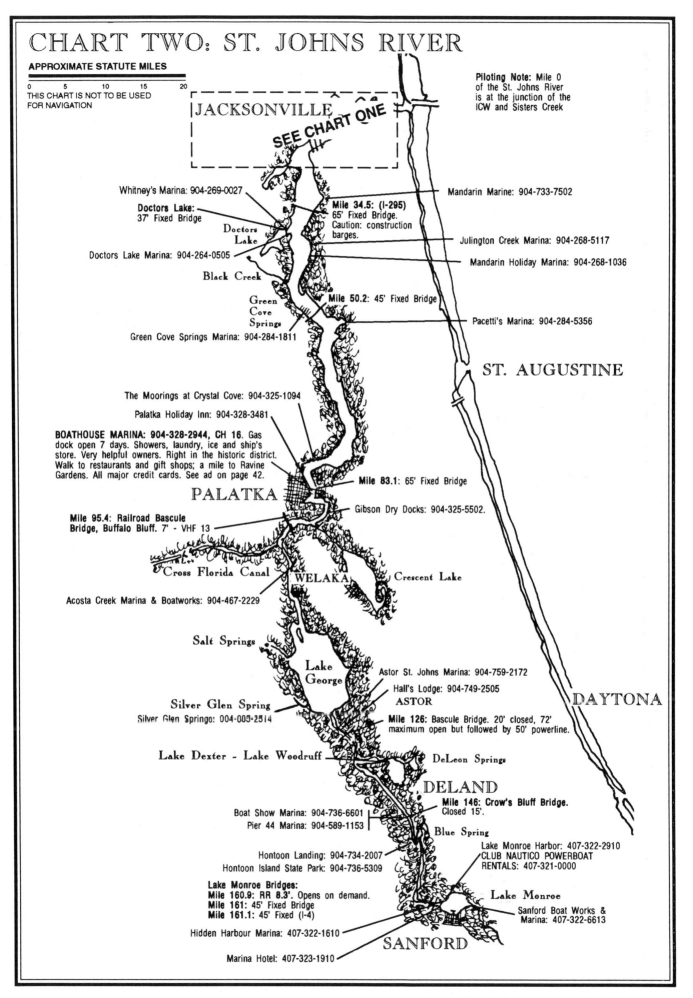

JACKSONVILLE

SEE CHART ONE

Piloting Note: Mile 0
of the St. Johns River
is at the junction of the
ICW and Sisters Creek

Whitney's Marina: 904-269-0027

Mandarin Marine: 904-733-7502

Doctors Lake:
37' Fixed Bridge

Doctors Lake

Mile 34.5: (I-295)
65' Fixed Bridge.
Caution: construction
barges.

Julington Creek Marina: 904-268-5117

Doctors Lake Marina: 904-264-0505

Mandarin Holiday Marina: 904-268-1036

Black Creek

Green Cove Springs

Mile 50.2: 45' Fixed Bridge

Pacetti's Marina: 904-284-5356

Green Cove Springs Marina: 904-284-1811

ST. AUGUSTINE

The Moorings at Crystal Cove: 904-325-1094

Palatka Holiday Inn: 904-328-3481

BOATHOUSE MARINA: 904-328-2944, CH 16. Gas
dock open 7 days. Showers, laundry, ice and ship's
store. Very helpful owners. Right in the historic district.
Walk to restaurants and gift shops; a mile to Ravine
Gardens. All major credit cards. See ad on page 42.

Mile 83.1: 65' Fixed Bridge

PALATKA

Gibson Dry Docks: 904-325-5502.

**Mile 95.4: Railroad Bascule
Bridge, Buffalo Bluff.** 7' - VHF 13

Cross Florida Canal

WELAKA

Crescent Lake

Acosta Creek Marina & Boatworks: 904-467-2229

Salt Springs

Lake George

Astor St. Johns Marina: 904-759-2172

Hall's Lodge: 904-749-2505

ASTOR

Silver Glen Spring

Silver Glen Springs: 904-685-2514

Mile 126: Bascule Bridge. 20' closed, 72'
maximum open but followed by 50' powerline.

DAYTONA

Lake Dexter - Lake Woodruff

DeLeon Springs

DELAND

Mile 146: Crow's Bluff Bridge.
Closed 15'.

Boat Show Marina: 904-736-6601

Pier 44 Marina: 904-589-1153

Blue Spring

Hontoon Landing: 904-734-2007

Hontoon Island State Park: 904-736-5309

Lake Monroe Harbor: 407-322-2910
**CLUB NAUTICO POWERBOAT
RENTALS: 407-321-0000**

Lake Monroe Bridges:
Mile 160.9: RR 8.3'. Opens on demand.
Mile 161: 45' Fixed Bridge
Mile 161.1: 45' Fixed (I-4)

Lake Monroe

Sanford Boat Works &
Marina: 407-322-6613

Hidden Harbour Marina: 407-322-1610

SANFORD

Marina Hotel: 407-323-1910

Matanzas Inlet

Marineland Marina: 904-471-0087

Treworgy Yachts: 904-445-5878

PALM COAST MARINA: 904-446-6370
800-874-2101, CH 16.
Fuel dock open 7-7 in Summer, 7-6 in Winter. Handles up to 165' with 7' draft. All resort amenities include golf, tennis, pools, bicycle rentals. Restaurant, marine store, convenience store and more on premises. Supermarket 2 miles. See ad on page 35.

St. Mile 803: Palm Coast Pkwy.
65' Fixed Bridge.

Sim-Par Marina: 904-439-2616

Flagler Marine: 904-439-0081

St. Mile 811: Flagler Beach Bridge.
Closed 14'. Apr.-May 31 & Oct. 1-Nov., 7AM-6PM opens on the hour and every 20 min. New 65' bridge under construction.

St. Mile 816: Bulow Bridge.
Closed 15'. Opens on demand.

Ormond Beach Bridge: 65' Fixed

Aloha Marina: 904-255-2345

Dixie Queen Marina: 904-257-1017

ENGLISH JIM'S MARINA: 904-253-5647
800-446-2823, CH 16. Gas & diesel fuel. Laundry, showers, phones, cable TV. See their advertisement on page 39.

DAYTONA BEACH

HALIFAX HARBOR MARINA: 904-253-0575,
800-343-2899. 300' fuel dock. Dockage for yachts to 150'. Dockage customers enjoy Halifax Harbor privileges at the oceanfront Marriott Hotel: shop, restaurants and special rates at health club, heated pool. See ad on page 35.

Daytona Marina & Boatworks: 904-252-6421

RIVERVIEW HOTEL & RESTAURANT: 904-428-5858, 800-945-7416
CH 16. Can take yachts up to 100' with 10' draft. Short walk to beach and shops. Besides the restored, charming old hotel, there's Riverview Charlie's Restaurant on site. See ad on page 38.

New Smyrna Beach

SeaFarer Marine: 904-427-4514

Florida Watercraft: 904-426-2628

Causeway Marine: 904-427-5267

Sea Harvest Marina: 904-428-8313

DAYTONA BEACH: 4 Bridges
St. Mile 829.1: Seabreeze Blvd. Closed 20'. Restricted Mon-Sat except holidays 7:30-8:30 AM and 4:30-5:30 PM. One opening during each restricted period at 8 AM and 5 PM. Construction starting on twin 65' bridges.
St. Mile 830: Main Street. Closed 22'. **& Broadway.** Closed 21'. Both open on demand.
St. Mile 830.6: Memorial Bridge. Closed 21'. Restricted Mon-Sat except holidays, 7:45-8:45 AM and 4:45-5:45 PM. One opening each period of restriction at 8:15 AM and 5:15 PM.

Seven Seas Marina & Boatyard: 904-761-3221

St. Mile 835: Port Orange. 65' Fixed Bridge

Adventure Yacht Harbor: 904-756-2180

PONCE DEEPWATER LANDING: 904-767-3266. A full service marina with fuel dock open from 7 AM to 7 PM. Can take boats up to 100' with 9' draft. Restaurant and marine store with ice and bait on site. Complete mechanical repairs and dry storage. See ad on page 35.

Sea Love Boat Works: 904-761-5434

Lighthouse Boatyard: 904-767-0683

Ponce de Leon Inlet

St. Mile 845: Coronado Beach Bridge. Closed 14'. Restricted all year, 7 AM-6 PM. Opens on the hour and every quarter hour. 30' bascule bridge under construction.

St. Mile 846.5: Harris Saxon Bridge. 65' Fixed

St. Mile 869: Allenhurst Bascule Bridge over the Haulover. Closed 27'. Opens on demand

St. Mile 877: Jay Jay RR Bridge. Closed 7'. Usually open.

Titusville Municipal Marina: 407-269-7255

Westland Marina: 407-267-1667

St. Mile 878.9: SR 402 Bridge. Closed 9'. Opens on signal except from 6-7:15 AM and 3:15-4:30 PM, Mon-Fri except federal holidays. No openings during restricted hours.

TITUSVILLE

Not shown at St. Mile 885: Addison Point Bridge. Closed 27'. Mon-Fri does not open 6:30-8 AM and 3:30-5 PM.

KENNEDY POINT MARINA & CLUB: 407-383-0280,
CH 16. Dockage to 60'. Diesel & gas, pool, jacuzzi, showers, laundry, weight room & racquet ball on site; stores and restaurants nearby. See ad on page 49.

Mosquito Lagoon

Shuttle Launch Pads

APPROXIMATE STATUTE MILES

0   5   10   15

THIS CHART IS NOT TO BE USED FOR NAVIGATION

CRUISING FLORIDA'S SPACE COAST

Somewhere above Titusville, as you cruise through the 18th Century on the Indian River Lagoon, the enormous Vehicle Assembly Building at Kennedy Space Center on Cape Canaveral looms into view to the south. It's your first clue that you're leaving the historic First Coast and entering the futuristic Space Coast.

Its namesake attraction is open every day and worth a visit. If you're fortunate enough to be in the area when a shuttle launch is scheduled, hang around and watch it — it's a guaranteed Life Experience and not to be missed.

The best view in the world is from the Banana River, which parallels the Indian River Lagoon and joins it at Indian Harbor Beach, just above Eau Gallie. About the only problem getting close to a launch may be the 36-foot fixed bridge on the Merritt Island Causeway across the Banana River and the fact that some drawbridges in the area may not open during a launch.

On the Indian River, the nearest docks to the Space Center are Kennedy Point Marina and the two marinas in Titusville — Titusville Municipal and Westland — or one of the facilities further south in Cocoa that include Whitley Marine.

If you're coming from the north and/or your boat requires more than 36 feet of clearance, you can use the Canaveral Barge Canal (with due care), which joins the ICW at Mile 893.6 and runs eastward into the Banana River at the south end of the Space Center's restricted area. During a launch you will not be allowed north of the Barge Canal and Port Canaveral Inlet.

If you're coming from the south and your boat needs less than five feet of depth and 36 feet of clearance, you can enter the Banana River at Dragon Point, at roughly Mile 914 — the landmark is a 30-foot green concrete dragon that was originally built as a playhouse. The channel from there to the Bennett Causeway is shallow and not well marked, but can be negotiated with care. You'll find several facilities on the east as you round Dragon Point, and farther north you'll find Banana River Marine and Coastal Marine on the Merritt Island side. Still farther north the area around the inlet is lined with facilities that include Cape Marina.

Between Cocoa Beach and the Bennett Causeway, which begins the restricted area, you have four or five miles of better depths and elbow room with a well-marked channel, room to anchor, spoil islands to beach

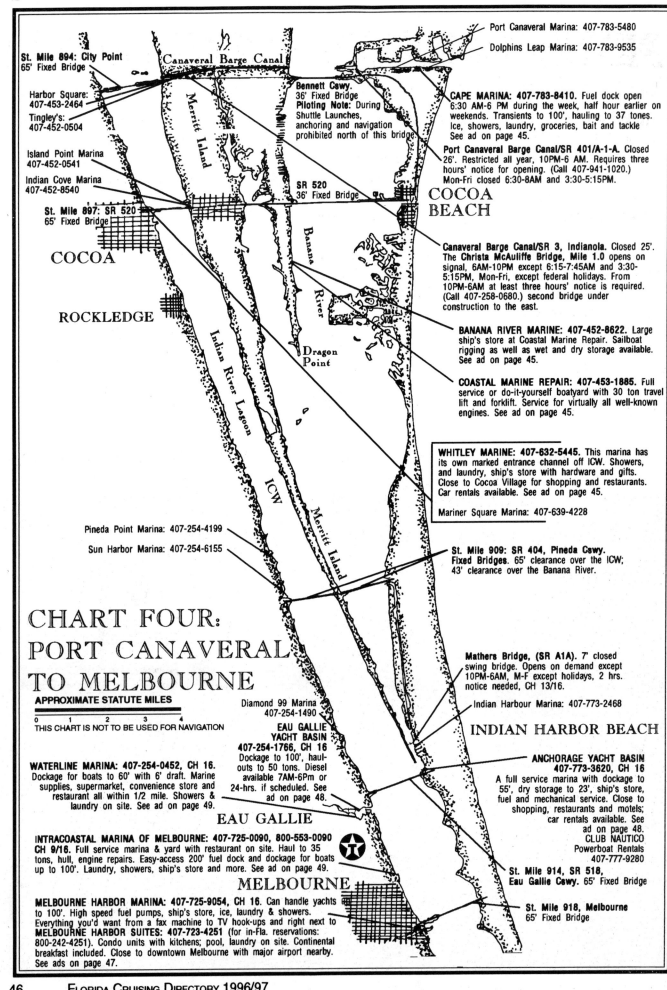

Port Canaveral Marina: 407-783-5480

Dolphins Leap Marina: 407-783-9535

St. Mile 894: City Point
65' Fixed Bridge

Harbor Square:
407-453-2464

Tingley's:
407-452-0504

Island Point Marina
407-452-0541

Indian Cove Marina
407-452-8540

St. Mile 897: SR 520
65' Fixed Bridge

COCOA

ROCKLEDGE

Canaveral Barge Canal

Bennett Cswy.
36' Fixed Bridge
Piloting Note: During Shuttle Launches, anchoring and navigation prohibited north of this bridge.

SR 520
36' Fixed Bridge

Merritt Island

Indian River Lagoon

Banana River

Dragon Point

ICW

Merritt Island

CAPE MARINA: 407-783-8410. Fuel dock open 6:30 AM-6 PM during the week, half hour earlier on weekends. Transients to 100', hauling to 37 tones. Ice, showers, laundry, groceries, bait and tackle See ad on page 45.

Port Canaveral Barge Canal/SR 401/A-1-A. Closed 26'. Restricted all year, 10PM-6 AM. Requires three hours' notice for opening. (Call 407-941-1020.) Mon-Fri closed 6:30-8AM and 3:30-5:15PM.

COCOA
BEACH

Canaveral Barge Canal/SR 3, Indianola. Closed 25'. The Christa McAuliffe Bridge, Mile 1.0 opens on signal, 6AM-10PM except 6:15-7:45AM and 3:30-5:15PM, Mon-Fri, except federal holidays. From 10PM-6AM at least three hours' notice is required. (Call 407-258-0680.) second bridge under construction to the east.

BANANA RIVER MARINE: 407-452-8622. Large ship's store at Coastal Marine Repair. Sailboat rigging as well as wet and dry storage available. See ad on page 45.

COASTAL MARINE REPAIR: 407-453-1885. Full service or do-it-yourself boatyard with 30 ton travel lift and forklift. Service for virtually all well-known engines. See ad on page 45.

WHITLEY MARINE: 407-632-5445. This marina has its own marked entrance channel off ICW. Showers, and laundry, ship's store with hardware and gifts. Close to Cocoa Village for shopping and restaurants. Car rentals available. See ad on page 45.

Mariner Square Marina: 407-639-4228

Pineda Point Marina: 407-254-4199

Sun Harbor Marina: 407-254-6155

St. Mile 909: SR 404, Pineda Cswy.
Fixed Bridges. 65' clearance over the ICW; 43' clearance over the Banana River.

CHART FOUR:
PORT CANAVERAL
TO MELBOURNE

APPROXIMATE STATUTE MILES

0   1   2   3   4
THIS CHART IS NOT TO BE USED FOR NAVIGATION

Mathers Bridge, (SR A1A). 7' closed swing bridge. Opens on demand except 10PM-6AM, M-F except holidays, 2 hrs. notice needed, CH 13/16.

Indian Harbour Marina: 407-773-2468

INDIAN HARBOR BEACH

Diamond 99 Marina
407-254-1490

EAU GALLIE YACHT BASIN
407-254-1766, CH 16
Dockage to 100', haul-outs to 50 tons. Diesel available 7AM-6Pm or 24-hrs. if scheduled. See ad on page 48.

WATERLINE MARINA: 407-254-0452, CH 16. Dockage for boats to 60' with 6' draft. Marine supplies, supermarket, convenience store and restaurant all within 1/2 mile. Showers & laundry on site. See ad on page 49.

ANCHORAGE YACHT BASIN
407-773-3620, CH 16
A full service marina with dockage to 55', dry storage to 23', ship's store, fuel and mechanical service. Close to shopping, restaurants and motels; car rentals available. See ad on page 48.
CLUB NAUTICO
Powerboat Rentals
407-777-9280

St. Mile 914, SR 518,
Eau Gallie Cswy. 65' Fixed Bridge

EAU GALLIE

INTRACOASTAL MARINA OF MELBOURNE: 407-725-0090, 800-553-0090 CH 9/16. Full service marina & yard with restaurant on site. Haul to 35 tons, hull, engine repairs. Easy-access 200' fuel dock and dockage for boats up to 100'. Laundry, showers, ship's store and more. See ad on page 49.

St. Mile 918, Melbourne
65' Fixed Bridge

MELBOURNE

MELBOURNE HARBOR MARINA: 407-725-9054, CH 16. Can handle yachts to 100'. High speed fuel pumps, ship's store, ice, laundry & showers. Everything you'd want from a fax machine to TV hook-ups and right next to **MELBOURNE HARBOR SUITES: 407-723-4251** (for in-Fla. reservations: 800-242-4251). Condo units with kitchens; pool, laundry on site. Continental breakfast included. Close to downtown Melbourne with major airport nearby. See ads on page 47.

MELBOURNE HARBOR

Great Facilities ⚓ Great Service ⚓ Great Location ⚓ Gateway to Central Florida

GREAT FACILITIES
- Protected Harbor/Dredged to 8'
- Open 7 Days Per Week
- 90 Modern Concrete Berths
- No Tides
- Vessels Up to 110'
- Transient & Permanent Slips
- Overnight Dockage for Power & Sail
- High Speed Gas & Diesel Pumps
- All Utilities: Phone Service/TV
- Clean, Private Rest Rooms and Showers
- Complete Laundry Facilities
- Marine Electronics Sales/Svc.
- Yacht Sales and Brokerage

GREAT LOCATION
Close To...
- Shopping/Theater/Art Galleries/Antiques
- Restaurants
- Motels/Hotels
- Banking
- Regional Airport
- Post Office/UPS/Fed Express
- Golf Course/Tennis Courts
- Sandy White Beaches

GREAT SERVICE
- Lowest Diesel/Gas Prices
- 24 Hour Security Service
- Mail Delivery
- Bagged Ice
- Car Rentals Available
- VHF 16 Monitored
- Channel 68 Working
- Facsimile Equipment

GATEWAY TO CENTRAL FLORIDA
Less Than 1 Hour to...
- Disney World/Epcot Center
- Universal Studios/Sea World
- Kennedy Space Center

Just South of the Melbourne Causeway Mile 918 Channel Marker 6 on the ICW
2210 South Front Street, Melbourne, Florida 32901 407.725.9054

Melbourne Harbor Suites

Spacious Condo Units for Four • Junior Kitchenettes for Two
- Fully Equipped Kitchens • Pool • Laundry On Site
- Historic Shopping District • Manatee Sanctuary • Muffins and Coffee Included

Private Marina Adjacent to Hotel • (407) 725-9054

Ask About Our Anniversary/Honeymoon Weekend Package

Hwy. 192 and U.S. 1 in Melbourne • Local # (407) 723-4251 • For reservations: (in FL) 1-800-242-4251

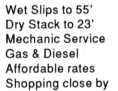
on and grass flats to fish. Above the causeway is a strict no-power zone, and the few anglers willing to row, paddle or sail a few miles north find fabulous fishing.

The Space Center is in fact such a big attraction that it distracts from the other pleasures and attractions of Space Coast waters, which are many.

On the mainland side, Titusville and Cocoa offer not only excellent dockage, shore facilities and shopping, but also are the gateways to Walt Disney World and the many other attractions in the Orlando area, which may qualify as "must-see" for many cruising families. You can rent a car or catch a shuttle bus for the 50-odd mile trip to Orlando, and any marina in the area can help you make the connection.

Facilities include the big Titusville Municipal Marina, and Kennedy Point, a yacht club open to the public and the marina nearest the Space Center. Further south, Harbor Square and Tingley's Marina are sheltered a mile or so inside the Canaveral Barge Canal, and in Cocoa, marinas cluster under the high bridge around Marker 897 and include Mariner Square and Whitley Marine, within walking distance of downtown Cocoa.

On the sea side, Cocoa Beach is the beginning of a stretch of beautiful and uncrowded beaches never very far from plentiful dockage on the waterway. On both sides and in the middle, fishing remains excellent all the way south, stocked with redfish, seatrout and other game species from the nursery waters of the restricted area. Dockside bait and tackle shops offer everything from guide service to advice for the cruising angler.

South of the Cape, and for nearly 120 miles to Vero Beach, the Indian River Lagoon is wide and deep and very popular with area sailors and anglers. There are a number of good marinas, including Diamond 99 Marina, logically enough at Marker 99 at Palm Shores.

Eau Gallie, across from Dragon Point at Mile 915, has been politically combined with Melbourne, but still stands as one of the oldest and prettiest harbors on the coast. Eau Gallie Yacht Basin is at the river mouth just south of the Causeway, and Waterline Marina is across the river near shopping and shore facilities. Anchorage Yacht Basin is across the Waterway at the east end of the causeway. Intracoastal Marina and Skipper's Restaurant are farther south between Eau Gallie and Melbourne.

Melbourne proper, at Mile 918, is the commercial heartland of the Space Coast and particularly convenient for boatmen, with facilities including Melbourne Harbor clustered below the causeway at the mouth of Crane Creek and restaurants, motels, fuel, transient dockage, and an airport with jet service to almost everywhere.

South of Melbourne, the Indian River continues wide and deep and dotted with dozens of inviting spoil islands, many of which are surrounded by deep water and offer good anchorages. If you're looking for more formal dockage, there are facilities spaced comfortably along the waterway — Pelican Harbor and Palm Bay Marina at Palm Bay, Sebastian River Marina and Boatyard (formerly Summit Landings), and Complete Yacht (North) at Micco, then Captain Hiram's opposite the inlet in Sebastian.

Farther southward through Pelican Island National Wildlife Refuge — the nation's first, established by President Theodore Roosevelt in 1904 — a wonderful scenic area called Indian River Narrows starts at the Wabasso bridge and runs along a series of islands and spoil banks for about four miles.

It marks the end of the Space Coast and the beginning of the Treasure Coast, the generally un-crowded and truly beautiful gateway to South Florida.

EDITOR's NOTE: This is based on the current list maintained by the Florida Department of Environmental Protection, and while it was updated shortly before press time, changes are constant and it's a good idea to check ramps in advance. Note that some ramps are in marinas, private clubs or condominiums where public access may be limited.

BREVARD COUNTY RAMPS

COCOA
Lee Wenner Park	300 Riveredge Dr.
McFarland Park	206 Indian River Dr.
Port St. John Boat Ramp	6650 N. US 1

COCOA BEACH
Cocoa Bch. Rec. Complex	Tom Warriner Blvd. at Minuteman Cswy. on Banana River
Ramp Road Park	Ramp Rd. on Banana River

GRANT
First Street Boat Ramp	4727 First St.
Jorgensen Landing	5045 US 1

INDIAN HARBOUR BEACH
Indian Harbour Marina	1399 Banana River Dr. on Banana River

MELBOURNE
Ballard Park	E. Thomas Barbour Dr. on Eau Gallie River
Diamond 99 Marina	4399 N. Harbor City Blvd. on Indian River
Eau Gallie Cswy. Park	Eau Gallie Cswy., SR 518 on Indian River; 4 areas: SW, SE, NW, NE
Front Street Civic Ctr.	S. Front St. on Indian River
Keels & Wheels	729 N. Harbor City Blvd. on Indian River (Reported: Very tight)
Melbourne Yacht Club	1202 E. River Dr. on Indian River
Pineda Landing	5995 US 1
Intracoastal Marina	705 S. Harbor City Blvd. on Indian River
Sun Harbor Marina	6155 N. Harbor City Blvd. on Indian River
Wheelhouse Marine	6175 N. Harbor City Blvd. on Indian River

MELBOURNE BEACH
Long Point Park	700 Long Point Rd.
Outdoor Resorts of America	3000 S. A1A
Sebastian Inlet State Rec. Area	9700 S. A1A on Inlet Brevard County Area.
South Beach Marina	9502 S. Hwy. A1A, Indian River Campbell Pocket

MERRITT ISLAND
Canaveral National Seashore	Mosquito Lagoon & Atlantic Ocean
Kelly Park	2550 N. Banana River Dr.
Merritt Island Ntnl. Wildlife Refuge	Off SR 405 on Indain River & Mosquito Lagoon Brevard County Area
Merritt Marine Center	582 S. Banana River Dr.
Tingley's Marina & Fish Camp	2750 Tingley Dr.

MICCO
Sebastian River Marina	4015 Main St. on Sebastian River

MIMS
Mims Boat Ramp	2010 Jones Ave.

PALM BAY
Alex J. Goode Park	1300 Bianca Dr. NE on Indian River
H. E. Pollak Park	Main St. NE on Indian River

PATRICK AFB
Patrick AFB	SSRO MWF Div. on A-1-A

PORT CANAVERAL
Central Park	9050 Flounder St.
Coghill's Marina	505 Commercial Dr.
Capt. John's Marina	Canaveral Peninsula on Atlantic
Dolphin's Leap Marina	505 Glen Cheek Dr.
Port's End Park	998 Mullet Dr.

PORT ST. JOHN
Manatee Hammock Park	7275 US 1

SATELLITE BEACH
Lake Shepard Boat Ramp	381 North Point Ct.

SCOTTSMOOR
Scottsmoore Landing	2400 Huntington Ave.

TITUSVILLE
Marina Park	451 Marina Rd.
Parrish Park	1 Max Brewer Pkwy., SR 402

INDIAN RIVER COUNTY BOAT RAMPS

MELBOURNE BEACH
Sebastian Inlet State Recreation Area	9700 S. A1A on Sebastian Inlet

ORCHID
CR 510 Wayside Park	CR 510 & US 1 on Indian River

OSLO
Oslo Boat Ramp	Oslo Rd. & US 1 on Indian River

SEBASTIAN
Dale Wimbrow Park	12305 Roseland Rd.
Main Street Dock	Main St. & Indian River Dr. on Indian River
Sebastian Yacht Club	820 Indian River

VERO BEACH
Bob Summers Park	Rio Viata & E. Indian River Dr. on Indian River
McWilliams Park	Beachland Blvd. & Old Bridge Rd. on Indian River

S. OF VERO BEACH
Round Island Beach Park	2200 S. A1A

WABASSO
Wabasso Cswy. Island Park	3105 Wabasso Rd.

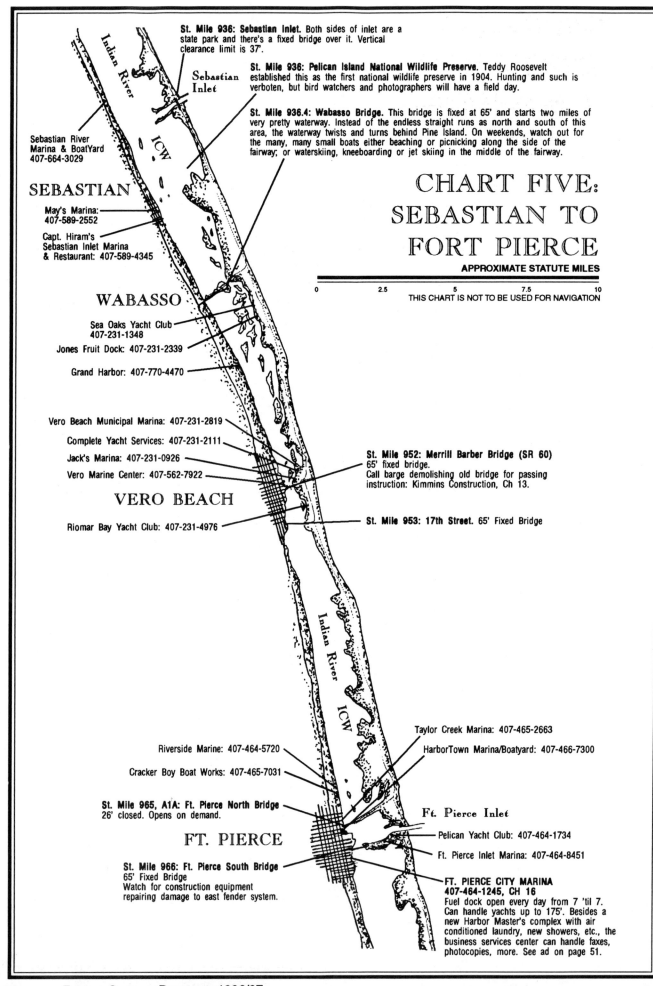

St. Mile 936: Sebastian Inlet. Both sides of inlet are a state park and there's a fixed bridge over it. Vertical clearance limit is 37'.

St. Mile 936: Pelican Island National Wildlife Preserve. Teddy Roosevelt established this as the first national wildlife preserve in 1904. Hunting and such is verboten, but bird watchers and photographers will have a field day.

St. Mile 936.4: Wabasso Bridge. This bridge is fixed at 65' and starts two miles of very pretty waterway. Instead of the endless straight runs as north and south of this area, the waterway twists and turns behind Pine Island. On weekends, watch out for the many, many small boats either beaching or picnicking along the side of the fairway; or waterskiing, kneeboarding or jet skiing in the middle of the fairway.

CHART FIVE: SEBASTIAN TO FORT PIERCE

APPROXIMATE STATUTE MILES

| 0 | 2.5 | 5 | 7.5 | 10 |

THIS CHART IS NOT TO BE USED FOR NAVIGATION

Sebastian Inlet

Indian River

ICW

Sebastian River
Marina & BoatYard
407-664-3029

SEBASTIAN

May's Marina:
407-589-2552

Capt. Hiram's
Sebastian Inlet Marina
& Restaurant: 407-589-4345

WABASSO

Sea Oaks Yacht Club
407-231-1348

Jones Fruit Dock: 407-231-2339

Grand Harbor: 407-770-4470

Vero Beach Municipal Marina: 407-231-2819

Complete Yacht Services: 407-231-2111

Jack's Marina: 407-231-0926

Vero Marine Center: 407-562-7922

VERO BEACH

Riomar Bay Yacht Club: 407-231-4976

St. Mile 952: Merrill Barber Bridge (SR 60)
65' fixed bridge.
Call barge demolishing old bridge for passing instruction: Kimmins Construction, Ch 13.

St. Mile 953: 17th Street. 65' Fixed Bridge

Indian River

ICW

Taylor Creek Marina: 407-465-2663

HarborTown Marina/Boatyard: 407-466-7300

Riverside Marine: 407-464-5720

Cracker Boy Boat Works: 407-465-7031

St. Mile 965, A1A: Ft. Pierce North Bridge
26' closed. Opens on demand.

FT. PIERCE

St. Mile 966: Ft. Pierce South Bridge
65' Fixed Bridge
Watch for construction equipment
repairing damage to east fender system.

Ft. Pierce Inlet

Pelican Yacht Club: 407-464-1734

Ft. Pierce Inlet Marina: 407-464-8451

**FT. PIERCE CITY MARINA
407-464-1245, CH 16**
Fuel dock open every day from 7 'til 7.
Can handle yachts up to 175'. Besides a
new Harbor Master's complex with air
conditioned laundry, new showers, etc., the
business services center can handle faxes,
photocopies, more. See ad on page 51.

CRUISING FLORIDA'S TREASURE COAST

The Treasure Coast is aptly named — in 1715 a Spanish treasure fleet was blown onto the reefs along the shore by a hurricane, scattering wrecks and their cargoes of gold, silver and artifacts for miles. Beachcombers still find occasional doubloons or pieces of eight after storms. Its origin is easier to pinpoint than its location, but the Treasure Coast is said to begin somewhere south of Cape Canaveral where the birds outnumber the airplanes.

Just south of the Pelican Island Preserve is State Road 150, a causeway that leads from the village of Wabasso on U.S. Highway One to a bridge over a stretch of water as pretty as any on the ICW. The channel meanders among islands bordered by tropical foliage and speckled with white sand beaches, and is very popular with area weekenders. Unfortunately, the area has also become very popular with developers, and its days of wild beauty may be numbered.

South of the Wabasso Bridge is the old Jones Fruit Dock, a vestige of Old Florida and long the only facility in the area. Sea Oaks Yacht Club is now just over a mile north, and more facilities are expected soon — development can have its benefits. If you'd rather avoid development, there's a peaceful anchorage in the creek mouth on Pine Island just north of Jones Dock. At Mile 122, the new marina at Grand Harbor resort shares its amenities with transient boats.

Eight miles farther south lies Vero Beach, where excellent facilities are a preview of the pleasures of the Gold Coast, and many a cruising boatman has succumbed to its many pleasures, stayed to enjoy them, and saved the Gold Coast for another year.

In Vero you will find a facility unique in Florida — moorings for rent. To control anchoring, Vero's town fathers planted moorings in Bethel Creek, the area's primary anchorage. Now instead of anchoring, which the town prohibits, you rent a mooring. But you don't have to spend your nights swinging to a mooring. Vero offers plenty of solid slips as well, and a couple of waterfront restaurants just west of the new high bridge for State Road 60. Facilities include the Municipal Marina, Complete Yacht (South) and Riomar Bay, the latter a yacht club that welcomes transients.

From Vero south, you'll find the Indian River wider and shallower, and the need to stay in the channel more important than it was farther north. The river averages more than a mile wide from below Vero to

Stuart, but the water on either side of the channel is often shallow enough to be waded by fishermen. You will see long strings of private markers leading at right angles from the channel toward private homes and public facilities alike.

Just north of Fort Pierce at Mile 963.5 you will see the village of Saint Lucie on the western shore. Saint Lucie was the original settlement in these parts, and although it is difficult to go ashore, you can enjoy its Old Florida architecture from the water. Immediately south, the river is dotted with spoil islands that are first-class locations for anchoring, shore picnics or overnight camping. Depths around the islands range from over your head to just over your shoetops, so you'll have to feel your way with care.

At Mile 965 you'll enter Fort Pierce, the largest town on the Treasure Coast, with its harbor, major all-weather inlet, and plenty of docking facilities, including modern Harbortown Marina. Opposite the inlet is the

expanded, rebuilt and renamed Fort Pierce City Marina, and a first-class facility in the heart of the city.

Pilot your boat past Fort Pierce Inlet and under the high southern bridge over the waterway with care. The considerable currents and tides in the area move the channel around from season to season, sometimes faster than markers and charts can keep up. When in doubt, follow a local boat. The inlet itself, on the other hand, is tamer and better maintained than others along the northern and central Florida coast, and is one of the best for access to the Atlantic. Mind the wind and tide, however — when they are in opposition they can produce a difficult chop.

Cruising southward from Fort Pierce, the next point of interest is Jensen Beach, a pretty little resort village at Mile 981.5. There are motels and shopping close by the waterfront and plenty of room to anchor south of the Jensen Beach Causeway. There are also a number of marinas as well as waterfront restaurants and watering holes. Just south of Jensen Beach, Outrigger Harbour Marina, once Frances Langford's Outrigger Resort, remains an attraction. All are reached via their own privately marked entrance channels from the ICW channel to the western shore.

If you like docking and living well, continue

southward to Mile 985, immediately south of the Stuart Causeway. There another privately marked channel leads eastward to the marina of the Indian River Plantation, which by anyone's measure is an outstanding resort. All of its first-class amenities and special services are available to marina guests.

Down the beach from the Plantation is the area's best-known historic site, the House of Refuge. One of nine built in the 1870s to provide shelter for shipwrecked sailors on the waterless coast, it is now a museum and sea turtle refuge, open daily except Monday, and there is a dock on the lagoon side for small craft. However you get to it, by land or sea, it's worth a visit for scenic as well as historic values. The Atlantic side of the barrier islands at this point is a ledge of eroded rock alternating with some of the finest stretches of uncrowded beach to be found anywhere. Thanks to the foresight of earlier residents, all are open and accessible to the public.

Along the ICW at this point are shoals, flats, sandbars and spoil islands interlaced with channels of varying depths, and the area is very popular with local fishermen for snook, seatrout and flounder, and with local boatmen for picnics, camping and watersports. Joining them in some of the better spots is tricky, and

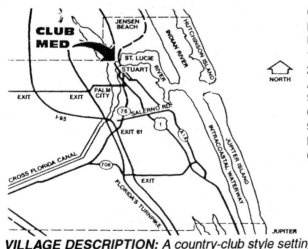

depths sometimes change on short notice, so you'll do well to ask — or follow — the locals.

At Mile 987.5 the waterway crosses the St. Lucie River at a place called The Crossroads. At this point, cruising boats have a number of options:

Number One is to go eastward out the St. Lucie Inlet to the Atlantic. The inlet has an absolutely terrible reputation for changing while your back is turned. If you don't know the inlet, follow a local boat. The mouth of the inlet, however, is famous for its snook fishing.

Option Number Two is to go westward into the St. Lucie River. The first point of interest on that route is the Manatee Pocket and Port Salerno on the south shore. More like a New England village than anything in Florida, it is wall-to-wall marine facilities and commercial and sport fishing docks, including Lowe's Boatyard, Mariner Cay, Pirate's Cove and others, and a nearly equal number of good restaurants and other stopping-places, all with docks. There is plenty of protected anchorage, but its use is limited to three days unless you're registered at Sandsprit Park at the mouth of the pocket.

Beyond Manatee Pocket the St. Lucie meanders northward and then turns west around downtown Stuart, opening up into a wonderful broad sailing area

in the process. There is an anchorage right off downtown as well as a city dock that you can use for a short time if you can get up the seawall. The bulk of Stuart marinas are east of the Roosevelt Bridge near U.S. Highway One. They include Pelican's Nest, Casa Rio, St. Lucie Marine, Waterside Place, and the Northside Marina, formerly the Stuart Yacht Club and Marina.

The Roosevelt Bridge is a busy one whose complex opening schedule is complicated by the fact that it is paralleled by a railroad bridge whose opening schedule is known only to God and the railroad dispatcher, who is probably a computer. The good news is that construction began on a new high bridge in 1995. The bad news is that the railroad bridge will remain.

Westbound past the bridges, you have yet another choice, since the St. Lucie splits at that point into its north and south forks.

You can go up the North Fork as far as White City, which is practically back to Fort Pierce, past Club Med Sandpiper, another full-fledged resort with dockage and all the amenities. North of there, cruising and fishing are excellent, but it's a jungle cruise with no facilities and a goodly population of large alligators.

The South Fork is the more developed and interesting. Only a mile or so upstream the river is

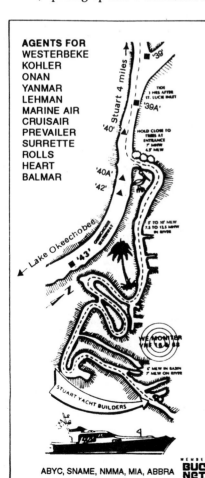

crossed by the Palm City Bridge with Woods Cove Marina at its eastern approach, lined with facilities and with shopping and restaurants within walking distance.

West and south of Stuart, the St. Lucie connects with the landcut of the Okeechobee Waterway, which goes all the way across the state to Fort Myers.

You also have yet another option of turning left and winding up the Old South Fork for fourteen-odd miles and back in time to Florida as it used to be. A nice surprise on that jungle cruise is the first-rate yard and facility at Stuart Yacht.

The final option is to continue southbound down the ICW, a course that will put you almost immediately alongside the channel to St. Lucie Inlet State Park, on the barrier island and accessible only by water. The reward is having most of the park's magnificent beach to yourself except on busy weekends and holidays.

A couple of miles farther south lies the prettiest anchorage on the entire ICW, at Peck Lake, a wide and mostly deep stretch of waterway created when a hurricane breached the barrier island. Shallows abound as usual, but if you turn off the ICW channel at Marker 19 you'll stay in deep water.

South of Peck Lake, the waterway passes through Hobe Sound, another beautiful stretch of water with a

bad case of schizophrenia. The mainland shore is mostly wildlife preserve, turning into marinas and the homes of ordinary mortals as you continue south toward Jupiter. The eastern shore, however, is Jupiter Island, possibly the most exclusive village in the United States. ("Hobe" is a Spanish pronunciation of Jove, which is another name for Jupiter, which with nearby Juno Beach ties all the towns in the area together. It's all in the family.)

Through all its length, Hobe Sound offers good off-channel anchoring between the sand bars and grass flats that extend from the shores, and the bars and little beaches offer great picnic spots. The fishing here is excellent, notably for seatrout and snook.

South toward Jupiter, the mainland shore becomes a series of marinas extending nearly all the way to the bridge connecting Jupiter Island to the mainland. They include Blowing Rocks and Seagate marinas at Mile 1002, then Jib Yacht Club at the Jupiter Island bridge and SeaSport Marina across the Loxahatchee River.

At that point the Indian River Lagoon ends and the waterway enters the Loxahatchee River with Jupiter Inlet to the east. Just west of the turn on the north shore is Jupiter Lighthouse. The classic red tower was built by Army Engineers under George Meade, the engineer who

This is how close the Gulf Stream comes to our island resort.

Anchored between the Atlantic Ocean and the Intracoastal Waterway, it's easy to find plenty of things to see and do. Besides outstanding deep sea fishing, Indian River Plantation offers Island Princess river boat cruises, 36 holes of golf, 13 tennis courts, 9 restaurants and lounges, deluxe hotel rooms and ocean front villas.

Our full service concrete 77 slip marina offers phone and cable TV hookups, electrical and water hookups and can accommodate boats up to 100 feet with six foot drafts. In addition we offer showers, laundry facilities, marine supplies and a gourmet market for your convenience.

Check Nautical Chart #11472. Look for our privately marked channel 1,000 feet south of the Stuart Causeway and one mile north of IWC Marker #229. This is how close an island resort comes to being perfect. For reservations or information call **1-800-444-3389** or **VHF Channel 16**.

555 N.E. Ocean Boulevard • Stuart, Florida 34996 • (407) 225-3700

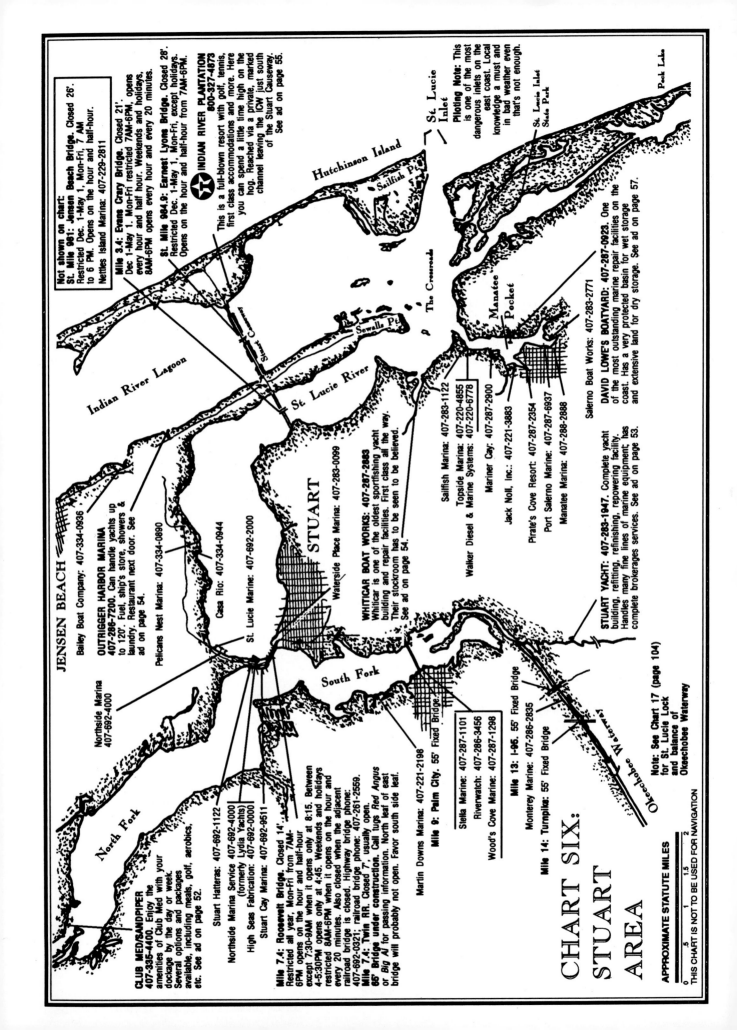

EDITOR's NOTE: This is based on the current list maintained by the Florida Department of Environmental Protection, and while it was updated shortly before press time, changes are constant and it's a good idea to check ramps in advance. Note that some ramps are in marinas, private clubs or condominiums where public access may be limited.

ST. LUCIE COUNTY BOAT RAMPS

FT. PIERCE

City of Ft. Pierce	1 Ave. A
Indian River Vets. Mem. Gdn.	600 N. Indian River Dr. on Indian River
Jaycee Park	S. Ocean Dr. & Maleleuca Dr.
North Causeway Island	County/DOT Wayside Park, SR A1A N.
Pelican Yacht Club	1120 Seaway Dr. on Indian River
South Causeway Island	County/DOT Wayside Park, SR A1A
Village Marina	Torpy Rd. on Indian River

JENSEN BEACH

Nettles Island Marina	9801 S. A1A on ICW

PORT ST. LUCIE

Rivergate	2200 SE Midport Rd.
Sandpiper Bay/Club Med	Morningside Blvd. on St. Lucie River

MARTIN COUNTY BOAT RAMPS

HOBE SOUND

Gleason Street Boat Ramp	Gleason St., ICW
Jonathan Dickinson State Park	16450 SE Federal Hwy, US 1, on Loxahatchee River

JENSEN BEACH

Casa Rio Boats & Motors	1050 NE Dixie Hwy. on St. Lucie River
Pelican Nest Marina	1009 NE Anchorage Dr. on St. Lucie River *(Private)*
Jensen Causeway Park	NE Causeway Blvd. on Indian River
Outdoor Resorts Campground	A1A & ICW
Jupiter Island	Hobe Sound Public Beach Park, 1 S. Bch. Rd.

PALM CITY

Leighton Park	2701 SW Cornell Ave. on St. Lucie River

PORT SALERNO

Charlie's Locker	4889 SE Dixie Hwy. on Manatee Pocket Sandsprit
Park	3443 SE St. Lucie Blvd. Indian River at Inlet

STUART

Bill's Place	4609 SE Manatee La. on Manatee Pocket
Phipp's Park	2175 SW Locks Rd. on St. Lucie Canal
Recreation Center & Park	71 Flagler Ave. on St. Lucie River
Sailfish Point	1755 SE Sailfish Point Blvd., Hutchinson Island on Atlantic Ocean, ICW & St. Lucie River
Shepard Park	US 1 & W. Ocean Blvd. on St. Lucie River
South River Condos Marina	4300 S. Kanner Hwy. on S. Fork St. Lucie River
Stuart Causeway Park	NE Ocean Blvd. & Stuart Cswy. on Indian River

went on to build most of the lights in the Keys and then to become the victor at Gettysburg.

The light presides over Jupiter Inlet, an inlet that can be a pussycat or a tiger depending on the force and direction of wind and tide. Unless the tide is slack and the wind is calm, or you have good local knowledge, we advise skipping Jupiter Inlet and enjoying the other pleasures of the area, which are legion. Primary among them are docking and eating at Charlie's Crab or docking at SeaSport Marina and eating at Harpoon Louie's, a very good double restaurant with one side for snowbirds and retirees and the other for beachcombers and the upwardly mobile.

For a great jungle cruise, head west under the 25-foot fixed Alternate A1A bridge and up the Loxahatchee River through Jonathan Dickenson State Park. It's a trip for the dinghy or a canoe rented at the park docks, up an ever-narrower and twistier river, but the scenery and wildlife are beautiful and the fishing is excellent.

Under the bridge at the confluence of the waterway with the Loxahatchee river, the remains of a marina mark what was once the landing for the steamboat from Titusville. It also marks the southern end of the Treasure Coast. Southward from there, you're going for the Gold.

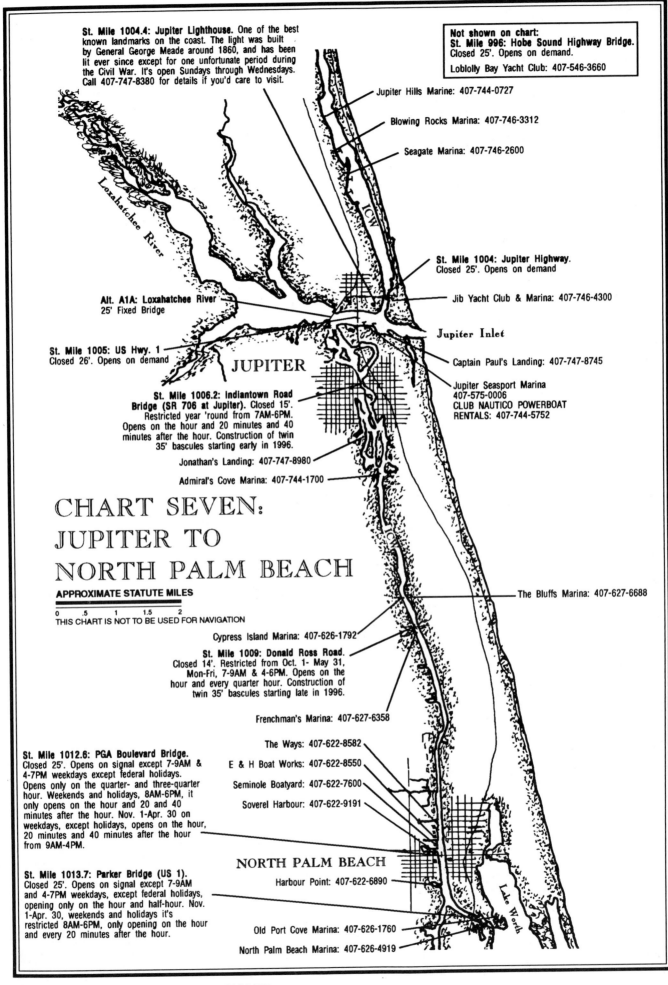

St. Mile 1004.4: Jupiter Lighthouse. One of the best known landmarks on the coast. The light was built by General George Meade around 1860, and has been lit ever since except for one unfortunate period during the Civil War. It's open Sundays through Wednesdays. Call 407-747-8380 for details if you'd care to visit.

Not shown on chart:
St. Mile 996: Hobe Sound Highway Bridge. Closed 25'. Opens on demand.

Loblolly Bay Yacht Club: 407-546-3660

Jupiter Hills Marine: 407-744-0727

Blowing Rocks Marina: 407-746-3312

Seagate Marina: 407-746-2600

ICW

St. Mile 1004: Jupiter Highway. Closed 25'. Opens on demand

Jib Yacht Club & Marina: 407-746-4300

Jupiter Inlet

Alt. A1A: Loxahatchee River 25' Fixed Bridge

Loxahatchee River

Captain Paul's Landing: 407-747-8745

St. Mile 1005: US Hwy. 1 Closed 26'. Opens on demand

JUPITER

Jupiter Seaport Marina
407-575-0006
CLUB NAUTICO POWERBOAT RENTALS: 407-744-5752

St. Mile 1006.2: Indiantown Road Bridge (SR 706 at Jupiter). Closed 15'. Restricted year 'round from 7AM-6PM. Opens on the hour and 20 minutes and 40 minutes after the hour. Construction of twin 35' bascules starting early in 1996.

Jonathan's Landing: 407-747-8980

Admiral's Cove Marina: 407-744-1700

CHART SEVEN: JUPITER TO NORTH PALM BEACH

APPROXIMATE STATUTE MILES

```
0    .5    1    1.5    2
```
THIS CHART IS NOT TO BE USED FOR NAVIGATION

The Bluffs Marina: 407-627-6688

Cypress Island Marina: 407-626-1792

St. Mile 1009: Donald Ross Road. Closed 14'. Restricted from Oct. 1- May 31, Mon-Fri, 7-9AM & 4-6PM. Opens on the hour and every quarter hour. Construction of twin 35' bascules starting late in 1996.

Frenchman's Marina: 407-627-6358

The Ways: 407-622-8582

St. Mile 1012.6: PGA Boulevard Bridge. Closed 25'. Opens on signal except 7-9AM & 4-7PM weekdays except federal holidays. Opens only on the quarter- and three-quarter hour. Weekends and holidays, 8AM-6PM, it only opens on the hour and 20 and 40 minutes after the hour. Nov. 1-Apr. 30 on weekdays, except holidays, opens on the hour, 20 minutes and 40 minutes after the hour from 9AM-4PM.

E & H Boat Works: 407-622-8550

Seminole Boatyard: 407-622-7600

Soverel Harbour: 407-622-9191

NORTH PALM BEACH

St. Mile 1013.7: Parker Bridge (US 1). Closed 25'. Opens on signal except 7-9AM and 4-7PM weekdays, except federal holidays, opening only on the hour and half-hour. Nov. 1-Apr. 30, weekends and holidays it's restricted 8AM-6PM, only opening on the hour and every 20 minutes after the hour.

Harbour Point: 407-622-6890

Lake Worth

Old Port Cove Marina: 407-626-1760

North Palm Beach Marina: 407-626-4919

CRUISING FLORIDA'S GOLD COAST

The Gold Coast of Florida represents 85 miles of the finest or worst urban cruising in the world, depending on your attitude about urban cruising. The Intracoastal Waterway leads right through the middle of it, past some of the finest marine and shore facilities and most beautiful resorts, residential and highrise communities in the country, through — or blessedly under — 44 bridges, past three major seaports, and through some of the heaviest commercial ship and recreational boat traffic imaginable. There are boatpeople who spend their free time exploring its endless waterways with pleasure, and others who make a long offshore detour to avoid it altogether. Of the two, the former are the more favored, for theirs is perhaps the most diverse and interesting cruising water to be found anywhere.

This fabled stretch of Waterway sneaks up on you after you turn southward at the mouth of the Loxahatchee River in Jupiter. The waterway changes from clear aquamarine to opaque brown and the shoreline scenery begins to take on a strong resemblance to a subtropical river. The waterway continues south through eight miles of channelized Lake Worth Creek to the PGA Boulevard bridge which marks the north end of Lake Worth. And at that point a large complex of marinas and marine facilities, several waterfront restaurants and a cluster of posh highrise condominium developments appear to mark the unmistakable gateway to the Gold Coast.

Just south of Harbor Point Marina at Mile 1012.4, the North Palm Beach Canal turns southward under a 15-foot fixed bridge and into a peaceful anchorage, albeit in a residential area where well-behaved transient boats are tolerated if not exactly welcome. Further east, passing between Old Port Cove and North Palm Beach Marinas and out into Lake Worth, a turn to the north leads to the head of the lake and a popular anchorage just a dinghy ride and a walk to supplies and shopping. An eight-foot fixed bridge on Highway A1A blocks the

New Port Cove Marine Center: 407-844-2504
New Port Cove Marine Center Boatyard: 407-848-0770

Old Slip Marina: 407-848-4669
Riviera Beach Municipal Marina: 407-842-7806
CLUB NAUTICO Powerboat Rentals: 407-863-8931
Cracker Boy Boat Works: 407-845-0357

Peanut Island
USCG

St. Mile 1017: Riviera Beach. 65' Fixed Bridge

Singer Island

Palm Beach Inlet

Piloting Note: Good all weather inlet used by large commercial vessels.

The Buccaneer: 407-842-1620

Cannonsport Marina: 407-848-7469

Sailfish Marina & Resort: 407-844-1724

 Rybovich Spencer Group: 407-844-1800

St. Mile 1021.9: Flagler Memorial Bridge. Closed 17'. Restricted Nov. 1-May 31, Mon-Fri except holidays. From 8AM to 5:45PM, it opens at 8:45AM, 4:15PM AND 5pm and on the hour and half-hour between 9:30AM-4PM.

Palm Beach Yacht Club Marina: 407-655-1944

PALM HARBOR MARINA: 407-655-4757 800-435-8051, CH 16. This is the downtown marina in Palm Beach. Thoroughly renovated, updated and a first class operation. Full services, store and convenient to everything West Palm has to offer. See ad on page 66.

PALM BEACH

WEST PALM BEACH

St. Mile: 1022.6: Royal Park Bridge. Closed 14'. Restricted Nov. 1-May 31, Mon-Fri except holidays. 8AM- 5:45PM, opens at 8:45AM and 4:15PM and on the quarter and three-quarter hour between 9:30AM & 3:30PM.

Australian/Brazilian/Peruvian Docks: 407-838-5463

St. Mile: 1024.7: Southern Boulevard Bridge. Closed 14'. Restricted Nov. 1-May 31, Mon-Fri except holidays, 7:30-9AM and 4:30-6:30PM. There is one opening during each period of restriction at 8:15AM and 5:30PM.

CHART EIGHT: LAKE WORTH

APPROXIMATE STATUTE MILES

0   2   4

THIS CHART IS NOT TO BE USED FOR NAVIGATION

Lake Worth

St. Mile 1029: Lake Avenue Bridge Closed 35'. Unrestricted.

 Gundlach's Marina: 407-582-4422

Murrelle Marine: 407-582-3213

St. Mile 1031: Lantana Ocean Avenue Bridge. Closed 13'. Dec.1-Apr. 30, Mon-Fri., 7AM-6PM; weekends and holidays, 10AM-6PM. Opens on the hour and every 15 minutes.

LANTANA

 Palm Beach Yacht Center: 407-588-9911

MANALAPAN

HYPOLUXO

Palm Beach Marina: 407-588-1211

Boynton Beach Inlet

Piloting Note: Small size and strong current make this a challenging inlet. Okay for fair weather use without local knowledge.

Water's Edge Marina: 407-736-8789
CLUB NAUTICO Powerboat Rentals: 407-738-1988.

BOYNTON BEACH

Two Georges' Marina/Restaurant: 407-732-4411

St. Mile 1035: Boynton Beach Avenue Bridge Closed 10'. Opens on demand.

way north into pretty Little Lake Worth for all but the smallest cruising boats.

Southward, 22-mile-long Lake Worth is not unlike the Indian River — wide and fairly shallow with the waterway channel dredged down the center (and good fishing on both sides), the area is full of no-wake and manatee zones and restricted anchorage, but the channel is mostly clean and green except for nine bridges as low as ten feet. Palm Beach Inlet, AKA Lake Worth Inlet, near the north end, is classed as all-weather, and there are a number of marine facilities and marinas in the area. Cannonsport, on Singer Island to the east, is one of three, and the mainland side has Riviera Beach Marina and a number of others. If you wish to dock in the thick of things, Palm Harbor Marina is right downtown on the West Palm Beach side.

Conceived in luxury and dedicated to the proposition that all men are not created equal, Palm Beach was for many years the ultimate winter resort, and West Palm Beach was built to house the help. Some idea of the old luxury can be seen at Henry Flagler's Whitehall Mansion, which is now a museum, Mar Lago, now owned by Donald Trump, and comparable mansions of the rich and famous that line the eastern shore.

At the south end of Lake Worth, Boynton Beach Inlet is a real bear best left to the local fishermen in small fast boats who use it heavily (because the fishing on both sides of the inlet is excellent).

South of the inlet, the waterway becomes a landcut again and passes through Boynton Beach and Delray Beach to Boca Raton with facilities and restaurants spaced nicely along its length, mostly around the frequent bridges. Just south of the Atlantic Avenue bridge above Mile 1040, Delray Harbor Club Marina welcomes transients with shopping close by. Boca itself is presided over by the landmark pink tower of the Boca Raton Resort and Club. Once called The Cloisters, it was the masterpiece of architect Addison Mizner's work, and is still one of the grande dames of South Florida hotels.

South of Boca the waterway continues as a landcut through Deerfield Beach, then past Hillsboro Inlet to Lighthouse Point and into Pompano Beach, and traffic takes a decided turn for the busier and faster — Claiborne Young called this area "the hotdog capital of the world". Indeed, from here to Port Everglades the only thing more common than no-wake zones are hotdogs in fast boats ignoring them. On weekends especially, the ocean is more peaceful — and often more safely navigable — than the waterway.

No welcome sign marks the northern entrance of Fort Lauderdale, the city that calls itself the Venice of America, but the welcome mat is out for boatpeople for the next 15 miles or so. You might debate whether its 300-odd miles of waterways qualify the city as a Venice,

RAMPS - BOAT RAMPS - BOAT RAMPS - BOAT R/

EDITOR's NOTE: This is based on the current list maintained by the Florida Department of Environmental Protection, and while it was updated shortly before press time, changes are constant and it's a good idea to check ramps in advance. Note that some ramps are in marinas, private clubs or condominiums where public access may be limited.

PALM BEACH COUNTY BOAT RAMPS

BOCA RATON
Red Reef Park	1111 N. Ocean Blvd. on Atlantic Ocean
Silver Palm Park Boat Ramp	600 E. Palmetto Park Rd. on ICW

BOYNTON BEACH
Boat Club Park	US 1 & NE 21st St. on Lake Worth
John Prince Memorial	Off Hypoluxo Rd.

DELRAY BEACH
Knowles Park	US 1 & SE 10th St. on ICW

JUNO BEACH
Juno Park	2090 Juno Rd. on ICW
Bert Winters Park	13436 Elllison Wilson Rd. on ICW

JUPITER
Blowing Rocks Marina	18487 US 1 on ICW
Burt Reynolds Park	800 N. US 1 on ICW at Jupiter Inlet

LAKE PARK
Lake Park Marina	Lake Shore Dr.

LANTANA
Boat Ramp	East Ocean Ave., ICW
Gundlach's Marina	870 Federal Hwy. on ICW
Sportsman's Park	300 Block of E. Ocean Ave.

RIVIERA BEACH
Phil Foster Memorial Park	900 E. Blue Heron Blvd. on ICW

WEST PALM BEACH
Currie Park	23rd St. & Flagler Dr. on Lake Worth

BOAT RAMPS - BOAT RAMPS - BOAT RAMPS - B

St. Mile 1038.7: NE 8th St. Bridge
Closed 9'. Restricted Nov. 1-May 31,
weekends and holidays, 11AM-6PM. Opens
on the hour and every 15 minutes.

Ocean City Marina: 407-272-9699

**St. Mile 1036: Briney
Breezes, SE 15th St. Bridge**
Closed 25'. Opens on demand.

St. Mile 1039.6: Atlantic Ave. Bridge
Closed 12'. Restricted Nov. 1-May 31, Mon-Fri.
10AM-6PM. Opens on the hour and half-hour.

Delray Beach Marina: 407-243-7250

DELRAY BEACH

DELRAY HARBOR CLUB MARINA: 407-276-0376, CH 16
Can handle up to 100'. Fuel dock open 8-5:30 in winter,
later in summer. Ship store, showers & pool on site, good
restaurants and shopping very nearby. Overnight security.
See ad on page 61.

Delray Beach Yacht Club: 407-272-2700

St. Mile 1041: Linton Blvd. Bridge
Closed 31.5' at the east fender. Opens
on demand.

CHART NINE:
DELRAY TO POMPANO BEACH

APPROXIMATE STATUTE MILES

0   2   4   6

THIS CHART IS NOT TO BE USED FOR NAVIGATION

St. Mile 1044.8: Spanish River Rd.
Closed 25'. Opens on demand.

Boca Inlet: 23' Bascule Bridge
Opens on demand.

Piloting Note:
Extremely dangerous
inlet. Continually
shoaling. Local
knowledge
suggested.

St. Mile 1047: Palmetto Pk. Rd.
Closed 19'. Opens on demand.

BOCA RATON

Boca Raton Resort & Club: 407-395-3000

Boca Raton Inlet

St. Mile 1048.2: Camino Real Bridge.
Closed 9'.Restricted all year 7AM-6PM.
Opens on the hour and every 15 minutes.

Hillsboro Drainage Canal Ramp

Deerfield Island Park
Reachable only by boat.

St. Mile 1050: Hillsboro Blvd. Bridge
Closed 21'. Restricted Oct. 1-May 31, 7AM-6PM.
Opens on the hour and every 20 minutes.

DEERFIELD BEACH

Cove Marina: 954-427-9747
CLUB NAUTICO Powerboat
Rentals: 954-431-4628

LIGHTHOUSE
POINT

Lighthouse Yacht & Racquet Club: 954-942-6688

Hillsboro Inlet Bridge. Closed 13'.
Restricted all year from 7AM-6PM.
Opens every twenty minutes.

Lighthouse Point Marina: 954-942-8118

Hillsboro Inlet

Piloting Note: While inlet
improvements continue, this
is still a fair weather inlet.
Caution in strong winds
from any easterly quadrant.

Merritt's Boat & Engine Works: 954-941-0118

St. Mile 1055: Pompano NE 14th St. Bridge
Closed 15'. Restricted all year from 7AM - 6PM.
Opens on the quarter-hour and three quarter-hour.

St. Mile 1056: Atlantic Blvd. Bridge. Closed 15'.
Restricted all year from 7AM - 6PM. Opens on
the hour and half-hour.

Sand's Harbor Hotel: 954-942-9100
CLUB NAUTICO Powerboat
Rentals: 954-942-3270

Lake Santa Barbara

POMPANO BEACH

Giannone Marine: 800-950-2628
954-784-9011

but there's no question that it lives up to its other billing — The Yachting Capital of the World.

It is doubtful that any spot on earth of equal size offers such an incredible concentration of marine facilities and services and such a population of pleasure boats and businesses that cater to them. The 12,000 boats stuffed into California's Marina del Rey fade in comparison to Broward County's 25,000 resident boats and the estimated 10,000 transient craft that visit there annually.

This didn't happen by accident. Long ago the city fathers decided to make the city attractive to the boating industry, and in 1954 they built the first municipally financed yachting center in the world at Bahia Mar. It has been copied and recopied all over the world, but remains one of the biggest, poshest, and best of all marine facilities.

Waterfront restaurants — including some of Florida's finest — line the ICW, with several of the most popular around the Oakland Park Boulevard bridge. On busy weekends boats raft halfway across the waterway from the half-dozen watering spots that line the east shore south of the bridge. If you want to pause for a taste of Fort Lauderdale highlife, this is the place.

Highrises alternate with palatial homes from there south, past Sunrise Boulevard to Los Olas Boule-

vard, the city docks, and the only legal anchorage in the area, just south of the Las Olas bridge on the west shore. Your first night is on the city; after that check in with the city dockmaster at 305-761-5423. North of the bridge to the west are the wide, deep, beautiful canals that separate the famous Nurmi Isles and boast hundreds of docks and some beautiful boats.

Fort Lauderdale has three excellent city docks, one under the Las Olas Boulevard bridge and a short stroll to the beach where the boys were, one up the New River in the middle of the city, and a third farther up the river at Cooley's Landing, in the heart of the beautiful new Riverwalk district.

A couple of miles south is Bahia Mar itself and the beginning of the center of marine activity that clusters around the 17th Street Causeway Bridge — the only bridge in the world with a painting under it — a huge Guy Harvey original of a leaping marlin, visible only to boats passing through the draw span.

On the north side of the causeway is the legendary Pier 66, now a Hyatt Regency property but still a world-class resort and marina with four diamonds on the AAA registry. Across the street is Pink City, a charming pink strip center that seems to house an unlimited number of yacht brokers and their wares as

well as Marina Inn and Yacht Harbor, which welcome transient craft when space permits. Across the causeway bridge, Marriott Hotel and Portside Marina welcome transients with every amenity. Megayachts too big to dock conventionally or too deep to enter the Waterway line both sides of the river.

Just north of the Marriott is the oldest marina in town, Lauderdale Marina, with the busiest gas dock and customs reporting station in the area - and one of the best seafood restaurants, Fifteenth Street Fisheries. The marina is owned by His Honor Bob Cox, the former mayor of Fort Lauderdale, who gets a lot of the credit for the city's excellent facilities for — and attitude about — boats and boatpeople.

The boats and facilities that line the ICW are only the obvious part of Fort Lauderdale's marine involvements. The New River, which winds for five or six miles west from the ICW just north of 17th Street, is a seemingly endless line of marine facilities from docks, including city docks, to engine shops to waterfront restaurants to boatyards capable of handling any type of boat or yacht. Somewhere along the New River you will find an example of every type, size, and value of boat that has ever been built, and all of the facilities it or you might ever require. Notable are Lauderdale Yacht Basin,

a full service yard that also caters to do-it-yourselfers, and Yacht Haven, a comfortable combination of marina and R/V park.

Right in the middle of the city, above the Andrews Avenue bridge and the "countdown" railroad bridge, is the Riverwalk area with the Center for the Performing Arts and the Museum of Science and Discovery on the north and the popular Shirttail Charlie's restaurant on the south. In all, we have counted 23 major marine facilities in the six or seven miles of winding river from the ICW turnoff to "Marina Mile", where the river forks, west as the North New River Canal and south as the South New River Canal.

The South Canal is a narrow and difficult ditch negotiable only by smaller boats, but eventually connects with the Dania Cutoff Canal, which runs past another dozen marinas and other facilities on its way to rejoin the ICW south of Port Everglades Inlet.

The western reaches of the canal are not navigable by boats that need more than eight or ten feet of clearance, which is a shame because it spoils a good side trip past some beautiful scenery and some equally beautiful facilities. Happily, those facilities are easily reached from the ICW end of the canal south of Port Everglades. *Continued on Page 71*

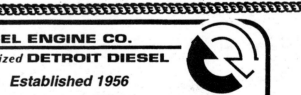

Because Location Is Everything.

HALL OF FAME
MARINA
Fort Lauderdale Beach

435 Seabreeze Boulevard, Fort Lauderdale, Florida 33316
(305) 764-3975

A WESTREC MARINA

The Best Yachting Address in the
Palm Beaches

Located In Downtown West Palm Beach. Across The Intracoastal Waterway From Palm Beach.

At Flashing Red Buoy #12

MARINA FACILITIES:
30, 50, and 100 Amp
Electric Service Available
Shower Rooms
Laundromat
Convenience Store
MasterCard, VISA, American Express
Credit Cards Honored
Private Telephone (Optional)
24-Hour Security
Private Parking
Brokerage Office on Premises
Fire Protection

Accommodations for crafts from 25'
to 150' in length and with drafts up to 10'
High speed diesel and gas pumps for
quick refueling
Texaco Fuel

SERVICES:
Mail Service
Tide and Weather Information
Assistance in entering and leaving your slip
Channel 16 VHF Monitoring
Cable TV
Close to Worth Avenue
Minutes to Airport

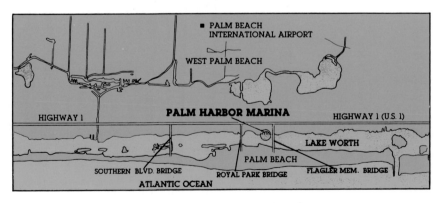

Palm Harbor Marina   -   400-A North Flagler Dr.   -   West Palm Beach, Florida 33401
Phone: 407 - 655-4757   1 - 800 - 435 - 8051   Fax: 407 - 659 - 0245

EDITOR's NOTE: This is based on the current list maintained by the Florida Department of Environmental Protection, and while it was updated shortly before press time, changes are constant and it's a good idea to check ramps in advance. Note that some ramps are in marinas, private clubs or condominiums where public access may be limited.

BROWARD COUNTY RAMPS

COCONUT CREEK
Donaldson Park — 900 NW 43th Ave. & Coconut Creek Pkwy.

DANIA
Houston Park/Dania Yacht Club — 850 NE 3rd St.
Lloyd Beach, State Rec. Area, — 6503 N. Ocean Dr., Atlantic & ICW

FORT LAUDERDALE
7th Ave. Boat Ramp — Cooley's Landing Marine Facility, 400 SW 7th Ave. on New River at SW 4th St.
15th St. Boat Ramp — 1770 SE 15th St. on Stranahan River
Broward Marine — 1601 SW 20th St. on New River
George English Park — 1101 Bayview Dr. & Sunrise Blvd. on Middle River
Joseph C. Carter Park — 1448 W. Sunrise Blvd. & NW 16th Ave.
Lauderdale Isles Yacht & Tennis — 2637 Whale Harbor La. on New River (Not usable)
Lou's Tackle & Marina — 3463 Griffin Rd.
Marina 84 — 3000 SR 84 on New River
New River Yacht Club — 3001 SR 84 on New River
Public Beach — South Beach Parking Lot (Catamarans)
Public Beach — NE 18th St.
Ramgoh Marina — 4500 SR 7 on New River
Riverbend Marine — 1515 SW 20th St. on New River
Small Boat Club — 1740 SW 42nd St.
Yacht Haven Park Marina — 2323 SR 84 on New River (Private)

HOLLYWOOD
Holland Park — Johnson St. & 6th Ave. on ICW
Hollywood Marina — 700 Polk St. on North Lake
Sailors Point — 9th Ave. & North Lake Dr. (Private)

OAKLAND PARK
City Boat Ramp — 2960 NE 12th Terr. (Fixed bridge)

POMPANO BEACH
Alsdorf Boat Launch Park — 2850 NE 14th St. Cswy.
Hillsboro Inlet Marina — 2635 N. Riverside Dr. on ICW
Pompano Fishing Pier — 222 Pompano Beach Blvd.

DADE COUNTY BOAT RAMPS

CORAL GABLES
Gables Waterway Towers — 90 Edgewater Dr. on Gables Waterway
Matheson Hammock Park — 9610 Old Cutler Rd.

HOMESTEAD
Black Point Park — SW 248th St. & SW 87th Ave. on Biscayne Bay
Homestead Bayfront Park — SW 328th St. & 97th Ave. 9698 SW N. Canal Dr.

KEY BISCAYNE
Key Biscayne Yacht Club — 180 Harbor Dr.
Key Marina — 3501 Rickenbacker Cswy. on Biscayne Bay
Marina Biscayne — 3301 Rickenbacker Cswy. on Biscayne Bay

MIAMI
Coral Reef Yacht Club — 2484 S. Bayshore Dr. on Biscayne Bay
Dinner Key Marina — 3400 Pan American Dr.
Eliz. Verrick Gym & Boat Ramp — 2600 S. Bayshore Dr. on Biscayne Bay
Florida International Univ. — University Park, N. Miami Complex, NE 151st St.
Fla. Power & Light Club Marina — 14925 SW 67th Ave. on Biscayne Bay
Homestead AFB — 31CJS-SS on Biscayne Bay & Mystic Lake
Legion Memorial Comm. Park — Biscayne Blvd. & NE 66th St. on Biscayne Bay
Miami Outboard Club — 1099 MacArthur Cswy.
Morningside Park — 850 NE 55th Terr.
Palm Bay Club — 780 NE 69th St. on Biscayne Bay
Pelican Harbor Marina — 79th St. Cswy. on Biscayne Bay
Snapper Creek Marina — 11190 Snapper Creek Rd.
Virginia Key Beach — Crandon Blvd., Virginia Key on Atlantic Ocean
Watson Island Park — 1050 MacArthur Cswy. on Biscayne Bay

MIAMI BEACH
Haulover Beach Park — 10800 Collins Ave. on Biscayne Bay & Atlantic Ocean
Island View Park — Purdy Ave. to Biscyane Bay & Dade Blvd. to 18th St. on Biscayne Bay

N. KEY BISCAYNE
Key Biscayne Golf Course — 6700 Crandon Blvd. on Biscayne Bay & Atlantic Ocean

S. MIAMI
Coral Reef Park — 9895 SW 152nd St. & 77th Ave. on Canal C-100C
Krome Ave. Launching Area — 1.5 miles n. of Trail, w. of Thompson Park (SR 27)

S. of FLORIDA CITY
Canal 111 Access Area Ramp — Off US 1 on C-111

THE ISLAND WITHIN.

4 Swimming Pools.
Refresh yourself in magnificent pools of every size and description from neo-classical to contemporary.

Choice of Golf Courses.
2 Robert Trent Jones courses are surrounded by tropical gardens and winding waterways.

24 Tennis Courts.
2 new multi-surface tennis complexes are home of Grand Slam Sports and resident pro, Fred Stolle.

Gourmet Dining.
11 private restaurants and lounges offer inspired choices from seaside casual to gourmet cuisine.

Private Ocean Club.
Relax on the powder-soft stretch of private beach along the Atlantic Ocean.

Spa & Fitness Center.
Pamper and challenge yourself with exotic treatments, the finest exercise equipment, and personal trainers.

Welcome to the Yacht Club & Marina at South Florida's luxurious Turnberry Isle Resort & Club. As a marina guest, all the amenities usually reserved exclusively for club members are at your command. The 119-slip marina, directly off the Intracoastal Waterway, accommodates vessels up to 200 feet, and features 30, 50 and 100-amp 3-phase electric service, cable television, two phone lines, mail service, showers, restrooms, and ice, plus a ship's store, Crew's Lounge and 24-hour security. And our European-trained staff redefines the meaning of excellent service. Slip inside the island within.

Turnberry Isle Resort & Club
A RAFAEL HOTEL

For information call: (305) 933-6934, Toll-Free 1-800-327-7028, Fax: (305) 932-9096.
MEMBER OF: *The Leading Hotels of the World* U·T·E·L·L INTERNATIONAL

RAFAEL HOTELS & RESORTS WORLDWIDE: NEW YORK / GENEVA / DUSSELDORF / MUNICH / MELBOURNE / BORA BORA / PHUKET / BALI / KUALA LUMPUR / COURCHEVEL / AMANUSA.

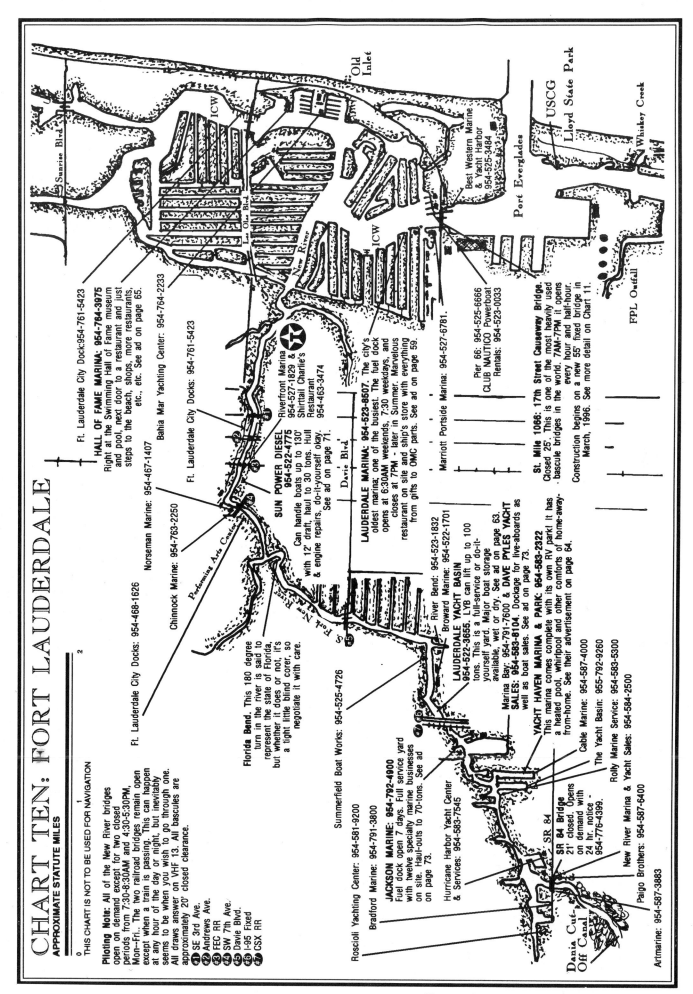

CHART TEN: FORT LAUDERDALE

APPROXIMATE STATUTE MILES

0   1   2

THIS CHART IS NOT TO BE USED FOR NAVIGATION

Piloting Note: All of the New River bridges open on demand except for two closed periods from 7:30-8:30AM and 4:30-5:30PM, Mon.-Fri.. The two railroad bridges remain open except when a train is passing. This can happen at any hour of the day or night, but inevitably seems to be when you wish to go through one. All draws answer on VHF 13. All bascules are approximately 20' closed clearance.

① SE 3rd Ave.
② Andrews Ave.
③ FEC RR
④ SW 7th Ave.
⑤ Davie Blvd.
⑥ I-95 Fixed
⑦ CSX RR

Ft. Lauderdale City Dock: 954-761-5423

HALL OF FAME MARINA: 954-764-3975
Right at the Swimming Hall of Fame museum and pool, next door to a restaurant and just steps to the beach, shops, more restaurants, etc., etc. See ad on page 65.

Bahia Mar Yachting Center: 954-764-2233

Norseman Marine: 954-467-1407

Ft. Lauderdale City Docks: 954-761-5423

Chinnock Marine: 954-763-2250

Ft. Lauderdale City Docks: 954-468-1626

SUN POWER DIESEL
954-522-4775
Can handle boats up to 130' with 12' draft, haul to 30 tons. Hull & engine repairs, do-it-yourself okay. See ad on page 71.

Riverfront Marina 954-527-1829 & Shirttail Charlie's Restaurant 954-463-3474

LAUDERDALE MARINA: 954-523-8507. The city's oldest marina; one of the busiest. The fuel dock opens at 6:30AM weekends, 7:30 weekdays, and closes at 7PM - later in Summer. Marvelous restaurant on site and ship's store with everything from gifts to OMC parts. See ad on page 59.

Marriott Portside Marina: 954-527-6781.

Best Western Marine & Yacht Harbor 954-525-3484

Pier 66: 954-525-6666
CLUB NAUTICO Powerboat Rentals: 954-523-0033

St. Mile 1066: 17th Street Causeway Bridge. Closed 25'. This is one of the most heavily used bascule bridges in the world. 7AM-7PM it opens every hour and half-hour. Construction begins on a new 55' fixed bridge in March, 1996. See more detail on Chart 11.

USCG
Lloyd State Park
954-525-3484

Florida Bend. This 180 degree turn in the river is said to represent the state of Florida, but whether it does or not, it's a tight little blind corer, so negotiate it with care.

Performing Arts Center

Summerfield Boat Works: 954-525-4726

River Bend: 954-523-1832
Broward Marine: 954-522-1701

LAUDERDALE YACHT BASIN
954-522-3655. LYB can lift up to 100 tons. This is a full-service or do-it-yourself yard. Major boat storage available, wet or dry. See ad on page 63. Marina Bay: 954-791-7600 & DAVE PYLES YACHT SALES: 954-583-8104. Dockage for live-aboards as well as boat sales. See ad on page 73.

YACHT HAVEN MARINA & PARK: 954-583-2322
This marina comes complete with its own RV park! It has a heated pool, whirlpool and other comforts of home-away-from-home. See their advertisement on page 64.

Cable Marine: 954-587-4000
The Yacht Basin: 955-792-9260
Rolly Marine Service: 954-583-5300
Rolly Marine & Yacht Sales: 954-584-2500

Roscioli Yachting Center: 954-581-9200

Bradford Marine: 954-791-3800

JACKSON MARINE: 954-792-4900
Fuel dock open 7 days. Full service yard with twelve specialty marine businesses on site. Haul-outs to 70-tons. See ad on page 73.

Hurricane Harbor Yacht Center & Services: 954-583-7545

SR 84
SR 84 Bridge 21' closed. Opens on demand with 24 hr. notice - 954-776-4399.

New River Marina & Yacht Sales: 954-587-6400

Paigo Brothers: 954-587-3883

Dania Cut-off Canal

Artmarine: 954-776-4399

Old Inlet
ICW
Las Olas Blvd.
New River
S. Fork New River
Davie Blvd
Port Everglades
FPL Outfall
Whiskey Creek
Sunrise Blvd

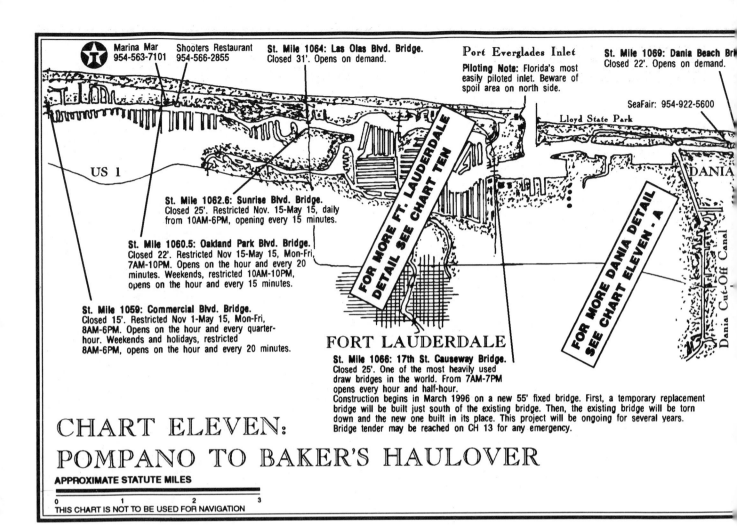

Marina Mar
954-563-7101

Shooters Restaurant
954-566-2855

St. Mile 1064: Las Olas Blvd. Bridge.
Closed 31'. Opens on demand.

Port Everglades Inlet

Piloting Note: Florida's most easily piloted inlet. Beware of spoil area on north side.

St. Mile 1069: Dania Beach Br
Closed 22'. Opens on demand.

Lloyd State Park

SeaFair: 954-922-5600

US 1

DANIA

FOR MORE FT. LAUDERDALE DETAIL SEE CHART TEN

FOR MORE DANIA DETAIL SEE CHART ELEVEN - A

Dania Cut-Off Canal

St. Mile 1062.6: Sunrise Blvd. Bridge.
Closed 25'. Restricted Nov. 15-May 15, daily from 10AM-6PM, opening every 15 minutes.

St. Mile 1060.5: Oakland Park Blvd. Bridge.
Closed 22'. Restricted Nov 15-May 15, Mon-Fri, 7AM-10PM. Opens on the hour and every 20 minutes. Weekends, restricted 10AM-10PM, opens on the hour and every 15 minutes.

St. Mile 1059: Commercial Blvd. Bridge.
Closed 15'. Restricted Nov 1-May 15, Mon-Fri, 8AM-6PM. Opens on the hour and every quarter-hour. Weekends and holidays, restricted 8AM-6PM, opens on the hour and every 20 minutes.

FORT LAUDERDALE

St. Mile 1066: 17th St. Causeway Bridge.
Closed 25'. One of the most heavily used draw bridges in the world. From 7AM-7PM opens every hour and half-hour.
Construction begins in March 1996 on a new 55' fixed bridge. First, a temporary replacement bridge will be built just south of the existing bridge. Then, the existing bridge will be torn down and the new one built in its place. This project will be ongoing for several years. Bridge tender may be reached on CH 13 for any emergency.

CHART ELEVEN:
POMPANO TO BAKER'S HAULOVER

APPROXIMATE STATUTE MILES

| 0 | 1 | 2 | 3 |

THIS CHART IS NOT TO BE USED FOR NAVIGATION

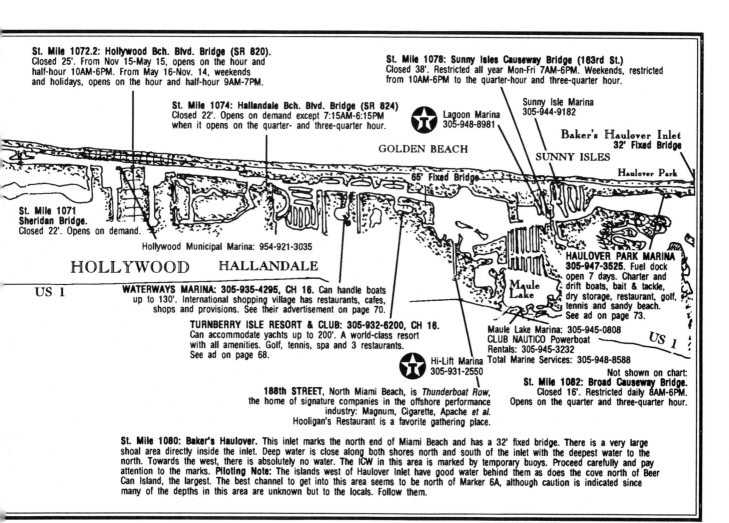

St. Mile 1072.2: Hollywood Bch. Blvd. Bridge (SR 820). Closed 25'. From Nov 15-May 15, opens on the hour and half-hour 10AM-6PM. From May 16-Nov. 14, weekends and holidays, opens on the hour and half-hour 9AM-7PM.

St. Mile 1074: Hallandale Bch. Blvd. Bridge (SR 824). Closed 22'. Opens on demand except 7:15AM-6:15PM when it opens on the quarter- and three-quarter hour.

St. Mile 1078: Sunny Isles Causeway Bridge (163rd St.) Closed 38'. Restricted all year Mon-Fri 7AM-6PM. Weekends, restricted from 10AM-6PM to the quarter-hour and three-quarter hour.

Lagoon Marina 305-948-8981

GOLDEN BEACH

Sunny Isle Marina 305-944-9182

Baker's Haulover Inlet 32' Fixed Bridge

SUNNY ISLES

Haulover Park

65' Fixed Bridge

St. Mile 1071 Sheridan Bridge. Closed 22'. Opens on demand.

Hollywood Municipal Marina: 954-921-3035

HOLLYWOOD   HALLANDALE

US 1

WATERWAYS MARINA: 305-935-4295, CH 16. Can handle boats up to 130'. International shopping village has restaurants, cafes, shops and provisions. See their advertisement on page 70.

TURNBERRY ISLE RESORT & CLUB: 305-932-6200, CH 16. Can accommodate yachts up to 200'. A world-class resort with all amenities. Golf, tennis, spa and 3 restaurants. See ad on page 68.

Hi-Lift Marina 305-931-2550

188th STREET, North Miami Beach, is *Thunderboat Row*, the home of signature companies in the offshore performance industry: Magnum, Cigarette, Apache *et al.* Hooligan's Restaurant is a favorite gathering place.

Maule Lake

HAULOVER PARK MARINA 305-947-3525. Fuel dock open 7 days. Charter and drift boats, bait & tackle, dry storage, restaurant, golf, tennis and sandy beach. See ad on page 73.

Maule Lake Marina: 305-945-0808 CLUB NAUTICO Powerboat Rentals: 305-945-3232 Total Marine Services: 305-948-8588

US 1

Not shown on chart: St. Mile 1082: Broad Causeway Bridge. Closed 16'. Restricted daily 8AM-6PM. Opens on the quarter and three-quarter hour.

St. Mile 1080: Baker's Haulover. This inlet marks the north end of Miami Beach and has a 32' fixed bridge. There is a very large shoal area directly inside the inlet. Deep water is close along both shores north and south of the inlet with the deepest water to the north. Towards the west, there is absolutely no water. The ICW in this area is marked by temporary buoys. Proceed carefully and pay attention to the marks. **Piloting Note:** The islands west of Haulover Inlet have good water behind them as does the cove north of Beer Can Island, the largest. The best channel to get into this area seems to be north of Marker 6A, although caution is indicated since many of the depths in this area are unknown but to the locals. Follow them.

South of the 17th Street Causeway the waterway jogs east through busy Port Everglades with its all-weather inlet and heavy commercial and recreational traffic. Ranking second among world cruise-ship ports, it's open, often windy and almost always rough, but it's an easy-enough passage except when a cruise ship or naval vessel with attending tugboats is filling it.

Between Everglades Inlet and the mouth of the Dania Cut-Off Canal, past the old turning basin and the warmwater outlet from Florida Power and Light's big generating plant, is some of the best urban sportfishing in the country. Big tarpon and snook come into the area to feed on the baitfish attracted by the nutrients in the warm water, and angler/weightlifters armed with heavy tackle gather in pursuit. Caution: It's also an area very popular with manatees, especially in cold weather.

Just south of the port at Mile 1067, Whiskey Creek leads off east into a favorite gunkhole and picnic spot for local small boatmen that's only a short walk from the beach. Southward from there the waterway passes through another landcut which lasts all the way to the north end of Biscayne Bay. The mainland side of the waterway is largely parks and residential areas; the barrier island side is wall-to-wall with restaurants, watering holes and other businesses catering to traffic on both the waterway and busy highway A1A all the way through Hollywood to North Miami and Biscayne Bay. Almost all have docks, and almost all are a block or so from the beach and Hollywood's "Boardwalk" —

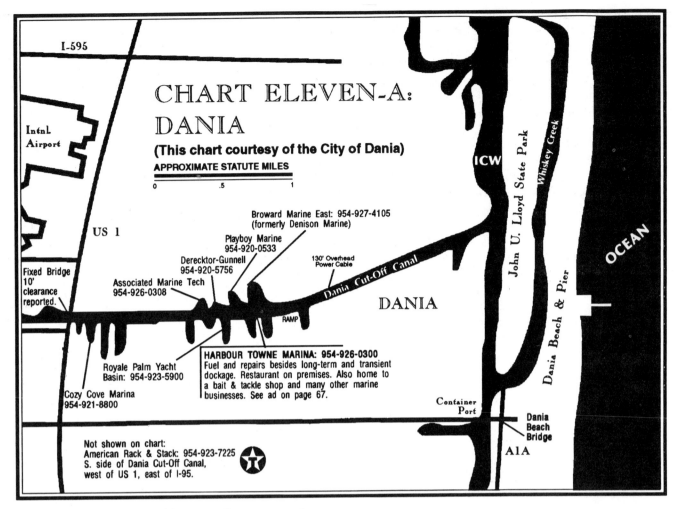

CHART ELEVEN-A: DANIA

(This chart courtesy of the City of Dania)

APPROXIMATE STATUTE MILES

I-595

Int'nl Airport

US 1

Fixed Bridge 10' clearance reported.

Associated Marine Tech 954-926-0308

Derecktor-Gunnell 954-920-5756

Playboy Marine 954-920-0533

Broward Marine East: 954-927-4105 (formerly Denison Marine)

130' Overhead Power Cable

Dania Cut-Off Canal

DANIA

RAMP

HARBOUR TOWNE MARINA: 954-926-0300
Fuel and repairs besides long-term and transient dockage. Restaurant on premises. Also home to a bait & tackle shop and many other marine businesses. See ad on page 67.

Royale Palm Yacht Basin: 954-923-5900

Cozy Cove Marina 954-921-8800

ICW

John U. Lloyd State Park

Whiskey Creek

OCEAN

Dania Beach & Pier

Container Port

Dania Beach Bridge

A1A

Not shown on chart:
American Rack & Stack: 954-923-7225
S. side of Dania Cut-Off Canal,
west of US 1, east of I-95.

actually blacktop but a lot of fun to stroll on anyway. A popular stop is Martha's, just above Mile 1070, and Hollwood Municipal Yacht Basin lies a couple of miles south on the mainland side.

Just after Marker 1075 the new Waterways Marina lies off the channel to the west. A favorite and unusual feature of the complex is the Unicorn natural foods market and restaurant. The elegant marina and world-class amenities of the Turnberry Isle Resort & Club lie further south on the right. Farther south at Mile 1077 a narrow canal leads west into Maule Lake and across the lake to its namesake marina.

Five miles farther south, the waterway opens into the headwaters of Biscayne Bay at Baker's Haulover, which marks the northern end of Miami Beach and is noted for the large shoal area between the waterway and the inlet. One of the shallowest parts of the ICW, it is mostly marked by temporary buoys that are moved around to follow the deeper water but never quite catch up. Approach and pass with care, and leave the inlet to the fishermen and go-fast boats that can handle it. Haulover Beach Park, north of the inlet on the east side, has a popular restaurant with temporary dockage.

South of Haulover, Biscayne Bay opens up before you approach the city of Miami. Like every other port city, Miami has its bad and even dangerous sections, and lately it's been getting terrible publicity, but it also has some of the finest facilities in the country for cruising

boatmen, and the two are seldom in the same neighborhood. If you like urban cruising, this is it.

Miami and Miami Beach are in the middle of a renaissance of marine facilities, speeded up somewhat by damage done by Hurricane Andrew in 1992. There is more good dockage available on Biscayne Bay today than there has been in many years, and a growing number of facilities and attractions to welcome cruising visitors. These include North Bay Landing on 79th Street and the Biscayne Marriott at the Venetian Causeway, and Sunset Harbor Marina further south on the Miami Beach side. Even the legendary Miami Beach resort hotels like the Doral, Eden Roc and Fontainbleau have docks along Indian Creek, one of the interesting channels inside the islands on the east side of the bay.

Just south of the Dodge Island Bridge on the mainland side is Miamarina, which was heavily damaged by Hurricane Andrew and received low priority among the rebuilding projects since. With renovations apparently stalled, it's a skeleton of its former self and can offer little more than a place to tie up in the protected harbor to visit Bayside, the collection of exotic shops and restaurants that surrounds the marina, or to board Miami's Metrorail system, which connects to almost anywhere in the city.

On the ocean side, right on Government Cut and distinguished by its signature lighthouse/office structure, is the big Miami Beach Marina, a steadily expanding and improving full-service facility that bills itself as The Gateway to the Caribbean. Amenities include a couple of excellent restaurants, market, ship's store, and proximity to the upscale South Beach district. It is sure to be easier to dock your boat there than to park your car on South Beach.

Across the bay on the mainland side is the Miami River, with the elegant duPont Plaza Hotel & Marina at its mouth and more than a dozen marinas and boatyards stretching four miles inland. Narrow but deep, criss-crossed by a dozen bridges, and bearing heavy traffic including small freighters, it was once a filthy sewer winding through slums and lined with wrecks and junk, but has undergone a renaissance of its own and is now a safer and more pleasant route for those visiting its facilities, which include such distinguished names as Richard Bertram and Merrill-Stevens.

Heading south from the river mouth, the bay opens up and the architecturally interesting towers of Brickell Avenue rise on the mainland shore, then subside as you pass under the Rickenbacker Causeway and give way to the elegant estates and parklike grounds that typify Coconut Grove and Coral Gables.

Notable among them is Viscaya, the landmark former home of International Harvester founder James Deering and now a museum open to the public. It is a Mediterranean palazzo which reportedly cost $5 million to build at the turn of the century and employed ten percent of the population of Miami in its construction. There are several other attractions of nautical interest in the area, including The Barnacle, the landmark home of Commodore Ralph Munro, who was one of the first settlers and leading yachtsmen of his time.

The largest yachting center in the Miami area is farther south on the west shore, at Dinner Key, roughly Mile 1094. Dinner Key was built as Pan Am's flying boat base for the Clippers. When the airline turned to wheels instead of hulls, they sold the property to the City of Miami, who used the terminal as city hall and built Dinner Key Marina, the biggest marina in Florida, on the surrounding property. Half a dozen other marinas and yacht clubs are clustered to the north. All are within walking distance of the pleasant facilities and pictur-esque attractions of the upscale village of Coconut Grove. If you'd rather stay out, there's an anchoring area just offshore that you can share with one of the most picturesque communities of bumboats in the southeast.

Opposite Dinner Key, across Rickenbacker Causeway, lie Virginia Key and Key Biscayne, which are actually the northernmost of the Florida Keys although

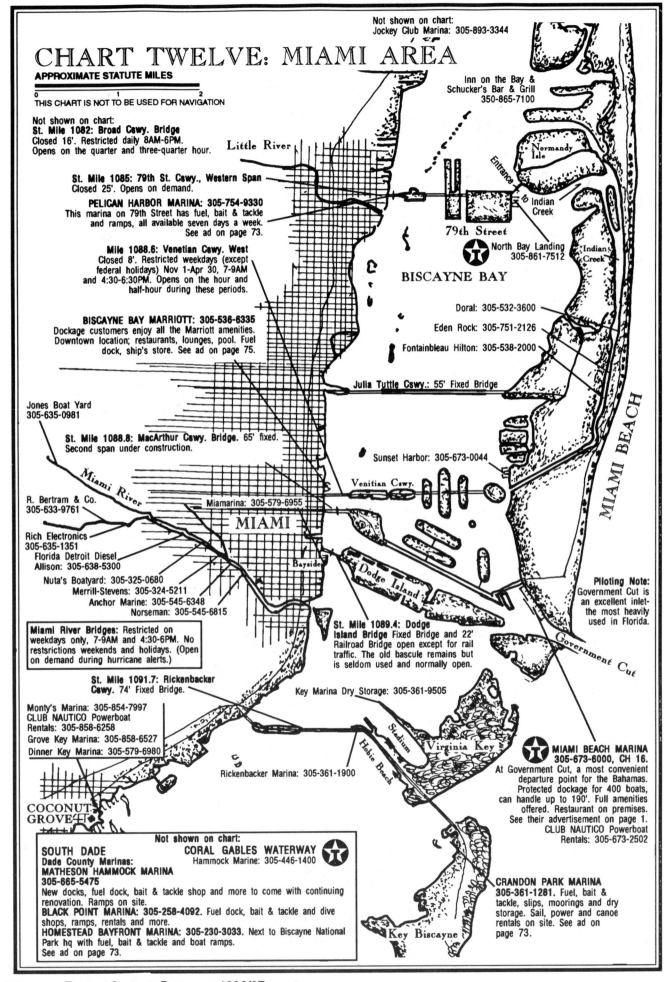

CHART TWELVE: MIAMI AREA

APPROXIMATE STATUTE MILES

0   1   2

THIS CHART IS NOT TO BE USED FOR NAVIGATION

Not shown on chart:
Jockey Club Marina: 305-893-3344

Inn on the Bay &
Schucker's Bar & Grill
350-865-7100

Not shown on chart:
St. Mile 1082: Broad Cswy. Bridge
Closed 16'. Restricted daily 8AM-6PM.
Opens on the quarter and three-quarter hour.

St. Mile 1085: 79th St. Cswy., Western Span
Closed 25'. Opens on demand.

PELICAN HARBOR MARINA: 305-754-9330
This marina on 79th Street has fuel, bait & tackle
and ramps, all available seven days a week.
See ad on page 73.

Mile 1088.6: Venetian Cswy. West
Closed 8'. Restricted weekdays (except
federal holidays) Nov 1-Apr 30, 7-9AM
and 4:30-6:30PM. Opens on the hour and
half-hour during these periods.

BISCAYNE BAY MARRIOTT: 305-536-6335
Dockage customers enjoy all the Marriott amenities.
Downtown location; restaurants, lounges, pool. Fuel
dock, ship's store. See ad on page 75.

Jones Boat Yard
305-635-0981

St. Mile 1088.8: MacArthur Cswy. Bridge. 65' fixed.
Second span under construction.

R. Bertram & Co.
305-633-9761

Rich Electronics
305-635-1351
Florida Detroit Diesel
Allison: 305-638-5300
Nuta's Boatyard: 305-325-0680
Merrill-Stevens: 305-324-5211
Anchor Marine: 305-545-6348
Norseman: 305-545-6815

Miami River Bridges: Restricted on
weekdays only, 7-9AM and 4:30-6PM. No
restrictions weekends and holidays. (Open
on demand during hurricane alerts.)

**St. Mile 1091.7: Rickenbacker
Cswy.** 74' Fixed Bridge.

Monty's Marina: 305-854-7997
CLUB NAUTICO Powerboat
Rentals: 305-858-6258
Grove Key Marina: 305-858-6527
Dinner Key Marina: 305-579-6980

COCONUT
GROVE

Not shown on chart:
SOUTH DADE
Dade County Marinas:
MATHESON HAMMOCK MARINA
305-665-5475
New docks, fuel dock, bait & tackle shop and more to come with continuing
renovation. Ramps on site.
BLACK POINT MARINA: 305-258-4092. Fuel dock, bait & tackle and dive
shops, ramps, rentals and more.
HOMESTEAD BAYFRONT MARINA: 305-230-3033. Next to Biscayne National
Park hq with fuel, bait & tackle and boat ramps.
See ad on page 73.

Not shown on chart:
CORAL GABLES WATERWAY
Hammock Marine: 305-446-1400

Little River

Normandy Isle

79th Street

North Bay Landing
305-861-7512

Entrance to Indian Creek

Indian Creek

BISCAYNE BAY

Doral: 305-532-3600
Eden Rock: 305-751-2126
Fontainbleau Hilton: 305-538-2000

Julia Tuttle Cswy.: 55' Fixed Bridge

MIAMI BEACH

Sunset Harbor: 305-673-0044

Venitian Cswy.

Miamarina: 305-579-6955

MIAMI

Bayside

Dodge Island

Piloting Note:
Government Cut is
an excellent inlet-
the most heavily
used in Florida.

**St. Mile 1089.4: Dodge
Island Bridge** Fixed Bridge and 22'
Railroad Bridge open except for rail
traffic. The old bascule remains but
is seldom used and normally open.

Government Cut

Key Marina Dry Storage: 305-361-9505

Miami River

Stadium

Hobie Beach

Virginia Key

Rickenbacker Marina: 305-361-1900

MIAMI BEACH MARINA
305-673-6000, CH 16.
At Government Cut, a most convenient
departure point for the Bahamas.
Protected dockage for 400 boats,
can handle up to 190'. Full amenities
offered. Restaurant on premises.
See their advertisement on page 1.
CLUB NAUTICO Powerboat
Rentals: 305-673-2502

CRANDON PARK MARINA
305-361-1281. Fuel, bait &
tackle, slips, moorings and dry
storage. Sail, power and canoe
rentals on site. See ad on
page 73.

Key Biscayne

Slip into something spectacular.

The Biscayne Bay Marriott Marina. Miami's most exceptional year-round dockage. Perfect location. Every convenience. Maximum value. Service and style by Marriott, of course.

- Located at ICW Mile Marker 48, close to Government Cut, gateway to the Keys and Bahamas
- 181 wet slips, davits, finger pier access
- Exercise Room
- 24-hour security
- Ship's store including liquor
- All the amenities of the Biscayne Bay Marriott Hotel
- Lounges
- Restaurants
- Pool
- Pizza Hut®

The spectacular awaits you. Call our Marina Manager for more information and reserve your space today.

BISCAYNE BAY
Marriott
HOTEL & MARINA®
We Make It Happen For You.

1633 N. Bayshore Drive, Miami, FL 33132 • (305)536-6335

Keys residents insist that Key Largo is the northern end of the chain. The islands still show the aftermath of the landfall of Hurricane Andrew, especially to their lush tropical vegetation, which is still in tatters in some areas.

Virginia Key is home to the Rosensteil School of Oceanography and Miami Seaquarium on the south shore and two marinas in a sheltered cove and popular anchorage north of the causeway between the excellent Rusty Pelican restaurant and the abandoned Marine Stadium. The north end of the island is a beach park still showing heavy damage from the hurricane — reported now to be out for bids to convert it to a commercial attraction, which will surely include a marine facility.

Across Bear Cut to the east, Key Biscayne is still a beauty spot divided about equally between parks, beaches and residential areas. The excellent municipal facility of Crandon Park Marina lies at the southwest corner of the island and the abandoned lighthouse at the east end marks Cape Florida and the outside route southward to the Keys via Hawk Channel.

South of Key Biscayne and Dinner Key, Biscayne Bay is a wide-open body that makes for great fishing and sailing, and is home to the annual Columbus Day Regatta, the largest such event in the world. At that point you officially leave The Gold Coast. The bay leads southward toward the Keys, and we will follow it there.

$19.95

Cruising Guide to the Florida Keys

NAUTICA INC.

NEW Revised 9th Edition

CONTENTS: PLACES TO GO, THINGS TO SEE, AERIAL SATELLITE PHOTOS, MARINAS, 42 DETAILED CHARTS, WEATHERS & TIDE INFORMATION, UNDERWATER ACTIVITIES

You Don't Have To Go Across The Gulfstream
- **Go Cruising Now**
- **Life's Too Short**
- **Get Your Main Squeeze**
- **Ride The Wind**
- **Get Your Food From the Sea**

Sail These Magic Islands, You Won't Want to Go Home! FULL COLOR This 256 page book will set you on your way to beautiful anchorages. Diving spots, fishing grounds, marinas, plus tide information. Things to do & see from the Keys to Tarpon Springs on the West Coast.

Send $19.95
Plus $2.00 Postage to:
Frank Papy
Box 263, Route 6
Ridgeland, SC 29936
(803) 521-9150

or contact Waterways Etc., Distributor

Name _____

Address _____

City _____ State _____ Zip _____

Dealer Inquiries Welcome

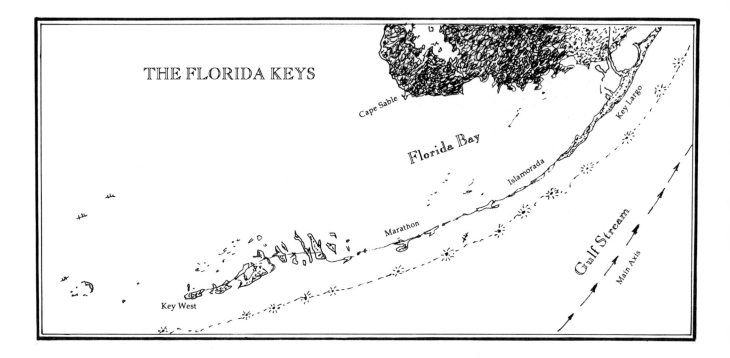

THE FLORIDA KEYS

Cape Sable

Florida Bay

Key Largo

Islamorada

Marathon

Gulf Stream

Main Axis

Key West

CRUISING THE FLORIDA KEYS

Cruising southward under the Rickenbacker Causeway, you find yourself in south Biscayne Bay and at the gateway to the Florida Keys, North America's most accessible — yet in many ways most unspoiled — cruising grounds. This directory's founder, Pete Smyth, described them accurately as "America's Out Islands - the Bahamas with channel markers and working telephones".

Note that while everyone speaks of the Keys as a chain, it is a curving one. Starting down the chain from Key Largo, your course will be almost due south, but by the time you reach Marathon it will be almost due west. Most cruising boatpeople simplify directions and speak in terms of "up" and "down" rather than compass points, a custom that we will often follow on these pages.

At that point southbound boats have two choices: The first is to continue inside the barrier islands on the ICW; the second is to go outside.

If you opt for the outside, you can follow the southern shore of Key Biscayne around Cape Florida or take Biscayne Channel out through the middle of Stiltsville, a gradually vanishing community of vacation homes perched on pilings. Hawk Channel runs along the ocean side of the Keys, protected by the reefs that parallel the shore all the way to Key West. Although its outside perimeter is one long reef - the second longest barrier reef in the Western Hemisphere — every hazard is well marked and you shouldn't have any difficulty — if you keep your eyes open.

The inside route, down the south bay, is wide open and pretty much of uniform and adequate depth until you get to Featherbed Bank at about Mile 1108. The bank, which extends nearly all the way across the bay, will be your first introduction to Keys-style skinny-water piloting with go-no-go depths and the need to learn to follow markers closely. Happily, the ICW channels are well marked, visibility is usually excellent in the clear water, and the prudent pilot who practices good eyeball navigation should have no trouble.

On the way south, good public facilities are spaced along the mainland shore. South of Dinner Key and its neighbor marinas, Matheson Hammock Marina, Black Point Marina, and Herbert Hoover Marina at Biscayne National Park are there if you need them and pleasant stops in any event. All are fully recovered, and indeed expanded and improved, after the damage caused by Hurricane Andrew in 1992.

For anglers, these are the fabled flats which are home to some of the biggest (and some say best-educated) bonefish on this side of the Gulf Stream as well as permit, tarpon, seatrout, snappers and other shallow-water gamefish. Fishermen, especially fly fishermen, come from all over the country to try for the elusive flats feeders, and support an active tackle, outfitting and guiding industry in the process.

Biscayne National Park occupies both sides of the lower half of the south bay (with a boundary detour around the landmark nuclear powerplant at Turkey

Point). The keys that line the eastern side of the bay are all part of the park, beginning with the Ragged Keys on the north (which could also be called the northernmost keys but aren't) and continuing southward to Boca Chica, Sands Key and the main island, Elliott Key. All are accessible only by boat. The Park Service maintains docks but only park facilities at Elliott Key. Sands Key and Elliott Key offer good anchorage, and protection from the elements is fine as long as the prevailing easterlies blow.

Elliott Key ends at Caesar's Creek, named for the notorious pirate Black Caesar. It offers passage out to Hawk Channel for boats clearing four feet. Further south, at the north end of Key Largo, is Angelfish Creek, the more favored of the two channels with another foot or so of depth.

On the ocean side just south of Angelfish Creek lies the very private and very prestigious Ocean Reef Club. Visitors and transients are not welcome, but reciprocal privileges are extended to members of accredited yacht clubs. Calling ahead is essential, especially in the winter season, because Ocean Reef is also very popular and can get very crowded.

Back on the bay side in Card Sound, you'll find Pumpkin Key at Mile 1122, entirely surrounded by

good, deep anchorage in winds from any direction. It's a very popular place and on a good weekend you may find yourself surrounded by boats.

At Mile 1125 you come to Card Bank, just below the Card Sound Bridge, then Barnes Sound. Barnes Sound is mostly open, but has some interesting corners for cruising folks to sneak into for a night or two. On the mainland side, south of Manatee Bay, you'll find Cross Key and several marinas, including The Moorings, Point Laura, and Manatee Bay Marina. Dockage and full services are readily available.

Cross Key ends at Jewfish Creek drawbridge over the ICW at Mile 1135, the point where the causeway from the mainland makes its landfall on Key Largo. Dockage with fuel, rooms, restaurants and supplies are available just south of the bridge, at Anchorage Resort & Yacht Club on the east side and Gilbert's Holiday Island on the west. The creaky old bascule bridge is scheduled for replacement by a high bridge in the near future, but Rob Cummings at Anchorage assures us that construction won't interfere with either navigation or his operation, which is good news.

Jewfish Creek is where local fishermen make a sharp turn to starboard and head across Florida Bay for the fabulous fishing from there to Flamingo, across the

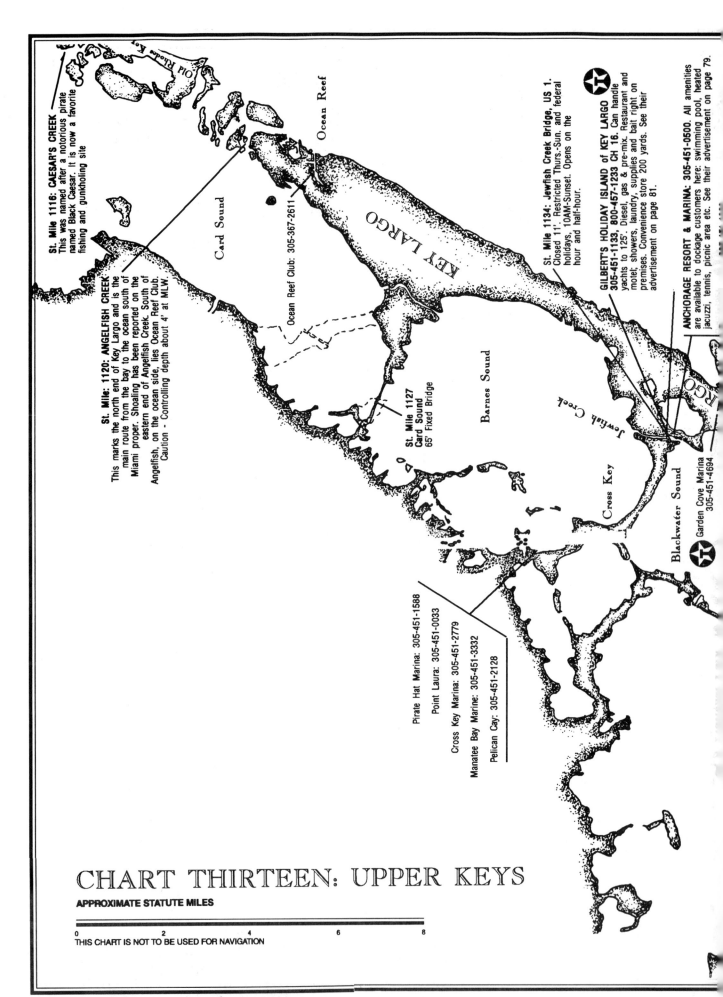

St. Mile 1116: CAESAR'S CREEK:
This was named after a notorious pirate named Black Caesar. It is now a favorite fishing and gunkholing site

St. Mile: 1120: ANGELFISH CREEK:
This marks the north end of Key Largo and is the main route from the bay to the ocean south of Miami proper. Shoaling has been reported on the eastern end of Angelfish Creek. South of Angelfish, on the ocean side, lies Ocean Reef Club. Caution - Controlling depth about 4' at MLW.

Card Sound

Ocean Reef Club: 305-367-2611

Ocean Reef

KEY LARGO

St. Mile 1127 Card Sound 65' Fixed Bridge

Barnes Sound

Jewfish Creek

Cross Key

Blackwater Sound

Garden Cove Marina 305-451-4694

St. Mile 1134: Jewfish Creek Bridge, US 1. Closed 11'. Restricted Thurs.-Sun. and federal holidays, 10AM-Sunset. Opens on the hour and half-hour.

GILBERT'S HOLIDAY ISLAND of KEY LARGO 305-451-1133, 800-457-1233 CH 16. Can handle yachts to 125'. Diesel, gas & pre-mix. Restaurant and motel; showers, laundry, supplies and bait right on premises. Convenience store 200 yards. See their advertisement on page 81.

ANCHORAGE RESORT & MARINA: 305-451-0500. All amenities are available to dockage customers here: swimming pool, heated jacuzzi, tennis, picnic area etc. See their advertisement on page 79.

Pirate Hat Marina: 305-451-1588

Point Laura: 305-451-0033

Cross Key Marina: 305-451-2779

Manatee Bay Marine: 305-451-3332

Pelican Cay: 305-451-2128

CHART THIRTEEN: UPPER KEYS

APPROXIMATE STATUTE MILES

| 0 | | 2 | | 4 | | 6 | | 8 |

THIS CHART IS NOT TO BE USED FOR NAVIGATION

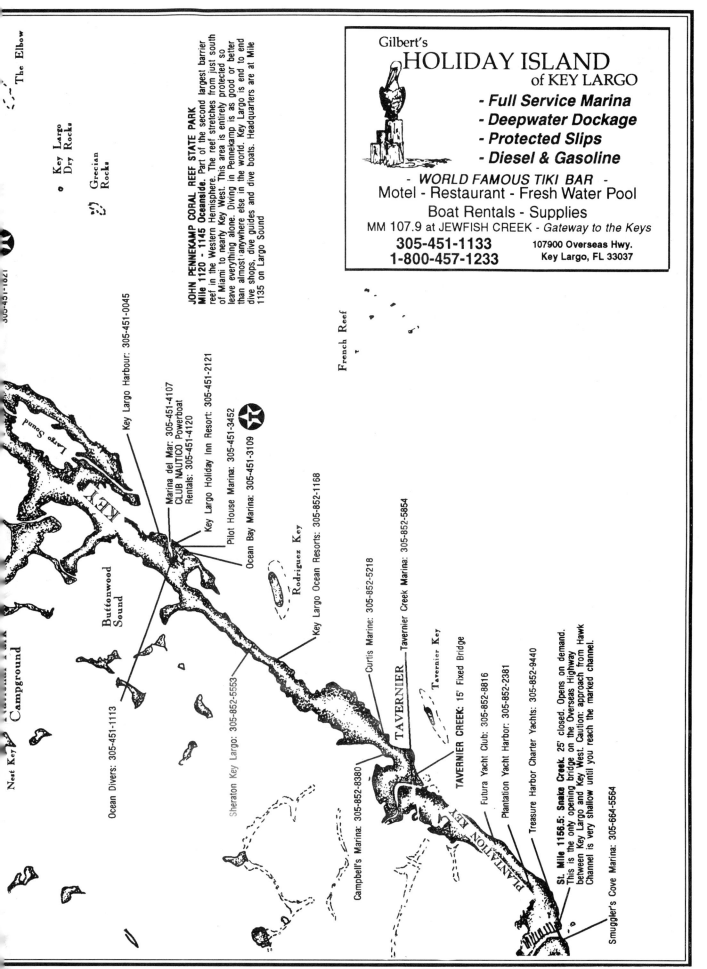

The Elbow

Key Largo Dry Rocks

Grecian Rocks

305-451-1021

JOHN PENNEKAMP CORAL REEF STATE PARK
Mile 1120 - 1145 Oceanside. Part of the second largest barrier reef in the Western Hemisphere. The reef stretches from just south of Miami to nearly Key West. This area is entirely protected so leave everything alone. Diving in Pennekamp is as good or better than almost anywhere else in the world. Key Largo is end to end dive shops, dive guides and dive boats. Headquarters are at Mile 1135 on Largo Sound

French Reef

Largo Sound

KEY LARGO

Buttonwood Sound

Next Key

Campground

Ocean Divers: 305-451-1113

Key Largo Harbour: 305-451-0045

Marina del Mar: 305-451-4107
CLUB NAUTICO Powerboat Rentals: 305-451-4120

Key Largo Holiday Inn Resort: 305-451-2121

Pilot House Marina: 305-451-3452

Ocean Bay Marina: 305-451-3109

Key Largo Ocean Resorts: 305-852-1168

Rodriguez Key

Sheraton Key Largo: 305-852-5553

Tavernier Creek Marina: 305-852-5854

Curtis Marine: 305-852-5218

TAVERNIER

Tavernier Key

TAVERNIER CREEK: 15' Fixed Bridge

Futura Yacht Club: 305-852-8816

Plantation Yacht Harbor: 305-852-2381

Treasure Harbor Charter Yachts: 305-852-9440

Campbell's Marina: 305-852-8380

PLANTATION KEY

St. Mile 1156.5: Snake Creek. 25' closed. Opens on demand. This is the only opening bridge on the Overseas Highway between Key Largo and Key West. Caution: approach from Hawk Channel is very shallow until you reach the marked channel.

Smuggler's Cove Marina: 305-664-5564

south shore of Everglades National Park. It's great fishing but no place for a cruising boat — shallow water over thin mud bottom with narrow channels marked mostly by sticks and branches stuck in the mud by fishermen (and just as often moved by other fishermen). Seen from the air, the shallows are crisscrossed by propeller tracks, and the watchword of the intrepid boatmen who do venture into the bay is "Steer clear of a standing bird with a dry butt".

On the ocean side, a couple of miles south of Jewfish Creek, a canal leads from Blackwater Sound across Key Largo and under two 14-foot fixed bridges to Largo Sound. It's an attractive and completely sheltered anchorage that is also easily accessed from either north or south on the ocean side, but as reported in Frank Papy's *Cruising Guide to the Keys*, the holding ground is "peculiar" — silt on top of limestone — which can make anchoring difficult.

On Largo Sound is the headquarters of Pennekamp Coral Reef State Park, which is one of the greatest natural wonders in Florida if not the continent. The park extends pretty much the entire length of Key Largo on the ocean side, and many divers believe that the variety and quality of marine life in Pennekamp is the equal of any in the world. As a result, much of the Key Largo waterfront is wall-to-wall dive boats, dive shops and related businesses, plus restaurants and shopping that serve its millions of visitors.

Key Largo is the largest of the Keys, one of the oldest named places in America, and one of the most hospitable places for the cruising boatman, with plenty of dockage and facilities, particularly at Key Largo Harbour, which welcomes transients and visitors to both the boatyard and the adjacent Pirate's Den restaurant. There are good anchorages on the bay side in Blackwater Sound, Tarpon Basin and Community Harbor and on the ocean side around Rodriguez and Tavernier Keys — except when the wind blows from the northeast.

Key Largo ends at Mile 1152, where Tavernier Creek meanders from bay to ocean. Tavernier Creek Marina and Plantation Key Marina a short distance to the west offer facilities and services.

On the bay side at Mile 1155 you'll find one of the largest marinas in the upper Keys, Plantation Yacht Harbor, which has everything you'd expect from a first-class marina and resort — rooms, dockside restaurant, dockage, fuel and much more. Directly offshore lies popular Cowpens Anchorage, so named for the pens built by the early settlers to keep captured sea cows — manatees — one of the staples of their meat-short diet.

A little farther down at Mile 1156.5, Snake Creek winds between bay and ocean and is spanned by the Overseas Highway's only remaining opening bridge. Why this spot was selected for a drawbridge is a mystery,

since it's reported that the channel beneath it now has less than four feet of depth.

In any event, a couple of miles further south is Whale Harbor Channel, at Mile 1158.9, which separates Windley Key from Upper Matecumbe Key, better known as Islamorada. The main emphasis on Islamorada is fishing, and Whale Harbor Inn on the west side and Holiday Isle Resort on the east have extensive charter and rental fleets. Both also offer a wide variety of marina services from dockage to bars and restaurants. Holiday Isle has a charter fleet, but it's also a full-bore resort with lodging, lounges, tiki bars, gift shops and acres of tourists baking in the sun.

Whale Harbor Channel marks the northern end of Upper Matecumbe/Islamorada. There are two anchorages of note on the bay side. The area directly inshore at Mile 1160 is the larger but less protected of the two; Little Basin to the west is shoaler but better protected. Local knowledge says the basin can float four feet, and it's bordered by a number of waterfront facilities including the Islamorada Yacht Basin and the Lorelei Restaurant, a favorite watering hole for local boatmen and anglers. At Mile 1162 on the ocean side you'll find Bud & Mary's Marina, a full service operation and a favorite among fishermen and the charter and guide boats for which Islamorada is famous.

The fishing out of Islamorada is regarded by many as the best and most varied in the continental United States. You can go offshore to troll for sailfish and blue and white marlin, fish deep for snapper and grouper, or work the waters around the reefs for a variety of sport fish. The flats on the ocean side are famous for bonefish and permit, and on the bay side for seatrout and redfish. Big tarpon and snook feed in the waters on both sides, making the bridges some of the best and most accessible fishing for shorebound anglers. When the wind and weather go bad on the ocean side, fishermen move to the bay side — and vice versa.

At Mile 1164 is Indian Key, which dates back to 1836 and was actually the site of Dade County's first courthouse. Originally settled by one Jacob Houseman, a Key Wester not well known for straight dealing, the island passed to Dr. Harry Perrine, who turned it into a tropical botanical garden. None of this impressed the local Caloosas, who attacked the key in 1840, destroyed everything and killed most of the inhabitants. Indian Key has a dock that's only accessible to small craft, but there's good anchorage offshore to dinghy in from, and it's still a botanical garden worth taking the time to visit.

At Mile 1164 on the gulf side is Lignumvitae Key, another botanical attraction and a state preserve with walking tours that feature now-rare native flora.

At Mile 1168, Matecumbe Bight on the bay side offers a decent anchorage except in a norther. Two miles

Key Colony Beach Marina

Safe Deep Water Dockage and Anchorage up to 120'

Commercial & Non-Commercial Diesel and Gasoline

FREE Overnight Dockage with 500 Gallons (Off Season)

- Restaurant and Bar
- Cabana Club & Pool and Beach Facility Available
- Airport & Golf Nearby
- Bicycle and Moped Rentals
- Pump Out Station • Boat Ramp

Call **289-1310**

We Monitor Channel 16

Channel Entrance - Bonefish Towers

BONEFISH TOWERS

farther south, the end of Lower Matecumbe Key is
marked on the ocean side by Caloosa Cove Resort,
another outstanding resort/marina complex. It offers
everything from service and repairs for boats to the care
and feeding of occupants.

Two miles farther south, at Mile 1170, you'll find
Channel Five, a great bay-to-ocean channel with plenty
of water and 65 feet of overhead clearance.

Mile 1180 on the gulf side brings you to Duck
Key, which has no anchorage but does have a well-
protected marina at the end of a very narrow, circuitous
channel limited to five feet of draft and plagued by
strong currents. It's worth the trouble, however, because
the marina is part of Hawk's Cay, one of the premier
resorts in the Keys. If you want overnight dockage with
a touch of class, an opportunity for shoreside recreation,
and some very good food, you may want to try it.

Next in the chain is Grassy Key, which is of only
limited interest to boatmen but is home to the Dolphin
Research Center, one of the few places that you can
actually get in the water and swim with dolphins, which
is a Life Experience. You can get recorded information at
305-289-1121 or you can talk to them at 305-289-0002.

From Mile 1185 to 1188 you'll find Fat Deer Key
and the city of Key Colony Beach, which occupies most
of its key. It is one of only three incorporated cities in the
Keys, the others being Key West and the tiny settlement
of Layton. It's also home of one of the really outstanding
sailfish tournaments in the area. Key Colony lies along
the southern rim of the island, and Key Colony Beach
Marina, a full-service deep-water facility where dockage
is free if you buy 500 gallons of fuel, lies inside the
sheltered bay between the Fat Deer and Vaca Keys.

Mile 1188 marks the beginning of Marathon, the
second largest settlement in the Keys and the hub of the
Middle Keys. Although it's perfectly normal to think of
Marathon as a city, it's also unincorporated. And note
that the surest way to be branded as a tourist is to call it
Marathon Key. The island is Vaca Key; the settlement is
Marathon.

The northern side of Marathon is filled with
resorts, marinas and boatyards, with a Coast Guard
station at Mile 1193. Just east of the station is Faro
Blanco, one of the leading resort and marina establish-
ments in all of the Keys. Faro Blanco now spreads across
Vaca Key to front both bay and ocean sides, and is
named for its landmark white lighthouse on the north
side of the island.

Southward from the western part of Vaca Key
lies Boot Key, and the space between the two is the best,
and perhaps the only, fully protected harbor anywhere
in the Keys. Boot Key has two entrances, which makes
access pretty easy, and the harbor has everything from
good haulout facilities to easy access to the stores and

A&B

IN THE HEART OF THE OLD TOWN OF

KEY WEST.

A & B is the friendliest marina in the heart of Key West's famous Old Town district, a stroll away from grocery stores, and everything you come to Key West to enjoy . . . restaurants, shopping, sunset at Mallory Square, ambience, a sense of history . . . boat, moped, bicycle, auto, ski rentals . . . tours by trolley, train, boat, bike and foot . . . parasailing, jetskiing . . . exciting nightlife, relaxing daylife, or perhaps the other way around.

Two restaurants on premises:
MC & Visa accepted.

For your safety, we monitor
VHF Channel 16 - 8 a.m. to 11 p.m.

A & B Marina is located in the Key West Bight, behind the rock jetty and Red Marker #4 (Chart 1145). Our 350' floating concrete dock accommodates yachts up to 180' with 40 slips for seasonal and transient rental. We provide 125V 30 amp and 250V 50 amp services, and TV on the dock.

A & B Lobster House & Marina is celebrating its _49th Year_. Owned and operated by the Felton Family.

---

(305) 294-2535 • Florida 1-800-223-8352

⚓ Lobster House & Marina

In the Heart of Old Town • 700 Front St., Key West, FL 33040

- Official Customs Clearing Center of Key West -

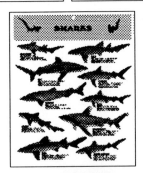
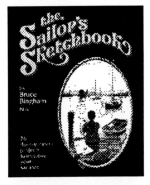

services of downtown Marathon. There are plenty of marinas, too - Sombrero Marina and Dockside Lounge, Sombrero Resort and Lighthouse Marina are at the eastern end, near the stores that line the Overseas Highway. Three more marinas and the hauling facility are at the western end; Faro Blanco Oceanside is the one nearest the bridge and in addition to the usual facilities offers floating hotel rooms and efficiencies on houseboats. Right next door is Pinellas Marina with a full range of services, and still further west at the harbor entrance is Marathon Marina, a hospitable and helpful full-service marina/boatyard with a good restaurant.

Directly offshore from Boot Key lies Sombrero Key Light, one of the most important on the reefs and one of the better diving and snorkeling sites. Directly inshore from Sombrero Key is Knights Key, at the extreme western end of the Marathon complex.

The famous Seven Mile Bridge begins at the west end of Knights Key. For purposes of reference, we'll place it at Mile 1197, which is where Moser Channel passes under the 65-foot-high bridge. The high bridge replaces an old drawbridge which will live in the memories of boatmen and motorists who spent hot summer afternoons waiting for its geriatric old span to open or close. Only the draw span is gone; the rest of the bridge was left to serve as a fishing pier.

Boats bound for Florida's Gulf Coast and bypassing Key West (a concept foreign to the editors) can turn northward from the west end of Vaca Key and take a compass course for Cape Sable with deep water all the way (eight feet is deep water in those parts). An earlier turnoff most suitable for shallow-draft boats and good weather turns northwest off Long Key and skirts the many banks up the west side of Florida Bay.

Those continuing to Key West have the option of continuing down the ICW among the lower keys or of heading out under Seven Mile Bridge and taking the Hawk Channel route down the ocean side. Weather and wind direction usually help make the choice.

A mile or so beyond the east end of the bridge lies Bahia Honda Key, where there is a beautiful state park and without doubt the best beach in the Keys. There's also a marina with fuel, although access is limited to boats that can clear the 20-foot highway bridge. Access to and from the ocean is now wide open with the removal of the old railroad bridge, but local information has it that you should use caution if you draw more than three feet.

At Mile 1215 on the ocean side is Newfound Harbor, the best and maybe the only decent harbor on the ocean side between Marathon and Key West. At the entrance to Newfound is the Little Palm Island Club, an elegant resort that was the setting for the filming of PT-109, the story of John F. Kennedy's heroics in the Pacific during World War II.

Newfound Harbor is formed by the Newfound Harbor Keys, the southern extension of Big Pine Key, which is the site of the National Key Deer Refuge. The park's namesake are the smallest and most endangered of all American deer.

From Mile 1220 to 1235 on the ocean side, the keys from Cudjoe to Boca Chica offer anchorages with varying degrees of shallowness and protection, none of which can be particularly recommended. But at Mile 1235 we're almost there — just a little farther south is Stock Island and its wall-to-wall marine facilities. One of the leading spots for cruising boatmen is the Key West Oceanside Marina.

At last we have, as they say, gone all the way and reached Key West. It's the end of both the ICW and the Overseas Highway, and the end of the line in more ways than one. For boatmen it offers the same thing it has offered seamen for ages — good, protected anchorage. Ashore, of course, it offers everything you can think of along with a great deal that may never even have crossed your mind.

The dockage situation in Key West has improved a great deal in recent years. The old submarine basin has become the first-class Truman Annex Marina, and top-shelf facilities are available in Key West Bight, including Galleon, A&B Marina and Key West Bight Marina, formerly Land's End. Further eastward on the island lies Garrison Bight, where the Key West Yacht Club, Key West Municipal Marina, and Garrison Bight Marinas have long held forth.

If you'd prefer to anchor out, there are plenty of places available. One favorite is near Christmas Tree Island, which is called Wisteria on the charts. The current is swift there, but the holding ground is good. There's plenty of anchorage, but the only place to land a dinghy legally is at the municipal dinghy landing at the foot of Simonton Street. And like the rest of Key West's waterfront, Simonton Street has become more and more congested and chancy. Secure both dinghy and gear.

Growth and development are affecting Key West in other ways as well. New and glamorous resort hotels, while beautiful and luxurious, add the risk of turning the southernmost city into little more than another link in a huge chain of homogenized destinations. But it hasn't happened yet, and — hopefully — Key West will remain unique for a long time.

Then again, thanks to its location, Key West has always been pretty much unique. It was originally settled by the Spanish, who called it Cayo Hueso, which means Isle of Bones. The English took it over in 1763 and promptly corrupted that to Key West.

In 1822 Key West and the rest of Florida became part of the United States, and the flag was raised by

EDITOR's NOTE: This is based on the current list maintained by the Florida Department of Environmental Protection, and while it was updated shortly before press time, changes are constant and it's a good idea to check ramps in advance. Note that some ramps are in marinas, private clubs or condominiums where public access may be limited.

MONROE COUNTY BOAT RAMPS

BIG PINE KEY

Bahia Honda State Recreation Area	US 1
Big Pine Key Fishing Lodge	Campground, US 1, MM 33
Old Wooden Bridge Fishing Camp	On Bogie Channel
Palmer's Place	on Gulf of Mexico
Sea Camp Assn.	Big Pine Ave.
Spanish Harbor Wayside Park	US 1 on Spanish Harbor
Watson Park	Key Deer Blvd., MM 31
Boca Chica Boat Ramp	On US 1 on Atlantic Ocean
Boat Ramp	Delmar Blvd.
Boat Ramp	SR 4
Riviera Village	Bay Dr.

CUDJOE KEY

Venture Out at Cudjoe Cay	Spanish Main Dr. on Cudjoe Key

E. STOCK ISLAND

Stock Island Boat Ramp	Off US 1, MM 5

EAST MARATHON

Crawl Key Boat Ramp	US 1 on Atlantic Ocean

FLAMINGO

Everglades National Park	Monroe County undesignated area, S. Main Park Rd. on Florida Bay
Flamingo Lodge Marina & Outpost Resort	SR 93/36 in Everglades National Park on Florida Bay & Buttonwood Canal

ISLAMORADA

Breezy Palms Resort	US 1, MM 80 Oceanside
Drop Anchor Resort Motel	MM 85, Oceanside
Gamefish Resort	75600 Overseas Hwy.
Goodtime Charlie's	US 1
Holiday Isle Resort & Marina	MM 84.1, Oceanside
Islamorada Yacht Basin	on Florida Bay
Lew's Marina	on Florida Bay
Papa Joe's Restaurant & Marina	79786 Overseas Hwy. on Florida Bay, MM 80
Pelican Cove Resort	Overseas Hwy., Oceanside MM 84.5
Pines & Palms Resort	
Plantation Yacht Harbor & Resort	87000 Overseas Hwy. on Florida Bay, MM 87
Ragged Edge Resort	MM 86.5, Treasure Harbor
Richmond's Landing	85500 Overseas Hwy. on Snake Creek, MM 85.5
Robby's Marina	on Gulf of Mexico
Sunset Inn	on Gulf of Mexico
Topsider Resort	75501 Overseas Hwy. on Lower Matecumbe Key
Tropic Air Resort	75790 Overseas Hwy.
Tropical Reef Resort	84997 Overseas Hwy. Oceanside, MM 85
Venetian Shores Marine	85920 Overseas Hwy. on Atlantic Ocean

KEY COLONY BEACH

Key Colony Beach Botel	17th St.
Key Colony Beach Marina	on Causeway

KEY LARGO

America Outdoor Gulfside Campground	US 1, MM 97.5
Blue Lagoon Motel	US 1 on Atlantic Ocean
Button Wood Condominiums	on Florida Bay
Calusa Camp Resort	325 Calusa, MM 101.5
Campers Cove	101640 N. Overseas Hwy. on Tarpon Basin
Captain Jax Travel Resort Marina	103620 Overseas Hwy. on Gulf of Mexico
Caribbean Club	MM 103
Gilberts Holiday Island	on Jewfish Creek, MM 107.9
John Pennekamp Coral Reef State Park	MM 102.5, US 1 Oceanside
Key Largo Harbour	MM 100, Oceanside
Key Largo Kampground & Marina	US 1, MM 101.5 Oceanside
Kings Campground & Marina	
Landings of Largo	9801 Windward Ave. on Buttonwood Sound
Little Blackwater Sound	MM 110, Everglades National Park, Bayside
Mandalay Marina	on Atlantic Ocean
Ocean Divers Marina	on Atlantic Ocean
Ocean Safari Marina	on Florida Bay
Point Laura Marina & Campground	999 Morris La. Oceanside, MM 112.5
Port Largo Yacht Club	Ocean Drive on Atlantic Ocean
Rock Harbor Club	1380 S. Overseas Hwy. on Florida Bay
Rowell's Marina	on Florida Bay, MM 105
Sunset Cove Motel	MM 99.5
Tahiti Village	US 1 on Largo Sound
Twin Harbor Motel & Campground	US 1, MM 103.5
Upper Keys Sailing Club	US 1 on Buttonwood Bay

KEY WEST

Blue Lagoon Marina	3101 N. Roosevelt Blvd. on Gulf of Mexico
Boca Chica NAS	On US 1 on Atlantic Ocean
Boyd's Campsites	S. Maloney Ave., US 1, MM 5
Cow Key Marina	5th Ave. on Stock Island on Gulf of Mexico
Geiger Key Marina & Travel Park	Hwy. 941
George Smathers Beach	S. Roosevelt Blvd. on Hawk Channel
Hornes Storage & Dockage	US 1 on Cow Key Channel
Key West Municipal Marina	US 1 on Garrison Bight
Key West Oceanside Marina	Maloney Ave. on Stock Island
Key West Seaside Resort	Boca Chica Rd., US 1
Key West Yacht Club Marina	2315 N. Roosevelt Blvd.
Murray Marine	Junior College Rd.
Simonton Boat Ramp & Park	1 Simonton St.
Sunset Harbor Marina	5th Ave. on Stock Island on Cow Key Channel

LITTLE DUCK KEY

Little Duck Key Boat Ramp	US 1 on Atlantic Ocean

LONG KEY

Atlantis Marina	105 Overseas Hwy. on Atlantic Ocean
Fiesta Key KOA Campground	MM 70, US 1
Outdoor Resorts at Long Key	US 1, MM 66

LOWER MATECUMBE KEY

Boy Scouts of Fla. Ntnl. High Adventure Sea Base	73800 Overseas Hwy.

LOWER SUGARLOAF KEY

Indian Mounds Boat Ramp	Indian Mound Rd., MM 19

MARATHON

Bonefish Harbor Marina	E. of Marathon
Buccaneer Lodge Resort	2600 Overseas Hwy. on Florida Bay
Coconut Grove Motel	4900 Overseas Hwy. on Atlantic Ocean
Faro Blanco Marine Resort	1996 Overseas Hwy. on Gulf of Mexico
Faro Blanco's Boot Key Marina	1000 15th St. on Atlantic Ocean
Galaway Bay Motel	1361 Overseas Hwy. on Atlantic Ocean
Hawk's Cay Resort & Marina	MM 61, Duck Key
Hidden Harbor Motel & Botel	2396 Overseas Hwy. on Gulf of Mexico
Holiday Inn & Marina	13201 Overseas Hwy., MM 54
Jolly Roger Travel Park	MM 59, US 1 on Grassy Key
Key RV Park	6099 Overseas Hwy. Oceanside
Kingsail Resort & Motel Marina	7050 Overseas Hwy. on Gulf of Mexico
Knight's Key Park & Marina	Knight's Key Blvd.
Lagoon Resort	7200 Aviation Blvd.
Marathon Recreation Complex	US 1 & 33rd St. on Gulf of Mexico
Ocean Isles Resort	10877 Overseas Hwy. on Vaca Key
Pelican Motel & Royal Hawaiian Motel/Botel	12020 Overseas Hwy., MM 53
SeaHorse Motel	7196 Overseas Hwy. on Gulf of Mexico, MM 51
Sombrero Resort & Lighthouse Marina	19 Sombrero Blvd.
Tarpon Marina	4590 Overseas Hwy. on Gulf of Mexico
The Reef Resort	6800 Overseas Hwy. on Gulf of Mexico

MARATHON SHORES

Ocean Isles Fishing Village	US 1 on Atlantic Ocean

MATECUMBE KEY

Teatable Channel Wayside Park & Ramp	US 1 on Atlantic Ocean

N. UPPER MATECUMBE KEY

Upper Matecumbe County Park	US 1, MM 81.5 on Atlantic Ocean

NE KEY LARGO

Blackwater Sound-Cross Key Boat Ramp	US 1 on Atlantic Ocean

OHIO KEY

Sunshine Key Camping Resort	US 1, MM 39 on Ohio Key

RAMROD KEY

Looe Key Reef Resort	On Atlantic Ocean

SHARK KEY

Shark Key Boat Ramp	On US 1 on Atlantic Ocean

SUGARLOAF KEY

Sugarloaf Key Campground	US 1, MM 20
Sugarloaf Lodge & Marina	MM 17 on Gulf of Mexico

SUMMERLAND KEY

Dolphin Marina	on Newfound Harbor
Summerland Key Yacht Harbor Marina	US 1 on Gulf of Mexico

TAVERNIER

Harry Harris County Park	MM 92.5 Oceanside
San Pedro Travel Park	on Atlantic Ocean
Summer Sea Condominiums	88500 Overseas Hwy. on Florida Bay

UPPER KEYS

Everglades National Park, shared with Monroe & Collier Counties	

WEST SUMMERLAND KEY

Boy Scout Camp Sawyer	West Summerland Key on Atlantic Ocean
Silver Shores Mobile Home Park	715 N. Jade Dr. on Atlantic Ocean

Matthew Perry, the man who later opened Japan to the outside world. He was followed by David Porter, who used a New York ferryboat to chase the pirates out of the Keys. He also established the naval base, and the military has been a dominant force in the area ever since.

The Key West of Porter's day was a cosmopolitan society that included Southerners, New Englanders, Tories, Bahamians, Spaniards, Greeks, Cubans, and a free-floating group of marine vagrants and hippies by whatever name. You could defend the argument that it is still much the same.

Key West was totally isolated except by sea until Henry Flagler's Overseas Railroad reached it in 1912. This connected the Keys to the mainland until the disastrous hurricane of 1935 destroyed the railroad. It wasn't until just before World War II that the Overseas Highway was built on Mr. Flagler's roadbed to open the Keys and Key West to the rest of the world by land.

Before that, salvaging ships wrecked along the reefs were the area's primary business. In one 18-month period some 324 ships went aground in the Keys, and at one time Key West had the highest per capita income in the United States as a result. It's little wonder that the government was moved to build the chain of lighthouses from Key West to Miami.

Key West is not, however, the end of the Keys for boatpeople whose ship and seamanship are equal to the extension. There's another sixty-odd miles to explore which will take you all the way out to the real end of the line, the Dry Tortugas.

Immediately west of Key West lies a string of shoals and keys that extend about 20 miles to the Marquesas Keys and which offer some of the best diving and fishing in the entire state of Florida. The nearer ones, Man and Woman Keys, are popular daytime beaching and snorkeling spots for local small craft. A bit farther on, at Boca Grande, there's a pretty good anchorage on the northwestern side. There are some interesting wrecks that you might want to explore, and the fishing is wonderful. Shoals around the entrance channel shift continually, so eyeball piloting is essential on the way in.

Further west, across choppy Boca Grande Channel, lie the Marquesas Keys, the closest thing to a tropical atoll you'll find in North America, although there are some convincing arguments that they were formed by a meteor strike rather than coral and mangroves. However formed, the islands are a naturalist's and fisherman's paradise but completely without facilities. For a perfect description, read Captain Jeffrey

CHART FOURTEEN: MIDDLE KEYS

APPROXIMATE STATUTE MILES

0   2   4   6

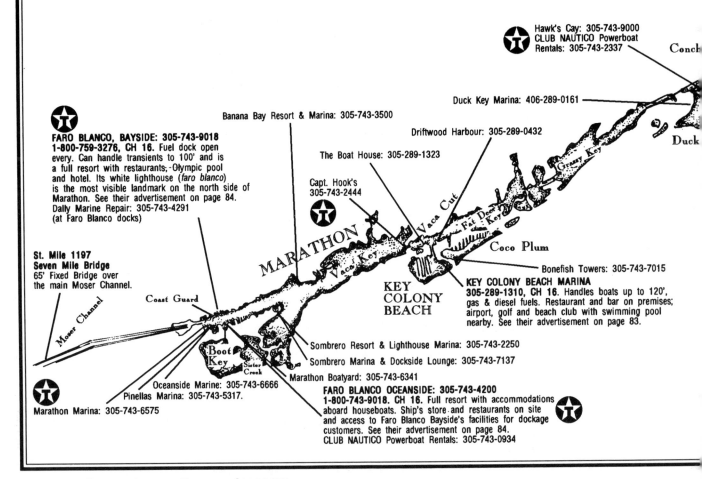

Mile 1185-1188: KEY COLONY BEACH. One of the three cities in the Keys. The others are Key West and Layton. Some that you would think of as cities are not incorporated. Key Colony Beach is the home of one of the most outstanding sailfish tournaments in the area. Outstanding in another sense in Bonefish Towers, which is the most clearly visible landmark for yachts coming down Hawk Channel.

Hawk's Cay: 305-743-9000
CLUB NAUTICO Powerboat
Rentals: 305-743-2337

Conch

Duck Key Marina: 406-289-0161

Duck

Banana Bay Resort & Marina: 305-743-3500

Driftwood Harbour: 305-289-0432

FARO BLANCO, BAYSIDE: 305-743-9018
1-800-759-3276, CH 16. Fuel dock open every. Can handle transients to 100' and is a full resort with restaurants, Olympic pool and hotel. Its white lighthouse (*faro blanco*) is the most visible landmark on the north side of Marathon. See their advertisement on page 84.
Dally Marine Repair: 305-743-4291
(at Faro Blanco docks)

The Boat House: 305-289-1323

Capt. Hook's
305-743-2444

St. Mile 1197
Seven Mile Bridge
65' Fixed Bridge over the main Moser Channel.

MARATHON

Vaca Key

Vaca Cut

Fat Deer Key

Grassy Key

Coco Plum

Bonefish Towers: 305-743-7015

KEY COLONY BEACH MARINA
305-289-1310, CH 16. Handles boats up to 120', gas & diesel fuels. Restaurant and bar on premises; airport, golf and beach club with swimming pool nearby. See their advertisement on page 83.

KEY COLONY BEACH

Coast Guard

Moser Channel

Boot Key

Sister Creek

Sombrero Resort & Lighthouse Marina: 305-743-2250

Sombrero Marina & Dockside Lounge: 305-743-7137

Marathon Boatyard: 305-743-6341

Oceanside Marine: 305-743-6666

Pinellas Marina: 305-743-5317.

FARO BLANCO OCEANSIDE: 305-743-4200
1-800-743-9018. CH 16. Full resort with accommodations aboard houseboats. Ship's store and restaurants on site and access to Faro Blanco Bayside's facilities for dockage customers. See their advertisement on page 84.
CLUB NAUTICO Powerboat Rentals: 305-743-0934

Marathon Marina: 305-743-6575

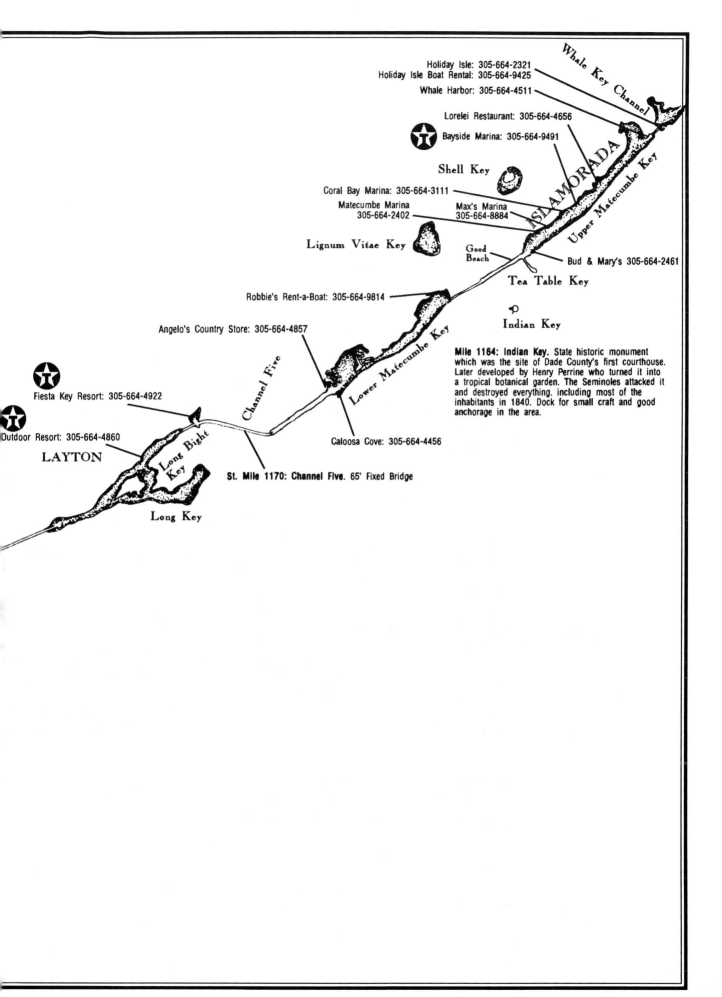

Holiday Isle: 305-664-2321
Holiday Isle Boat Rental: 305-664-9425
Whale Harbor: 305-664-4511

Lorelei Restaurant: 305-664-4656

Bayside Marina: 305-664-9491

Shell Key

Coral Bay Marina: 305-664-3111

Matecumbe Marina
305-664-2402

Max's Marina
305-664-8884

Lignum Vitae Key

Good
Beach

Bud & Mary's 305-664-2461

Tea Table Key

Robbie's Rent-a-Boat: 305-664-9814

Angelo's Country Store: 305-664-4857

Indian Key

Mile 1164: Indian Key. State historic monument
which was the site of Dade County's first courthouse.
Later developed by Henry Perrine who turned it into
a tropical botanical garden. The Seminoles attacked it
and destroyed everything. including most of the
inhabitants in 1840. Dock for small craft and good
anchorage in the area.

Fiesta Key Resort: 305-664-4922

Outdoor Resort: 305-664-4860

LAYTON

Caloosa Cove: 305-664-4456

St. Mile 1170: Channel Five. 65' Fixed Bridge

Long Bight Key

Long Key

CHART FIFTEEN: LOWER KEYS

APPROXIMATE STATUTE MILES

0   2   4   6

THIS CHART IS NOT TO BE USED FOR NAVIGATION

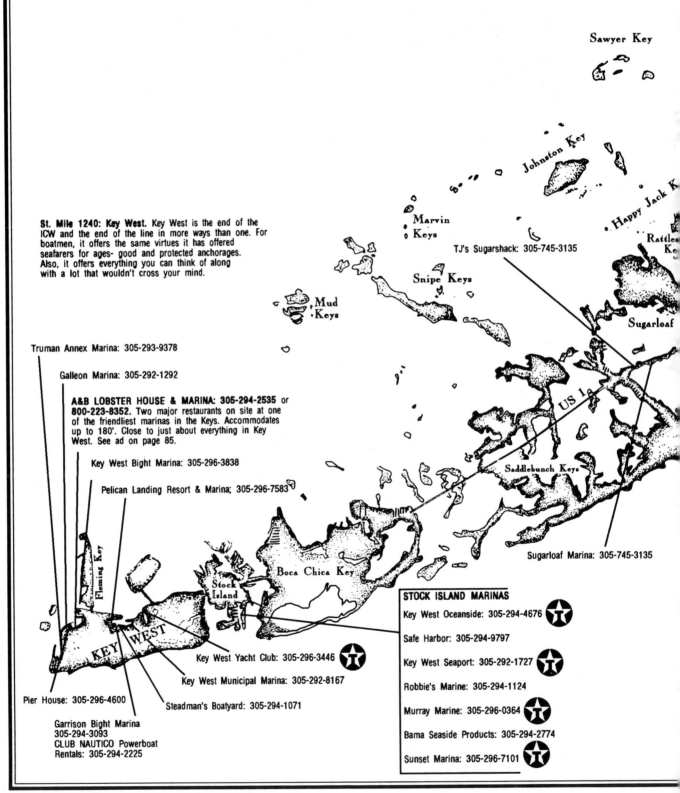

St. Mile 1240: Key West. Key West is the end of the ICW and the end of the line in more ways than one. For boatmen, it offers the same virtues it has offered seafarers for ages- good and protected anchorages. Also, it offers everything you can think of along with a lot that wouldn't cross your mind.

Sawyer Key

Johnston Key

Happy Jack K

Marvin Keys

TJ's Sugarshack: 305-745-3135

Rattle Ke

Snipe Keys

Sugarloaf

Mud Keys

Truman Annex Marina: 305-293-9378

Galleon Marina: 305-292-1292

US 1

A&B LOBSTER HOUSE & MARINA: 305-294-2535 or **800-223-8352.** Two major restaurants on site at one of the friendliest marinas in the Keys. Accommodates up to 180'. Close to just about everything in Key West. See ad on page 85.

Key West Bight Marina: 305-296-3838

Pelican Landing Resort & Marina; 305-296-7583

Saddlebunch Keys

Sugarloaf Marina: 305-745-3135

Fleming Key

Stock Island

Boca Chica Key

STOCK ISLAND MARINAS

Key West Oceanside: 305-294-4676

Safe Harbor: 305-294-9797

Key West Yacht Club: 305-296-3446

KEY WEST

Key West Seaport: 305-292-1727

Key West Municipal Marina: 305-292-8167

Robbie's Marine: 305-294-1124

Murray Marine: 305-296-0364

Pier House: 305-296-4600

Steadman's Boatyard: 305-294-1071

Bama Seaside Products: 305-294-2774

Garrison Bight Marina
305-294-3093
CLUB NAUTICO Powerboat
Rentals: 305-294-2225

Sunset Marina: 305-296-7101

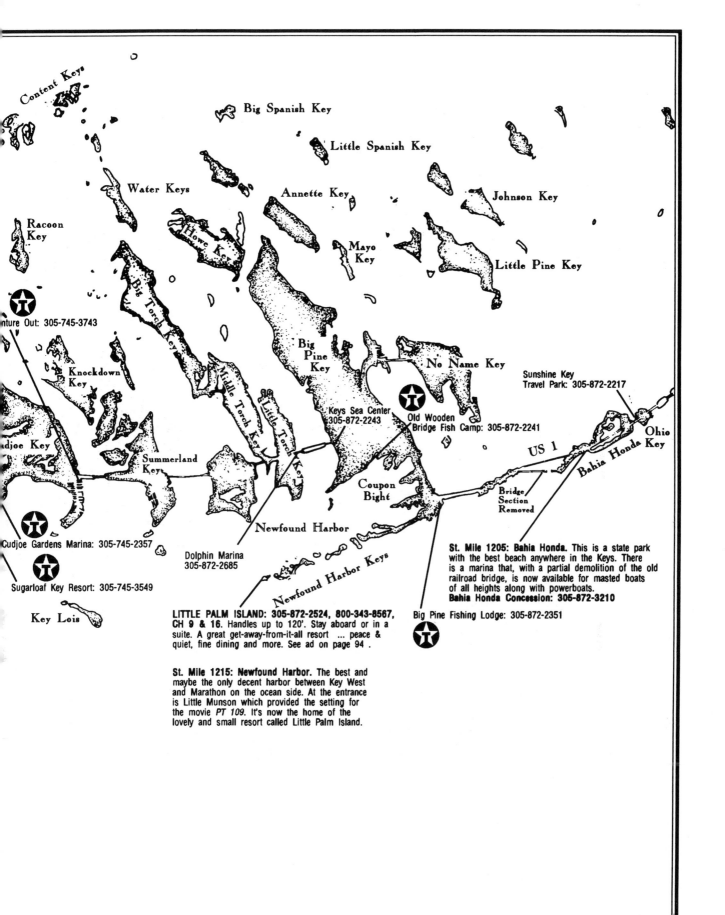

Content Keys

Big Spanish Key

Little Spanish Key

Water Keys

Annette Key

Johnson Key

Racoon Key

Howe Key

Mayo Key

Little Pine Key

[star] nture Out: 305-745-3743

Big Torch Key

Knockdown Key

Big Pine Key

No Name Key

Sunshine Key
Travel Park: 305-872-2217

Middle Torch Key

Keys Sea Center
305-872-2243

Old Wooden
Bridge Fish Camp: 305-872-2241

Ohio Key

djoe Key

Little Torch Key

Summerland Key

Coupon Bight

US 1

Bahia Honda Key

[star] Cudjoe Gardens Marina: 305-745-2357

Newfound Harbor

Bridge Section Removed

Dolphin Marina
305-872-2685

[star] Sugarloaf Key Resort: 305-745-3549

Newfound Harbor Keys

St. Mile 1205: Bahia Honda. This is a state park with the best beach anywhere in the Keys. There is a marina that, with a partial demolition of the old railroad bridge, is now available for masted boats of all heights along with powerboats.
Bahia Honda Concession: 305-872-3210

Key Lois

LITTLE PALM ISLAND: 305-872-2524, 800-343-8567, CH 9 & 16. Handles up to 120'. Stay aboard or in a suite. A great get-away-from-it-all resort ... peace & quiet, fine dining and more. See ad on page 94 .

Big Pine Fishing Lodge: 305-872-2351

[star]

St. Mile 1215: Newfound Harbor. The best and maybe the only decent harbor between Key West and Marathon on the ocean side. At the entrance is Little Munson which provided the setting for the movie *PT 109*. It's now the home of the lovely and small resort called Little Palm Island.

Cardenas' beautiful little book *Marquesa*. It's a *Walden* for the 90s, available in any good bookstore or fly shop, or from the author's own fly shop in Key West.

The Marquesas are another end of the line for everyone but self-sufficient cruising boats capable of handling the passage to the Dry Tortugas, another 40 miles west. The 60 miles from Key West past the Marquesas and on to the Tortugas is completely devoid of food, water, or facilities of any kind, and only those equipped and prepared for 120 miles of cruising and all contingencies including unpredictable weather should even think about the trip. Yet despite their isolation, or maybe because of it, hundreds of yachtsmen cruise every year to this most southerly of National Parks. Other hundreds head out of Key West for the fabulous fishing in the same waters. Charter and party boats fish those waters from as far away as Naples and Fort Myers, a hundred miles north on the Gulf Coast.

Fort Jefferson is the main attraction of the Dry Tortugas. Started in 1846 to guard the entrance to the Gulf, the fort was never finished and never saw battle. During the Civil War it was used to house Confederate prisoners of war, who included the unfortunate Dr. Samuel Mudd, wrongly convicted of treason for treating the broken leg of John Wilkes Booth as he fled after the assassination of Abraham Lincoln. The island was abandoned in 1874, later preserved as a National Monument, and elevated to National Park status in 1992.

To the west, there are good anchorages around Garden Key and Loggerhead Key. Frank Papy suggests you ask the park rangers which anchorage is best for the prevailing weather, take their advice, then use your dinghy to explore the other keys. Be aware that some are off limits, especially when hundreds of thousands of sooty terns and other sea birds nest on Bush Key and other islets in the area. The entire area is patrolled constantly by sea and air and wildlife regulations are vigorously enforced.

At Loggerhead Key, you have reached the real end of the line. From Loggerhead there is nothing to the west but 900 miles of open water between you and the coast of Mexico and nothing to the north for cruising boats but 80 miles of open Gulf to The Sun Coast.

Let's go there...

CRUISING FLORIDA'S SUN COAST

From the Dry Tortugas it's an 80-odd-mile run northward, either direct or coastwise via Cape Sable, to Florida's Sun Coast. The route skirts the shallows of Florida Bay, the western Everglades and Ten Thousand Islands — and some of the finest fishing in North America. The flats inside Florida Bay are off limits to all but the shallowest craft and most experienced skippers, but up the Gulf side of the Bay, into Flamingo in Everglades National Park, and northward up the Everglades shoreline is a wilderness cruise to be remembered. The ten-mile side trip in to the marina and visitors facilities at Flamingo is one of the finest in Florida for nature lovers. West of Flamingo the beautiful wild beach at Cape Sable offers wonderful beachcombing to those willing to anchor off and dinghy in.

Heading northward, the route skirts the wilderness coast for 50 miles to the facilities at Everglades City and Chokoloskee Island and another ten to Marco Island and the southern end of the Sun Coast proper. Along the way, Ponce de Leon Bay at the mouth of the Shark River offers sheltered anchorages among many mangrove islands once inside the shoaling entrance — and no end of opportunities to explore the Everglades for those so inclined. Thirty miles above the Shark River, Daybeacon #1 on Indian Key marks the entrance to Chokoloskee Bay, the facilities at the Rod & Gun Club and Barron River Marina in Everglades City. Five miles further up the inland route, or in from Daybeacon #3 off Gomez Point, you can take the channelized Faka Union River into Port of the Islands Resort and a full-service marina.

Cruising northward toward the Sun Coast, you enter Gullivan Bay and at Coon Key you have the option of taking an inside passage to the hospitable fishing village of Goodland, from where a well-marked channel of the Big Marco River leads to Marco Island and Naples. Vertical clearance is set by the 55-foot fixed bridge. Goodland offers full-service marinas including The Barge at Goodland Bridge, a number of good restaurants, and an Old Florida scene that contrasts with the development further north.

The alternative is to go around Cape Romano to Marco Island or further north to Gordon Pass below Naples. Our correspondent in the area, Commander Edward Beckhorn of the USCG Auxiliary, warns that the decision to turn inland at Coon Key or head outside around Cape Romano must be made well south of Coon

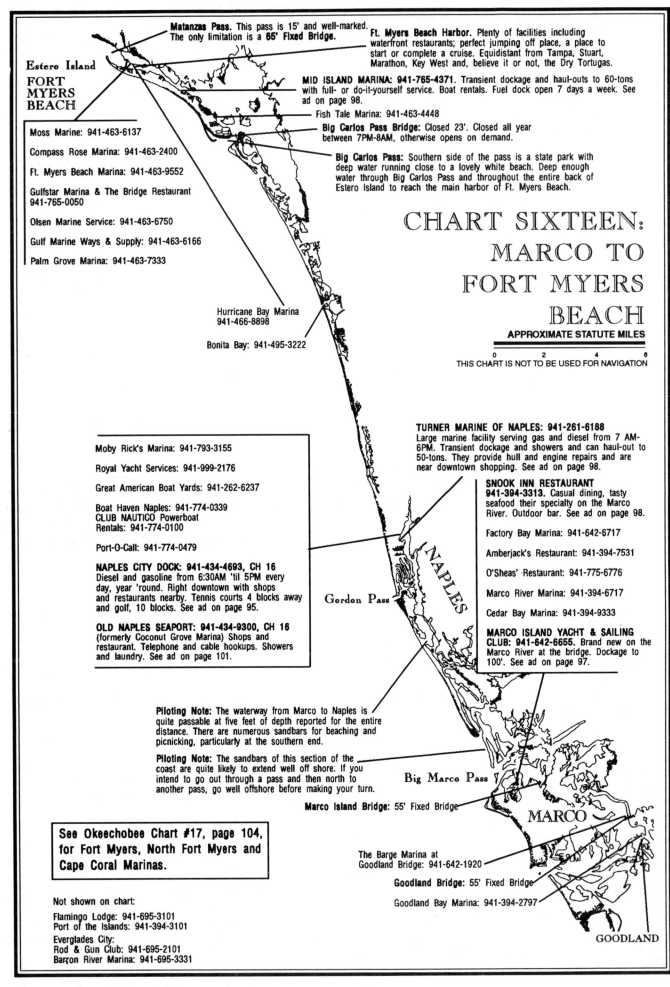

Matanzas Pass. This pass is 15' and well-marked. The only limitation is a **65' Fixed Bridge.**

Estero Island
FORT
MYERS
BEACH

Ft. Myers Beach Harbor. Plenty of facilities including waterfront restaurants; perfect jumping off place, a place to start or complete a cruise. Equidistant from Tampa, Stuart, Marathon, Key West and, believe it or not, the Dry Tortugas.

MID ISLAND MARINA: 941-765-4371. Transient dockage and haul-outs to 60-tons with full- or do-it-yourself service. Boat rentals. Fuel dock open 7 days a week. See ad on page 98.

Fish Tale Marina: 941-463-4448

Big Carlos Pass Bridge: Closed 23'. Closed all year between 7PM-8AM, otherwise opens on demand.

Big Carlos Pass: Southern side of the pass is a state park with deep water running close to a lovely white beach. Deep enough water through Big Carlos Pass and throughout the entire back of Estero Island to reach the main harbor of Ft. Myers Beach.

Moss Marine: 941-463-6137

Compass Rose Marina: 941-463-2400

Ft. Myers Beach Marina: 941-463-9552

Gulfstar Marina & The Bridge Restaurant
941-765-0050

Olsen Marine Service: 941-463-6750

Gulf Marine Ways & Supply: 941-463-6166

Palm Grove Marina: 941-463-7333

Hurricane Bay Marina
941-466-8898

Bonita Bay: 941-495-3222

CHART SIXTEEN: MARCO TO FORT MYERS BEACH

APPROXIMATE STATUTE MILES

```
0        2        4        6
```
THIS CHART IS NOT TO BE USED FOR NAVIGATION

TURNER MARINE OF NAPLES: 941-261-6188 Large marine facility serving gas and diesel from 7 AM-6PM. Transient dockage and showers and can haul-out to 50-tons. They provide hull and engine repairs and are near downtown shopping. See ad on page 98.

SNOOK INN RESTAURANT
941-394-3313. Casual dining, tasty seafood their specialty on the Marco River. Outdoor bar. See ad on page 98.

Factory Bay Marina: 941-642-6717

Amberjack's Restaurant: 941-394-7531

O'Sheas' Restaurant: 941-775-6776

Marco River Marina: 941-394-6717

Cedar Bay Marina: 941-394-9333

MARCO ISLAND YACHT & SAILING CLUB: 941-642-6655. Brand new on the Marco River at the bridge. Dockage to 100'. See ad on page 97.

Moby Rick's Marina: 941-793-3155

Royal Yacht Services: 941-999-2176

Great American Boat Yards: 941-262-6237

Boat Haven Naples: 941-774-0339
CLUB NAUTICO Powerboat
Rentals: 941-774-0100

Port-O-Call: 941-774-0479

NAPLES CITY DOCK: 941-434-4693, CH 16 Diesel and gasoline from 6:30AM 'til 5PM every day, year 'round. Right downtown with shops and restaurants nearby. Tennis courts 4 blocks away and golf, 10 blocks. See ad on page 95.

OLD NAPLES SEAPORT: 941-434-9300, CH 16 (formerly Coconut Grove Marina) Shops and restaurant. Telephone and cable hookups. Showers and laundry. See ad on page 101.

Gordon Pass

NAPLES

Big Marco Pass

MARCO

Piloting Note: The waterway from Marco to Naples is quite passable at five feet of depth reported for the entire distance. There are numerous sandbars for beaching and picnicking, particularly at the southern end.

Piloting Note: The sandbars of this section of the coast are quite likely to extend well off shore. If you intend to go out through a pass and then north to another pass, go well offshore before making your turn.

Marco Island Bridge: 55' Fixed Bridge

The Barge Marina at
Goodland Bridge: 941-642-1920

Goodland Bridge: 55' Fixed Bridge

Goodland Bay Marina: 941-394-2797

GOODLAND

See Okeechobee Chart #17, page 104, for Fort Myers, North Fort Myers and Cape Coral Marinas.

Not shown on chart:

Flamingo Lodge: 941-695-3101
Port of the Islands: 941-394-3101
Everglades City:
Rod & Gun Club: 941-695-2101
Barron River Marina: 941-695-3331

NOW THE ISLAND IS COMPLETE.

The magnificent 13,000 square foot clubhouse will feature a lounge and grill room on the first floor and formal dining and function rooms on the second level.

The spacious covered outdoor dining area is complete with its own bar and grill and overlooks the Marco River.

One hundred twenty slips range in size from 40 to 100 feet, featuring a state-of-the art floating dock system. Cable, water, electricity and pump-out facility are available.

For Slip Sales, Leases and Yacht Club Membership Information Call: 941-642-4444. Ext 500.

Marco Beach Realty, Inc. REALTOR®

Marco Island's Real Estate Center

900 North Collier Boulevard. Box 8088. Marco Island, Florida 33969-8088. 941/394-2505

1-800/237-8817 In Fla. 1-800/637-8817. FAX 941/642-5895

Key to clear the extensive shoals south and west of Cape Romano. He also warns deep-draft boats to use the channel from Coon Key to Caxambas pass with great care and local information if available.

To visit Marco Island, bypass the island and the shallows around Big Marco Pass well offshore, enter through Capri Pass and double back to Marco. This route has the advantage of near-ten-foot depths in contrast to the shallow inside course around Coon Key.

Marco is rich in facilities and waterfront restaurants to choose from. The marinas are largely concentrated in the Factory Bay area on the north end of the island, and include Cedar Island, Marco River and Factory Bay Marinas and dockage at O'Sheas' Restaurant and the popular Snook Inn. A new marina under construction at the foot of Jolley Bridge may be in service as the Marco Island Yacht & Sailing Club by the time you read this.

The inside waterway from Marco to Naples is well marked, and it is reported that you can carry five feet through the entire route. Much of the way, particularly the southern end, is marked by lovely coves and cul de sacs that you can sneak into although most of the beaches are a little too steep for easy beaching. Of note

are anchorages at Johnson Bay and Little Marco Island.

If you elect to go offshore, note that the sandbars in this area extend well offshore. Distance from shore and water depth are not necessarily related.

The beautiful city of Naples is the next port of call. If you enter Naples from the open Gulf through Gordon Pass, follow the markers and note that the deep water lies on the south side of the pass. Once inside you can wind your way up the waterway past the many proper and prosperous properties to the town itself. It's chockablock with marinas, clustered right downtown and including the excellent Municipal Marina and Turner Marine, where you can dock and find full service and repair facilities and shore attractions within easy walking distance. Just north of there is Old Marco Seaport, also with a restaurant and shopping onsite.

If you plan to cruise northward from Naples, you have to go outside — the short inside passage runs only from Coon Key Pass to Naples and there is no inside channel to the north until you reach the southern end of the Gulf ICW at San Carlos Bay. It's a pleasant 40-mile passage in good weather, but good weather is essential — it's a rough one in an onshore wind and there is only one viable port in case you change your mind.

OH GIVE ME A HOME WHERE
THE SPORTFISHERMEN ROAM

Since before the turn of the century, privileged sportsmen have come to Southwest Florida to enjoy the region's fabulous fishing, pristine coastal waters and abundant wildlife. Now there is a community designed for those individuals who desire the same . . . Gulf Harbour Yacht & Country Club. This 547-acre habitat is located just off the Intracoastal Waterway in Fort Myers, just minutes from the tropical islands of Sanibel & Captiva and the blue-green waters of the Gulf. In addition to a 190-slip, full-service marina which accommodates vessels up to 90 feet, residents enjoy an 18-hole championship golf course, tennis complex and spectacular country club with a fitness center and fine dining. The homes of Gulf Harbour are equally impressive with an array of custom estate homes, villas and waterfront penthouse homes priced from the $130s to over $1 million.

We invite you to discover the lifestyle of a lifetime at Gulf Harbour.

Harbour Landings Now
Selling From $350,000.

NOAA Chart #11427 Ft. Myers to Charlotte Harbor & Wiggens Pass. Latitude 26 degrees 32-19.0 North, Longitude 81 degrees 56-19.0 West.

GULF HARBOUR
YACHT & COUNTRY CLUB

Developed By Florida Design Communities

15000 McGregor Boulevard • Fort Myers, Florida 33908 • Sales (800) 216-9317 • Marina (941) 437-0881

Twelve miles up the coast, Wiggins Pass at the mouth of the Cocohatchee River offers shelter and good anchorage inside. Wiggins Pass Marina is not geared for large boats or overnight dockage, but has fuel, service, a ship's store and a hospitable attitude if you need help.

The next place of interest is Estero Island, better known as Fort Myers Beach. There are passes at both ends of the island. The southerly one is Big Carlos Pass, less used because of shoals offshore and better left to the fishermen and smaller boats. For craft of shallower draft, however, the southern side of the pass has deep water close to a wonderful stretch of white sand beach.

The more popular entrance to Fort Myers Beach is Matanzas Pass at the north end of the island. (We know there's another Matanzas Pass on the east coast south of St. Augustine. Matanzas is Spanish for massacre, and there were a lot of massacres in Florida in pioneer days.) Deep and well marked, Matanzas Pass is restricted only by a fixed bridge with 65-foot clearance.

Inside, you'll find Fort Myers Beach, a well protected harbor with a multitude of marinas and repair facilities on both sides of the bridge, including Palm Grove, Moss Marine, Compass Rose and Fort Myers Beach Marinas. The full-service facilities at Hurricane Bay are on the other side of San Carlos Island, reached through a smaller cut just north of the Pass. Shore facilities and restaurants in the area are many but scattered, and you can find almost anything along San Carlos and Estero Boulevards if you don't mind walking or cadging a lift for a few blocks.

The inside waters of Estero Bay between Estero Island and the mainland are navigable with only some difficulty by shallower-draft boats all the way back to Big Carlos Pass with excellent fishing, a pleasant anchorage inside Black Island, and a pretty shoreline along Carl Johnson State Park.

Heading north, the routes fork just north of the bridge connecting Sanibel Island with the mainland and you have another of those no-lose choices — up the Caloosahatchee River to Fort Myers or on up the Gulf ICW to Sanibel Island and Pine Island Sound.

Fort Myers itself is a first-class destination port — a beautiful and historic old city with excellent facilities and accessible downtown shopping, reached by a pleasant 15-mile run up the Caloosahatchee and with plenty of dockage if not many places to anchor out.

Notable is the Fort Myers Yacht Basin, an exemplary municipal marina between the city's two bridges, deserving of its claim of "friendliest place on the waterway". Across the river, MarinaTown Marina and Harbor Village both enjoy a reputation for hospitality — and actually welcome live-aboards. Several other facilities line the left bank of the Caloosahatchee, including Landings Marina below the Cape Coral bridge, then Deep Lagoon Marina inside Deep Lagoon and the posh new Gulf Harbour Yacht & Country Club, which has a 190-slip full-service marina with country club community amenities. Cape Coral Yacht Basin is opposite on Redfish Point, and Tarpon Point Marina lies in a sheltered cove at the mouth of the river.

Back out in San Carlos Bay, you will find yourself at Mile Zero of the Gulf Intracoastal Waterway — and in what local boatmen call Misery Mile, a mixmaster caused by tides and river currents meeting at right angles and demanding close attention to both course and steerageway through the area.

Once through that mile or two, however, you enter Pine Island Sound, which may be the loveliest cruising area on the Gulf Coast. It's another of those areas whose combination of beauty and convenience has cut short many a longer float plan. You can easily spend an entire vacation cruising between Pine Island on the east and the barrier chain of Sanibel, Captiva, North Captiva and Cayo Costa on the west.

The east shore of Pine Island Sound is Pine Island, which might have been another St. Augustine

EDITOR's NOTE: This is based on the current list maintained by the Florida Department of Environmental Protection, and while it was updated shortly before press time, changes are constant and it's a good idea to check ramps in advance. Note that some ramps are in marinas, private clubs or condominiums where public access may be limited.

LEE COUNTY BOAT RAMPS

ALVA
County Ramp — Davis Blvd. at Rt. 31
BOCA GRANDE
Inn Motel/Boatel — Gasparilla Island on Gulf of Mexico'
BOKEELIA
Al & Jean's Fish Camp — 16489 Tortuga St., NW on Charlotte Harbor
Four Winds Marina — 16501 Stringfellow Rd.
Harbor Hideaway — 7290 Barrancas Ave. on Charlotte Harbor
Silver Tarpon Lodge — on Jack Creek
BONITA SPRINGS
Bonita Beach Trailer Park — 17800 Meadowlark La.
Fish Trap Marina — 4794 Bonita Bch. Rd. on Fish Trap Bay
CAPE CORAL
Burnt Store Boat Ramp — N. Burnt Store Rd. & SW 3rd Terr.
Cape Coral Yacht & Racquet Comm. Park — 5819 Driftwood Pkwy. on Caloosahatchee River
Herman Horton Memorial Park — SE 26th Pl. & Everest Pkwy. on Caloosahatchee River
Matlacha Park — 2577 Pine Island Rd. on Matlacha Pass
CAPTIVA ISLAND
Bayside Marina — on Pine Island Sound
South Seas Plantation — Captiva Rd. on Gulf of Mexico
Tween Waters Inn — 15951 Captiva Rd.
ESTERO
Koreshan State Historic Site — US 41 on Estero River
Tahiti Mobile Village — 20518 Tahitian Blvd. on San Carlos Pass
FT. MYERS
Coastal Marine Mart — 5605 Palm Beach Blvd.
Fort Myers Sailing Club
Landing Racquet & Golf Club — 4420 Flagship Dr. on Caloosahatchee River
Landings Marina — 5200 S. Landings Dr.
Marina 31 — 17281 SR 31
Mullock Creek Marina — 18501 Mullock Creek La.
Orange Harbor Mobile Home & RV Park — 5749 Palm Beach Blvd. on Orange River
Palm Grove Marina — 2500 Main St.
Punta Rassa Boat Ramp — 18500 McGregor Blvd. on San Carlos Bay
FT. MYERS BEACH
Carl Johnson Regional Park — 24340 Estero Blvd. on Black Island on Gulf of Mexico
Ebb Tide Travel Park — 1725 Main St.
Snug Harbor Marina — 6455 San Carlos Blvd. on Matanzas Pass
MATLACHA
Lee County Matlacha Boat Ramp — Matlacha Park
McDonnell's Matlacha Marina — Pine Island Rd. on Matlacha Pass
N. FT. MYERS
Boatland — 1021 N. Tamiami Trail
Ft. Myers Sailing Club — Moody Rd. on Caloosahatchee River
North Bay Marina — 1016 N. Tamiami Tr. on Caloosahatchee River
Old Bridge Mobile Home Park — Marina, 1776 New Post Rd. on Caloosahatchee
Upriver Campground — 17021 Upriver Dr.
PINELAND
Pineland Marina & Campground — 13921 Waterfront Dr. on Pine Island Sound
PUNTA GORDA
Burnt Store Marina & Country Club — 5000 Burnt Store Rd.
SANIBEL ISLAND
The Castaways at Blind Pass — 6460 Sanibel-Captiva Rd.
Darling National Wildlife Refuge — 1 Wildlife Dr. on Pine Island Sound
Sanibel Boat Ramp — S. end of Sanibel Causeway
Sanibel Inn — 937 E. Gulf Dr.
Timmy's Nook Marina — 915 Palm St. on Pine Island Sound
ST. JAMES CITY
Gulf Haven Fish Camp & Marina — SR 767 on Monroe Canal
St. James Marina — 3157 Stringfellow Rd.

CHARLOTTE COUNTY BOAT RAMPS

BOCA GRANDE
Uncle Henry's — Gasparilla Rd. on Gulf of Mexico
CHARLOTTE HARBOR
Charlotte Harbor Camp & Travel Park — 4838 Tamiami Tr., Peace River (Small boats - Bridge)
EL JOBEAN
El Jobean Park — SR 771 on Myakka River
ENGLEWOOD
Chuck's Marina — 1990 Placida Rd. on ICW
Tamarind Gulf & Bay Condos — 2955 North Beach Rd. on Lemon Bay (Private)
PLACIDA
Eldreds Marina — Gasparilla Sound
Gasparilla Marina — 15001 Gasparilla Rd.
PORT CHARLOTTE
Port Charlotte Beach Complex — 111 SW Colleen St.on Charlotte Harbor
PUNTA GORDA
Darst Ave. Boat Ramp — on Shell Creek
Emerald Pointe Condominiums — 25188 E. Marion Ave. on Charlotte Harbor (Private)
Howard Johnson's Resort — 33 Tamiami Tr. on Peace River
Laishley Park — US 41 & Retta Esplanade on Peace River
Ponce de Leon Park — 326 W. Marion on Charlotte Harbor
Punta Gorda RV Resort — 3701 Baynard Dr. on Alligator Creek (Private)
Punta Gorda Windmill Village — 215 Rio Villa Dr. on Alligator Creek (Private)
Riviera Marina — 5600 Deltona Dr., Alligator Creek off Charlotte Harbor
RIDGE HARBOR
Riverside Park & Boat Ramp — Riverside Dr. & Darst St. on Shell Creek

COLLIER COUNTY BOAT RAMPS

CHOKOLOSKEE
Chokoloskee Island Park — Hamilton Ave.
EAST NAPLES
Bayview Park — Danford St. on Naples Bay
EVERGLADES CITY
Barron River Resort — 803 Collier Ave.
Fisherman's Cove — 777 Copeland Ave. S.
Glades Haven Rec. Resort
GOODLAND
Goodland Bay Marina — 604 E. Palm Ave.
MARCO ISLAND
Caxambas Park & Boat Ramp — End of SR 951 on Caxambus Pass
Moran's Barge Marina & Motel — Goodland Bridge
Port of the Islands Resort & Marina — US 41
State Road 951 Boat Ramp — SR 951 on Big Marco Pass
NAPLES
Bay Marina — 854 River Point Dr.
Bluebill Avenue Boat Ramp — Bluebill Ave.
Boat Haven Naples — 1484 5th Ave. S.
Briggs Nature Center — 401 Shell Island Rd.
Brookside Marina — 2023 Davis Blvd on Gordon River
Collier-Seminole State Park — 20200 E. Tamiami Tr. on Blackwater Creek
Delnor-Wiggins Pass State Rec. Area — 11100 Gulf Shore Dr. N., SR 864 on Gulf of Mexico
Greystone Park Campground — 13300 E. Tamiami Tr., US 41 S.
Isle of Capri Marina — Dockside Marine, 231 Capri Blvd., Johnson Bay
KOA Naples Campground — 1700 Barefoot Williams Rd. on Henderson Creek
Naples Landing — 9th St. & 11th Ave. on Naples Bay
Pelican Bay — 801 Laurel Oak Dr. on Gulf of Mexico
Port of the Islands — 25000 Tamiami Trail E.

SARASOTA COUNTY BOAT RAMPS

ENGLEWOOD
Indian Mound Park — Winston St. on Lemon Bay
NOKOMIS
Nokomis Beach — on Dona Bay
OSPREY
Blackburn Point Park — on Sarasota Bay (Canoes only)
Captain's Cove
SARASOTA
Centennial Park — 1059 N. Trail on Sarasota Bay
Ken Thompson — 1700 Ken Thompson Pkwy., Lido Key on Sarasota Bay
Civic Center Park — US Hwy. 41 between 6th & 10th Sts.
Pinecraft Park — Bahia Vista on Phillippi Creek
Turtle Beach — Midnight Pass Rd., Siesta Key on Little Sarasota Bay
SIESTA KEY
Midnight Pass Marina — 8865 Midnight Pass Rd. on Little Sarasota Bay
SOUTH VENICE
Manasota Beach — Manasota Bch. Rd. on Manasota Key
VENICE
Higel Marine Park — Tarpon Center Dr. on Roberts Bay

had not Ponce de Leon been killed by hostile Caloosas when he landed on the island in 1513. As it is, the area is relatively undeveloped with fine beaches and small islands that are popular with local boatmen on weekends and holidays but fairly empty the rest of the time.

On the east side of Pine Island, a protected route runs through Matlacha Pass and northward to Charlotte Harbor between equally interesting mangrove shorelines visited mostly by fishermen. The channel twists and turns, passage is restricted by four-foot depths and a reported 32-foot overhead cable, and facilities are lacking, but the reward is having the water and excellent fishing pretty much to yourself. Note that many of the islands are within Pine Island Sound Aquatic Preserve. Stand at least 50 yards off and don't go ashore.

Sanibel and Captiva, on the west side of the sound, are laid-back resort islands justly famous for their shelling, and are Siamese twins separated only by the nearly nonexistent Blind Pass. Cruising boatmen will find the full-service Sanibel Island Marina between the lighthouse at Point Ybel and the western end of the bridge/causeway to the mainland. There is also a good anchorage just inside Point Ybel. From Lighthouse Point Park you can take a trolley to Sanibel shore attractions or just to tour the island.

Further exploration to the north requires passing under the 26-foot fixed bridge or an end run toward Punta Rassa and the draw span at the east end of the causeway. It's worth it; further up the coast of Sanibel Island is the beautiful protected anchorage off the wilderness shore of Ding Darling National Wildlife Refuge. From there a side trip by dinghy into shallow Tarpon Bay is a birdwatcher's dream.

Further north, in a cove on Captiva protected by Buck Island, are two marinas, Jensen's Twin Palms and the larger 'Tween Waters. The latter is a full-fledged resort where dockage includes access to its many amenities, and the marina also offers anchorage and access to shore facilities to transients for a modest fee. At the north end of Captiva is the world-class resort of South Seas Plantation with a full-service marina, three excellent restaurants, and every amenity.

Northward past Redfish Pass at the north end of Captiva is North Captiva, a beautiful but wholly private island, then Cayo Costa, an island state park and one of the most pleasant you will find to visit. Its Gulf side is endless beach; the sound side has a deep anchorage close onshore at the southern end, and the north end is Johnson Shoals, a complex of sandbars passable by smaller boats and providing great anchorage if you can get in. A careful approach through Pelican Pass will take you into comfortable and protected anchorage in Pelican Bay, inside Punta Blanca Island. The entire area is enormously popular with local watersports enthusiasts, especially on weekends, but it's big enough that you can always find a space for yourself.

About halfway up Cayo Costa is the wonderful little island of Cabbage Key. The original home of author Mary Roberts Reinhart has been converted into an exceptionally friendly little marina, restaurant and inn where a visit is almost mandatory. Although Cabbage Key Inn is accessible only by water, it's so popular that it's always a good idea to call ahead for reservations.

Right across the channel from Cabbage Key is Useppa, another private island and famous residence.

Continued on Page 106

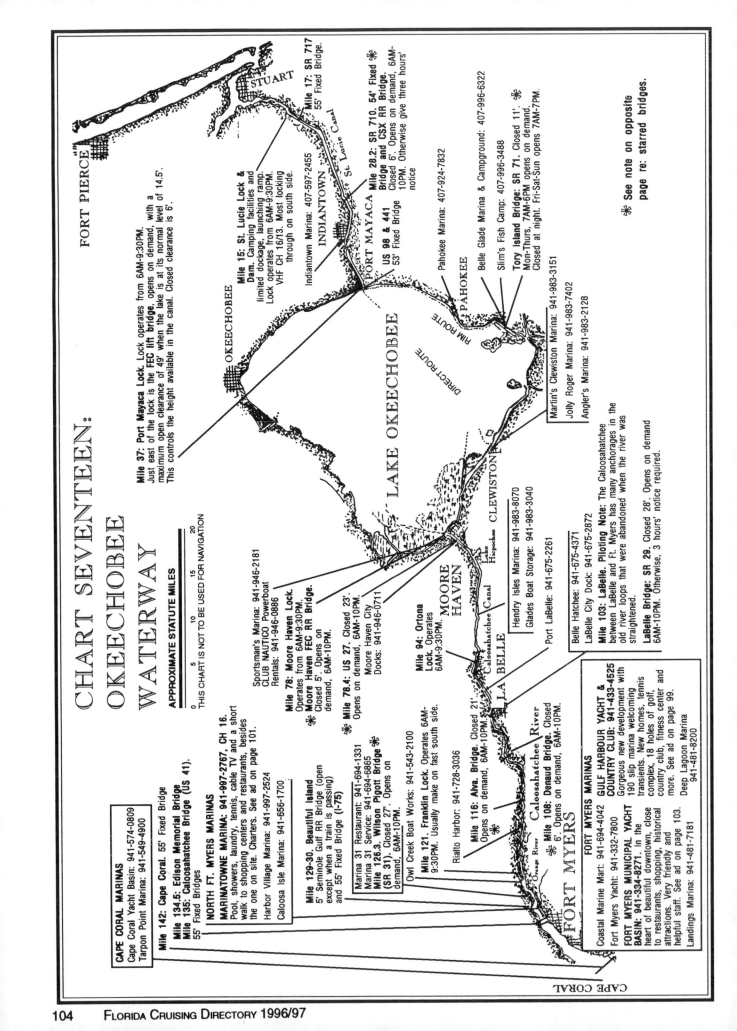

CHART SEVENTEEN: OKEECHOBEE WATERWAY

FORT PIERCE

STUART

OKEECHOBEE

INDIANTOWN

St. Lucie Canal

PORT MAYACA

LAKE OKEECHOBEE

PAHOKEE

RIM ROUTE

DIRECT ROUTE

CLEWISTON

Lake Hicpochee

Caloosahatchee Canal

MOORE HAVEN

LA BELLE

Caloosahatchee River

Orange River

FORT MYERS

CAPE CORAL

APPROXIMATE STATUTE MILES

0 5 10 15 20

THIS CHART IS NOT TO BE USED FOR NAVIGATION

Mile 37: Port Mayaca Lock. Lock operates from 6AM-9:30PM. Just east of the lock is the FEC lift bridge, opens on demand, with a maximum open clearance of 49' when the lake is at its normal level of 14.5'. This controls the height available in the canal. Closed clearance is 6'.

Mile 15: St. Lucie Lock & Dam. Camping facilities and limited dockage, launching ramp. Lock operates from 6AM-9:30PM. VHF CH 16/13. Most locking through on south side.

Indiantown Marina: 407-597-2455

Mile 17: SR 717 55' Fixed Bridge.

Mile 28.2: SR 710. 54' Fixed Bridge and CSX RR Bridge. Closed 6'. Opens on demand, 6AM-10PM. Otherwise give three hours' notice

US 98 & 441 53' Fixed Bridge

Pahokee Marina: 407-924-7832

Belle Glade Marina & Campground: 407-996-6322

Slim's Fish Camp: 407-996-3488

Tory Island Bridge: SR 71. Closed 11'. Mon-Thurs, 7AM-6PM opens on demand. Closed at night. Fri-Sat-Sun opens 7AM-7PM.

Martin's Clewiston Marina: 941-983-3151

Jolly Roger Marina: 941-983-7402

Angler's Marina: 941-983-2128

❋ **See note on opposite page re: starred bridges.**

Sportsman's Marina: 941-946-2181
CLUB NAUTICO Powerboat Rentals: 941-946-0886

Mile 78: Moore Haven Lock. Operates from 6AM-9:30PM.
❋ **Moore Haven FEC RR Bridge.** Closed 5'. Opens on demand, 6AM-10PM.

Mile 78.4: US 27. Closed 23'. Opens on demand, 6AM-10PM.

Moore Haven City Docks: 941-946-0711

Mile 94: Ortona Lock. Operates 6AM-9:30PM.

Hendry Isles Marina: 941-983-8070
Glades Boat Storage: 941-983-3040

Port LaBelle: 941-675-2261

Belle Hatchee: 941-675-4371
LaBelle City Dock: 941-675-2872

Mile 103: LaBelle. Piloting Note: The Caloosahatchee between LaBelle and Ft. Myers has many anchorages in the old river loops that were abandoned when the river was straightened.

LaBelle Bridge: SR 29. Closed 28'. Opens on demand 6AM-10PM. Otherwise, 3 hours' notice required.

CAPE CORAL MARINAS
Cape Coral Yacht Basin: 941-574-0809
Tarpon Point Marina: 941-549-4900

Mile 142: Cape Coral. 55' Fixed Bridge

Mile 134.5: Edison Memorial Bridge
Mile 135: Caloosahatchee Bridge (US 41). 55' Fixed Bridges

NORTH FT. MYERS MARINAS
MARINATOWNE MARINA: 941-997-2767, CH 16. Pool, showers, laundry, tennis, cable TV and a short walk to shopping centers and restaurants, besides the one on site. Charters. See ad on page 101.

Harbor Village Marina: 941-997-2524
Caloosa Isle Marina: 941-656-1700

Mile 129-30. Beautiful Island 5' Seminole Gulf RR Bridge (open except when a train is passing) and 55' Fixed Bridge (I-75)

Marina 31 Restaurant: 941-694-1331
Marina 31 Service: 941-694-6865
❋ **Mile 126.3: Wilson Pigott Bridge (SR 31).** Closed 27'. Opens on demand, 6AM-10PM.

Owl Creek Boat Works: 941-543-2100

Mile 121. Franklin Lock. Operates 6AM-9:30PM. Usually make on fast south side.

Rialto Harbor: 941-728-3036

❋ **Mile 116: Alva. Bridge.** Closed 21'. Opens on demand, 6AM-10PM.

❋ **Mile 108: Denaud Bridge.** Closed 6'. Opens on demand, 6AM-10PM.

FORT MYERS MARINAS
Coastal Marine Mart: 941-694-4042
Fort Myers Yacht: 941-332-7800
FORT MYERS MUNICIPAL YACHT BASIN: 941-334-8271. In the heart of beautiful downtown, close to restaurants, shopping, historical attractions. Very friendly and helpful staff. See ad on page 103.
Landings Marina: 941-481-7181

GULF HARBOUR YACHT & COUNTRY CLUB: 941-433-4525 Gorgeous new development with 190 slip marina welcoming transients. New homes, tennis complex, 18 holes of golf, country club, fitness center and more. See ad on page 99.

Deep Lagoon Marina 941-481-8200

CRUISING THE OKEECHOBEE WATERWAY

The 152-mile Okeechobee Waterway, which crosses Florida from Stuart to the Gulf at Fort Myers, can be divided into three parts like Caesar's Gaul.

From "The Crossroads" at the mouth of the St. Lucie River in Stuart, it's ten miles up the river and around the city, then up the South Fork of the St. Lucie River and under the high bridges of Interstate 95 and Florida's Turnpike to the start of the waterway at St. Lucie Lock at Mile 15. It's the first of five locks that raise your boat the 12-16 feet from sea level to Lake Okeechobee level and back to sea level again. The locks monitor Channels 13 or 16 and respond to a two-long-two-short horn signal. All of them operate from 0600 to 2130 daily, but before you commit to the Waterway it's essential to find out about any restrictions or temporary special hours, which are frequent. Start with a call the Clewiston Operations office of the Corps of Engineers at 813-983-8101, and ask lockmasters for current conditions as you pass each lock.

At the St. Lucie lock is a nice little county park with dock, ramp, picnic and campsites. Just east of the lock is a complete facility at Monterrey Marine.

From there to the second lock at Port Mayaca is the first part of the waterway, a fairly straight landcut that runs past Indiantown and friendly Indiantown Marina near Mile 30, which has been called the second cleanest in the world. No, we don't know the cleanest.

Nine miles west at the lake entrance there's a lift bridge at Port Mayaca with a maximum clearance of 49 feet when the lake is at its normal level of 14.5 feet (if the lake is higher, the clearance is less and vice versa; call ahead), then through Port Mayaca Lock at Mile 38 and almost immediately into the second part of the waterway, the Lake Okeechobee crossing.

At this point you must make the decision whether to cross Lake Okeechobee by the 25-mile direct route to Clewiston or to take the more circuitous and better protected rim route which follows the edge of the lake. There may not be enough water to change your mind and cross between the two routes, so your decision can be relatively final.

Lake Okeechobee is big, shallow, and can be mean when the wind is up. The direct route has a controlling depth of eight feet and is a straight run except for a channel which must be used to get safely through a rock reef in the middle of the lake.

The rim route channel is a fringe benefit of the building of Hoover Dike to prevent recurrence of the terrible flooding caused by the hurricane of 1928. It's 12 miles longer than the direct route to Clewiston and has a controlling depth of only six feet, but runs around islands and through cuts that offer both shelter and anchorage possibilities. The only facilities on the rim route are small marinas at Pahokee and Belle Glade, better suited to small boats but near the towns.

If you leave the channel, go slowly and eyeball the water carefully for snags and shallows. Anchoring bow and stern is a good idea to prevent swinging into trouble in the night. Some of the best bass fishing in the area is to be found between the rim route channel and the boulders along the lakeshore between Canal Point and Kreamer and Torry Islands.

The two routes meet again at about Mile 65 at Clewiston, the largest town on the canal, which offers ample facilities up a short canal at a very nice marina/motel/restaurant/shop complex owned by Roland Martin of video fishing fame.

From Clewiston, the channel continues along the edge of the lake to Moore Haven at Mile 77, which has two marinas, a nice municipal dock and a big park/launching ramp. From Moore Haven, the route heads down the Caloosahatchee Canal to the Ortona Lock at Mile 94 and into the third part of the waterway, the Caloosahatchee River — one of the prettiest and most easily navigable of rivers.

Going downriver — westward — from Moore Haven, the waterway runs through shallow Lake Hicpochee and down an eight-mile cut, past Hendry Isles Marina and Glade Boat Storage at Mile 89, then through Ortona Lock to the pretty resort town of LaBelle at Mile 103. A mile or so east of town is Port LaBelle Marina and a charming cove that's good for anchoring out. In LaBelle, there's Belle Hatchee Marina and a city dock with a good number of stores close by. 20 miles down-waterway is the town of Alva with Alva Supply & Marina, and further downstream is the full-service facility of Rialto Harbor Docks.

From there downriver to Fort Myers, the river becomes gradually more natural and less channelized. Where engineers cut off oxbow bends of the old river-bed, they created wonderful anchorages along the way.

Seven miles below Alva you are eased back down to sea level at Franklin Lock at Mile 121, which also has dockage and hookups. Four miles downstream there's a cluster of facilities at Fort Myers Shores that includes Owl Creek Boat Works and popular Marina 31 Restaurant, which has dockage and facilities for transients.

Five miles further, past the wilderness shores of Caloosahatchee Wildlife Refuge on the north shore and Beautiful Island on the south, the river opens up onto the Fort Myers waterfront. The Waterway continues through the city and its excellent facilities (which are described in the Sun Coast section of this directory) and meets the Gulf Intracoastal Waterway in San Carlos Bay.

✳ **Three hours' notice required for after-hours bridge openings. Numbers to call:**

Florida DOT (Dept. of Transportation)
941-656-7800

CSX Railroad: - 813-664-6240

Bridges controlled by FEC RR and Seminole Gulf RR normally remain open except when a train is scheduled to cross.

Originally an Indian midden and the highest point in the area, it was the lair of Jose Gaspar, one of the nastier pirates, then became the private fishing club of Barron Collier, who developed much of the area and for whom Collier County is named. His home is now Useppa Island Club, a private resort which accepts transient cruising boats but only by reservation. You can enjoy the beauty of the island from a distance from two good anchorages, one directly opposite Cabbage Key and the other at the northwest end of the island, but do not attempt to land anywhere on the island.

At this point you can turn eastward and make the side trip around the north end of Pine Island and into Charlotte Harbor, a broad 20-mile estuary which leads to the mouths of the Peace and Myakka Rivers. On the way there are two marinas on Jug Creek, sheltered inside Bokeelia Island. One is largely private, but the other, Four Winds Marina, is justly popular with those who can manage the approach over four-foot depths.

Halfway to Punta Gorda, in a creek mouth south of Key Point, Burnt Store Marina and Resort is one of the largest on the Gulf and offers all the amenities of a luxury resort. Further upstream at the mouth of the Peace River, several facilities are clustered around the bridge between Port Charlotte and Punta Gorda, including the popular Fisherman's Village on the Punta Gorda side, which is hard alongside a big indoor shopping and restaurant complex that boasts no less then seven restaurants.

From there you can venture up the Peace River for several miles with a shallow draft and a careful pilot and see the agricultural and ranching heart of Florida, or by small boat up the Myakka River for the world-class birdwatching and fishing the area is famous for.

Back along the Gulf ICW across Boca Grande Inlet north of Cayo Costa lies Gasparilla Island, named for the notorious pirate Jose Gaspar, who is something of an icon in these parts despite his reputation as a plunderer, ladies' man and Bluebeard or perhaps

because of it. The seat of Gasparilla Island is the comfortable old resort village of Boca Grande, the gathering place for the elite anglers who seek the area's giant tarpon and compete in its many fishing tournaments. As a result the island boasts half a dozen marine facilities, among them the Boca Grande Pass Marina on the south and Gasparilla Inn and Cottages sheltered in Boca Grande Bayou. On the north, where the causeway crosses to the mainland, the popular Uncle Henry's Marina Resort holds forth on the site of the old Boca Grande Club with dockage and many amenities.

Northward above Gasparilla Pass, the waterway runs through Placida Harbor, then narrows at Cape Haze, where there's a popular protected anchorage northwest of Daybeacon 30, and through a couple of miles of narrow cut before it opens into Lemon Bay. Just south of the opening lies Palm Island Resort, another of those pleasant resort marinas where transients are permitted use of the amenities.

The waterway runs northward through Lemon Bay to Englewood and Venice and some of the best cruising and most hospitable facilities on the Sun Coast. The entire Lemon Bay area is pierced by little passes and delightful gunkholes for exploring and anchoring. Like Pine Island Sound to the south, it's another area with so many attractions that you could forget your float plan and spend all the available time exploring right here.

A favorite spot in the area is around Stump Pass, where you can have your cake and eat it, too — shuttle from remote anchorages around the Charlotte Beach State Recreation Area across the bay to Stump Pass Marina at Grove City and enjoy every service known to the marine industry and the hospitality for which the Gulf Coast is justly famous.

From Stump Pass, the route north is another choice of inviting anchorages along Englewood Beach on the barrier island and toward Englewood on the mainland side. There the same kind of shuttle route runs to the mainland and the facilities at Chadwick Cove.

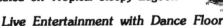

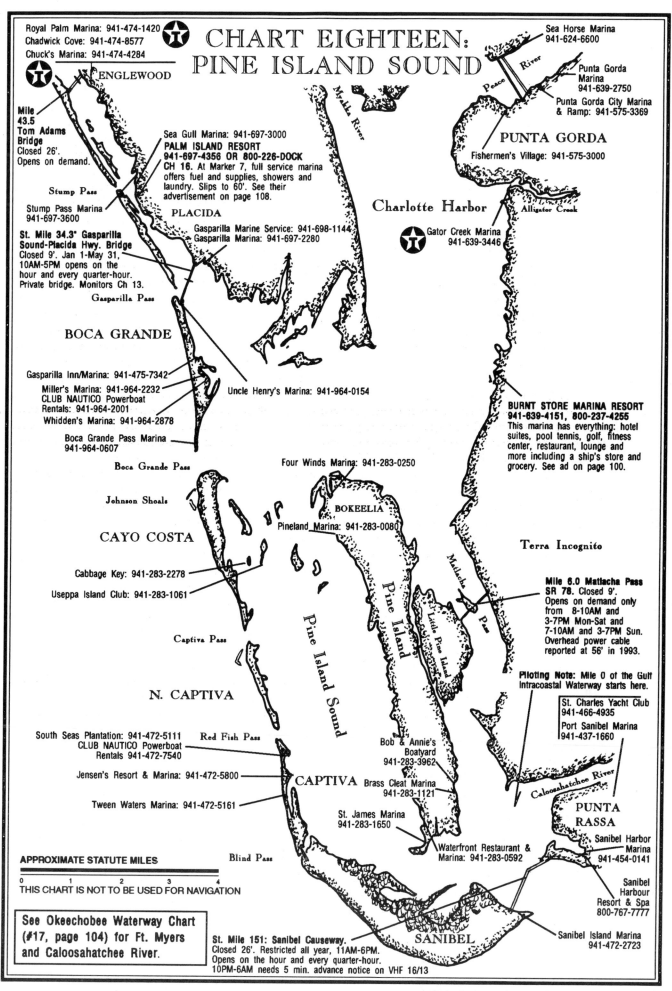

CHART EIGHTEEN: PINE ISLAND SOUND

Royal Palm Marina: 941-474-1420
Chadwick Cove: 941-474-8577
Chuck's Marina: 941-474-4284

ENGLEWOOD

Mile 43.5 Tom Adams Bridge
Closed 26'.
Opens on demand.

Stump Pass

Stump Pass Marina
941-697-3600

St. Mile 34.3" Gasparilla Sound-Placida Hwy. Bridge
Closed 9'. Jan 1-May 31, 10AM-5PM opens on the hour and every quarter-hour. Private bridge. Monitors Ch 13.

Gasparilla Pass

BOCA GRANDE

Gasparilla Inn/Marina: 941-475-7342
Miller's Marina: 941-964-2232
CLUB NAUTICO Powerboat Rentals: 941-964-2001
Whidden's Marina: 941-964-2878
Boca Grande Pass Marina 941-964-0607

Boca Grande Pass

Johnson Shoals

CAYO COSTA

Cabbage Key: 941-283-2278
Useppa Island Club: 941-283-1061

Captiva Pass

N. CAPTIVA

South Seas Plantation: 941-472-5111
CLUB NAUTICO Powerboat Rentals 941-472-7540
Jensen's Resort & Marina: 941-472-5800
Tween Waters Marina: 941-472-5161

Red Fish Pass

Blind Pass

Sea Gull Marina: 941-697-3000
PALM ISLAND RESORT
941-697-4356 OR 800-226-DOCK
CH 16. At Marker 7, full service marina offers fuel and supplies, showers and laundry. Slips to 60'. See their advertisement on page 108.

PLACIDA

Gasparilla Marine Service: 941-698-1144
Gasparilla Marina: 941-697-2280

Uncle Henry's Marina: 941-964-0154

Four Winds Marina: 941-283-0250

BOKEELIA

Pineland Marina: 941-283-0080

Myakka River

Peace River

Sea Horse Marina 941-624-6600

Punta Gorda Marina 941-639-2750

Punta Gorda City Marina & Ramp: 941-575-3369

PUNTA GORDA

Fishermen's Village: 941-575-3000

Charlotte Harbor

Alligator Creek

Gator Creek Marina 941-639-3446

BURNT STORE MARINA RESORT
941-639-4151, 800-237-4255
This marina has everything: hotel suites, pool tennis, golf, fitness center, restaurant, lounge and more including a ship's store and grocery. See ad on page 100.

Terra Incognito

Mile 6.0 Matlacha Pass
SR 78. Closed 9'.
Opens on demand only from 8-10AM and 3-7PM Mon-Sat and 7-10AM and 3-7PM Sun. Overhead power cable reported at 56' in 1993.

Piloting Note: Mile 0 of the Gulf Intracoastal Waterway starts here.

St. Charles Yacht Club 941-466-4935
Port Sanibel Marina 941-437-1660

Pine Island

Little Pine Island

Matlacha Pass

Pine Island Sound

Bob & Annie's Boatyard 941-283-3962

CAPTIVA

Brass Cleat Marina 941-283-1121

St. James Marina 941-283-1650

Waterfront Restaurant & Marina: 941-283-0592

PUNTA RASSA

Caloosahatchee River

Sanibel Harbor Marina 941-454-0141

Sanibel Harbour Resort & Spa 800-767-7777

Sanibel Island Marina 941-472-2723

SANIBEL

APPROXIMATE STATUTE MILES

0 1 2 3 4

THIS CHART IS NOT TO BE USED FOR NAVIGATION

See Okeechobee Waterway Chart (#17, page 104) for Ft. Myers and Caloosahatchee River.

St. Mile 151: Sanibel Causeway.
Closed 26'. Restricted all year, 11AM-6PM. Opens on the hour and every quarter-hour. 10PM-6AM needs 5 min. advance notice on VHF 16/13

North of Englewood, Lemon Bay narrows and eventually turns into a four-mile cut that detours inland around Venice to Roberts Bay and Venice Inlet. You'll find plenty of hospitality and facilities in that friendly resort and retirement town, where Ringling Brothers Circus winters and where more anchorages abound inside the inlet. Among the marine facilities are Fisherman's Wharf & Marina a mile south of the inlet and Crow's Nest Marina with its restaurant and tavern right inside the inlet in downtown Venice.

Blackburn Point, at Mile 62.4, is the site of the last swing bridge in these parts and home to several marinas clustered at the south end of Little Sarasota Bay. A couple of miles north of Blackburn Point is Midnight Pass, the subject of much controversy some years ago. The forces of nature were gradually moving the pass northward, endangering the homes of some people influential enough to get the pass filled in. Taking exception, local boatmen tried to dig it out one night. They did not succeed, but their efforts created a nice little cove and beach. Beware — at low tide some spots can be as shallow as two or three feet.

Northward, the waterway transits Little Sarasota Bay, winds through the narrows at Siesta Key, then opens into Roberts Bay and Sarasota Bay proper. If Pine

Island Sound is an escape from civilization and Lemon Bay is a wonderful combination of undeveloped anchorages and friendly facilities within easy reach, Sarasota Bay is a return to the Twentieth Century with a sparkling modern city on the mainland side, luxurious homes and resorts on the barrier islands, and wonderful cruising waters between with excellent facilities and great restaurants at every turn along its shores. It is urban cruising at its very best.

Sarasota lies at Mile 73, and is one of the prettiest cities to be found anywhere, site of more shore attractions than space permits us to list, and home to any number of marinas and docking facilities. Three are clustered at either end of the John Ringling Causeway to Lido and Longboat Keys. The largest is Marina Operations, right downtown on the mainland side and home to Marina Jack's restaurant and a pantheon of shore facilities. It's also adjacent to a very large anchoring area that's an easy commute to the shore attractions.

Across Sarasota Bay is Longboat Key with Sarasota Yacht Club and several fine anchorages sheltered by Bird, Otter, St. Armand's and Lido Key.

Northward on the mainland side, Holiday Inn Marina and Yacht Basin is sheltered in a cove at the mouth of Bowlee's Creek. Across the bay on the barrier island is the notable marina and resort complex at Longboat Key Moorings, where transient boatmen can enjoy the services and amenities of the resort.

Longboat Key ends at Longboat Pass, Mile 85, one of the prettiest places in an area known far and wide for its pretty places. There's plenty of room to anchor and places to dock, facilities at Buccaneer Inn Restaurant and Marina, and nearby Moore's Stone Crab Restaurant is one of the finest eating places on the coast.

North of Longboat Pass, the waterway narrows between Bradenton Beach and the fishing village of Cortez and passes Bradenton Beach Marina on the barrier island end of the bridge. On the mainland north of the bridge is the Seafood Shack Restaurant and Marina. Like the Buccaneer further south, it's one of the few facilities to give the word "restaurant" top billing over "marina", both for good reason.

North of Cortez the waterway crosses Anna Maria Sound to the laid-back little community on Anna Maria Island before entering Tampa Bay. Facilities on the island include Crabby Bill's restaurant and marina, formerly Pete Reynard's, and Galati Marine. To the east lies the mouth of the Manatee River and a pleasant five-mile cruise up a wild estuary and past good anchorage opportunities to the marine facilities and shore attractions of Bradenton and Palmetto. Boca del Rio Marina is right at the river mouth, and at the Highway 41 bridge further upstream you have a choice of the Bradenton Pier and Yacht Basin on the south and the full-service Regatta Pointe Marina on the north.

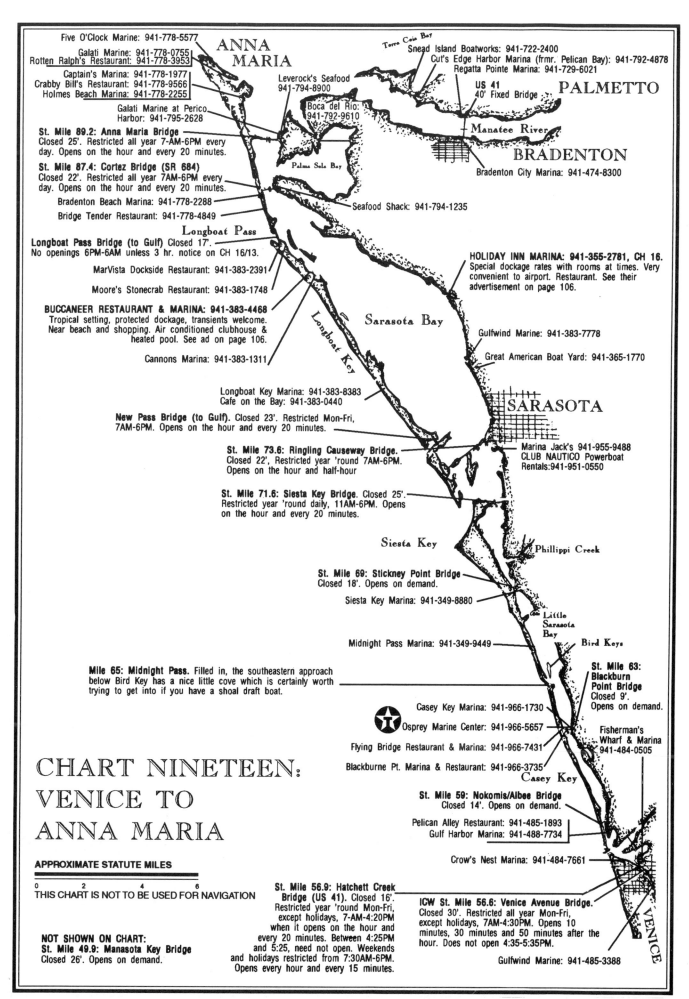

Five O'Clock Marine: 941-778-5577
Galati Marine: 941-778-0755
Rotten Ralph's Restaurant: 941-778-3953
Captain's Marina: 941-778-1977
Crabby Bill's Restaurant: 941-778-9566
Holmes Beach Marina: 941-778-2255
Galati Marine at Perico
Harbor: 941-795-2628

ANNA MARIA

Torre Ceia Bay
Snead Island Boatworks: 941-722-2400
Cut's Edge Harbor Marina (frmr. Pelican Bay): 941-792-4878
Regatta Pointe Marina: 941-729-6021

US 41
40' Fixed Bridge

PALMETTO

Leverock's Seafood
941-794-8900

Boca del Rio:
941-792-9610

Manatee River

BRADENTON

St. Mile 89.2: Anna Maria Bridge
Closed 25'. Restricted all year 7-AM-6PM every
day. Opens on the hour and every 20 minutes.

St. Mile 87.4: Cortez Bridge (SR 684)
Closed 22'. Restricted all year 7AM-6PM every
day. Opens on the hour and every 20 minutes.

Palma Sola Bay

Bradenton City Marina: 941-474-8300

Bradenton Beach Marina: 941-778-2288
Bridge Tender Restaurant: 941-778-4849

Seafood Shack: 941-794-1235

Longboat Pass

Longboat Pass Bridge (to Gulf) Closed 17'.
No openings 6PM-6AM unless 3 hr. notice on CH 16/13.

MarVista Dockside Restaurant: 941-383-2391

Moore's Stonecrab Restaurant: 941-383-1748

BUCCANEER RESTAURANT & MARINA: 941-383-4468
Tropical setting, protected dockage, transients welcome.
Near beach and shopping. Air conditioned clubhouse &
heated pool. See ad on page 106.

Cannons Marina: 941-383-1311

Sarasota Bay

HOLIDAY INN MARINA: 941-355-2781, CH 16.
Special dockage rates with rooms at times. Very
convenient to airport. Restaurant. See their
advertisement on page 106.

Gulfwind Marine: 941-383-7778

Great American Boat Yard: 941-365-1770

Longboat Key

Longboat Key Marina: 941-383-8383
Cafe on the Bay: 941-383-0440

New Pass Bridge (to Gulf). Closed 23'. Restricted Mon-Fri,
7AM-6PM. Opens on the hour and every 20 minutes.

St. Mile 73.6: Ringling Causeway Bridge.
Closed 22', Restricted year 'round 7AM-6PM.
Opens on the hour and half-hour

St. Mile 71.6: Siesta Key Bridge. Closed 25'.
Restricted year 'round daily, 11AM-6PM. Opens
on the hour and every 20 minutes.

SARASOTA

Marina Jack's 941-955-9488
CLUB NAUTICO Powerboat
Rentals:941-951-0550

Siesta Key

Phillippi Creek

St. Mile 69: Stickney Point Bridge
Closed 18'. Opens on demand.

Siesta Key Marina: 941-349-8880

Midnight Pass Marina: 941-349-9449

Little
Sarasota
Bay

Bird Keys

Mile 65: Midnight Pass. Filled in, the southeastern approach
below Bird Key has a nice little cove which is certainly worth
trying to get into if you have a shoal draft boat.

**St. Mile 63:
Blackburn
Point Bridge**
Closed 9'.
Opens on demand.

Casey Key Marina: 941-966-1730
Osprey Marine Center: 941-966-5657
Flying Bridge Restaurant & Marina: 941-966-7431
Blackburne Pt. Marina & Restaurant: 941-966-3735

Fisherman's
Wharf & Marina
941-484-0505

Casey Key

CHART NINETEEN: VENICE TO ANNA MARIA

St. Mile 59: Nokomis/Albee Bridge
Closed 14'. Opens on demand.

Pelican Alley Restaurant: 941-485-1893
Gulf Harbor Marina: 941-488-7734

Crow's Nest Marina: 941-484-7661

APPROXIMATE STATUTE MILES

0   2   4   6
THIS CHART IS NOT TO BE USED FOR NAVIGATION

NOT SHOWN ON CHART:
St. Mile 49.9: Manasota Key Bridge
Closed 26'. Opens on demand.

**St. Mile 56.9: Hatchett Creek
Bridge (US 41).** Closed 16'.
Restricted year 'round Mon-Fri,
except holidays, 7-AM-4:20PM
when it opens on the hour and
every 20 minutes. Between 4:25PM
and 5:25, need not open. Weekends
and holidays restricted from 7:30AM-6PM.
Opens every hour and every 15 minutes.

ICW St. Mile 56.6: Venice Avenue Bridge.
Closed 30'. Restricted all year Mon-Fri,
except holidays, 7AM-4:30PM. Opens 10
minutes, 30 minutes and 50 minutes after the
hour. Does not open 4:35-5:35PM.

Gulfwind Marine: 941-485-3388

VENICE

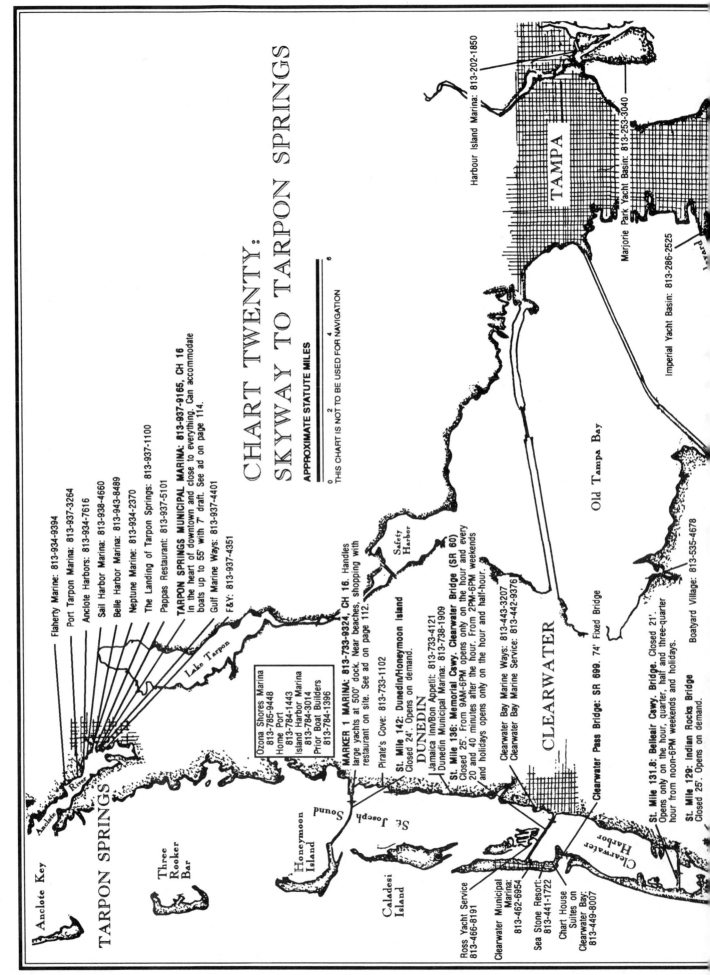

CHART TWENTY: SKYWAY TO TARPON SPRINGS

APPROXIMATE STATUTE MILES

0   2   4   6

THIS CHART IS NOT TO BE USED FOR NAVIGATION

Anclote Key

TARPON SPRINGS

Three Rooker Bar

Honeymoon Island

Caladesi Island

St. Joseph Sound

Honeymoon Island

Safety Harbor

Old Tampa Bay

TAMPA

CLEARWATER

Clearwater Harbor

Lake Tarpon

Anclote River

Flaherty Marine: 813-934-9394

Port Tarpon Marina: 813-937-3264

Anclote Harbors: 813-934-7616

Sail Harbor Marina: 813-938-4660

Belle Harbor Marina: 813-943-8489

Neptune Marine: 813-934-2370

The Landing of Tarpon Springs: 813-937-1100

Pappas Restaurant: 813-937-5101

TARPON SPRINGS MUNICIPAL MARINA: 813-937-9165, CH 16 In the heart of downtown and close to everything. Can accommodate boats up to 55' with 7' draft. See ad on page 114.

Gulf Marine Ways: 813-937-4401

F&Y: 813-937-4351

Ozona Shores Marina 813-785-9448
Home Port
Island Harbor Marina 813-784-1443
813-784-3014
Prior Boat Builders 813-784-1396

MARKER 1 MARINA: 813-733-9324, CH 16. Handles large yachts at 500' dock. Near beaches, shopping with restaurant on site. See ad on page 112.

Pirate's Cove: 813-733-1102

St. Mile 142: Dunedin/Honeymoon Island Closed 24'. Opens on demand.

DUNEDIN

Jamaica Inn/Bon Appetit: 813-733-4121
Dunedin Municipal Marina: 813-738-1909

St. Mile 136: Memorial Cswy. Clearwater Bridge (SR 60) Closed 25'. From 9AM-6PM opens only on the hour and every 20 and 40 minutes after the hour. From 2PM-6PM weekends and holidays opens only on the hour and half-hour.

Clearwater Bay Marine Ways: 813-443-3207
Clearwater Bay Marine Service: 813-442-9376

Clearwater Pass Bridge: SR 699. 74' Fixed Bridge

St. Mile 131.8: Belleair Cswy. Bridge. Closed 21'. Opens only on the hour, quarter, half and three-quarter hour from noon–6PM weekends and holidays.

St. Mile 129: Indian Rocks Bridge Closed 25'. Opens on demand.

Ross Yacht Service 813-466-8191

Clearwater Municipal Marina: 813-462-6954

Sea Stone Resort: 813-441-1722

Chart House Suites on Clearwater Bay: 813-449-8007

Boatyard Village: 813-535-4678

Harbour Island Marina: 813-202-1850

Marjorie Park Yacht Basin: 813-253-3040

Imperial Yacht Basin: 813-286-2525

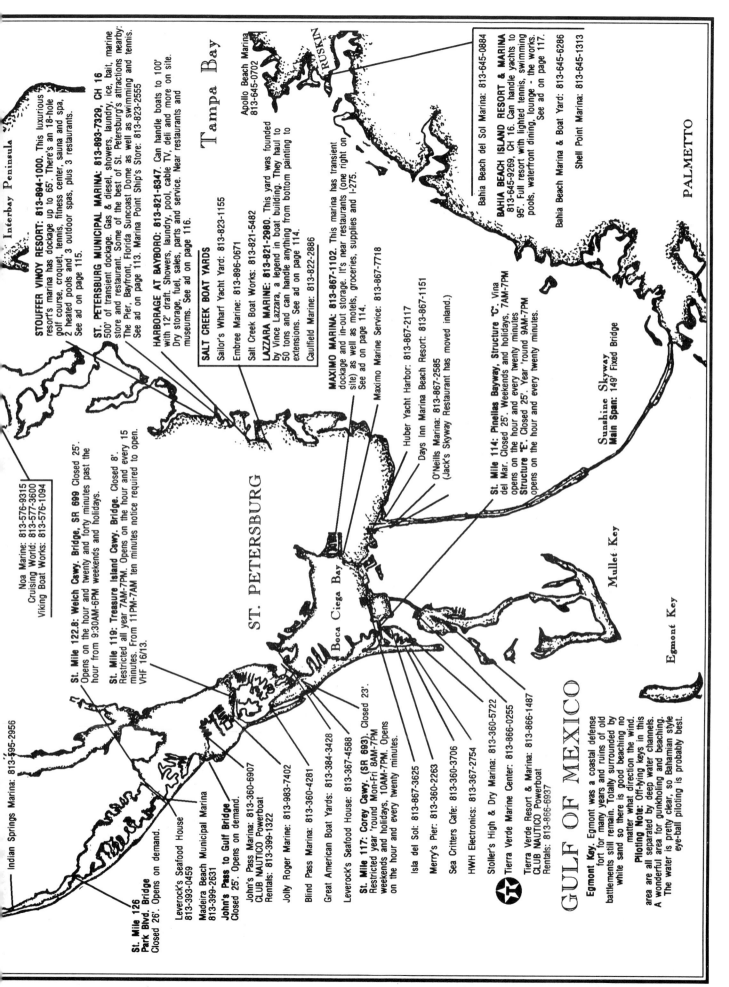

STOUFFER VINOY RESORT: 813-894-1000. This luxurious resort's marina has dockage up to 65'. There's an 18-hole golf course, croquet, tennis, fitness center, sauna and spa, 2 heated pools and 3 outdoor spas, plus 3 restaurants. See ad on page 115.

ST. PETERSBURG MUNICIPAL MARINA: 813-893-7329, CH 16 500' of transient dockage. Gas & diesel, showers, laundry, ice, bait, marine store and restaurant. Some of the best of St. Petersburg's attractions nearby: The Pier, Bayfront, Florida Suncoast Dome as well as swimming and tennis. See ad on page 113. Marina Point Ship's Store: 813-823-2555

HARBORAGE AT BAYBORO: 813-821-6347. Can handle boats to 100' with 12' draft. Showers, laundry, pool, cable TV, deli and more on site. Dry storage, fuel, sales, parts and service. Near restaurants and museums. See ad on page 116.

Tampa Bay

Apollo Beach Marina
813-645-0702

RUSKIN

SALT CREEK BOAT YARDS
Sailor's Wharf Yacht Yard: 813-823-1155
Embree Marine: 813-896-0671
Salt Creek Boat Works: 813-821-5482
LAZZARA MARINE: 813-821-2980. This yard was founded by Vince Lazzara, a legend in boat building. They haul to 50 tons and can handle anything from bottom painting to extensions. See ad on page 114.
Caulfield Marine: 813-822-2886

Bahia Beach del Sol Marina: 813-645-0884

BAHIA BEACH ISLAND RESORT & MARINA 813-645-9269, CH 16. Can handle yachts to 95'. Full resort with lighted tennis, swimming pools, waterfront dining, lounge - the works. See ad on page 117.

Bahia Beach Marina & Boat Yard: 813-645-6286
Shell Point Marina: 813-645-1313

PALMETTO

MAXIMO MARINA: 813-867-1102. This marina has transient dockage and in-out storage. It's near restaurants (one right on site) as well as motels, groceries, supplies and I-275. See ad on page 114.

Maximo Marine Service: 813-867-7718

Huber Yacht Harbor: 813-867-2117

Days Inn Marina Beach Resort: 813-867-1151

O'Neills Marina: 813-867-2585
(Jack's Skyway Restaurant has moved inland.)

St. Mile 114: Pinellas Bayway, Structure "C", Vina del Mar. Closed 25'. Weekends and holidays, 7AM-7PM opens on the hour and every twenty minutes **Structure "E".** Closed 25'. Year 'round 9AM-7PM opens on the hour and every twenty minutes.

Sunshine Skyway
Main Span: 149' Fixed Bridge

Noa Marine: 813-576-9315
Cruising World: 813-577-3600
Viking Boat Works: 813-576-1094

St. Mile 122.8: Welch Cswy. Bridge, SR 699 Closed 25'. Opens on the hour and twenty and forty minutes past the hour from 9:30AM-6PM weekends and holidays.

St. Mile 119: Treasure Island Cswy. Bridge. Closed 8'. Restricted all year 7AM-7PM. Opens on the hour and every 15 minutes. From 11PM-7AM ten minutes notice required to open. VHF 16/13.

Indian Springs Marina: 813-595-2956

St. Mile 126 Park Blvd. Bridge Closed 26'. Opens on demand.

Leverock's Seafood House
813-393-0459

Madeira Beach Municipal Marina
813-399-2631

John's Pass to Gulf Bridge Closed 25'. Opens on demand.

John's Pass Marina: 813-360-6907
CLUB NAUTICO Powerboat
Rentals: 813-399-1322

Jolly Roger Marine: 813-983-7402

Blind Pass Marina: 813-360-4281

Great American Boat Yards: 813-384-3428

Leverock's Seafood House: 813-367-4588

St. Mile 117: Corey Cswy. (SR 693). Closed 23'. Restricted year 'round Mon-Fri 8AM-7PM weekends and holidays, 10AM-7PM. Opens on the hour and every twenty minutes.

Isla del Sol: 813-867-3625

Merry's Pier: 813-360-2263

Sea Critters Cafe: 813-360-3706

HWH Electronics: 813-367-2754

Stoller's High & Dry Marina: 813-360-5722

Tierra Verde Marine Center: 813-866-0255

Tierra Verde Resort & Marina: 813-866-1487
CLUB NAUTICO Powerboat
Rentals: 813-866-6937

ST. PETERSBURG

Boca Ciega Bay

Mullet Key

Egmont Key

GULF OF MEXICO

Egmont Key. Egmont Key was a coastal defense fort for many years and ruins of old battlements still remain. Totally surrounded by white sand so there is good beaching no matter what direction the wind. **Piloting Note:** Off-lying keys in this area are all separated by deep water channels. A wonderful area for gunkholing and beaching. The water is pretty clear, so Bahamian style eye-ball piloting is probably best.

North of Bradenton and eastward under the beautiful Sunshine Skyway Bridge, Tampa Bay is a cruising grounds unto itself, a very large and very commercial harbor port which also supports a huge boating community and a fine sportfishery. The bay contains quite a few places worth visiting and a couple that have a "must see" rating.

Turning into the bay under the Skyway Bridge and going counterclockwise around the shore, the Little Manatee River enters ten miles from the Skyway, and two miles up the shallowish river is Shell Point Marina. North of the river mouth is Bahia Beach, a resort community with three marinas — Bahia Beach Island, Bahia del Sol and Bahia Beach, and a secluded anchorage in a protected basin off Crab Creek. There is another nice anchorage to the north at Apollo Beach with a waterfront restaurant nearby, but the only dockage is at a private club and available only to members of reciprocating clubs.

The northeastern arm of Tampa Bay is Hillsborough Bay, and the major urban marine attraction is Harbour Island (Must-See #1), right in downtown Tampa, a beautiful modern marina complex with restaurants and night clubs, shops and a luxury hotel, all connected to downtown Tampa by a people mover. If you like action and excitement, Harbour Island is your kind of place. Even if it's not,

it's worth a visit, and visiting boatpeople are as welcome here as anywhere in Florida. Wrapped around the complex is the beautiful new Harbor Island Marina, where transient guests enjoy the use of the hotel's amenities. For quieter dockage, transients are sometimes welcome at Marjorie Park Yacht Basin across Seddon Channel on Davis Island.

Continuing counterclockwise around the Interbay Peninsula, you enter the northern reaches of Tampa Bay, best known as Old Tampa Bay, which is crisscrossed by bridge/causeways with low clearances, has few anchorages or facilities, and is not ratable as a cruising grounds. Most visiting boats cut off Old Tampa Bay and head westward, venturing no further north than the channel that parallels the Gandy bridge/causeway across the mouth of the bay. There is Imperial Yacht Center, at the east foot of the causeway, a facility more devoted to resident powerboats but which welcomes transients.

At the other end of the causeway, however, is St. Petersburg, known all over the world as Sailing City and once the home of a major portion of the sailboat builders in the United States. The next few miles are wall-to-wall with excellent and hospitable facilities, beginning with three boatyards at the west foot of the Gandy Bridge, then concentrating right downtown with the first-class facilities of the restored Stouffer Vinoy Resort, the St. Petersburg Municipal Marina with Marina Point — a huge facility right in the heart of everything — and St. Petersburg Yacht Club, all clustered north of the airport that juts out into the bay, and the Harborage at Bayboro, south of the airport peninsula at the mouth of Salt Creek.

For all of the urban development in the area, there is also good anchorage in the North Yacht Basin if you register at the Municipal Marina nearby. There is a pleasant and less urban anchorage in Coffeepot Bayou, south of Snell Isle and just north of Stouffer Vinoy's basin entrance.

In the middle of all this, at the end of Municipal Pier, stands The Pier (Must-See #2), a five-level inverted glass pyramid housing an observation deck, museum, art gallery, a spectacular aquarium, several restaurants and bars, shops and boutiques, a meeting and banquet facility that can seat 450, and outdoor attractions that include pierside miniature golf. Visiting boats will find dockage at the Municipal Docks on the south side, from where a tram serves The Pier.

Farther around the counterclock, Salt Creek leads off to the southwest just south of the Harborage at Bayboro, and is lined with marine facilities, including the Salt Creek Boat Works, Jopie and Sandy Helsen's Sailor's Wharf, and several others,

Chart Your Course

... for Sunsational St. Petersburg. Within footsteps of the St. Petersburg Municipal Marina, discover miles of lush, green waterfront parks, world-renowned museums, captivating sports events, first class hotels, restaurants, outdoor cafes and shops — and the world famous St. Petersburg Pier.

610 slips • Accommodates vessels of up to 100 feet • 500-ft. transient dock • 10-ft. depth • Electric, water, phone & cable T.V. • mail delivery • laundry & showers • Ship's store • gas & repairs • 24-hour security • boat ramps • picnic and playgrounds • charters • sailing center.

For a free brochure or further information, call toll free 1-800-782-8350.

St. Petersburg MARINA

300 Second Avenue S.E., St. Petersburg, FL 33701 (813) 893-7329

Where Boaters Come
To Get The Wind Back In Their Sails.

On the coast of the St. Petersburg peninsula, you'll find an elegant way to shelter yourself from the ordinary: The Vinoy Resort Marina. Here, shimmering Tampa Bay is the backdrop for 74 slips, each featuring complimentary power, phone hookup, cable television, water, ice, and 24-hour security. And your personal Dockmaster will see that you and your guests are equally well attended to.

On land, our resort is a beautiful vessel itself, harboring luxury amenities like oversized rooms, elegant dining options, a fully equipped fitness center, and turn-of-the-century glamour. Fourteen tennis courts, tournament croquet, and world-class golf are at your disposal. For reservations, call your travel agent or 1-800-HOTELS-1.

RENAISSANCE®
VINOY RESORT

501 5th Avenue, N.E., St. Petersburg, FL 33701. Tel: (813) 894-1000.

including Lazzara Marine, the full-service and do-it-yourself yard founded by legendary boatbuilder Vince Lazzara.

Heading out of Tampa Bay and back to the Gulf ICW, the northbound cruiser has two options:

The first is an inside route that rounds Pinellas Point and goes under the Sunshine Skyway into Maximo Channel, then under Pinellas Bayway and into Boca Ciega Bay. The mainland shore has several facilities, including the Marina Beach Resort/Days Inn/Annapolis Sailing School complex at the east approach of the Skyway, and O'Neill's Marina inside Maximo Point on the west. Marina Beach is on Maximo Channel south of the Pinellas Bayway. Maximo Marina and Maximo Marine Service are up a canal just north of the Maximo Point Bridge. Gulfport City Marina is further north in Gulfport Harbor and Great American Boatyard is further west at the north end of Boca Ciega Bay.

A more adventurous and scenic outside route runs southwest under the Skyway to Egmont Key, where the ruins of an old coastal defense fort is totally surrounded by a white sand beach. You can pick a lee anchorage and go ashore no matter what direction the wind is blowing from. (Cruising boatmen who opt not to enter Tampa Bay will find Egmont directly north of Anna Maria Island across the main Southwest Channel.)

North of Egmont Key are Fort DeSoto, Mullet Key and a whole complex of low-lying keys joined by a causeway to the mainland and separated by deep-water channels which extend north to Pass-a-Grille. There are plenty of places to anchor or gunkhole, but currents through the mouth of Tampa Bay change the bottom so constantly that you're better off piloting by eyeball than by any chart or guide.

Running northward inside Pass-a-Grille on the way to rejoin the Gulf ICW, the route passes half a dozen facilities, including Tierra Verde Resort & Marina and Tierra Verde Marine Center on Tierra Verde Island north of Cabbage Key, Merry's Pier and Stoller's on Pass-a-Grille.

From Pass-a-Grille, the inside and outside routes merge in Boca Ciega Bay and the Gulf ICW continues northward between the Pinellas Peninsula and a perfect chain of protective barrier islands that stretches 25 miles to Honeymoon Island and St. Joseph Sound. In that 25 miles, and the ten miles further to Anclote Keys and Tarpon Springs, lies the most remarkable concentration of marinas, boatyards, marine facilities and water-accessible attractions in Florida or possibly anywhere. Marinas and boatyards alone number around 50 — more than one per mile — and the restaurants, hotels and businesses along the way with some kind of dockage have probably never been counted. Everything is a stone's throw from the beautiful Gulf beaches that are the primary attraction of this part of Florida the year around. To list them all would take another directory, so we will touch the high points as we cruise northward and hope the others will forgive us.

Surprisingly, there are also peaceful anchorages and wild spots along the way where you can spend the night if you don't mind being overlooked by residents on their highrise balconies — this is urban cruising at its very best, and might be exactly the place to get the bulb changed in that masthead light.

North of the St. Petersburg Beach Causeway at the end of Long Key is Blind Pass Marina. Further north under Treasure Island Causeway the waterway widens to Tom Stuart Causeway at Bay Pines, where there is a cluster of marinas and boatyards including Johns Pass, Snug Harbor and Madiera Beach Municipal Marina with a Leverock's restaurant with dockage nearby. Northward, Boca Ciega Bay continues another four

EDITOR's NOTE: This is based on the current list maintained by the Florida Department of Environmental Protection, and while it was updated shortly before press time, changes are constant and it's a good idea to check ramps in advance. Note that some ramps are in marinas, private clubs or condominiums where public access may be limited.

MANATEE COUNTY BOAT RAMPS

ANNA MARIA
Galati's Boats — 900 South Bay Blvd.
BRADENTON
Bayshore Gardens Park & Rec. Dist. — 6919 26th St. W. on Sarasota Bay
Braden Castle Assn. — 1 Office Dr. on Manatee River
Braden River Shores Boat Ramp — E. Manatee Ave. (SR 64) on Braden River
Manatee River RV Park — 800 Key Rd. NE on Manatee River & Gulf of Mexico
Palma Sola Cswy. County Park — E. Manatee Ave. (SR 64) on Palma Sola Bay
Paradise Bay Boat Club — 10315 Cortez Rd. W. on Little Sarasota Bay *(Private)*
Trailer Estates Marina — 2303 Pennsylvania Ave. *(Private)*
Warner's Bayou Boat Ramp — NW Riverview Blvd., Warners Bayou at Manatee River
BRADENTON BEACH
Bradenton Beach Marina — 402 Church Ave. on Sarasota Bay
Coquina Beach & Bayside Park — SR 789 on Anna Maria
CORTEZ
Holiday Cove Travel Trailer Resort — SR 634 on ICW *(Private)*
ELLENTON
Bob & Mary's Place — 5717 18th St. E.
Colony Cove Mobile Home Park — 7520 US 301 N. on Manatee River
Highland Shores Boat Ramp — Off SR 43 on Manatee River
HOLMES BEACH
63rd Street Memorial Park — East terminus 63rd St.
Island Bay Marina — 5501 Marina Dr. on ICW
Kingfish Ramp — W. Manatee Ave. (SR 64) on Sarasota Bay
LONGBOAT KEY
Buccaneer Rest. & Marina — 595 Dream Isl. Rd. on Sarasota Bay
Cannon's Marina — 6040 Gulf of Mexico Dr.
Linley Street — 755 Linley St.
PALMETTO
Bradenton Yacht Club — 4307 Snead Island Rd. on Manatee River *(Private)*
Fisherman's Cove Resort — 100 Palm View Rd.
Jet Mobile Home Park — 506 5th Ave. W.
Palmetto Boat Ramp — Riverside Dr. & Green Bridge

HILLSBOROUGH COUNTY BOAT RAMPS

APOLLO BEACH
Apollo Beach Golf & Sea Club — 801 Gold & Sea Blvd. on Tampa Bay
MACDILL AFB
Recreation Services — Rec. 6 SVS/SVR, 1904 Golf Cse. Ave.
RIVERVIEW
Alafia River Boat Ramp — 4014 Alafia Blvd.
Alafia River RV Resort — 9812 Gibsonton Dr.
Hidden River Travel Resort — 12500 McMullen Loop on Alafia River
Riverview Civic Center — 11020 Park Dr.
Williams Park — 9425 S. US 41
RUSKIN
Bahia Beach Marina — 3301 Sea Grape Dr.
Cockroach Bay Boat Ramp — Cockroach Bay Rd.
Domino Boat Ramp — 22nd & 8th Ave. on Marsh Branch
E.G. Simmons Park — 19th St. NW on Tampa Bay
Hawaiian Isles Travel Resort — 2600 Cockroach Bay Rd. on Tampa Bay
Ruskin Commongood Park — 1st Ave. NW
Shell Point Fishing Lodge & Marina — 3324 W. Shell Point Rd. on Tampa Bay
Sun City Heritage Park — 3030 S. US 41
Wildcat Creek Park — Off Fairmount on Little Manatee River
TAMPA
Ballast Point Park — 5223 Interbay Blvd.
Bayshore Blvd. Marina — 312 Bayshore Blvd.
Courtney Campbell Cswy. Ramp — SR 60 (W-Bound) on Old Tampa Bay
Davis Island Boat Ramp — Severn Ave. on Hillsborough Bay
DOT Wayside Park & Boat Ramp — 22nd St. Cswy. (N-Bound) on McKay Bay
DOT Wayside Park & Boat Ramp — 22nd St. Cswy. (S-Bound) on McKay Bay
Gandy Boat Ramp — Gandy & Westshore Blvds. on Old Tampa Bay
Marjorie Park & Marina — 115 Columbia Dr. on Hillsborough Bay
Picnic Island Beach & Park — 1409 Picnic Island Blvd.

PINELLAS COUNTY BOAT RAMPS

BELLEAIR BEACH
Bay Park #2 — 7th St.
Belleair Beach Cswy. Ramp — SR 686 on West Bay Dr., Clearwater Harbor
CLEARWATER
Seminole Boat Landing — Seminole St. on Clearwater Harbor
CLEARWATER BEACH
CB Recreation Complex — Bay Esplanade on Clearwater Harbor
E. of CLEARWATER
Campbell Cswy. Wyside. Pk. — Westbound SR 60 on Old Tampa Bay
DUNEDIN
Edgewater Park & Marina — Edgewater Dr. & Main St. on Clwtr. Harbor
GULFPORT
Gulfport Marina Complex — 4630 29th Ave. S. on Boca Ciega Bay
INDIAN ROCKS BEACH
Indian Rocks Beach Boat Ramp — 15th Ave. on Clearwater Harbor
Indian Rocks Beach Boat Ramp — 3rd Ave. on Clearwater Harbor
INDIAN SHORES
Park Blvd. Boat Ramp — 18651 Gulf & Park Blvds. on ICW
MADEIRA BEACH
Madeira Beach Municipal Marina — 503 150th Ave. on Boca Ciega Bay
MULLET KEY
Fort DeSoto Park — SR 679 at mouth of Tampa Bay
NORTH REDINGTON
Tides Hotel & Bath Club — 16700 Gulf Blvd.
OLDSMAR
Greentree Marina — 1011 St. Petersburg Dr. on Tampa Bay
OZONA
George's Marina — 139 Shore Dr. on Smith Bayou
Pat's Landing — 297 Old Bayshore Dr. on St. Joseph Sound
Speckled Trout Marina — 315 Bayshore Dr. on St. Joseph Sound
SAFETY HARBOR
Philippe Park — Off SR 590 on Safety Harbor
Safety Harbor Marina & Pier — 750 Main St. on Old Tampa Bay
SOUTH PASADENA
South Pasadena Marina — 6810 Gulfport Blvd. on Boca Ciega Bay
SOUTH ST. PETERSBURG
O'Neill's Skyway Boat Basin — 6701 34th St. on Boca Ciega Bay
ST. PETERSBURG
Bay Vista Park — 500 Pinellas Point Dr. & 4th St. on Tampa Bay
Coffee Pot Bayou — E. end of 31st Ave. N. on Coffee Pot Bayou at 1st St.
Crisp Park — Poplar St. & 35 Av. N., Smacks Bayou off Tampa Bay
Demens Landing South — 2nd Ave. S., 2 blks. E. of 1st St. on Tampa Bay
DeNarvaez Park & Jungle Prada Pier — Park St. & Elbow La. N. on Boca Ciega Bay
Eckerd College — 4600 54th Ave. S. on Boca Ciega Bay
Gandy Bridge Marina — 13050 Gandy Blvd. on Tampa Bay
Grandview Park — 6th St. & 38th Ave. S. on Big Bayou off Tampa Bay
Lassing Park — Beach Dr. & 15th Ave. on Tampa Bay
Lake Maggiore — 9th St. & 38th Ave. S.
Maximo Park — 34th St. S. & Pinellas Point Dr.
St. Petersburg Campground — 5400 95th St. N. on Long Bayou
Sunlit Cove — Bay St. NE & Sunlit Cove Dr.
University of South Florida — 140 7th Ave. S. on Bayboro Harbor
War Vets Memorial Park — 9600 Bay Pines Blvd. (US Alt. 19) on ICW
Weedon Island State Rec. Area — 1500 Weedon Dr. on Tampa Bay
ST. PETERSBURG BCH.
Bay Winds Marina — 60 Corey Ct. Circle, Corey Av. & Bay St. Boca Ciega Bay
Egan Park — 9101 Blind Pass Rd.
Pass-a-Grille Wayside Public Ramp — W. Marietana Dr. & Pass-a-Grille Way Boca Ciega Bay
St. Petersburg Bch. Ramp — E. 33rd Ave.
TARPON SPRINGS
A. L. Anderson Park
Craig Park — Spring Blvd. & Bath St.
Linger Longer Resort — 355 Anclote Rd. off Alt. US 19 on Gulf of Mexico
Sunset Beach — Gulf Rd. on Gulf of Mexico
TREASURE ISLAND
123rd Ave.Ramp — 123rd Ave. & Lagoon Lane
John's Pass Marina — 12795 King Fish Dr. on John's Pass
Municipal Marina — 120 108th Ave. on Boca Ciega Bay
Treasure Island Public Boat Ramp — 100th Ave. on Boca Ciega Bay
Treasure Island Public Boat Ramp — 84th Ave. on Boca Ciega Bay

miles to Redington Shores on Island Key, and at Mile 126 you enter "The Narrows" a claustrophobic four mile stretch in which currents can be strong, idle-speed and no-wake zones are practically end to end, enforcement is vigilant and marine facilities are few, but a pleasant-enough passage if you relax and enjoy it — you can chat with boat-watchers on shore without raising your voice.

The narrow section begins to open up at Mile 130, where it passes the full-service facility of Indian Springs Marina and Hamlin's Landing Resort and Marina south of the Indian Rocks Bridge, then opens into Clearwater Harbor.

The harbor and the waterway to the north are dotted with spoil islands formed when the channel was dredged, and they provide pretty good beaching and anchoring. Some have fairly deep water around them; others don't. Pick your way with a bit of care.

Clearwater starts at Mile 135, has a very good pass to the Gulf, and is home to a number of marine facilities. Leading the list is Clearwater Municipal Marina, an excellent city-owned facility on the barrier island at the foot of the causeway. Ross Marine Service is on an island off the west end of the causeway. Clearwater Bay Marine Service, a full-service and self-service facility, and Clearwater Bay Marine Ways, separate facilities with similar names, are on the mainland side north of the causeway, next door to the Clearwater Municipal Launching Ramp.

Just east of the channel, south of the Clearwater Causeway, is another of those nice urban anchorages completely surrounded by a highrise development.

North of Clearwater on the mainland side is the pleasant — and much quieter — town of Dunedin with a fine municipal marina inside a sheltered basin near a number of waterfront restaurants. Marker 1 Marina and Jesse's Restaurant are just south of the causeway bridge.

A couple of miles further north, on the Gulf side at Mile 140.5, is Caladesi Island, a state park which can only be reached by boat or by park ferry from Honeymoon Island. There's a nice state-operated marina inside Seven Mouth Creek which welcomes transients and it's an easy walk to the island's famous shelling beach.

Honeymoon Island is a state recreation area with a nice beach. The causeway area is a favorite gathering place for windsurfers, Hobie Catters, jet skiers and other watersportspeople. The Hurricane Pass area between Honeymoon and Caladesi Islands is superb cruising and offers any number of opportunities for anchoring and beaching, although the pass itself is shallow and subject to constant shoaling. Pirate's Cove and Marker One Marinas are across the bay at the mouth of Curlew Creek and the foot of the Honeymoon Island causeway.

Just north of Honeymoon Island is one of the world's largest sandbars with the interesting name of Three Rooker Bar. The shelling and fishing are among the best in the area, and there are any number of places to beach or anchor off and wade in. The entire area is very popular with local boatpeople, but there's enough water and shoreline to accommodate a lot of boats and picnics without crowding.

Five miles north of Three Rooker Bar an old lighthouse marks Anclote Key, the northernmost of the barrier islands protecting the waterway. They say that navigating Anclote is a snap, which must be why so many boats go aground there. There is a swash channel around the south end of the island, but between that channel and the main body of water is a semicircular shoal. To get into the swash channel from the south you have to stay in the ICW until you get to Marker 7X, then do a 180 around the marker and into the deeper water.

Anclote Key is a state preserve, so leave the wild things alone. It also has the reputation of having an interior full of snakes, which tends to make leaving the wild things alone no problem at all. Snakes or no snakes, the island is a lovely wild place.

Just inshore from Anclote Key is the mouth of the Anclote River and Tarpon Springs, which has to be one of the greatest places in Florida to visit any time. The town was settled almost entirely by Greeks, led by sponge divers who came from the old country in search of the golden fleece. Their Old World values extend to the marine community, where service and repair work is pretty much impeccable. The Anclote River is lined with good marine facilities capable of building or taking care of anything from a dinghy to an 80-foot shrimp boat.

One tourist attraction in Tarpon Springs is the sponge docks; the other is Louis Pappas' restaurant, which has grown since 1925 from the town cafe into an enormous and elaborate riverside palace dedicated to Greek cuisine and seating well over a thousand. They have a small dock, and the food and the experience are worth a stop. They're also right alongside Tarpon Springs Municipal Marina, another of the Gulf Coast's excellent municipal facilities.

One of the best things about Tarpon Springs for cruising boatmen is that it's easy to find. The entrance to the Anclote River is marked by a tall powerhouse smokestack lighted by strobe lights at night. Shoals on a spoil bank on the south side of the fairway extend well offshore, so if you are coming from the south, stay off until you reach the lighted marker at the beginning of the entrance channel before turning toward the smoke-stack. You can then follow the very pretty meanderings of the Anclote River upstream and to the picturesque sponge docks right along the main street of the city.

The Sun Coast ends above Tarpon Springs, and so does the Gulf Intracoastal Waterway for the 120 miles to its continuation off Carrabelle in the Panhandle. There's no way north but offshore by your choice of three routes through what we call The Other Florida.

"THE OTHER FLORIDA"

The cruising waters of the Gulf Coast of Florida divide themselves naturally into four distinctly different sections.

We've skirted the western Everglades and Ten Thousand Islands on our way from Key West to the Sun Coast, since those difficult and largely wilderness waters are of more interest to fishermen than cruising boatmen.

We've offered rather extensive observations on the Sun Coast, which is what most people think of when thinking about the west coast of Florida, and which includes some of the finest cruising waters and most hospitable facilities in the state.

But there are two more sections and they make up another Florida: The Big Bend Coast and the Panhandle.

Let's head northward from Tarpon Springs, where the protected southern portion of the Gulf ICW ends, and look at these two very different coastlines:

CRUISING FLORIDA'S BIG BEND COAST

Short cuts are always attractive but they are rarely romantic. That was never more true than for boatmen cruising the Big Bend coast of Florida — an area unique for undeveloped shorelines, beautiful rivers and estuaries, fine cruising and fishing, charming ports nicely spaced, steadily-improving facilities for cruising boats, and unmatched southern-style hospitality for those who take the time to explore and enjoy it.

The name "Big Bend" is geographically accurate, describing as it does the Gulf Coast as it bends from northbound up the peninsula to westbound across the Panhandle, but it hardly describes the area's wild charm. The new name of "Nature Coast" does a better job, and is fast gaining in acceptance and usage.

For our purposes, we might use the name "Big Test" to describe the area, since the Gulf Intracoastal Waterway ends at Tarpon Springs and does not pick up again until Carrabelle, 120-odd miles northwest. On the charts it is a daunting gap, but in fact it is more of an invitation to a new experience in cruising. The Big Bend Coast is unique, not just to Florida, but to anywhere else

on the Intracoastal Waterway, and it offers a quality of experience not available anywhere else.

You can, of course, just make the 120-odd-mile Rhumb Line passage from Anclote to Carrabelle on St. George Sound in the Panhandle, where the Gulf ICW starts again, and save miles and minutes. But it's an offshore run that demands a seaworthy boat, good weather, good navigation, good visibility and constant vigilance, especially of the weather, which can change in the blink of an eye.

For skippers less pressed for time, less confident and/or less well equipped, yet still trying to make miles toward the Panhandle, the Big Bend buoyage system is a great compromise. You can start at Marker #10 off Gulf Harbors just north of Anclote, proceed to #12 off Cedar Key, and so on, buoy-hopping offshore at an average of ten miles a hop, in comfortable depths but within easy reach of safe harbor or at least shelter if the weather goes bad, which it can.

The buoyage system route, curving to follow the shoreline, is longer than the direct route, but makes the

CHART TWENTY-ONE: BIG BEND

ST. MARKS

Apalachee Bay

Keaton Beach Marina: 904-578-2897

APPROXIMATE STATUTE MILES

0   10   20   30
THIS CHART IS NOT TO BE USED FOR NAVIGATION

KEATON BEACH

Piney Point

Mike's Marine Ways: 904-925-5685
Full service yard for power & sail.
See ad on page 125.

Shields Marina: 904-925-6158

Sellers Marine: 904-925-6813

Riverside Marine: 904-925-6157

Steinhatchee River

Riverhaven Marina: 352-498-0709
(formerly Sportsman's Marina)

West Wind Fish Camp: 352-498-5254

Palm Grove Lodge: 352-498-3721

Ideal Fish Camp & Motel: 352-498-3877

Deadman Bay

Pepperfish Keys

Horseshoe Point

Horseshoe Marina: 352-498-5687

Dockside Marina: 352-498-5768

Suwannee River

Suwannee Shore Marina: 352-542-7482

MILLER'S MARINA
352-542-7349, CHs 16 & 70
Fina gas & diesel from 8 to 5 every
day. Can handle boats to 60', haul to
12-tons. Engine and generator repairs.
Boat rentals and campground. See
ad on page 123..

ISLAND ROOM RESTAURANT
352-543-6520 Dining in the
charming "old Florida" of Cedar Key.
See ad on page 122.

Cedar Key Municipal Dock
352-543-5560

Cedar Keys

Yankeetown Boat Co.
352-447-2529

Waccasassa Bay

Withlacoochee River

Knox Bait House & Marina
352-795-2771
Bay Point Dive Center
352-563-1040
King's Bay Marine/Pete's Pier
352-795-3302

CRYSTAL RIVER

TWIN RIVERS MARINA
352-795-3552 Crystal Bay
. Overnight dockage and
gas & diesel fuels. Haul
to 35-tons for repairs.
Outboard sales & service.
See ad on page 124.

HOMOSASSA

GULF OF MEXICO

MacRae's: 352-628-2602
Riverhaven
352-628-5545

Riverside Inn Resort
352-628-2474

Chassahowitzka River

BAYPORT

Hernando Beach Marina
352-596-2952

Skeleton Key Marina
813-868-3411

American Marina
813-842-4065

HUDSON

Leverock's Seafood House
813-849-8000
A-B-Sea Harborage Marina
813-845-1726

PORT RICHEY

GULF HARBORS

Anclote Keys

TARPON SPRINGS

trip much easier on both navigating skills and peace of mind. It starts at flashing red #10 north of Anclote Key and proceeds by even-numbered flashing red markers to #26, in Apalachee Bay off St. Marks. It only takes nine markers. The passage looks easier already.

The big trouble with both of those routes is that they only get you across the void. In doing so they bypass the series of rivers and bays and villages and towns that are the attraction of Big Bend cruising. The area is not altogether wilderness. As the chart shows, there are plenty of places for fuel, dockage, food and supplies, more or less evenly spaced so that cruising from one to the next requires only a short hop. All of them deserve attention, particularly by those who love nature and wildlife and truly getting away from it all. For anglers, the fishing, especially around the river mouths and particularly the tarpon fishing at Homosassa, is legendary.

The big trouble with the inshore waters is that they're shallow. Sometimes really shallow. Boats comfortable in four feet of water at low tide can cruise inshore with a little care for tides and charts; boats needing more water than that are often restricted to narrow and often twisting channels and careful research to use the area's three-foot tidal range to advantage.

Hopping northward along the coast:

The resort city of Gulf Harbors occupies a peninsula that juts into the Gulf just north of Anclote Keys. At the end of the two-mile canal that serves as its harbor there's dockage at A-B Sailing Charters and your last chance at the northernmost Leverock's waterfront restaurant.

The Pithlachascotee (they shorten it to "Cotee") River at Port Richey, just north of Gulf Harbors, has fairly comfortable depths, good channel marking, and several marinas and shore facilities although it lacks the cruising and exploring aspects of rivers further north. American Marina, right inside the river mouth, accommodates transients and is within easy distance of shopping and several restaurants. Two other marinas are geared more to small boats.

Hudson, just up the coast, offers a good small harbor once inside the entrance, which can be shallower than four feet at low tide. Dockage and full service is available at Skeleton Key Marina, and restaurants and shore facilities are nearby.

Hernando Beach lacks a major river but makes up for it with a well-marked if narrow approach channel best entered at high tide. Developers have not discovered the town, but it offers full services at Gulfstar and Hernando Beach Marinas with a good restaurant and shopping nearby.

The mouth of the Chassahowitzka River has great fishing and shallow gunkholing in the coastal wilderness of the Chassahowitzka National Wildlife Refuge, but it's more outboard than cruiser country. The four-mile run upriver to the town of the same name is pretty much limited to outboards and stern drives and there are no facilities for cruising boats.

The Homosassa River offers world-famous fishing for huge tarpon at its mouth and world-class scenery for those willing to wind six or seven miles upriver to Homosassa Springs. Facilities in the area are mostly geared to smaller craft, but MacRae's and the

Riverside Inn & Marina can accommodate cruising boats and there are several waterfront restaurants with dockage as well.

The route northward from Homosassa is a 15-mile end run around the shallow wilderness shoreline of the Chassahowitzka Refuge to Crystal Bay and the mouth of the Crystal River, a beautiful spring-fed stream largely protected from development at the mouth, with comfortable approach depths around six feet in the channel and a good sheltered harbor. Diving in the clear waters, often with the river's many manatees for company, is excellent. If you're nervous about big nuclear power plants, the one on the north shore of the river will make you uncomfortable but its warm outflow makes the area one of the great fishing and manatee watching spots in Florida. Twin Rivers Marina, near the river mouth at the confluence with Salt River, offers full services and overnight dockage. The cruise upstream to King's Bay is pretty, and King's Bay Marina (AKA Pete's Pier) lies at the end in the village of Crystal River, where at least basic supplies are within walking distance.

Eight miles north of Crystal Bay, the Withlacoochee River is rated by many as the most beautiful on the Big Bend, and one of the deepest, with approach depths of eight feet although in a rather narrow channel you may have to share with a lot of commercial fishing traffic. Seven miles upstream, full service is available at Yankeetown Boat Company. Further up, dockage but no services are available at the Riverside Marina, and you can dock overnight at the restored Isaak Walton Lodge and visit their justly popular restaurant. The ten-foot bridge at Inglis prevents

further exploration up the river and into Lake Rosseau, a scenic area very popular with area bass fishermen.

Twenty miles northwest of the Withlacoochee, Cedar Key is the halfway point of the Big Bend cruise, and a trip back in time to an island fishing village that has tried to turn itself into a tourist mecca and artists colony but hasn't quite succeeded yet — some visitors say that it's what Key West was like in the Good Old Days. It's a charming combination — picturesque Old Florida but with a municipal dock, hotels, restaurants, shopping and shore attractions that are often restored old homes and businesses. Cedar Key is more geared to tourists by land than by boat, however, and has no marine facilities worthy of note. The municipal dock is old, high and rough, and area boatmen most often anchor off and join the tourists ashore by dinghy.

(A particular attraction for the Smyth family on Cedar Key is The Island Room, a waterfront restaurant at Cedar Cove Beach and Yacht Club owned by Pete's nephew and namesake Peter Stefani and his partner Dustin Meuse. It's popular but a little tricky to reach — they talk guests in on Channel 16, and the adjacent small harbor offers some of the few transient slips in the area.)

A short run north of Cedar Key is the world-famous Suwannee (not Swannee) River and the town of Suwannee, a short run upstream with three marinas, several restaurants and shore facilities, and many good places to anchor in the protected harbor. Miller's Marine, a mile and a half upriver, offers service and transient facilities and will rent you a fishing boat or houseboat to explore the river upstream; Suwannee Shores Marina further upstream is more geared for

small craft but has dockage, a restaurant, and a good attitude. The entry channel can be as shallow as four feet and should be approached with care and attention to the tide, but once inside the river itself is wide, deep, wild and beautiful for more than 20 miles inland. How much further upstream you venture depends on the size of your boat and your appetite for absolutely beautiful southern river scenery.

Twelve miles north of the Suwannee, the little town of Horseshoe Beach lies on Horseshoe Point, an isolated point on a shallow shoreline but with the full-service Dockside Marina inside the sheltered harbor.

Twenty miles further north, the Steinhatchee River requires a careful approach up a long channel and under a fixed bridge variously measured at 25 and 28 feet, but the reward is six feet of depth to the hospitable fishing village of Steinhatchee, one of the least developed on the Big Bend. Marine facilities at Riverhaven

and Palm Grove Lodge are geared to smaller craft, but the basics are available and there are both docks and anchorage along the river with pretty much everything in town within walking distance.

From Deadman Bay at the mouth of the Steinhatchee, it's a long swing along a shallow and nearly deserted coast as it bends westward toward the Panhandle. The area is beautiful, wild, and nearly uninhabited; there is only the marina at Keaton Beach midway and no other facilities along the coast for 45 miles.

At the end of that run, however, a beautiful old white lighthouse easily identifies St. Marks, on the St. Marks and Wakulla Rivers, one of the most historic towns in the state. It was here that the Spanish gave up on Florida and ceded the colony to the British in 1763.

St. Marks is either the end of the Big Bend Coast or the beginning of Florida's Panhandle, or maybe both.

Let's head there...

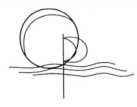

EDITOR's NOTE: This is based on the current list maintained by the Florida Department of Environmental Protection, and while it was updated shortly before press time, changes are constant and it's a good idea to check ramps in advance. Note that some ramps are in marinas, private clubs or condominiums where public access may be limited.

DIXIE COUNTY BOAT RAMPS
CHIEFLAND
Lower Suwannee National Wildlife Refuge Dixie County Area
HORSESHOE BEACH
Dockside Marina Hwy. 351 on Gulf of Mexico
Horseshoe Beach County Park SR 351
Shired Island Boat Ramp SR 357 on Shired Creek (6 mi. s. of Horseshoe Bch.)
JENA
Rocky Creek Boat Ramp Off SR 361 on Rocky Creek (5 mi. s. of Jena)
OLD TOWN
Suwannee Gables Motel US 19 on Suwannee River
STEINHATCHEE
Pat Johnson's Fish Camp Jena Rd. on SR 368 on Steinhatchee River
SUWANNEE
Jon's Holiday Marina 171-8 Canal St. on Suwannee River
Miller's Marine County Rd. 349 on Suwannee River
Moores' Suwannee Marina SR 349 on Suwannee River
Suwannee River Boat Ramp #L26 Off SR 349 on Suwannee River

PASCO COUNTY BOAT RAMPS
ANCLOTE
Anclote River Park CR 595A & Seminole St. on Anclote River (at Gulf)
HUDSON
Hudson Beach W. Clark Ave. on Gulf of Mexico
Staley's Hudson Marina 6625 Clark St. on Hudson Channel
PORT RICHEY
Nick's Park Off Bayview Rd. on Pithlachascotee River
Port Richey Marina 218 Bayview St. on Cotee River

SUWANNEE COUNTY BOAT RAMPS
LIVE OAK
Suwannee River Boat Ramp Off S-795 on Suwannee River

HERNANDO COUNTY BOAT RAMPS
BAYPORT
Bayport Park Off SR 50 on Gulf of Mexico
HERNANDO BEACH
Hernando Beach Cortez Blvd.
Hernando Beach Park 6400 Shoal Line Blvd.
WEEKI WACHEE
Jenkins Creek Park CR 597

CITRUS COUNTY BOAT RAMPS
HOMOSASSA
Camp 'n Water Campground 11465 W. Priest La.
Mason Creek Boat Ramp Mason Creek Rd.
CRYSTAL RIVER
Barge Canal Boat Ramp US 19 on Cross Fla. Barge Canal (7 mi. n. of Crystal River)
Fort Island Gulf Beach Country Rd. 44 on Crystal Bay
Lake Rousseau Campground 10811 N. Coveview Terr.
OZELLO
Ozello Park County Rd. 494 on Crystal Bay (n. of Ozello)
Ozello Park John Brown Rd. off County Rd. 494

LEVY COUNTY BOAT RAMPS
CEDAR KEY
Cedar Key City Park SR 24 at #4 Channel
N. of CEDAR KEY
Shell Mound County Park Pff CR 347, end of CR 326 on Suwannee Sound. 6 mi. n. of Cedar Key
CHIEFLAND
Lower Suwannee National Wildlife Refuge, Levy County Area

TAYLOR COUNTY
KEATON BEACH
Fishermen's Marina on Gulf of Mexico
PERRY
Aucilla Wildlife Management Area West of Perry, Taylor County Area US 98 on Aucilla River
Buckeye Cellulose Recreation Areas 17 Miles SW of Perry Hickory Mount Impoundment, Off US 98 on Gulf of Mexico
Buckeye Cellulose Recreation Areas 35 Miles S. of Perry, Dallas Creek Landing, Off SR 361 on Dallas Creek
Spring Warrior Fish Camp Spring Warrior Rd. on Spring Warrior Creek
ST. MARKS NATIONAL WILDLIFE REFUGE
US 98 on Gulf of Mexico in Jefferson, Taylor & Wakulla Counties
STEINHATCHEE
Wood's Gulf Breeze Park Hwy. 51 on Gulf of Mexico

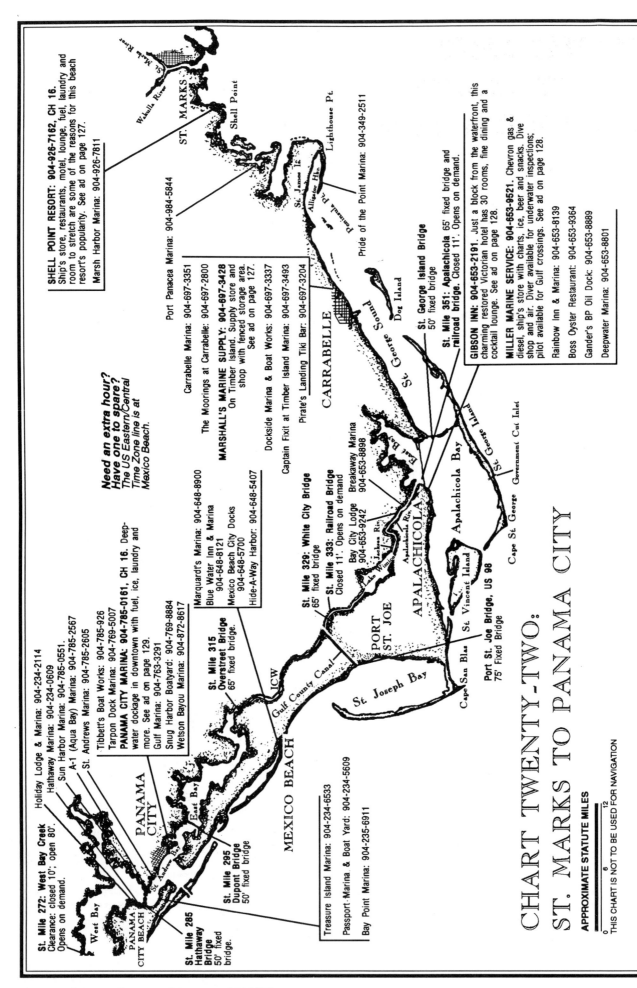

SHELL POINT RESORT: 904-926-7162, CH 16. Ship's store, restaurants, motel, lounge, fuel, laundry and room to stretch are some of the reasons for this beach resort's popularity. See ad on page 127.

Marsh Harbor Marina: 904-926-7811

Port Panacea Marina: 904-697-3351

Carrabelle Marina: 904-697-3351

The Moorings at Carrabelle: 904-697-2800

MARSHALL'S MARINE SUPPLY: 904-697-3428 On Timber Island. Supply store and shop with fenced storage area. See ad on page 127.

Dockside Marina & Boat Works: 904-697-3337

Captain Fixit at Timber Island Marina: 904-697-3493

Pirate's Landing Tiki Bar: 904-697-3204

St. George Island Bridge 50' fixed bridge

St. Mile 351: Apalachicola 65' fixed bridge and **railroad bridge.** Closed 11'. Opens on demand.

GIBSON INN: 904-653-2191. Just a block from the waterfront, this charming restored Victorian hotel has 30 rooms, fine dining and a cocktail lounge. See ad on page 128.

MILLER MARINE SERVICE: 904-653-9521. Chevron gas & diesel, ship's store with charts, ice, beer and snacks. Dive shop and air. Diver available for underwater inspections; pilot available for Gulf crossings. See ad on page 128.

Rainbow Inn & Marina: 904-653-8139

Boss Oyster Restaurant: 904-653-9364

Gander's BP Oil Dock: 904-653-8889

Deepwater Marina: 904-653-8801

Need an extra hour? Have one to spare? The US Eastern/Central Time Zone line is at Mexico Beach.

Marquardt's Marina: 904-648-8900

Blue Water Inn & Marina 904-648-8121

Mexico Beach City Docks 904-648-5700

Hide-A-Way Harbor: 904-648-5407

St. Mile 329: White City Bridge 65' fixed bridge

St. Mile 333: Railroad Bridge Closed 11'. Opens on demand

Breakaway Marina 904-653-8898

Bay City Lodge 904-653-9242

St. Mile 272: West Bay Creek Clearance: closed 10'; open 80'. Opens on demand.

Holiday Lodge & Marina: 904-234-2114

Hathaway Marina: 904-234-0609

Sun Harbor Marina: 904-785-0551.

A-1 (Aqua Bay) Marina: 904-785-2567

St. Andrews Marina: 904-785-2605

Tibbett's Boat Works: 904-785-926

Tarpon Dock Marina: 904-769-5007

PANAMA CITY MARINA: 904-785-0161, CH 16. Deepwater dockage in downtown with fuel, ice, laundry and more. See ad on page 129.

Gulf Marina: 904-763-3291

Snug Harbor Boatyard: 904-769-8884

Wetson Bayou Marina: 904-872-8617

St. Mile 315 **Overstreet Bridge** 65' fixed bridge.

St. Mile 295 **Dupont Bridge** 50' fixed bridge

St. Mile 265 **Hathaway Bridge** 50' fixed bridge.

Treasure Island Marina: 904-234-6533

Passport Marina & Boat Yard: 904-234-5609

Bay Point Marina: 904-235-6911

Port St. Joe Bridge, US 98 75' Fixed Bridge

CHART TWENTY-TWO: ST. MARKS TO PANAMA CITY

APPROXIMATE STATUTE MILES

0   6   12

THIS CHART IS NOT TO BE USED FOR NAVIGATION

Note: ICW MILEAGE ON THIS CHART IS EAST OF HARVEY LOCK.

CRUISING FLORIDA'S PANHANDLE

Florida's Panhandle is a unique geopolitical feature, gerrymandered westward from Tallahassee along the Gulf shore for 230 miles as the coastal crow flies, blocking Georgia from the Gulf and nearly landlocking Alabama in the process. It owes its existence to the former state of West Florida with its capitol in Pensacola, separate and different from the state of East Florida with its capitol in Jacksonville.

For cruising boatpeople, the Panhandle is a long series of beautiful and diverse waters, often with a choice of staying inland, cruising the bays inside the barrier islands, or running offshore along some of the most beautiful beaches in the world. Either route leads past some of the most hospitable ports in Florida, and represents a cruising grounds of unique beauty and charm far removed from the highrise canyons of the Gold Coast and the wilderness coast of the Big Bend.

Beyond any question, the outstanding physical feature of the Panhandle is its beaches. Built of finely pulverized quartz deposited by the receding glaciers at the end of the last ice age, they stretch along the entire coastline from Alligator Point on the east to beyond Alabama on the west. Sometimes these beaches are on the mainland but more often they form the seaward side of the other outstanding feature of the Panhandle — the barrier islands that create a sheltered waterway and create a veritable cornucopia of bays to explore and anchorages to enjoy. Most of the islands are state preserves or parks or have been designated as National Seashore, and so will remain out of reach of the develop-

ers who have stacked so much Florida waterfront with condominiums.

If you are westbound and have taken the scenic route up the Big Bend shore, your Panhandle begins at St. Marks. If you follow the buoyage system or take the rhumb line, it starts further west at Carrabelle — and you have missed one of the nicest ports in Florida.

About 30 miles up the empty Big Bend coast from Keaton, you can turn northward into the St. Mark's River, past the remains of its historic white lighthouse, and eight miles upriver to the historic city of St. Mark's, with full services available at Shields Marina and Riverside Marina and service at Mike's Marine Ways, with shopping and restaurants within easy walking distance. You can anchor off and visit Fort San Marcos, and a short distance up the St. Mark's River is a pretty anchorage well away from everything.

Heading westward from St. Marks, Shell Point juts into the Gulf and the marina at Shell Point Resort offers full services and welcomes transients. At Panacea, on Dickerson Bay, there is Port Panacea Marina, then across Apalachee Bay and around Lighthouse point is Alligator Point, where you'll find both shelter and welcome at Pride of the Point Marina in Alligator Harbor, although only after you circle South Shoal, negotiate Bay Mouth Bar, and approach from the west.

Carrabelle, about ten miles farther west, is at the mouth of the New River, sheltered by the first, most easterly barrier island, Dog Island, and has facilities at Carrabelle Marina and The Moorings inside its sheltered

harbor and at Dockside Marina and Captain Fixit on Timber Island. There is good anchorage on the inside of Dog Island, notably at Tyson's Harbor on the east end.

The Gulf Intracoastal Waterway officially begins just west of Carrabelle with the barrier islands of St. George, Little St. George and St. Vincent. Only St. George is connected to the mainland; the others are isolated and very much worth exploring. Little St. George, where you can visit the 1833 lighthouse, is separated from St. George by Government Cut, the primary entrance channel into Apalachicola.

Apalachicola was, at one point, a primary port for shipping cotton. The town is very old and picturesque and well supplied with marinas — a municipal marina plus Miller's Marine Service and Rainbow Marina, the latter with accommodations and dockside dining next door at Boss Oyster — all pretty much clustered at the western foot of Gorie Memorial Bridge.

Apalachicola is another trip back in time. To walk the town's streets of an evening is to go back a hundred years or more to gracious Victorian times. Outstanding among the remarkable buildings is the Gibson Inn, a fully restored hotel and restaurant. The whole area specializes in seafood, especially the wonderful local oysters, and if you're lucky enough to be there in the first week of November for their Seafood Fest or the first week of May for their Spring Fiesta, you can join the tens of thousands of other seafood lovers who come from all over the southeast for their pigouts.

From Apalachicola, which is at Mile 350, or 350 miles EHL — east of Harvey Lock at New Orleans — the Gulf ICW leaves the coast and travels up the Apalachicola River, a beautiful wild stream with many anchorage opportunities along its banks. Fill up and stock up before leaving; there are no facilities and no fuel docks on the 55 miles of waterway to Panama City.

About three miles upstream, the Apalachicola turns northward while the waterway turns west into the Jackson River. Adventurous boatpeople can follow the Apalachicola upstream for several miles through heavily wooded swampland to the St. Marks, East and Brothers Rivers with good depths, and the really adventurous can follow it all the way to Jim Woodruff Dam at Chattahoochee on the Georgia border. The river is famous for its big saltwater striped bass.

Back on the westbound waterway, you cross Lake Wimico, a beautiful if a bit shallow five-mile-long body much favored by local fishermen. There's good sheltered anchorage in an oxbow loop of an old river bed at the west end of the lake.

The head of Lake Wimico is at mile 335 and from there to mile 312, you'll be in either landcut or canalized creeks and rivers, whose canalization has created a number of sheltered oxbows that provide good anchorage. The only stopping place on this route is at White City, where there is a dock but no facilities for cruising boats. White City is best known as the spot where you change from Eastern to Central Time or vice versa. Tall ships will celebrate the new 65' bridge on Highway 71.

A mile or so further west, at mile 328, you can turn off to the southwest on the Gulf County Canal. This will take you to St. Josephs Bay and Port St. Joe, a side trip you ought to take if you like beaches and scallops and don't need marine facilities, which are lacking. Happily, they exist just five miles to the west at Mexico Beach, where there is a municipal marina, Mexico Beach

Marina (under new ownership), Blue Water Inn and Marina and Marquardt Marina, the latter unfortunately protected by a 12-foot fixed bridge.

If the weather permits an outside passage toward Panama City, that course will lead you to St. Andrew Sound, inside Crooked Island, one of the most beautiful anchorages on the Gulf coast when Tyndall Air Force Base activities let it be used.

From Cape San Blas west to Pensacola and the Alabama border you will find signs of the damage caused by Hurricanes Erin and Opal in 1995 (See Pages 6-7). The storms devastated the beaches and barrier islands of the Panhandle, but caused surprisingly little damage on the mainland side in some areas. By the time you read this and reach there, most of the area's marine facilities will be restored to at least near-normal, but be aware that some new shallows and bars have been created that may not have been remarked.

Back in the Gulf ICW, at Mile 312, the waterway runs down Wetappo Creek and enters East Bay, which leads directly to Panama City and the first marine facilities of consequence west of Apalachicola.

Approaching the city from the east, the waterway passes Pitt Bayou, Watson Bayou, and Massalina Bayou, all offering good shelter and adequate marine facilities, then reaches St. Andrews Bay and Panama City, which features some of the best marine facilities, shopping and shore attractions in the Panhandle — and maintains a great attitude toward visiting boatmen as well.

Panama City is sheltered inside the barrier island of Shell Island, opposite the main pass from the Gulf into St. Andrews Bay, one of the best deep-water channels on the Gulf Coast. Facilities on the Panama City side of the bay include an excellent City Marina at the mouth of Massalina Bayou and St. Andrews and Sun Harbor Marinas right downtown.

Immediately inside and west of St. Andrews Inlet is Grand Lagoon, where you'll find several marinas, including Bay Point at the Marriott Resort on the north shore and Passport Marina and the Lighthouse Restaurant and Treasure Island Marinas further west.

Hurricane damage in the protected bays and on the mainland was minimal from all reports although the beachfront took a beating from Opal's tidal surge.

If you choose to anchor out, you will find so many places on St. Andrews Bay that being crowded is virtually impossible. And finding a place where deep, blue, gin-clear water laps along a bone-white sand beach is easy. In fact, you'll find deep water alongside beaches almost everywhere. Of particular interest is the anchorage at Land's End on the eastern end of Shell Island.

Cruising west from Panama City, the Intracoastal passes under Hathaway Bridge and crosses North Bay and West Bay to (roughly) Mile 270. The Hathaway Marina and a restaurant and dive shop are at the bridge.

At that point the Waterway enters West Bay Creek, then leads through a narrow 20-mile landcut to the eastern end of Choctawhatchee Bay. At this point, you're 20-plus miles short of Destin, but you can turn off the waterway at Mile 240 and spend a little time in Baytowne Marina at Sandestin Resort, inside Hogtown Bayou on the south side of the bay, or in the bayous nearby. Joe's Bayou, just off the waterway at the northern end of Destin, is a very popular sheltered anchorage with good depths. Across the bay on the north shore, Rocky Bayou and Boggy Bayou offer good

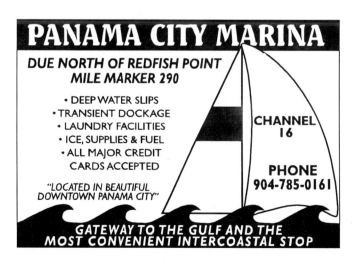

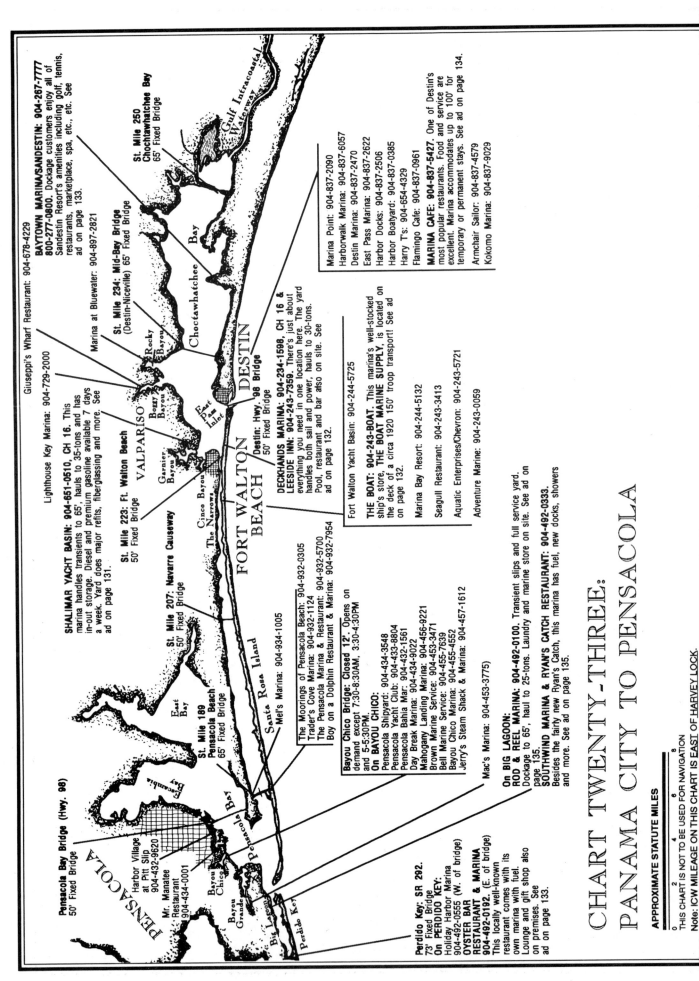

CHART TWENTY-THREE: PANAMA CITY TO PENSACOLA

APPROXIMATE STATUTE MILES

0 2 4 6 8

THIS CHART IS NOT TO BE USED FOR NAVIGATION

Note: ICW MILEAGE ON THIS CHART IS EAST OF HARVEY LOCK.

BAYTOWN MARINA/SANDESTIN: 904-267-7777, 800-277-0800. Dockage customers enjoy all of Sandestin Resort's amenities including golf, tennis, restaurants, marketplace, spa, etc., etc. See ad on page 133.

Giuseppi's Wharf Restaurant: 904-678-4229

Lighthouse Key Marina: 904-729-2000

Marina at Bluewater: 904-897-2821

St. Mile 250 Choctawhatchee Bay 65' Fixed Bridge

St. Mile 234: Mid-Bay Bridge (Destin-Niceville), 65' Fixed Bridge

SHALIMAR YACHT BASIN: 904-651-0510, CH 16. This marina handles transients to 65', hauls to 35-tons and has in-out storage. Diesel and premium gasoline available 7 days a week. Yard does major refits, fiberglassing and more. See ad on page 131.

St. Mile 223: Ft. Walton Beach 50' Fixed Bridge

St. Mile 207: Navarre Causeway 50' Fixed Bridge

St. Mile 189 Pensacola Beach 65' Fixed Bridge

Mel's Marina: 904-934-1005

DECKHANDS MARINA: 904-234-1598, CH 16 & LEESIDE INN: 904-243-7359. There's just about everything you need in one location here. The yard handles both sail and power, hauls to 30-tons. Pool, restaurant and bar also on site. See ad on page 132.

Fort Walton Yacht Basin: 904-244-5725

THE BOAT: 904-243-BOAT. This marina's well-stocked ship's store, **THE BOAT MARINE SUPPLY,** is located on the deck of a circa 1920 150' troop transport! See ad on page 132.

Marina Bay Resort: 904-244-5132

Seagull Restaurant: 904-243-3413

Aquatic Enterprises/Chevron: 904-243-5721

Adventure Marine: 904-243-0059

Marina Point: 904-837-2090
Harborwalk Marina: 904-837-6057
Destin Marina: 904-837-2470
East Pass Marina: 904-837-2622
Harbor Docks: 904-837-2506
Harbor Boatyard: 904-837-0385
Harry T's: 904-654-4329
Flamingo Cafe: 904-837-0961

MARINA CAFE: 904-837-5427. One of Destin's most popular restaurants. Food and service are excellent. Marina accommodates up to 100' for temporary or permanent stays. See ad on page 134.

Armchair Sailor: 904-837-4579
Kokomo Marina: 904-837-9029

The Moorings of Pensacola Beach: 904-932-0305
Trader's Cove Marina: 904-932-1124
The Pensacola Marina & Restaurant: 904-932-5700
Boy on a Dolphin Restaurant & Marina: 904-932-7954

Bayou Chico Bridge: Closed 12'. Opens on demand except 7:30-8:30AM, 3:30-4:30PM and 4-5:30PM.

On BAYOU CHICO:
Pensacola Shipyard: 904-434-3548
Pensacola Yacht Club: 904-433-8804
Pensacola Bahia Mar: 904-432-1561
Day Break Marina: 904-434-9022
Mahogany Landing Marina: 904-456-9221
Brown Marine Service: 904-453-3471
Bell Marine Service: 904-455-7639
Bayou Chico Marina: 904-455-4552
Jerry's Steam Shack & Marina: 904-457-1612

Mac's Marina: 904-453-3775)

On BIG LAGOON:
ROD & REEL MARINA: 904-492-0100. Transient slips and full service yard. Dockage to 65', haul to 25-tons. Laundry and marine store on site. See ad on page 135.

SOUTHWIND MARINA & RYAN'S CATCH RESTAURANT: 904-492-0333. Besides the fairly new Ryan's Catch, this marina has fuel, new docks, showers and more. See ad on page 135.

Pensacola Bay Bridge (Hwy. 98) 50' Fixed Bridge

Harbor Village at Pitt Slip 904-432-9620

Mr. Manatee Restaurant 904-434-0001

Perdido Key: SR 292. 73' Fixed Bridge.
On PERDIDO KEY:
Holiday Harbor Marina 904-492-0555 (W. of bridge)

OYSTER BAR RESTAURANT & MARINA 904-492-0192. (E. of bridge) This locally well-known restaurant comes with its own marina with fuel. Lounge and gift shop also on premises. See ad on page 133.

Destin: Hwy. 98 Bridge 50' Fixed Bridge

Rocky Bayou
Boggy Bayou
Garnier Bayou
Cinco Bayou
The Narrows
East Pass Inlet

DESTIN
VALPARISO
FORT WALTON BEACH
Choctawhatchee Bay
Santa Rosa Island
East Bay
Pensacola Bay
Escambia Bay
Bayou Chico
Bayou Grande
Big Lagoon
Perdido Key
PENSACOLA
Gulf Intracoastal Waterway

SHALIMAR
YACHT BASIN

QUALITY
- SERVICE
- STORAGE
- SECURITY
- SALES

REPAIRS: Major or Minor on Engines; Generators; A/C; Props; Shafts; Steering; Fiberglass

YARD WORK: Haul; Clean; Paint; Sandblast; Gelstrip & Blister Removal; Canvas Shop; Welding

DOCKAGE: On Our Safe & Secure Cove; Dock Master; Fuel (Diesel & Premium, Fast Pumps, Street Prices); Pumpout Service Station FREE With Fill-up

SLIPS: Dry Rack to 30 ft.; Wet Covered to 40 ft.; Open Wet to 60 ft.; Longest Vessel, 100 ft.; Rental by Day or Month; Electrical Service 110 Volt Twin 30-Amp Connectors; Courtesy Dock Carts; Telephone & TV Hookups Available

AMENITIES: Marine Store & Supplies; Custom Rod & Reel Shop; Ice; Showers; Laundromat; Convenience, Grocery, Deli Stores and Many Dining Choices Nearby; All Shopping Within 5 Minutes; Local Rental Cars; VHF Channel 16 Monitored; Approach Depth 18 ft.; Dockside Depth 8 ft.; 5 Transient Berths

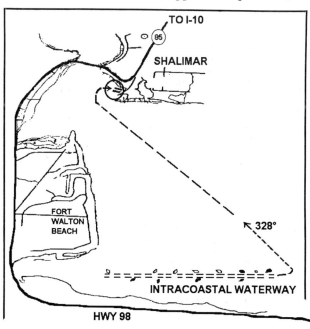

SHALIMAR YACHT BASIN
P.O. Box 189 • Shalimar, FL 32579
Call: (904) 651-0510

A pleasant, professional and friendly atmosphere. Expect to be treated with courtesy, kindness, respect and understanding. Come see us—you'll **enjoy** it!

Just 2 miles by water from *Sugar White* beaches & *Emerald Water*. Nearby, the famous Destin **sportfishing fleet** for an *unforgettable* fishing experience.

LOCATION: 100 Old Ferry Road, Shalimar, Florida

From Hwy 98: North on Hwy 85 to Shalimar bridge; take first right; 1 block on right.

From Hwy I-10: Take Hwy 85 South, Exit 12 through Niceville/Valparaiso to Shalimar; third stoplight turn left; 1/2 mile on right.

anchorages and facilities, including Bluewater Bay marina on Rocky and Lighthouse Marina and Giuseppi's Wharf restaurant on Boggy.

Destin lies just north and east of East Pass Inlet, on the peninsula that shelters Choctawhatchee Bay on the south, and is a resort and sportfishing city offering many marinas, waterfront hotels and restaurants, with shore facilities within easy distance. The area from Destin west to Navarre Beach took the worst damage from Hurricane Opal, but our sources in the area report that all but a few facilities will be offering full services by early 1996.

Note that the fixed bridges at Destin, Fort Walton Beach and Navarre are all listed at 50' clearance, but sources tell us that all three are closer to 48' at high tide with the Destin bridge the worst offender. If you need more than 48', approach all three with care.

The main dockage area in Destin lies just south and east of the fixed bridge over East Pass. After passing through the bridge, turn sharply east to enter Destin Harbor between the mainland and the protective sandbar to the south. The channel is narrow, but the harbor is open and protected. Facilities line the northern shore and include Destin Marine north of the bridge and Marina Point at the harbor entrance, Kokomo Marina and East Pass Marine, Harbor Boatyard and the popular Marina Cafe. Destin Harbor facilities were particularly hard hit by Opal, and a call ahead is a good idea.

Outside East Pass lie the famous beaches of Santa Rosa Island. Although the dunes were reduced in many places by Opal's tidal surge, they are still among the most beautiful on the Gulf. Five miles west, at the western end of Choctawhatchee Bay, lies Fort Walton Beach, which offers a number of marinas with full services, plenty of motels, restaurants, and shops. Available marine facilities include Shalimar Yacht Basin at the entrance to Garnier Bayou, about three miles north of the waterway at Mile 225 and a worthwhile short side trip. Garnier Bayou itself, and Cinco Bayou to the southwest, offer some very pleasant protected anchorages. Back on the waterway, just east of Fort Walton Beach, are Deckhands Marina and Leeside Inn with a motel and restaurant onsite.

Passing under the Fort Walton Beach bridges the waterway leaves the open waters of Choctawhatchee Bay and enters narrow Santa Rosa Sound. Its eastern stretch, called The Narrows, is a continuation of Fort Walton Beach. The Narrows is well named and particularly constricted, and local boatmen recommend listening to Channel 16 for barge traffic when transiting the area. The good news is that the eastern end of that stretch is lined with marine and shore attractions, including Marina Bay and The Boat Marina (named for

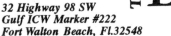

its office and ship's store, which is built into the concrete hull of what was once a 150-foot troop carrier) and Fort Walton Yacht Basin on the north shore. Hurricane damage was heavy in the Narrows area, but services are being restored; call ahead for advice on conditions.

Santa Rosa Sound leads westward from Fort Walton Beach almost as narrow as The Narrows, and offers a number of nice coves and good anchorages along the way with the welcome opportunity to pick your shore according to wind direction. The anchorages, however, tend to be shallow until you get south of Hurlburt Field. Sam's Oyster Bar, at Mile 206 in Navarre, was at ground zero when Hurricane Opal came ashore, and lost their docks and half of their building, but they're still open while rebuilding. If they have a dock by the time you get there, it's worth a meal stop.

Pensacola, at mile 185, is the end of the line for our Gulf Coast cruise. A cosmopolitan city and deep-water port, Pensacola offers many marinas, repair facilities, motels and restaurants and is easily worth a layover for there is much to do and see.

That follows, since Pensacola is the first place the Spanish tried to found a North American colony. They were followed in order by the French, British, Spanish again, the Confederacy and United States, and the legacy of each is a lesson in American history and architecture. Of note in this regard are Fort Pickens, Fort McRae, Fort Barrancas, the Pensacola Lighthouse and the restored Seville Square Historical District. Another notable attraction is the Naval Air Museum with its collection of aircraft from the old NC-4 to the latest jet fighters.

After 62 years without a hurricane, the Pensacola area suffered damage from both Erin and Opal, but has rebounded quickly and most of its facilities are reported to be in pre-hurricane condition.

Approaching the city from the east, you encounter the first interesting harbor and facilities at the south end of the 65' Pensacola Beach Bridge in Little Sabine Bay, a protected harbor with a full-service marina, The Moorings, and the notable Trader Cove restaurant. Both were damaged by a fire before the hurricane, but may be back in service by the time you read this.

Just east of there, at Fishing Bend on Pensacola Beach, is a most unusual facility— Quietwater Mall, which has docks. The novelty of tying up at a shopping mall is almost enough to be worth feeling your way in.

West of the bridge, turning northward around the point at Gulf Breeze and into Pensacola Bay, you find facilities in every direction. Right downtown, at the foot of the Historic District, Harbour Village at Pitt Slip offers full service and welcomes transients, who can walk from there into downtown Pensacola and its many restaurants, historic and urban attractions.

A mile or so west is Bayou Chico, a sheltered downtown harbor practically lined with marine facilities and so popular that transients are urged to call ahead and reserve dock space. Notable among them are Mahogany Landing, Daybreak and Bayou Chico Marinas. Admiral Zack's Marine provides service but is not a marina.

Another hop west and south leads to Grande Bayou, which separates the city from Pensacola Naval Air Station to the south. Larger and far less developed than Bayou Chico, Grande Bayou is guarded by a 14-foot fixed bridge at the entrance and served by only one small marina, Mac's on the north shore. But for boats that can get under 14 feet and need less than 5 feet of water, the area offers good anchorage possibilities.

Turning back to the north and east of the city and under the Pensacola Bay Bridge, you can turn north into Escambia Bay and up the Escambia River, where there are no facilities but fine cruising and many opportunities to anchor in relative seclusion. Further east is East Bay and the Blackwater River, where again you will find beautiful cruising water and good anchorages for five or six miles to the low bridge at Milton, but no marine facilities and few docks for cruising-sized boats.

Back in the waterway south and west of Pensacola, you pass through the turning basin and inlet area, where you share water with the Navy, then pick up the ICW again south of the point occupied by the Naval Air Station. Following the Waterway west, you pass Fort Pickens to the south, cross the inlet (with an eye out for its swells), then follow a short landcut into Big Lagoon, where many of the local boatmen spend their weekends and holidays on the water and the beach.

Big Lagoon is an attractive body of completely sheltered water — Perdido Key on the south is undeveloped, part of the Gulf Islands National Seashore, and narrow enough to dinghy ashore and walk across to the Gulf beaches. But less than a mile across on the north shore are the facilities and comforts of two good marinas, Rod & Reel Marina and Southwind Marina with Ryan's Catch Restaurant. Rod & Reel is particularly noted as friendly and helpful to cruising boatpeople and to this Directory as well.

There are good anchorages east of Redfish Point and inside Spanish Point, and another at the west end across from the Big Lagoon State Recreation Area on the north shore. Hurricane tidal surges washed completely over Perdido Key in many places and destroyed what park facilities were there, but the beaches are still beautiful and the marinas on Big Lagoon are fully operational again. West of Big Lagoon, damage was minimal except for the loss of many dunes.

At the west end of the lagoon, near the high Gulf Beach/Perdido Key bridge, is the Oyster Bar Marina and Restaurant, a popular seafood place with overnight dockage for transients and a great view of the waterway. The Oyster Bar and its near-neighbor, Holiday Harbor Marina, share the distinction of being the westernmost facilities on the Waterway in Florida, and therefore the last in this Directory.

West of there the waterway winds through yet another narrows, past the Old River and some inviting anchorage possibilities, then into Perdido Bay. You can continue northward to the upper bay and the Perdido River. The Florida-Alabama border runs down the center of the river — and marks the end of our territory.

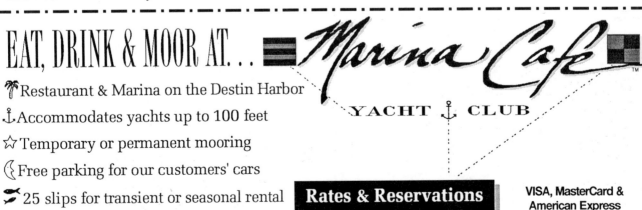

Good News for Westbound Boatmen:

You don't drop off the edge of the world when you cross the Florida/Alabama line in Perdido Bay, although Les Westerman at the Rod & Reel Marina on Big Lagoon might suggest it. In addition to being spokesman for the region's Marine Industry Association, Les is a vehement objector to the use of a once-popular nickname for the Panhandle, which we hope he notices is no longer used in this Directory even in jest.

Actually, you just sail off the edge of Florida and onto the edge of Alabama, and good cruising water continues to stretch out westward ahead of you.

But this is the *Florida Cruising Directory*, and that, as they say, is all, folks! We've circumnavigated the entire state, from the Georgia line above Fernandina on the east to the Alabama line in Perdido Bay. We've traveled deep into the interior on the beautiful Saint Johns River and we've crossed the state on the Okeechobee Waterway.

We've cruised some 1300 miles, farther than the distance from Fernandina to New York, but we've been in Florida all the way. We've also taken the ultimate side trip – a look out to the wonderful and almost limitless cruising grounds of the Bahamas.

Florida is indeed an amazing state, and the possibilities it offers for boating and cruising are almost literally endless.

Go now, cruise – and enjoy!   **The Editors**

EDITOR's NOTE: This is based on the current list maintained by the Florida Department of Environmental Protection, and while it was updated shortly before press time, changes are constant and it's a good idea to check ramps in advance. Note that some ramps are in marinas, private clubs or condominiums where public access may be limited.

BAY COUNTY BOAT RAMPS

CALLAWAY

Callaway Community Center	600 Beulah Ave.& Omoco St. on Callaway Bayou

LYNN HAVEN

Leslie Porter Wayside Park	SR 77 & 3rd St. on North Bay

MEXICO BEACH

Hideaway Harbor Yacht Basin	37th St. on Gulf
Marquardt's Marina	40th St.
Municipal Boat Ramp	Circle Dr. off US 98 on Gulf
Public Boat Ramp	US 98 & 37th St. on Gulf

PANAMA CITY

Bob George Park	East Ave. & First Plaza
Carl Gray/Richard Simpson Pk.	Collegiate Dr.
Etheridge Marina	112-A 3rd Ct. on Masalina Bayou
Gulf Marina	1500 E. Bus. 98. on St. Andrews Bay
Naval Coastal Systems Ctr.	US 98 & Hathaway Bridge on St. Andrews Bay Recreation Office T2025
Panama City Marina	Gov't. & Harrison Aves. on St. Andrews Bay
Panama City Marina Service	1 Harrison Ave. on St. Andrews Bay
St. Andrews Marina	Bayview & 10th St. on St. Andrews Bay
St. Andrews State Rec. Area	4607 State Park La., Shell Island on Gulf
Sun Harbor Lodge & Marina	5505 W. Hwy. 98 on St. Andrews Bay
Tibbetts Boat Works	305 E. Beach Dr. on Bayou
Tyndall AFB	US 98 on East Bay & St. Andrews Bay on Alligator & Felix Lakes

PANAMA CITY BEACH

Bay Point Resort	100 Dellwood Bch. Rd. on Gulf
CJ's Bayside Marina	6325 Big Daddy Dr. on Gulf
Holiday Lodge Marina	6400 US 98 West on St. Andrews Bay
Mystic Street Boat Ramp	Mystic St., Grand Lagoon
Oriole Street Boat Dock	Oriole St., Grand Lagoon
Passport Marina	5325 N. Lagoon Dr.
Port Lagoon Yacht Basin	5201 N. Lagoon Dr.
Safari Street Boat Ramp	Safari St.on Grand Lagoon
Treasure Island Marina	3605 S. Thomas Dr.
Venture Out	4345 Thomas Dr.

PARKER

Donaldson Point Boat Ramp	Dover Rd.
Earl Gilbert Park	Oakshore Dr.

SOUTHPORT

Fanning Bayou Boat Ramp	SR 77A on Fanning Bayou
McKenzie Road Boat Ramp	McKenzie Rd. on North Bay

WAKULLA COUNTY RAMPS

CRAWFORDVILLE

Fiddlers Point Boat Ramp	(Small)

SHELL POINT

Marsh Harbor Marina	on Gulf of Mexico (Not paved)
Shell Point Marina	on Shell Point Beach

PANACEA

Bayside Marina	on Ochlockonee River
Levy Bay Boat Ramp	SR 372B at Levy Bay
Mashes Sands Park	CR 372 on Ochlockonee Bay & Gulf of Mexico, s. of Panacea
Wakulla County Ramp	Dickerson Bay at Port Panacea Marina, Rock Landing Rd., Hwy 98
Wakulla County Ramp	SR 372 at Ochlockonee River at new bridge

ST. MARKS

Shields Marina	Riverside Dr. on St. Marks River
St. Marks Ntnl. Wildlife Refuge	Lighthouse Point Recreation Site, SR 59 on Gulf of Mexico
St. Marks Park	Canal & 1st Sts. at San Marcos de Apalachee on St. Marks River

GULF COUNTY

INDIAN PASS

Indian Pass Boat Ramp	End of SR 308 on Indian Lagoon

PORT ST. JOE

City Park	5th & Baltzell Sts. on St. Joseph Bay
Frank Pate Jr. Park	Baltzell Ave.
St. Joseph Peninsula State Park¹	T.H. Stone Memorial SR 30E on Gulf of Mexico

FRANKLIN COUNTY

APALACHICOLA

Battery Park & Marina	Ave. B., Market St. & Bay Ave. on Apalachicola Bay
Bay City Marina & Lodge	Bay City Rd. (SR 384) on Apalachicola River
Breakaway Lodge	200 Waddell Rd.
Rainbow Inn & Marina	123 Water St.

CARRABELLE

Carrabelle Marina	Hyw. 98
City Boat Ramp	4th St. W. & US 98
The Moorings at Carrabelle	US 98 (Private)

EASTPOINT

Ferry Park Ramp	SR 65 on East Bay
Sportsman's Lodge & Marina	Off US 98 on East Bay

PANACEA/ALLIGATOR POINT

Alligator Point Campground	SR. 370, Alligator Point
Pride of the Point Marina	Hwy. 370, Alligator Point

ST. GEORGE ISLAND

County Boat Ramp	Corner G1A & SR 300
Dr. Julian G. Bruce	St, George Island State Park

ST. THERESA

St. Theresa Wayside Park & Boat Ramp	Off US 98

WALTON COUNTY

CHOCTAWHATCHEE BEACH

Choctawhatchee Beach Wayside Park	SR 331 on Choctawhatchee Bay, n. & s. of bridge

FREEPORT

Fort Rucker Recreation Area	Off Hwy. 20 on Choctawhatchee Bay
Gene's Marina	on Choctawhatchee Bay
Wheeler Point Wayside Park	SR 83 on Choctawhatchee Bay s. of Freeport

OKALOOSA COUNTY LINE

Choctaw Beach Park	South side of SR 20, 1.5 mi. e. Okaloosa County Line

SANTA ROSA BEACH

Charles E. Cessna Park	SR 393 off US 98 at Hogtown Bayou on Choctawhatchee Bay
Grayton Bch. State Rec. Area	CR 30A on Western Lake/Gulf of Mexico (Sometimes open to Gulf but often not)

ESCAMBIA COUNTY RAMPS

GULF BEACH HEIGHTS

	Galvez Rd. & Cruzat

GULF BREEZE

Seaside 76	on Little Sabine Bay

PENSACOLA

Baird Fish Camp	4080 Indigo Dr.
Bayou Texar Boat Ramp	Stanley & Cervantes Sts. on Bayou Texar
Bayview Park	20th Ave. & Mallory St. on Pensacola Bay
Big Lagoon State Rec. Area	12301 Gulf Beach Hwy. SR 293 on Big Lagoon/ICW
Blue Angel Navy Rec. Park.	2100 Bronson Field Rd.
Grand Lagoon Yacht Club	10653 Gulf Beach Hwy., on Big Lagoon
Navy Point	from Sunset Ave to Cousineau Rd. on Bayou Grande
Pensacola Naval Air Station	on Pensacola Bay at Sherman Cove & Sherman Pond
Pensacola Yacht Club	1897 W. Cypress St.
Rod & Reel Marina	10045 Sinton Dr. on Big Lagoon ICW
Sanders Beach Center	Sonia & I Sts. on Pensacola Bay (Not recommended)
Seafarer Dock	16401 Perdido Key Dr. on Gulf of Mexico
Wayside Park	US 98 at Pensacola Bay Bridge
Windward Dock	16777 Perdido Key Dr. on Old River

PENSACOLA BEACH

Quietwater Beach Rec. Area	SR 399 & Pensacola Bch. Blvd. on Gulf of Mexico
Sabine Yacht & Racquet Club	300 Ft. Pickens Rd. on Gulf of Mexico
Unnamed Park	Ft. Pickens Rd. on Santa Rosa Sound, outside fort gate (Good for catamarans)

SANTA ROSA COUNTY

BAGDAD

Bagdad Boat Ramp	Off SR 191-C on Blackwater Ba
Garcon Point Boat Ramp	12 mi. S. of Bagdad, SR 191 on Escambia Bay
Nichols Seaside Marina	Hwy. 191 S. on Blackwater Ba

GULF BREEZE

Seaside 76	on Little Sabine Bay
Shoreline Park	Shoreline Dr., SR 399, EnglishNavyCreek
Gulf Breeze Wayside Park	US 98 on Pensacola Bay SW corner of 3-Mile Bridge

HOLLEY

Holley Boat Ramp #1	Off SR 87 on East Bay
Holley Boat Ramp #2	Off SR 87 on East Bay

MARY ESTHER

Navarre Family Campground	US 98 1.5 mi. E. of Navarre Bri Santa Rosa Sound

MILTON

Angel's Bay RV Park	W. Hwy. 90
Bill Perry Marina	110 Quinn St. on Quinn Bayou
Covey's Fish Camp	SR 89 on Yellow River

NAVARRE

Navarre Park	US 98 & SR 87 on Santa Rosa

NAVARRE BEACH

Navarre Beach Campground	Rt. 98 on Santa Rosa Sound

PACE

Avalon Boat Ramp #3	4 Miles SE of Pace off SR 281
Mulatto Bay	
Bayview Heights Park	SR 197 & US 90 on Escambia
Floridatown Park	Floridatown Rd. & Park St. on Escambia Bay
Indian Bayou Boat Ramp	7 Miles SE of Pace, Garcon Point Rd. on Indian Bayou
Jim's Fish Camp	Hwy. 90 on Escambia River

SANTA ROSA ISLAND

Island View KOA Campground	Hwy. 399 on Santa Rosa Soun

WOODLAWN BEACH

Woodlawn Beach	Woodlawn Bch. Rd. Santa Rosa Sound

OKALOOSA COUNTY

CINCO BAYOU

Cinco Bayou Sea Way	Sea Way at 5-Mile Bayou

DESTIN

Destin Marina	104 Calhoun Ave., Choctawhatc Bay
East Pass Marina	US 98 on Gulf of Mexico
Joe's Bayou	Beach Dr. (Parking limited)
Sandpiper Cove Club	On Old Pass Lagoon (Private)

EGLIN AIR FORCE BASE

Eglin AFB	Between I-10 & SR 20, Okaloos County Area 3201 ABG/SSR o Choctawhatchee Bay

FT. WALTON BEACH

Aquatic Enterprises	Hwy. 98 at Brooks Bridge
Colony Estates Park	Cinco Bayou off Pocahontas Ave
Ft. Walton Yacht Club	180 Ferry Rd. NE on Choctawha Bay
Garniers Beach Park	Beachview Dr. & Marshall on Choctawhatchee Bay
Gulf Islands Ntl. Seashore	Okaloosa County Area, US 98 o Santa Rosa Island on Gulf of M (atDeckhands Marina)
Howard Johnson Motel	314 Miracle Strip Pkwy. SW on S Rosa Sound
Liza M. Jackson Park	US 98 & Driftwood Ave. on Sant Rosa Sound
Mohl's Marina	14 Mariner Dr. on Garnier's Bay
Ross Marler Park	Off US 98 E. of Bridge over Sou

HURLBURT FIELD NAB

Naval Air Base	834 CSG/SSRO Outdoor Recre

MARY ESTHER

Mary Esther Dock	Misty Water La. on Santa Rosa

NICEVILLE

Bluewater Bay Marina	200 Yacht Club Dr. on Choctawh Bay
Fred Gannon Rocky Bayou State Rec. Area	SR 20 on Choctawhatchee Bay
Lions Park	Bayshore Dr. & 27th St. on Bog Bayou
Niceville City Boat Ramp	S. Magnolia Ave. on Tom's Bayo

SHALIMAR

Poquito Bayou Cnty. Park	End of Bay St. on Little Bayou

VALPARAISO

Florida Park	230 Grandview Ave.
Glenn Park	184 John Sims Pkwy.
Lincoln Park	Bayshore Dr.

FLORIDA CRUISING DIRECTORY
CLASSIFIED LISTINGS
REGIONS

Bahamas

First Coast & St. Johns River
 (Fernandina to New Smyrna
 & St. Johns River)

Indian River Lagoon
 (Titusville to Jensen Beach)

Stuart to Boca Raton

Broward County

Dade County

Keys

Marco Island to Placida
 & the Okeechobee Waterway

Englewood to Skyway

Skyway to Tarpon Springs

Northwest
 (Homosassa to Pensacola)

CATEGORIES

Air Conditioning/
 Refrigeration
Batteries/Electrical
 Equipment & Services
Boat Builders
Canvas Products
Carpentry
Charters & Rentals
Charts & Books
Cleaning & Maintenance
Clubs & Associations
CNG Fuels/Propane
Compass Adjusting
Customizers,
 Custom Fabrications
Dealers, Powerboats
Dealers, Sailboats
Designers, Interior
Designers, Yacht
 & Naval Architects

Dive Boats/Dive Shops/Divers
Documentation
Education
Electronics
Engines, Diesel
Engines, Gasoline
Engines, Outboard
Fiberglass & Plastics
Finance Companies, Banks
Fishing Tackle/Bait/
 Taxidermists/Tournaments
Generators
Heads & MSDs
Hydraulic Equipment
Inflatables/Life Rafts/Safety
 & Survival Equipment
Insurance
Lumber & Plywood

Machine Shop Services
Marine Stores, Retail
Miscellaneous
Mooring/Dock
 Products/Lifts
Painting & Refinishing
 Materials & Services
Plating & Metal
 Refinishing
Propellers/Shafts/Bearings
Sailing Supplies:
 Sails, Rigging, Hardware
Shoes & Shoe Repair
Surveyors
Towing & Salvage
Transmissions
Video Services
Water Purification Systems
Water Taxi Service
Yacht Brokers

AIR CONDITIONING, REFRIGERATION

BAHAMAS

Running Mon Marina & Resort
Kelly Court & Knotts Blvd.
Freeport 800 315 6054

FIRST COAST & ST. JOHNS

The Boat Show
2999 SR 44 W.
Deland 904-736-6601

Jacksonville Yacht Basin
14603 Beach Blvd.
Jacksonville Bch. 904-223-4511

Marine Electrical Power
11232-2 St. Johns Industrial Pky.
Jacksonville 904 928 9203

Treworgy Yachts
5658 N. Oceanshore Blvd.
Palm Coast 904-445-5878

INDIAN RIVER LAGOON

Bethel Marine Corp.
1225 E. New Haven
Melbourne 407-727-0088

Cape Marina
800 Scallop Dr.
Cape Canaveral 407-783-8410
See advertisement on page 45.

Helseth Marine Services
3611 Rio Vista Blvd.
Vero Beach 407 234 3560

C. Huntress Marine
407 Ave. H
Ft. Pierce 407-461-3993

STUART TO BOCA RATON

Eastern Marine Corporation
2381 SE Dixie Hwy.
Stuart 407-288-4291

Irwin Oster Marine Service
Harbour Point Marina
2225 Monet Rd.
Palm Bch. Gdns.
407-627-1244

Stuart Yacht
450 SW Salerno Rd.
Stuart 407-283-1947
See advertisement on page 53.

BROWARD COUNTY

ARW Maritime
961 S. E. 20th St. B2
Ft. Lauderdale 954 463 0110

Rich Beers Marine
201 SW 7th Ave.
Ft. Lauderdale 954-764-6192

Beard Marine Air Conditioning
624 W. SR 84
Ft. Lauderdale 954 463 2288

Leonard De Layo Marine
5673 N. W. 39th Ave #A
Coconut Creek 954 429 8550

Lunaire Marine/Sail Kool
201 SW 20th St.
Ft. Lauderdale 954 525 4018

Marine Air Systems
2000 N. Andrews Ave. Ext.
Pompano Bch. 954 973 2477

Neptune Air
718 SE 17th St.
Ft. Lauderdale 954 463 3005

Polar Marine Air Conditioning
 & Refrigeration
3200 S. Andrews Ave.
Ft. Lauderdale 954 463 7637

Raritan Engineering Co.
3101 SW 2nd Ave.
Ft. Lauderdale 954 525 0378

T.K. Alley
1991 Tigertail Blvd.
Dania 954 920 0300

DADE COUNTY

Aqua-Air Div. of J.D. Nall
1050 E. 9th St.
Hialeah 305-884-8363

Bo Jean Boat Yard
3041 NW So. River Dr.
Miami 305-633-8919

KEYS

Hagopian
99353 Overseas Hwy.
Key Largo 305-451-2525

MARCO ISLAND TO PLACIDA

Boat/U.S.
12901 MacGregor Blvd.
Ft. Myers 941 481-7447

Custom Coolers
1401 Westview Dr.
Naples 941 643-1988

Glades Boat Storage
Boatyard Dr.
Moore Haven 941 983 3040

Mermaid Mfg. Co.
2651 Park Windsor Dr.
Fort Myers 941 418 0535

Rose Boat & Engine Works
4427 Mercantile Ave.
Naples 941 643-6657

ENGLEWOOD TO SKYWAY

AC Marine, Inc.
2012 Whitefield Pk. Dr.
Sarasota 941 755-8053

Shoreline
1825 30th Ave. W.
Bradenton 941 745-2554

West Florida Marine Elect.
3104 N. Tamiami Trail
Sarasota 941 351 3332

SKYWAY TO TARPON SPRINGS

AAA Marine Products
4022 54th Ave. North
St. Petersburg 813 521-1385

AIR CONDITIONING, REFRIGERATION

Boat/U.S.
11477 US Hwy. 19 S
Clearwater 813 573-2678
8203 N. Dale Mabry Hwy.
Tampa 813 933-5515

King-Air
6425 125th Ave. N.
Largo 813 536 7658

Marine ACR Systems
2625 46th St. S.
St. Petersburg 813 321-9676

Marine Engineering Specialists
3301 34th Ave. N.
St. Petersburg 813 526-7875

Marina Point Ships Store
500 1st Ave S.E.
St. Petersburg 813 823-2555

NORTHWEST

Brown Marine Services
40 Audusson Ave.
Pensacola 904-453-3471

Climate Control of Pensacola
3310 Barrancas Ave.
Pensacola 904-453-6066

Deckhand's Marina
1350 Miracle Strip Pkwy.
Ft. Walton Bch. 904-243-7359
See advertisement on page 132.

Holiday Harbor Marina
14050 Canal-a-Way
Pensacola 904-492-0555

Treasure Island Marina
3605 Thomas Dr.
Panama City Bch. 904-234-6533

BATTERIES, ELECTRICAL EQUIPMENT & SERVICES

FIRST COAST & ST. JOHNS

The Boat Show
2999 SR 44 W.
Deland 904-736-6601

Florida Watercraft
177 North Cswy.
New Smyrna Bch. 904-426-2628

Julington Creek Marina
12807 San Jose Blvd.
Jacksonville 904 268 5117

Mandarin Holiday Marina
12796 San Jose Blvd.
Jacksonville 904-268-1036

Marine Electric
630 Aurora St. S.
Daytona Bch. 904-761-3108

Palm Coast Marina
200 Clubhouse Dr.
Palm Coast 904-446-6370
See advertisement on page 35.

Sea Love Boatworks
4877 Front St.
Ponce Inlet 904-761-5434

West Marine
4415 Roosevelt Blvd.
Jacksonville 904-388-7510

INDIAN RIVER LAGOON

Cape Marina
800 Scallop Dr.
Cape Canaveral 407-783-8410
See advertisement on page 45.

Harbor Town Marina/Boatyard
1936 HarborTown Dr.
Ft. Pierce 407-466-7300

Indian Cove Marina
14 Myrtice Ave.
Merritt Island 407-452-8540

Intracoastal Marina of Melbourne
705 S. US 1
Melbourne 407-725-0090
See advertisement on page 48.

Pineda Point Marina
6175 N. Harbor City Blvd.
Melbourne 407-254-4199

Whitley Marine
93 Delannoy Ave.
Cocoa 407-632-5445
See advertisement on page 45.

STUART TO BOCA RATON

Dietz Enterprises
1501 Decker Ave.
Stuart 407 286 6282

Marine Diesel Analysts
2851 SE Monroe St.
Stuart 407-288-3208

Northside Marina
400 NW Alice Ave.
Stuart 407-692-4000

Irwin Oster Marine Service
Harbour Point Marina
2225 Monet Rd.
Palm Bch. Gdns. 407-627-1244

Larry Smith Electronics
1619 Broadway
Riviera Beach 407-844-3592

Offshore Marine Electronics
8459 Garden Gate Place
Boca Raton 407 849 6302

Rapco Auto Electric
3025 SE Dixie Hwy.
Stuart 407-286-1855

Stuart Yacht
450 SW Salerno Rd.
Stuart 407-283-1947
See advertisement on page 53.

West Marine
12189 U.S. Hwy. 1, #23
North Palm Beach
407-775-1434

Whiticar Boat Works
3636 SE Old St. Lucie Blvd.
Stuart 407-287-2883
See advertisement on page 54.

BROWARD COUNTY

A&M Marine Electric
2033 W. McNab Rd., T
Pompano Bch. 954 968-1995

American Battery & Alternator
3101 Davie Blvd.
Ft. Lauderdale 954-583-2470

Rich Beers Marine
201 SW 7th Ave.
Ft. Lauderdale 954-764-6192

Brunner & Assoc.
5200 SW 34th St.
Ft. Lauderdale 954-463-3645

Concord Marine Electronic
2233 S. Federal Hwy.
Ft. Lauderdale 954 779 1100

Eastern Marine Service
4270 N. W. 19th Ave. #C
Pompano Bch 954 784 0950

Florida Battery
1260 W. Sunrise Blvd.
Ft. Lauderdale 954-764-6911

Island Marine
775A Taylor Lane
Dania 954 9227077

Jeff's Marine Electric
1126 S. Federal Hwy. #330
Ft. Lauderdale 954-792-2622

Lauderdale Battery
Marine & General Battery
301 S. W. 25th St.
Ft. Lauderdale 954 525 2046

Raritan Engineering Co.
3101 SW 2nd Ave.
Ft. Lauderdale 954-525-0378

Raz Marine
281 SW 33rd St.
Ft. Lauderdale 954-525-5513

Royale Palm Yacht Basin
629 NE 3rd St.
Dania 954-923-5900

Ward's Marine Electric
630 SW Flagler Ave.
Ft. Lauderdale 954-523-2815
See advertisement on page 63.

West Marine
2300 S. Federal Hwy.
Ft. Lauderdale 954-527-5540

DADE COUNTY

Anchor Marine
96 NW 7th St.
Miami 305-545-6348

Atlantic Radio Telephone
2495 NW 35th Ave
Miami 305-633-9636

Bo Jean Boat Yard
3041 NW So. River Dr.
Miami 305-633-8919

R.B. Grove
261 SW 6th St.
Miami 305-854-5420

West Marine
3635 S. Dixie Hwy.
Miami 305-444-5520

KEYS

The Boat House
12411 Overseas Hwy.
Marathon 305-289-1323

Curtis Marine
229 Banyan La.
Tavernier 305-852-5218

Italian Fishermen Marina
MM 104 US 1
Key Largo 305-451-3726

Key West Electrical Repair & Supply
311 Margaret St.
Key West 305-296-8548

Pete's Electric
1779 Overseas Hwy.
Marathon 305-743-8328

MARCO ISLAND TO PLACIDA

Compass Rose Marina
1195 Main St.
Ft. Myers 941 463-2400

Hurricane Bay Marine
18850 San Carlos Blvd.
Ft. Myers 941 466-8898

Pineland Marina
13951 Waterfront Dr.
Pineland 941 283-0080

Owl Creek Boat Works
8251 Owl Creek Dr.
Alva 941 543-2100

Rose Boat & Engine Works
4427 Mercantile Ave.
Naples 941 643-6657

Tony's Dock Side Service
Marco Island 941 642-0204

Turner Marine of Naples
899 10th St. S.
Naples 941 262-5973
See advertisement on page 98.

ENGLEWOOD TO SKYWAY

Alternator & Starter Rebuilders
208 Warfield Ave.
Venice 941 488-5355

Battery Sale & Supply
4106 S. Tamiami Tr.
Sarasota 941 924-8665

Gulfwind Marine
1485 S. Tamiami Trail
Venice 941 485-3388

Mid-Island Marina
4756 Ester Blvd.
Ft. Myers 941 765 4371
See advertisement on page 98.

Roman Electric
401 Mango St.
Sarasota 941 366-4089

SKYWAY TO TARPON SPRINGS

Interstate Battery Systems
11347 43rd St. N.
Clearwater 813-577-9431

Gulf Coast Marine Services
12756 Daniel Rd.
Clearwater 813-573-1996

Marina Point Ships Store
500 1st Ave. SE
St. Petersburg 813-896-2641

Tamrad
618 N 13th St.
Tampa 813-229-0080

West Marine
5001 34th Street South
St. Petersburg 813-867-5700

NORTHWEST

Holiday Harbor Marina
14050 Canal-a-Way
Pensacola 904-492-0555

Marshall Marine Ways
Timber Island Rd.
Carrabelle 904-697-3428
See advertisement on page 127.

Miller Marine
119 Water St.
Apalachicola 904-653-9521
See advertisement on page 128.

Pride of the Point Marina
Rt. 1 Box 3461
Panacea 904-349-2517

Rod & Reel Marina
10045 Sinton Dr.
Pensacola 904-492-0100
See advertisement on page 135.

Shell Point Resort
Rt. 2, Box 4361-1
Crawfordville 904-926-7162
See advertisement on page 127.

Treasure Island Marina
3605 Thomas Dr.
Panama City Bch. 904-234-6533

BUILDERS

FIRST COAST & ST. JOHNS

Huckins Yacht Corp.
3482 Lakeshore Blvd.
Jacksonville 904-389-1125

Hunter Marine Corp.
Box 1030, Hwy. 441
Alachua 800 771 9463

Luhrs Corp.
255 Diesel Rd.
St. Augustine 904-829-0500

Treworgy Yachts
5658 N. Oceanshore Blvd.
Palm Coast 904-445-5878

INDIAN RIVER LAGOON

Regal Marine Industries
2300 Jetport Dr.
Orlando 407-851-4360

Sea Ray Boats
100 Sea Ray Blvd.
Merritt Island 407-452-6710

STUART TO BOCA RATON

Beachcomber Fiberglass Tech.
2850 SE Market Place
Stuart 407-283-0200

W. L. Knowles & Co.
3190 SE Slater St.
Stuart 407-286-5663

Stuart Yacht
450 SW Salerno Rd.
Stuart 407-283-1947
See advertisement on page 53.

Whiticar Boat Works
3636 SE Old St. Lucie Blvd.
Stuart 407-287-2883
See advertisement on page 54.

BROWARD COUNTY

Blackfin Yacht Corp.
3391 SE 14th Ave.
Ft. Lauderdale 954-525-6314

Broward Marine
1601 SW 20th St.
Ft. Lauderdale 954-522-1701

Dusky Marine
110 N. Bryan Rd.
Dania 954-922-8890

DADE COUNTY

Answer Marine
9500 NW 36th Ave.
Miami 305-836-1033

Bertram Yacht
3663 NW 21st St.
Miami 305-633-8011

Cigarette Racing Team
3131 NE 188th St.
N. Miami Bch. 305-931-4564

Florida Bay Boat Co.
7095 SW 47th St.
Miami 305-666-3003

Magnum Marine Corp.
2900 NE 188th St.
N. Miami Bch. 305-931-4292

Mako Marine
4355 NW 128th St.
Miami 305-685-6591

Norseman Shipbuilding
437 NW S. River Dr.
Miami 305-545-6815

Phoenix Marine Ent.
1775 W Okeechobee Rd.
Hialeah 305-887-5625

VIP Marine
950 NW 72nd St.
Miami 305-696-3232

KEYS

Tiki Watersports
& Glander Boats
MM 94.5 US 1
Key Largo 305-852-9298

MARCO ISLAND TO PLACIDA

Shamrock Marine
905 SE 9th Terr.
Cape Coral 941-574-2800

ENGLEWOOD TO SKYWAY

Boca Grande
3604 Osprey
Sarasota 941-365-3387

Chris-Craft
8161 15th St. E.
Sarasota 941-351-4900

Ski Supreme
1651 Whitfield Ave.
Sarasota 941-755-5800

Sea-N-Sport
6065 17th St. East
Bradenton 941 753 9429

Wellcraft Marine
1651 Whitfield Ave.
Sarasota 941-753 7811

SKYWAY TO TARPON SPRINGS

Endeavor International
6021 142nd Ave. N.
Clearwater 813-729 2248

Hutchins/Compac Sailboats
1195 Kapp Dr.
Clearwater 813-443-4408

Island Packet Yachts
1979 Wild Acres Rd.
Largo 813-535-6431

Stamas Yacht Inc.
300 Pampas Ave.
Tarpon Springs 800- 782-6271

NORTHWEST

Baha Cruisers
Hwy. 51 N
Mayo 904-294-2431

Monterey Boats
Archer 352-495-3624

P-C Marine
6001 East Hwy. 98
Panama City 904-871-4805

Pro-Line Boats
S. Coast Blvd.
Crystal River 352-795-4111

CANVAS PRODUCTS, COVERS

FIRST COAST & ST. JOHNS

The Boat Show
2999 SR 44 West
Deland 904-736-6601

Boatswain's Locker
4565 Lake Shore Dr.
Jacksonville 904-388-0231

Custom Marine Components
13755 Atlantic Blvd.
Jacksonville 904 221 6412

Daytona Marina & Boat Works
645 S. Beach St.
Daytona Bch. 904-252-6421

Florida Watercraft
177 North Cswy.
New Smyrna Bch. 904-426-2628

Hidden Harbor Marina
4370 Carraway Place
Sanford 407 322 1610

Tops 'n Covers
500 Ballough Rd.
Daytona Bch. 904-255-2620

INDIAN RIVER LAGOON

Cape Marina
800 Scallop Dr.
Cape Canaveral 407-783-8410
See advertisement on page 45.

DeFreitas Marine Canvas
14 Myrtice Ave.
Merritt Island 407 453 4912

Harbor Town Marina/Boatyard
1936 HarborTown Dr.
Ft. Pierce 407-466-7300

Intracoastal Marina of Melbourne
705 S. US 1
Melbourne 407-725-0090
See advertisement on page 48.

Pineda Point Marina
6175 N. Harbor City Blvd.
Melbourne 407-254-4199

STUART TO BOCA RATON

AA Boat Tops
508 S. H St.
Lake Worth 407-588-8677

Anchor Canvas
2391 SE Dixie Hwy.
Stuart 407-287-7440

Custom Yacht Tenders
508 N. G St.
Lake Worth 407-585-9696

Poly-Steel Shelters
1209 E. Ocean Blvd.
Stuart 407-287-9294

Wilmark Sailmakers
2400 E. Tamarind Ave.
West Palm Bch. 407-833-4824

Yacht Service
909 Hillcrest Ave.
Stuart 407-286-5334

BROWARD COUNTY

Atkinson Marine
235 SW 32nd Ct.
Ft. Lauderdale 954-763-1652

Beaver-Brand Canvas
205 S. W. 7th Ave.
Ft. Lauderdale 954 763 7423

Canvas Factory
1061 N. E. 28th Ave.
Pompano Beach 954 781 1970

Cruisin' Canvas
1500 W. Broward Blvd.
Ft. Lauderdale 954-467-2722

General Fabrics
621 S. W. 2nd Ave.
Fort Lauderdale 954-522-5253

Hurricane Canvas
2001 S.W. 20th St.
Ft. Lauderdale 954 771 2978

Sail Cleaners
4910 NE 11th Ave.
Ft. Lauderdale 954-491-3327

DADE COUNTY

Bo Jean Boat Yard
3041 NW So. River Dr.
Miami 305-633-8919

Smitty's Boat Tops
727 S. Krome Ave.
Homestead 305-245-0229

KEYS

Canvas Creations
14 Key Lime Square
Key West 305-294-8216

Captain Canvas
135 Madeira Ave.
Islamorada 305-664-4766

Key Largo Harbour
100 Ocean Dr.
Key Largo 305-451-0045

Key Quality Canvas
5101 Overseas Hwy.
Marathon 305-743-4252

Nanci's Canvas
106000 US 1
Key Largo 305-451-2138

Toucan Canvas
4699 Overseas Hwy.
Marathon 305-763-6707

ENGLEWOOD TO SKYWAY

Atlas Custom Canvas
1303 Main St.
Sarasota 941-364-8222

Canvas King
2880 Siesta Dr.
Venice 941-493-0986

MARCO ISLAND TO PLACIDA

Fish Tale Marina
7225 Estero Blvd.
Ft. Myers Bch. 941-463-4448

Pineland Marina
13951 Waterfront Dr.
Pineland 941-283-0080

Scotties North Bay Marina
Tamiami Tr.
N. Ft. Myers 941-995-7479

SKYWAY TO TARPON SPRINGS

Clearwater Canvas
1575 S. Missouri Ave.
Clearwater 813-442-7551

JSI/Johnson Sails
3000 Gandy Blvd.
St. Petersburg 813-577-3220

Lippincott Marine Canvas
301 14th Ave. South
St. Petersburg 813 821 5949

Marine Sewing
6801 Gulfport Blvd. S.
South Pasadena 813-345-6994

Rip Shop
1663 1st Ave. S.
St. Petersburg 813-896-2313

CARPENTRY

NORTHWEST

Aquatic Ent. Inc.
1201A Hwy. Miracle Strip E.
Ft. Walton Beach 904-243-5721

Bob's Top Shop
2135 5th St.
Panama City 904-763-1683

Canvas Specialties
1201 C Hwy 98 E
Ft. Walton Bch. 904 664 6200

Chico Marina
3009 Barrancas Ave.
Pensacola 904 458 5804

Leeward Time, Inc.
26 A Beal Pkwy. N.W.
Fort Walton Beach 904 243 2738

Redish Canvas/Awning
3840 Navy Blvd.
Pensacola 904-456-1096

Sabre Sails
38 Miracle Pkwy.
Ft. Walton Bch. 904 244 0001

Treasure Island Marina
3605 Thomas Dr.
Panama City Bch. 904-234-6533

CARPENTRY

FIRST COAST & ST. JOHNS

Daytona Marina & Boat Works
645 S. Beach St.
Daytona Bch. 904-252-6421

Florida Watercraft
177 North Cswy.
New Smyrna Bch. 904-426-2628

Treworgy Yachts
5658 N. Oceanshore Blvd.
Palm Coast 904-445-587

INDIAN RIVER LAGOON

Cape Marina
800 Scallop Dr.
Cape Canaveral 407-783-8410
See advertisement on page 45.

Coastal Marine Repair
1357 S. Banana River Dr.
Merritt Island 407-453-1885
See advertisement on page 45.

Harbor Town Marina/Boatyard
1936 HarborTown Dr.
Ft. Pierce 407-466-7300

Indian Cove Marina
14 Myrtice Ave.
Merritt Island 407-452-8540

STUART TO BOCA RATON

Bruno's Marine Service
2868 SE Iris St.
Stuart 407-283-0790

Maritime Lumber Supply
2393 SE Dixie Hwy.
Stuart 407-287-2919

Whiticar Boat Works
3636 SE Old St. Lucie Blvd.
Stuart 407-287-2883
See advertisement on page 54.

CARPENTRY

BROWARD COUNTY

Chinnock Marine
518 W. Las Olas Blvd.
Ft. Lauderdale 954-763-2250

Custom Marine Woodworking, Inc.
2554 Key Largo Lane
Ft. Lauderdale 954-791-5457

Down East Boatworks
1431 SW 1st Ave.
Fort Lauderdale 954-729-9291

Craig L. Duncan Custom Yacht Carpentry
1915 SW 21st Ave
Fort Lauderdale 954 792-7551

River Bend Marina
1515 SW 20th St.
Ft. Lauderdale 954-523-1832

Seafarer Marine
3100 SW 3rd Ave.
Ft. Lauderdale 954-763-4263

Wood Chuck Workshop
at Harbour Towne Marina
Dania 954 922 3221

DADE COUNTY

Bo Jean Boat Yard
3041 NW So. River Dr.
Miami 305-633-8919

Danish Craftsman
17201 Biscayne Blvd.
N. Miami Bch. 305-944-4899

Smitty's Boat Tops
727 S. Krome Ave.
Homestead 305-245-0229

KEYS

Manatee Bay Marine
99 Morris Ln
Key Largo 305-451-3332

MARCO ISLAND TO PLACIDA

Mid-Island Marina
4756 Ester Blvd.
Ft. Myers 941 765 4371
See advertisement on page 98.

Olsen Marine Service
1100 Main St.
Ft. Myers Bch. 941-463-6750

Owl Creek Boat Works
Route 2, Box 298
Alva 941-543-2100

Rose Boat & Engine Works
4427 Mercantile Ave.
Naples 941-643-6657

ENGLEWOOD TO SKYWAY

Bradenton Beach Marina
402 Church Ave.
Bradenton Bch. 941-778-2288

Royal Palm Marina
779 W. Wentworth
Englewood 941 474-1420

SKYWAY TO TARPON SPRINGS

Out Island Woodworks
2145 Capri
Clearwater 813-736-5918

Pete's Boatworks
4709-B 96th St.
St. Petersburg 813 393 5732

Sailor's Wharf
1421 Bay St. SE
St. Petersburg 813-823-1155

NORTHWEST

B&B Enterprises
666 Myrick St.
Pensacola 904-434-5015

Deckhand's Marina
1350 Miracle Strip Pkwy.
Ft. Walton Bch. 904-243-7359
See advertisement on page 132.

Hardwood Sales
721 N. T St.
Pensacola 904-432-8238

Hernando Beach Marina
4139 Shoal Hill Blvd.
Spring Hill 352-596-2952

Passport Marina & Boat Yard
5323 N. Lagoon Dr.
Panama City 904-234-5609

Pride of the Point Marina
Rt. 1 Box 3461
Panacea 904-349-2517

Wood Furniture Craftworks
721 N. T St.
Pensacola 904-432-8238

CHARTERS & RENTALS

ALL REGIONS

Club Nautico
850 NE 3rd St.
Dania 954-927-9800

BAHAMAS
(Also see Bahamas Marinas)

Boat Harbour
Abaco 809-367-2736

Brendal's Dive Shop
Green Turtle Cay
Abaco 809-359-6226

Conch Inn Resort & Marina
Marsh Harbour
Abaco 809-367-2800

Elbow Cay Beach Inn
Hope Town 809-367-2748

Green Turtle Club
Green Turtle Cay
809-365-4271
See advertisement on page 26.

Island Marine
Parrott Cay
Abaco 809-367-2822

Man O War Marina
Abaco 809-365-6008

Seahorse Boat Rentals
POB AB20013 Marsh Harbour
Abaco 809-367-2513

Triple J Marina
Bay St.
Marsh Harbour 809-367-2163

Walker's Cay
Abaco 954-522-1469

Weech's Dock
Bimini 809-347-2028

FIRST COAST & ST. JOHNS

The Boat Show
2999 SR 44 West
Deland 904-736-6601

Florida Watercraft
177 North Cswy.
New Smyrna Bch. 904-426-2628

Hontoon Landing
2317 River Ridge Rd.
Deland 904-734-2007

Lighthouse Charters
3074 Harbor Drive
St. Augustine 904 825 1985

Palm Coast Marina
200 Clubhouse Dr.
Palm Coast 904-446-6370
See advertisement on page 35.

Pier 68 Marina
8137 N. Main St.
Jacksonville 904-764-2053.

St. Augustine Sailing
3040 Harbor Dr.
St. Augustine 904-829-2294

Sanford Boat Rental
Hidden Harbor Marina
Sanford 800-237-5105

INDIAN RIVER LAGOON

Action Sail & Sport Center
5465 N. US 1
Melbourne 407-242-26284

Cape Marina
800 Scallop Dr.
Cape Canaveral 407-783-8410
See advertisement on page 45.

Harbor Town Marina/Boatyard
1936 HarborTown Dr.
Ft. Pierce 407-466-7300

Pelicans Nest Marina
1009 NE Anchorage Dr.
Jensen Beach 407-334-0890

STUART TO BOCA RATON

Palm Beach Yacht Brokerage
800 N. Flagler Dr.
West Palm Bch 407-833-8633

Indian River Plantation
55 NE Ocean Blvd.
Hutchinson Island
Stuart 407-225-3700
1-800-444-3389
See advertisement on page 55.

Inlet Rentals
255 E. 22nd Ct.
Riviera Bch. 407-844-2504

Jupiter Hills Lighthouse Marina
18261 US Hwy. 1
Jupiter 407-744-0727

Northside Marina
400 NW Alice Ave.
Stuart 407-692-4000

River Sport Boat Rentals
US 1 at Roosevelt Bridge
Stuart 407-692-9746

Sailfish Marina
3565 SE St. Lucie Blvd.
Stuart 407-283-1122

Sailfish Marina & Resort
98 Lake Dr.
Palm Bch. Shores 407-844-8460

Singer Island Sailboat Rental
Phil Foster Park
Riviera Bch. 407-848-2628

BROWARD COUNTY

Castlemain
300 SW 2nd St.
Ft. Lauderdale 954-760-4730

C.P. Irwin Yacht Brokerage
801 Seabreeze Blvd.
Ft. Lauderdale 954-463-6302

Fun in the Sun Charters
U. S. Route #1
Dania 954 923 2808

Rex Yacht Sales
2152 SE 17th St., #202
Ft. Lauderdale 954-463-8810

Southeast Yachting School & Charters
2170 SE 17th St., #304
Ft. Lauderdale 954-523-2628

Windridge Yacht Charters
1700 E. Las Olas Blvd., #203
Ft. Lauderdale 954-525-7724

Yacht Management Group
at Harbour Towne Marina
Dania 954 929 6900

DADE COUNTY

Action Bay Boat Rentals
163rd & Collins
Miami Bch. 305-945-2628

American Bahamas Charters
3265 Virginia St.
Miami 305-858-8023

Barefoot Island Cruises
Watson Island Marina
Miami 305-379-8069

Cruzan Yacht Charters
3400 Pan American Dr.
Coconut Grove 305-858-2822

Easy Sailing
3400 Pan American Dr.
Coconut Grove 305-858-4001

Florida Sailing Charter Club
3650 N. Bayhomes Dr.
Miami 305-662-2667

Florida Yacht Charters & Sales
1290 5th St.
Miami Bch. 305-532-8600

Haulover Marina
10800 Collins Ave.
Miami 305 947 3525
See advertisement on page 73.

Key Biscayne Boat Rentals
3301 Rickenbacker Cswy.
Key Biscayne 305-361-1024

Matheson Hammock Marina
9610 Old Cutler Rd.
Miami 305-665-5475

Merrill-Stevens Yacht Sales
1270 NE 11th St.
Miami 305-858-5911

Paradise Yacht Charters
3632 Stewart Ave.
Miami 305-285-1001

Turnberry Isle Resort & Club
19755 NE 36th Ct.
Aventura 305-932-6200
See advertisement on page 68.

KEYS

A- B- Sea Harborage Marina
MM 48 (at Faro Blanco)
Marathon 305 289 0373

The Boat House
12411 Overseas Hwy.
Marathon 305-289-1323

Bud 'n Mary's Marina
Islamorada 305-664-2461

Caloosa Fishing Boat
Key Largo 305-852-3200

Clyde's 7 Mile Marina
900 Overseas Hwy.
Marathon 305-743-7712

Cross Key Marina
MM 112.5
Key Largo 305-451-2779

Cudjoe Gardens Marina
802 Drost Dr. MM 21
Cudjoe Key 305-745-2357

Duck Key Marina
MM 61
Marathon 305-289-0161

Egan's Waterway
106690 Overseas Hwy.
Key Largo 305-451-1929.

Fish or Dive Boat Rentals
Boot Key/1000 15th St.
Marathon 305-743-0372

Hawk's Cay Resort & Marina
MM 61, Duck Key
Marathon 305-743-7000

Florida Keys Charters
Key Largo 305-451-2221

Garrison Bight Marina
711 Eisenhower Dr.
Key West 305-294-3093

Gilbert's Holiday Island of Key Largo
107900 Overseas Hwy.
Key Largo 305-451-1133
See advertisement on page 81.

Holiday Isle Boat Rental
Islamorada 305-664-9425
FL 1-800-432-2875
Ntnl. 1-800-327-7070

Houseboat Vacations
MM 85.9/85944 Overseas Hwy.
Islamorada 305-664-4009

Italian Fishermen Marina
Overseas Hwy. MM 104
Key Largo 305-451-3726

Key Largo Holiday Inn Resort
99701 Overseas Hwy.
Key Largo 305-451-2121

Key West Bight Marina
201 William St.
Key West 305-296-3838

Lime Tree Bay
MM 68.5
Long Key 305-664-4744

Ocean Divers
522 Caribbean Dr.
Key Largo 305-451-1113

Perdue Dean
2 Fishing Village Dr.
Key Largo 305-367-2661

Pilot House Marina
15 No. Channel Dr.
Key Largo 305 451 3452

Plantation Key Marina
MM 90.5 US 1
Plantation Key 305-852-5424

Robbie's Rent-A-Boat
MM 77.5 Overseas Hwy.
Islamorada 305-664-4196

Ron's Houseboat Rentals
196 Harborview Dr.
Tavernier 305-852-3486

Smugglers Blues
177 Star Lane
Key West 305 744 7334

Southernmost Sailing
P.O. Box 369
Key West 305 293 1883

Treasure Harbor Marine
 at Ragged Edge Resort
200 Treasure Harbor Drive
Islamorada 305-852-2458

MARCO ISLAND TO PLACIDA

The Barge Marina
San Marco Rd. (SR 92)
Goodland 941-642-1920

Blind Pass Marina
6486 Sanibel-Captiva Rd.
Sanibel Island 941-472-1020

Captain Russ' Boat Rentals
Whidden's Marina
Boca Grande 941-697-5152

Fish Tale Marina
7225 Estero Blvd.
Ft. Myers Bch. 941-463-4448

Fishermen's Village Yacht Basin
1200 W. Retta Esplanade
Punta Gorda 941-639-3232

Fort Myers Beach Marina
703 Fisherman's Wharf
Ft. Myers Bch 941 463 9557

Ft. Myers Yacht Charters
14341 Port Comfort Rd.
Ft. Myers 941 466 1800

Goodland Bay
Boat Rentals
Goodland 941-394-2797

Goodlife Charter Services
3444 Marinatown Lane
N. Ft. Myers 941 995 0505

Jensen's Twin Palm Resort
Captiva 941-472-5800

Marco Island Marina
Rental Boats
Marco Island 941-394-2502
Naples 941-597-3549

Moss Marine
Harbor Ct.
Ft. Myers Bch. 941-463-6137

Palm Grove Marina
 Powerboat Rentals
2500 Main St.
Ft.Myers Bch. 941-463-7333

Pineland Marina
13951 Waterfront Dr.
Pineland 941-283-0080

Port-O-Call Marina
550 Port-O-Call Way
Naples 941 774 0479

Sanibel Island Marina
634 N. Yachtsman Dr.
Sanibel 941-472-2723

Southwest Florida Yachts
3444 Marinatown La.
N. Ft. Myers 941-656-1339
1-800-262-SWFY

Tarpon Bay
Canoe & Boat Rentals
Sanibel Island 941-472-8900

ENGLEWOOD TO SKYWAY

Cannon's Marina Boat Rentals
6051 Gulf of Mexico Dr.
Longboat Key 941-383-1311

Chitwood Charters
Sarasota 941-957-1530

Don & Mike's Boat & Ski Rental
Island Park Dr.
Sarasota 941-366-6659

Dona Bay Marine
504 S. Tamiami Tr.
Nokomis 941-484-2324

Englewood Bait House
1450 Beach Rd.
Englewood 941-475-4511

O'Leary's Sailing School
Island Park, Bayfront
Sarasota 941-953-7505

VIP Boat Club
Fisherman's Wharf
Venice 941-488-2789

Weston's Fish & Fun Resort
985 Gulf Blvd.
Englewood 941-474-3431

SKYWAY TO TARPON SPRINGS

Bay Island Charters
Clearwater Beach Marina
Clearwater 813-449-0602

Beach Motor Boat Rentals
Clearwater Beach Marina
Clearwater 813-446-5503

Bon Appetit
148 Marine Plaza
Dunedin 813-733-2151

Cobb & Allen Offshore Yachts
603 Pinellas St.
Clearwater 813-441-2066

Days Inn Marina Beach Resort
6800 34th St. S.
St. Petersburg 813-867-1151

Florida West Coast Charters
12030 Gandy Blvd.
St. Petersburg 813-576-3801

Gulf Charters
408.5 Riverside Dr.
Tarpon Springs 813-934-4036

Harbour Island Marina
777 S. Harbour Isl. Blvd. #270
Tampa 813-229-5324

Marina Point Ships Store
500 1st Ave SE
St. Petersburg 813-823-2555

Redington Shores Marina
17811 Gulf Blvd.
Redington Shores 813-391-1954

Royalty Yacht Charters
220 1st Ave. N.
St. Petersburg 813-898-0100.

St. Petersburg Yacht Charters &
Sales
500 1st Ave. SE
St. Petersburg 813-823-2555

Tampa Westshore Water Sports
6200 Courtney Campbell Cswy.
Tampa 813-873-2021

VIP Boat Club
Marker 1 Marina
343 Causeway Blvd
Dunedin 813-734-5969

West Wind Charters
1300 Beach Tr.
Indian Rocks Bch.
813-596-3836

NORTHWEST

A-B-Sea Marina
4995 U.S. Hwy. 19
New Port Richey 813 845 1726

Ahoy Charters
New Port Richey 813-942-2086

Baytowne Marina at Sandestin
5500 Hwy. 98 E.
Destin 904-267-7777
See advertisement on page 133.

Bluewater Charters
Marker Dock/Hwy. 98
Destin 904-837-6148

Capt. Anderson Cruise Boat
Grand Lagoon
Panama City Bch. 904-234-5940

Captain Dan Welch
Pensacola 904-968-1898

Deep Sea Fishing Headquarters
Pensacola 904-432-7536

Deckhand's Marina
1350 Miracle Strip Pkwy.
Ft. Walton Bch. 904-243-7359
See advertisement on page 132.

Hathaway Landings Marina
6426 W. Hwy. 98
Panama City Bch 904 234 0609

Holiday Harbor Marina
14050 Canal-a-Way
Pensacola 904-492-0555

Kelly Dock Charter Service
Destin 904-837-2343

Marquardt's Marina
Hwy. 98
Mexico Bch. 904-648-8900

Miller's Marina
PO Box 280
Suwannee 352-542-7349
See advertisement on page 123.

**Oyster Bar Restaurant
& Marina**
13700 River Road
Perdido Key 904 492 0192
See advertisement on page 133.

Pontoon Boat Rentals
Mary Esther 904-243-4488

Pride of the Point Marina
Rt. 1 Box 3461
Panacea 904-349-2517

Rainbow Inn & Marina
123 Water St.
Apalachicola 904-653-8139

S&S Sailing
Hwy. 98 E
Ft. Walton Bch. 904-243-2022

Sailing South
Hwy. 98 & Benning Dr.
Destin 904-837-7245

Shell Point Resort
Rt. 2, Box 385
Crawfordville 904-926-7162
See advertisement on page 127.

Southwind Marina
10121 Sinton Dr.
Pensacola 904-492-0333
See advertisement on page 135.

Treasure Island Marina
3605 Thomas Dr.
Panama City Bch. 904-234-6533

CHARTS & BOOKS

FIRST COAST & ST. JOHNS

The Boat Show
2999 SR 44 W.
Deland 904-736-6601

Boathouse Marina
329 River St.
Palatka 904-328-2944
See advertisement on page 42.

Daytona Marina & Boat Works
645 S. Beach St.
Daytona Bch. 904-252-6421

Florida Watercraft
177 North Cswy.
New Smyrna Bch. 904-426-2628

Palm Coast Marina
200 Clubhouse Dr.
Palm Coast 904-446-6370
See advertisement on page 35.

Pier 17
4619 Roosevelt Blvd.
Jacksonville 904-387-4669

Shaws Yacht Brokerage
& Marine Supply
728 Ballough Rd.
Daytona Bch. 904-255-0495

**St. Augustine
Municipal Marina**
111 Avenida Menendez
St. Augustine 904 825 1026
See advertisement on page 38.

INDIAN RIVER LAGOON

Banana River Marine Service
1360 S. Banana River Drive
Merritt Island 407-452-8622
See advertisement on page 45.

Cape Marina
800 Scallop Dr.
Cape Canaveral 407-783-8410
See advertisement on page 45.

Marina at Ft. Pierce
219 Fisherman's Wharf
Ft. Pierce 407-461-1266

**Melbourne Harbor
Ship's Store**
2210 S. Front St.
Melbourne 407-725-9054
See advertisement on page 47.

Whitley Marine
93 Delannoy Ave.
Cocoa 407-632-5445
See advertisement on page 45.

STUART TO BOCA RATON

C. Foster Marine Supplies
3385 Se Dixie Hwy.
Stuart 407-286-2118

Sailfish Marina
98 Lake Dr.
Palm Bch. Shores 407-844-8460

BROWARD COUNTY

Bluewater Books & Charts
1481 SE 17th St.
Ft. Lauderdale 954-763-6533
1-800-942-2583
See advertisement on page 142.

Lauderdale Marina
1900 SE 15th St.
Ft. Lauderdale 954-523-8507
See advertisement on page 59.

Pier 66 Dockstore
17th St. Causeway
Ft. Lauderdale 954-525-6666

DADE COUNTY

American Nautical Services
 Navigation Center
254 NE 4th St.
Miami 305-358-1414

Cruising Gear Intnl.
2751 SW 27th Ave.
Miami 305-854-7600

CHARTS & BOOKS

KEYS

The Boat House
12411 Overseas Hwy.
Marathon 305-289-1323

Key West Marine Hardware
818 Caroline St.
Key West 305-294-3425
See advertisement on page 89.

Perkins & Son
901 Fleming St.
Key West 305-294-7635

Tugboat's
2211 Overseas Hwy.
Marathon 305-743-4585

MARCO ISLAND TO PLACIDA

Fish Tale Marina
7225 Estero Blvd.
Ft. Myers Bch. 941-463-4448

Pineland Marina
13951 Waterfront Dr.
Pineland 941-283-0080

Sanibel Island Marina
634 N. Yachtsman Dr.
Sanibel 941-472-2723

ENGLEWOOD TO SKYWAY

Turner Marine
826 13th St. W.
Bradenton 941-746-3456

SKYWAY TO TARPON SPRINGS

Marina Point Ship's Store
500 1st Ave. SE
St. Petersburg 813-896-2641

Marker 1 Marina
343 Causeway Blvd.
Dunedin 813 733 9324
See advertisement on page 112.

Poston Marine
109 N. Meridian
Tampa 813 229 1836

NORTHWEST

Armchair Sailor Books & Charts
546 Hwy. 98 E.
Destin 904-837-1579

Baytowne Marina at Sandestin
5500 Hwy. 98 E.
Destin 904-267-7777
See advertisement on page 133.

Hathaway Landings Marina
6426 W. Hwy. 98
Panama City Bch 904 234 0609

Holiday Harbor Marina
14050 Canal-a-Way
Pensacola 904-492-0555

Johnson Supply Co.
50 S. E Street
Pensacola 904-434-7103

Miller Marine
119 Water St.
Apalachicola 904-653-9521
See advertisement on page 128.

Miller's Marina
PO Box 280
Suwannee 352-542-7349
See advertisement on page 123.

Rod & Reel Marina
10045 Sinton Dr.
Pensacola 904 492 0100
See Advertisement on page 135.

Sailors Supply
231 E. Beach Dr.
Panama City 904-769-5007

Treasure Island Marina
3605 Thomas Dr.
Panama City Bch. 904-234-6533

CLEANING & MAINTENANCE

FIRST COAST & ST. JOHNS

The Boat Show
2999 SR 44 W.
Deland 904-736-6601

Florida Watercraft
177 North Cswy.
New Smyrna Bch. 904-426-2628

Palm Coast Marina
200 Clubhouse Dr.
Palm Coast 904-446-6370
See advertisement on page 35.

Ponce Deepwater Landing
133 Inlet Harbor Rd.
Ponce Inlet 904-767-3266
See advertisement on page 35.

First Mate Yacht Services
212 Yacht Club Dr.
St. Augustine 904-829-0184

INDIAN RIVER LAGOON

Cape Marina
800 Scallop Dr.
Cape Canaveral 407-783-8410
See advertisement on page 45.

Casa Rio
1050 N. E. Dixie Hwy.
Jensen Beach 407 334 0944

Harbor Town Marina/Boatyard
1936 HarborTown Dr.
Ft. Pierce 407-466-7300

Pineda Point Marina
6175 N. Harbor City Blvd.
Melbourne 407-254-4199

Whitley Marine
93 Delannoy Ave.
Cocoa 407-632-5445
See advertisement on page 45.

STUART TO BOCA RATON

Boca Raton Resort & Club
501 E. Camino Real
Boca Raton 407-395-3000

Palm Beach Yacht Club Marina
800 N. Flagler Dr.
West Palm Bch. 407-655-1944

Mer-Maid Yacht Services
10190 Boca Entrada Blvd., #210
Boca Raton 407-451-2118

Sailfish Marina & Resort
98 Lake Dr.
Palm Bch. Shores 407-844-8460

Shurhold Products
P.O. Box 1068
Palm City 407-287-1313

Stain Busters
10458 Riverside Dr.
Palm Bch. Gdns. 407 625 6700

BROWARD COUNTY

Century Marine Services
1024 Tyler St.
Hollywood 954-925-0796

Capt. Walt Harrison Yacht Maint.
5361 NE 17th Ave.
Ft. Lauderdale 954-771-5436

Need Charts?
Call Bluewater

- Over 35,000 nautical books and charts
- Worldwide nautical chart coverage
- Charts from all major chart publishers
- Electronic charts—all major brands in stock
- World's largest selection of cruising guides
- Over 2,000 courtesy flags in stock
- Same day shipping—we ship worldwide

Ask our friendly experts for help!

Bluewater
BOOKS & CHARTS

Southport Center
1481 SE 17th Street Causeway
Fort Lauderdale, FL 33316 USA
Tel. 954-763-6533 ☎ *Fax. 954-522-2278*

Toll Free Orders 1-800-942-2583

While you're in Palm Beach County, be sure to sample some of the best water in the world.

Fishing, diving, sailing, yachting, canoeing, waterskiing, windsurfing or whatever ...
Palm Beach County has it.
And our members can help you enjoy the water better than anyone else.

Businesses
"Safeguarding Enjoyable Boating"

For boating information and a free guide
to services, call or write today.

**The Marine Industries Association
of Palm Beach County, Inc.**
Post Office Box 12661
Lake Park, Florida 33403
(407) 624-9092

Harbormaster International
4701 N. Federal Hwy.
Lighthouse Pt. 954-943-5203

Sail Cleaners
4910 NE 11th Ave.
Ft. Lauderdale 954-491-3327

Yachting Bliss
801 Seabreeze Blvd.
Ft. Lauderdale 954 779 3506
See advertisement on page 143.

Yeager Marine Associates
1126 S. Federal Hwy., Ste. # 424
Ft. Lauderdale 954-523-3872
See advertisement on page 76.

DADE COUNTY

Bo Jean Boat Yard
3041 NW So. River Dr.
Miami 305-633-8919

Cleanse A Yacht
3221 NE 165th St.
N. Miami Bch. 305-944-2541

Smitty's Boat Tops
727 S. Krome Ave.
Homestead 305-245-0229

MARCO ISLAND TO PLACIDA

Compass Rose Marina
1195 Main St.
Ft. Myers 941-463-2400

Moss Marine
Harbor Ct.
Ft. Myers Bch. 941-463-6137

Nautical Services
3155 Placida Rd.
Grove City 941-697-7155

Owl Creek Boat Works
18251 Owl Creek Dr.
Alva 941-543-2100

Pineland Marina
13951 Waterfront Dr.
Pineland 941-283-0080

ENGLEWOOD TO SKYWAY

Finish Care Services
Bradenton 941-745-2925

Fleetside Maintenance
Sarasota 941-378-5516

SKYWAY TO TARPON SPRINGS

Marina Point Ships Store
500 1st Ave S.E.
St. Petersburg 813-823-2555

The Teak Doctor
St. Petersburg 813-397-4165

NORTHWEST

Bayou Chico Marina
806 Lakewood Rd.
Pensacola 904-455-4552

Baytowne Marina at Sandestin
5500 Hwy. 98 E.
Destin 904-267-7777
See advertisement on page 133.

Deckhand's Marina
1350 Miracle Strip Pkwy.
Ft. Walton Bch. 904-243-7359
See advertisement on page 128.

Engineering Specialties
Pensacola 904-968-6769

Holiday Harbor Marina
14050 Canal-a-Way
Pensacola 904-492-0555

Marshall Marine Ways
Timber Island Rd.
Carrabelle 904-697-3428
See advertisement on page 127.

Mike's Marine Ways
St. Marks 904-925-6585
See advertisement on page 125.

Port Panacea Marina
Rocklanding Rd.
Panacea 904-349-2454

Treasure Island Marina
3605 Thomas Dr.
Panama City Bch. 904-234-6533

Zack's Marine Service
Pensacola Shipyard Marina
Pensacola 904 469 0005

CLUBS & ASSOCIATIONS

ALL REGIONS

Marine Industries Assn. of
Florida
PO Box 172
Tallahassee, 32302
904-668-5665

World Yacht Club Intnl.
11111 Biscayne Blvd.
Miami 305-285-1001

BAHAMAS

International Power & Sail
P. O. Box 10985
Nassau 800 333 3244

Staniel Cay Yacht Club
Exumas 809-355-2011

FIRST COAST & ST. JOHNS

Captain's Club
14603 Beach Blvd.
Jacksonville 904-233-5494

Hidden Harbour Marina
4370 Carraway Pl.
Sanford 407-322-1610

Queen's Harbour Yacht &
Country Club
701 Queen's Harbour Blvd.
Jacksonville 904-221-2605

INDIAN RIVER LAGOON

Club Med/Sandpiper
Morningside Blvd.
Port St. Lucie 407-335-4400
See advertisement on page 52.

Ft. Pierce Sportfishing Club
PO Box 4051 Zip: 34948
Ft. Pierce 407-464-5066

Kennedy Point Marina & Club
4747 S. Washington Ave.
Titusville 407 383 0280
See advertisement on page 49.

Riomar Bay Yacht Club
2345 S. Hwy. A1A
Vero Bch. 407-231-5466

STUART TO BOCA RATON

Cannonsport Marina
178 Lake Dr.
Palm Bch. Shores
407-848-7469

Loblolly Bay Yacht Club
8000 S.E. Little Harbor Dr.
Hobe Sound 407 546 3660

Marine Industries Assn.
of Palm Beach County
PO Box 12661, Zip:33403
West Palm Bch. 407-642-9092
See advertisement on page 142.

Palm Beach Yacht Club
& Marina
800 N. Flagler Dr.
West Palm Bch. 407-655-1944

Norine Rouse Scuba Club
4708 N. Dixie Hwy.
W. Palm Bch. 407-844-2466

Stuart Sailfish Club
Stuart 407-286-9373

BROWARD COUNTY

Lauderdale Small Boat Club
1740 SW 42nd St.
Ft. Lauderdale 954-359-7659

Marine Industries Assn.
of South Florida
2312 S. Andrews Ave.
Ft. Lauderdale 954-524-2733

World Yacht Club
2698 SW 23rd Ave.
Ft. Lauderdale 954-587-3387
1-800-45-FLOAT

DADE COUNTY

Eastern Shores Yacht Club
251 174th St. Apt. 1205
Miami Bch. 305-932-0856

Jockey Club
11111 Biscayne Blvd.
Miami 305-893-3344

Turnberry Isle Resort & Club
19755 NE 36th Ct.
Aventura 305-932-6200
See advertisement on page 68.

KEYS

Marathon Intnl. Bonefish
Tournament Club
POB 2509
Marathon Shores 33050

Marathon Yacht Club
825 33rd St. Gulf
Marathon 305-743-6739

ENGLEWOOD TO SKYWAY

Bradenton Yacht Club
4307 Snead Island Rd.
Palmetto 941-748-7930

Florida Assoc. of Canoe
Liveries & Outfitters
PO Box 1764
Arcadia

SKYWAY TO TARPON SPRINGS

Boat Club of America III
26 Madonna Blvd.
Tierra Verde 813-866-0068

Clearwater Yacht Club
830 Bayway Blvd.
Clearwater Beach 813-447-6000

Harbour Island Marina
777 S. Harbour Isl. Blvd. #270
Tampa 813-229-5324

St. Petersburg Yacht Club
St. Petersburg 813-822-3873

Stouffer Vinoy Resort's
Vinoy Club
501 5th Ave. NE
St. Petersburg 813-894-1000
See ad on page 115.

Tierra Verde Yacht Club
Tierra Verde 813-864-3490

VIP Boat Club
343 Causeway Blvd.
Dunedin 813 734 5969

NORTHWEST

Fort Walton Bch. Yacht Club
Yacht Club Drive
Fort Walton Bch. 904 243 7102

Grand Lagoon Yacht Club
10603 Gulf Beach Hwy.
Pensacola 904 492 0255

Marine Industries Association
of Florida
PO Box 172
Tallahassee, 32302
904-668-5665

Pensacola Yacht Club
Bayou Chico
Pensacola 904-433-8804

St. Andrews Bay Yacht Club
Panama City 904-433-8804

CNG FUELS/ PROPANE

BAHAMAS

Lucayan Marina Village
PO Box F-42654
Freeport, Grand Bahama
809 373 8888
See advertisement on page 27.

FIRST COAST & ST. JOHNS

Mobile Gas Co.
Jacksonville 904-733-9533

Shaws Yacht Brokerage
& Marine Supply
728 Ballough Rd.
Daytona Bch. 904-255-0495

Stuart Marine
St. Augustine 904-824-1601

INDIAN RIVER LAGOON

Banana River Marine Service
1360 S. Banana River Drive
Merritt Island 407-452-8622
See advertisement on page 45.

CNG FUELS/PROPANE

STUART TO BOCA RATON

C. Foster Marine Supplies
3385 SE Dixie Hwy.
Stuart 407-286-2118

Palm Harbor Marina
400-A N. Flagler Dr.
West Palm Bch. 407-655-4757
See advertisement on page 66.

BROWARD COUNTY

Boye's Gas Service
404 N. Federal Hwy.
Ft. Lauderdale 954 763 4545

Lauderdale Marina
1900 SE 15th St.
Ft. Lauderdale 954-523-8507
See advertisement on page 59.

Marine Hardware
& Equipment
1530 N. Federal Hwy.
Pompano Bch. 954-782-2280

DADE COUNTY

Miami Beach Marina
300 Alton Rd.
Miami Bch. 305-673-6000
See advertisement on page 1.

KEYS

Key West Marine Hardware
818 Caroline St.
Key West 305-294-3425
See advertisement on page 89.

Marathon Boat Yard
2055 Overseas Hwy.
Marathon 305-743-6341

Marathon Marina
1021 11th St. Oceanside
Marathon 305-743-6595

Mid Keys Marine Supply
2055 Overseas Hwy.
Marathon 305-743-6020

Perkins & Son
901 Fleming
Key West 305-296-7075

Tugboat's
2211 Overseas Hwy.
Marathon 305-743-4585

MARCO ISLAND TO PLACIDA

Atlantis Yacht Corp.
Punta Gorda 941-332-5552

Fort Myers Yacht Basin
1300 Lee St.
Ft. Myers 941-334-8271
See advertisement on page 103.

Palm Grove Marina
2500 Main St.
Ft. Myers Bch. 941-463-7333

Turner Marine of Naples
899 10th St. S.
Naples 941-262-5973
See advertisement on page 98.

ENGLEWOOD TO SKYWAY

Gaspar Marine Supplies
Englewood 941-697-2556

Marina Operations
at Marina Jack's
Sarasota 941-955-9488

SKYWAY TO TARPON SPRINGS

Marina Point Ship's Store
500 1st Ave. SE.
St. Petersburg 813-823 2555

Pass-A-Grille Bait & Tackle
801 Pass-A-Grille Way
St. Petersburg Bch. 813 360 6606

Ross Yacht Service
279 Windward Passage
Clearwater 813-446-8191

Sigma Marine Supply
950 Roosevelt Ave.
Tarpon Springs 813-934-0794

NORTHWEST

J. V. Gander
319 Water St.
Apalachicola 904-653-8889

Miller Marine
119 Water St.
Apalachicola 904-653-9521
See advertisement on page 128.

Miller's Marina
PO Box 280
Suwannee 352-542-7349
See Advertisement on page 123.

Rod & Reel Marina
10045 Sinton Dr.
Pensacola 904-492-0100
See Advertisement on page 135.

COMPASS ADJUSTING

INDIAN RIVER LAGOON

Morelco Marine Electronics
1432 N. Harbor City Blvd.
Melbourne 407-254-8855

STUART TO BOCA RATON

E&H Boat Works
2180 Idlewilde Rd.
Palm Bch. Gdns. 407-622-8550

BROWARD COUNTY

Bee Marine Service
234 SW 30th St.
Ft. Lauderdale 954-467-3911

Magnetic Compass Co.
1011 Arizona Ave.
Ft. Lauderdale 954-584-3833

DADE COUNTY

American Nautical Services
Navigation Center
254 NE 4th St.
Miami 305-358-1414

KEYS

Cayo Hueso Ship's Store
2318 N. Roosevelt Blvd.
Key West 305-294-1365

Maritime Mart
5800 Overseas Hwy.
Marathon 305-743-3321

MARCO ISLAND TO PLACIDA

Nautical Service Technologies
Ste. 202, 3798 Tamiami Trail N.
Naples 941-263-8246

ENGLEWOOD TO SKYWAY

Galati Perico Harbor Marina
12310 Manatee Ave. West
Bradenton 941-795-2628

SKYWAY TO TARPON SPRINGS

C&R Marine
3671 131 Ave. N.
Clearwater 813-573-9105

HWH Electronics
4215 Gulf Blvd.
St. Petersburg 813-367-2754

CUSTOMIZERS, CUSTOM FABRICATIONS

FIRST COAST & ST. JOHNS

Custom Marine Components
1884 Mealy St.
Atlantic Bch. 904-247-1880

Daytona Marina & Boat Works
645 South Beach St.
Daytona Bch. 904-252-6421

Coquina Marina
256 Riberia St.
St. Augustine 904-824-2520

St. Augustine Marine
404 S. Riberia St.
St. Augustine 904-824-4394
See advertisement on page 37.

INDIAN RIVER LAGOON

Seabrite Stainless
424 S. DeLeon Ave.
Titusville 407-269-7812

STUART TO BOCA RATON

Beachcomber Fiberglass Tech.
2850 SE Market Pl.
Stuart 407-283-0200

Birdsall Marine Design
4521 Georgia Ave.
West Palm Bch. 407-369-0686

Bluewater Towers
1240 W. Industrial Ave.
Boynton Bch. 407-369-0686

Diesel Mechanics Co-op
2628 NW 2nd Ave.
Boca Raton 407-391-8143

High Seas Fabrication
272 N. Flagler Ave.
Stuart 407 692 0000

Maritime Lumber Supply
2393 SE Dixie Hwy.
Stuart 407-287-2919

Whiticar Boat Works
3636 SE Old St. Lucie Blvd.
Stuart 407-287-2883
See advertisement on page 54.

BROWARD COUNTY

Atkinson Marine
235 SW 32nd Ct.
Ft. Lauderdale 954-763-1652

John P. Downs Company
800 Old Griffin Rd.
Dania 954-921-0800

Hanlon & Wilson Co.
2881 NE 7th Ave.
Pompano Bch. 954-942-8321

Marine Welding &Fabricating
241 S. W. 31st St.
Ft. Lauderdale 954 525 0348

PipeWelders Marine,
2965 State Rd. 84
Ft. Lauderdale 954-587-8400

KEYS

Marathon Boat Yard
2055 Overseas Hwy.
Marathon 305-743-6341

MARCO ISLAND TO PLACIDA

All Marine
4008 Wholesale G. NW
North Ft. Myers 941-995-7990

Owl Creek Boat Works
18251 Owl Creek Dr.
Alva 941-543-2100

Seaworthy Towers & Marine
4427 Mercantile Ave.
Naples 941-643-0199

SKYWAY TO TARPON SPRINGS

Flaherty Marine
761 Anclote Rd.
Tarpon Springs 813-934-9394

Wood Company
4161 118th Ave. N.
Clearwater 813-573-3611
1-800-288-3611

NORTHWEST

Deckhand's Marina
1350 Miracle Strip Pkwy.
Ft. Walton Bch. 904-243-7359
See advertisement on page 132.

J.J.'s Marine Service
2505 Thomas Dr.
Panama City 904-234-8048

Marshall Marine Ways
Timber Island Rd.
Carrabelle 904-697-3428
See advertisement on page 127.

Passport Marina & Boat Yard
5325 N. Lagoon Dr.
Panama City 904-234-5609

DEALERS, POWERBOATS

FIRST COAST & ST. JOHNS

Advance Marine
9451 Craven Rd.
Jacksonville 904 730 3332

The Boat Show
2999 SR 44 West
Deland 904-736-6601

Daytona Marina & Boat Works
645 S. Beach St.
Daytona Bch. 904-252-6421

Eagle Yachts,
721 Ballough Rd.
Daytona Bch. 904-258-7578

First Coast Marine
2100 Florida Blvd.
Neptune Bch 904-246-1614

Florida Watercraft
177 North Cswy.
New Smyrna Bch. 904-426-2628

Gerry's Marina
157 N. Causeway
New Smyrna Bch. 904-428-2341

Hontoon Marina
2728 W. Hwy. 44
Deland 904-734-4301

Jacksonville Yacht Basin
14603 Beach Blvd.
Jacksonville Bch. 904-223-4511

Julington Creek Marina
12807 San Jose Blvd.
Jacksonville 904 268 5117

Killarney Boat Center
750 N. US 17-92
Longwood 407-830-9985

Offshore Yacht & Ship Bkrs.
404 Riberia St.
St. Augustine 904-829-9224

Pablo Creek Marina
13846 Atlantic Blvd.
Jacksonville 904-221-4228

Pete Loftin's Outboard Inc.
6424 Arlington Exp.
Jacksonville 904-724-1400

Pier 68
8137 N. Main St.
Jacksonville 904 765 9925

INDIAN RIVER LAGOON

Boatland
125 Fisherman's Wharf
Ft. Pierce 407-465-8800
703 S. US 1
Melbourne 407-984-8800

Boats 'n Motors
4676 N. U.S. 1
Vero Bch. 407-562-5943

Brevard Marine Service,
150 E. Merritt Island Cswy.
Merritt Island 407-452-8250

Casa Rio
1050 N. E. Dixie Hwy.
Jensen Beach 407 334 0944

Complete Yacht Services
3599 E. Indian River Dr.
Vero Beach 407-231-2111

Indian Harbour Marina
1399 Banana River Dr.
Indian Harb. Bch. 407-773-2468

Miner's Marina
8685 N. US 1
Sebastian 407-664-8500

St. Lucie Outboard Marine
3312 Orange Ave.
Ft. Pierce 407-464-1440

Taylor Creek Marina
1600 N 2nd St.
Ft. Pierce 407-465-2663

Harbor Yacht Sales & Charters
2210 S. Front St.
Melbourne 407-729-8400

Vero Marine Center
12 Royal Palm Blvd.
Vero Bch. 407-562-7922

Winter Park Marine
1031 S. Orlando Ave.
Winter Park 407-647-6262

STUART TO BOCA RATON

Allied Marine Group
260 N. Federal Hwy.
Stuart 407 692 1123
2401 PGA Blvd.
Palm Bch. Gdns. 407 775 3531

Basset Boat Company
1050 N. E. Dixie Highway
Jensen Beach 407 334 0999

Boatland
290 N. Federal Hwy.
Stuart 407-692-2900

Casa Rio Boat & Motor Sales
1050 NE Dixie Hwy.
Jensen Bch. 407-334-0944

Coastal Marine
705 SE Monterey Road
Stuart 407-283-7733

Power Plus Marine
5400 S. Dixie Hwy.
W. Palm Bch. 407 588 7088

Stuart Cay Marina
290 N. Federal Hwy.
Stuart 407-692-9511

Ocean Yachts of Palm Bch.
1200 US 1
N. Palm Bch. 407-627-0100

Stuart Hatteras
110 N Federal Hwy.
Stuart 407-692-1122

Stuart Yacht
450 SW Salerno Rd.
Stuart 407-283-1947
See advertisement on page 53.

BROWARD COUNTY

Alexander Yachts
2150 SE 17th St.
Ft. Lauderdale 954-763-7676

Allied Marine Group
1445 S.E. 16th St.
Ft. Lauderdale 954 462 5527

Angler's Boat Center
7390 State Road 84
Ft. Lauderdale 954-475-9024

Bassett Boat Co. of Florida
700 S. Federal Hwy.
Pompano Bch. 954-783-9555

Boat Center
1771 S State Road 7
Ft. Lauderdale 954-581-4300

Boat Fair
301 SW 7th Ave.
Ft. Lauderdale 954-463-6432

Cozy Cove Marina
300 N Federal Hwy.
Dania 954-921-8800

Everglades Marina
1801 SE 17th St.
Ft. Lauderdale 954-763-3030

Hal Jones & Co.
1900 SE 15th St.
Ft. Lauderdale 954-527-1778

Lauderdale Marina
1900 SE 15th St.
Ft. Lauderdale 954-523-8507
See advertisement on page 59.

Mullers Boat & Yacht Sales
2501 So. Federal Hwy.
Ft. Lauderdale, 954 763 3823

Ocean Yachts of South Florida
1535 SE 17th St.
Ft. Lauderdale 954-522-5843

Paigo Brothers Marine
3000 State Road 84
Ft. Lauderdale 954-587-6400

Pompano Beach Marine Center
701 S Federal Hwy.
Pompano Bch. 954-946-1450

Walsh Yachts
1900 SE 15th St.
Ft. Lauderdale 954-525-7447

DADE COUNTY

Allied Marine Group
2550 S. Bayshore Dr.
Coconut Grove 305 854 1100

Bayflite Marine
17800 Biscayne Blvd.
North Miami 305-935-3521

Fisherman's Paradise
2727 NW 38th St.
Miami 305-635-2445,
3800 NW 27th Ave.
Miami 305-634-1578

Bob Hewes Boats
12565 NW 7th Ave.
North Miami 305-681-6602

Hi-Lift Marina
2890 NE 187th St.
North Miami Bch. 305-931-2550

Johnson-Kirby
5566 S Dixie Hwy.
South Miami 305-666-1806

Langer's Marine
520 West Ave.
Miami Bch. 305-672-2227

KEYS

The Boat House
12411 Overseas Hwy.
Marathon 305-289-1323

Caribee Boat Sales & Storage
Islamorada 305-664-3431

Duck Key Marina
Duck Key 305-289-0161

Inflatable Boats
of the Florida Keys
2601 Overseas Hwy.
Marathon 305-743-7085

Italian Fisherman Marina
MM103 Overseas Hwy.
Key Largo 305-451-3726

Key Largo Harbour
100 Ocean Dr.
Key Largo 305-451-0045

Keys Sea Center Inc.
Big Pine Key 305-872-2243

Perdue-Dean Co. Inc.
Ocean Reef, 2 Fishing Vlg. Dr.
Key Largo 305-367-2661,

Plantation Key Marina
MM 90.5 US 1
Plantation Key 305-852-5424

MARCO ISLAND TO PLACIDA

Allied Marine Group
895 10th St. So.
Naples 941 262 6500

Bonita Boat Center
27760 Tamiami Trail SW
Bonita Springs 941-992-5777

Boat Haven Naples Inc.
1484 5th Ave S.
Naples 941-774-0339

Fish Tale Marina
7225 Estero Blvd.
Ft. Myers Bch. 941-463-4448

Fort Myers Beach Marina
703 Fisherman's Wharf
Ft. Myers Bch 941 463 9557

Gulf Liner Marine
Fisherman's Wharf & Marina
601 N. Tamiami Tr.
Venice 941-488-5150

Ireland Yacht Sales
14025 S. Tamiami Trail
Ft. Myers 941 433 2111
634 N. Yachtsman
Sanibel 941 472 2723

Ingman Marine
1189 Tamiami Trail
Port Charlotte 941 255 1555

Sea Horse Marina
4999 Tamiami Trail
Charlotte Harbor 941 624 6600

Jack's Marine South
2200 Marine Park Dr.
Ft. Myers 941-694-2708

ENGLEWOOD TO SKYWAY

Chuck's Marina
1990 Placida Rd.
Englewood 941-474-4284

Five O'clock Marine
412 Pine Ave.
Anna Maria Island 941 778 5577

Gulfwind Marine
at Perico Harbor
11911 Manatee Ave. W.
Bradenton 941-795-2628
1485 S. Tamiami Trail
Venice 941-485-3388

Holmes Beach Marina
202 52nd St.
Homes Bch. 941-778-2255

Offshore Marine Inc.
302 N. Orange Ave.
Sarasota 941 951 0099

Osprey Marine Center
480 Blackburn Pt. Rd.
Osprey 941-966-5657

Shark's Tooth Marine
115 N. US 41 By-Pass
Venice 941 486 0112

Sunshine Marine
3225 Placida Rd.
Englewood 941 698 1616

Stump Pass Marina
3060 Placida Rd.
Englewood 941-697-3600

Venice Boat Sales
505 S. Tamiami Trail
Nokomis 941 488 7884

DEALERS, POWERBOATS

SKYWAY TO TARPON SPRINGS

Bahia Beach Island Resort
Harbormaster Yachts
611 Destiny Dr.
Ruskin 813-645-9269
See advertisement on page 117.

Capt. Hubbard's Marina
150 - 128th Ave.
Madeira Beach 813 393 1947

Gulf Coast Yacht Sales
1260 US 19 S.
Clearwater 813-536-7999

Gulfwind Marine
1665 US 19 South
Clearwater 813-536-9489

Harborage at Bayboro
1110 3rd St. South
St. Petersburg 813 821 6347
See Advertisement on page 116.

John's Pass Marina
12795 Kingfish Dr.
Treasure Island 813-360-6907

Kenyon Power Boats
19400 US 19 N.
Clearwater 813 539 7444

Mariner Yacht Sales
Gandy Blvd.
St. Petersburg 813-576-3307

O'Neill's Marina
No. end of Skyway
St. Petersburg 813 867 2585

R & M Marine
5980 66th St. N.
St. Petersburg 813 544 3975

Ross Yacht Service
279 Windward Passage
Clearwater 813-446-8191

Stoller Marine
12126 1st Ave. So.
St. Petersburg 813 821 4676

Tampa Boat Mart
3431 Henderson Blvd.
Tampa 813-877-1273

NORTHWEST

Aquatic Enterprises
1201A Hwy. Miracle Strip E.
Ft. Walton Beach 904-243-5721

Auer Marine
33 Beal Pkwy.
Ft. Walton Bch. 904-243-7163

Boats 'n Motors
2453 W. Tennessee St.
Tallahassee 904-576-2171

Baytowne Marina at Sandestin
5500 Hwy. 98 E.
Destin 904-267-7777
See advertisement on page 133.

Coastmarine
230 Eglin Pkwy. SE.
Ft. Walton Beach 904 244 3333
Holiday Harbor Marina
Perdido Key 904-492-4500
Thomas Dr.
Panama City Bch. 904-233-1300

Crystal River Marine
990 N. Suncoast Blvd.
Crystal River 904-795-2597

Economy Marine
6205 North 'W' St.
Pensacola 904-479-2447

Holiday Harbor Marina
14050 Canal-a-Way
Pensacola 904-492-0555

Hudson Marine Corp.
9 Marina Dr.
Ft. Walton 904-862-3165

Killinger Marine
6015 N. Old Palafox Hwy.
Pensacola 904-477-1112

Marquardt's Marina
Hwy. 98
Mexico Beach 904-648-8900

Riverhaven Marina
490 West
Homosassa Spgs. 352-628-5545

Sailfish Boat Sales
3009 Barrancas Ave.
Pensacola 904-457-1493

Sandpiper Yacht Sales
600 S. Barracks St. Ste. 102
Pensacola 904-434-0050

Shalimar Yacht Basin
PO Box 189, Zip: 32579
Shalimar 904 651 0510
See Advertisement on Page 131.

Treasure Island Marina
3605 Thomas Dr.
Panama City Bch. 904-234-6533

DEALERS, SAILBOATS

FIRST COAST & ST. JOHNS

Ortega Yacht Sales
3420 Lakeshore Blvd.
Jacksonville 904-388-5547

Ortega River Boat Yard
4451 Herschel St.
Jacksonville 904-387-5538

St. Augustine Yacht Sales
Camachee Cove
St. Augustine 904-829-2294

Whitney Sail Center
3027 US Hwy 17 South
Orange Park 904-269-0027

INDIAN RIVER LAGOON

Barrett & Sons Sailing Center
4503 N. Orange Blossom Trail
Orlando 407-295-0117

Diamond 99 Marina
& Yacht Sales
4399 N Harbor City Blvd.
Melbourne 407-254-1490

Indian Cove Marina
14 Myrtice Ave.
Merritt Island 407-452-8540

Whitley Marine
93 Delannoy Ave.
Cocoa 407-632-5445
See advertisement on page 45.

STUART TO BOCA RATON

Eastern Yacht Sales
1177 Ave. C
Riviera Bch. 407-844-1100

BROWARD COUNTY

Cabo Rico Yachts
2258 S. E. 17th St.
Ft. Lauderdale 954 462 6699

Rex Yacht Sales
2152 SE 17th St.
Ft. Lauderdale 954-463-8810

Spinnaker Cay
1500 Cordova Rd.
Ft. Lauderdale 954-525-6397

Summerfield Boat Works
1500 SW 17th St.
Ft. Lauderdale 954-525-4726

DADE COUNTY

Florida Yacht Charters & Sales
1290 5th St.
Miami Bch. 305-532-8600

KEYS

Lime Tree Bay Sailboats
Long Key 305-664-4256

New Wave Marine
82883 US 1
Islamorada 305-664-5526

MARCO ISLAND TO PLACIDA

Boat Mart
US 41 at Midway
Port Charlotte 941-743-7040

SKYWAY TO TARPON SPRINGS

Mariner Yachts
Gandy Blvd.
St. Petersburg 813-576-3307

Marine Concepts
Alt. 19 N. of Anclote River
Tarpon Springs 800 881 1525

Ross Yacht Service
279 Windward Passage
Clearwater 813-446-8191

Sail, Inc.
607 N. Ft. Harrison
Clearwater 813-447-1814

Sailor's Wharf
1421 Bay St. S.E.
St. Petersburg 813 879 2244

NORTHWEST

Keys Sailing
500 Quietwater Bch. Rd. #14B
Pensacola 904-932-5520

Ahoy Yachts
32 Miracle Strip Pkwy. SW
Destin 904-244-2722

Odyssey Sales
3009 Barracuda Ave.
Pensacola 904 453 8863

Sailors Supply Co.
231 E. Beach Dr.
Panama City 904-769-5007

DESIGNERS, INTERIOR

FIRST COAST & ST. JOHNS

Daytona Marina & Boat Works
645 S. Beach St.
Daytona Bch. 904-252-6421

Oceanic Designs
100 S. Beach St.
Daytona Bch. 904-258-6061

Sea Love Boatworks
4877 Front St.
Ponce Inlet 904-761-5434

STUART TO BOCA RATON

Bernard's Carpet & Draperies
200 US 1
Juno Bch. 407-626-1110

Dalton Designs
2480 PGA Blvd.
Palm Bch. Gardens
407-622-6299

Home Works & Boat Works
4340 SE Commerce Ave.
Stuart 407-286-5967

Rowell Interiors
4343 SE US 1
Stuart 407-283-6390

BROWARD COUNTY

Broward Interiors
515 SW 1st Ave.
Ft. Lauderdale 954-764-1118

Harrill House International
428 NE 3rd Ave.
Ft. Lauderdale 954-761-3624

IKD Yacht Interior Design
850 N. E. 3rd St. Suite 113
Dania 954 922 9220

Plachter Interior Design
1263 E. Las Olas Blvd.
Ft. Lauderdale 954-524-9070

Puleo, Inc.
2101 S. Andrews Ave.
Ft. Lauderdale 954-522-0173

True's Marine Glass & Mirror
101 S. W. 15th St.
Ft. Lauderdale 954 467 7005

Yacht Interiors by Shelley
2050 S. Federal Hwy.
Ft. Lauderdale 954 525 3111

MARCO TO PLACIDA

Dockside Interiors
340 Tamiami Trail North
Naples 941-262-7943

ENGLEWOOD TO SKYWAY

The Yacht Boutique
1303 Main Street
Sarasota 941-364-8222

DESIGNERS, YACHT & NAVAL ARCHITECTS

FIRST COAST & ST. JOHNS

Huckins Yacht Corp.
3482 Lakeshore Blvd.
Jacksonville 904-389-1125

St. Augustine Marine
404 S. Riberia St.
St. Augustine 904-824-4394
See advertisement on page 37.

Treworgy Yachts
5658 N. Oceanshore Blvd.
Palm Coast 904-445-5878

STUART TO BOCA RATON

Coyle Yacht Design
188 Alice Ave.
Jensen Bch. 407-692-0454

Stuart Yacht
450 SW Salerno Rd.
Stuart 407-283-1947
See advertisement on page 53.

BROWARD COUNTY

Gries Marine Technology
2170 SE 17th St. #307
Ft. Lauderdale 305-467-2940

DADE COUNTY

Richard C. Cole
19701 Whispering Pines Rd.
Miami 305-255-3863

MARCO ISLAND TO PLACIDA

Tradewinds Yacht Design
8595 Redwood Drive
St. James City 941 283 3403

SKYWAY TO TARPON SPRINGS

Glen Henderson Yacht Design
14231 60th St. N.
Clearwater 813-530-4277

Charles Morgan Associates
200 2nd Ave. S.
St. Petersburg 813-894-7027

DIVE BOATS, DIVE SHOPS, DIVERS

BAHAMAS
(Also see Bahamas Marinas)

Brendal's Dive Shop
Green Turtle Cay
809 365 4411

Green Turtle Club
Green Turtle Cay
809-365-4271
See advertisement on page 26.

Man-O-War Marina
Man-O-War Cay
809-365-6998

FIRST COAST & ST. JOHNS

Adventure Divers
3127 S. Ridgewood Ave.
Daytona Bch. 904-788-8050

American Divers
6255 Merrill Rd.
Jacksonville 904-743-7234

First Coast Divers
St. Augustine Rd.
Mandarin 904-260-0422

Florida Watercraft
177 North Cswy.
New Smyrna Bch. 904-426-2628

Mayport Marine
4852 Mayport Rd.
Jacksonville 904-246-8929

Scuba World
1941 S. Woodland Blvd.
Deland 904-734-3483

INDIAN RIVER LAGOON

Deep Six Dive & Watersports
416 Miracle Mile
Vero Bch. 407-562-2891

Dive Center
1716 N. US 1
Sebastian 407-589-4500

Dixie Divers
1717 S. US 1
Ft. Pierce 407-451-4488

Hatt's Diving Headquarters
2006 Front St.
Melbourne 407-723-5932

Scuba Shack
2485 NE Dixie Hwy.
Jensen Bch. 407-334-8808

Under Sea World
521 N. US 1
Ft. Pierce 407-465-4114

STUART TO BOCA RATON

Adventure Scuba
150 N. US 1
Tequesta 407-746-1555

American Dive Center
1888 N. W. 2nd Ave.
Boca Raton 407 393 0621

Dixie Divers
1843 SE Federal Hwy.
Stuart 407-283-5588

Frank's Dive Shop
301 E. Blue Heron Blvd.
Riviera Bch. 407-848-7632

Reef Dive Shop
304 E Ocean Ave.
Lantana 407-585-1425

Seafari Dive & Surf
75 E. Indiantown Rd. #603
Jupiter 407 747 6115

Sub-Sea Aquatics
at Seagate Marina
18701 SE Federal Hwy.
Jupiter 407-744-6674

BROWARD COUNTY

Adventure Divers
923 SE 20th St.
Ft. Lauderdale 954-523-8354

Aquatic Divers
1327 S. Federal Hwy.
Dania 954-920-7627

Blue Water Scuba
5846 Stirling Rd.
Hollywood 954 967 6529

Divers' Den
2333 S. University Dr.
Ft. Lauderdale 954 473 9455

Divers' Haven
1530 Cordova Rd.
Ft. Lauderdale 954-524-2112

Divers Unlimited
6023 Hollywood Blvd.
Hollywood 954-981-0156

Mrs. G. Diving
6536 Flagler St.
Hollywood 954-983-1998
(Commercial)

Lauderdale Diver
1334 SE 17th St.
Ft. Lauderdale 954-467-2822

Pro Dive
Bahia Mar
Ft. Lauderdale 954-761-3413

U. S. #1 Scuba
15 N. Federal Hwy.
Pompano Beach 954 946 6055

DADE COUNTY

Crandon Park Marina
4000 Collins Ave.
Key Biscayne 305 361 1281
See advertisement on page 73.

Divers' Den
12614 N. Kendall Dr.
Miami 305-595-3483

Miami Beach Marina
300 Alton Rd.
Miami Beach 305-673-6000
See advertisement on page 1.

Sunset Harbour Marina
1928 Purdy Ave.
Miami Bch. 305-673-0044

KEYS

Admiral Dive
MM 103
Key Largo 305-451-1114

Atlantis Marina Dive Shop
MM 68.5
Long Key 305-665-5180

Buccaneer Resort Hotel
2600 Overseas Hwy.
Marathon 305-743-9071
1-800-237-3329

Cudjoe Gardens Marina
802 Drost Dr. MM 21
Cudjoe Key 305-745-2357

Divers' Den
102965 Overseas Hwy.
Key Largo 305 451 3483

Divers World
MM 99.5
Key Largo 305-451-3200

The Diving Site
MM 53.5
Marathon 305-289-1021

Key West Oceanside Marina
5950 Maloney Ave.
Key West 305-294-4676

Lady Cyana Divers
MM 85.9
Islamorada 305-664-8717

Looe Key Dive Center
MM 27
Ramrod Key 305-872-2215

Ocean Quest
87000 Overseas Hwy.
Islamorada 305-852-8770

Pelican Landing Resort & Marina
915 Eisenhower Dr.
Key West 305-296-7583

Pinellas Marina
1200 Ocean Ave.
Marathon 305-743-5317

Quiesence Diving Services
MM 103.5
Key Largo 305-451-2440

Reef Raiders
109 Duval St.
Key West 305-294-3635
US 1, Stock Island
Key West 305-294-0660
Galleon Marina
Key West 305-294-0442

Sea Dwellers Sports Center
MM 100
Key Largo 305-451-3640

Underseas
MM 30.5
Big Pine Key 305-872-2700

MARCO ISLAND TO PLACIDA

ABC Sports
1915 Linhart Ave.
Ft. Myers 941-334-4616

Del Rey Divers (East)
Naples 941-263-2319

Dolphin World
2671 Edison Ave. Ste #1
Ft. Myers 800 945 5521

Factory Bay Marina
1079 Bald Eagle Dr.
Marco Island 941-642-6717

The Dive Station
15065 McGregor Blvd.
Ft. Myers 941-489-1234

Pieces of Eight Dive Center
Captiva 941-472-9424

South Seas Plantation Resort
Captiva Island 941-472-5111

ENGLEWOOD TO SKYWAY

Aqua Sports
2401-D Tamiami Tr.
Port Charlotte 941-627-3454

Coral Kings Pro Dive Shop
5770 S.Tamiami Tr.
Sarasota 941-922-3338

Sea Trek Divers
7014 Cortez Rd. W.
Bradenton 941-753-3483

SKYWAY TO TARPON SPRINGS

Boat Club of America III
26 Madonna Blvd.
Tierra Verde 813-866-0068

Dan's Scuba School
1754 Drew St.
Clearwater 813-446-8275

Scuba World of Tampa
7010 Sheldon Rd.
Tampa 813-887-1089

Sports Unlimited
4545 W. Hillsborough Ave.
Tampa 813-886-0591

Treasure Island Divers
111 108th Ave.
Treasure Island 813-360-6669

NORTHWEST

Aquanaut
24 Hwy. 98
Destin 904-837-0359

Blue Dolphins
363 Brooks St. SE
Ft. Walton Bch 904-243-6212

Captain Black's Marine
Port St. Joe 904-229-6330

Crystal Lodge Dive Center
US 19 North
Crystal River 352-795-6798

Dive Mart
5501 Duval St.
Pensacola 904-479-3456

Diver's Den
4720 E. Bus. Hwy. 98
Panama City 1-800-272-4777

Fantasea Scuba
1 Hwy. 98
Destin 904-837-0732

Holiday Scuba Center
5505 W. Hwy. 98
Panama City 904-769-7482

Miller Marine
119 Water St.
Apalachicola 904-653-9521
See advertisement on page 128.

Port Paradise Dive Center
1610 SE Paradise Cir.
Crystal River 352-795-7437

Scuba Den
3375 Shoal Line Blvd.
Hernando Bch. 352-596-3365

EDUCATION

Scuba Shack
719 S. Palafox
Pensacola 904-433-4319

Snorkeling Adventures
Hwy. 98
Destin 904-837-9029

Treasure Island Marina
3605 Thomas Dr.
Panama City Bch. 904-234-6533

DOCUMENTATION

FIRST COAST & ST. JOHNS

Peggy Vann
Yacht Documentation
8139 Chimney Oak Dr.
Jacksonville 904-778-1309

INDIAN RIVER LAGOON

Sharon Netzley
Satellite Bch. 407-777-4083

STUART TO BOCA RATON

Lance Marine Documentation
1616 Crandon Ave.
West Palm Bch. 407 844 2287

BROWARD COUNTY

Jan Saxton Yacht
Documentation
1525 S. Andrews Ave.
Ft. Lauderdale 954-764-6702

Silverado International, Inc.
1975 E. Sunrise Blvd.
Ft. Lauderdale 954-462-1401

DADE COUNTY

SeaVeyors
695 NE 123 St.
N. Miami 305-891-2120

SKYWAY TO TARPON SPRINGS

Gloria Rector
Vessel Documentation
Brandon 813-689-5140

Specialized Yacht Services
9300 5th St. N.
St. Petersburg 813-577-6100

NORTHWEST

Hathaway Landings Marina
6426 W. Hwy. 98
Panama City Bch 904 234 0609

West Florida Vessel
Documentation
1324 N. Z St.
Pensacola 904-433-8870

EDUCATION

FIRST COAST & ST. JOHNS

American Marine Institute
3042 W. Intnl. Speedway Blvd.
Daytona Bch. 904-255-0295

Cleveland Ski School
Rt. 3, Box 66
Hawthorne 352-481-2152

EDUCATION

Sail Amelia Sailing School
5 N. 6th St.
Fernandina Bch. 904-261-9125

St. Augustine Sailing
3040 Harbor Dr.
St. Augustine 904-829-2294

INDIAN RIVER LAGOON

Diamond 99 Marina
4399 N. US 1
Melbourne 407-254-1490

Marine Mechanics Institute
9751 Delegates Drive
Orlando 407 240 2422

Maritime & Yachting Museum
9801 S. Ocean Blvd.
Jensen Beach 407 334 7733

STUART TO BOCA RATON

Chapman School of Seamanship
4343 SE St. Lucie Blvd.
Stuart 800 225 2841

Palm Beach Maritime
 Training Center
636 US 1, #107
N. Palm Bch. 407-881-5590

BROWARD COUNTY

Boat Handling Co.
629 NE 3rd St.
Dania 954-975-7633

Institute of Marine Science
1428 SW 12th Ave.
Pompano Bch. 954-943-5875

Maritime Professional
1921 S. Andrews Ave.
Fort Lauderdale 954 525 1014

Nova University
3301 College Ave.
Ft. Lauderdale 954-475-7417

On-Board Boating Academy
Capt. Bob Armstrong
850 N. E. 3rd St. #204
Dania 954 927 9800

Sea School
712 SE 17th St.
Ft. Lauderdale 954-463-7001

Southeast Yachting School &
Charters
2170 SE 17th St. #304
Ft. Lauderdale 954-523-2628

World Yacht Club
2698 SW 23rd Ave.
Ft. Lauderdale 954-587-3387

DADE COUNTY

Florida Detroit Diesel-Allison
2277 NW 14th St.
Miami 305-634-3541

Houston Marine Training Center
2560 S. Bayshore Dr.
Coconut Grove 305-858-4674

KEYS

Florida Keys Sailing School
l85944 US Hwy. 1
Islamorada 305-664-4009

MARCO ISLAND TO PLACIDA

Houston Marine Training Ctr.
3106 Tamiami Tr., N.
Naples 941-261-6824

Maritime Services Group
P. O. Box 8989
Naples 941 262 5159

National Women's Sail. Club
P.O. Box 08044
Ft. Myers 800 566 6972

NAVTECH
13430 McGregor
Ft. Myers 1-800-245-4425

ENGLEWOOD TO SKYWAY

Club Carib
Regatta Pointe Marina
Palmetto 941-723-1610

O'Leary's Sailing School
Island Park - Bayfront
Sarasota 941-953-7505

Women for Sail
5181 Hidden Harbor Rd.
Sarasota 1-800-346-6404

SKYWAY TO TARPON SPRINGS

Annapolis Sailing School
6800 Sunshine Skyway Lane
St. Petersburg 800 638 9192

Sea School
3770 16th St. N
St. Petersburg 813-577-3992

NORTHWEST

Apalachicola Maritime Inst.
PO Box 625
Apalachicola 904-653-8708

Cleveland Ski School & Training
Route 3 Box 66
Hawthorne 352-481-2152

Houston Marine Training Ctr.
301 Hwy. 98
Destin 904-654-1616
 5514 N. Davis Hwy. Suite 112
Pensacola 904-474-1577

Sea School (Panama City)
2015 W. Hwy. 98
Panama City 904-871-4662

ELECTRONICS: SALES & SERVICE

FIRST COAST & ST. JOHNS

Barnaclean/The Clean Seas Co.
1301 Riverplace Blvd. Ste. 1904
Jacksonville 904-396-0985

The Boat Show
2999 SR 84 W.
Deland 904-736-6601

Daytona Marine Electronics
94 Dunlawton Ave.
Daytona Beach 904 760 2466

Florida Watercraft
177 North Cswy.
New Smyrna Bch. 904-426-2628

Jackson Electronics
3358 Lakeshore Blvd.
Jacksonville 904-384-7006

Marineland Marina
176 Marina Dr.
Marineland 904-471-0087

Matanzas Marine
5658 N. Ocean Shore
Flagler Bch. 904-445-5878

Seacoast Electronics
240 Tallyrand Ave.
Jacksonville 904-355-0343

Sebastian Harbor Marina
975 S. Ponce de Leon Blvd.
St. Augustine 904-825-4008

INDIAN RIVER LAGOON

Bethel Marine Corp.
1225 E New Haven Ave.
Melbourne 407-727-0088

Boater's World
Market Place Square
3193 N.W. Federal Hwy.
Jensen Beach 407-692-1150

Canaveral Marine Electronics
Port Canaveral 407-784-3817

Cape Marina
800 Scallop Dr.
Cape Canaveral 407-783-8410
See advertisement on page 45.

Harbor Marine Electronics
Ft. Pierce 407-466-3300

Harbor Town Marina/Boatyard
1936 HarborTown Dr.
Ft. Pierce 407-466-7300

Hatley's Electronics
404 Center St.
Cocoa 407-632-8930

Marelco Marine Electronics
1432 N. Harbor Blvd.
Melbourne 407-254-8855

Mazza Marine
414 Richard Road
Rockledge 407-636-5725

Pineda Point Marina
6175 N. Harbor City Blvd.
Melbourne 407-254-4199

Randy's Marine Electronics
Port St. Lucie 407-879-1841

RGM Industries
3342-A Lillian Blvd.
Titusville 407-269-0063
See advertisements on pages 45 & 148.

Sea-Tronics
Melbourne Bch. 407-777-8729

STUART TO BOCA RATON

Avalon Marine
48 E. Blue Heron
Riviera Beach 407-863-4496

Boater's World
at Ritz South Congress Plaza
3678 S. Congress Ave.
Lake Worth 407-967-1937

Coral Reef Electronics
2532 SE Clayton St.
Stuart 407-283-3340

Consolidated Electronic Dist.
1300 Clearmount St. N.E. #201
Palm Bay Beach 407-729-6706

Harbour Marine Electronics
2208 Idlewilde Rd.
Palm Bch. Gdns. 407-622-5802

Industrial Marine Electronics
Stuart 407-286-3527

Marker 1 Electronics
 18733 SE Federal Hwy.
Jupiter 407-575-1011
 2300 Idlewilde Ct.
Palm Bch. Gdns. 407 626 1101

Monterey Marine
6800 SW Jack James Rd.
Stuart 407-286-2835

Northside Marine Electronics
400 N. W. Alice Ave.
Stuart 407 692 5111

Rich Electronics
221 E. Blue Heron Blvd.
Riviera Bch. 407-848-5400

Larry Smith Electronics
1619 Broadway
Riviera Bch. 407-844-3592

Stuart Yacht
450 SW Salerno Rd.
Stuart 407-283-1947
See advertisement on page 53.

BROWARD COUNTY

ACR Electronics
5757 Ravenswood Rd.
Ft. Lauderdale 954-981-3333

Avalon Marine Electronics
1598 Cordova Rd.
Ft. Lauderdale 954-527-4047

Bluewater Books & Charts
1481 SE 17th St.
Ft. Lauderdale 954-763-6533
See advertisement on page 142.

Boater's World
960 North Federal Hwy
Pompano Bch. 781-0007.

Commercial Marine Electronics
2830 N.E. 7th Ave.
Pompano Bch. 954-943-6343

Concord Marine Electronics
2233 S. Federal Hwy.
Ft. Lauderdale 954 779 1100

Custom Navigation South
3200 S. Andrews Ave. #100.
Ft. Lauderdale 954-761-3678

Electronics Unlimited
South Andrews Marine Plaza
3229 S Andrews Ave.
Ft. Lauderdale 954-467-2695

High Seas Technology
2965 W. St. Rd. 84
Ft. Lauderdale 954 587 8400

D. S. Hull Co.
3320 SW 3rd Ave.
Ft. Lauderdale 954-463-4307

Island Marine Electric
775-A Taylor La.
Dania 954-922-7077

Navigator Marine Electronics
632 SW 4th Ave.
Ft. Lauderdale 954-462-0280

Radio Holland USA, BV
1509 S. W. 1st Ave
Ft. Lauderdale 954-764-0130

Sealand Marine, Inc.
2696 East Atlantic Blvd.
Pompano Beach 954-943-1008

Skipper Marine Electronics
5053 NW 10th Terr.
Ft. Lauderdale 954-493-8255

Al Stuckey Marine
Ft. Lauderdale 954-523-8488

Tropic Aero Marine
1090 N. W. 53rd St.
Ft. Lauderdale 954 491 6355

DADE COUNTY

Atlantic Radio Telephone
2495 NW 35th Ave.
Miami 305-633-9636

Crook & Crook
2795 S.W. 27th Ave.
Miami 305-854-0005

Diaz Marine Electronics
260-A S.W. 6th St.
Miami 305-858-7588

Dockside Marine Electronics
2215 N.W. 14th St.
Miami 305-635-0105

Electro-Marine
Miami 305-856-1924

Elite Marine
12280 NE 14th Ave.
N. Miami 305-895-6908

L. B. Harvey Marine
152 SW 8th St.
Miami 305-856-1583

Johnson Electronics
2051 NW 11th St. Ste. 100
Miami 305-642-7370

Langer-Krell Marine Electronics
533 West Ave.
Miami Bch. 305-672-3421

The Marine Depot
6917 NW 82nd Ave.
Miami 305-477-3330

Navatech
3103 NW 20th St.
Miami 305-633-6491

R&M Electronics/
Elite Marine Electronics
12280 NE 14th Ave.
N. Miami 305-666-7155

Rich Electronics
3300 NW 21st St.
Miami 305-635-1351

Southern Marine Research
1401 NW 89th Ct.
Miami 305-591-9433

Tiger Direct Inc.
910 S, Dayland Blvd. #1500
Miami 305 529 3434

KEYS

The Boat House
12411 Overseas Hwy.
Marathon 305-289-1323

Jon Johnson Marine Electronics
11530 Overseas Hwy.
Marathon 305-743-4049

Key West Electronics
Key West 305-294-4210

Mid Keys Marine Supply
2055 Overseas Hwy.
Marathon 305-743-6020

Milt's Marine Electronics
81650 Overseas Hwy.
Islamorada 305 664 4786

Maritime Mart
5800 Overseas Hwy.
Marathon 305-743-3419

Milt's Marine Electronics
81650 Overseas Hwy.
Islamorada 305-664-4786

Seamark Electronics Inc.
2994 Overseas Hwy. St.
Marathon 305-743-6633

MARCO ISLAND TO PLACIDA

AAA Electronic Repair Center
4896 Golden Gate Pkwy.
Naples 941-455-1411

Felix Marine Electronics
5240 Bank St. Ste. 14
Ft. Myers 941-936-6463
3470 Bayshore Dr.
Naples 941 732 0101

Gulfcoast Marine Electronics
2378 Linwood Ave.
Naples 941-775-2224

HWH Electronics Corporation
1146 6th Ave. South
Naples 941 394 8700

Southern Marine Electronic Serv.
4712 del Prado Blvd.
Cape Coral 941-945-0787

Marine Electronic Services
19190 San Carlos Blvd,
Ft. Myers Beach 941-463-4451

ENGLEWOOD TO SKYWAY

Jaytron
2635 Manatee Ave. E.
Bradenton 941-746-6385

Tradyne
1312 Main St.
Sarasota 941-366-6759

SKYWAY TO TARPON SPRINGS

Consolidated Electronic
Distributors
2227 Brevard Rd. N.E.
St. Petersburg 813-729-6706

ETS Marine Electronics
1107 No. Ward St.
Tampa 813-289-1819
3840 Tanner Rd.
Dover 813 659 1859

Gulf Coast Marine Electronics
4243 N. Westshore Blvd.
Tampa 813 879 9714

HWH Electronics
4215 Gulf Blvd.
St. Petersburg Bch.
813-367-2754

Island Yacht Services
3671 131st Ave. N., Ste. B
Clearwater 813-573-7755

Johnson Sails
St. Petersburg 813-577-3220

Navico
2381 114th Ave. N.
Largo 813-546-4300

Sigma Marine Supplies
950 Roosevelt Blvd.
Tarpon Springs 813-934-0794

Si-Tex Marine Electronics
14000 Roosevelt Blvd.
Clearwater 813-535-4681

Sound Marine Electronic
1204 S 22nd St.
Tampa 813-247-7195

Suncoast Electronics
Largo 813-584-7055

Tamrad
618 N. 13th St.
Tampa 813-229-0080

NORTHWEST

Anything Marine
1129 Beck Ave.
Panama City 904-785-0630

Deckhand's Marina
1350 Miracle Strip Pkwy.
Ft. Walton Bch. 904-243-7359
See advertisement on page 132.

D&D Marine Electronics
1803 W. Garden St.
Pensacola 904-433-6214

J. V. Gander
319 Water St.
Apalachicola 904-653-8889

George's Marine Electronics
Hwy. 19 S.
Crystal River 352-795-6861

George's Marine Electronics
628 New Warrington Rd.
Pensacola 904-456-4553

Harbor Communications
Panama City 904-785-9679

Marine Electronics Company
2807 West 12th St.
Panama City 904-763-5658

Marshall Marine Ways
Timber Island Rd.
Carrabelle 904-697-3428
See advertisement on page 127.

Miller Marine
119 Water St.
Apalachicola 904-653-9521
See advertisement on page 128.

Redmond Marine Electronics
126 Hwy. 98
Destin 904-837-9092

RMS Marine Supply
Rt. 1, Box 3670 - Crawfordville
Medart 904-926-3114

Perdido Marine Electronics
10281 Gulf Breeze Hwy.
Pensacola 904-492-0451

Treasure Island Marina
3605 Thomas Dr.
Panama City Bch. 904-234-6533

ENGINES, SALES & SERVICE, DIESEL

FIRST COAST & ST. JOHNS

The Boat Show
2999 SR 84 W.
Deland 904-736-6601

Daytona Marina & Boat Works
645 S. Beach St.
Daytona Bch. 904-252-6421

Sea Love Boatworks
4877 Front St.
Ponce Inlet 904-761-5434

Sea-Farer Marine
248 North Causeway
New Smyrna 904-427-4514

Southeastern Power
2060 W 21st St.
Jacksonville 904-335-3437

Treworgy Yachts
5658 N. Oceanshore Blvd.
Palm Coast 904-445-5878

INDIAN RIVER LAGOON

Anchorage Yacht Basin
96 E. Eau Gallie Cswy.
Melbourne 407-773-3620
See advertisement on page 42.

Cape Marina
800 Scallop Dr.
Cape Canaveral 407-783-8410
See advertisement on page 45.

Coastal Marine Repair
1357 S. Banana River Dr.
Merritt Island 407-453-1885
See advertisement on page 45.

E & B Marine Supply
1024 S. Harbor City Blvd.
Melbourne 407-723-1878

Indian Harbor Marina
1399 Banana River Dr.
Indian Harbor Bch. 407 773 2468

**Intracoastal Marina
of Melbourne**
705 S. US 1
Melbourne 407-725-0090
See advertisement on page 48.

Merit Marine Center
582 S Banana River Dr.
Merritt Island 407-453-5912

Pineda Point Marina
6175 N. Harbor City Blvd.
Melbourne 407-254-4199

Southern Yacht Services
971 N. E. Industrial Blvd.
Jensen Beach 407 334 5214

STUART TO BOCA RATON

David Lowe's Boatyard
4550 SE Boatyard Dr.
PO Box L, Rocky Point
Port Salerno 407-287-0923
See advertisement on page 57.

Diesel Engine
& Marine Service
2848 Iris St.
Stuart 407-283-7040

Diesel Injection Service
2201 SE Indian St. M-2
Stuart 407-283-8999

Diesel Mechanics Co-op
2604 NW 2nd Ave.
Boca Raton 407-391-8143

Kikos Marine Service
1027 Aspin Rd.
West Palm Bch. 407-683-7730

Marine Diesel Analysts
2851 S. E. Monroe St.
Stuart 407 286 8145

Sailfish Marina
3565 SE St. Lucie Blvd.
Stuart 407-288-6292

Seminole Boat Yard
Gold Coast Diesel Service
2208 Idlewilde Rd.
Lake Park 407-844-9660

Nick's Marine
611 Commerce Way
Jupiter 407-746-1656

Performance Diesel Service
SPS Industrial Park
3079 SE Monroe St.
Stuart 407-283-2424

Phil's Motor Repair
Port Salerno 407-287-2653

Stuart Yacht
450 SW Salerno Rd.
Stuart 407-283-1947
See advertisement on page 53.

Whiticar Boat Works
3636 SE Old St. Lucie Blvd.
Stuart 407-287-2883
See advertisement on page 54.

BROWARD COUNTY

Bomac Marine Power Corp.
271 SW 33rd St.
Ft. Lauderdale 954-766-2625

ENGINES, DIESEL

Clymer Diesel Power Services
1903 W. McNab Rd.
Pompano Bch. 954-971-6600

Everglades Diesel
Injection Service
243 SW 33rd Ct.
Ft. Lauderdale 954-522-1780

Expert Diesel
4700 Oakes Rd.
Ft. Lauderdale 954-462-5290

Global Maritime Services
247 SW 33rd Ct.
Ft. Lauderdale 954-522-1489

K. W. Diesel
5441 N. E. 1st Terrace
Ft. Lauderdale 954 239 3583

Ted Hettler Yacht Services
301 Bayberry Dr.
Plantation 954-587-7282

Marine Gear & Power Systems
2901 SW 2nd Ave.
Ft. Lauderdale 954-763-6433

Merritt's Boat & Engine Works
2931 NE 16th St.
Pompano 954-941-5207

O-K Generators & Diesel
373 N. River Ave.
Deerfield Bch. 954-428-9990

On-Site Diesel Repair
4974 SW 105th Terr.
Cooper City 954-434-5449

Rolly Marine
2551 State Road 84
Ft. Lauderdale 954-583-5300

Royale Palm Yacht Basin
629 NE 3rd St.
Dania 954-923-5900

RPM Diesel Engine Co.
2555 State Road 84
Ft. Lauderdale 954-587-1620
See advertisement on page 64.

Sun Power Diesel
413 SW 3rd Ave.
Ft. Lauderdale 954-522-4775
See advertisement on page 71.

DADE COUNTY

Anchor Marine
961 NW 7th St.
Miami 305-545-6348

Bo Jean Boat Yard
3041 NW So. River Dr.
Miami 305-633-8919

R. Bertram & Co.
3660 NW 21st St.
Miami 305-633-9763

Florida Detroit Diesel-Allison
2277 NW 14th St.
Miami 305-633-5028

R.B. Grove
261 SW 6th St.
Miami 305-854-5420

Pantropic Power Products
8205 NW 58th St.
Miami 305-592-4944

KEYS

Cadiz Diesel Service
9699 Overseas Hwy.
Marathon 305-743-3771

Coral Bay Marina
601 Mastic St.
Islamorada 305-664-3111

Dally Marine Repair
at Faro Blanco Docks
Marathon 305-743-4291

Jim Mander's Yacht Shop
MM 106.6 Bayside
Key Largo 305-451-3891

Lower Keys Diesel Repair
120 Barbuda Lane
Ramrod Key 305-872-2722

MARCO ISLAND TO PLACIDA

Ft. Myers Cummins Southeast.
2671 Edison Ave.
Ft. Myers 941-337-1211

General Engine & Equipment
2305 Rockhill Rd.
Ft. Myers 941-983-8177

Hurricane Bay Marine
18850 San Carlos Blvd.
Ft. Myers 941-466-8898

Rose Boat & Engine Works
4427 Mercantile Ave.
Naples 941-643-6657

ENGLEWOOD TO SKYWAY

Anchor Marine Products Inc.
4320 15th St.
E. Bradenton 941-685-5786

Brownies Diesel Service
311 13th Ave. W.
Palmetto 941 729 1615

Cavanagh Marine Repair
5327 14th W.
Bradenton 941 727 7905

Fowler Marine
635 Palmetto Pt. Dr.
Palmetto 941 722 8475

Galati's Marina
900 S. Bay Blvd.
Anna Maria 941-778-0755

Great American Boat Yards
1889 N. Tamiami Trail
Sarasota 941-365-1770

Holiday Inn/Sarasota
7150 N. Tamiami Trail
Sarasota 941 355 2781
See advertisement on page 106.

Otmar's Diesel Engines
1242 N. Lime Ave.
Sarasota 941-366-2470

Royal Palm Marina Inc.
779 W. Wentworth
Englewood 941-474-1420

SKYWAY TO TARPON SPRINGS

Cummins Southeastern Power
5910 E. Hillsborough Ave.
Tampa 813-626-1101

Diesel Energy Systems
7855 N. 126th Ave.
Largo 813-536-9979

General Engine & Equipment
8311 Sabal Industrial Blvd.
Tampa 813-621-7591

Great American Boat Yards
6810 Gulfport Blvd.
St. Petersburg 813-384-3428

Marina Point Ships Store
500 1st Ave S.E.
St. Petersburg 813-823-2555

Mastry Engine Center
2895 46th Ave. N.
St. Petersburg 813-522-9471

Ringhaver Equip Co.
Tampa 813 671 3700

Stuart Diesel Service
6515 Adamo Dr.
Tampa 813-623-1551

NORTHWEST

Brown Marine Services
40 Audusson Ave.
Pensacola 904-453-3471

Bell Marine Service
18 Audusson Ave.
Pensacola 904-455-7639

Captain Fixit Marine
Timber Island Marina
Carrabelle 904 697 3493

Holiday Marine
1126 No. Blvd. E.
Leesburg 352 787 4824

Gulf Coast Marine Service
Hwy 490
Homosassa Spgs. 352-628-5885

Hernando Beach Marina
4139 Shoal Hill Blvd.
Spring Hill 352-596-2952

Holiday Harbor Marina
14050 Canal-a-Way
Pensacola 904-492-0555

Miller's Marina
PO Box 280
Suwannee 352-542-7349
See advertisement on page 123.

Passport Marina
5325 N. Lagoon Dr.
Panama City Bch 904 234 5609

Perdido Marine Electronics
3731- A W Navy Blvd.
Pensacola 904 457 6116

Posner Marine Service
610 New Warrington Rd.
Pensacola 904-453-8182

Treasure Island Marina
3605 Thomas Dr.
Panama City Bch 904-234-6533

ENGINES, SALES & SERVICE, GASOLINE

FIRST COAST & ST. JOHNS

The Boat Show
2999 SR 84 W.
Deland 904-736-6601

Daytona Marina & Boat Works
645 S. Beach St.
Daytona Bch. 904-252-6421

First Coast Marine
2100 Florida Blvd.
Neptune Bch 904-246-1614

Florida Watercraft
177 North Cswy.
New Smyrna Bch. 904-426-2628

Julington Creek Marina
12807 San Jose Blvd.
Jacksonville 904 268 5117

Lighthouse Marine
5434 San Juan Ave.
Jacksonville 904-384-6995

Pablo Creek Marina
13846 Atlantic Blvd.
Jacksonville 904-221-4228

Ponce Deepwater Landing
133 Inlet Harbor Road
Ponce Inlet 904-767-3266
See advertisement on page 35.

Sea Love Boatworks
4877 Front St.
Ponce Inlet 904-761-5434

Treworgy Yachts
5658 N. Oceanshore Blvd.
Palm Coast 904-445-5878

INDIAN RIVER LAGOON

Anchorage Yacht Basin
96 E. Eau Gallie Cswy.
Melbourne 407-773-3620
See advertisement on page 48.

Banana River Marine Service
1360 S. Banana River Drive
Merritt Island 407-452-8622
See advertisement on page 45.

Cape Marina
800 Scallop Dr.
Cape Canaveral 407-783-8410
See advertisement on page 45.

Harbor Town Marina/Boatyard
1936 HarborTown Dr.
Ft. Pierce 407-466-7300

Pineda Point Marina
6175 N. Harbor City Blvd.
Melbourne 407-254-4199

STUART TO BOCA RATON

Champion Engines
3326 SE Dixie Hwy.
Stuart 407-283-6788

JAS Marine
1917 N. Dixie Hwy.
West Palm Bch. 407-835-8190

TC's Marine Service
846 N. Dixie Hwy.
Lantana 407-588-5889

Whiticar Boat Works
3636 SE Old St. Lucie Blvd.
Stuart 407-287-2883
See advertisement on page 54.

BROWARD COUNTY

Atlas Marine Engine Supply
4641 Ravenswood Rd.
Ft. Lauderdale 954-983-3029

Chinnock Marine
518 W. Las Olas Blvd.
Ft. Lauderdale 954-763-2250

Florida Marine Engines
580 N. Federal Hwy.
Deerfield Bch. 954-428-2895

Harbor 1 Hi-Performance Marine
1495 Old Griffin Rd.
Dania 954-920-4555

Ted Hettler Yacht Service
301 Bayberry Dr.
Plantation 954-587-7282

Jerry's Marine Service
100 SW 16th St.
Ft. Lauderdale 954-525-0311

Lighthouse Point Marine Serv.
2901 NE 28th Ct.
Lighthouse Pt. 954-941-6166

DADE COUNTY

Anchor Marine
961 NW 7th St.
Miami 305-545-6348

Florida Marine Service
300 SW 6th St.
Miami 305-285-0359

R.B. Grove
261 SW 6th St.
Miami 305-854-5420

Performance Marine
7701 NW 54th St.
Miami 305-592-1702

KEYS

The Boat House
12411 Overseas Hwy.
Marathon 305-289-1323

Coral Bay Marina
601 Mastic St.
Islamorada 305 664 3111

Oceanside Marine Service
1015 15th St.
Marathon 305-743-6666

MARCO ISLAND TO PLACIDA

Fish Tale Marina
7225 Estero Blvd.
Ft. Myers Bch. 941-463-4448

Hurricane Bay Marine
18850 San Carlos Blvd.
Ft. Myers 941-466-8898

Moss Marine
Harbor Ct.
Ft. Myers Bch. 941-463-6137

Rose Boat & Engine Works
4427 Mercantile Ave.
Naples 941-643-6657

Royal Palm Marina Inc.
779 W. Wentworth
Englewood 941-474-1420

Sanibel Island Marina
634 N. Yachtsman Dr.
Sanibel 941-472-2723

ENGLEWOOD TO SKYWAY

Cavanagh Marine Repair
5327 14th St. W.
Bradenton 941 727 7905

Osprey Marine Center
480 Blackburn Pt. Rd.
Osprey 941-443-3207

SKYWAY TO TARPON SPRINGS

Clearwater Bay Marine Service
900 N. Osceola
Clearwater 813-442-9376

Marina Point Ships Store
500 1st Ave S.E.
St. Petersburg 813-823-2555

Mastry Engine Center
2895 46th Ave. N.
St. Petersburg 813-522-9471

Maximo Marine Service
3701 1/2 50th Ave. S.
St. Petersburg 813-867-7718

Prior Boat Builders
4100 Bayshore Blvd.
Dunedin 813-784-1396

NORTHWEST

Aquatic Enterprises
1201A Hwy. Miracle Strip E.
Ft. Walton Beach 904-243-5721

Brown Marine Services
40 Audusson Ave.
Pensacola 904-453-3471

Economy Marine
6205 North 'W' St.
Pensacola 904-479-2447

Holiday Harbor Marina
14050 Canal-a-Way
Pensacola 904-492-0555

Holiday Marine
1126 No. Blvd. E.
Leesburg 352 787 4824

Marquardt's Marina
Hwy. 98
Mexico Beach 904-648-8900

Miller's Marina
PO Box 280
Suwannee 352-542-7349
See advertisement on page 123.

Passport Marina & Boat Yard
5323 N. Lagoon Dr.
Panama City 904-234-5609

Shields Marina
PO Box 218 Riverside Dr.
St. Marks 904-925-6158

Treasure Island Marina
3605 Thomas Dr.
Panama City Bch 904-234-6533

ENGINES, SALES & SERVICE, OUTBOARD

BAHAMAS

Sea Horse Marine
Hope Town 809-366-0023

FIRST COAST & ST. JOHNS

Albritton Marine
25th & Main St.
Jacksonville 904-356-2344

The Boat Show
2999 SR 84 W.
Deland 904-736-6601

Daytona Marina & Boat Works
645 S. Beach St.
Daytona Bch. 904-252-6421

First Coast Marine
2100 Florida Blvd.
Neptune Bch 904-246-1614

Julington Creek Marina
12807 San Jose Blvd.
Jacksonville 904 268 5117

Florida Watercraft
177 North Cswy.
New Smyrna Bch. 904-426-2628

Pete Loftin's Outboard
6424 Arlington Expwy.
Jacksonville 904-724-1400

Ormond Marina
1618 John Anderson Dr.
Ormond Bch. 904-441-0650

Ponce Deepwater Landing
133 Inlet Harbor Rd.
Ponce Inlet 904-767-3266
See advertisement on page 35.

Red Bay Marina
209 Bulkhead Dr.
Green Cove Spg. 904-284-1155

Sea Love Boatworks
4877 Front St.
Ponce Inlet 904-761-5434

Treworgy Yachts
5658 N. Oceanshore Blvd.
Palm Coast 904-445-5878

INDIAN RIVER LAGOON

Cape Marina
800 Scallop Dr.
Cape Canaveral 407-783-8410
See advertisement on page 45.

Casa Rio
1050 N. E. Dixie Hwy.
Jensen Beach 407 334 0944

Coastal Marine Repair
1357 S. Banana River Dr.
Merritt Island 407-453-1885
See advertisement on page 45.

Pineda Point Marina
6175 N. Harbor City Blvd.
Melbourne 407-254-4199

STUART TO BOCA RATON

Certified Marine
2655 S. Federal Hwy.
Stuart 407-288-2626

Power Plus Marine
5400 South Dixie Hwy
West Palm Beach 407 588 7088

Stella Marine
250 S. W. Monterey Rd.
Stuart 407 287 1101
2361 PGA Blvd. Ste. C Box 7
Palm Beach Gdns. 407 624 9950

BROWARD COUNTY

Dusky Marine
110 N. Bryan Rd.
Dania 954-922-8890

Everglades Marina
1801 SE 17th St.
Ft. Lauderdale 954-763-3030

Joel's Outboard Service
615 N. Andrews Ave.
Ft. Lauderdale 954-763-7729

Lauderdale Marina
1900 SE 15th St.
Ft. Lauderdale 954-523-8507
See advertisement on page 59.

Pompano Beach Marine Center
701 S. Federal Hwy.
Pompano Bch. 954-946-1450

Riverfront Marina
420 SW 3rd Ave.
Ft. Lauderdale 954-527-1829

Thunderboat Marina
2051 Griffin Rd.
Ft. Lauderdale 954-963-2660

DADE COUNTY

Causeway 79
724 NE 79th St.
Miami 305-757-7671

Fisherman's Paradise
3800 NW 27th Ave,
Miami 305-635-2445

Hi-Lift Marina
2890 NE 187th St.
N. Miami Bch. 305-931-2550

Johnson-Kirby
5966 S. Dixie Hwy.
S. Miami 305-666-1806

Langer's Marine
520 West Ave.
Miami Beach 305-672-2227

KEYS

The Boat House
12411 Overseas Hwy.
Marathon 305-289-1323

Duck Key Marina
Rt. 1, Box 1149
Duck Key 305-289-0161

Gulfside 59 Marina
US 1
Marathon 305-743-3372

Marx Marine Service
3800 Overseas Hwy.
Marathon 305-743-9208

Perdue Dean Co.
2 Fishing Village Dr.
Key Largo 305 367 2611

Performance Outboard
MM 101.5 Oceanside
Key Largo 305-451-3078

MARCO ISLAND TO PLACIDA

Anchorman
502 King St.
Punta Gorda 941-637-7474

Dolphin Marina
1506 SE 46th St.
Cape Coral 941-542-7097

Fish Tale Marina
7225 Estero Blvd.
Ft. Myers Bch. 941-463-4448

ENGINES, OUTBOARD

Gulf Coast Marine
2550 Tamiami Tr.
Port Charlotte 941-629-5300

Gulf Liner Marine
601 N. Tamiami Tr.
Venice 941 488 5150

Ingman Marine
1189 Tamiami Trail
Pt. Charlotte 941 255 1555

Inn Marina
891 8th St.
Boca Grande 941 964 2777

Moss Marine
Harbor Ct.
Ft. Myers Bch. 941-463-6137

Pineland Marina
13951 Waterfront Dr.
Pineland 941-283-0060

Sanibel Island Marina
634 N. Yachtsman Dr.
Sanibel 941-472-2723

ENGLEWOOD TO SKYWAY

Osprey Marine Center
480.5 Blackburn Pt. Rd.
Osprey 941-966-5657

Stump Pass Marina
3060 Placida Rd.
Englewood 941 697-3600

Royal Palm Marina Inc.
779 W. Wentworth
Englewood 941-474-1420

SKYWAY TO TARPON SPRINGS

Clearwater Outboard
603 S. Missouri
Clearwater 813-441-1097

Harborage at Bayboro
1500 2nd St. So.
St. Petersburg 813 821 6347
See advertisement on page 116.

H&H Marine Sales
10220 San Martin Blvd.
St. Petersburg 813-576-0923

Jack's Interbay Marine
4810 McElroy Ave.
Tampa 813-831-3000

Piper's Marine
8888 W. Hillsborough Ave.
Tampa 813-886-0967

Suncoast Marine Center
1300 Seminole Blvd.
Largo 813-581-6248

Warren's Marine Service
at Port Tarpon Marina
Tarpon Springs 813-938-3322

NORTHWEST

Adventure Marine
1201B Miracle Strip Pkwy.
Ft. Walton Bch. 904-243-0059

Hernando Beach Marina
4139 Shoal Hill Blvd.
Spring Hill 352-596-2952

Holiday Harbor Marina
14050 Canal-a-Way
Pensacola 904-492-0555

Lou's Marine
3408 Gulf Breeze Pkwy
Pensacola 904-932-0701

Mike's Marine Supply
Box 429, Hwy. 98
Panacea 904-984-5637

Marine Services of
Apalachicola
Hwy. 98 West
Apalachicola 904-653-9296

Marquardt's Marina
Hwy. 98
Mexico Bch. 904-648-8900

Shalimar Yacht Basin
PO Box 189, Zip: 32579
Shalimar 904 651 0510
See Advertisement on Page 131.

Shields Marina
Riverside Drive
St. Marks 904 925 6158

Treasure Island Marina
3605 Thomas Dr.
Panama City Bch 904-234-6533

Wells Marine of Pensacola
2725 W. Cervantes
Pensacola 904-432-2383

FIBERGLASS & PLASTIC SUPPLIES

FIRST COAST & ST. JOHNS

Baer Marine
299 San Marco
St. Augustine 904-824-3240

The Boat Show
2999 SR 84 W.
Deland 904-736-6601

Daytona Marina & Boat Works
645 S. Beach St.
Daytona Bch. 904-252-6421

Florida Marine Chemical
88 Riberia St. Suite 10
St. Augustine 904 829 3807

Florida Watercraft
177 North Cswy.
New Smyrna Bch. 904-426-2628

Monroe Harbour Marina
531 Palmetto
Sanford 407-322-2910

Pier 68 Marina
8137 N. Main St.
Jacksonville 904-765-9925

Treworgy Yachts
5658 N. Oceanshore Blvd.
Palm Coast 904-445-5878

INDIAN RIVER LAGOON

Cape Marina
800 Scallop Dr.
Cape Canaveral 407-783-8410
See advertisement on page 45.

Cocoa Beach Marina
307 Cocoa Bch. Cswy.
Cocoa Bch. 407-783-8972

Indian Cove Marina
14 Myrtice Ave.
Merritt Island 407-452-8540

Intracoastal Marina
of Melbourne
705 S. US 1
Melbourne 407-725-0090
See advertisement on page 48.

Pineda Point Marina
6175 N. Harbor City Blvd.
Melbourne 407-254-4199

Westland Marine
419 Washington
Titusville 407-327-0703

Whitley Marine
93 Delannoy Ave.
Cocoa 407-632-5445
See advertisement on page 45.

STUART TO BOCA RATON

Beachcomber Fiberglass Tech.
2850 SE Market Place
Stuart 407-287-0200

Glue Products
4015 Georgia Ave.
West Palm Bch. 407-833-1863

BROWARD COUNTY

River Bend Marina
1515 SW 20th St.
Ft. Lauderdale 954-523-1832

DADE COUNTY

Smitty's Boat Tops
727 S. Krome Ave.
Homestead 305-245-0229

KEYS

Steadman's Boatyard
701 Palm Ave.
Key West 305-294-1071

Tugboat's
2211 Overseas Hwy.
Marathon 305-743-4585

Tiki Water Sports
MM 94.5
Key Largo 305-852-9298

MARCO ISLAND TO PLACIDA

Harbor Hideaway
7290 Barrancas Ave. NW
Bokeelia 941-283-1167

Hurricane Bay Marine
18850 San Carlos Blvd.
Ft. Myers 941-466-8898

Mid-Island Marina
4756 Ester Blvd.
Ft. Myers 941 765 4371
See advertisement on page 98.

Owl Creek Boat Works
18251 Owl Creek Dr.
Alva 941-543-2100

Rose Boat & Engine Works
4427 Mercantile Ave.
Naples 941-643-6657

ENGLEWOOD TO SKYWAY

Bradenton Fiberglass Co.
5925 17th St. E.
Bradenton 941 753 9621

Classic Boat Works
2249 Industrial Blvd.
Sarasota 941-351-3004

Fiberglass Services
5612-A Lawton Dr.
Sarasota 941 923 8112

SKYWAY TO TARPON SPRINGS

Brown's Marine
500-A Anclote Rd.
Tarpon Springs 813-934-7576

Flaherty Marine
761 Anclote Rd.
Tarpon Springs 813-934-9394

Fiberglass Coatings
3201 28th St. N.
St. Petersburg 813 327 8117

Kardol
1954 Carroll St.
Clearwater 1-800-252-7365

Marina Point Ship's Store
500 1st Ave. SE
St. Petersburg 813-896-2641

Ross Yacht Service
279 Windward Passage
Clearwater 813-446-8191

NORTHWEST

Aquatic Enterprises
1201-A Hwy. Miracle Strip E.
Ft. Walton Bch. 904-243-5721

Brown Marine Service
40 Audusson Ave.
Pensacola 904-453-3471

Key Sailing
500 Quietwater Bch. Rd.
Gulf Breeze 904-932-5520

Marshall Marine Ways
Timber Island Rd.
Carrabelle 904-697-3428
See advertisement on page 127.

Mike's Marine Ways
St. Marks 904 925 5685

Passport Marina & Boat Yard
5325 N. Lagoon Dr.
Panama City 904-234-5609

RMS Marine Supply
Rt. 1, Box 3670
Crawfordville/Medart
904-926-3114

Sellers Marine Service
St. Marks 904-925-6813

FINANCE COMPANIES

FIRST COAST & ST. JOHNS

The Boat Show
2999 SR 84 W.
Deland 904-736-6601

First New England Financial
5555 Playa Way
Jacksonville 904-744-4210

Florida Watercraft
177 North Cswy.
New Smyrna Bch. 904-426-2628

INDIAN RIVER LAGOON

First National Bank & Trust
Vero Beach 407 569 4000

STUART TO BOCA RATON

American Marine Financial
34 E. 5th St. Suite #2
Stuart 407 223 9909

First National Bank
Stuart 407-287-4000
Ft. Pierce 407 465 4000

First Union Bank
301 E. Ocean Blvd.
Stuart 407-287-4200

BROWARD COUNTY

Atlantic Financial Southeast
Ft. Lauderdale 954-771-3393

Barnett Bank of So. Florida
910 SE 17th St.
Pompano Bch. 954-765-1752

Essex Credit Corp.
2101 S. Andrews Ave. #204
Ft. Lauderdale 954-763-7450

First New England Financial
1535 S. E. 17th St. #103
Ft. Lauderdale 954-763-1089

First Union National Bank
1710 S. Andrews Ave.
Ft. Lauderdale 954 467 5306

Ganis Credit Corporation
2170 S. E. 17th St.
Ft. Lauderdale 954 527 2888
See advertisement on page 63.

Maritime Financial
1300 S. E. 17th St. Suite 214
Ft. Lauderdale 800 380 6644

Nations Bank Of Florida N. A.
One Financial Plaza
Ft. Lauderdale 954 765 2226

Offshore Financial Corp.
2190 S. E. 17th St. #303
Ft. Lauderdale 954 462 7773

DADE COUNTY

Centrust Savings Bank
101 E. Flagler St.
Miami 1-800-468-4638

Equitable Financial Companies
2875 NE 191st St.
N. Miami Bch. 305-937-0800

MARCO ISLAND TO PLACIDA

Boat/U.S.
12901 MacGregor Blvd.
Ft. Myers 941-481-7447

ENGLEWOOD TO SKYWAY

Island Bank
5327 Gulf Dr.
Holmes Beach 941-778-2224

SKYWAY TO TARPON SPRINGS

Barnett Bank of
 Pinellas County
3100 Central Ave.
St. Petersburg 813-892-1105

C&S National Bank
804 Central Ave.
St. Petersburg 813-821-1111

Essex Credit Corp.
9620 Executive Ctr. Dr. Suite 125
St, Petersburg 813 576 2407

First New England Financial
9500 Kroger Blvd., #202
St. Petersburg 813-576-0042

Ganis Credit Corp.
146 2nd St. N. Ste. 107
St. Petersburg 800 234 4446
3001 N. Rocky Pt. Rd. E #335
Tampa 800 937 9114

Sun Bank
301 4th St. N
St. Petersburg 813-823-4181

FISHING SUPPLIES, TACKLE, BAIT, TAXIDERMISTS, TOURNAMENTS

BAHAMAS

Bimini Big Game Club
P. O Box 699
Bimini 800-327-4149

Green Turtle Club
Green Turtle Cay
809-365-4271
See advertisement on page 26.

Lucayan Marina Village
PO Box F-42654
Freeport, Grand Bahama
809 373 8888
See advertisement on page 27.

Walker's Cay
Abaco
FL: 800-432-2092
US: 800-327-3714

FIRST COAST & ST. JOHNS

A-1-A Discount Bait & Tackle
2893 Hwy. A-1-A
Mayport 904-247-4424

Andy's Bait & Tackle
15 Ferry Pl.
St. Augustine 904-825-1139

Brad's Taxidermy
13401 Beach Blvd.
Jacksonville 904-223-1570

Bridgetender Live Bait & Tackle
820 Moody Blvd. (Rear)
Flagler Bch. 904-439-0440

Florida Watercraft
177 North Cswy.
New Smyrna Bch. 904-426-2628

Frank's Bait & Tackle
854 Mason Ave.
Daytona Bch. 904-253-4078

Harold's Sport Center
124 N. Causeway
New Smyrna Bch. 904-428-2841

Homer's Bait & Tackle
12807 San Jose Blvd.
Mandarin 904-262-5771

Howard's
92 Dunlawton Ave.
Port Orange 904-761-8478

Julington Creek Marina
12807 San Jose Blvd.
Jacksonville 904 268 5117

Palm Coast Marina
200 Clubhouse Dr.
Palm Coast 904-446-6370
See advertisement on page 35.

Ponce Deepwater Landing
133 Inlet Harbor Rd.
Ponce Inlet 904-767-3266
See advertisement on page 35.

Riverside Marine & Tackle
111 N. Riverside Dr.
New Smyrna Bch. 904-427-3434

Sebastian Harbor Marina
975 S. Ponce de Leon Blvd.
St. Augustine 904-825-4008

INDIAN RIVER LAGOON

Cape Marina
800 Scallop Dr.
Cape Canaveral 407-783-8410
See advertisement on page 45.

Captain Jack's Tackle
 & Marine Supply
780 Mullet Rd.
Port Canaveral 407-783-3694

DeBrooks Fishing Corner
107 Fisherman's Wharf
Ft. Pierce 407-464-5066

Dolphin's Leap
505 Glen Cheek Dr.
Port Canaveral 407-783-9535

Jack's Marina
1 Beachland Blvd.
Vero Bch. 407-231-0926

Pelicans Nest Marina
1009 NE Anchorage Dr.
Jensen Bch. 407-334-0890

STUART TO BOCA RATON

Tony Acceta & Sons
932 Ave. E
Riviera Bch. 407-844-3441

Ande Monofilament
1310 53rd St.
West Palm Bch. 407-842-2474

Boca Raton Resort & Club
501 E. Camino Real
Boca Raton 407-395-3000

Gone Fishing Bait & Tackle
8195 N. Military Tr.
Palm Bch. Gdns. 407-694-9369

Murray Bros.
211 E. Blue Heron Blvd.
Riviera Bch. 407-845-1043

Pompanette
2361 PGA Blvd.
Palm Bch. Gdns. 407-624-0111

Riviera Beach Marina
200 E. 13th St.
Riviera Bch. 407-842-7806

Rupp Marine
4761 Anchor Ave.
Port Salerno 407-286-5300

Sailfish Marina
3565 SE St. Lucie Blvd.
Stuart 407-283-1122

Sailfish Marina & Resort
98 Lake Dr.
Palm Bch. Shores 407-844-8460

Tuppen's
1002 N. Dixie Hwy.
Lake Worth 407-582-9012

BROWARD COUNTY

Beach Bait & Tackle
1112 Las Olas Blvd.
Ft. Lauderdale 954-524-3302

Big Blue Sea Chests
818 NW 8th Ave.
Ft. Lauderdale 954-467-0077

Boyd's Tackle Shop
508 N. Andrews Ave.
Ft. Lauderdale 954-462-8366

Bud's Place
Fish City Docks
Pompano Bch. 954-946-6712

Ft. Laud. Billfish Tournament
849 S. W. 11th Court
Ft. Lauderdale 954 563 0385

Hillsboro Rod & Reel
2507 N. Ocean Blvd.
Pompano Bch. 954-946-9023

Kingsbury & Sons Tackle
1801 S. Federal Hwy.
Ft. Lauderdale 954-467-3474

J. T. Reese, Taxidermist
1918 S. Andrews Ave.
Ft. Lauderdale 954-524-4369

Pompanette
1515 SE 16th St.
Ft. Lauderdale 954-525-6367

Pompano Bch. Fishing Rodeo
P. O. Box 5584
Lighthouse Pt. 954 942 4513

So. Florida Fishing Classic
P. O. Box 5042
Lighthouse Pt. 954 942 3204

DADE COUNTY

Caribbean Marine Taxidermy
10715 SW 190 St., #25
Miami 305-253-5225

Crandon Park Marina
4000 Crandon Blvd.
Key Biscayne 305-361-1281
See advertisement on page 70.

El Capitan Sport Center
1590 NW 27th Ave.
Miami 305-635-7500

Fisherman's Paradise
3800 NW 27th Ave.
Miami 305-625-2445

Watson Island
1050 MacArthur Cswy
Miami 305 371 2378

KEYS

Abel's Tackle Box
MM 84.5
Islamorada 305-664-2521

Bluewater Tackle
100460 Overseas Hwy.
Key Largo 305-451-5875

The Boat House
12411 Overseas Hwy.
Marathon 305-289-1323

Dolphin Marina
MM 28.5, US 1
Rt. 4, Box 1038
Little Torch Key 305-872-2685

Key Colony Beach Marina
Key Colony Beach Cswy.
Key Colony Bch. 305-289-1310
See advertisement on page 83.

Gilbert's Holiday Island of Key Largo
107900 Overseas Hwy.
Key Largo 305-451-1133
See advertisement on page 81.

Holiday Isle Marina
84001 US 1
Islamorada 305-664-2321

Key West Bight Marina
201 William St.
Key West 305-296-3838

Key West Marine Hardware
818 Caroline St.
Key West 305-294-3425
See advertisement on page 89.

Little Palm Island
Box 1036 Rt. 4
Little Torch Key 305-872-2524
1-800-343-8567
See advertisement on page 94.

Miller's Tackle Shop
US 1
Big Pine 305-872-2304

Pflueger Marine Taxidermy
88976 U.S. Hwy. 1 Tavernier
Marathon 305-852-5528

Pinellas Marina
1200 Ocean Ave.
Marathon 305-743-5317

Sugarloaf Marina
MM 17
Sugarloaf Shrs. 305-745-3135

World Class Angler
at Faro Blanco Resort
Marathon 305-743-6139

MARCO ISLAND TO PLACIDA

Back Bay Marina
4751 Bonita Bch. Rd.
Bonita Springs 941-992-2601

Bait Box
1041 Periwinkle Way
Sanibel Island 941-472-1618

Deebold's Marina Fishing Trips
Ft. Myers Bch. 941-466-3525

Factory Bay Marina
1079 Bald Eagle Dr.
Marco Island 941-642-6717

Fish Tale Marina
7225 Estero Blvd.
Ft. Myers Bch. 941-463-4448

Fisherman's Wharf Tackle Shop
509 N. Tamiami Tr.
Venice 941-484-8430

Fishermen's World
17195 San Carlos Blvd.
Ft. Myers 941-466-8686

Fort Myers Beach Marina
703 Fisherman's Wharf
Ft. Myers Bch 941 463 9557

J&J Marine
2757 E. Tamiami Tr.
Naples 941-774-6612

Moss Marine
Harbor Ct.
Ft. Myers Bch. 941-463-6137

Naples Sporting Goods
779-5th Ave. South
Naples 941 262 6752

Pineland Marina
13951 Waterfront Dr.
Pineland 941-283-0080

Roland Martin's Marina
920 E. del Monte Ave.
Clewiston 941-983-3151

Paul's Bait & Tackle
26107 Hickory Blvd.
Bonita Bch. 941-992-0167

Prime Line Bait & Tackle
12016 Matlacha Blvd.
Cape Coral 941-283-1335

Sanibel Island Marina
634 N. Yachtsman Dr.
Sanibel 941-472-2723

Ike Shaw & Co. Taxidermy
2717 N. Tamiami Trail
N. Ft. Myers 941-995-4444

World Record Taxidermy
723 E. Sugarland Hwy.
Clewiston 941-983-6800

FISHING

ENGLEWOOD TO SKYWAY

Captain's Cove Bait & Tackle
801 Blackburn Pt. Rd.
Osprey 941-966-1771

Cecil's Bait & Tackle
2005 S. Tamiami Trail
Venice 941-497-0436

Economy Tackle
6018 S.Tamiami Trail
Sarasota 941-924-2785

Englewood Bait House
1450 Beach Rd.
Englewood 941-475-4511

Fisherman's Edge
4425 Placida Rd.
Grove City 941-697-7595

General Store
307 Pine Ave.
Anna Maria 941-778-4656

King Bait & Tackle
2011 Placida Rd.
Englewood 941-475-4905

Mr. B's Fishin' Hole
5919 Palmer Rd.
Sarasota 941-377-2706

Osprey Marine Center
480.5 Blackburn Pt. Rd.
Osprey 941-966-5657

Rio Villa Bait & Tackle
113 Rio Villa Dr.
Punta Gorda 941-639-7166

Stump Pass Marina
3060 Placida Rd.
Englewood 941-697-3600

SKYWAY TO TARPON SPRINGS

Big Pier 50
Clearwater Bch. 813-446-0060

Dunedin Bait & Tackle
1307 Bayshore Blvd.
Dunedin 813-738-3474

Madeira Bch. Municipal Marina
503 150th Ave.
Madeira Bch. 813-399-2631

Marina Point Ship's Store
500 1st Ave. SE
St. Petersburg 813-896-2641

Patti's Bait Shop
8924 W. Hillsborough Ave.
Tampa 813-889-8519

Tarpon Fisherman's Supply
332 Anclote Rd.
Tarpon Springs 813 938 4337

NORTHWEST

Aquatic Enterprises
1201A Hwy. Miracle Strip E.
Ft. Walton Bch. 904-243-5721

Bayou Chico Marina
806 Lakewood Rd.
Pensacola 904-455-4552

Blue Water Bait & Tackle
4065 S. Suncoast Bl.
Homosassa Spgs. 352-628-0414

Destin Fishin' Hole
240 Miracle Strip Pkwy.
Destin 904-837-9043
323 Page Rd.
Mary Esther 904-243-7191

Dockside Marine
Hwy. 351 POB 80
Horseshoe Bch. 352-498-5768

Dolphin Bait & Tackle
600 S. Barracks Ste. 112
Pensacola 904-438-3242

Gulf Breeze Bait & Tackle
2206 Thomas Dr.
Gulf Breeze 904-932-6789

Half Hitch Tackle
2206 Thomas Dr.
Panama City 904-234-2621

Hathaway Landings Marina
6426 W. Hwy. 98
Panama City Bch. 904 234 0609

Holiday Harbor Marina
14050 Canal-a-Way
Pensacola 904-492-0555

Howell Marine Supply
3100 W. Hwy. 98
Panama City 904-785-8548

Knox's Bait House
558 NW 3rd Ave.
Crystal River 352-795-2771

Marshall Marine Ways
Timber Island Rd.
Carrabelle 904-697-3428
See advertisement on page 127.

Miller's Marina
PO Box 280
Suwannee 904-542-7349
See advertisement on page 123.

Outcast Bait & Tackle
3520 Barrancas Ave.
Pensacola 904-457-1450

Panama City Marina
One Harrison Ave.
Panama City 904-785-0161
See advertisement on page 129.

Port Panacea Marina
Rocklanding Rd.
Panacea 904-349-2454

Rileys Bait & Tackle
Carrabelle 904-697-3777

Dockside Marina
Horseshoe 352-498-5768

Rod & Reel Marina
10045 Sinton Dr.
Pensacola 904-492-0100
See advertisement on page 135.

Shell Island Fish Camp
St. Marks 904-925-6226

Shell Point Resort
Rt. 2 Box 4361-1
Crawfordville 904-926-7162
See advertisement on page 127.

Smith Bait & Tackle
6813 Pine Forest Rd.
Pensacola 904-944-6396

The Tackle Shop
3317 Shoal Line Blvd.
Hernando Bch. 352-596-4638

Southwind Marina
10121 Sinton Dr.
Pensacola 904-492-0333
See advertisement on page 135.

Treasure Island Marina
3605 Thomas Dr.
Panama City Bch. 904-234-6533

Wright Tackle Shop
620 E. Wright St.
Pensacola 904-432-4558

GENERATORS, SALES & SERVICE

FIRST COAST & ST. JOHNS

The Boat Show
2999 SR 84 W.
Deland 904-736-6601

First Mate Yacht Services
212 Yacht Club Dr.
St. Augustine 904-829-0184

Southeastern Power
2060 W 21st St.
Jacksonville 904-355-3437

Daytona Marina & Boat Works
645 S. Beach St.
Daytona Bch. 904-252-6421

INDIAN RIVER LAGOON

Cape Marina
800 Scallop Dr.
Cape Canaveral 407-783-8410
See advertisement on page 45.

C. Huntress Marine
407 Ave. H
Ft. Pierce 407-461-3993

STUART TO BOCA RATON

Dietz Enterprises
281 SE Monterey Rd.
Stuart 407-286-6282

Stuart Yacht
450 SW Salerno Rd.
Stuart 407-283-1947
See advertisement on page 53.

Whiticar Boat Works
3636 SE Old St. Lucie Blvd.
Stuart 407-287-2883
See advertisement on page 54.

BROWARD COUNTY

Alaska Diesel Electric
1405 SW 6th Ct.
Pompano Bch. 954-946-7601

Complete Yacht Service
200 NW 33rd St.
Ft. Lauderdale 954-462-6977

Generator Plus
1123 SE 2nd Ave.
Deerfield Bch. 954-429-8724

Don Hillman
2501 State Road 84
Ft. Lauderdale 954-581-2376

Kilo-Pak
190 S. Bryan Road
Dania 954 925 6300

O-K Generators
373 N. River Ave.
Deerfield Bch. 954-428-9990

Sun Power Diesel
413 SW 3rd Ave.
Ft. Lauderdale 954-522-4775
See advertisement on page 71.

DADE COUNTY

R.B. Grove
261 SW 6th St.
Miami 305-854-5420

KEYS

Chris Carson's Marine
Service & Supply
Mile Marker 98.6 Bayside
Key Largo 305-852-2725

MARCO ISLAND TO PLACIDA

Hurricane Bay Marine
18850 San Carlos Blvd.
Ft. Myers 941-466-8898

Gulf Coast Marine Electric
1148 Main St.
Ft. Myers Bch 941-765-6600

Owl Creek Boat Works
18251 Owl Creek Dr.
Alva 941-543-2100

Rose Boat & Engine Works
4427 Mercantile Ave.
Naples 941-643-6657

ENGLEWOOD TO SKYWAY

AC Marine Inc.
2012 Whitfield Park Dr.
Bradenton 941-755-8053

Economy Supply
Venice 941-485-1430

Marine Installation Services
Bradenton 941-758-1587

SKYWAY TO TARPON SPRINGS

AAA Marine Products
4022 54th Ave. N.
St. Petersburg 813-521-1385

Diesel Energy Systems
7855 126th Ave. N.
Largo 813-536-9979

Marine A/CR Systems
2625 46th St. S.
St. Petersburg 813-321-9676

NORTHWEST

Bell Marine Service
18 Audusson Ave.
Pensacola 904-455-7639

Marine Services
801 S. Pace Blvd.
Pensacola 904-438-6454

Miller's Marina
PO Box 280
Suwannee 352-542-7349
See advertisement on page 123.

Posner Marine Service
610 New Warrington Rd.
Pensacola 904-453-8182

HEADS & MSDs

FIRST COAST & ST. JOHNS

The Boat Show
2999 SR 84 W.
Deland 904-736-6601

Daytona Marina & Boat Works
645 S. Beach St.
Daytona Bch. 904-252-6421

Florida Watercraft
177 North Cswy.
New Smyrna Bch. 904-426-2628

Sea Love Boatworks
4877 Front St.
Ponce Inlet 904-761-5434

Treworgy Yachts
5658 N. Oceanshore Blvd.
Palm Coast 904-445-5878

INDIAN RIVER LAGOON

Cape Marina
800 Scallop Dr.
Cape Canaveral 407-783-8410
See advertisement on page 45.

Pineda Point Marina
6175 N. Harbor City Blvd.
Melbourne 407-254-4199

Whitley Marine
93 Delannoy Ave.
Cocoa 407-632-5445
See advertisement on page 45.

STUART TO BOCA RATON

Irwin Oster Marine Service
Harbour Point Marina
2225 Monet Rd.
Palm Bch. Gdns. 407-627-1244

BROWARD COUNTY

Headhunter
214 SW 21st Terr.
Ft. Lauderdale 954-581-6996

Paul B. Murphy Co.
921 SE 20th St.
Ft. Lauderdale 954-522-2626

Raz Marine
281 SW 33rd St.
Ft. Lauderdale 954-525-5513

Raritan Engineering
3101 SW 2nd Ave.
Ft. Lauderdale 954-525-0378

DADE COUNTY

Bo Jean Boat Yard
3041 NW So. River Dr.
Miami 305-633-8919

KEYS

Marathon Boat Yard
2055 Overseas Hwy.
Marathon 305-743-6341

MARCO ISLAND TO PLACIDA

Hurricane Bay Marine
18850 San Carlos Blvd.
Ft. Myers 941-466-8898

Owl Creek Boat Works
18251 Owl Creek Dr.
Alva 941-543-2100

Palm Grove Marina
2500 Main St.
Ft. Myers Bch. 941-463-7333

Rose Boat & Engine Works
4427 Mercantile Ave.
Naples 941-643-6657

SKYWAY TO TARPON SPRINGS

Harbour Island Marina
777 S. Harbour Isl. Blvd. #270
Tampa 813-229-5324

Seafarer Marine Supply
12270 Ulmerton Rd.
Largo 813-595-8813

NORTHWEST

Brown Marine Services
40 Audusson Ave.
Pensacola 904-453-3471

Deckhand's Marina
1350 Miracle Strip Pkwy.
Ft. Walton Bch. 904-243-7359
See advertisement on page 132.

Engineering Specialties
Pensacola 904-968-6769

Miller's Marina
PO Box 280
Suwannee 352-542-7349
See advertisement on page 123.

Ship Shape Marina
8 Audussan Ave.
Pensacola 904-456-4000

Treasure Island Marina
3605 Thomas Dr.
Panama City Bch. 904-234-6533

Walker's Marine Service
F27C Park La.
Destin 904-837-9711

HYDRAULIC EQUIPMENT
FIRST COAST & ST. JOHNS

Circuit Engineering
8421 Atlantic Blvd.
Jacksonville 904-721-1414

Florida Watercraft
177 North Cswy.
New Smyrna Bch. 904-426-2628

Treworgy Yachts
5658 N. Oceanshore Blvd.
Palm Coast 904-445-5878

STUART TO BOCA RATON

E & H Boat Works
2180 Idlewilde Rd.
Palm Bch. Gdns. 407-622-8550

Florida Rigging & Hydraulics
3905 Investment Ln.
Riviera Bch. 407-863-7444

BROWARD COUNTY

C.L. Associates
260 SW 32nd Ct.
Ft. Lauderdale 954-525-9846

Latham Marine
280 SW 32nd Ct.
Ft. Lauderdale 954-462-9545

DADE COUNTY

Bo Jean Boat Yard
3041 NW So. River Dr.
Miami 305-633-8919

KEYS

H&H Marine Supplies
US 1, Stock island
Key West 305-294-1008

Manatee Bay Boatyard
99 Morris Lane
Key Largo 305-451-3332

Peninsular Marine Ent.
7 Peninsula Ave.
Key West 305-296-8110

Sirco Hardware & Marine
314 McDonald Ave. Stock Isl.
Key West 305-294-2537

MARCO ISLAND TO PLACIDA

Owl Creek Boat Works
18251 Owl Creek Dr.
Alva 941-543-2100

Hurricane Bay Marine
18850 San Carlos Blvd.
Ft. Myers Bch. 941-466-8898

Rose Boat & Engine Works
4427 Mercantile Ave.
Naples 941-643-6657

NORTHWEST

Brown Marine Service
40 Audusson Ave.
Pensacola 904-453-3471

INFLATABLES/ LIFE RAFTS SAFETY & SURVIVAL EQUIPMENT
FIRST COAST & ST. JOHNS

Boat/U.S.
8595 Beach Blvd.
Jacksonville 904-642-6238

Datrex
618 Tallyrand Ave.
Jacksonville 904-355-1401
See advertisement on page 33.

Florida Watercraft
177 North Cswy.
New Smyrna Bch. 904-426-2628

Pier 17 Marina
4619 Roosevelt Blvd.
Jacksonville 904-387-4669

Shaws Yacht Marine Supply
728 Ballough Rd.
Daytona Bch. 904-255-0495

INDIAN RIVER LAGOON

Cape Marina
800 Scallop Dr.
Cape Canaveral 407-783-8410
See Advertisement on page 45.

McLaughlin Marine
465 Ballard Dr.
Melbourne 407-242-2342

Modern Marine
515 N. U.S. 1
Fort Pierce 407 461 7285

STUART TO BOCA RATON

A Sailor's Place
2389 SE Dixie Hwy.
Stuart 407-283-9990

Boat/U.S.
Palm Bch. Marketplace
1900 B Okeechobee Blvd.
West Palm Bch. 407-684-490

Holiday Harbor Marina
14050 Canal-a-Way
Pensacola 904-492-0555

Inflatables International
West Palm Beach 407-881-1901

International Watercraft
2389 SE Dixie Hwy.
Stuart 407-283-0933

Zodiac Palm Beach
2240 Broadway
Riviera Beach 407-844-9399

BROWARD COUNTY

Boat/U.S.
505 W. Broward Blvd.
Ft. Lauderdale 954-523-2570

Inflatable Experts
2226 S Fed. Hwy.
Ft. Lauderdale 954 764 1161

Inflatable Repair Services
Ft. Lauderdale 954-462-6208

Inflatable Services/
84 Boat Works
990 W. St. Rd. 84
Ft. Lauderdale 954-779-7000

Lauderdale Marina
1900 SE 15th St.
Ft. Lauderdale 954-523-8507
See advertisement on page 59.

Marine Medical Center
17th St. Causeway
Ft. Lauderdale 954-527-9355

Pneumatic Craft
1020 W. Sunrise Blvd.
Ft. Lauderdale 954-46-5811
See advertisement on page 155.

DADE COUNTY

Boat/U.S.
6848 S.W. 40th Street
(Bird Road)
Miami 305-663-5745

Datrex
3795 NW 25th St.
Miami 305-638-8220

Eastern Aero Marine
3650 NW 25th St.
Miami 305-871-4050
1-800-THE-RAFT

Lifeline Inflatable Service
1584 N.W. 29th St.
Miami 305 636 1970

KEYS

The Boat House
12411 Overseas Hwy.
Marathon 305-289-1323

Inflatable Boats of
the Florida Keys
2601 Overseas Hwy.
Marathon 305-743-7085

Key West Inflatables
6000 Peninsular Ave.
Key West 305 293 0348

Marathon Boat Yard
2055 Overseas Hwy.
Marathon 305-743-6341

MARCO TO PLACIDA

Boat/U.S.
Bridge Plaza Shopping Ctr.
12901 McGregor Blvd.
Ft. Myers 941-481-9350
3808 E Tamiami Trail
Naples 941-774-3233

The Dinghy Shop
12011 Americus Drive
Ft. Myers 941 275 2040

Fish Tale Marina
7225 Estero Blvd.
Ft. Myers Bch. 941-463-4448

Inflatable Boat Center
11990 Cleveland Ave.
Ft. Myers 941-275-8555

ENGLEWOOD TO SKYWAY

Boat/U.S.
4229 S. Tamiami Trail
Sarasota 941-481-9350

Galati Perico Harbor Marina
12310 Manatee Ave. West
Bradenton 941-795-2628

Winslow Marine Products
928 S. Tamiami Tr.
Osprey 941-966-9791

INFLATABLES

SKYWAY TO TARPON SPRINGS

Avon Marine
4740 126th Ave. N.
Clearwater 800 642 AVON

Boat Doc
4971 110th Ave. No.
Clearwater 813 572 4317

Boat/U.S.
11477 U.S. Hwy. 19 N
Clearwater 813-573-1319

Bonnanni
107 N. 11th St.
Tampa 813-229-6411

D'Angelo Marine
905 E. Skagway
Tampa 813 933 7006

Harbour Island Marina
777 S. Harbour Isl. Blvd. #270
Tampa 813-229-5324

Survival Technologies
6418 US 41
Apollo Bch. 813-645-4515

NORTHWEST

Inflatable-boat
1103 S. Fairfield Dr.
Pensacola 904 455 8607

Marshall Marine Ways
Timber Island Rd.
Carrabelle 904-697-3428
See advertisement on page 127.

Pride of the Point Marina
Rt. 1 Box 3461
Panacea 904-349-2517

Shell Point Resort
Rt. 2
Crawfordville 904-926-7162
See advertisement on page 127.

Treasure Island Marina
3605 Thomas Dr.
Panama City Bch. 904-234-6533

INSURANCE

FIRST COAST & ST. JOHNS

Thompson, Bailey, Baker Agcy.
31 Cordova St.
St. Augustine 904-824-1631

INDIAN RIVER LAGOON

Rick Carroll Insurance
Jensen Bch. 407-334-3181

Pruitt Insurance
33 N. Babcock St.
Melbourne 407-254-3639

Warren T. Zeuch Insurance
2156 Ponce de Leon Circle
Vero Bch. 407-562-6581

BROWARD

C. A. Hansen Corp.
1650 SE 17th St., #205
Ft. Lauderdale 954-467-6432

Compass Financial Group
9540 N. Fed. Hwy. #208
Lighthouse Pt. 954 946 8505

The Loomis Company
2929 E. Commercial Blvd., #705
Ft. Lauderdale 954-772-0448

Maritime Insurance Group
2500 Hollywood #405
Hollywood 954 923 5582

Nederlanden Insurance
2413 E. Atlantic Blvd.
Pompano Bch. 954-941-0900

World Marine Underwriters
1600 SE 17th St.
Ft. Lauderdale 954-761-8500

DADE COUNTY

AmerInsurance
3401 NW 82nd Ave.
Miami 305-470-2011

The Kolisch Companies
90 Almeria Ave.
Coral Gables 305-447-8600

Royal Marine Yacht
Underwriters
8300 Executive Ctr. Dr., #102
Miami 305-477-3755

Seaward Marine Insurance
925 Arthur Godfrey Rd.
Miami Beach 305 538 0474

ENGLEWOOD TO SKYWAY

Florida Marine Insurance
Agency
240 No. Washington Blvd.
Sarasota 941 953 2255

SKYWAY TO TARPON SPRINGS

Acordia
311 Parkway Blvd.
Clearwater 813 796 6666

Allstate Insurance
1141 2nd Ave. S.
Tierra Verde 813-381-1758

Allied Specialty Insurance
10451 Gulf Coast Blvd.
Treasure Island 813-367-6900

Essex Credit Corp.
9620 Executive Center Dr.
St. Petersburg 813 576 2407

Tampa Bay Underwriters
750 94th Ave. N., #212
St. Petersburg 813-576-1682

Wiseley Marine Insurance
9300 Fifth St. North
St. Petersburg 813 579 9579

NORTHWEST

Harmon Gilmore
215 Mountain Dr., 103
Destin 904-837-6186

Treasure Island Marina
3605 Thomas Dr.
Panama City Bch. 904-234-6533

LUMBER & PLYWOOD

FIRST COAST & ST. JOHNS

Daytona Marina & Boat Works
645 S. Beach St.
Daytona Bch. 904-252-6421

Treworgy Yachts
5658 N. Oceanshore Blvd.
Palm Coast 904-445-5878

INDIAN RIVER LAGOON

Custom Docks Marine Lumber
Cocoa Bch. 407-452-5940

Gator Lumber
9555 S. US 1
Sebastian 407-589-8976

STUART TO BOCA RATON

Maritime Lumber Supply
2393 SE Dixie Hwy.
Stuart 407-287-2919

Southern Pine Lumber Co.
4436 SW Honey Tree Terr.
Stuart 407-283-6041

Teak Connection
2391 SE Dixie Hwy.
Stuart 800 274 8325

Whiticar Boat Works
3636 SE Old St. Lucie Blvd.
Stuart 407-287-2883
See advertisement on page 54.

BROWARD COUNTY

Seafarer Marine
3100 SW 3rd Ave
Ft. Lauderdale 954-763-4263

DADE COUNTY

Amazon Lumber & Trading
319 NE 59th Terr.
Miami 305-757-1943

Shell Lumber
2733 SW 27th Ave.
Miami 305-856-6401

Smitty's Boat Tops
727 S. Krome Ave.
Homestead 305-245-0229

KEYS

Marathon Woodworks
203 107th St. Gulf
Marathon 305-743-6401

MARCO TO PLACIDA

Owl Creek Boat Works
18251 Owl Creek Dr.
Alva 941-543-2100

SKYWAY TO TARPON SPRINGS

Wood Company
4161 118th Ave. N.
Clearwater 813-573-3611
1-800-288-3611

NORTHWEST

Bristol Woodworking
511-B Hwy. 98 E.
Destin 904-654-1001

Brown Marine Service
40 Audusson Ave.
Pensacola 904-453-3471

Destin Lumber & Supply
Hwy 98
Destin 904-837-2176

Hodges Bros. Lumber
437 N. Eglin Pkwy.
Ft. Walton Bch. 904-862-1555

MACHINE SHOP SERVICES

FIRST COAST & ST. JOHNS

The Boat Show
2999 SR 44 W.
Deland 904-736-6601

Daytona Marina & Boat Works
645 S. Beach St.
Daytona Bch. 904-252-6421

Treworgy Yachts
5658 N. Oceanshore Blvd.
Palm Coast 904-445-5878

INDIAN RIVER LAGOON

Harbor Town Marina/Boatyard
1936 HarborTown Dr.
Ft. Pierce 407-466-7300

Helseth Marine Services
3611 Rio Vista Blvd
Vero Beach 407 234 3560

Hydraulic Service
660 Oleander St.
Merritt Island 407-453-4673

Seabrite Stainless Steel
of Florida
424 S. DeLeon Ave.
Titusville 407-459-1282

STUART TO BOCA RATON

Bobby Soles Prop. Services
1730 Hill Ave.
W. Palm Bch. 407 848 6678

Champion Engines
3326 SE Dixie Hwy.
Stuart 407-283-6788

Diesel Mechanics Co-op
2608 NW 2nd Ave.
Boca Raton 407-391-8143

Performance Diesel Service
SPS Industrial Park
3079 SE Monroe St.
Stuart 407-283-2424

BROWARD COUNTY

American Marine Products
1790 SW 13th Ct.
Pompano Bch. 954-782-1400

Atkinson Marine, Inc.
235 SW 32nd Ct.
Ft. Lauderdale 954-763-1652

Chinnock Marine
518 W. Las Olas Blvd.
Ft. Lauderdale 954-763-2250

Clymer Diesel Power Services
1903 W. McNab Rd.
Pompano Bch. 954-971-6600

DeAngelo Marine Exhaust
150 SW 33rd St.
Ft. Lauderdale 954-763-3005

Derecktor-Gunnell
775 Taylor La.
Dania 954-920-5756

Lyman Automotive Mach.
220 S.W. 20th St.
Ft. Lauderdale 954 766 2565

Motor Services
3131 SW 2nd Ave.
Ft. Lauderdale 954-763-3660

DADE COUNTY

B & B Welding & Machine
6995 NW 32nd Ave.
Miami 305-696-3621

Power Propeller Co.
2611 N. W. 21st Terrace
Miami 800 662 3111

Smitty's Boat Tops
727 S. Krome Ave.
Homestead 305-245-0229

KEYS

Andrews Marine
3rd St. & 3rd Ave.
Key West 305-296-8887

Manatee Bay Boatyard
99 Morris Lane
Key Largo 305-451-3332

Mandalay Marine Repair
80 E. 2nd St.
Key Largo 305-852-5450

Peninsular Marine Enterprises
6000 Peninsula Ave
Key West 305-296-8110

Propeller Service
Key West 305-296-8887

MARCO ISLAND TO PLACIDA

Coast Engine Rebuilders
16163 Old US 1
Ft. Myers 941-482-7070

D & D Machine Specialties Inc.
2089 Central Ave.
Ft. Myers 941-334-4868

ENGLEWOOD TO SKYWAY

Deane Machine & Supply
614 7th Ave. W.
Bradenton 941-746-2115

General Propeller Co.
1415 Ninth Avenue East
Bradenton 1-800-282-3181

Rayco Manufacturing
1430 9th Ave. E
Bradenton 941-747-2728

SKYWAY TO TARPON SPRINGS

A to Z Machine & Welding
Unit C 1985 Sherwood
Clearwater 813-441-9776

Aquarius Marine
9 Oscar Hill Road
Tarpon Springs 813 938 5951

Bob's Machine Shop
1501 33rd St., SE
Ruskin 813-645-3966

Gulf Marine Ways
950 Dodecanese Blvd.
Tarpon Springs 813-937-4401

NORTHWEST

Brown Marine Service
40 Audusson Ave.
Pensacola 904-453-3471

Pride of the Point Marina
Rt. 1 Box 3461
Panacea 904-349-2517

MARINE STORES, RETAIL BAHAMAS

Running Mon Marina & Resort
Kelly Court & Knotts Blvd.
Freeport 800 315 6054

FIRST COAST & ST. JOHNS

Amelia Island Yacht Basin
999 First Coast Hwy., West
Amelia Island 904-277-4615

Baer Marine
299 San Marco
St. Augustine 904-824-3240

The Boat House
30 S. 2nd St.
Fernandina Bch. 904 261 0167

The Boat Show
2999 SR 84 W.
Deland 904-736-6601

Boat/U.S.
8595 Beach Blvd.
Jacksonville 904-642-6238

Boater's World
303 E. Altamonte Dr. Ste. 1000
Altamonte Spring 407-767-5788
9501 Arlington Expw, Unit E-51
Jacksonville 904-724-3601

Boathouse Marina
329 River St.
Palatka 904-328-2944
See advertisement on page 42.

Celia Lester's Ship Store
1202 Beach Blvd.
Jacksonville Bch. 904-247-5229
See advertisement on page 157.

Coquina Marina
256 Riberia St.
St. Augustine 904 824 2520

E & B Marine
5951 University Blvd. W.
Jacksonville 904-737-4360
8102 Blanding Blvd. W.
Jacksonville 904-777-4600

Fernandina Harbour Marina
One Front St.
Fernandina Beach 904 261 0355

First Mate Yacht Services
235 Yacht Club Dr.
St. Augustine 904-829-0184

Florida Watercraft
177 North Causeway
New Smyrna Bch. 904-426-2628

Halifax Harbor Marina
450 Basin St.
Daytona Bch. 904-253-0575
See advertisement on page 35.

Julington Creek Marina
12807 San Jose Blvd.
Jacksonville 904 268 5117

Palm Coast Marina
200 Clubhouse Dr.
Palm Coast 904-446-6370
See advertisement on page 35.

Pier 68 Marina
8137 N. Main St.
Jacksonville 904-765-9925

Pier 17 Marina
4619 Roosevelt Blvd.
Jacksonville 904-387-4669

Ponce Deepwater Landing
133 Inlet Harbor Rd.
Ponce Inlet 904-767-3266
See advertisement on page 35.

Sanford Boatworks Marina
4130 Celery Ave.
Sanford 407 222 6613

Sea Love Boat Works
4877 Front St.
Ponce Inlet 904 761 5434

Sebastian Harbor Marina
975 S. Ponce de Leon Blvd.
St. Augustine 904-825-4008

Seven Seas Marina& Boatyard
3300 S. Peninsula Dr.
Daytona Bch 904-761-3221

Shaws Yacht Marine Supply
728 Ballough Rd.
Daytona Bch. 904-255-0495

St. Augustine Municipal Marina
111 Avenida Menendez
St. Augustine 904 825 1026
See advertisement on page 38.

West Marine
4415 Roosevelt Blvd.
Jacksonville 904-388-7510

MARINE STORES

INDIAN RIVER LAGOON

Anchorage Yacht Basin
96 E. Eau Gallie Cswy.
Melbourne 407-773-3620
See advertisement on page 48.

Banana River Marine Service
1360 S. Banana River Drive
Merritt Island 407-452-8622
See advertisement on page 45.

Cape Marina
800 Scallop Dr.
Cape Canaveral 407-783-8410
See advertisement on page 45.

Diamond 99 Marina
4399 N. US 1
Melbourne 407-254-1490

Eau Gallie Yacht Basin
587 Young St.
Melbourne 407 254 1766
See Advertisement on page 48.

E & B Marine
1024 S. Harbor City Blvd.
Melbourne 407-723-1878
5135 Adanson St.
Orlando 407-644-8557
3523 NW Federal Hwy.
Jensen Bch. 407-692-3092

Fort Pierce City Marina
1 Avenue A
Fort Pierce 407 464 1245
See advertisement on page 51.

Harbor Town Marina/Boatyard
1936 HarborTown Dr.
Ft. Pierce 407-466-7300

Indian Cove Marina
14 Myrtice Ave.
Merritt Island 407-452-8540

Lake Marine Harbor
531 N. Palmetto Ave.
Sanford 407-322-2910

McLaughlin Marine
465 Ballard Dr.
Melbourne 407-242-2342

Melbourne Harbor
2210 S. Front St.
Melbourne 407 725 9054
See advertisement on page 47.

Modern Discount Marine
515 N. US 1
Ft. Pierce 407-461-7285

West Marine
1509 N. Harbor City Blvd.
Melbourne 407 242 9600

Whitley Marine
93 Delannoy Ave.
Cocoa 407-632-5445
See advertisement on page 45.

STUART TO BOCA RATON

Abscoa
373 SE Monterey Rd.
Stuart 407-286-9600

Boca Raton Resort & Club
501 E. Camino Real
Boca Raton 407-395-3000

Bluewater Marine Supply
1557 Cypress Dr.
Jupiter 407-744-3676

Boat Owners Warehouse
2230 Broadway (U.S. 1)
Riviera Bch. 407-845-7777

Boat/U.S.
Palm Bch. Marketplace
1900 B Okeechobee Blvd.
West Palm Bch. 407-684-490

Cannonsport Marina
178 Lake Drive
Palm Beach Shores 407 848 7469

C. Foster Marine Supplies
3385 SE Dixie Hwy.
Stuart 407-286-2118

Delray Harbor Club Marina
1035 S. Federal Hwy.
Delray Beach 407 276 0376
See advertisement on page 61.

E & B Marine
1401 Old Dixie Hwy.
Lake Park 407-863-1440

Hopkins Marine Hardware
207 6th St.
West Palm Bch. 407-832-4206

Jib Yacht Club & Marina
46 Beach Rd.
Tequesta 407-746-4300

Northside Marina
400 NW Alice Ave.
Stuart 407-692-4000

Palm Harbor Marina
400-A N. Flagler Dr.
West Palm Bch. 407-655-4757
See advertisement on page 66.

Rybovich Spencer
4200 Poinsettia Ave.
W. Palm Beach 407 844 1800

Sailfish Marina & Resort
98 Lake Dr.
Palm Bch. Shores 407-844-8460

West Marine
12189 US Hwy 1, #23
N. Palm Bch 407-775-1434

Whiticar Boat Works
3636 SE Old St. Lucie Blvd.
Stuart 407-287-2883
See advertisement on page 54.

BROWARD COUNTY

Boat Owners Warehouse
311 SW 24th St.
Ft. Lauderdale 954-522-7998
1720 E. Hallandale Bch. Blvd.
Hallandale 954-457-5081
750 E. Sample Rd.
Pompano Bch. 954-942-0477

Boat/U.S.
505 W. Broward Blvd.
Ft. Lauderdale 954-523-7993

Charlie's Locker
1445 SE 17th St.
Ft. Lauderdale 954-523-3350

E & B Marine Supply
2111 N. Federal Hwy.
Hollywood 954-921-1800
1951 W. Copans Rd.
Pompano Bch. 954-960-0560

Hildebrand Marine
3330 N. Federal Hwy.
Lighthouse Pt. 954-946-7840

KMC Marine
3856 N. U.S.1
Lighthouse Point 954-941-9193

Lauderdale Marina
1900 SE 15th St.
Ft. Lauderdale 954-523-8507
See advertisement on page 59.

Marine Hardware &
Equipment of Pompano
1530 N. Federal Hwy.
Pompano Bch. 954-782-2280

Sailorman
350 E. State Rd. 84
Ft. Lauderdale 954 522 6716

West Marine
2300 S. Federal Hwy.
Ft. Lauderdale 954-527-5540
110 N. Federal Hwy.
Deerfield Bch. 954-427-6165

DADE COUNTY

B & F Marine
1991 NW 27th Ave.
Miami 305-638-3614

Biscayne Bay Marriott
1633 N. Bayshore Dr.
Miami 305-374-4900
See advertisement on page 75.

Boating Mart
724 NE 79th St.
Miami 305-757-7671

Bo Jean Boat Yard
3041 NW So. River Dr.
Miami 305-633-8919

E & B Marine
18766 S. Dixie Hwy.
Miami 305-232-0811
8240 W. Flagler
Miami 305-225-9417

Florida Marine Service
227 SW 6th St.
Miami 305-285-0359

Hopkins-Carter Hardware Co.
3701 NW 21st St.
Miami 305 653 7377
300 Alton Rd.
(at Miami Beach Marina)
Miami Bch. 305 534 0300

Marine Express
2737 NW 17th St.
Miami 305-635-1064

River Marine Supply
260 SW 6th St.
Miami 305-856-0080

Ship & Shore
541 West Ave.
Miami Beach 305 534 4137

Turnberry Ship's Store
19755 Turnberry Way
N. Miami Bch. 305-932-6200
See advertisement on page 68.

West Marine
3635 S. Dixie Hwy.
Miami 305-444-5520

KEYS

The Boat House
12411 Overseas Hwy.
Marathon 305-289-1323

Caloosa Cove Marina
MM 73
Lwr. Matecumbe 305-664-4455

Curtis Marine
229 Banyan La.
Tavernier 305-852-5218

Faro Blanco
Oceanside & Bayside
MM 48.5
Marathon 305-743-9016
See advertisement on page 84.

Hawk's Cay Marina
MM 61 US 1
Marathon 305-743-9000

Key Largo Marine Supply
105960 US 1
Key Largo 305-451-5211

Key West Marine Hardware
818 Caroline St.
Key West 305-294-3425
See advertisement on page 89.

Manatee Bay Marine
99 Morris Ln
Key Largo 305-451-3332

Mariners Cove
MM 103.2
Key Largo 305-451-1030
4711 Overseas Hwy.
Marathon 305-743-0029

Mid Keys Marine Supply
2055 Overseas Hwy.
Marathon 305-743-6020

Oceanside Marina
6950 Maloney Ave.
Key West 305-294-4676

Perkins & Son Chandlery
901 Fleming St.
Key West 305-294-7635

Pinellas Marina
1200 Oceanview Ave.
Marathon 305-743-5317

Plantation Key Marina
MM 90.5 US 1
Plantation Key 305-852-5424

Tugboat's
2211 Overseas Hwy.
Marathon 305-743-4585

West Marine
2055 Overseas Hwy
Marathon 305 289 1009
725 Caroline St.
Key West 305 295 0999

MARCO ISLAND TO PLACIDA

Boat/U.S.
12901 MacGregor Blvd.
Ft. Myers 941-481-7447
3808 E. Tamiami Tr.
Naples 941-774-3233

Boater's World
12001 US Hwy 41
Ft. Myers 941-278-5500
2144 Tamiami Tr. N.
Naples 941-262-1575

Burnt Store Marina
Ship & Grocery
3150 Matecumbe Key Rd.
Punta Gorda 941 639 0225
See advertisement on page 100.

Crow's Nest Marina Restaurant
1968 Tarpon Circle Drive
Venice 941 484 7661

Deep Lagoon Marina
14070 McGregor Blvd.
Fort Myers 941 481 8200

E & B Marine Supply
4350 Fowler St.
Ft. Myers 941-275-5939

Factory Bay Marina
1079 Bald Eagle Dr.
Marco Island 941-642-6717

Fish Tale Marina
7225 Estero Blvd.
Ft. Myers Bch. 941-463-4448

Marine Surplus
2901 Palm Beach Blvd.
Ft. Myers 941 332 0909

Naples Ships Store
830 12th Ave. S.
Naples 941-649-0899

Palm Grove Marina
2500 Main St.
Ft. Myers Bch. 941-463-7333

Pineland Marina
13951 Waterfront Dr.
Bokeelia 941-283-0080

Port of the Islands
25000 Tamiami Trail East
Naples 941-394-3101

Rialto Harbor Docks
1901 Balsey Road
Alva 941 728 3036

Sanibel Island Marina
634 N. Yachtsman Dr.
Sanibel 941-472-2723

Shell Point Marina
3334 Shell Point Rd.
Ruskin 941-645-1313

Turner Marine of Naples
899 10th St. S.
Naples 941-262-5973
See advertisement on page 98.

West Marine
1520 Colonial Blvd.
Ft. Myers 941-275-6077
915 Taylor Rd.
Punta Gorda 941 637 0000

ENGLEWOOD TO SKYWAY

Boat /US
4229 S. Tamiami Tr.
Sarasota 941-925-7361

E & B Marine Supply
3140 Tamiami Tr.
Sarasota 941-351-3431

Gulf Coast Hardware
975 S. McCall Rd.
Englewood 941-474-1703

Gulfwind Marine
1485 S. Tamiami Trail
Venice 941-485-3388

Longboat Key Marina
2800 Harbourside Dr.
Longboat Key 941-383-8383

Marine Surplus
7070 15th St. E.
Sarasota 941-758-3552

Osprey Marine Center
480-1/2 Blackburn Pt. Rd.
Osprey 941-966-5657

Stump Pass Marina
3060 Placida Rd.
Englewood 941-697-3600

Turner Marine Supply
826 13th St. W.
Bradenton 941-746-3456

SKYWAY TO TARPON SPRINGS

Beacon Marine Supply
6801 Gulfport Blvd.
South Pasadena 813-345-6994

Boat/U.S.
 8203 N. Dale Mabry Hwy.
Tampa 813-933-5515
 11477 U.S. Hwy. 19 N
Clearwater 813-573-2678

Boater's World
 10500 Ulmerton Rd. #202
Largo 813-584-8500
 9931 Adamo Dr. E.
Tampa 813-620-0997

E & B Marine
 18891 US 19 N.
Clearwater 813-536-4002
 2000 34th St. N.
St. Petersburg 813-327-0072
 8245B N. Florida Ave.
Tampa 813-935-0449
 4750 US 19 N.
New Port Richey 813-841-7176

Harborage at Bayboro
1500 2nd St. So.
St. Petersburg 813 821 6347
See advertisement on page 116.

Kenyon Parts Superstore
19666 U.S. 19 N.
Clearwater 813-539-7444

Marina Point Ships Store
500 1st Ave S.E.
St. Petersburg 813-823-2555
See advertisement on page 113.

Marine Surplus
1142 34th St. South
St. Petersburg 813 321 0359

Marker 1 Marina
343 Causeway Blvd.
Dunedin 813 733 9324
See advertisement on page 112.

Prior Boat Builders
4100 Bayshore Blvd.
Dunedin 813-784-1396

Ross Yacht Service
279 Windward Passage
Clearwater 813-446-8191

Shell Point Marina
3324 W. Shell Pt. Rd.
Ruskin 813 645 1313

West Marine
5001 34th St. South
St. Petersburg 813-867-5700

NORTHWEST

Anything Marine
1129 Beck Ave.
Panama City 904-785-0630

Aquatic Enterprises
1201A Hwy. Miracle Strip E.
Ft. Walton Beach 904-243-5721

Baytowne Marina at Sandestin
5500 Hwy. 98 E.
Destin 904-267-7777
See advertisement on page 133.

Bayou Chico Marina
806 Lakewood Rd.
Pensacola 904-455-4552

The Boat Marine Supply
32 Hwy. 98 W
Ft. Walton Bch. 904-243-2628
See advertisement on page 132.

Crum's Mini-Mall
Hwy. 98
Panacea 904-984-0281

E & B Marine
 218 Eglin Pkwy. NE
Ft. Walton Bch. 904-664-2254
 1326 W. 15th St.
Panama City 904-763-1844
 618 New Warrington Rd.
Pensacola 904 456-7305

J. V. Gander
319 Water St.
Apalachicola 904-653-8889

Holiday Harbor Marina
14050 Canal-a-Way
Pensacola 904-492-0555

Marshall Marine
Timber Island Rd.
Carrabelle 904-697-3428
See advertisement on page 127.

Marquardt's Marina
Hwy. 98
Mexico Beach 904-648-8900

Mike's Marine Supply
Hwy. 98
Panacea 904-984-5637

Miller Marine
119 Water St.
Apalachicola 904-653-9521
See advertisement on page 128.

Moorings of Pensacola Beach
655 Pensacola Bch. Blvd.
Pensacola 904-932-0305

Panama City Marina
1 Harrison Ave.
Panama City 904-785-0161

Port Panacea Marina
Rocklanding Rd.
Panacea 904-349-2454

Pride of the Point Marina
Rt. 1 Box 3461
Panacea 904-349-2517

Sailors Supply Co.
231 E. Beach Dr.
Panama City 904-769-5007

Shell Point Resort
Rt. 2 Box 4361-1
Crawfordville 904-926-7162
See advertisement on page 127.

Shields Marina
PO Box 218, Riverside Dr.
St. Marks 904-925-6158

Skidmore's Sports Center
999 Hwy 44 E.
Crystal River 352-795-4033

Suncoast Marine & Outdoor
3784 S. Suncoast Blvd..
Homosassa Spgs. 352-628-9220

Treasure Island Marina
3605 Thomas Dr.
Panama City 904-234-6533

Twin Rivers Marina
3 Miles East of the Gulf
Crystal River 352 795 3552
See Advertisement on page 124.

Yachties of Florida
511-A Hwy. 98 E.
Destin 904-837-4900

Wefing's
Water St.
Apalachicola 904-653-9218

MISCELLANEOUS PRODUCTS & SERVICES

OUT OF STATE

Cruising Guide to the Florida Keys
Frank Papy
PO Box 263, Rt. 1
Ridgeland, SC 29936
803-726-3962
See advertisement on page 77.

Log Book Publications Living Aboard Magazine
141 N. Roadway
New Orleans 504 283 1312
See advertisement on page 14.

Trim Master Marine
3081 Mercantile Industrial Dr.
St. Charles, MO 63301
314-949-8746
See advertisement on page 9.

FIRST COAST & ST. JOHNS

Camachee Cove Yacht Harbor
3070 Harbor Dr.
St. Augustine 904-829-5676
Waterfront Property
See advertisement on page 38.

INDIAN RIVER LAGOON

Compton & Assoc., P. A.
117 Queen Christina Court
Ft. Pierce 407 466 918
Attorneys

RGM Industries
3342-A Lillian Blvd.
Titusville 407-269-0063
See advertisements on
 pages 45 & 149.

STUART TO BOCA RATON

William E. Guy, Jr.
P.O. Box 3386
Stuart 407-286-7322
Attorney

High Seas Fabrication
272 N. Flagler Ave.
Stuart 407 692 0000
Metal Work

Lift-All Crane Service
3873 SW Bruner Terr.
Stuart 407-283-5765

Poly-Steel Shelters
1209 E. Ocean Blvd.
Stuart 407-287-9294
Shelters, boat sheds

Yacht Shots
Photography by Rick Friese
PO Box 31658 Zip: 33420
Palm Bch. Gdns. 407-627-8989

BROWARD COUNTY

Abask Alarms
209 N. E. 33rd St.
Ft. Lauderdale 954 563 0758

Anchor Petroleum
Ft. Lauderdale 954-764-2407
Dockside fuel delivery service

American Lubri-Car
3087 NW 28th St.
Ft. Lauderdale 954-731-3200
Dockside oil & lube service

Bell South Mobility
Ft. Lauderdale 800-243-3000
See advertisement on
 inside cover.

Bright Ideas Advertising
108 S.E. 8th Ave.
Ft. Lauderdale, 954 763 5777
Marine Advertising Agency

Chowel
by Exmoor Co.
Ft. Lauderdale 800-749-8151
Fitted Chaise Lounge Cover
See advertisement on page 180.

Chris Pollock
 Bookkeeping Services
Ft. Lauderdale 954-726-2770

Clearsight
1378 S. E. 17th St.
Fort Lauderdale 954 761 3937
Opticians

Crew Unlimited
2065 S. Federal Hwy.
Ft. Lauderdale 954-462-4624
Crew Placement/Yacht Deliveries

MISCELLANEOUS

Drum Reality
1900 S. E. 15th St.
Ft. Lauderdale 954 764 4242
Marine oriented real estate

Mark Ercolin
901 S.E. 17th St., Ste. 210
Fort Lauderdale 954 792 5425
Attorney

Federal Marine Consignment
2501 So. Federal Hwy.
Ft. Lauderdale 954 779 7559

Great Southern Insulation
923 SE 20th St.
Ft. Lauderdale 954-763-1844
Yacht Soundproofing

Hassel Free - Crew Services
1550 SE 17th St., #5
Ft. Lauderdale 954-763-1841

International Marina Resources
300 SW 2nd St.
Ft. Lauderdale 954-764-2064
Marina Mgt., Consultants

Island Express
Terminal 3, Ft. Laud. Airport
Ft. Lauderdale 954 359 0380
Airline to the Bahamas

Lady Bug Pest Control
PO Box 22031
Ft. Lauderdale 954-764-4936

Marine Medical Center
1493 SE 17th St.
Ft. Lauderdale 954-527-9355

The Marine Web
515 Seabreeze Blvd.
Ft. Lauderdale 954 463 4125
See advertisement on page 15.

Marine Welding & Fabricating
241 S. W. 31st. St.
Ft. Lauderdale 954 525 0348

**Mayhue's Super Liquor
 Spirits Delivery**
1645 Cordova Rd.
Ft. Lauderdale 954-525-6565
See ad on page 159.

Mike Whitt Photography
1550 S. E. 17th St. #3
Ft. Lauderdale 954 463 8249

World Yacht Club
2698 SW 23rd Ave.
Ft. Lauderdale 954-587-3387
1-800-45-FLOAT
Computer filing of Float Plans

Waterfront News
1523 S. Andrews Ave.
Ft. Lauderdale 954-524-9450
See advertisement on page 76.

**Waterfront Publishing
Waterway Times Magazine**
7 SW 15th Terr.
Ft. Lauderdale 954-761-1937
See advertisement on page 13.

Yachting Promotions
1315 N. E. 9th Ave.
Ft. Lauderdale 954 764 7642
Boat shows

DADE COUNTY

Bahamas Tourist Office
Aventura 800 327 7678
See advertisement on page 21.

JT's Marine Engine Service
4370 SW 13th Terr.
Miami 305-443-4192
Gas, diesel & electrical repairs

Mitchell, Harris, Horr & Assoc.
2650 Biscayne Blvd.
Miami 305-358-1405
Attorneys

KEYS

Dolphin Research Center
MM 59 Gulfside
Marathon 305-289-1121

Key West
Seaplane Service
Key West 305-294-6978

Pilot House Marina
15 No. Channel Dr.
Key Largo 305 451 3452
Auto Rentals

MARCO ISLAND TO PLACIDA

Dri-Dek Corporation
2706 S. Horseshoe Dr.
Naples 1-800-348-2398
Compartment Liner

ENGLEWOOD TO SKYWAY

Mote Marine Laboratory
1600 City Island Park
Sarasota 941-388-4441
Boat donations

Ship to Shore
Ft. Myers 941-945-0535
Fuel delivery

SKYWAY TO TARPON SPRINGS

Quickload Boat Trailers
2901 44th Ave. N.
St. Petersburg 813-527-5078

NORTHWEST

Apalachicola Maritime Institute
Apalachicola 904-653-8708
1877 Workboat & Museum

The Destin Fishing Museum
1 Block East of Destin Bridge
Destin 904-654-1011

MOORING & DOCK PRODUCTS, LIFTS

FIRST COAST & ST. JOHNS

Florida Floats
1813 Dennis St.
Jacksonville 904-358-3362

Florida Watercraft
177 North Cswy.
New Smyrna Bch. 904-426-2628

Gator Dock & Marine
Sanford 1-800-621-2207

Halifax Marine Construction
945 Duncan Rd. S.
Daytona 904-767-4972

Keibler Tech
967 NE Industrial Park
Jensen Bch. 407-334-7025

Mooring Products
1189 N. US #1
Ormond Beach 904 676 9447

INDIAN RIVER LAGOON

Sidewinder Boat Lifts
962 Industrial Park
Jensen Beach 407 334 7025

Whitley Marine
93 Delannoy Ave.
Cocoa 407 632 5445
See advertisement on page 45.

STUART TO BOCA RATON

Boca Dock & Seawall
160 So. Dixie Hwy.
Boca Raton 407 750 4255

Hi-Tide Marine Const.
3191 SE Waaler St.
Stuart 407-283-9354

BROWARD COUNTY

Atlantic Boatlifts
1111 Old Griffin Rd.
Dania 954-524-2000

Flexmaster Dock Fenders
Dania 954-922-0610

Hemisphere Marine
1900 S. E. 15th St.
Ft. Lauderdale 954 523 8507

Mar-Quipt
231 SW 5th St.
Pompano Bch. 954-942-0440

Mooring Products
 of Florida
1590 N. Federal Hwy.
Pompano Bch. 954-942-0200

DADE COUNTY

Aqua Lift
18524 NW 67th Ave.
Miami 305-556-8299

KEYS

The Boat House
12411 Overseas Hwy.
Marathon 305-289-1323

Marathon Boat Yard
2055 Overseas Hwy.
Marathon 305-743-6341

Marathon Marina
1021 11th St. Oceanside
Marathon 305-743-6595

Smokey Stover, Inc.
Sugarloaf Key 305-745-1114

MARCO ISLAND TO PLACIDA

Dolphin Boat Lifts
114 5th St., Page Pk.
Ft. Myers 941-936-1782

ENGLEWOOD TO SKYWAY

Ace Boat Hoist
2211 South Tamiami Trail
Venice 941-493-8100

Casey Key Marina
482 Blackburn Pt. Rd.
Osprey 941 966 1730

Galati Perico Harbor Marina
12310 Manatee Ave. West
Bradenton 941-795-2628

SKYWAY TO TARPON SPRINGS

Davit Master
5560 Ulmerton Rd.
Clearwater 813-573-4414

Lucas Manufacturing
12875 58th St. North
Clearwater 813-535-2174

Nautical Structures
13161 56th Ct.
Clearwater 813-573-4414

Shell Point Marina
3324 Shell Point Rd.
Ruskin 813-645-1313

NORTHWEST

Bailey Marine Construction
Pensacola 904-432-5909

The Moorings at Carrabelle
1000 U. S. Hwy. 98
Carrabelle 904 697 3950

Posner Marine Services, Inc.
 610 New Warrington Rd.
Pensacola 904-453-8182

Treasure Island Marina
3605 Thomas Dr.
Panama City Bch. 904-234-6533

PAINTING & REFINISHING-MATERIALS & SERVICES

FIRST COAST & ST. JOHNS

Amelia Island Yacht Basin
999 First Coast Hwy., West
Amelia Island 904-277-4615

Miller's Marina
PO Box 280
Suwannee 352-542-7349
See advertisement on page 123.

Pier 68 Marina
8137 N. Main St.
Jacksonville 904-765-9925

Sea Love Boat Works
4877 Front St.
Ponce Inlet 904 761 5434

INDIAN RIVER LAGOON

Cape Marina
800 Scallop Dr.
Cape Canaveral 407-783-8410
See advertisement on page 45.

Coastal Marine Repair
1357 S. Banana River Dr.
Merritt Island 407-453-1885
See advertisement on page 45.

Pineda Point Marina
6175 N. Harbor City Blvd.
Melbourne 407-254-4199

Whitley Marine
93 Delannoy Ave.
Cocoa 407-632-5445
See advertisement on page 45.

STUART TO BOCA RATON

David Lowe's Boatyard
4550 SE Boatyard Dr.
PO Box L, Rocky Point
Port Salerno 407-287-0923
See advertisement on page 57.

Monterey Marine
6800 SW Jack James Dr.
Stuart 407-286-2835

Jack Noll, Inc.
4715 SE DeSoto Ave.
Stuart 407-221-3883

Whiticar Boat Works
3636 SE Old St. Lucie Blvd.
Stuart 407-287-2883
See advertisement on page 54.

BROWARD COUNTY

Summerfield Boat Works
1500 SW 17th St.
Ft. Lauderdale 954-525-4726

DADE COUNTY

Anchor Marine
96 NW 7th St.
Miami 305-545-6348

Bo Jean Boat Yard
3041 NW So. River Dr.
Miami 305-633-8919

KEYS

The Boat House
12411 Overseas Hwy.
Marathon 305-289-1323

Marathon Boat Yard
2055 Overseas Hwy.
Marathon 305-743-6341

Mid Keys Marine Supply
2055 Overseas Hwy.
Marathon 305-743-6020

MARCO ISLAND TO PLACIDA

All Marine
4800 Wholesale G N.W.
North Ft. Myers 941-995-7990

Gulf Marine Ways & Supply
1148 Main St.
Ft. Myers Bch. 941-463-6166

Rose Boat & Engine Works
4427 Mercantile Ave.
Naples 941-643-6657

ENGLEWOOD TO SKYWAY

Gulfwind Marine
1485 S. Tamiami Trail
Venice 941-485-3388

SKYWAY TO TARPON SPRINGS

Indian Springs Marina
15151 113th Ave. N.
Largo 813-595-2956

Maximo Marine Service
3701 1/2 50th Ave. S.
St. Petersburg 813-867-7718

New Nautical Coatings
4242 31st St. N.
St. Petersburg 813 528 0997

Prior Boat Builders
4100 Bayshore Blvd.
Dunedin 813-784-1396

NORTHWEST

Deckhand's Marina
1350 Miracle Strip Pkwy.
Ft. Walton Bch. 904-243-7359
See advertisement on page 132.

Hardwood Sales
721 N. T St.
Pensacola 904-432-8238

Williams Boat Yard
720 S. C St.
Pensacola 904-432-4191

PLATING & METAL REFINISHING

FIRST COAST & ST. JOHNS

Sea Love Boatworks
4877 Front St.
Ponce Inlet 904-761-5434

BROWARD COUNTY

Gulf Plating
518 SW 1st Ave.
Ft. Lauderdale 305-467-9751

KEYS

Marathon Boat Yard
2055 Overseas Hwy.
Marathon 305-743-6341

MARCO ISLAND TO PLACIDA

Owl Creek Boat Works & Storage
18251 Owl Creek Dr.
Alva 941-543-2100

SKYWAY TO TARPON SPRINGS

Galati Perico Harbor Marina
12310 Manatee Ave. West
Bradenton 813-795-2628

PROPELLERS, SHAFTS & BEARINGS

FIRST COAST & ST. JOHNS

Ellis Propeller Co.
2900 Phoenix Ave.
Jacksonville 904-354-8233

Daytona Marina & Boat Works
645 S. Beach St.
Daytona Bch. 904-252-6421

Florida Watercraft
177 North Cswy.
New Smyrna Bch. 904-426-2628

Hidden Harbor Marina
4370 Carraway Place
Sanford 407 322 1610

Jacksonville Propeller & Mach.
520 E 8th St.
Jacksonville 407-353-6213

Sea Love Boatworks
4877 Front St.
Ponce Inlet 904-761-5434

Treworgy Yachts
5658 N. Oceanshore Blvd.
Palm Coast 904-445-5878

INDIAN RIVER LAGOON

Cape Marina
800 Scallop Dr.
Cape Canaveral 407-783-8410
See advertisement on page 45.

Harbor City Marine Service
982 Aurora Rd.
Melbourne 407-259-1206

Indian Cove Marina
14 Myrtice Ave.
Merritt Island 904-452-8540

Intracoastal Marina of Melbourne
705 S. US 1
Melbourne 407-725-0090
See advertisement on page 48.

Pineda Point Marina
6175 N. Harbor City Blvd.
Melbourne 407-254-4199

Whitley Marine
93 Delannoy Ave.
Cocoa 407-632-5445
See advertisement on page 45.

STUART TO BOCA RATON

Bobby Soles Propeller
3009 SE Monroe St.
Stuart 407-283-1453
1730 Hill Ave. Mangonia Park
West Palm Bch. 407-848-6678

Jack Noll, Inc.
4715 SE DeSoto Ave.
Stuart 407-221-3883

Motor Fuelers Inc.
Box 33743
St. Petersburg 813-527-4701

Stuart Propeller & Marine
4340 SE Commerce Ave.
Stuart 407-286-7343

BROWARD COUNTY

Frank & Jimmie's Prop Shop
100 SW 6th St.
Ft. Lauderdale 954-467-7723

High Seas Marine Parts & Props
5046 NE 12th Ave.
Ft. Lauderdale 954-771-9668

Lauderdale Propeller Service
755A Taylor Lane
Dania 954-921-5002

DADE COUNTY

Bo Jean Boat Yard
3041 NW So. River Dr.
Miami 305-633-8919

Miami Propeller Co.
2051 NW 11th St.
Miami 1-800-433-7767

Power Propeller Co.
2611 N. W. 21st Terrace
Miami 800 662 3111

KEYS

The Boat House
12411 Overseas Hwy.
Marathon 305-289-1323

Coral Bay Marina
601 Mastic St.
Islamorada 305 664 3111

Keys Propeller & Marine Supply
MM 102.5
Key Largo 305-451-0031

Manatee Bay Marine
99 Morris Lane
Key Largo 305-451-3332

MARCO ISLAND TO PLACIDA

Deep Lagoon Marina
14070 McGregor Blvd.
Fort Myers 941 481 8200

Del Rey Divers (East)
Naples 941-263-2319

East Trail Marine
11572 Tamiami Trail E.
Naples 941-775-6111

Hurricane Bay Marine
18850 San Carlos Blvd.
Ft. Myers Bch. 941-466-8898

Marine Propeller Service
1115 SE 12th Ct.
Cape Coral 941-772-3222

Owl Creek Boat Works
18251 Owl Creek Dr.
Alva 941-543-2100

ENGLEWOOD TO SKYWAY

Galati Perico Harbor Marina
12310 Manatee Ave. West
Bradenton 941-795-2628

General Propeller Co.
1415 Ninth Avenue East
Bradenton 1-800-282-3181

Gulfwind Marine
1485 S. Tamiami Trail
Venice 941-485-3388

Hill Propellers
1950 Whitfield Park Dr.
Sarasota 941 755 8277

Osprey Marine Center
480.5 Blackburn Pt. Rd.
Osprey 941-966-5657

Royal Palm Marina Inc.
779 W. Wentworth
Englewood 941-474-1420

SKYWAY TO TARPON SPRINGS

Admiral C&B
6235 S. Manhattan Ave.
Tampa 813 837 9476
10491 75th St. N.
Largo 813 545 2767

Maximo Marine Service
3701 1/2 50th Ave. S.
St. Petersburg 813-867-7718

The Prop Exchange
26 1st St North
St. Petersburg 813-894-1882

NORTHWEST

Brown Marine Service
40 Audusson Ave.
Pensacola 904-453-3471

Engineering Specialties
Pensacola 904-968-6769

Gator Propeller Service
Rt. 3 Box 423
Perry 904-584-6727

Holiday Marine
1126 No. Blvd. E.
Leesburg 352 787 4824

Marine Wheels Inc.
2902 W. 12th St.
Panama City 904-763-2889

Marquardt's Marina
Hwy. 98
Mexico Bch. 904-648-8900

Marshall Marine
Timber Island Rd.
Carrabelle 904-697-3428
See advertisement on page 127.

Panama Props
7431 E. Hwy. 22
Panama City 904-871-3431

Passport Marina
5325 N. Lagoon Dr.
Panama City Bch. 904 234 5609

Prop Shop
801 S. Pace Blvd.
Pensacola 904 469 0600

Treasure Island Marina
3605 Thomas Dr.
Panama City Bch. 904-234-6533

SAILING SUPPLIES: SAILS, RIGGING & HARDWARE

FIRST COAST & ST. JOHNS

Lynn's Canvas Shop
2403 Market St.
Jacksonville 904-353-0306

Amelia Island Yacht Basin
999 First Coast Hwy., West
Amelia Island 904-277-4615

Daytona Marina & Boat Works
645 S. Beach St.
Daytona Bch. 904-252-6421

Florida Watercraft
177 North Cswy.
New Smyrna Bch. 904-426-2628

Sea Love Boatworks
4877 Front St.
Ponce Inlet 904-761-5434

St. Augustine Marine
404 S. Riberia St.
St. Augustine 904-824-4394
See advertisement on page 37.

INDIAN RIVER LAGOON

Banana River Marine Service
1360 S. Banana River Drive
Merritt Island 407-452-8622
See advertisement on page 45.

Diamond 99 Marina & Yacht Sales
4399 N. US 1
Melbourne 407-254-1490

Indian Cove Marina
14 Myrtice Ave.
Merritt Island 407-452-8540

McLaughlin Marine
465 Ballard Dr.
Melbourne 407-242-2342

Pineda Point Marina
6175 N. Harbor City Blvd.
Melbourne 407-254-4199

Sails by Morgan
14 Myrtrice Ave..
Merritt Island 407-452-6689

Whitley Marine
93 Delannoy Ave.
Cocoa 407-632-5445
See advertisement on page 45.

STUART TO BOCA RATON

Boca Raton Resort & Club
501 E. Camino Real
Boca Raton 407-395-3000

Mack Sails
3129 SE Dominica Terr.
Stuart 407-283-2306

Wilmark Sailmakers
2400 E. Tamarind Ave.
West Palm Bch. 407-833-4824

SAILING

BROWARD COUNTY

Beaver-Brand Canvas
205 S. W. 7th Ave
Ft. Lauderdale 305 763 7423

Hood Sailmakers
100 SW 15th St.
Ft. Lauderdale 305-522-4663

Nance & Underwood Sails
& Rigging
262 SW 33rd St.
Ft. Lauderdale 305-764-6001

Norseman Marine
516 W. Las Olas Blvd.
Ft. Lauderdale 305-467-1407

Sail Cleaners
4910 NE 11th Ave.
Ft. Lauderdale 305-491-3327

Super Sailmakers
503 N. Andrews Ave.
Ft. Lauderdale 305-763-6621

DADE COUNTY

Bo Jean Boat Yard
3041 NW So. River Dr.
Miami 305-633-8919

Neil Pryde - Fowler Sails
2210 NW 14th St., #10
Miami 305-638-8885

Sailing Services
2560 SW 27th Ave.
Miami 305-444-4774

Shore Sails
615 SW 2nd Ave.
Miami 305-858-3000

KEYS

Abaco Sails
11215 US 1
Marathon 305-743-0337

Tugboat's
2211 Overseas Hwy.
Marathon 305-743-4585

Cayo Hueso Sails
& Ship Store
2318 N. Roosevelt Blvd.
Key West 305-294-1365

Curtis Marine
229 Banyan La.
Tavernier 305-852-5218

Key Largo Harbour
100 Ocean Dr.
Key Largo 305-451-0045

Key West Marine Hardware
818 Caroline St.
Key West 305-294-3425
See advertisement on page 89.

MARCO ISLAND TO PLACIDA

Advanced Sailing Services
1000 San Carlos Blvd.
Ft. Myers Beach 941-466-2700

Seaworthy Sails
400 South Road
Ft. Myers 941-275-0555

Turner Marine of Naples
899 10th St. S.
Naples 941-262-5973
See advertisement on page 98.

ENGLEWOOD TO SKYWAY

Atlantic Sail Traders
2062 Harvard St.
Sarasota 941 351 6023

Sailmakers
417 10th Ave. W.
Palmetto 941 723 0802

Sailor's Marine Supply, Ltd.
238 Tamiami Trail South
Venice 941-485-9774

The Sail Exchangers
2062 Harvard
Sarasota 941-955-7600

Ullman Sails
957 N. Lime Ave
Sarasota 941-951-0189

SKYWAY TO TARPON SPRINGS

Advanced Sails
107 15th Ave. S. E.
St. Petersburg 813 896 7245

Doyle Sailmakers
4320 Gandy Blvd.
Tampa 813 837 0966

Hood Sailmakers Inc./
Hood Yacht Systems
107 SE 15th Ave.
St. Petersburg 813-823-3392

Johnson Sails
3000 Gandy Blvd.
St. Petersburg 813-577-3220

Marina Point Ships Store
500 1st Ave S.E.
St. Petersburg 813-823-2555

North Sails
1320 20th St. No.
St. Petersburg 813 898 1123

The Rip Shop
1663 1st Ave. S.
St. Petersburg 813-896-2313

Ross Yacht Service
279 Windward Passage
Clearwater 813-446-8191

Sailor's Wharf
1421 Bay St. SE
St. Petersburg 813-823-1155

UK Sailmaker
1211 N. Betty La.
Clearwater 813-461 0022

NORTHWEST

C. B. Sails
5308 East Hwy. 98
Panama City 800 334 8854

Pride of the Point Marina
Rt. 1 Box 3461
Panacea 904-349-2517

Schurr Sails
490 S. L St.
Pensacola 904-438-9354

Tarpon Dock Marina
231 E. Beach Dr.
Panama City 904 769 5007

SHOES & SHOE REPAIR

FIRST COAST & ST. JOHNS

Palm Coast Marina
200 Clubhouse Dr.
Palm Coast 904-446-6370
See advertisement on page 35.

The Shaws YB & Marine
728 Ballough Rd.
Daytona Bch. 904-255-0495

STUART TO BOCA RATON

Maus & Hoffman
Worth Ave.
Palm Bch. 407-655-1141
Royal Palm Plaza
Boca Raton 407-368-9983

BROWARD COUNTY

Dockside Cobbler
1376 SE 17th St.
Ft. Lauderdale 954-763-4057

Lounge Lizards
Las Olas Blvd.
Ft. Lauderdale 954-561-5689

Maus & Hoffman
800 E. Las Olas Blvd.
Ft. Lauderdale 800-628-6287

Modern Shoe Repair
1421 S. Andrews Ave.
Ft. Lauderdale 954-524-9409

DADE COUNTY

Marks Athletic Soles
4028 SW 57th Ave.
Miami 305-665-8601

Maus & Hoffman
Bal Harbour Shops
Bal Harbour 305-865-7411

SKYWAY TO TARPON SPRINGS

Marina Point Ships Store
500 1st Ave S.E.
St. Petersburg 813-823-2555

SURVEYORS

FIRST COAST & ST. JOHNS

Dan LaBry
Jacksonville 904-737-6669

Pascoe & Bass
10536 Inverness Dr.
Jacksonville 904-262-4015

Society of Accredited
Marine Surveyors
4163 Oxford Ave.
Jacksonville 800-344-9077

INDIAN RIVER LAGOON

James C. Harper & Associates
300 Magnolia Ave. Ste. 3
Merritt Island 407-452-5091

South Sails
101 Central Rd.
Indian Harbor Bch. 407 777 9555

Capt. Warren Sheffield
Melbourne 407-259-5681

STUART TO BOCA RATON

Thomas Price
9418 SE Sharon St.
Hobe Sound 407-546-0928

Seese Marine Surveyors
2303 N. US Hwy. 1, #4
Ft. Pierce 407-465-0425

BROWARD COUNTY

Pascoe & Associates
1721 SE 4th Ave.
Ft. Lauderdale 954-524-8661

Ed Rowe & Assoc.
1821 S. W. 22nd Ave.
Ft. Lauderdale 954 792 6092

Mike Rhodes, Marine Surveyor
PO Box 50163
Lighthouse Point 954-946-6671

Gerald Slakoff, Marine Surveyor
1525 N. Andrews Ave.
Ft. Lauderdale 954-525-7930

Southeast Fire & Marine Assoc.
PO Box 805 New River Station
Ft. Lauderdale 954-527-1981

The Marine Surveyors
120 E. Oakland Park Blvd. #202
Ft. Lauderdale 954-566-6806

DADE COUNTY

Dave Alter & Assoc.
POB 560-532
Miami Zip: 33256
305-667-0326

American Nautical Services
Navigation Center
250 NE 3rd St.
Miami 305-358-1414

Brett Carlson Marine
1002 N. E. 105th St.
Miami Shores 305 891 0445

KEYS

Deep 6 Marine Surveyors
300 Morris Lane
Key Largo 305-451-2817

Osprey Marine Services
4650 Overseas Hwy.
Marathon 305-743-4435

MARCO ISLAND TO PLACIDA

Independent Marine Surveyors
18400 San Carlos Blvd.
Ft. Myers Bch. 941-466-4544

ENGLEWOOD TO SKYWAY

R. C. Buckles Associates
Sarasota 941-924-3013
(Tampa Bay to Marco)

SKYWAY TO TARPON SPRINGS

Coral Marine Services
St. Petersburg 813 527 6653

ITS Marine Surveyors
10051 5th St. N.
St. Petersburg 813-578-4003

NORTHWEST

Richard M. Everett III
P. O. Box 13512
Pensacola 904 934 3783

Marine Surveyors
Panama City 904-769-7323

Pride of the Point Marina
Rt. 1 Box 3461
Panacea 904-349-2517

Treasure Island Marina
3605 Thomas Dr.
Panama City Bch. 904-234-6533

TOWING & SALVAGE

FIRST COAST & ST. JOHNS

Daytona Marina & Boat Works
645 S. Beach St.
Daytona Bch. 904-252-6421

First Mate Yacht Services
212 Yacht Club Dr.
Camachee Cove Yacht Harbor
St. Augustine 904-829-0184

STUART TO BOCA RATON

E & H Boat Works
2180 Idlewilde Rd.
Palm Bch. Gdns. 407-622-8550

Jack Noll, Inc.
4715 SE DeSoto Ave.
Stuart 407-221-3883

Sailfish Marina
3565 SE St. Lucie Blvd.
Stuart 407-283-1122

TowBoat/U.S.
P. O. 718
Port Salerno 407 283 5077

BROWARD COUNTY

Cape Ann Towing
Ft. Lauderdale 954 463-2527

Gahagen's Diving & Towing Co.
1490 SW 18th Terr.
Ft. Lauderdale 954-463-7845

Koch Towing Co.
1614 SW 18th Ave.
Ft. Lauderdale 954-467-3500

DADE COUNTY

Atlantis Marine
3400 Pan American Dr.
Miami 305-854-6198

Sealift
2999 NW 2nd Ave.
Miami 305-576-2151

KEYS

Dolphin Marina
MM 28.5, US 1
Rt. 4, Box 1038
Little Torch Key 305-872-2685

**Gilbert's Holiday Island
of Key Largo**
107900 Overseas Hwy.
Key Largo 305-451-1133
See advertisement on page 81.

Key West Harbor Service
901 Fleming St.
Key West 305-296-7075

Manatee Bay Marine
99 Morris Lane
Key Largo 305-451-3332

MARCO ISLAND TO PLACIDA

Deep Lagoon Marina
14070 McGregor Blvd.
Fort Myers 941 481 8200

Gulf Coast Marine
   Towing & Salvage
820 12th Ave. S.
Naples 941-261-7599

Moss Marine
Harbor Ct.
Ft. Myers Bch. 941-463-6137

Pineland Marina
13951 Waterfront Dr.
Pineland 941-283-0080

Smitty's Marine
   Towing & Salvage
414 Crescent
Ft. Myers Bch. 941-765-1444

ENGLEWOOD TO SKYWAY

Terry's Marine Services
Englewood 941 697 3459

Maritime Safety
Bradenton 941-756-3422

SKYWAY TO TARPON SPRINGS

Bay Towing
1305 Shoreline Dr.
Tampa 813-247-1552

Gulfwind Towing
202 22nd St.
Tampa 813-248-8697

NORTHWEST

Brown Marine Service
40 Audusson Ave.
Pensacola 904-453-3471

Deckhand's Marina
1350 Miracle Strip Pkwy.
Ft. Walton Bch. 904-243-7359
See advertisement on page 132.

Destin Marine Salvage
646Hwy. 98
Destin 904-837-9401

Pride of the Point Marina
Rt. 1 Box 3461
Panacea 904-349-2517

Treasure Island Marina
3605 Thomas Dr.
Panama City Bch. 904-234-6533

Undertow
31 Newman Ave.
Pensacola 904 453 3775

TRANSMISSIONS

FIRST COAST & ST. JOHNS

Daytona Marina & Boat Works
645 S. Beach St.
Daytona Bch. 904-252-6421

Peyton's Marine Engineering
140 Riverside Dr.
Holly Hill 904-252-6008

Sea Love Boatworks
4877 Front St.
Ponce Inlet 904-761-5434

Treworgy Yachts
5658 N. Oceanshore Blvd.
Palm Coast 904-445-5878

INDIAN RIVER LAGOON

**Banana River
   Marine Service**
1360 S. Banana River Drive
Merritt Island 407-452-8622
See advertisement on page 45.

Cape Marina
800 Scallop Dr.
Cape Canaveral 407-783-8410
See advertisement on page 45.

Harbor Town Marina/Boatyard
1936 HarborTown Dr.
Ft. Pierce 407-466-7300

STUART TO BOCA RATON

Marine Diesel Analysts
2851 SE Monroe St.
Stuart 407-288-3208

Marine Propulsion Corp.
3201 SE Railroad Ave.
Stuart 407-283-6486

National Transmissions
502 NE 3rd St.
Boynton Bch. 407-737-7551

BROWARD COUNTY

Marine Gear & Power Systems
2901 SW 2nd Ave.
Ft. Lauderdale 954-763-6433

River Bend Marina
1515 SW 20th St.
Ft. Lauderdale 954-523-1832

Transmission Marine
223 SW 33rd Ct.
Ft. Lauderdale 954-467-1540

Tuit Power
225 SW 33rd Ct.
Ft. Lauderdale 954-467-1508
See advertisement on page 163.

DADE COUNTY

Bo Jean Boat Yard
3041 NW So. River Dr.
Miami 305-633-8919

Champion Marine
19055 Biscayne Blvd.
Miami 305-947-8485

Florida Detroit Diesel-Allison
2277 NW 14th St.
Miami 305-633-5028

Miami Transmission
4406 Ponce De Leon Blvd.
Coral Gables 305-443-3749

KEYS

**Gilbert's Holiday Island
of Key Largo**
107900 Overseas Hwy.
Key Largo 305-451-1133
See advertisement on page 81.

Oceanside Marine
1025 25th St.
Marathon 305-743-6666

MARCO ISLAND TO PLACIDA

Flagship Marine Engine
200 E. Ann St.
Punta Gorda 941-639-3738

Hurricane Bay Marine
18850 San Carlos Blvd.
Ft. Myers Bch. 941-466-8898

Owl Creek Boat Works
18251 Owl Creek Dr.
Alva 941-543-2100

Rose Boat & Engine Works
4427 Mercantile Ave.
Naples 941-643-6657

ENGLEWOOD TO SKYWAY

Gulfwind Marine
1485 S. Tamiami Trail
Venice 941-485-3388

Innovation Marine
2331B Whitfield Indus. Way
Sarasota 941-756-4337

SKYWAY TO TARPON SPRINGS

Gerald's Marine Service
2235 1st Ave. So.
St. Petersburg 813-321-4589

Prior Boat Builders
4100 Bayshore Blvd.
Dunedin 813-784-1396

Ringhaver Power Systems
9797 Gibsonton Dr.
Riverview 813-671-3700

NORTHWEST

Bell Marine Service
18 Audusson ave.
Pensacola 904-455-7639

Paul's Marine
1023 Harrison Ave.
Panama City 904-785-3258

Pride of the Point Marina
Rt. 1 Box 3461
Panacea 904-349-2517

Treasure Island Marina
3605 Thomas Dr.
Panama City Bch. 904-234-6533

VIDEO SERVICES

ALL REGIONS

Compass Rose Productions
1323 SE 17th St., #605
Ft. Lauderdale 954-728-9821

Video Workshop
1661 E. Sample Rd.
Pompano Bch. 954-942-3199
See advertisement on page 164.

Waterways Video
Production:
   Video Workshop
   1661 E. Sample Rd.
   Pompano Bch. 954-942-3199
Distribution:
   Waterways Etc.
   POB 21586
   Ft. Lauderdale 954-462-8151
   1-800-749-8151

WATER PURIFICATION SYSTEMS

FIRST COAST & ST. JOHNS

Sea Love Boatworks
4877 Front St.
Ponce Inlet 904-761-5434

INDIAN RIVER LAGOON

Cape Marina
800 Scallop Dr.
Cape Canaveral 407-783-8410
See advertisement on page 45.

C. Huntress Marine
407 Ave. H
Ft. Pierce 407-461-3993

STUART TO BOCA RATON

Whiticar Boat Works
3636 SE Old St. Lucie Blvd.
Stuart 407-287-2883
See advertisement on page 54.

BROWARD COUNTY

Amtech
3100 S. Andrews Ave.
Ft. Lauderdale 305 463 7637

Astro- Pure
S. Andrews Ave.
Ft. Lauderdale 305-832-0630

WATER PURIFICATION

Matrix Desalination
3295 SW 11th Ave.
Ft. Lauderdale 305-524-5120

Raz Marine
281 SW 33rd St.
Ft. Lauderdale 305-525-5513

Ultra Pure
1842 Adventure Pl.
N. Lauderdale 305-722-7839

Village Marine Tec.
804 S. E. 17th St.
Ft. Lauderdale 305 523 4900
800-625-8802
See advertisement on page 164.

Watermakers
2233 S. Andrews Ave.
Ft. Lauderdale 305-467-8920

DADE COUNTY

Rich Electronics
3300 NW 21st St.
Miami 305-635-1351

Merrill-Stevens
1270 NW 11th St.
Miami 305-324-5211

WATER TAXI SERVICE

BAHAMAS

Lucayan Marina Village
PO Box F-42654
Freeport, Grand Bahama
809 373 8888
See advertisement on page 27.

STUART TO BOCA RATON

Palm Beach Water Taxi
PGA Blvd & Intracoastal
N. Palm Beach 407-775-2628

BROWARD COUNTY

Water Taxi of Ft. Lauderdale
1900 SE 15th St.
Ft. Lauderdale 954-565-5507

DADE COUNTY

Miami by Water Taxi
Miami/Miami Beach
305-858-6292

MARCO ISLAND TO PLACIDA

Boca Grand Charters
881 Belcher Rd.
Boca Grande 941-964-1100

Naples Water Taxi
Naples 941-774-7277

Pineland Marina
13951 Waterfront Dr.
Pineland 941-283-0080

SKYWAY TO TARPON SPRINGS

Caladesi Clearwater
 Ferry Service
210 Drew
Clearwater 813-442-7433

Clearwater Marina
25 Causeway Blvd.
Clearwater Beach 813 462 6954

Harbour Island Marina
777 S. Harbour Isl. Blvd. #270
Tampa 813-229-5324

NORTHWEST

Ruby B
Dog Island Passenger Ferry
POB 648
Carrabelle 904-697-3434

YACHT BROKERS

FIRST COAST & ST. JOHNS

Daytona Marina & Boat Works
645 S. Beach St.
Daytona Bch. 904-252-6421

First Coast Yacht Sales
Camachee Cove Harbour
St. Augustine 904-824-7293

Florida Watercraft
177 North Cswy.
New Smyrna Bch. 904-426-2628

Roger Hansen Yacht Sales
3344 Lakeshore Blvd.
Jacksonville 904-384-3113
See advertisement on page 33

Huckins Yacht Brokerage
3482 Lakeshore Blvd.
Jacksonville 904-389-1125

H & H Yacht Sales
450 Basin St.
Daytona Bch. 904-255-0744

Jacksonville Yacht Sales
4451 Herschel St.
Jacksonville 904 387 5530

Offshore Yacht & Ship Brokers
404 Riberia St.
St. Augustine 904-829-9224

The Shaws Yacht Brokerage
728 Ballough Rd.
Daytona Bch. 904-255-0495

St. Augustine Yacht Center
3040 Harbor Dr.
St. Augustine 904-829-2294

INDIAN RIVER LAGOON

Diamond 99 Marina &
 Yacht Sales
4399 N. US 1
Melbourne 407-254-1490

Eagle Yachts
14 Myrtice Ave.
Merritt Island 407 453 2202

East-West Yachts
10 Avenue A
Ft. Pierce 407-466-1240

Harbor Town Marina/Boatyard
1936 HarborTown Dr.
Ft. Pierce 407-466-7300

Melbourne Harbor
2210 S. Front St.
Melbourne 407 725 9054
See advertisement on page 47.

Noel Yachts
515 Glen Creek Dr.
Port Canaveral 407 783 1126

Waterline Marina
905 N. Harbor City Blvd.
Melbourne 407 254 0452
See advertisement on page 49.

STUART TO BOCA RATON

Richard Bertram & Co.
2885 PGA Blvd
Palm Bch. Gdns. 407-625-1045

Gilman Yachts
1212A U.S. Hwy 1
N. Palm Bch. 407-655-1790

David Lowe's Boatyard
4550 SE Boatyard Dr.
PO Box L, Rocky Point
Port Salerno 407-287-0923
See advertisement on page 57.

Palm Beach Yacht Club
 & Marina
800 N. Flagler Dr.
West Palm Bch. 407-655-1944

Stuart Cay Marina
290 N. Federal Hwy.
Stuart 407 692 9511

Tabor Yachts
Pirates Cove Marina
4307 S.E. Bayview St.
Port Salerno 407 288 7466

Topside Marine Sales
3585 S. E. St. Lucie Blvd.
Stuart 407 220 4853

Rybovich Spencer
4200 Poinsettia Ave.
W. Palm Beach 407 844 1800

Sailfish Marina and Resort
98 Lake Dr.
Palm Bch. Shores 407-844-8460

Stuart Yacht
450 SW Salerno Rd.
Stuart 407-283-1947
See advertisement on page 53.

BROWARD COUNTY

Alexander Yacht Brokers
2150 SE 17th St.
Ft. Lauderdale 954-763-7676

Ardell Yacht & Ship Brokers
1550 SE 17th St.
Ft. Lauderdale 954-525-7637

Bonnie Castle Yachts
111 Briny Ave.
Pompano Beach 954 946 4359

Bradford International
3151 SR 84
Ft. Lauderdale 954-791-2600

C. P Irwin Yacht Brokerage
801 Seabreeze Blvd.
Ft. Lauderdale 954-463-6302

Dave D'Onofrio Yacht Sales
1875 SE 17th St.
Ft. Lauderdale 954-527-4848

Dave Pyles Yacht Sales
2596 SW 23rd Terr.
Ft. Lauderdale 954-583-8104
See advertisement on page 73.

Emerald Yacht-Ship Inc.
2170 SE 17th St.
Ft. Lauderdale 954-522-0556

Fraser Yachts
2230 S. E. 17th St.
Ft. Lauderdale 954-463-0600

Hal Jones & Co.
1900 SE 15th St.
Ft. Lauderdale 954-527-1778

HMY Yacht Sales
850 NE 3rd St. #203
Dania 954-926-0400

Jackson Marine Center
1915 SW 21st Ave.
Ft. Lauderdale 954 792 4900
See advertisement on page 73.

Luke Brown & Assoc.
1500 Cordova Rd. #200
Ft. Lauderdale 954-525-6617

Marine Unlimited
232 Basin Drive
Lauderdale-by-the-Sea
954-491-0430

Pilot Yachts
1635 Miami Rd.
Ft. Lauderdale 954-525-5711

Rex Yacht Sales
2152 S.E. 17th St.
Ft. Lauderdale 954 463 8810

Richard Bertram & Co.
651 Seabreeze Blvd.
Ft. Lauderdale 954-467-8405

Summerfield Yacht Sales
1700 S.W. 17th St.
Fort Lauderdale 954 522 7716

United/Derecktor Gunnell Yachts
901 SE 17th St.
Ft. Lauderdale 954-524-4616

Walsh Yachts
1900 SE 15th St.
Ft. Lauderdale 954-525-7447

Woods & Oviatt
2301 S. E. 17th St.
Ft. Lauderdale 954 463 5606

DADE COUNTY

Merrill-Stevens
 Yacht Brokerage
 2701 S. Bayshore Dr., #605
Miami 305-858-5911
 1270 N. W. 11th St.
Miami 305 547 2650

Richard Bertram & Co.
3660 NW 21st St.
Miami 305-633-9761

KEYS

Richard Bertram & Co.
2 Fishing Village Dr.
Key Largo 305-367-3267

MARCO ISLAND TO PLACIDA

Bain Yacht Sales
1200 W. Retta Esplanade
Punta Gorda 941 637 1335

Great American Boat Yards
 1310 Lee St.
Ft. Myers 941-334-8622
 1146 6th Ave. S.
Naples 941-262-6137

International Yachting Services
 at Old Naples Seaport
1001 10th Ave. S.
Naples 941-262-8411

Naples Yacht Brokerage
774 12th Ave.
Naples 941 434 8338

Palm Grove Marina
2500 Main St.
Ft. Myers Bch. 941-463-7333

Sanibel Island Marina
634 N. Yachtsman Dr.
Sanibel 941-472-2723

Southwest Florida Yachts
3444 Marinatown La.
N. Ft. Myers 941-656-1339

Starboard Yacht
2805 S. Tamiami Trail
Punta Gorda 941 637 7788

Yacht Registry
343 Causeway Blvd
Dunedin 941-733-0334

ENGLEWOOD TO SKYWAY

Carson Yacht Brokerage
1065 Riverside Dr.
Palmetto 941-723-1825

Great American Boat Yards
1889 Tamiami Trail N.
Sarasota 941-365-1770

Massey Yacht Sales
Regatta Point Marina
Palmetto 941 723 1610

Sarasota Bay Yacht Sales
1303 Main St.
Sarasota 941-364-8222

Sarasota Yacht & Ship
1306 Main St.
Sarasota 941-365-9095

Venice Boat Sales
505 S. Trail
Nokomis 941 488 7884

SKYWAY TO TARPON SPRINGS

Anchor Yachts International
98114 Pinellas Bayway Dr.
Tierra Verde 813-867-8027

Capt. Jack's
101 16th Ave. S.
St. Petersburg 813 825 0757

Clearwater Yacht Sales
401 2nd St.
Indian Rocks Bch. 813-596-7701

Marina Point Ships Store
500 1st Ave S.E.
St. Petersburg 813-823-2555

Maximo Marina
4801 37th St. S.
St. Petersburg 813 867 1102
See advertisement on page 114.

Charles Morgan Associates
200 2nd Ave. S.
St. Petersburg 813-894-7027

Ross Yachts
279 Windward Passage
Clearwater 813-446-8191

Sailors Wharf, Inc.
1421 Bay St. S. E.
St. Petersburg 813 823 1155

D. M. Savage Yacht & Ship Bkg.
4326 Central Ave.
St. Petersburg 813-327-1288

Snug Harbor Yacht Sales
10121 Snug Harbor Rd.
St. Petersburg 813-577-3392

St. Petersburg Yacht Charters
 & Sales
500 1st Ave. SE
St. Petersburg 813-896-2641

Wayne Winther & Associates
4935 34th St. S.
St. Petersburg 813-866-3168

West Florida Yachts
4880 37th St. S.
St. Petersburg 813 864 0310

NORTHWEST

ABC Yachts
at Mel's Marina
Gulf Breeze 904 932 3226

Ahoy Yachts
The Boat Marina
32 Hwy. 98
Ft. Walton Bch. 904-244-2722

Deckhand's Marina
1350 Miracle Strip Pkwy.
Ft. Walton Bch. 904-243-7359
See advertisement on page 132.

Grand Lagoon
3706 Thomas Drive
Panama City Bch 904 233 4747

Melvin B. Gaines
Yacht Brokerage, Inc.
520 Commerce Dr.
Panama City Bch 800-245-1210

Miller's Marina
PO Box 280
Suwannee 352-542-7349
See advertisement on page 123.

Odyssey Marine Sales
3009 Barrancas Ave.
Pensacola 904-453 8863

Sailfish Boat Sales
3009 Barrancas Ave.
Pensacola 904-457-1493

Treasure Island Marina
3605 Thomas Dr.
Panama City Bch. 904-234-6533

Yachties of Florida
511-A Hwy. 98 E.
Destin 904-837-4900

TIDE TABLES: FERNANDINA BEACH, AMELIA RIVER, FLORIDA

Times & Heights of High and Low Waters

(All times given are Eastern Standard Time and may differ because of wind conditions.)

Feb. 1996

Day	Time (h m)	Height (ft)	Height (cm)
16 F	0621 1220 1837	7.1 -0.4 6.5	216 -12 198
17 Sa	0032 0719 1314 1935	-0.8 7.4 -0.7 6.9	-24 226 -21 210
18 Su ●	0129 0813 1406 2030	-1.1 7.5 -1.0 7.1	-34 229 -30 216
19 M	0222 0903 1454 2122	-1.2 7.6 -1.2 7.3	-37 232 -37 223
20 Tu	0313 0952 1540 2211	-1.2 7.4 -1.1 7.3	-37 226 -34 223
21 W	0402 1039 1626 2259	-0.9 7.1 -0.9 7.1	-27 216 -27 216
22 Th	0450 1124 1711 2346	-0.6 6.8 -0.6 6.8	-18 207 -18 207
23 F	0540 1208 1759	-0.1 6.3 -0.2	-3 192 -6
24 Sa	0032 0633 1253 1849	6.5 0.4 5.9 0.2	198 12 180 6
25 Su	0120 0729 1340 1943	6.1 0.7 5.5 0.5	186 21 168 15
26 M ◐	0211 0827 1431 2038	5.9 1.0 5.3 0.7	180 30 162 21
27 Tu	0306 0924 1527 2133	5.7 1.1 5.1 0.8	174 34 155 24
28 W	0405 1019 1626 2228	5.6 1.1 5.1 0.7	171 34 155 21
29 Th	0503 1111 1723 2320	5.7 1.0 5.3 0.6	174 30 162 18

March 1996

Day	Time (h m)	Height (ft)	Height (cm)
1 F	0555 1159 1815	5.9 0.8 5.5	180 24 168
2 Sa	0010 0643 1244 1903	0.4 6.1 0.5 5.8	12 186 15 177
3 Su	0056 0726 1324 1947	0.2 6.3 0.3 6.0	6 192 9 183
4 M	0139 0808 1402 2029	-0.1 6.4 0.0 6.2	-3 195 0 189
5 Tu ○	0220 0847 1438 2109	-0.2 6.5 -0.1 6.3	-6 198 -3 192
6 W	0259 0926 1514 2147	-0.3 6.4 -0.3 6.4	-9 195 -9 195
7 Th	0339 1004 1550 2226	-0.4 6.4 -0.3 6.4	-12 195 -9 195
8 F	0420 1043 1628 2306	-0.3 6.3 -0.3 6.5	-9 192 -9 198
9 Sa	0504 1124 1711 2350	-0.2 6.1 -0.3 6.4	-6 186 -9 195
10 Su	0554 1210 1800	0.0 5.9 -0.2	0 180 -6
11 M	0039 0650 1300 1857	6.4 0.2 5.8 0.0	195 6 177 0
12 Tu ◑	0135 0753 1357 2001	6.3 0.3 5.7 0.0	192 9 174 0
13 W	0240 0857 1502 2107	6.3 0.2 5.7 0.0	192 6 174 0
14 Th	0351 1000 1613 2213	6.3 0.1 5.8 -0.2	192 3 177 -6
15 F	0500 1100 1720 2317	6.5 -0.2 6.1 -0.4	198 -6 186 -12
16 Sa	0603 1158 1822	6.7 -0.5 6.5	204 -15 198
17 Su	0018 0700 1252 1918	-0.7 6.9 -0.8 6.9	-21 210 -24 210
18 M	0114 0752 1342 2011	-0.9 7.0 -1.0 7.1	-27 213 -30 216
19 Tu ●	0206 0841 1429 2100	-1.0 7.0 -1.1 7.3	-30 213 -34 223
20 W	0255 0927 1513 2147	-1.0 6.9 -1.0 7.2	-30 210 -30 219
21 Th	0341 1012 1556 2232	-0.8 6.7 -0.8 7.0	-24 204 -24 213
22 F	0427 1055 1639 2315	-0.5 6.4 -0.5 6.7	-15 195 -15 204
23 Sa	0512 1137 1723 2358	-0.1 6.0 -0.1 6.4	-3 183 -3 195
24 Su	0600 1219 1809	0.3 5.7 0.3	9 174 9
25 M	0041 0651 1303 1900	6.1 0.7 5.4 0.7	186 21 165 21
26 Tu ◐	0127 0745 1351 1955	5.8 1.0 5.2 0.9	177 30 158 27
27 W	0218 0840 1445 2052	5.6 1.1 5.1 1.0	171 34 155 30
28 Th	0315 0934 1544 2149	5.5 1.1 5.1 0.9	168 34 155 27
29 F	0413 1026 1643 2243	5.5 1.0 5.3 0.8	168 30 162 24
30 Sa	0510 1115 1738 2336	5.7 0.8 5.6 0.6	174 24 171 18
31 Su	0601 1201 1828	5.9 0.5 5.9	180 15 180

April 1996

Day	Time (h m)	Height (ft)	Height (cm)
1 M	0025 0649 1245 1915	0.3 6.1 0.2 6.2	9 186 6 189
2 Tu	0111 0733 1326 1959	0.0 6.2 0.0 6.5	0 189 0 198
3 W ○	0155 0817 1406 2041	-0.2 6.4 -0.3 6.7	-6 195 -9 204
4 Th	0238 0859 1445 2124	-0.4 6.4 -0.4 6.9	-12 195 -12 210
5 F	0320 0941 1525 2206	-0.5 6.4 -0.5 6.9	-15 195 -15 210
6 Sa	0404 1025 1607 2251	-0.5 6.3 -0.5 6.9	-15 192 -15 210
7 Su	0450 1111 1653 2338	-0.3 6.2 -0.4 6.9	-9 189 -12 210
8 M	0541 1159 1744	-0.2 6.1 -0.2	-6 186 -6
9 Tu	0030 0637 1252 1843	6.8 0.0 6.0 0.0	207 0 183 0
10 W ◑	0126 0738 1351 1948	6.6 0.1 5.9 0.2	201 3 180 6
11 Th	0229 0841 1455 2055	6.5 0.1 6.0 0.2	198 3 183 6
12 F	0336 0941 1602 2201	6.4 0.0 6.2 0.1	195 0 189 3
13 Sa	0441 1039 1707 2304	6.5 -0.2 6.5 -0.1	198 -6 198 -3
14 Su	0542 1135 1806	6.6 -0.4 6.8	201 -12 207
15 M	0003 0637 1227 1900	-0.3 6.7 -0.5 7.1	-9 204 -15 216
16 Tu	0058 0728 1316 1950	-0.4 6.7 -0.7 7.3	-12 204 -21 223
17 W ●	0149 0816 1402 2037	-0.5 6.7 -0.7 7.4	-15 204 -21 226
18 Th	0236 0901 1446 2122	-0.5 6.6 -0.6 7.3	-15 201 -18 223
19 F	0320 0944 1527 2204	-0.4 6.4 -0.4 7.1	-12 195 -12 216
20 Sa	0403 1026 1608 2245	-0.1 6.2 0.0 6.9	-3 189 0 210
21 Su	0445 1107 1649 2324	0.2 5.9 0.3 6.6	6 180 9 201
22 M	0528 1147 1731	0.6 5.7 0.7	18 174 21
23 Tu	0005 0613 1230 1818	6.3 0.9 5.5 1.0	192 27 168 30
24 W	0047 0702 1315 1911	6.1 1.1 5.4 1.2	186 34 165 37
25 Th ◐	0134 0754 1406 2008	5.9 1.2 5.4 1.3	180 37 165 40
26 F	0225 0847 1501 2106	5.8 1.2 5.5 1.3	177 37 168 40
27 Sa	0321 0937 1559 2203	5.7 1.1 5.6 1.2	174 34 171 37
28 Su	0418 1027 1656 2257	5.8 0.9 5.9 0.9	177 27 180 27
29 M	0514 1115 1750 2350	5.9 0.6 6.3 0.7	180 18 192 21
30 Tu	0606 1202 1839	6.1 0.4 6.7	186 12 204

May 1996

Day	Time (h m)	Height (ft)	Height (cm)
1 W	0040 0656 1248 1927	0.3 6.3 0.1 7.0	9 192 3 213
2 Th	0129 0744 1333 2014	0.0 6.5 -0.2 7.3	0 198 -6 223
3 F ○	0215 0831 1418 2101	-0.2 6.6 -0.4 7.5	-6 201 -12 229
4 Sa	0301 0919 1503 2148	-0.4 6.6 -0.5 7.6	-12 201 -15 232
5 Su	0348 1008 1549 2238	-0.4 6.6 -0.4 7.6	-12 201 -12 232
6 M	0436 1059 1638 2329	-0.3 6.6 -0.3 7.5	-9 201 -9 229
7 Tu	0528 1151 1732	-0.2 6.5 0.0	-6 198 0
8 W	0021 0624 1246 1833	7.3 0.0 6.5 0.3	223 0 198 9
9 Th	0117 0723 1344 1938	7.1 0.1 6.5 0.5	216 3 198 15
10 F ◑	0216 0823 1446 2044	6.9 0.2 6.6 0.6	210 6 201 18
11 Sa	0317 0921 1549 2148	6.7 0.1 6.7 0.5	204 3 204 15
12 Su	0419 1017 1651 2249	6.6 0.1 6.9 0.5	201 3 210 15
13 M	0518 1110 1748 2346	6.6 0.0 7.2 0.4	201 0 219 12
14 Tu	0612 1201 1840	6.6 -0.1 7.4	201 -3 226
15 W	0040 0703 1250 1929	0.3 6.5 -0.1 7.5	9 198 -3 229
16 Th	0130 0750 1336 2014	0.2 6.5 0.0 7.5	6 198 0 229
17 F ●	0216 0835 1419 2057	0.2 6.4 0.1 7.4	6 195 3 226
18 Sa	0258 0917 1500 2137	0.3 6.3 0.2 7.3	9 192 6 223
19 Su	0339 0958 1539 2216	0.4 6.2 0.5 7.1	12 189 15 216
20 M	0418 1038 1618 2254	0.6 6.1 0.7 6.9	18 186 21 210
21 Tu	0457 1119 1658 2333	0.9 6.0 1.0 6.7	27 183 30 204
22 W	0538 1200 1742	1.1 5.9 1.3	34 180 40
23 Th	0013 0622 1243 1830	6.5 1.2 5.8 1.5	198 37 177 46
24 F	0055 0708 1329 1925	6.3 1.3 5.8 1.6	192 40 177 49
25 Sa ◐	0141 0758 1419 2023	6.2 1.3 5.9 1.6	189 40 180 49
26 Su	0232 0848 1514 2121	6.1 1.2 6.1 1.5	186 37 186 46
27 M	0327 0939 1611 2218	6.1 1.0 6.4 1.3	186 30 195 40
28 Tu	0425 1029 1708 2314	6.2 0.8 6.7 1.0	189 24 204 30
29 W	0522 1121 1803	6.3 0.5 7.1	192 15 216
30 Th	0008 0617 1212 1855	0.7 6.5 0.2 7.5	21 198 6 229
31 F	0101 0711 1303 1947	0.3 6.6 0.0 7.8	9 201 0 238

June 1996

Day	Time (h m)	Height (ft)	Height (cm)
1 Sa ○	0152 0804 1353 2039	0.0 6.8 -0.3 8.1	0 207 -9 247
2 Su	0242 0858 1443 2131	-0.2 6.9 -0.4 8.2	-6 210 -12 250
3 M	0331 0951 1533 2224	-0.3 7.0 -0.4 8.2	-9 213 -12 250
4 Tu	0421 1045 1625 2316	-0.3 7.1 -0.2 8.0	-9 216 -6 244
5 W	0512 1140 1720	-0.2 7.1 0.1	-6 216 3
6 Th	0009 0607 1235 1820	7.8 0.0 7.1 0.4	238 0 216 12
7 F	0102 0704 1331 1924	7.5 0.1 7.1 0.7	229 3 216 21
8 Sa ◑	0157 0802 1430 2029	7.2 0.2 7.1 0.9	219 6 216 27
9 Su	0255 0858 1530 2132	6.9 0.3 7.1 0.9	210 9 216 27
10 M	0353 0952 1630 2231	6.6 0.3 7.2 0.9	201 9 219 27
11 Tu	0451 1044 1726 2327	6.5 0.3 7.3 0.9	198 9 223 27
12 W	0545 1135 1818	6.4 0.4 7.4	195 12 226
13 Th	0020 0636 1224 1906	0.8 6.4 0.4 7.5	24 195 12 229
14 F	0109 0723 1310 1951	0.8 6.4 0.4 7.5	24 195 12 229
15 Sa ●	0154 0808 1353 2032	0.7 6.3 0.5 7.4	21 192 15 226
16 Su	0236 0851 1434 2112	0.7 6.3 0.6 7.3	21 192 18 223
17 M	0314 0932 1513 2150	0.8 6.3 0.7 7.2	24 192 21 219
18 Tu	0352 1012 1551 2227	0.9 6.2 0.9 7.1	27 189 27 216
19 W	0428 1051 1630 2304	1.0 6.1 1.1 6.9	30 186 34 210
20 Th	0505 1131 1710 2341	1.1 6.1 1.3 6.8	34 186 40 207
21 F	0543 1212 1755	1.2 6.1 1.5	37 186 46
22 Sa	0021 0625 1254 1846	6.6 1.2 6.1 1.6	201 37 186 49
23 Su	0103 0711 1340 1943	6.5 1.1 6.2 1.6	198 34 189 49
24 M ◐	0150 0801 1432 2042	6.3 1.0 6.4 1.6	192 30 195 49
25 Tu	0243 0854 1528 2142	6.3 0.9 6.6 1.4	192 27 201 43
26 W	0340 0949 1629 2241	6.2 0.7 6.9 1.1	189 21 210 34
27 Th	0442 1044 1729 2339	6.3 0.4 7.3 0.8	192 12 223 24
28 F	0543 1141 1828	6.4 0.2 7.7	195 6 235
29 Sa	0035 0642 1237 1924	0.4 6.7 -0.1 8.0	12 204 -3 244
30 Su ○	0129 0740 1332 2019	0.0 6.9 -0.4 8.3	0 210 -12 253

July 1996

Day	Time (h m)	Height (ft)	Height (cm)
1 M	0221 0837 1425 2113	-0.3 7.1 -0.5 8.4	-9 216 -15 256
2 Tu	0312 0934 1518 2207	-0.5 7.3 -0.5 8.3	-15 223 -15 253
3 W	0402 1029 1611 2259	-0.5 7.4 -0.4 8.2	-15 226 -12 250
4 Th	0452 1123 1706 2350	-0.4 7.4 -0.1 7.9	-12 226 -3 241
5 F	0545 1218 1804	-0.3 7.4 0.3	-9 226 9
6 Sa	0042 0639 1312 1906	7.5 -0.1 7.3 0.6	229 -3 223 18
7 Su ◑	0134 0735 1408 2009	7.1 0.1 7.2 0.9	216 3 219 27
8 M	0228 0831 1506 2111	6.7 0.3 7.1 1.0	204 9 216 30
9 Tu	0324 0925 1604 2209	6.4 0.4 7.0 1.1	195 12 213 34
10 W	0421 1018 1701 2305	6.2 0.5 7.0 1.1	189 15 213 34
11 Th	0517 1109 1753 2357	6.0 0.5 7.0 1.0	183 15 213 30
12 F	0608 1158 1841	6.0 0.6 7.1	183 18 216
13 Sa	0045 0656 1245 1926	1.0 6.0 0.6 7.1	30 183 18 216
14 Su	0130 0741 1329 2007	0.9 6.1 0.5 7.1	27 186 15 216
15 M ●	0211 0824 1411 2046	0.8 6.1 0.5 7.1	24 186 15 216
16 Tu	0248 0906 1450 2124	0.7 6.1 0.6 7.0	21 186 18 213
17 W	0324 0946 1527 2200	0.7 6.1 0.7 6.9	21 186 21 210
18 Th	0358 1024 1605 2236	0.7 6.1 0.8 6.8	21 186 24 207
19 F	0432 1102 1643 2312	0.7 6.1 0.9 6.6	21 186 27 201
20 Sa	0507 1141 1725 2350	0.7 6.1 1.1 6.5	21 186 34 198
21 Su	0546 1221 1813	0.7 6.2 1.2	21 189 37
22 M	0031 0630 1305 1908	6.3 0.7 6.2 1.3	192 21 189 40
23 Tu ◐	0116 0720 1355 2008	6.2 0.6 6.3 1.2	189 18 192 37
24 W	0208 0816 1452 2110	6.0 0.5 6.5 1.1	183 15 198 34
25 Th	0306 0915 1556 2212	6.0 0.3 6.7 0.8	183 9 204 24
26 F	0410 1016 1702 2312	6.0 0.1 7.0 0.5	183 3 213 15
27 Sa	0516 1116 1804	6.2 -0.2 7.4	189 -6 226
28 Su	0011 0620 1216 1904	0.1 6.5 -0.5 7.7	3 198 -15 235
29 M	0107 0720 1313 2000	-0.3 6.8 -0.7 8.0	-9 207 -21 244
30 Tu ○	0159 0818 1409 2054	-0.7 7.1 -0.9 8.1	-21 216 -27 247
31 W	0250 0914 1502 2146	-0.9 7.3 -1.0 8.0	-27 223 -30 244

Aug. 1996

Day	Time (h m)	Height (ft)	Height (cm)
1 Th	0339 1009 1555 2237	-1.0 7.4 -0.8 7.8	-30 226 -24 238
2 F	0428 1102 1648 2327	-0.9 7.4 -0.5 7.4	-27 226 -15 226
3 Sa	0518 1154 1743	-0.7 7.2 -0.1	-21 219 -3
4 Su	0017 0610 1247 1842	7.0 -0.4 7.0 0.3	213 -12 213 9
5 M	0107 0704 1340 1944	6.5 -0.1 6.8 0.7	198 -3 207 21
6 Tu ◑	0158 0800 1436 2045	6.1 0.2 6.6 0.9	186 6 201 27
7 W	0253 0856 1533 2143	5.8 0.3 6.4 1.0	177 9 195 30
8 Th	0349 0949 1630 2238	5.6 0.4 6.3 1.0	171 12 192 30
9 F	0446 1042 1724 2330	5.5 0.5 6.4 0.9	168 15 195 27
10 Sa	0539 1132 1813	5.5 0.4 6.4	168 12 195
11 Su	0017 0628 1220 1857	0.8 5.6 0.4 6.5	24 171 12 198
12 M	0102 0714 1305 1939	0.6 5.8 0.3 6.6	18 177 9 201
13 Tu	0142 0758 1347 2018	0.4 5.9 0.2 6.6	12 180 6 201
14 W ●	0219 0839 1427 2056	0.3 6.0 0.1 6.6	9 183 3 201
15 Th	0254 0919 1504 2132	0.2 6.0 0.1 6.5	6 183 3 198

Time meridian 75° W. 0000 is midnight. 1200 is noon.
Heights are referred to mean lower low water which is the chart datum of soundings.

TIDE TABLES: FERNANDINA BEACH, AMELIA RIVER, FLORIDA

Times & Heights of High and Low Waters

(All times given are Eastern Standard Time and may differ because of wind conditions.)

Aug. 1996

Day	Time (h m)	Height (ft)	Height (cm)
16 F	0327	0.1	3
	0957	6.0	183
	1542	0.2	6
	2208	6.4	195
17 Sa	0400	0.1	3
	1034	6.0	183
	1620	0.3	9
	2244	6.2	189
18 Su	0435	0.1	3
	1112	6.0	183
	1701	0.4	12
	2322	6.0	183
19 M	0512	0.1	3
	1151	6.0	183
	1747	0.6	18
20 Tu	0004	5.9	180
	0556	0.1	3
	1236	6.0	183
	1841	0.7	21
21 W ◐	0050	5.7	174
	0648	0.1	3
	1326	6.1	186
	1942	0.7	21
22 Th	0142	5.6	171
	0747	0.1	3
	1425	6.2	189
	2046	0.6	18
23 F	0242	5.6	171
	0850	0.0	0
	1532	6.3	192
	2149	0.4	12
24 Sa	0349	5.6	171
	0955	-0.3	-9
	1641	6.6	201
	2250	0.0	0
25 Su	0458	5.9	180
	1058	-0.5	-15
	1745	6.9	210
	2348	-0.4	-12
26 M	0602	6.2	189
	1159	-0.8	-24
	1844	7.2	219
27 Tu	0044	-0.8	-24
	0702	6.6	201
	1258	-1.1	-34
	1940	7.4	226
28 W ○	0137	-1.1	-34
	0759	6.9	210
	1353	-1.3	-40
	2032	7.5	229
29 Th	0226	-1.4	-43
	0853	7.1	216
	1446	-1.3	-40
	2123	7.4	226
30 F	0314	-1.4	-43
	0946	7.2	219
	1537	-1.2	-37
	2213	7.1	216
31 Sa	0401	-1.3	-40
	1037	7.1	216
	1627	-0.9	-27
	2301	6.8	207

September 1996

Day	Time (h m)	Height (ft)	Height (cm)
1 Su	0448	-1.0	-30
	1127	6.9	210
	1719	-0.4	-12
	2349	6.3	192
2 M	0537	-0.6	-18
	1217	6.6	201
	1814	0.0	0
3 Tu	0036	5.9	180
	0629	-0.2	-6
	1308	6.3	192
	1912	0.4	12
4 W ◑	0126	5.5	168
	0724	0.1	3
	1400	6.0	183
	2012	0.7	21
5 Th	0218	5.2	158
	0821	0.3	9
	1455	5.8	177
	2111	0.8	24
6 F	0314	5.0	152
	0918	0.4	12
	1552	5.7	174
	2205	0.8	24
7 Sa	0412	5.0	152
	1012	0.4	12
	1647	5.7	174
	2256	0.6	18
8 Su	0507	5.1	155
	1103	0.3	9
	1738	5.8	177
	2344	0.5	15
9 M	0558	5.3	162
	1152	0.2	6
	1824	5.9	180
10 Tu	0027	0.3	9
	0645	5.5	168
	1238	0.0	0
	1906	6.1	186
11 W	0108	0.0	0
	0729	5.7	174
	1322	-0.2	-6
	1947	6.2	189
12 Th ●	0146	-0.2	-6
	0810	5.9	180
	1403	-0.3	-9
	2026	6.2	189
13 F	0221	-0.3	-9
	0850	6.0	183
	1442	-0.3	-9
	2104	6.1	186
14 Sa	0256	-0.4	-12
	0929	6.0	183
	1520	-0.3	-9
	2141	6.0	183
15 Su	0330	-0.5	-15
	1007	6.0	183
	1559	-0.3	-9
	2219	5.9	180
16 M	0406	-0.5	-15
	1046	6.0	183
	1641	-0.1	-3
	2259	5.7	174
17 Tu	0445	-0.4	-12
	1128	6.0	183
	1727	0.0	0
	2343	5.5	168
18 W	0531	-0.3	-9
	1215	6.0	183
	1821	0.2	6
19 Th	0032	5.4	165
	0624	-0.2	-6
	1308	6.0	183
	1922	0.2	6
20 F ◐	0126	5.3	162
	0726	-0.2	-6
	1408	6.0	183
	2026	0.2	6
21 Sa	0228	5.3	162
	0833	-0.2	-6
	1515	6.1	186
	2129	-0.1	-3
22 Su	0337	5.5	168
	0940	-0.4	-12
	1624	6.2	189
	2229	-0.4	-12
23 M	0445	5.8	177
	1044	-0.7	-21
	1727	6.5	198
	2327	-0.7	-21
24 Tu	0548	6.2	189
	1145	-0.9	-27
	1825	6.7	204
25 W	0021	-1.1	-34
	0646	6.6	201
	1243	-1.2	-37
	1919	6.8	207
26 Th ○	0113	-1.4	-43
	0741	6.9	210
	1337	-1.4	-43
	2010	6.9	210
27 F	0202	-1.6	-49
	0833	7.1	216
	1428	-1.4	-43
	2059	6.8	207
28 Sa	0248	-1.6	-49
	0922	7.1	216
	1517	-1.2	-37
	2146	6.5	198
29 Su	0333	-1.4	-43
	1011	6.9	210
	1605	-0.9	-27
	2233	6.2	189
30 M	0418	-1.0	-30
	1058	6.7	204
	1653	-0.5	-15
	2319	5.8	177

October 1996

Day	Time (h m)	Height (ft)	Height (cm)
1 Tu	0504	-0.6	-18
	1145	6.3	192
	1743	-0.1	-3
2 W	0004	5.5	168
	0552	-0.2	-6
	1232	6.0	183
	1836	0.3	9
3 Th	0051	5.1	155
	0645	0.2	6
	1320	5.7	174
	1933	0.6	18
4 F ◑	0141	4.9	149
	0742	0.5	15
	1412	5.4	165
	2031	0.7	21
5 Sa	0235	4.8	146
	0840	0.6	18
	1506	5.3	162
	2125	0.7	21
6 Su	0333	4.8	146
	0936	0.5	15
	1602	5.3	162
	2216	0.6	18
7 M	0430	5.0	152
	1030	0.4	12
	1655	5.5	168
	2303	0.4	12
8 Tu	0523	5.2	158
	1120	0.2	6
	1744	5.6	171
	2347	0.2	6
9 W	0612	5.5	168
	1208	0.0	0
	1829	5.8	177
10 Th	0029	-0.1	-3
	0657	5.8	177
	1254	-0.2	-6
	1912	5.9	180
11 F	0109	-0.3	-9
	0740	6.1	186
	1337	-0.4	-12
	1954	6.0	183
12 Sa ●	0147	-0.5	-15
	0822	6.3	192
	1418	-0.5	-15
	2035	6.0	183
13 Su	0225	-0.7	-21
	0902	6.4	195
	1459	-0.6	-18
	2115	5.9	180
14 M	0303	-0.7	-21
	0943	6.4	195
	1540	-0.5	-15
	2157	5.8	177
15 Tu	0342	-0.7	-21
	1026	6.4	195
	1624	-0.4	-12
	2241	5.7	174
16 W	0425	-0.6	-18
	1112	6.4	195
	1712	-0.3	-9
	2329	5.6	171
17 Th	0513	-0.5	-15
	1201	6.3	192
	1806	-0.1	-3
18 F	0021	5.5	168
	0609	-0.3	-9
	1256	6.2	189
	1906	0.0	0
19 Sa ◐	0117	5.4	165
	0712	-0.2	-6
	1356	6.1	186
	2009	0.0	0
20 Su	0220	5.5	168
	0820	-0.1	-3
	1501	6.1	186
	2110	-0.2	-6
21 M	0327	5.7	174
	0927	-0.2	-6
	1607	6.2	189
	2209	-0.5	-15
22 Tu	0433	6.0	183
	1031	-0.4	-12
	1708	6.3	192
	2305	-0.7	-21
23 W	0535	6.4	195
	1131	-0.6	-18
	1805	6.4	195
	2358	-1.0	-30
24 Th	0631	6.8	207
	1228	-0.8	-24
	1858	6.5	198
25 F	0049	-1.2	-37
	0723	7.0	213
	1321	-1.0	-30
	1947	6.5	198
26 Sa ○	0137	-1.3	-40
	0812	7.2	219
	1411	-1.0	-30
	2035	6.4	195
27 Su	0223	-1.2	-37
	0900	7.1	216
	1457	-0.9	-27
	2121	6.2	189
28 M	0306	-1.0	-30
	0945	7.0	213
	1542	-0.6	-18
	2205	6.0	183
29 Tu	0349	-0.7	-21
	1029	6.7	204
	1626	-0.3	-9
	2249	5.7	174
30 W	0432	-0.3	-9
	1112	6.4	195
	1712	0.1	3
	2332	5.4	165
31 Th	0516	0.1	3
	1155	6.1	186
	1759	0.5	15

November 1996

Day	Time (h m)	Height (ft)	Height (cm)
1 F	0016	5.2	158
	0604	0.5	15
	1239	5.8	177
	1850	0.8	24
2 Sa	0103	5.0	152
	0658	0.8	24
	1326	5.6	171
	1944	0.9	27
3 Su ◑	0154	5.0	152
	0756	0.9	27
	1416	5.4	165
	2037	0.9	27
4 M	0249	5.0	152
	0854	0.9	27
	1510	5.4	165
	2128	0.8	24
5 Tu	0347	5.2	158
	0950	0.8	24
	1605	5.5	168
	2216	0.6	18
6 W	0443	5.5	168
	1043	0.6	18
	1658	5.6	171
	2302	0.3	9
7 Th	0535	5.8	177
	1134	0.4	12
	1748	5.8	177
	2347	0.1	3
8 F	0623	6.1	186
	1222	0.1	3
	1836	5.9	180
9 Sa	0031	-0.2	-6
	0709	6.5	198
	1309	-0.1	-3
	1921	6.0	183
10 Su ●	0114	-0.4	-12
	0754	6.7	204
	1354	-0.4	-12
	2006	6.1	186
11 M	0157	-0.6	-18
	0838	6.9	210
	1438	-0.5	-15
	2052	6.2	189
12 Tu	0239	-0.8	-24
	0923	7.0	213
	1523	-0.5	-15
	2138	6.1	186
13 W	0323	-0.8	-24
	1010	7.0	213
	1609	-0.5	-15
	2227	6.1	186
14 Th	0409	-0.7	-21
	1059	7.0	213
	1657	-0.4	-12
	2318	6.0	183
15 F	0500	-0.5	-15
	1151	6.8	207
	1751	-0.2	-6
16 Sa	0012	6.0	183
	0557	-0.2	-6
	1245	6.7	204
	1849	-0.1	-3
17 Su ◐	0109	6.0	183
	0701	0.0	0
	1343	6.5	198
	1950	-0.1	-3
18 M	0210	6.0	183
	0808	0.2	6
	1444	6.4	195
	2050	-0.2	-6
19 Tu	0315	6.2	189
	0914	0.1	3
	1546	6.3	192
	2147	-0.3	-9
20 W	0419	6.5	198
	1017	0.1	3
	1647	6.3	192
	2242	-0.5	-15
21 Th	0519	6.7	204
	1117	-0.1	-3
	1744	6.3	192
	2335	-0.6	-18
22 F	0614	7.0	213
	1213	-0.2	-6
	1836	6.3	192
23 Sa	0026	-0.7	-21
	0706	7.2	219
	1305	-0.3	-9
	1925	6.3	192
24 Su ○	0114	-0.7	-21
	0753	7.3	223
	1353	-0.3	-9
	2012	6.3	192
25 M	0159	-0.6	-18
	0838	7.2	219
	1438	-0.3	-9
	2056	6.2	189
26 Tu	0242	-0.5	-15
	0921	7.1	216
	1520	-0.1	-3
	2139	6.0	183
27 W	0323	-0.3	-9
	1002	6.9	210
	1601	0.1	3
	2220	5.8	177
28 Th	0403	0.0	0
	1042	6.6	201
	1641	0.4	12
	2302	5.7	174
29 F	0444	0.4	12
	1121	6.4	195
	1723	0.7	21
	2343	5.5	168
30 Sa	0527	0.7	21
	1201	6.2	189
	1807	0.9	27

December 1996

Day	Time (h m)	Height (ft)	Height (cm)
1 Su	0026	5.4	165
	0615	1.0	30
	1243	6.0	183
	1854	1.0	30
2 M	0113	5.4	165
	0709	1.2	37
	1328	5.8	177
	1943	1.0	30
3 Tu ◑	0203	5.4	165
	0807	1.3	40
	1418	5.7	174
	2034	1.0	30
4 W	0258	5.5	168
	0905	1.2	37
	1511	5.7	174
	2124	0.8	24
5 Th	0355	5.8	177
	1001	1.1	34
	1608	5.7	174
	2214	0.6	18
6 F	0452	6.1	186
	1056	0.8	24
	1704	5.8	177
	2304	0.3	9
7 Sa	0546	6.4	195
	1149	0.5	15
	1758	6.0	183
	2354	0.0	0
8 Su	0637	6.8	207
	1240	0.2	6
	1849	6.2	189
9 M	0043	-0.3	-9
	0727	7.2	219
	1330	-0.1	-3
	1940	6.3	192
10 Tu ●	0131	-0.5	-15
	0816	7.4	226
	1418	-0.4	-12
	2030	6.5	198
11 W	0219	-0.7	-21
	0906	7.6	232
	1505	-0.5	-15
	2121	6.6	201
12 Th	0307	-0.8	-24
	0956	7.7	235
	1552	-0.6	-18
	2213	6.6	201
13 F	0356	-0.7	-21
	1047	7.6	232
	1641	-0.5	-15
	2306	6.7	204
14 Sa	0449	-0.5	-15
	1138	7.4	226
	1733	-0.4	-12
15 Su	0000	6.6	201
	0545	-0.2	-6
	1231	7.1	216
	1829	-0.2	-6
16 M	0056	6.6	201
	0648	0.1	3
	1325	6.8	207
	1927	-0.1	-3
17 Tu ◐	0155	6.6	201
	0753	0.4	12
	1423	6.6	201
	2026	-0.1	-3
18 W	0257	6.6	201
	0858	0.5	15
	1523	6.3	192
	2123	-0.1	-3
19 Th	0400	6.7	204
	1001	0.5	15
	1623	6.2	189
	2219	-0.1	-3
20 F	0500	6.9	210
	1100	0.5	15
	1721	6.2	189
	2312	-0.1	-3
21 Sa	0556	7.0	213
	1156	0.4	12
	1815	6.2	189
22 Su	0003	-0.1	-3
	0648	7.1	216
	1247	0.3	9
	1904	6.2	189
23 M	0052	-0.2	-6
	0735	7.2	219
	1335	0.2	6
	1950	6.2	189
24 Tu ○	0138	-0.1	-3
	0818	7.2	219
	1418	0.2	6
	2034	6.2	189
25 W	0220	-0.1	-3
	0859	7.1	216
	1458	0.3	9
	2115	6.1	186
26 Th	0300	0.0	0
	0937	7.0	213
	1536	0.4	12
	2155	6.0	183
27 F	0339	0.2	6
	1014	6.8	207
	1613	0.5	15
	2234	5.9	180
28 Sa	0417	0.4	12
	1050	6.6	201
	1649	0.6	18
	2312	5.8	177
29 Su	0456	0.7	21
	1127	6.4	195
	1726	0.8	24
	2352	5.8	177
30 M	0538	0.9	27
	1205	6.2	189
	1806	0.9	27
31 Tu	0033	5.7	174
	0626	1.2	37
	1246	6.0	183
	1850	0.9	27

January 1997

Day	Time (h m)	Height (ft)	Height (cm)
1 W ◑	0121	5.7	174
	0723	1.3	40
	1335	5.9	180
	1943	1.0	30
2 Th	0211	5.8	177
	0822	1.3	40
	1426	5.8	177
	2036	0.8	24
3 F	0308	5.9	180
	0921	1.2	37
	1522	5.7	174
	2131	0.7	21
4 Sa	0409	6.2	189
	1020	1.0	30
	1623	5.8	177
	2226	0.4	12
5 Su	0510	6.5	198
	1118	0.7	21
	1723	6.0	183
	2322	0.1	3
6 M	0608	6.9	210
	1213	0.3	9
	1822	6.2	189
7 Tu	0017	-0.3	-9
	0704	7.3	223
	1307	-0.1	-3
	1917	6.5	198
8 W ●	0110	-0.6	-18
	0757	7.7	235
	1358	-0.4	-12
	2012	6.7	204
9 Th	0202	-0.9	-27
	0849	7.9	241
	1447	-0.7	-21
	2105	6.9	210
10 F	0253	-1.0	-30
	0941	8.0	244
	1535	-0.8	-24
	2158	7.1	216
11 Sa	0344	-1.0	-30
	1031	7.9	241
	1624	-0.8	-24
	2252	7.1	216
12 Su	0437	-0.7	-21
	1122	7.7	235
	1714	-0.7	-21
	2345	7.1	216
13 M	0532	-0.4	-12
	1213	7.3	223
	1807	-0.5	-15
14 Tu	0039	7.0	213
	0631	0.0	0
	1305	6.9	210
	1903	-0.2	-6
15 W ◐	0135	6.8	207
	0734	0.3	9
	1400	6.5	198
	2001	0.0	0
16 Th	0234	6.7	204
	0838	0.6	18
	1457	6.2	189
	2059	0.1	3
17 F	0336	6.6	201
	0941	0.7	21
	1557	6.0	183
	2155	0.2	6
18 Sa	0438	6.6	201
	1040	0.7	21
	1657	5.8	177
	2250	0.2	6
19 Su	0535	6.6	201
	1136	0.7	21
	1752	5.8	177
	2342	0.2	6
20 M	0627	6.7	204
	1227	0.6	18
	1843	5.9	180
21 Tu	0032	0.2	6
	0714	6.8	207
	1314	0.5	15
	1929	6.0	183
22 W	0118	0.1	3
	0757	6.8	207
	1357	0.4	12
	2012	6.0	183
23 Th ○	0201	0.1	3
	0837	6.8	207
	1436	0.3	9
	2053	6.1	186
24 F	0240	0.1	3
	0914	6.8	207
	1511	0.3	9
	2132	6.1	186
25 Sa	0318	0.1	3
	0950	6.7	204
	1546	0.4	12
	2209	6.0	183
26 Su	0355	0.3	9
	1025	6.5	198
	1619	0.4	12
	2245	6.0	183
27 M	0431	0.4	12
	1100	6.4	195
	1653	0.5	15
	2322	5.9	180
28 Tu	0510	0.6	18
	1136	6.2	189
	1728	0.6	18
29 W	0000	5.9	180
	0553	0.8	24
	1214	6.0	183
	1809	0.6	18
30 Th	0041	5.9	180
	0643	1.0	30
	1257	5.9	180
	1856	0.6	18
31 F ◑	0128	5.9	180
	0741	1.0	30
	1346	5.7	174
	1950	0.6	18

Feb. 1997

Day	Time (h m)	Height (ft)	Height (cm)
1 Sa	0222	6.0	183
	0843	1.0	30
	1441	5.6	171
	2049	0.5	15
2 Su	0326	6.1	186
	0945	0.8	24
	1544	5.7	174
	2151	0.3	9
3 M	0434	6.4	195
	1046	0.5	15
	1651	5.8	177
	2252	0.0	0
4 Tu	0540	6.7	204
	1145	0.2	6
	1755	6.1	186
	2352	-0.4	-12
5 W	0640	7.1	216
	1242	-0.3	-9
	1855	6.5	198
6 Th	0050	-0.8	-24
	0736	7.5	229
	1335	-0.7	-21
	1952	6.8	207
7 F ●	0146	-1.1	-34
	0830	7.7	235
	1425	-1.0	-30
	2047	7.1	216
8 Sa	0239	-1.3	-40
	0922	7.8	238
	1514	-1.2	-37
	2140	7.3	223
9 Su	0330	-1.3	-40
	1012	7.7	235
	1602	-1.2	-37
	2233	7.4	226
10 M	0422	-1.1	-34
	1102	7.5	229
	1651	-1.1	-34
	2325	7.3	223
11 Tu	0515	-0.7	-21
	1151	7.1	216
	1741	-0.8	-24
12 W	0017	7.1	216
	0611	-0.3	-9
	1241	6.7	204
	1835	-0.4	-12
13 Th	0110	6.8	207
	0711	0.2	6
	1333	6.2	189
	1931	-0.1	-3
14 F ◐	0206	6.5	198
	0814	0.5	15
	1428	5.8	177
	2030	0.2	6
15 Sa	0306	6.3	192
	0915	0.7	21
	1527	5.6	171
	2127	0.3	9

Time meridian 75° W. 0000 is midnight. 1200 is noon.
Heights are referred to mean lower low water which is the chart datum of soundings.

TIDE TABLES: MAYPORT, FLORIDA

Times & Heights of High and Low Waters

(All times given are Eastern Standard Time and may differ because of wind conditions.)

Feb. 1996

Day	Time (h m)	Height (ft)	Height (cm)
16 F	0613 1211 1834	4.9 -0.7 4.3	149 -21 131
17 Sa	0022 0710 1305 1930	-1.1 5.1 -1.0 4.5	-34 155 -30 137
18 Su ●	0118 0802 1355 2023	-1.3 5.1 -1.2 4.7	-40 155 -37 143
19 M	0212 0852 1444 2113	-1.4 5.1 -1.3 4.8	-43 155 -40 146
20 Tu	0304 0940 1531 2202	-1.3 5.0 -1.3 4.9	-40 152 -40 149
21 W	0355 1027 1618 2249	-1.1 4.8 -1.1 4.8	-34 146 -34 146
22 Th	0446 1113 1705 2338	-0.8 4.6 -0.8 4.7	-24 140 -24 143
23 F	0538 1200 1754	-0.4 4.3 -0.5	-12 131 -15
24 Sa	0027 0633 1248 1845	4.5 0.0 4.1 -0.1	137 0 125 -3
25 Su	0119 0731 1340 1940	4.3 0.3 3.8 0.2	131 9 116 6
26 M ◐	0215 0830 1435 2038	4.2 0.6 3.7 0.4	128 18 113 12
27 Tu	0314 0929 1533 2135	4.1 0.7 3.6 0.5	125 21 110 15
28 W	0413 1024 1630 2230	4.1 0.6 3.7 0.4	125 18 113 12
29 Th	0507 1114 1723 2320	4.2 0.5 3.8 0.3	128 15 116 9

March 1996

Day	Time (h m)	Height (ft)	Height (cm)
1 F	0557 1158 1811	4.3 0.3 3.9	131 9 119
2 Sa	0005 0642 1239 1855	0.1 4.4 0.1 4.1	3 134 3 125
3 Su	0046 0723 1315 1936	-0.1 4.5 -0.1 4.2	-3 137 -3 128
4 M	0124 0801 1350 2015	-0.2 4.5 -0.2 4.3	-6 137 -6 131
5 Tu ○	0201 0838 1423 2052	-0.3 4.5 -0.3 4.4	-9 137 -9 134
6 W	0237 0914 1456 2128	-0.4 4.5 -0.4 4.5	-12 137 -12 137
7 Th	0315 0950 1531 2205	-0.3 4.4 -0.4 4.6	-9 134 -12 140
8 F	0355 1027 1610 2245	-0.3 4.4 -0.4 4.6	-9 134 -12 140
9 Sa	0440 1107 1653 2330	-0.1 4.3 -0.3 4.6	-3 131 -9 140
10 Su	0530 1153 1743	0.0 4.2 -0.2	0 128 -6
11 M	0022 0628 1247 1840	4.6 0.2 4.0 0.0	140 6 122 0
12 Tu ◐	0123 0735 1351 1946	4.6 0.3 3.9 0.0	140 9 119 0
13 W	0234 0846 1503 2059	4.5 0.3 4.0 0.0	137 9 122 0
14 Th	0348 0955 1616 2209	4.6 0.1 4.1 -0.2	140 3 125 -6
15 F	0457 1057 1722 2314	4.7 -0.2 4.3 -0.5	143 -6 131 -15
16 Sa	0558 1153 1821	4.9 -0.5 4.6	149 -15 140
17 Su	0012 0653 1244 1914	-0.7 5.0 -0.8 4.8	-21 152 -24 146
18 M	0107 0743 1333 2004	-1.0 5.0 -1.0 5.0	-30 152 -30 152
19 Tu ●	0158 0831 1419 2052	-1.1 5.0 -1.1 5.1	-34 152 -34 155
20 W	0247 0917 1503 2137	-1.0 4.9 -1.0 5.1	-30 149 -30 155
21 Th	0334 1001 1547 2221	-0.8 4.7 -0.8 5.0	-24 143 -24 152
22 F	0421 1044 1631 2306	-0.6 4.5 -0.5 4.8	-18 137 -15 146
23 Sa	0509 1128 1716 2351	-0.2 4.3 -0.2 4.6	-6 131 -6 140
24 Su	0559 1213 1803	0.2 4.1 0.2	6 125 6
25 M	0039 0651 1300 1855	4.5 0.5 3.9 0.5	137 15 119 15
26 Tu ◐	0130 0748 1352 1952	4.3 0.8 3.8 0.8	131 24 116 24
27 W	0226 0845 1449 2052	4.2 0.9 3.8 0.9	128 27 116 27
28 Th	0325 0940 1547 2150	4.2 0.9 3.9 0.8	128 27 119 24
29 F	0422 1030 1642 2243	4.2 0.8 4.0 0.7	128 24 122 21
30 Sa	0514 1115 1733 2331	4.3 0.6 4.2 0.5	131 18 128 15
31 Su	0602 1156 1819	4.4 0.3 4.4	134 9 134

April 1996

Day	Time (h m)	Height (ft)	Height (cm)
1 M	0014 0645 1234 1902	0.2 4.5 0.1 4.6	6 137 3 140
2 Tu	0055 0727 1311 1943	0.0 4.5 -0.1 4.7	0 137 -3 143
3 W ○	0135 0807 1347 2023	-0.2 4.6 -0.3 4.9	-6 140 -9 149
4 Th	0215 0846 1425 2103	-0.3 4.6 -0.5 5.0	-9 140 -15 152
5 F	0256 0927 1505 2145	-0.4 4.5 -0.5 5.1	-12 137 -15 155
6 Sa	0340 1009 1548 2230	-0.3 4.5 -0.4 5.1	-9 137 -12 155
7 Su	0428 1055 1635 2319	-0.2 4.4 -0.3 5.0	-6 134 -9 152
8 M	0521 1146 1728	0.0 4.3 -0.1	0 131 -3
9 Tu	0014 0621 1244 1829	4.9 0.1 4.2 0.1	149 3 128 3
10 W ◐	0117 0727 1349 1939	4.8 0.2 4.2 0.2	146 6 128 6
11 Th	0226 0835 1459 2052	4.7 0.2 4.3 0.2	143 6 131 6
12 F	0335 0940 1606 2202	4.7 0.1 4.4 0.1	143 3 134 3
13 Sa	0440 1038 1709 2305	4.7 -0.1 4.7 -0.2	143 -3 143 -6
14 Su	0539 1132 1805	4.8 -0.4 4.9	146 -12 149
15 M	0001 0633 1222 1857	-0.4 4.8 -0.6 5.1	-12 146 -18 155
16 Tu	0053 0722 1308 1944	-0.6 4.8 -0.7 5.2	-18 146 -21 158
17 W ●	0142 0809 1352 2029	-0.7 4.8 -0.8 5.2	-21 146 -24 158
18 Th	0228 0853 1435 2113	-0.7 4.6 -0.7 5.2	-21 140 -21 158
19 F	0313 0935 1517 2154	-0.5 4.5 -0.5 5.1	-15 137 -15 155
20 Sa	0357 1016 1558 2236	-0.3 4.4 -0.2 4.9	-9 134 -6 149
21 Su	0441 1057 1639 2317	0.0 4.2 0.1 4.7	0 128 3 143
22 M	0526 1139 1722	0.3 4.1 0.4	9 125 12
23 Tu	0001 0613 1224 1809	4.6 0.6 4.0 0.7	140 18 122 21
24 W	0047 0703 1312 1902	4.4 0.8 3.9 1.0	134 24 119 30
25 Th ◐	0138 0755 1404 2001	4.3 0.9 4.0 1.1	131 27 122 34
26 F	0232 0848 1500 2102	4.2 1.0 4.0 1.1	128 30 122 34
27 Sa	0328 0938 1555 2158	4.2 0.8 4.2 0.9	128 24 128 27
28 Su	0422 1024 1648 2249	4.2 0.6 4.4 0.7	128 18 134 21
29 M	0513 1107 1737 2337	4.3 0.4 4.6 0.4	131 12 140 12
30 Tu	0602 1149 1824	4.4 0.1 4.8	134 3 146

May 1996

Day	Time (h m)	Height (ft)	Height (cm)
1 W	0023 0648 1231 1910	0.1 4.4 -0.2 5.0	3 134 -6 152
2 Th	0107 0733 1313 1955	-0.2 4.5 -0.4 5.2	-6 137 -12 158
3 F ○	0153 0819 1356 2040	-0.4 4.5 -0.6 5.3	-12 137 -18 162
4 Sa	0239 0905 1442 2128	-0.5 4.5 -0.6 5.3	-15 137 -18 162
5 Su	0327 0954 1530 2218	-0.5 4.5 -0.6 5.3	-15 137 -18 162
6 M	0419 1045 1622 2311	-0.4 4.5 -0.4 5.2	-12 137 -12 158
7 Tu	0514 1140 1719	-0.3 4.4 -0.2	-9 134 -6
8 W	0008 0613 1240 1823	5.1 -0.1 4.4 0.0	155 -3 134 0
9 Th	0109 0716 1343 1934	4.9 0.0 4.4 0.2	149 0 134 6
10 F ◐	0213 0820 1448 2045	4.8 0.0 4.5 0.2	146 0 137 6
11 Sa	0317 0920 1552 2152	4.7 -0.1 4.7 0.2	143 -3 143 6
12 Su	0420 1017 1652 2252	4.6 -0.2 4.9 0.0	140 -6 149 0
13 M	0517 1109 1747 2347	4.6 -0.3 5.0 -0.1	140 -9 152 -3
14 Tu	0610 1157 1837	4.5 -0.4 5.1	137 -12 155
15 W	0037 0659 1243 1924	-0.3 4.5 -0.5 5.2	-9 137 -15 158
16 Th	0124 0745 1327 2008	-0.4 4.4 -0.5 5.2	-12 134 -15 158
17 F ●	0209 0828 1408 2049	-0.4 4.3 -0.4 5.1	-12 131 -12 155
18 Sa	0252 0909 1448 2129	-0.3 4.2 -0.3 5.0	-9 128 -9 152
19 Su	0333 0949 1527 2209	-0.2 4.1 -0.1 4.8	-6 125 -3 146
20 M	0414 1029 1606 2248	0.0 4.1 0.2 4.7	0 125 6 143
21 Tu	0454 1109 1646 2327	0.2 4.0 0.4 4.6	6 122 12 140
22 W	0535 1150 1728	0.5 4.0 0.7	15 122 21
23 Th	0008 0618 1234 1815	4.4 0.6 4.0 0.9	134 18 122 27
24 F	0051 0703 1321 1908	4.3 0.7 4.0 1.0	131 21 122 30
25 Sa ◐	0138 0750 1412 2007	4.2 0.8 4.1 1.1	128 24 125 34
26 Su	0229 0839 1505 2107	4.2 0.7 4.2 1.0	128 21 128 30
27 M	0324 0928 1600 2204	4.1 0.5 4.4 0.8	125 15 134 24
28 Tu	0420 1017 1654 2259	4.1 0.2 4.6 0.5	125 6 140 15
29 W	0515 1106 1747 2351	4.2 -0.1 4.9 0.1	128 -3 149 3
30 Th	0609 1154 1838	4.2 -0.4 5.1	128 -12 155
31 F	0041 0702 1243 1930	-0.2 4.3 -0.6 5.3	-6 131 -18 162

June 1996

Day	Time (h m)	Height (ft)	Height (cm)
1 Sa ○	0131 0754 1332 2021	-0.5 4.4 -0.8 5.4	-15 134 -24 165
2 Su	0222 0846 1423 2113	-0.7 4.4 -0.9 5.5	-21 134 -27 168
3 M	0314 0939 1516 2206	-0.8 4.5 -0.8 5.4	-24 137 -24 165
4 Tu	0407 1033 1611 2300	-0.7 4.5 -0.7 5.3	-21 137 -21 162
5 W	0502 1130 1711 2356	-0.7 4.5 -0.4 5.1	-21 137 -12 155
6 Th	0600 1228 1815	-0.5 4.6 -0.2	-15 140 -6
7 F	0054 0659 1329 1923	4.9 -0.4 4.6 0.0	149 -12 140 0
8 Sa ◐	0154 0758 1431 2031	4.7 -0.3 4.7 0.2	143 -9 143 6
9 Su	0254 0857 1532 2136	4.5 -0.3 4.7 0.2	137 -9 143 6
10 M	0355 0952 1631 2235	4.4 -0.2 4.8 0.1	134 -6 146 3
11 Tu	0452 1044 1726 2329	4.3 -0.3 4.9 0.0	131 -9 149 0
12 W	0545 1133 1816	4.2 -0.3 5.0	128 -9 152
13 Th	0019 0635 1219 1903	-0.1 4.2 -0.3 5.0	-3 128 -9 152
14 F	0105 0721 1302 1946	-0.1 4.1 -0.4 5.0	-3 125 -12 152
15 Sa ●	0149 0804 1344 2027	-0.2 4.1 -0.3 4.9	-6 125 -9 149
16 Su	0230 0845 1423 2106	-0.2 4.0 -0.2 4.8	-6 122 -6 146
17 M	0309 0924 1501 2144	-0.1 4.0 -0.1 4.8	-3 122 -3 146
18 Tu	0347 1002 1538 2221	0.0 4.0 0.1 4.7	0 122 3 143
19 W	0423 1040 1614 2257	0.1 4.0 0.3 4.5	3 122 9 137
20 Th	0459 1118 1652 2333	0.3 4.0 0.5 4.4	9 122 15 134
21 F	0535 1158 1734	0.4 4.0 0.7	12 122 21
22 Sa	0010 0613 1240 1822	4.3 0.5 4.1 0.9	131 15 125 27
23 Su	0051 0657 1326 1917	4.2 0.5 4.2 0.9	128 15 128 27
24 M ◐	0137 0745 1417 2018	4.1 0.4 4.3 0.9	125 12 131 27
25 Tu	0230 0838 1513 2122	4.1 0.3 4.5 0.7	125 9 137 21
26 W	0329 0933 1613 2224	4.0 0.1 4.7 0.5	122 3 143 15
27 Th	0432 1029 1714 2322	4.0 -0.2 4.9 0.1	122 -6 149 3
28 F	0534 1124 1813	4.1 -0.5 5.1	125 -15 155
29 Sa	0018 0635 1219 1909	-0.3 4.2 -0.8 5.3	-9 128 -24 162
30 Su ○	0112 0732 1313 2004	-0.6 4.3 -1.0 5.5	-18 131 -30 168

July 1996

Day	Time (h m)	Height (ft)	Height (cm)
1 M	0205 0828 1408 2058	-0.8 4.5 -1.1 5.5	-24 137 -34 168
2 Tu	0257 0923 1503 2151	-1.0 4.6 -1.0 5.5	-30 140 -30 168
3 W	0350 1018 1559 2244	-1.0 4.7 -0.9 5.4	-30 143 -27 165
4 Th	0444 1113 1658 2338	-0.9 4.8 -0.6 5.2	-27 146 -18 158
5 F	0538 1209 1800	-0.8 4.8 -0.3	-24 146 -9
6 Sa	0033 0634 1307 1905	4.9 -0.6 4.8 0.0	149 -18 146 0
7 Su ◐	0129 0731 1406 2010	4.7 -0.4 4.8 0.2	143 -12 146 6
8 M	0227 0829 1507 2114	4.4 -0.2 4.8 0.3	134 -6 146 9
9 Tu	0326 0924 1605 2213	4.2 -0.1 4.8 0.4	128 -3 146 12
10 W	0424 1018 1701 2307	4.1 -0.1 4.8 0.3	125 -3 146 9
11 Th	0518 1108 1753 2357	4.0 0.0 4.9 0.2	122 0 149 6
12 F	0609 1156 1840	4.0 -0.1 4.9	122 -3 149
13 Sa	0043 0656 1240 1924	0.1 4.0 -0.1 4.9	3 122 -3 149
14 Su	0126 0739 1321 2004	0.0 4.1 -0.1 4.9	0 125 -3 149
15 M ●	0206 0819 1400 2043	0.0 4.1 -0.1 4.9	0 125 -3 149
16 Tu	0243 0858 1437 2119	0.0 4.1 0.0 4.8	0 125 0 146
17 W	0318 0935 1512 2154	0.0 4.1 0.1 4.7	0 125 3 143
18 Th	0350 1011 1546 2227	0.1 4.2 0.3 4.6	3 128 9 140
19 F	0422 1047 1622 2300	0.2 4.2 0.5 4.5	6 128 15 137
20 Sa	0455 1123 1702 2335	0.3 4.3 0.6 4.4	9 131 18 134
21 Su	0531 1202 1747	0.3 4.3 0.8	9 131 24
22 M	0013 0613 1245 1840	4.4 0.4 4.4 0.9	134 12 134 27
23 Tu ◐	0057 0702 1337 1941	4.3 0.4 4.5 0.9	131 12 137 27
24 W	0150 0757 1436 2048	4.2 0.3 4.6 0.8	128 9 140 24
25 Th	0252 0858 1542 2155	4.1 0.2 4.8 0.6	125 6 146 18
26 F	0400 1000 1649 2258	4.1 -0.1 5.0 0.3	125 -3 152 9
27 Sa	0510 1102 1753 2357	4.2 -0.3 5.2 -0.1	128 -9 158 -3
28 Su	0614 1201 1853	4.4 -0.6 5.4	134 -18 165
29 M	0053 0714 1258 1948	-0.5 4.6 -0.9 5.6	-15 140 -27 171
30 Tu ○	0146 0811 1354 2041	-0.8 4.8 -1.0 5.7	-24 146 -30 174
31 W	0238 0905 1450 2133	-1.0 5.0 -1.0 5.6	-30 152 -30 171

Aug. 1996

Day	Time (h m)	Height (ft)	Height (cm)
1 Th	0329 0958 1545 2224	-1.0 5.1 -0.8 5.5	-30 155 -24 168
2 F	0420 1051 1642 2315	-0.9 5.1 -0.6 5.3	-27 155 -18 162
3 Sa	0511 1145 1740	-0.7 5.1 -0.2	-21 155 -6
4 Su	0007 0605 1240 1841	5.0 -0.4 5.0 0.1	152 -12 152 3
5 M	0101 0700 1337 1944	4.7 -0.1 5.0 0.5	143 -3 152 15
6 Tu ◐	0156 0757 1436 2046	4.5 0.1 4.9 0.7	137 3 149 21
7 W	0254 0854 1535 2146	4.3 0.3 4.8 0.8	131 9 146 24
8 Th	0353 0950 1633 2241	4.2 0.4 4.9 0.8	128 12 149 24
9 F	0449 1043 1726 2331	4.2 0.4 4.9 0.7	128 12 149 21
10 Sa	0541 1132 1814	4.2 0.4 5.0	128 12 152
11 Su	0017 0628 1217 1857	0.6 4.3 0.3 5.0	18 131 9 152
12 M	0058 0711 1259 1938	0.4 4.4 0.3 5.1	12 134 9 155
13 Tu	0137 0752 1337 2016	0.3 4.5 0.2 5.1	9 137 6 155
14 W ●	0212 0830 1413 2052	0.2 4.5 0.2 5.0	6 137 6 152
15 Th	0244 0907 1447 2126	0.2 4.6 0.3 5.0	6 140 9 152

Time meridian 75° W. 0000 is midnight. 1200 is noon.
Heights are referred to mean lower low water which is the chart datum of soundings.

TIDE TABLES: MAYPORT, FLORIDA

Times & Heights of High and Low Waters

(All times given are Eastern Standard Time and may differ because of wind conditions.)

Aug. 1996

Day	Time (h m)	Height (ft)	Height (cm)
16 F	0315 0942 1521 2159	0.2 4.6 0.4 4.9	6 140 12 149
17 Sa	0346 1016 1556 2231	0.3 4.7 0.5 4.8	9 143 15 146
18 Su	0419 1051 1635 2305	0.3 4.8 0.7 4.7	9 146 21 143
19 M	0456 1129 1720 2343	0.4 4.8 0.8 4.6	12 146 24 140
20 Tu	0539 1214 1813	0.5 4.9 1.0	15 149 30
21 W ◐	0029 0629 1307 1914	4.5 0.6 4.9 1.1	137 18 149 34
22 Th	0124 0728 1410 2024	4.4 0.6 5.0 1.0	134 18 152 30
23 F	0230 0833 1521 2134	4.4 0.5 5.1 0.8	134 15 155 24
24 Sa	0343 0942 1632 2240	4.4 0.3 5.3 0.5	134 9 162 15
25 Su	0455 1047 1738 2339	4.6 0.0 5.5 0.1	140 0 168 3
26 M	0600 1149 1837	4.8 -0.3 5.7	146 -9 174
27 Tu	0034 0658 1247 1931	-0.2 5.1 -0.5 5.8	-6 155 -15 177
28 W ○	0125 0753 1342 2023	-0.5 5.4 -0.7 5.8	-15 165 -21 177
29 Th	0215 0845 1435 2112	-0.7 5.5 -0.7 5.8	-21 168 -21 177
30 F	0304 0936 1528 2201	-0.7 5.6 -0.5 5.6	-21 171 -15 171
31 Sa	0352 1026 1621 2250	-0.6 5.6 -0.3 5.4	-18 171 -9 165

September 1996

Day	Time (h m)	Height (ft)	Height (cm)
1 Su	0441 1117 1715 2339	-0.3 5.5 0.1 5.1	-9 168 3 155
2 M	0531 1209 1812	0.0 5.4 0.5	0 165 15
3 Tu	0029 0624 1303 1912	4.8 0.4 5.2 0.9	146 12 158 27
4 W ◑	0123 0721 1400 2013	4.6 0.7 5.1 1.1	140 21 155 34
5 Th	0219 0820 1459 2113	4.5 0.9 5.0 1.3	137 27 152 40
6 F	0318 0919 1558 2209	4.4 1.1 5.0 1.3	134 34 152 40
7 Sa	0415 1014 1652 2259	4.5 1.1 5.1 1.2	137 34 155 37
8 Su	0508 1105 1741 2344	4.6 1.0 5.1 1.0	140 30 155 30
9 M	0556 1151 1825	4.7 0.9 5.2	143 27 158
10 Tu	0025 0640 1233 1906	0.8 4.8 0.7 5.3	24 146 21 162
11 W	0102 0721 1311 1945	0.7 5.0 0.6 5.3	21 152 18 162
12 Th ●	0136 0800 1347 2021	0.5 5.1 0.6 5.3	15 155 18 162
13 F	0208 0836 1422 2056	0.5 5.2 0.5 5.2	15 158 15 158
14 Sa	0240 0912 1457 2130	0.4 5.2 0.6 5.1	12 158 18 155
15 Su	0312 0947 1534 2205	0.4 5.3 0.7 5.1	12 162 21 155
16 M	0348 1024 1615 2242	0.5 5.3 0.8 5.0	15 162 24 152
17 Tu	0427 1106 1702 2324	0.6 5.3 0.9 4.9	18 162 27 149
18 W	0513 1153 1756	0.7 5.3 1.1	21 162 34
19 Th	0013 0606 1250 1859	4.8 0.8 5.3 1.2	146 24 162 37
20 F ◐	0113 0708 1356 2009	4.7 0.9 5.3 1.2	143 27 162 37
21 Sa	0222 0819 1509 2119	4.7 0.9 5.4 1.0	143 27 165 30
22 Su	0336 0931 1619 2223	4.8 0.7 5.5 0.7	146 21 168 21
23 M	0445 1038 1722 2320	5.0 0.5 5.6 0.4	152 15 171 12
24 Tu	0547 1139 1820	5.3 0.1 5.8	162 3 177
25 W	0013 0643 1236 1913	0.0 5.6 -0.1 5.9	0 171 -3 180
26 Th ○	0103 0735 1329 2002	-0.2 5.8 -0.3 5.8	-6 177 -9 177
27 F	0151 0825 1420 2050	-0.4 6.0 -0.3 5.7	-12 183 -9 174
28 Sa	0237 0913 1509 2137	-0.4 6.0 -0.2 5.6	-12 183 -6 171
29 Su	0323 1001 1559 2223	-0.2 5.9 0.1 5.4	-6 180 3 165
30 M	0409 1048 1649 2309	0.1 5.8 0.4 5.1	3 177 12 155

October 1996

Day	Time (h m)	Height (ft)	Height (cm)
1 Tu	0457 1136 1742 2357	0.4 5.6 0.8 4.9	12 171 24 149
2 W	0547 1227 1837	0.8 5.4 1.2	24 165 37
3 Th	0047 0641 1320 1935	4.8 1.1 5.2 1.4	146 34 158 43
4 F ◑	0141 0740 1417 2034	4.6 1.4 5.1 1.6	140 43 155 49
5 Sa	0238 0841 1514 2129	4.6 1.5 5.1 1.6	140 46 155 49
6 Su	0335 0939 1609 2219	4.7 1.5 5.1 1.5	143 46 155 46
7 M	0430 1032 1700 2304	4.8 1.4 5.2 1.3	146 43 158 40
8 Tu	0519 1119 1746 2344	5.0 1.3 5.2 1.1	152 40 158 34
9 W	0605 1202 1829	5.2 1.1 5.3	158 34 162
10 Th	0022 0647 1242 1909	0.9 5.3 0.9 5.3	27 162 27 162
11 F	0057 0727 1320 1948	0.7 5.5 0.7 5.3	21 168 21 162
12 Sa ●	0131 0806 1357 2026	0.5 5.6 0.6 5.3	15 171 18 162
13 Su	0206 0844 1436 2104	0.4 5.6 0.6 5.2	12 171 18 158
14 M	0242 0923 1516 2143	0.4 5.7 0.6 5.1	12 174 18 155
15 Tu	0322 1005 1601 2225	0.4 5.7 0.7 5.1	12 174 21 155
16 W	0406 1051 1650 2313	0.5 5.7 0.8 5.0	15 174 24 152
17 Th	0455 1142 1746	0.7 5.6 1.0	21 171 30
18 F	0007 0552 1242 1849	4.9 0.8 5.5 1.1	149 24 168 34
19 Sa ◐	0110 0658 1348 1957	4.9 1.0 5.4 1.1	149 30 165 34
20 Su	0219 0811 1457 2104	4.9 1.0 5.4 0.9	149 30 165 27
21 M	0328 0924 1604 2205	5.1 0.9 5.5 0.7	155 27 168 21
22 Tu	0434 1030 1705 2301	5.3 0.6 5.5 0.4	162 18 168 12
23 W	0533 1129 1801 2352	5.6 0.4 5.6 0.1	171 12 171 3
24 Th	0627 1224 1853	5.8 0.1 5.6	177 3 171
25 F	0041 0718 1315 1942	-0.1 6.0 0.0 5.5	-3 183 0 168
26 Sa ○	0127 0806 1403 2028	-0.2 6.0 0.0 5.4	-6 183 0 165
27 Su	0212 0851 1450 2113	-0.2 6.0 0.0 5.3	-6 183 0 162
28 M	0256 0936 1537 2157	0.0 5.9 0.2 5.1	0 180 6 155
29 Tu	0339 1020 1623 2240	0.2 5.7 0.5 4.9	6 174 15 149
30 W	0424 1105 1710 2325	0.5 5.5 0.8 4.8	15 168 24 146
31 Th	0509 1150 1800	0.9 5.3 1.1	27 162 34

November 1996

Day	Time (h m)	Height (ft)	Height (cm)
1 F	0011 0559 1238 1852	4.7 1.2 5.1 1.4	143 37 155 43
2 Sa	0100 0654 1329 1946	4.6 1.5 5.0 1.5	140 46 152 46
3 Su ◑	0154 0753 1423 2039	4.6 1.6 4.9 1.5	140 49 149 46
4 M	0249 0853 1517 2129	4.6 1.7 4.9 1.5	140 52 149 46
5 Tu	0344 0949 1610 2215	4.8 1.6 4.9 1.3	146 49 149 40
6 W	0436 1039 1659 2257	4.9 1.4 4.9 1.1	149 43 149 34
7 Th	0524 1125 1746 2337	5.1 1.2 4.9 0.8	155 37 149 24
8 F	0610 1209 1830	5.3 0.9 5.0	162 27 152
9 Sa	0016 0653 1251 1914	0.5 5.5 0.6 5.0	15 168 18 152
10 Su ●	0055 0736 1333 1956	0.3 5.6 0.4 5.0	9 171 12 152
11 M	0135 0819 1416 2040	0.1 5.7 0.3 5.0	3 174 9 152
12 Tu	0218 0904 1501 2125	0.0 5.8 0.2 5.0	0 177 6 152
13 W	0303 0951 1549 2213	0.0 5.8 0.2 4.9	0 177 6 149
14 Th	0351 1041 1641 2305	0.1 5.7 0.3 4.9	3 174 9 149
15 F	0444 1135 1737	0.3 5.6 0.5	9 171 15
16 Sa	0002 0544 1233 1838	4.8 0.5 5.4 0.5	146 15 165 15
17 Su ◐	0104 0652 1336 1942	4.9 0.7 5.3 0.6	149 21 162 18
18 M	0210 0804 1441 2045	4.9 0.8 5.2 0.5	149 24 158 15
19 Tu	0316 0915 1545 2145	5.1 0.7 5.1 0.3	155 21 155 9
20 W	0419 1019 1645 2240	5.3 0.5 5.1 0.1	162 15 155 3
21 Th	0517 1118 1741 2331	5.4 0.3 5.1 0.0	165 9 155 0
22 F	0611 1211 1833	5.6 0.1 5.0	171 3 152
23 Sa	0019 0701 1300 1921	-0.2 5.7 0.0 4.9	-6 174 0 149
24 Su ○	0105 0747 1347 2007	-0.2 5.7 0.0 4.9	-6 174 0 149
25 M	0149 0832 1432 2050	-0.2 5.6 0.0 4.8	-6 171 0 146
26 Tu	0231 0914 1515 2132	-0.1 5.5 0.1 4.6	-3 168 3 140
27 W	0313 0955 1558 2213	0.1 5.3 0.3 4.5	3 162 9 137
28 Th	0354 1036 1640 2254	0.3 5.2 0.5 4.4	9 158 15 134
29 F	0435 1117 1723 2336	0.6 5.0 0.7 4.4	18 152 21 134
30 Sa	0519 1158 1807	0.9 4.8 0.9	27 146 27

December 1996

Day	Time (h m)	Height (ft)	Height (cm)
1 Su	0020 0605 1242 1852	4.3 1.1 4.7 1.1	131 34 143 34
2 M	0107 0658 1328 1940	4.3 1.3 4.6 1.1	131 40 140 34
3 Tu ◑	0157 0755 1418 2028	4.4 1.4 4.5 1.1	134 43 137 34
4 W	0251 0854 1511 2116	4.5 1.4 4.4 1.0	137 43 134 30
5 Th	0345 0951 1604 2204	4.6 1.2 4.4 0.7	140 37 134 21
6 F	0438 1043 1658 2250	4.8 1.0 4.4 0.4	146 30 134 12
7 Sa	0530 1133 1749 2337	5.0 0.6 4.4 0.1	152 18 134 3
8 Su	0620 1221 1840	5.2 0.3 4.5	158 9 137
9 M	0023 0709 1309 1929	-0.2 5.3 0.0 4.6	-6 162 0 140
10 Tu ●	0110 0758 1357 2019	-0.4 5.5 -0.2 4.6	-12 168 -6 140
11 W	0158 0848 1446 2109	-0.6 5.6 -0.4 4.7	-18 171 -12 143
12 Th	0248 0938 1536 2201	-0.6 5.6 -0.4 4.7	-18 171 -12 143
13 F	0340 1030 1628 2255	-0.5 5.5 -0.4 4.7	-15 168 -12 143
14 Sa	0436 1124 1724 2352	-0.4 5.4 -0.3 4.7	-12 165 -9 143
15 Su	0537 1220 1821	-0.1 5.2 -0.2	-3 158 -6
16 M	0051 0643 1319 1922	4.7 0.1 4.9 -0.1	143 3 149 -3
17 Tu ◐	0154 0752 1420 2022	4.8 0.3 4.7 -0.1	146 9 143 -3
18 W	0257 0900 1522 2121	4.8 0.3 4.6 -0.1	146 9 140 -3
19 Th	0400 1004 1623 2217	4.9 0.3 4.5 -0.1	149 9 137 -3
20 F	0459 1102 1720 2310	5.0 0.2 4.4 -0.2	152 6 134 -6
21 Sa	0553 1155 1813 2359	5.1 0.0 4.4 -0.3	155 0 134 -9
22 Su	0643 1244 1901	5.1 -0.1 4.3	155 -3 131
23 M	0045 0730 1330 1946	-0.4 5.1 -0.2 4.3	-12 155 -6 131
24 Tu ○	0129 0813 1413 2028	-0.4 5.1 -0.2 4.2	-12 155 -6 128
25 W	0210 0853 1453 2109	-0.3 5.0 -0.2 4.2	-9 152 -6 128
26 Th	0250 0932 1532 2147	-0.2 4.9 -0.1 4.2	-6 149 -3 128
27 F	0328 1009 1610 2225	-0.1 4.8 0.0 4.1	-3 146 0 125
28 Sa	0406 1046 1646 2303	0.1 4.6 0.2 4.1	3 140 6 125
29 Su	0443 1122 1722 2341	0.4 4.5 0.4 4.1	12 137 12 125
30 M	0523 1159 1759	0.6 4.4 0.5	18 134 15
31 Tu	0022 0607 1238 1840	4.1 0.8 4.2 0.6	125 24 128 18

January 1997

Day	Time (h m)	Height (ft)	Height (cm)
1 W ◑	0109 0701 1326 1930	4.1 1.0 4.1 0.6	125 30 125 18
2 Th	0159 0800 1416 2021	4.1 1.0 4.0 0.5	125 30 122 15
3 F	0255 0902 1513 2115	4.2 0.9 3.9 0.3	128 27 119 9
4 Sa	0354 1003 1613 2210	4.4 0.6 3.9 0.1	134 18 119 3
5 Su	0454 1101 1714 2305	4.6 0.3 4.0 -0.3	140 9 122 -9
6 M	0552 1156 1812 2358	4.8 -0.1 4.1 -0.6	146 -3 125 -18
7 Tu	0648 1248 1908	5.0 -0.4 4.2	152 -12 128
8 W ●	0051 0741 1340 2002	-0.9 5.2 -0.7 4.4	-27 158 -21 134
9 Th	0143 0833 1430 2055	-1.1 5.4 -1.0 4.5	-34 165 -30 137
10 F	0236 0925 1521 2147	-1.2 5.4 -1.1 4.6	-37 165 -34 140
11 Sa	0330 1016 1613 2241	-1.1 5.3 -1.1 4.7	-34 162 -34 143
12 Su	0426 1109 1706 2336	-1.0 5.1 -1.0 4.7	-30 155 -30 143
13 M	0525 1202 1801	-0.7 4.9 -0.8	-21 149 -24
14 Tu	0033 0628 1258 1858	4.7 -0.4 4.6 -0.6	143 -12 140 -18
15 W ◐	0132 0734 1357 1957	4.6 -0.1 4.4 -0.4	140 -3 134 -12
16 Th	0234 0840 1457 2057	4.6 0.1 4.1 -0.3	140 3 125 -9
17 F	0337 0944 1558 2154	4.6 0.1 4.0 -0.2	140 3 122 -6
18 Sa	0437 1043 1657 2249	4.6 0.1 3.9 -0.2	140 3 119 -6
19 Su	0533 1136 1751 2340	4.6 0.0 3.9 -0.3	140 0 119 -9
20 M	0624 1225 1840	4.6 -0.1 3.9	140 -3 119
21 Tu	0027 0711 1310 1925	-0.4 4.7 -0.2 3.9	-12 143 -6 119
22 W	0111 0753 1351 2007	-0.4 4.7 -0.3 4.0	-12 143 -9 122
23 Th ○	0152 0832 1430 2046	-0.4 4.6 -0.3 4.0	-12 140 -9 122
24 F	0230 0910 1506 2123	-0.4 4.6 -0.3 4.0	-12 140 -9 122
25 Sa	0306 0945 1540 2159	-0.3 4.5 -0.2 4.0	-9 137 -6 122
26 Su	0341 1019 1612 2234	-0.1 4.4 -0.1 4.0	-3 134 -3 122
27 M	0415 1052 1644 2308	0.0 4.3 0.0 4.0	0 131 0 122
28 Tu	0451 1125 1717 2345	0.2 4.2 0.1 4.0	6 128 3 122
29 W	0531 1201 1755	0.4 4.0 0.2	12 122 6
30 Th	0025 0618 1241 1840	4.1 0.6 3.9 0.2	125 18 119 6
31 F ◑	0111 0714 1329 1932	4.1 0.6 3.8 0.2	125 18 116 6

Feb. 1997

Day	Time (h m)	Height (ft)	Height (cm)
1 Sa	0207 0818 1426 2031	4.2 0.6 3.7 0.1	128 18 113 3
2 Su	0311 0926 1533 2134	4.3 0.5 3.7 -0.1	131 15 113 -3
3 M	0420 1031 1642 2237	4.4 0.2 3.8 -0.4	134 6 116 -12
4 Tu	0526 1131 1747 2337	4.6 -0.2 4.0 -0.7	140 -6 122 -21
5 W	0627 1227 1848	4.9 -0.6 4.2	149 -18 128
6 Th	0034 0723 1319 1944	-1.1 5.1 -1.0 4.5	-34 155 -30 137
7 F ●	0129 0816 1411 2037	-1.3 5.2 -1.3 4.7	-40 158 -40 143
8 Sa	0224 0908 1501 2130	-1.5 5.3 -1.4 4.8	-46 162 -43 146
9 Su	0318 0958 1551 2222	-1.4 5.2 -1.4 4.9	-43 158 -43 149
10 M	0413 1049 1642 2314	-1.2 5.0 -1.2 4.9	-37 152 -37 149
11 Tu	0509 1140 1734	-0.9 4.7 -1.0	-27 143 -30
12 W	0009 0608 1233 1829	4.8 -0.6 4.5 -0.7	146 -18 137 -21
13 Th	0106 0711 1330 1927	4.6 -0.2 4.2 -0.4	140 -6 128 -12
14 F ◐	0206 0815 1429 2028	4.5 0.1 3.9 -0.1	137 3 119 -3
15 Sa	0308 0918 1530 2128	4.4 0.2 3.8 0.0	134 6 116 0

Time meridian 75° W. 0000 is midnight. 1200 is noon.
Heights are referred to mean lower low water which is the chart datum of soundings.

TIDE TABLES: MIAMI, FLORIDA

Times & Heights of High and Low Waters

(All times given are Eastern Standard Time and may differ because of wind conditions.)

Feb. 1996

Day	Time (h m)	Height (ft)	Height (cm)
16 F	0545 1154 1801	2.7 -0.3 2.7	82 -9 82
17 Sa	0019 0640 1249 1857	-0.7 2.8 -0.5 2.8	-21 85 -15 85
18 Su ●	0113 0731 1341 1950	-0.8 2.9 -0.6 2.9	-24 88 -18 88
19 M	0204 0819 1430 2041	-0.8 3.0 -0.7 3.0	-24 91 -21 91
20 Tu	0253 0906 1518 2130	-0.8 3.0 -0.7 2.9	-24 91 -21 88
21 W	0341 0952 1605 221[illegible]	-0.6 2.9 -0.7 2.8	-18 88 -21 85
22 Th	0428 1037 1652 2308	-0.5 2.7 -0.5 2.6	-15 82 -15 79
23 F	0516 1123 1740 2359	-0.2 2.5 -0.4 2.4	-6 76 -12 73
24 Sa	0606 1211 1830	0.0 2.3 -0.2	0 70 -6
25 Su	0052 0659 1302 1924	2.3 0.2 2.1 0.0	70 6 64 0
26 M ◐	0150 0757 1359 2022	2.1 0.4 2.0 0.1	64 12 61 3
27 Tu	0251 0859 1459 2122	2.0 0.4 1.9 0.1	61 12 58 3
28 W	0352 1001 1600 2219	2.0 0.4 1.9 0.1	61 12 58 3
29 Th	0447 1056 1655 2311	2.1 0.4 2.0 0.1	64 12 61 3

March 1996

Day	Time (h m)	Height (ft)	Height (cm)
1 F	0535 1144 1744 2358	2.2 0.3 2.1 0.0	67 9 64 0
2 Sa	0617 1226 1828	2.3 0.1 2.2	70 3 67
3 Su	0040 0656 1304 1908	-0.1 2.4 0.0 2.4	-3 73 0 73
4 M	0119 0732 1340 1947	-0.2 2.5 -0.1 2.5	-6 76 -3 76
5 Tu ○	0157 0807 1416 2025	-0.2 2.5 -0.2 2.6	-6 76 -6 79
6 W	0234 0842 1452 2103	-0.2 2.6 -0.3 2.6	-6 79 -9 79
7 Th	0312 0918 1529 2143	-0.2 2.6 -0.3 2.6	-6 79 -9 79
8 F	0351 0955 1609 2226	-0.2 2.5 -0.3 2.6	-6 76 -9 79
9 Sa	0432 1036 1652 2312	-0.1 2.5 -0.3 2.5	-3 76 -9 76
10 Su	0519 1122 1742	0.0 2.4 -0.3	0 73 -9
11 M	0005 0612 1216 1838	2.4 0.1 2.3 -0.2	73 3 70 -6
12 Tu ◑	0105 0714 1319 1944	2.4 0.2 2.3 -0.1	73 6 70 -3
13 W	0212 0823 1429 2054	2.4 0.2 2.3 -0.1	73 6 70 -3
14 Th	0322 0934 1542 2204	2.4 0.1 2.4 -0.2	73 3 73 -6
15 F	0428 1040 1649 2308	2.5 0.0 2.5 -0.3	76 0 76 -9
16 Sa	0528 1139 1750	2.7 -0.2 2.7	82 -6 82
17 Su	0006 0621 1233 1845	-0.4 2.8 -0.4 2.9	-12 85 -12 88
18 M	0058 0711 1322 1935	-0.5 2.9 -0.5 3.0	-15 88 -15 91
19 Tu ●	0147 0757 1409 2023	-0.5 3.0 -0.6 3.0	-15 91 -18 91
20 W	0234 0841 1454 2109	-0.5 2.9 -0.6 3.0	-15 88 -18 91
21 Th	0319 0924 1537 2154	-0.4 2.9 -0.5 2.9	-12 88 -15 88
22 F	0403 1007 1621 2239	-0.2 2.7 -0.4 2.7	-6 82 -12 82
23 Sa	0447 1050 1705 2325	0.0 2.5 -0.2 2.6	0 76 -6 79
24 Su	0533 1134 1750	0.2 2.4 0.0	6 73 0
25 M	0014 0622 1222 1840	2.4 0.4 2.2 0.2	73 12 67 6
26 Tu ◐	0106 0716 1317 1936	2.2 0.5 2.1 0.3	67 15 64 9
27 W	0204 0816 1417 2036	2.1 0.6 2.0 0.4	64 18 61 12
28 Th	0304 0918 1521 2137	2.1 0.6 2.0 0.4	64 18 61 12
29 F	0401 1014 1619 2233	2.2 0.5 2.1 0.3	67 15 64 9
30 Sa	0452 1104 1711 2322	2.2 0.4 2.2 0.2	67 12 67 6
31 Su	0537 1148 1757	2.4 0.2 2.4	73 6 73

April 1996

Day	Time (h m)	Height (ft)	Height (cm)
1 M	0007 0617 1228 1839	0.1 2.5 0.0 2.6	3 76 0 79
2 Tu	0049 0656 1306 1920	0.0 2.6 -0.1 2.7	0 79 -3 82
3 W ○	0129 0733 1344 2000	-0.1 2.7 -0.2 2.8	-3 82 -6 85
4 Th	0208 0811 1423 2040	-0.1 2.7 -0.3 2.9	-3 82 -9 88
5 F	0248 0850 1503 2123	-0.1 2.8 -0.4 2.9	-3 85 -12 88
6 Sa	0330 0932 1546 2207	-0.1 2.7 -0.4 2.9	-3 82 -12 88
7 Su	0415 1017 1633 2256	0.0 2.7 -0.3 2.8	0 82 -9 85
8 M	0504 1107 1725 2350	0.1 2.6 -0.2 2.7	3 79 -6 82
9 Tu	0600 1204 1824	0.2 2.5 -0.1	6 76 -3
10 W ◑	0050 0703 1309 1930	2.6 0.2 2.5 0.0	79 6 76 0
11 Th	0156 0811 1421 2041	2.6 0.3 2.5 0.0	79 9 76 0
12 F	0305 0920 1533 2150	2.6 0.2 2.5 0.0	79 6 76 0
13 Sa	0409 1025 1639 2254	2.6 0.0 2.7 0.0	79 0 82 0
14 Su	0508 1122 1738 2350	2.7 -0.1 2.8 -0.1	82 -3 85 -3
15 M	0600 1214 1831	2.8 -0.3 3.0	85 -9 91
16 Tu	0042 0648 1301 1919	-0.2 2.9 -0.4 3.0	-6 88 -12 91
17 W ●	0129 0733 1346 2004	-0.2 2.9 -0.4 3.1	-6 88 -12 94
18 Th	0213 0815 1428 2047	-0.1 2.9 -0.4 3.0	-3 88 -12 91
19 F	0255 0856 1509 2129	-0.1 2.8 -0.3 2.9	-3 85 -9 88
20 Sa	0337 0937 1550 2211	0.0 2.7 -0.2 2.8	0 82 -6 85
21 Su	0419 1018 1631 2253	0.2 2.5 -0.1 2.7	6 76 -3 82
22 M	0502 1100 1714 2338	0.3 2.4 0.1 2.5	9 73 3 76
23 Tu	0548 1146 1800	0.5 2.3 0.3	15 70 9
24 W	0025 0638 1238 1852	2.4 0.6 2.1 0.4	73 18 64 12
25 Th ◐	0118 0733 1336 1949	2.3 0.6 2.1 0.5	70 18 64 15
26 F	0214 0831 1438 2050	2.2 0.6 2.1 0.5	67 18 64 15
27 Sa	0310 0927 1538 2148	2.2 0.5 2.2 0.5	67 15 67 15
28 Su	0402 1018 1632 2241	2.3 0.4 2.3 0.4	70 12 70 12
29 M	0450 1105 1721 2329	2.4 0.2 2.5 0.3	73 6 76 9
30 Tu	0534 1148 1807	2.5 0.0 2.7	76 0 82

May 1996

Day	Time (h m)	Height (ft)	Height (cm)
1 W	0015 0617 1231 1850	0.2 2.6 -0.2 2.9	6 79 -6 88
2 Th	0058 0659 1313 1934	0.1 2.8 -0.3 3.0	3 85 -9 91
3 F ○	0142 0742 1356 2018	0.0 2.8 -0.4 3.1	0 85 -12 94
4 Sa	0226 0826 1441 2104	-0.1 2.9 -0.5 3.1	-3 88 -15 94
5 Su	0312 0912 1528 2151	-0.1 2.9 -0.5 3.1	-3 88 -15 94
6 M	0401 1002 1618 2242	0.0 2.8 -0.4 3.0	0 85 -12 91
7 Tu	0453 1056 1713 2337	0.0 2.7 -0.3 2.9	0 82 -9 88
8 W	0550 1156 1813	0.1 2.6 -0.1	3 79 -3
9 Th	0037 0652 1302 1918	2.8 0.1 2.6 0.0	85 3 79 0
10 F ◑	0140 0758 1411 2027	2.7 0.1 2.6 0.1	82 3 79 3
11 Sa	0245 0904 1521 2134	2.6 0.1 2.6 0.1	79 3 79 3
12 Su	0347 1006 1625 2236	2.6 0.0 2.7 0.1	79 0 82 3
13 M	0444 1102 1722 2332	2.7 -0.1 2.8 0.1	82 -3 85 3
14 Tu	0536 1153 1814	2.7 -0.2 2.9	82 -6 88
15 W	0022 0624 1239 1901	0.1 2.7 -0.3 2.9	3 82 -9 88
16 Th	0108 0707 1322 1944	0.1 2.7 -0.3 2.9	3 82 -9 88
17 F ●	0151 0749 1403 2025	0.1 2.7 -0.3 2.9	3 82 -9 88
18 Sa	0232 0829 1442 2105	0.1 2.6 -0.2 2.8	3 79 -6 85
19 Su	0312 0909 1521 2144	0.2 2.6 -0.1 2.7	6 79 -3 82
20 M	0353 0949 1601 2224	0.3 2.5 0.0 2.6	9 76 0 79
21 Tu	0434 1030 1642 2305	0.3 2.3 0.1 2.5	9 70 3 76
22 W	0517 1115 1725 2348	0.4 2.2 0.2 2.4	12 67 6 73
23 Th	0603 1203 1813	0.5 2.2 0.4	15 67 12
24 F	0035 0652 1257 1905	2.3 0.5 2.1 0.5	70 15 64 15
25 Sa ◐	0125 0744 1355 2002	2.3 0.5 2.1 0.5	70 15 64 15
26 Su	0217 0838 1453 2100	2.3 0.4 2.2 0.5	70 12 67 15
27 M	0309 0930 1550 2156	2.3 0.3 2.3 0.4	70 9 70 12
28 Tu	0401 1021 1643 2249	2.4 0.1 2.5 0.3	73 3 76 9
29 W	0450 1109 1733 2339	2.5 -0.1 2.7 0.2	76 -3 82 6
30 Th	0539 1157 1821	2.6 -0.3 2.8	79 -9 85
31 F	0028 0627 1245 1909	0.1 2.7 -0.5 3.0	3 82 -15 91

June 1996

Day	Time (h m)	Height (ft)	Height (cm)
1 Sa ○	0117 0716 1333 1957	-0.1 2.8 -0.6 3.1	-3 85 -18 94
2 Su	0205 0805 1422 2046	-0.1 2.9 -0.6 3.1	-3 88 -18 94
3 M	0255 0856 1512 2136	-0.2 2.9 -0.6 3.1	-6 88 -18 94
4 Tu	0347 0949 1605 2228	-0.2 2.9 -0.5 3.1	-6 88 -15 94
5 W	0441 1046 1701 2323	-0.2 2.8 -0.4 2.9	-6 85 -12 88
6 Th	0537 1146 1800	-0.1 2.7 -0.2	-3 82 -6
7 F	0020 0637 1249 1902	2.8 -0.1 2.6 -0.1	85 -3 79 -3
8 Sa ◑	0120 0740 1356 2007	2.7 -0.1 2.6 0.1	82 -3 79 3
9 Su	0221 0842 1503 2112	2.6 -0.1 2.5 0.2	79 -3 76 6
10 M	0321 0943 1606 2214	2.5 -0.1 2.6 0.2	76 -3 79 6
11 Tu	0418 1039 1703 2310	2.5 -0.2 2.6 0.2	76 -6 79 6
12 W	0510 1129 1754	2.5 -0.2 2.6	76 -6 79
13 Th	0001 0558 1216 1841	0.2 2.5 -0.2 2.7	6 76 -6 82
14 F	0047 0643 1259 1923	0.2 2.5 -0.2 2.7	6 76 -6 82
15 Sa ●	0129 0724 1339 2003	0.2 2.5 -0.2 2.7	6 76 -6 82
16 Su	0210 0804 1418 2041	0.2 2.4 -0.2 2.7	6 73 -6 82
17 M	0249 0844 1456 2119	0.2 2.4 -0.1 2.6	6 73 -3 79
18 Tu	0327 0923 1534 2156	0.2 2.4 -0.1 2.6	6 73 -3 79
19 W	0406 1004 1613 2234	0.2 2.3 0.0 2.5	6 70 0 76
20 Th	0446 1046 1654 2313	0.3 2.2 0.1 2.4	9 67 3 73
21 F	0527 1130 1737 2355	0.3 2.2 0.2 2.3	9 67 6 70
22 Sa	0612 1219 1825	0.3 2.1 0.3	9 64 9
23 Su	0039 0659 1312 1917	2.3 0.3 2.1 0.4	70 9 64 12
24 M ◐	0128 0750 1409 2013	2.2 0.2 2.2 0.4	67 6 67 12
25 Tu	0220 0844 1508 2112	2.2 0.1 2.3 0.4	67 3 70 12
26 W	0315 0939 1606 2211	2.3 0.0 2.4 0.3	70 0 73 9
27 Th	0411 1034 1701 2307	2.4 -0.2 2.6 0.2	73 -6 79 6
28 F	0507 1128 1755	2.5 -0.4 2.8	76 -12 85
29 Sa	0001 0601 1221 1847	0.0 2.7 -0.6 2.9	0 82 -18 88
30 Su ○	0054 0655 1313 1938	-0.1 2.8 -0.7 3.1	-3 85 -21 94

July 1996

Day	Time (h m)	Height (ft)	Height (cm)
1 M	0146 0748 1406 2028	-0.3 2.9 -0.7 3.1	-9 88 -21 94
2 Tu	0238 0842 1458 2119	-0.4 3.0 -0.7 3.1	-12 91 -21 94
3 W	0331 0937 1551 2211	-0.4 3.0 -0.6 3.1	-12 91 -18 94
4 Th	0424 1032 1646 2304	-0.4 2.9 -0.5 3.0	-12 88 -15 91
5 F	0519 1130 1742 2358	-0.4 2.8 -0.3 2.8	-12 85 -9 85
6 Sa	0616 1231 1841	-0.3 2.7 -0.1	-9 82 -3
7 Su ◑	0054 0715 1334 1943	2.7 -0.2 2.5 0.1	82 -6 76 3
8 M	0153 0815 1438 2046	2.5 -0.1 2.5 0.2	76 -3 76 6
9 Tu	0252 0915 1541 2148	2.4 -0.1 2.4 0.3	73 -3 73 9
10 W	0349 1012 1639 2245	2.3 -0.1 2.4 0.3	70 -3 73 9
11 Th	0444 1104 1732 2338	2.3 -0.1 2.5 0.3	70 -3 76 9
12 F	0534 1152 1819	2.3 -0.1 2.5	70 -3 76
13 Sa	0024 0619 1236 1901	0.3 2.3 -0.1 2.6	9 70 -3 79
14 Su	0107 0702 1316 1939	0.3 2.4 -0.1 2.6	9 73 -3 79
15 M ●	0146 0742 1355 2016	0.2 2.4 -0.1 2.6	6 73 -3 79
16 Tu	0224 0821 1432 2052	0.2 2.4 -0.1 2.6	6 73 -3 79
17 W	0301 0859 1509 2128	0.2 2.4 -0.1 2.6	6 73 -3 79
18 Th	0337 0938 1547 2203	0.1 2.4 0.0 2.5	3 73 0 76
19 F	0414 1018 1625 2239	0.2 2.4 0.1 2.5	6 73 3 76
20 Sa	0452 1059 1705 2317	0.2 2.3 0.2 2.4	6 70 6 73
21 Su	0533 1144 1749 2358	0.2 2.3 0.3 2.4	6 70 9 73
22 M	0617 1234 1838	0.2 2.3 0.4	6 70 12
23 Tu ◐	0045 0708 1330 1933	2.3 0.1 2.3 0.5	70 3 70 15
24 W	0138 0804 1431 2035	2.3 0.1 2.3 0.4	70 3 70 12
25 Th	0238 0904 1533 2138	2.4 0.0 2.5 0.4	73 0 76 12
26 F	0340 1006 1634 2240	2.5 -0.2 2.6 0.2	76 -6 79 6
27 Sa	0442 1105 1732 2339	2.6 -0.3 2.8 0.1	79 -9 85 3
28 Su	0542 1202 1827	2.8 -0.5 3.0	85 -15 91
29 M	0035 0639 1257 1919	-0.1 2.9 -0.6 3.1	-3 88 -18 94
30 Tu ○	0128 0734 1351 2010	-0.3 3.1 -0.7 3.2	-9 94 -21 98
31 W	0220 0828 1443 2100	-0.4 3.2 -0.6 3.3	-12 98 -18 101

Aug. 1996

Day	Time (h m)	Height (ft)	Height (cm)
1 Th	0312 0921 1535 2150	-0.5 3.2 -0.6 3.2	-15 98 -18 98
2 F	0403 1015 1627 2240	-0.4 3.1 -0.4 3.1	-12 94 -12 94
3 Sa	0455 1110 1720 2331	-0.4 3.0 -0.2 2.9	-12 91 -6 88
4 Su	0549 1206 1815	-0.2 2.8 0.1	-6 85 3
5 M	0025 0644 1305 1913	2.7 -0.1 2.7 0.3	82 -3 82 9
6 Tu ◑	0120 0743 1407 2015	2.6 0.0 2.5 0.4	79 0 76 12
7 W	0219 0842 1510 2117	2.4 0.1 2.5 0.5	73 3 76 15
8 Th	0319 0942 1611 2218	2.3 0.2 2.4 0.6	70 6 73 18
9 F	0416 1037 1705 2312	2.3 0.2 2.5 0.6	70 6 76 18
10 Sa	0509 1127 1752 2359	2.4 0.2 2.5 0.5	73 6 76 15
11 Su	0556 1211 1834	2.4 0.2 2.6	73 6 79
12 M	0041 0639 1252 1912	0.4 2.5 0.1 2.7	12 76 3 82
13 Tu	0120 0720 1331 1948	0.3 2.6 0.1 2.7	9 79 3 82
14 W ●	0156 0758 1408 2023	0.3 2.6 0.1 2.8	9 79 3 85
15 Th	0231 0835 1444 2057	0.2 2.7 0.1 2.8	6 82 3 85

Time meridian 75° W. 0000 is midnight. 1200 is noon.
Heights are referred to mean lower low water which is the chart datum of soundings.

TIDE TABLES: MIAMI, FLORIDA

Times & Heights of High and Low Waters

(All times given are Eastern Standard Time and may differ because of wind conditions.)

Aug. 1996

Day	Time (h m)	Height (ft)	Height (cm)
16 F	0306 0913 1520 2131	0.2 2.7 0.2 2.7	6 82 6 82
17 Sa	0341 0950 1557 2206	0.2 2.7 0.3 2.7	6 82 9 82
18 Su	0418 1030 1636 2242	0.2 2.7 0.4 2.7	6 82 12 82
19 M	0457 1113 1718 2323	0.2 2.6 0.5 2.6	6 79 15 79
20 Tu	0542 1202 1807	0.2 2.6 0.6	6 79 18
21 W ◐	0011 0633 1258 1903	2.6 0.3 2.6 0.6	79 9 79 18
22 Th	0107 0732 1400 2007	2.5 0.3 2.6 0.6	76 9 79 18
23 F	0211 0837 1507 2114	2.6 0.2 2.7 0.6	79 6 82 18
24 Sa	0319 0944 1612 2220	2.7 0.1 2.8 0.4	82 3 85 12
25 Su	0426 1048 1712 2321	2.8 0.0 3.0 0.2	85 0 91 6
26 M	0528 1147 1808	3.0 -0.2 3.2	91 -6 98
27 Tu	0018 0626 1243 1900	0.0 3.2 -0.3 3.3	0 98 -9 101
28 W ○	0111 0721 1335 1950	-0.2 3.4 -0.3 3.4	-6 104 -9 104
29 Th	0201 0813 1426 2038	-0.3 3.5 -0.3 3.5	-9 107 -9 107
30 F	0250 0904 1515 2126	-0.3 3.5 -0.2 3.4	-9 107 -6 104
31 Sa	0339 0954 1605 2213	-0.3 3.4 -0.1 3.3	-9 104 -3 101

September 1996

Day	Time (h m)	Height (ft)	Height (cm)
1 Su	0428 1045 1654 2302	-0.2 3.3 0.1 3.1	-6 101 3 94
2 M	0518 1138 1746 2352	0.0 3.1 0.4 2.9	0 94 12 88
3 Tu	0610 1233 1841	0.2 2.9 0.6	6 88 18
4 W ◐	0045 0706 1331 1940	2.7 0.4 2.7 0.8	82 12 82 24
5 Th	0143 0805 1433 2043	2.6 0.5 2.6 0.9	79 15 79 27
6 F	0245 0906 1535 2145	2.5 0.6 2.6 0.9	76 18 79 27
7 Sa	0346 1004 1630 2240	2.5 0.6 2.6 0.9	76 18 79 27
8 Su	0442 1057 1719 2328	2.5 0.6 2.7 0.8	76 18 82 24
9 M	0531 1143 1801	2.6 0.5 2.8	79 15 85
10 Tu	0010 0614 1225 1840	0.7 2.8 0.5 2.9	21 85 15 88
11 W	0048 0654 1304 1916	0.5 2.9 0.4 3.0	15 88 12 91
12 Th ●	0124 0732 1341 1950	0.4 3.0 0.4 3.0	12 91 12 91
13 F	0159 0810 1418 2025	0.4 3.1 0.4 3.1	12 94 12 94
14 Sa	0234 0847 1454 2059	0.3 3.1 0.4 3.1	9 94 12 94
15 Su	0310 0925 1531 2134	0.3 3.1 0.5 3.0	9 94 15 91
16 M	0347 1005 1611 2213	0.3 3.1 0.6 3.0	9 94 18 91
17 Tu	0428 1048 1654 2256	0.3 3.1 0.7 2.9	9 94 21 88
18 W	0514 1137 1744 2346	0.4 3.0 0.8 2.9	12 91 24 88
19 Th	0607 1234 1842	0.5 2.9 0.8	15 88 24
20 F ◐	0046 0709 1338 1948	2.8 0.5 2.9 0.9	85 15 88 27
21 Sa	0154 0818 1446 2058	2.8 0.5 3.0 0.8	85 15 91 24
22 Su	0306 0928 1552 2205	2.9 0.5 3.1 0.6	88 15 94 18
23 M	0415 1034 1653 2306	3.1 0.4 3.2 0.4	94 12 98 12
24 Tu	0518 1134 1749	3.3 0.2 3.4	101 6 104
25 W	0001 0614 1228 1840	0.2 3.5 0.1 3.5	6 107 3 107
26 Th ○	0052 0707 1319 1928	0.0 3.6 0.1 3.6	0 110 3 110
27 F	0141 0756 1407 2015	-0.1 3.7 0.1 3.6	-3 113 3 110
28 Sa	0227 0845 1454 2100	-0.1 3.7 0.2 3.5	-3 113 6 107
29 Su	0313 0932 1541 2145	0.0 3.6 0.3 3.4	0 110 9 104
30 M	0359 1019 1628 2230	0.1 3.5 0.5 3.2	3 107 15 98

October 1996

Day	Time (h m)	Height (ft)	Height (cm)
1 Tu	0446 1107 1716 2318	0.3 3.3 0.7 3.1	9 101 21 94
2 W	0534 1158 1807	0.5 3.1 0.9	15 94 27
3 Th	0009 0626 1252 1903	2.9 0.7 2.9 1.0	88 21 88 30
4 F ◐	0105 0722 1350 2004	2.7 0.9 2.8 1.1	82 27 85 34
5 Sa	0207 0824 1450 2106	2.6 1.0 2.8 1.1	79 30 85 34
6 Su	0310 0924 1547 2202	2.6 1.0 2.8 1.1	79 30 85 34
7 M	0409 1020 1638 2251	2.7 0.9 2.9 0.9	82 27 88 27
8 Tu	0459 1109 1722 2334	2.8 0.9 3.0 0.8	85 27 91 24
9 W	0544 1153 1802	3.0 0.8 3.1	91 24 94
10 Th	0013 0625 1234 1839	0.7 3.1 0.7 3.1	21 94 21 94
11 F	0050 0704 1312 1916	0.5 3.3 0.6 3.2	15 101 18 98
12 Sa ●	0126 0743 1350 1952	0.4 3.4 0.6 3.3	12 104 18 101
13 Su	0203 0821 1429 2029	0.3 3.4 0.6 3.3	9 104 18 101
14 M	0241 0901 1508 2108	0.3 3.5 0.6 3.3	9 107 18 101
15 Tu	0322 0943 1550 2150	0.3 3.4 0.7 3.2	9 104 21 98
16 W	0405 1029 1636 2237	0.3 3.4 0.8 3.2	9 104 24 98
17 Th	0454 1119 1729 2331	0.4 3.3 0.8 3.1	12 101 24 94
18 F	0550 1216 1828	0.5 3.2 0.9	15 98 27
19 Sa ◐	0034 0654 1320 1935	3.0 0.6 3.1 0.9	91 18 94 27
20 Su	0144 0804 1427 2044	3.0 0.7 3.1 0.8	91 21 94 24
21 M	0257 0914 1533 2150	3.1 0.7 3.2 0.6	94 21 98 18
22 Tu	0405 1020 1634 2250	3.2 0.6 3.3 0.5	98 18 101 15
23 W	0506 1119 1729 2344	3.4 0.5 3.4 0.3	104 15 104 9
24 Th	0602 1213 1819	3.6 0.4 3.5	110 12 107
25 F	0033 0652 1302 1906	0.1 3.7 0.4 3.5	3 113 12 107
26 Sa ○	0120 0740 1349 1951	0.0 3.7 0.4 3.5	0 113 12 107
27 Su	0205 0825 1434 2034	0.0 3.7 0.4 3.5	0 113 12 107
28 M	0248 0909 1518 2117	0.1 3.6 0.5 3.3	3 110 15 101
29 Tu	0331 0953 1601 2201	0.2 3.5 0.7 3.2	6 107 21 98
30 W	0414 1037 1646 2245	0.4 3.3 0.8 3.0	12 101 24 91
31 Th	0459 1123 1734 2333	0.6 3.1 0.9 2.8	18 94 27 85

November 1996

Day	Time (h m)	Height (ft)	Height (cm)
1 F	0546 1211 1825	0.8 3.0 1.0	24 91 30
2 Sa	0026 0639 1304 1921	2.7 0.9 2.9 1.1	82 27 88 34
3 Su ◐	0125 0736 1400 2019	2.6 1.0 2.8 1.1	79 30 85 34
4 M	0227 0837 1456 2115	2.6 1.1 2.8 1.0	79 34 85 30
5 Tu	0327 0935 1548 2206	2.7 1.0 2.8 0.9	82 30 85 27
6 W	0421 1028 1635 2252	2.8 1.0 2.9 0.7	85 30 88 21
7 Th	0509 1116 1719 2334	3.0 0.9 3.0 0.6	91 27 91 18
8 F	0553 1159 1800	3.1 0.8 3.1	94 24 94
9 Sa	0014 0635 1241 1840	0.4 3.3 0.7 3.2	12 101 21 98
10 Su ●	0055 0716 1323 1921	0.3 3.4 0.6 3.2	9 104 18 98
11 M	0135 0757 1404 2002	0.1 3.5 0.5 3.3	3 107 15 101
12 Tu	0217 0840 1448 2046	0.1 3.5 0.5 3.3	3 107 15 101
13 W	0302 0925 1534 2133	0.1 3.5 0.5 3.3	3 107 15 101
14 Th	0349 1013 1623 2224	0.1 3.4 0.5 3.2	3 104 15 98
15 F	0441 1105 1717 2321	0.2 3.3 0.6 3.1	6 101 18 94
16 Sa	0537 1201 1816	0.3 3.2 0.6	9 98 18
17 Su ◐	0024 0640 1303 1921	3.0 0.5 3.1 0.6	91 15 94 18
18 M	0134 0748 1407 2027	3.0 0.6 3.1 0.5	91 18 94 15
19 Tu	0244 0858 1512 2132	3.0 0.6 3.1 0.4	91 18 94 12
20 W	0352 1003 1612 2231	3.1 0.6 3.1 0.3	94 18 94 9
21 Th	0453 1102 1707 2325	3.2 0.5 3.1 0.1	98 15 94 3
22 F	0547 1156 1758	3.3 0.5 3.2	101 15 98
23 Sa	0014 0637 1245 1844	0.0 3.4 0.4 3.2	0 104 12 98
24 Su ○	0100 0723 1330 1929	0.0 3.4 0.4 3.2	0 104 12 98
25 M	0144 0806 1414 2011	0.0 3.4 0.4 3.1	0 104 12 94
26 Tu	0225 0848 1456 2052	0.0 3.3 0.5 3.0	0 101 15 91
27 W	0306 0928 1537 2134	0.1 3.2 0.5 2.9	3 98 15 88
28 Th	0346 1009 1619 2216	0.3 3.1 0.6 2.8	9 94 18 85
29 F	0427 1050 1702 2300	0.4 2.9 0.7 2.6	12 88 21 79
30 Sa	0511 1133 1748 2349	0.5 2.8 0.8 2.5	15 85 24 76

December 1996

Day	Time (h m)	Height (ft)	Height (cm)
1 Su	0557 1219 1837	0.7 2.7 0.8	21 82 24
2 M	0041 0649 1308 1929	2.4 0.8 2.6 0.8	73 24 79 24
3 Tu ◐	0139 0745 1400 2022	2.4 0.9 2.5 0.7	73 27 76 21
4 W	0238 0843 1453 2115	2.5 0.9 2.5 0.6	76 27 76 18
5 Th	0335 0940 1544 2205	2.5 0.8 2.6 0.5	76 24 79 15
6 F	0428 1033 1633 2253	2.7 0.7 2.7 0.3	82 21 82 9
7 Sa	0517 1123 1721 2340	2.8 0.6 2.8 0.1	85 18 85 3
8 Su	0604 1210 1807	3.0 0.5 2.9	91 15 88
9 M	0025 0650 1256 1854	-0.1 3.2 0.3 3.0	-3 98 9 91
10 Tu ●	0111 0735 1343 1941	-0.2 3.3 0.2 3.1	-6 101 6 94
11 W	0158 0822 1430 2030	-0.3 3.3 0.1 3.1	-9 101 3 94
12 Th	0246 0909 1518 2120	-0.3 3.3 0.1 3.1	-9 101 3 94
13 F	0336 0958 1609 2214	-0.3 3.3 0.0 3.1	-9 101 0 94
14 Sa	0429 1050 1703 2311	-0.2 3.2 0.1 3.0	-6 98 3 91
15 Su	0525 1144 1801	0.0 3.1 0.1	0 94 3
16 M	0012 0625 1243 1902	2.9 0.1 2.9 0.1	88 3 88 3
17 Tu ◐	0118 0730 1344 2006	2.8 0.3 2.8 0.1	85 9 85 3
18 W	0226 0837 1446 2109	2.7 0.3 2.7 0.1	82 9 82 3
19 Th	0333 0942 1547 2210	2.7 0.4 2.7 0.0	82 12 82 0
20 F	0435 1043 1644 2305	2.8 0.4 2.7 -0.1	85 12 82 -3
21 Sa	0531 1138 1737 2355	2.8 0.3 2.7 -0.1	85 9 82 -3
22 Su	0621 1228 1824	2.9 0.3 2.7	88 9 82
23 M	0041 0706 1313 1909	-0.2 2.9 0.3 2.7	-6 88 9 82
24 Tu ○	0124 0748 1355 1951	-0.2 2.9 0.2 2.7	-6 88 6 82
25 W	0204 0827 1435 2031	-0.2 2.9 0.2 2.6	-6 88 6 79
26 Th	0243 0905 1513 2110	-0.1 2.8 0.2 2.6	-3 85 6 79
27 F	0321 0942 1552 2150	0.0 2.8 0.3 2.5	0 85 9 76
28 Sa	0400 1019 1631 2231	0.1 2.7 0.3 2.4	3 82 9 73
29 Su	0439 1057 1711 2314	0.2 2.6 0.3 2.3	6 79 9 70
30 M	0521 1137 1753	0.3 2.4 0.3	9 73 9
31 Tu	0001 0606 1219 1839	2.2 0.4 2.3 0.3	67 12 70 9

January 1997

Day	Time (h m)	Height (ft)	Height (cm)
1 W ◐	0054 0658 1310 1932	2.2 0.5 2.3 0.3	67 15 70 9
2 Th	0150 0754 1401 2026	2.2 0.6 2.2 0.3	67 18 67 9
3 F	0249 0853 1456 2121	2.2 0.5 2.3 0.1	67 15 70 3
4 Sa	0348 0952 1552 2216	2.3 0.5 2.3 0.0	70 15 70 0
5 Su	0444 1049 1647 2309	2.5 0.3 2.4 -0.2	76 9 73 -6
6 M	0536 1142 1741	2.7 0.2 2.6	82 6 79
7 Tu	0001 0627 1234 1833	-0.4 2.8 0.0 2.7	-12 85 0 82
8 W ●	0052 0716 1324 1925	-0.6 3.0 -0.2 2.9	-18 91 -6 88
9 Th	0142 0805 1414 2016	-0.7 3.1 -0.3 3.0	-21 94 -9 91
10 F	0233 0853 1504 2109	-0.7 3.1 -0.4 3.0	-21 94 -12 91
11 Sa	0324 0943 1555 2202	-0.7 3.1 -0.5 2.9	-21 94 -15 88
12 Su	0416 1034 1648 2258	-0.6 3.0 -0.4 2.8	-18 91 -12 85
13 M	0510 1126 1743 2356	-0.4 2.9 -0.4 2.7	-12 88 -12 82
14 Tu	0608 1221 1841	-0.2 2.7 -0.3	-6 82 -9
15 W ◐	0058 0708 1320 1942	2.6 0.0 2.5 -0.2	79 0 76 -6
16 Th	0204 0813 1421 2044	2.5 0.1 2.4 -0.2	76 3 73 -6
17 F	0310 0918 1522 2146	2.4 0.2 2.3 -0.2	73 6 70 -6
18 Sa	0414 1022 1622 2244	2.4 0.2 2.3 -0.2	73 6 70 -6
19 Su	0512 1119 1717 2336	2.4 0.2 2.3 -0.2	73 6 70 -6
20 M	0603 1210 1806	2.4 0.2 2.3	73 6 70
21 Tu	0023 0648 1255 1851	-0.2 2.5 0.1 2.3	-6 76 3 70
22 W	0105 0728 1335 1932	-0.3 2.5 0.1 2.3	-9 76 3 70
23 Th ○	0145 0806 1413 2011	-0.3 2.5 0.0 2.3	-9 76 0 70
24 F	0222 0841 1450 2049	-0.3 2.5 0.0 2.3	-9 76 0 70
25 Sa	0259 0916 1525 2127	-0.2 2.5 0.0 2.3	-6 76 0 70
26 Su	0335 0951 1601 2205	-0.2 2.4 0.0 2.3	-6 73 0 70
27 M	0412 1025 1638 2244	-0.1 2.4 0.0 2.2	-3 73 0 67
28 Tu	0450 1101 1716 2326	0.0 2.3 0.0 2.2	0 70 0 67
29 W	0531 1140 1758	0.1 2.2 0.0	3 67 0
30 Th	0013 0616 1223 1845	2.1 0.2 2.1 0.0	64 6 64 0
31 F ◐	0105 0709 1313 1938	2.1 0.3 2.1 0.0	64 9 64 0

Feb. 1997

Day	Time (h m)	Height (ft)	Height (cm)
1 Sa	0204 0808 1411 2038	2.1 0.4 2.1 -0.1	64 12 64 -3
2 Su	0307 0912 1514 2140	2.1 0.3 2.1 -0.2	64 9 64 -6
3 M	0410 1016 1617 2241	2.3 0.2 2.3 -0.3	70 6 70 -9
4 Tu	0509 1116 1718 2339	2.5 0.0 2.4 -0.5	76 0 73 -15
5 W	0604 1212 1815	2.7 -0.2 2.6	82 -6 79
6 Th	0034 0656 1304 1910	-0.7 2.8 -0.4 2.8	-21 85 -12 85
7 F ●	0126 0746 1356 2003	-0.8 3.0 -0.6 2.9	-24 91 -18 88
8 Sa	0218 0835 1446 2055	-0.9 3.0 -0.7 3.0	-27 91 -21 91
9 Su	0309 0924 1536 2147	-0.9 3.0 -0.8 3.0	-27 91 -24 91
10 M	0400 1013 1627 2240	-0.8 3.0 -0.7 2.9	-24 91 -21 88
11 Tu	0452 1103 1719 2336	-0.6 2.8 -0.6 2.7	-18 85 -18 82
12 W	0546 1155 1814	-0.3 2.6 -0.5	-9 79 -15
13 Th	0034 0643 1251 1912	2.5 -0.1 2.4 -0.3	76 -3 73 -9
14 F ◐	0136 0744 1350 2013	2.4 0.1 2.2 -0.2	73 3 67 -6
15 Sa	0241 0850 1453 2117	2.2 0.2 2.1 -0.1	67 6 64 -3

Time meridian 75° W. 0000 is midnight. 1200 is noon.
Heights are referred to mean lower low water which is the chart datum of soundings.

TIDE TABLES: KEY WEST, FLORIDA

Times & Heights of High and Low Waters

(All times given are Eastern Standard Time and may differ because of wind conditions.)

Feb. 1996

Day	Time (h m)	Height (ft)	Height (cm)
16 F	0128 0817 1252 1947	-0.4 1.0 0.1 1.8	-12 30 3 55
17 Sa	0216 0859 1351 2043	-0.5 1.1 0.0 1.9	-15 34 0 58
18 Su ●	0300 0938 1447 2134	-0.5 1.2 -0.2 1.8	-15 37 -6 55
19 M	0341 1016 1539 2223	-0.5 1.4 -0.3 1.8	-15 43 -9 55
20 Tu	0420 1052 1631 2310	-0.4 1.5 -0.3 1.6	-12 46 -9 49
21 W	0459 1129 1723 2356	-0.3 1.5 -0.3 1.4	-9 46 -9 43
22 Th	0537 1206 1816	-0.1 1.5 -0.3	-3 46 -9
23 F	0043 0615 1244 1912	1.2 0.0 1.5 -0.2	37 0 46 -6
24 Sa	0132 0655 1325 2014	1.0 0.1 1.5 -0.1	30 3 46 -3
25 Su	0228 0739 1412 2123	0.8 0.3 1.4 0.0	24 9 43 0
26 M ◐	0342 0834 1510 2237	0.7 0.4 1.3 0.0	21 12 40 0
27 Tu	0519 0942 1623 2346	0.7 0.4 1.3 0.0	21 12 40 0
28 W	0638 1055 1739	0.7 0.4 1.3	21 12 40
29 Th	0043 0727 1159 1842	0.0 0.8 0.4 1.4	0 24 12 43

March 1996

Day	Time (h m)	Height (ft)	Height (cm)
1 F	0129 0802 1253 1932	-0.1 0.9 0.3 1.4	-3 27 9 43
2 Sa	0206 0833 1338 2015	-0.1 1.0 0.2 1.5	-3 30 6 46
3 Su	0238 0901 1419 2055	-0.1 1.1 0.1 1.5	-3 34 3 46
4 M	0307 0930 1457 2133	-0.2 1.2 0.0 1.5	-6 37 0 46
5 Tu ○	0334 0959 1535 2212	-0.2 1.3 -0.1 1.5	-6 40 -3 46
6 W	0401 1029 1614 2251	-0.1 1.4 -0.2 1.5	-3 43 -6 46
7 Th	0430 1058 1654 2332	-0.1 1.5 -0.3 1.4	-3 46 -9 43
8 F	0500 1129 1739	0.0 1.5 -0.3	0 46 -9
9 Sa	0015 0533 1203 1829	1.2 0.1 1.6 -0.3	37 3 49 -9
10 Su	0105 0610 1242 1926	1.1 0.2 1.6 -0.2	34 6 49 -6
11 M	0203 0653 1330 2034	0.9 0.3 1.6 -0.2	27 9 49 -6
12 Tu ◑	0318 0749 1432 2150	0.8 0.4 1.6 -0.2	24 12 49 -6
13 W	0448 0902 1552 2305	0.8 0.4 1.6 -0.2	24 12 49 -6
14 Th	0608 1026 1720	0.9 0.4 1.6	27 12 49
15 F	0010 0706 1144 1838	-0.2 1.0 0.3 1.6	-6 30 9 49
16 Sa	0103 0751 1251 1943	-0.2 1.1 0.1 1.7	-6 34 3 52
17 Su	0149 0831 1349 2039	-0.2 1.3 -0.1 1.7	-6 40 -3 52
18 M	0231 0908 1443 2129	-0.2 1.5 -0.3 1.7	-6 46 -9 52
19 Tu ●	0310 0943 1532 2215	-0.2 1.6 -0.4 1.6	-6 49 -12 49
20 W	0347 1018 1620 2259	-0.1 1.7 -0.4 1.5	-3 52 -12 46
21 Th	0424 1051 1707 2342	0.0 1.7 -0.4 1.3	0 52 -12 40
22 F	0500 1125 1754	0.1 1.7 -0.3	3 52 -9
23 Sa	0024 0536 1201 1844	1.2 0.2 1.7 -0.2	37 6 52 -6
24 Su	0108 0614 1239 1938	1.0 0.3 1.6 -0.1	30 9 49 -3
25 M	0157 0656 1324 2039	0.9 0.4 1.5 0.0	27 12 46 0
26 Tu ◐	0258 0748 1418 2149	0.8 0.5 1.4 0.1	24 15 43 3
27 W	0418 0900 1527 2258	0.8 0.6 1.3 0.1	24 18 40 3
28 Th	0541 1024 1649 2356	0.8 0.5 1.3 0.1	24 15 40 3
29 F	0636 1135 1803	0.9 0.5 1.3	27 15 40
30 Sa	0043 0715 1232 1902	0.1 1.1 0.3 1.4	3 34 9 43
31 Su	0120 0748 1319 1951	0.1 1.2 0.2 1.4	3 37 6 43

April 1996

Day	Time (h m)	Height (ft)	Height (cm)
1 M	0152 0818 1401 2035	0.1 1.3 0.1 1.5	3 40 3 46
2 Tu	0222 0849 1440 2117	0.1 1.5 -0.1 1.5	3 46 -3 46
3 W ○	0251 0919 1519 2158	0.1 1.6 -0.2 1.5	3 49 -6 46
4 Th	0321 0950 1559 2241	0.1 1.7 -0.3 1.4	3 52 -9 43
5 F	0353 1022 1641 2324	0.1 1.8 -0.4 1.3	3 55 -12 40
6 Sa	0427 1057 1727	0.2 1.8 -0.4	6 55 -12
7 Su	0011 0504 1135 1817	1.2 0.3 1.9 -0.4	37 9 58 -12
8 M	0103 0546 1219 1914	1.1 0.3 1.8 -0.3	34 9 55 -9
9 Tu	0202 0635 1312 2018	1.0 0.4 1.8 -0.2	30 12 55 -6
10 W ◑	0313 0738 1418 2129	1.0 0.5 1.7 -0.1	30 15 52 -3
11 Th	0430 0900 1541 2238	1.0 0.5 1.6 0.0	30 15 49 0
12 F	0539 1028 1713 2338	1.1 0.4 1.5 0.0	34 12 46 0
13 Sa	0634 1146 1833	1.2 0.3 1.5	37 9 46
14 Su	0030 0720 1251 1938	0.0 1.4 0.1 1.5	0 43 3 46
15 M	0115 0800 1347 2033	0.0 1.6 -0.1 1.5	0 49 -3 46
16 Tu	0156 0836 1437 2122	0.1 1.7 -0.3 1.5	3 52 -9 46
17 W ●	0235 0911 1523 2206	0.1 1.8 -0.3 1.4	3 55 -9 43
18 Th	0312 0944 1607 2248	0.2 1.9 -0.4 1.4	6 58 -12 43
19 F	0349 1017 1650 2327	0.2 1.9 -0.4 1.3	6 58 -12 40
20 Sa	0425 1050 1733	0.3 1.9 -0.3	9 58 -9
21 Su	0006 0501 1125 1818	1.2 0.4 1.8 -0.2	37 12 55 -6
22 M	0046 0538 1203 1905	1.1 0.4 1.7 -0.1	34 12 52 -3
23 Tu	0131 0619 1247 1959	1.0 0.5 1.6 0.1	30 15 49 3
24 W	0223 0710 1337 2058	1.0 0.6 1.5 0.2	30 18 46 6
25 Th ◐	0326 0821 1439 2159	1.0 0.6 1.4 0.2	30 18 43 6
26 F	0434 0948 1554 2255	1.0 0.6 1.3 0.3	30 18 40 9
27 Sa	0532 1105 1713 2342	1.1 0.5 1.3 0.3	34 15 40 9
28 Su	0617 1205 1823	1.2 0.4 1.3	37 12 40
29 M	0022 0655 1255 1921	0.3 1.4 0.2 1.3	9 43 6 40
30 Tu	0058 0731 1338 2012	0.3 1.5 0.0 1.4	9 46 0 43

May 1996

Day	Time (h m)	Height (ft)	Height (cm)
1 W	0132 0805 1420 2059	0.3 1.7 -0.1 1.4	9 52 -3 43
2 Th	0206 0839 1501 2145	0.3 1.8 -0.3 1.4	9 55 -9 43
3 F ○	0242 0915 1544 2231	0.3 2.0 -0.4 1.4	9 61 -12 43
4 Sa	0319 0953 1629 2317	0.3 2.0 -0.5 1.3	9 61 -15 40
5 Su	0358 1033 1717	0.3 2.1 -0.5	9 64 -15
6 M	0006 0442 1118 1807	1.2 0.3 2.1 -0.4	37 9 64 -12
7 Tu	0057 0530 1207 1902	1.2 0.4 2.0 -0.3	37 12 61 -9
8 W	0154 0627 1304 2001	1.1 0.5 1.8 -0.2	34 15 55 -6
9 Th	0256 0738 1412 2103	1.1 0.5 1.7 -0.1	34 15 52 -3
10 F ◑	0401 0903 1533 2204	1.2 0.5 1.5 0.1	37 15 46 3
11 Sa	0503 1029 1702 2300	1.3 0.4 1.4 0.1	40 12 43 3
12 Su	0558 1145 1824 2351	1.5 0.2 1.3 0.2	46 6 40 6
13 M	0645 1248 1931	1.6 0.0 1.3	49 0 40
14 Tu	0037 0727 1341 2026	0.2 1.8 -0.1 1.3	6 55 -3 40
15 W	0120 0805 1429 2114	0.3 1.9 -0.2 1.3	9 58 -6 40
16 Th	0200 0841 1512 2156	0.3 1.9 -0.3 1.3	9 58 -9 40
17 F ●	0239 0915 1553 2235	0.3 2.0 -0.3 1.2	9 61 -9 37
18 Sa	0317 0948 1633 2311	0.4 2.0 -0.3 1.2	12 61 -9 37
19 Su	0353 1023 1713 2347	0.4 1.9 -0.2 1.2	12 58 -6 37
20 M	0430 1059 1754	0.4 1.9 -0.2	12 58 -6
21 Tu	0025 0509 1137 1836	1.1 0.5 1.8 -0.1	34 15 55 -3
22 W	0106 0551 1219 1920	1.1 0.6 1.7 0.0	34 18 52 0
23 Th	0151 0641 1305 2007	1.1 0.6 1.5 0.1	34 18 46 3
24 F	0241 0746 1400 2057	1.1 0.6 1.4 0.2	34 18 43 6
25 Sa ◐	0335 0906 1505 2146	1.2 0.6 1.3 0.3	37 18 40 9
26 Su	0427 1025 1621 2233	1.3 0.5 1.2 0.3	40 15 37 9
27 M	0516 1130 1740 2318	1.4 0.4 1.2 0.4	43 12 37 12
28 Tu	0600 1225 1850	1.5 0.2 1.2	46 6 37
29 W	0001 0642 1313 1950	0.4 1.7 0.0 1.2	12 52 0 37
30 Th	0042 0723 1359 2042	0.4 1.9 -0.2 1.2	12 58 -6 37
31 F	0124 0804 1445 2131	0.4 2.0 -0.4 1.3	12 61 -12 40

June 1996

Day	Time (h m)	Height (ft)	Height (cm)
1 Sa ○	0207 0847 1530 2219	0.3 2.1 -0.5 1.3	9 64 -15 40
2 Su	0251 0932 1617 2306	0.3 2.2 -0.5 1.2	9 67 -15 37
3 M	0337 1019 1705 2353	0.3 2.2 -0.5 1.2	9 67 -15 37
4 Tu	0427 1109 1754	0.3 2.2 -0.4	9 67 -12
5 W	0042 0522 1201 1845	1.3 0.3 2.0 -0.3	40 9 61 -9
6 Th	0133 0625 1259 1937	1.3 0.4 1.8 -0.2	40 12 55 -6
7 F	0228 0738 1404 2031	1.3 0.4 1.6 0.0	40 12 49 0
8 Sa ◑	0325 0900 1520 2125	1.4 0.4 1.4 0.1	43 12 43 3
9 Su	0422 1022 1647 2219	1.5 0.3 1.2 0.2	46 9 37 6
10 M	0518 1136 1810 2311	1.6 0.2 1.1 0.3	49 6 34 9
11 Tu	0609 1239 1920	1.8 0.0 1.1	55 0 34
12 W	0000 0656 1332 2017	0.4 1.8 -0.1 1.1	12 55 -3 34
13 Th	0046 0738 1418 2103	0.4 1.9 -0.2 1.1	12 58 -6 34
14 F	0130 0816 1500 2143	0.4 1.9 -0.2 1.1	12 58 -6 34
15 Sa ●	0211 0853 1539 2218	0.4 2.0 -0.2 1.1	12 61 -6 34
16 Su	0250 0928 1617 2252	0.4 2.0 -0.2 1.1	12 61 -6 34
17 M	0329 1003 1654 2325	0.4 1.9 -0.2 1.2	12 58 -6 37
18 Tu	0407 1040 1730	0.4 1.9 -0.1	12 58 -3
19 W	0000 0447 1117 1806	1.2 0.5 1.8 -0.1	37 15 55 -3
20 Th	0036 0529 1157 1842	1.2 0.5 1.7 0.0	37 15 52 0
21 F	0115 0617 1240 1919	1.2 0.5 1.6 0.1	37 15 49 3
22 Sa	0157 0714 1328 1958	1.3 0.6 1.4 0.2	40 18 43 6
23 Su	0241 0823 1426 2040	1.3 0.5 1.3 0.3	40 15 40 9
24 M ◐	0328 0939 1536 2126	1.4 0.5 1.1 0.4	43 15 34 12
25 Tu	0416 1050 1659 2216	1.5 0.3 1.1 0.4	46 9 34 12
26 W	0506 1153 1821 2308	1.6 0.2 1.0 0.5	49 6 30 15
27 Th	0557 1249 1929 2359	1.8 0.0 1.1 0.4	55 0 34 12
28 F	0648 1340 2026	2.0 -0.2 1.1	61 -6 34
29 Sa	0050 0739 1429 2116	0.4 2.1 -0.4 1.2	12 64 -12 37
30 Su ○	0141 0830 1516 2202	0.4 2.2 -0.5 1.2	12 67 -15 37

July 1996

Day	Time (h m)	Height (ft)	Height (cm)
1 M	0232 0920 1602 2247	0.3 2.3 -0.5 1.3	9 70 -15 40
2 Tu	0324 1011 1648 2331	0.2 2.3 -0.5 1.3	6 70 -15 40
3 W	0419 1102 1734	0.2 2.2 -0.4	6 67 -12
4 Th	0016 0516 1155 1820	1.4 0.2 2.0 -0.2	43 6 61 -6
5 F	0102 0619 1251 1906	1.5 0.2 1.8 -0.1	46 6 55 -3
6 Sa	0151 0729 1352 1954	1.6 0.3 1.5 0.1	49 9 46 3
7 Su ◑	0242 0846 1502 2044	1.6 0.3 1.3 0.3	49 9 40 9
8 M	0338 1005 1625 2137	1.7 0.2 1.1 0.4	52 6 34 12
9 Tu	0436 1119 1753 2233	1.7 0.2 1.0 0.5	52 6 30 15
10 W	0534 1223 1906 2327	1.8 0.1 1.0 0.5	55 3 30 15
11 Th	0627 1318 2003	1.8 0.0 1.0	55 0 30
12 F	0018 0715 1404 2047	0.5 1.9 0.0 1.1	15 58 0 34
13 Sa	0106 0758 1445 2123	0.5 1.9 -0.1 1.1	15 58 -3 34
14 Su	0150 0837 1522 2155	0.5 2.0 -0.1 1.2	15 61 -3 37
15 M ●	0231 0913 1557 2225	0.5 2.0 -0.1 1.2	15 61 -3 37
16 Tu	0311 0949 1630 2256	0.4 1.9 -0.1 1.3	12 58 -3 40
17 W	0350 1024 1701 2327	0.4 1.9 0.0 1.3	12 58 0 40
18 Th	0429 1101 1732	0.4 1.8 0.0	12 55 0
19 F	0000 0510 1139 1802	1.4 0.4 1.7 0.1	43 12 52 3
20 Sa	0035 0555 1219 1833	1.4 0.5 1.6 0.2	43 15 49 6
21 Su	0111 0646 1304 1907	1.5 0.5 1.5 0.3	46 15 46 9
22 M	0149 0746 1357 1945	1.5 0.5 1.3 0.4	46 15 40 12
23 Tu ◐	0232 0857 1504 2030	1.6 0.4 1.2 0.5	49 12 37 15
24 W	0322 1012 1629 2125	1.7 0.3 1.1 0.6	52 9 34 18
25 Th	0419 1123 1759 2226	1.8 0.2 1.0 0.6	55 6 30 18
26 F	0522 1226 1912 2328	1.9 0.0 1.1 0.6	58 0 34 18
27 Sa	0624 1321 2008	2.1 -0.1 1.2	64 -3 37
28 Su	0029 0724 1411 2055	0.5 2.2 -0.2 1.3	15 67 -6 40
29 M	0126 0820 1458 2139	0.4 2.3 -0.3 1.4	12 70 -9 43
30 Tu ○	0222 0913 1542 2220	0.3 2.3 -0.3 1.5	9 70 -9 46
31 W	0317 1005 1625 2301	0.2 2.3 -0.2 1.6	6 70 -6 49

Aug. 1996

Day	Time (h m)	Height (ft)	Height (cm)
1 Th	0412 1056 1707 2342	0.1 2.2 -0.1 1.7	3 67 -3 52
2 F	0509 1147 1748	0.1 2.0 0.0	3 61 0
3 Sa	0024 0608 1239 1831	1.8 0.2 1.7 0.2	55 6 52 6
4 Su	0109 0712 1335 1915	1.8 0.2 1.5 0.3	55 6 46 9
5 M	0156 0822 1439 2002	1.8 0.3 1.3 0.5	55 9 40 15
6 Tu ◑	0249 0937 1558 2056	1.8 0.3 1.1 0.6	55 9 34 18
7 W	0350 1052 1729 2157	1.8 0.3 1.1 0.7	55 9 34 21
8 Th	0456 1200 1846 2300	1.8 0.3 1.1 0.7	55 9 34 21
9 F	0600 1257 1941 2358	1.9 0.3 1.1 0.7	58 9 34 21
10 Sa	0655 1344 2021	1.9 0.2 1.2	58 6 37
11 Su	0050 0741 1423 2054	0.6 2.0 0.2 1.3	18 61 6 40
12 M	0136 0822 1458 2123	0.6 2.0 0.2 1.3	18 61 6 40
13 Tu	0218 0859 1529 2151	0.5 2.0 0.1 1.4	15 61 3 43
14 W ●	0257 0934 1558 2220	0.5 2.0 0.2 1.5	15 61 6 46
15 Th	0335 1010 1626 2250	0.4 2.0 0.2 1.6	12 61 6 49

Time meridian 75° W. 0000 is midnight. 1200 is noon.
Heights are referred to mean lower low water which is the chart datum of soundings.

TIDE TABLES: KEY WEST, FLORIDA

Times & Heights of High and Low Waters

(All times given are Eastern Standard Time and may differ because of wind conditions.)

Tide tables for Aug. 1996 through Feb. 1997, listing Time (h.m) and Height (ft and cm) of high and low waters for each day.

Aug. 1996

Day	Time	Height (ft)	Height (cm)
16 F	0413 1046 1653 2320	0.4 0.2 1.9 1.6	12 6 58 49
17 Sa	0452 1124 1721 2351	0.4 0.3 1.8 1.7	12 9 55 52
18 Su	0534 1204 1750	0.7 0.4 1.7	21 12 52
19 M	0024 0622 1248 1823	1.7 0.9 0.5 1.6	52 27 15 49
20 Tu	0100 0717 1340 1900	1.8 1.2 0.6 1.6	55 37 18 49
21 W	0143 0824 1446 1947	1.8 1.3 0.7 1.6	55 40 21 49
22 Th	0236 0941 1612 2047	1.9 1.2 0.8 1.6	58 37 24 49
23 F	0343 1057 1744 2159	2.0 1.2 0.8 1.7	61 37 24 52
24 Sa	0458 1204 1853 2312	2.1 1.0 0.7 1.9	64 30 21 58
25 Su	0611 1301 1945	2.2 0.7 0.5	67 21 15
26 M	0716 1349 2029	0.6 0.5 1.5	18 15 46
27 Tu	0120 0815 1433 2110	2.3 0.4 0.3 2.3	70 12 9 70
28 W	0217 0908 1515 2148	2.3 0.3 0.2 2.3	70 9 6 70
29 Th	0311 0958 1555 2226	2.3 0.2 0.2 2.0	70 6 6 61
30 F	0405 1047 1634 2305	2.1 0.2 0.3 2.0	64 6 9 61
31 Sa	0457 1135 1711 2344	0.1 0.2 2.1	3 6 64

September 1996

Day	Time	Height (ft)	Height (cm)
1 Su	0552 1224 1753	0.1 0.3 1.8	3 9 55
2 M	0025 0649 1315 1834	2.1 0.2 0.6 1.6	64 6 18 49
3 Tu	0109 0751 1412 1920	2.0 0.4 0.7 1.4	61 12 21 43
4 W	0159 0901 1524 2016	2.0 0.4 0.8 1.3	61 12 24 40
5 Th	0300 1016 1654 2123	1.9 0.5 0.9 1.3	58 15 27 40
6 F	0412 1127 1814 2236	1.9 0.5 0.9 1.3	58 15 27 40
7 Sa	0527 1228 1907 2342	1.9 0.5 0.8 1.4	58 15 24 43
8 Su	0630 1312 1945	2.0 0.4 0.7	61 12 21
9 M	0036 0720 1350 2015	1.6 0.5 0.5	49 15 15
10 Tu	0123 0803 1423 2044	2.2 0.4 0.6 1.5	67 12 18 46
11 W	0204 0841 1452 2112	2.3 0.4 0.4 1.7	70 12 12 52
12 Th	0243 0918 1519 2140	2.3 0.3 0.4 1.8	70 9 12 55
13 F	0319 0955 1546 2209	2.1 0.2 0.3 2.0	64 6 9 61
14 Sa	0356 1032 1613 2239	2.0 0.1 0.3 2.0	61 3 9 61
15 Su	0435 1111 1641 2310	0.1 0.4 2.0	3 12 61

October 1996

Day	Time	Height (ft)	Height (cm)
1 Tu	0603 1253 1756 2353	0.3 0.8 2.3	9 24 70
2 W	0026 0719 1344 1841	2.2 0.4 1.5 0.9	67 12 46 27
3 Th	0113 0822 1446 1936	2.1 0.6 1.4 0.8	64 18 43 24
4 F	0210 0932 1603 2049	2.0 0.7 1.4 0.9	61 21 43 27
5 Sa	0321 1042 1722 2211	1.9 0.7 1.1	58 21 34
6 Su	0442 1148 1818 2323	1.9 0.7 0.9 1.0	58 21 27 30
7 M	0554 1228 1857	1.9 0.6 0.8	58 18 24
8 Tu	0020 0651 1306 1929	1.9 0.6 0.6	58 18 18
9 W	0107 0738 1338 2000	2.0 0.6 0.6	61 18 18
10 Th	0148 0820 1407 2029	2.1 0.6 0.6 2.0	64 18 18 61
11 F	0225 0900 1434 2059	2.1 0.5 0.6 2.1	64 15 18 64
12 Sa	0302 0940 1504 2130	2.0 0.3 0.7 2.2	61 9 21 67
13 Su	0340 1020 1534 2201	1.9 0.3 0.8 2.3	58 9 24 70
14 M	0419 1101 1606 2235	1.7 0.2 1.0 2.3	52 6 30 70
15 Tu	0502 1145 1640 2311	0.2 0.8 2.2	6 24 67

November 1996

Day	Time	Height (ft)	Height (cm)
1 F	0035 0735 1406 1900	2.1 0.6 1.4 1.0	64 18 43 30
2 Sa	0126 0841 1507 2011	2.0 0.9 1.4 1.0	61 27 43 30
3 Su	0229 0944 1613 2137	1.8 1.0 1.6 0.7	55 30 49 21
4 M	0344 1041 1711 2254	1.7 0.7 1.5 0.8	52 21 46 24
5 Tu	0441 1130 1758 2355	1.7 0.7 1.3 0.8	52 21 40 24
6 W	0612 1210 1837	1.7 0.6 0.8	52 18 24
7 Th	0044 0709 1246 1912	1.9 0.6 0.7	58 18 21
8 F	0126 0757 1319 1947	2.0 0.6 0.7 2.4	61 18 21 73
9 Sa	0206 0842 1357 2021	0.5 0.7 2.2	15 21 67
10 Su	0245 0925 1424 2056	1.7 0.3 0.7 2.2	52 9 21 67
11 M	0324 1008 1459 2132	0.1 0.9 2.4	3 27 73
12 Tu	0406 1052 1537 2211	1.7 0.1 1.0 2.4	52 3 30 73
13 W	0450 1140 1617 2253	1.6 0.1 1.3 2.4	49 3 40 73
14 Th	0538 1225 1703 2340	1.4 0.2 1.4 2.3	43 6 43 70
15 F	0629 1318 1756	1.4 0.3 1.7	43 9 52

December 1996

Day	Time	Height (ft)	Height (cm)
1 Su	0053 0748 1415 1933	1.8 0.4 1.3 1.0	55 12 40 24
2 M	0146 0838 1506 2050	1.6 0.5 1.4 0.8	49 15 43 24
3 Tu	0250 0928 1600 2217	1.5 0.5 1.4 0.7	46 15 43 21
4 W	0405 1018 1652 2317	1.4 0.6 1.6 0.6	43 18 49 18
5 Th	0525 1104 1739	1.3 0.6 1.9	40 18 58
6 F	0013 0636 1147 1823	0.4 0.6 2.1	12 18 64
7 Sa	0100 0734 1228 1905	1.4 0.4 0.8 2.1	43 12 24 64
8 Su	0144 0825 1307 1947	1.6 0.4 0.8	49 12 24
9 M	0227 0911 1350 2029	0.2 0.9 2.1	6 27 64
10 Tu	0309 0955 1432 2112	1.8 0.1 1.0 2.3	55 3 30 70
11 W	0353 1039 1516 2157	1.7 0.0 1.4 2.3	52 0 43 70
12 Th	0438 1124 1604 2245	1.6 0.0 1.4 2.3	49 0 43 70
13 F	0529 1209 1655 2335	1.4 0.0 1.7 2.1	43 0 52 64
14 Sa	0612 1256 1753	1.4 0.2 1.8	43 6 55
15 Su	0030 0702 1347 1900	2.0 0.4 1.4	61 12 43

January 1997

Day	Time	Height (ft)	Height (cm)
1 W	0209 0821 1459 2114	1.2 0.3 1.3 0.4	37 9 40 12
2 Th	0316 0908 1549 2229	1.1 0.4 1.3 0.3	34 12 40 9
3 F	0439 0959 1643 2335	1.0 0.4 1.5 0.1	30 12 46 3
4 Sa	0603 1053 1737	1.0 0.5 1.6	30 15 49
5 Su	0031 0713 1145 1829	0.0 0.5 1.7	0 15 52
6 M	0122 0809 1236 1921	1.7 -0.1 0.6 1.9	52 -3 18 58
7 Tu	0209 0857 1325 2010	1.7 -0.2 0.7 2.0	52 -6 21 61
8 W	0254 0941 1415 2100	1.7 -0.2 0.8 2.1	52 -6 24 64
9 Th	0339 1023 1504 2149	1.6 -0.1 1.2 2.1	49 -3 37 64
10 F	0423 1105 1556 2239	1.5 -0.2 1.3 2.1	46 -6 40 64
11 Sa	0507 1147 1650 2330	1.3 0.0 1.3 1.9	40 0 40 58
12 Su	0552 1230 1748	1.2 0.3 1.6	37 9 49
13 M	0024 0636 1316 1853	1.7 0.4 1.4	52 12 43
14 Tu	0122 0723 1405 2004	1.5 0.6 1.3	46 18 40
15 W	0228 0812 1459 2122	1.2 0.7 1.3 0.2	37 21 40 6

Feb. 1997

Day	Time	Height (ft)	Height (cm)
1 Sa	0400 0856 1544 2253	0.8 0.3 1.4	24 9 43
2 Su	0534 1000 1649	0.8 0.4 1.5	24 12 46
3 M	0000 0652 1107 1757	-0.2 0.4 1.6	-6 12 49
4 Tu	0058 0750 1210 1900	-0.3 0.9 1.7	-9 27 52
5 W	0148 0836 1308 1958	-0.5 1.0 1.9	-15 30 58
6 Th	0235 0918 1403 2052	-0.6 1.1 1.9	-18 34 58
7 F ●	0318 0958 1457 2144	-0.6 1.3 1.9	-18 40 58
8 Sa	0401 1037 1550 2234	-0.6 1.3 1.9	-18 40 58
9 Su	0442 1116 1645 2325	-0.5 1.1 1.7	-15 34 52
10 M	0523 1156 1741	-0.4 1.0 1.5	-12 30 46
11 Tu	0016 0604 1238 1840	1.5 -0.2 0.9	46 -6 27
12 W	0111 0647 1323 1945	1.3 -0.1 1.2	40 -3 37
13 Th	0212 0733 1412 2057	1.0 0.0 1.1 -0.1	30 0 34 -3
14 F	0326 0825 1620 2213	0.8 0.2 1.5 -0.1	24 6 46 -3
15 Sa	0458 0928 1628 2328	0.7 0.3 1.4 -0.1	21 9 43 -3

Time meridian 75° W. 0000 is midnight. 1200 is noon.
Heights are referred to mean lower low water which is the chart datum of soundings.

TIDE TABLES: ST. PETERSBURG, FLORIDA

Times & Heights of High and Low Waters

(All times given are Eastern Standard Time and may differ because of wind conditions.)

Monthly tables for Feb. 1996, March 1996, April 1996, May 1996, June 1996, July 1996, and Aug. 1996. Each day lists Time (h m) and Height (ft / cm) for successive high and low waters.

Feb. 1996

Day	Time	Height (ft)	Height (cm)
16 F	0615 / 1346 / 1733 / 2337	-0.7 / 1.2 / 0.9 / 2.2	-21 / 37 / 27 / 67
17 Sa	0719 / 1410 / 1833	-0.7 / 1.3 / 0.7	-21 / 40 / 21
18 Su ●	0033 / 0757 / 1457 / 1927	2.2 / -0.4 / 1.4 / 0.5	67 / -13 / 43 / 15
19 M	0126 / 0831 / 1541 / 2019	2.1 / -0.1 / 1.5 / 0.3	64 / -3 / 46 / 9
20 Tu	0217 / 0903 / 1621 / 2110	1.9 / 0.3 / 1.6 / 0.1	58 / 9 / 49 / 3
21 W	0308 / 0933 / 1548 / 2202	1.7 / 0.7 / 1.8 / -0.1	52 / 21 / 55 / -3
22 Th	0401 / 1001 / 1617 / 2256	1.5 / 1.0 / 1.8 / -0.2	46 / 30 / 55 / -6
23 F	0457 / 1049 / 1649 / 2355	1.3 / 1.3 / 1.8 / -0.1	40 / 40 / 55 / -3
24 Sa	0600 / 1148 / 1725	1.0 / 1.6 / 1.9	30 / 49 / 58
25 Su	0101 / 0720 / 1302 / 1807	0.0 / 0.9 / 1.7 / 2.0	0 / 27 / 52 / 61
26 M	0218 / 1858	0.0 / 1.8	0 / 55
27 Tu	0340 / 2005	-0.1 / 1.7	-3 / 52
28 W	0450 / 2124	-0.1 / 1.7	-3 / 52
29 Th	0543 / 1318 / 1619 / 2235	-0.2 / 1.1 / 1.0 / 1.8	-6 / 34 / 30 / 55

March 1996

Day	Time	Height (ft)	Height (cm)
1 F	0623 / 1328 / 1723 / 2329	-0.3 / 0.9 / 0.9 / 1.8	-9 / 27 / 27 / 55
2 Sa	0655 / 1340 / 1812	-0.3 / 1.3 / 0.7	-9 / 40 / 21
3 Su	0013 / 0723 / 1352 / 1855	1.8 / -0.2 / 1.4 / 0.6	55 / -6 / 43 / 18
4 M	0052 / 0749 / 1403 / 1934	1.8 / -0.2 / 1.4 / 0.4	55 / -6 / 43 / 12
5 Tu ○	0131 / 0821 / 1418 / 2014	1.7 / 0.1 / 1.5 / 0.3	52 / 3 / 46 / 9
6 W	0217 / 0839 / 1438 / 2055	1.7 / 0.4 / 1.6 / 0.1	52 / 12 / 49 / 3
7 Th	0255 / 0905 / 1503 / 2138	1.6 / 0.8 / 1.8 / 0.0	49 / 24 / 55 / 0
8 M	0343 / 0931 / 1532 / 2227	1.5 / 1.2 / 1.9 / -0.1	46 / 37 / 58 / -3
9 Sa	0439 / 0957 / 1606 / 2322	1.4 / 1.5 / 2.0 / -0.2	43 / 46 / 61 / -6
10 Su	0543 / 1038 / 1645	1.2 / 1.9 / 2.1	37 / 58 / 64
11 M	0027 / 1049 / 1831	-0.2 / 0.9 / 2.1	-6 / 30 / 64
12 Tu	0144 / 0906 / 1114 / 1947	-0.2 / 1.0 / 0.9 / 2.0	-6 / 30 / 27 / 61
13 W	0305 / 2113	-0.3 / 2.0	-9 / 61
14 Th	0419 / 1212 / 1505 / 2213	-0.3 / 1.1 / 1.0 / 1.9	-9 / 34 / 30 / 58
15 F	0520 / 1235 / 1634 / 2235	-0.4 / 1.3 / 1.0 / 2.0	-12 / 40 / 30 / 61
16 Sa	0609 / 1258 / 1741 / 2342	-0.4 / 2.0 / 0.7 / 2.0	-12 / 43 / 21 / 61
17 Su	0649 / 1320 / 1837	-0.3 / 1.5 / 0.5	-9 / 46 / 15
18 M	0039 / 0723 / 1341 / 1927	2.0 / -0.1 / 1.7 / 0.3	61 / -3 / 52 / 9
19 Tu ●	0130 / 0753 / 1402 / 2014	1.9 / 0.2 / 1.8 / 0.1	58 / 6 / 55 / 3
20 W	0219 / 0821 / 1425 / 2059	1.7 / 0.7 / 1.9 / 0.0	52 / 21 / 58 / 0
21 Th	0308 / 0847 / 1451 / 2145	1.6 / 1.1 / 2.0 / 0.0	49 / 34 / 61 / 0
22 F	0358 / 0912 / 1519 / 2232	1.4 / 1.6 / 2.1 / -0.1	43 / 48 / 64 / -3
23 Sa	0452 / 0936 / 1552 / 2324	1.2 / 2.0 / 2.1 / -0.1	37 / 61 / 64 / -3
24 Su	0552 / 0957 / 1628	1.1 / 2.1 / 2.1	34 / 64 / 64
25 M	0022 / 1805	0.0 / 2.0	0 / 61
26 Tu ○	0128 / 1805	0.1 / 1.9	3 / 58
27 W	0242 / 1916	0.1 / 1.8	3 / 55
28 Th	0351 / 1156 / 1437 / 2043	0.1 / 1.2 / 1.1 / 1.7	3 / 37 / 34 / 52
29 F	0448 / 1208 / 1608 / 2207	0.0 / 1.3 / 1.0 / 1.8	0 / 40 / 30 / 55
30 Sa	0532 / 1223 / 1711 / 2311	0.1 / 1.5 / 0.7 / 1.9	3 / 46 / 21 / 58
31 Su	0607 / 1237 / 1801	0.1 / 1.6 / 0.7	3 / 49 / 21

April 1996

Day	Time	Height (ft)	Height (cm)
1 M	0002 / 0637 / 1250 / 1843	1.8 / 0.0 / 1.8 / 0.4	55 / 0 / 55 / 12
2 Tu	0046 / 0708 / 1304 / 1922	1.8 / 0.3 / 1.7 / 0.2	55 / 9 / 52 / 6
3 W ○	0128 / 0731 / 1322 / 2002	1.7 / 0.7 / 1.9 / 0.1	52 / 21 / 58 / 3
4 Th	0212 / 0757 / 1345 / 2043	1.6 / 1.1 / 2.0 / 0.1	49 / 34 / 61 / 3
5 F	0259 / 0823 / 1413 / 2128	1.5 / 1.6 / 2.2 / -0.1	46 / 49 / 67 / -3
6 Sa	0353 / 0850 / 1447 / 2217	1.3 / 2.0 / 2.3 / -0.3	40 / 61 / 70 / -9
7 Su	0454 / 0919 / 1526 / 2312	1.4 / 2.2 / 2.3 / -0.3	43 / 67 / 70 / -9
8 M	0604 / 0948 / 1612	1.3 / 2.3 / 2.4	40 / 70 / 73
9 Tu	0015 / 0729 / 1025 / 1706	-0.3 / 1.2 / 2.0 / 2.3	-9 / 37 / 61 / 70
10 W ○	0126 / 0911 / 1128 / 1814	-0.2 / 1.2 / 1.2 / 2.2	-6 / 37 / 37 / 67
11 Th	0239 / 1027 / 1937	-0.1 / 1.5 / 2.0	-3 / 46 / 61
12 F	0346 / 1108 / 1643 / 2111	0.0 / 1.6 / 1.2 / 2.0	0 / 49 / 37 / 61
13 Sa	0427 / 1138 / 1650 / 2244	0.2 / 2.1 / 0.9 / 2.2	6 / 64 / 27 / 67
14 Su	0507 / 1127 / 1741 / 2346	0.3 / 1.8 / 0.5 / 2.0	9 / 55 / 15 / 61
15 M	0607 / 1205 / 1838	0.3 / 1.9 / 0.3	9 / 58 / 9
16 Tu	0047 / 0639 / 1250 / 1924	1.8 / 0.1 / 2.0 / 0.1	55 / 3 / 61 / 3
17 W	0138 / 0708 / 1312 / 2006	1.7 / 0.6 / 1.7 / -0.1	52 / 18 / 67 / -3
18 Th	0226 / 0734 / 1335 / 2047	1.6 / 0.7 / 2.2 / -0.1	49 / 21 / 67 / -3
19 F	0313 / 0800 / 1402 / 2128	1.5 / 1.2 / 2.3 / -0.2	46 / 37 / 70 / -6
20 Sa	0401 / 0824 / 1431 / 2211	1.4 / 1.9 / 2.4 / -0.2	40 / 58 / 73 / -6
21 Su	0453 / 0850 / 1505 / 2258	1.3 / 2.3 / 2.4 / -0.3	40 / 70 / 73 / -9
22 M	0550 / 0919 / 1548 / 2348	1.3 / 2.4 / 2.3 / -0.3	37 / 73 / 70 / -9
23 Tu	0653 / 0955 / 1631	1.3 / 2.4 / 2.3	40 / 73 / 70
24 W	0044 / 0804 / 1043 / 1727	-0.3 / 1.3 / 2.0 / 2.1	-9 / 40 / 61 / 64
25 Th ○	0126 / 0915 / 1128 / 1836	-0.2 / 1.2 / 1.1 / 2.0	-6 / 37 / 34 / 61
26 F	0245 / 1007 / 1421 / 1959	-0.1 / 1.5 / 1.2 / 1.9	-3 / 46 / 37 / 58
27 Sa	0339 / 1106 / 1541 / 2127	0.1 / 1.7 / 1.2 / 1.8	3 / 52 / 37 / 55
28 Su	0427 / 1106 / 1650 / 2244	0.3 / 2.0 / 0.8 / 1.8	9 / 61 / 24 / 55
29 M	0507 / 1127 / 1741 / 2346	0.5 / 2.1 / 0.6 / 1.9	15 / 64 / 18 / 58
30 Tu	0542 / 1826	0.6 / 0.3	18 / 9

May 1996

Day	Time	Height (ft)	Height (cm)
1 W	0038 / 0613 / 1208 / 1908	1.7 / 0.7 / 2.1 / 0.1	52 / 21 / 64 / 3
2 Th	0128 / 0643 / 1233 / 1950	1.7 / 0.8 / 2.3 / -0.1	52 / 24 / 70 / -3
3 F ○	0219 / 0711 / 1302 / 2034	1.6 / 1.0 / 2.4 / -0.3	49 / 30 / 73 / -9
4 Sa	0313 / 0739 / 1336 / 2114	1.5 / 1.1 / 2.5 / -0.4	46 / 34 / 76 / -12
5 Su	0410 / 0758 / 1415 / 2154	1.5 / 1.1 / 2.6 / -0.4	46 / 34 / 79 / -12
6 M	0413 / 0811 / 1415 / 2235	1.4 / 1.2 / 2.6 / -0.4	43 / 37 / 79 / -12
7 Tu	0518 / 0847 / 1501 / 2305	1.4 / 1.4 / 2.4 / -0.4	43 / 43 / 73 / -12
8 W	0624 / 0933 / 1555	1.4 / 2.0 / 2.3	43 / 40 / 70
9 Th	0003 / 0729 / 1038 / 1656	-0.3 / 1.3 / 1.9 / 2.1	-9 / 40 / 58 / 64
10 F ○	0104 / 0911 / 1212 / 1809	-0.1 / 1.3 / 1.3 / 1.9	-3 / 40 / 37 / 58
11 Sa	0204 / 1003 / 1356 / 2109	0.0 / 1.6 / 1.2 / 1.9	0 / 49 / 37 / 58
12 Su	0302 / 0911 / 1529 / 2109	0.2 / 1.9 / 1.0 / 1.7	6 / 58 / 30 / 52
13 M	0353 / 1003 / 1646 / 2239	0.4 / 1.9 / 0.7 / 1.7	12 / 58 / 21 / 52
14 Tu	0438 / 1112 / 1747 / 2359	0.6 / 2.1 / 0.4 / 1.7	18 / 64 / 12 / 52
15 W	0516 / 1140 / 1836	0.7 / 2.2 / 0.2	21 / 67 / 6
16 Th	0152 / 0620 / 1208 / 1958	1.5 / 0.7 / 2.1 / 0.1	46 / 21 / 64 / 3
17 F ●	0240 / 0648 / 1257 / 2036	1.5 / 0.8 / 2.3 / -0.1	46 / 24 / 70 / -6
18 Sa	0325 / 0715 / 1325 / 2114	1.4 / 1.0 / 2.4 / -0.2	43 / 30 / 73 / -6
19 Su	0414 / 1758 / 2154	1.4 / 2.5 / -0.2	43 / 76 / -6
20 M	0454 / 0818 / 1435 / 2235	1.4 / 2.0 / 2.4 / -0.4	43 / 61 / 73 / -12
21 Tu	0539 / 0900 / 1517 / 2318	1.4 / 2.4 / 2.3 / -0.4	43 / 73 / 70 / -12
22 W	0623 / 0952 / 1605	1.4 / 2.4 / 2.3	43 / 73 / 70
23 Th	0004 / 0707 / 1058 / 1700	-0.3 / 1.4 / 2.1 / 2.1	-9 / 43 / 64 / 64
24 F	0052 / 0750 / 1212 / 1804	-0.1 / 1.3 / 1.3 / 1.9	-3 / 40 / 40 / 58
25 Sa ○	0141 / 0832 / 1352 / 1919	0.0 / 1.6 / 1.3 / 1.9	0 / 49 / 37 / 58
26 Su	0230 / 0911 / 1513 / 2044	0.2 / 1.9 / 1.0 / 1.7	6 / 58 / 30 / 52
27 M	0317 / 0946 / 1620 / 2212	0.4 / 1.9 / 0.7 / 1.7	12 / 58 / 21 / 52
28 Tu	0401 / 1018 / 1717 / 2330	0.6 / 2.1 / 0.5 / 1.6	18 / 64 / 15 / 49
29 W	0441 / 1049 / 1807	0.7 / 2.2 / 0.2	21 / 67 / 6
30 Th	0036 / 0518 / 1120 / 1853	1.5 / 1.0 / 2.4 / 0.0	46 / 30 / 73 / 0
31 F	0135 / 0552 / 1154 / 1939	1.6 / 1.0 / 2.6 / -0.3	49 / 37 / 79 / -9

June 1996

Day	Time	Height (ft)	Height (cm)
1 Sa ○	0233 / 0623 / 1253 / 2026	1.5 / 1.2 / 2.7 / -0.4	46 / 37 / 82 / -12
2 Su	0331 / 0703 / 1313 / 2113	1.5 / 1.3 / 2.8 / -0.5	46 / 40 / 85 / -15
3 M	0428 / 0746 / 1400 / 2203	1.5 / 1.3 / 2.8 / -0.4	46 / 40 / 85 / -12
4 Tu	0521 / 0838 / 1452 / 2253	1.5 / 1.3 / 2.7 / -0.3	46 / 40 / 82 / -9
5 W	0608 / 0942 / 1551 / 2343	1.5 / 1.3 / 2.6 / -0.2	46 / 40 / 79 / -6
6 Th	0652 / 1050 / 1655	1.6 / 1.2 / 2.3	49 / 40 / 70
7 F	0033 / 0734 / 1223 / 1806	0.0 / 1.6 / 2.0 / 2.0	0 / 52 / 37 / 61
8 Sa	0123 / 0817 / 1354 / 1928	0.3 / 1.7 / 1.8 / 1.8	9 / 58 / 30 / 55
9 Su	0209 / 0859 / 1523 / 2105	0.5 / 2.0 / 1.5 / 1.5	15 / 61 / 46 / 46
10 M	0256 / 0941 / 1640 / 2249	0.7 / 2.1 / 1.1 / 1.4	21 / 64 / 34 / 43
11 Tu	0340 / 1021 / 1742	0.9 / 2.3 / 0.9	30 / 70 / 9
12 W	0015 / 0422 / 1057 / 1832	1.4 / 1.2 / 2.4 / 0.3	43 / 37 / 73 / 9
13 Th	0120 / 0501 / 1138 / 1914	1.5 / 1.4 / 2.5 / 0.0	46 / 43 / 76 / 0
14 F ●	0212 / 0537 / 1213 / 1951	1.5 / 1.2 / 2.7 / -0.1	46 / 37 / 82 / -3
15 Sa ●	0256 / 0610 / 1232 / 2026	1.4 / 1.4 / 2.9 / -0.4	43 / 40 / 88 / -12
16 Su	0333 / 0645 / 1304 / 2100	1.4 / 1.3 / 2.9 / -0.1	43 / 40 / 88 / -3
17 M	0405 / 0723 / 1339 / 2135	1.4 / 1.3 / 2.5 / -0.1	43 / 40 / 76 / -3
18 Tu	0435 / 0806 / 1418 / 2211	1.5 / 1.3 / 2.5 / -0.1	46 / 40 / 85 / -12
19 W	0505 / 0856 / 1502 / 2324	1.5 / 1.3 / 2.5 / -0.3	46 / 37 / 76 / -9
20 Th	0535 / 0950 / 1549 / 2324	1.6 / 1.2 / 2.3 / 0.0	49 / 40 / 70 / 0
21 F	0607 / 1050 / 1642	1.7 / 1.2 / 2.1	52 / 37 / 64
22 Sa	0003 / 0641 / 1159 / 1740	0.3 / 1.7 / 2.1 / 2.0	9 / 52 / 34 / 58
23 Su	0042 / 0716 / 1316 / 1848	0.4 / 1.9 / 1.9 / 1.8	12 / 58 / 30 / 55
24 M	0123 / 0754 / 1434 / 2009	0.6 / 2.0 / 1.6 / 1.5	18 / 61 / 49 / 46
25 Tu	0207 / 0834 / 1546 / 2145	0.8 / 2.1 / 1.5 / 1.4	24 / 64 / 46 / 43
26 W	0250 / 1000 / 1658 / 2323	0.9 / 2.3 / 1.0 / 1.2	30 / 70 / 15 / 46
27 Th	0340 / 1000 / 1749	1.4 / 2.4 / 0.1	43 / 40 / 3
28 F	0043 / 0426 / 1044 / 1841	1.5 / 1.3 / 2.5 / -0.1	46 / 40 / 76 / -3
29 Sa	0146 / 0511 / 1129 / 1930	1.5 / 1.4 / 2.7 / -0.3	46 / 42 / 82 / -9
30 Su	0239 / 0558 / 1216 / 2017	1.5 / 1.3 / 2.9 / -0.4	46 / 40 / 88 / -12

July 1996

Day	Time	Height (ft)	Height (cm)
1 M	0325 / 0649 / 1305 / 2103	1.5 / 1.3 / 2.9 / -0.4	46 / 40 / 88 / -12
2 Tu	0407 / 0744 / 1357 / 2147	1.5 / 1.3 / 2.8 / -0.3	46 / 40 / 85 / -9
3 W	0445 / 0844 / 1451 / 2230	1.5 / 1.2 / 2.7 / -0.2	49 / 37 / 82 / -6
4 Th	0521 / 0949 / 1551 / 2312	1.7 / 1.1 / 2.5 / 0.1	52 / 34 / 76 / 3
5 F	0556 / 1058 / 1654 / 2353	1.8 / 1.0 / 2.2 / 0.3	55 / 30 / 67 / 9
6 Sa	0633 / 1214 / 1801	1.9 / 0.9 / 1.9	58 / 27 / 58
7 Su ○	0032 / 0713 / 1337 / 1919	0.6 / 2.0 / 0.8 / 1.6	18 / 64 / 24 / 49
8 M	0112 / 0756 / 1503 / 2100	0.8 / 2.1 / 0.8 / 1.4	24 / 67 / 24 / 43
9 Tu	0154 / 0843 / 1624 / 2303	1.0 / 2.3 / 0.5 / 1.3	30 / 70 / 15 / 40
10 W	0240 / 0933 / 1730	1.2 / 2.4 / 0.3	37 / 73 / 3
11 Th	0039 / 0332 / 1021 / 1822	1.4 / 1.3 / 2.6 / 0.1	43 / 40 / 76 / 3
12 F	0138 / 0424 / 1105 / 1904	1.4 / 1.5 / 2.7 / 0.0	43 / 43 / 82 / -3
13 Sa	0218 / 0512 / 1145 / 1940	1.4 / 1.4 / 2.8 / -0.1	43 / 43 / 85 / -3
14 Su	0246 / 0557 / 1221 / 2011	1.5 / 1.4 / 2.6 / 0.0	46 / 40 / 79 / 0
15 M ●	0309 / 0640 / 1256 / 2042	1.5 / 1.3 / 2.6 / 0.0	46 / 40 / 79 / 0
16 Tu	0329 / 0722 / 1332 / 2111	1.5 / 1.2 / 2.9 / 0.1	46 / 37 / 88 / 3
17 W	0348 / 0806 / 1411 / 2141	1.6 / 1.2 / 2.8 / -0.4	49 / 37 / 85 / -12
18 Th	0410 / 0853 / 1453 / 2212	1.6 / 1.2 / 2.7 / -0.2	52 / 34 / 82 / -6
19 F	0435 / 0941 / 1538 / 2243	1.7 / 1.1 / 2.5 / 0.1	55 / 34 / 76 / 3
20 Sa	0504 / 1033 / 1723 / 2315	1.8 / 1.0 / 2.2 / 0.3	58 / 30 / 67 / 9
21 Su	0535 / 1132 / 1723 / 2348	2.0 / 0.9 / 1.9 / 0.2	61 / 27 / 58 / 18
22 M	0609 / 1239 / 1828	2.1 / 0.8 / 1.7	64 / 24 / 52
23 Tu ○	0022 / 0648 / 1355 / 1948	0.8 / 2.2 / 0.8 / 1.4	24 / 67 / 24 / 43
24 W	0101 / 0732 / 1513 / 2133	1.0 / 2.3 / 0.5 / 1.3	30 / 70 / 15 / 40
25 Th	0147 / 0824 / 1627 / 2331	1.2 / 2.4 / 0.3 / 1.2	37 / 73 / 9 / 46
26 F	0233 / 0922 / 1732	1.4 / 2.6 / 0.0	43 / 40 / 79
27 Sa	0048 / 0353 / 1022 / 1827	1.4 / 1.5 / 2.7 / -0.3	43 / 40 / 76 / 3
28 Su	0137 / 0457 / 1145 / 1916	1.6 / 1.4 / 2.7 / 0.0	49 / 43 / 82 / 0
29 M	0218 / 0556 / 1213 / 2001	1.6 / 1.3 / 2.9 / -0.2	49 / 40 / 88 / -6
30 Tu ○	0247 / 0653 / 1306 / 2042	1.7 / 1.3 / 2.6 / 0.0	46 / 40 / 79 / -6
31 W	0317 / 0749 / 1359 / 2121	1.7 / 1.3 / 2.8 / 0.0	52 / 40 / 85 / -12

Aug. 1996

Day	Time	Height (ft)	Height (cm)
1 Th	0348 / 0846 / 1453 / 2158	1.8 / 0.9 / 2.6 / 0.2	55 / 27 / 79 / 6
2 F	0419 / 0945 / 1550 / 2233	1.9 / 0.8 / 2.4 / 0.4	58 / 24 / 73 / 12
3 Sa	0452 / 1047 / 1650 / 2306	2.0 / 0.8 / 2.1 / 0.7	61 / 24 / 64 / 21
4 Su	0528 / 1154 / 1754 / 2339	2.1 / 0.7 / 1.8 / 0.9	64 / 21 / 55 / 27
5 M	0607 / 1154 / 2339	2.2 / 0.7 / 1.6	67 / 21 / 49
6 Tu	0012 / 0652 / 1430 / 2058	1.1 / 2.3 / 0.6 / 1.4	34 / 70 / 18 / 43
7 W ○	0048 / 0744 / 1555 / 2327	1.2 / 2.5 / 0.5 / 1.4	37 / 76 / 15 / 43
8 Th	0140 / 0846 / 1707	1.3 / 2.3 / 0.4	40 / 70 / 12
9 F	0049 / 0258 / 0952 / 1802	1.5 / 1.4 / 2.4 / 0.3	46 / 43 / 73 / 9
10 Sa	0121 / 0421 / 1051 / 1844	1.6 / 1.4 / 2.4 / 0.2	49 / 43 / 73 / 6
11 Su	0147 / 0510 / 1138 / 1917	1.6 / 1.4 / 2.5 / 0.2	49 / 43 / 76 / 6
12 M	0203 / 0558 / 1218 / 1946	1.6 / 1.3 / 2.7 / -0.2	49 / 37 / 85 / 0
13 Tu	0219 / 0641 / 1254 / 2013	1.7 / 1.2 / 2.5 / 0.3	52 / 34 / 76 / 0
14 W ●	0248 / 0722 / 1330 / 2039	1.7 / 1.1 / 2.9 / -0.2	52 / 34 / 88 / -6
15 Th	0248 / 0802 / 1407 / 2106	1.8 / 1.1 / 2.8 / 0.0	55 / 30 / 85 / 12

Time meridian 75° W. 0000 is midnight. 1200 is noon.

Heights are referred to mean lower low water which is the chart datum of soundings.

TIDE TABLES: ST. PETERSBURG, FLORIDA

Times & Heights of High and Low Waters

(All times given are Eastern Standard Time and may differ because of wind conditions.)

Aug. 1996

Day	Time (h m)	Height (ft)	Height (cm)
16 F	0307 0844 1446 2133	1.9 0.9 2.4 0.5	58 27 73 15
17 Sa	0332 0927 1530 2200	2.0 0.8 2.2 0.6	61 24 67 18
18 Su	0400 1014 1619 2229	2.1 0.7 2.1 0.8	64 21 64 24
19 M	0432 1106 1715 2258	2.2 0.7 1.9 0.9	67 21 58 27
20 Tu	0507 1208 1821 2329	2.3 0.6 1.7 1.1	70 18 52 34
21 W ◐	0549 1323 1944	2.4 0.6 1.6	73 18 49
22 Th	0005 0641 1445 2142	1.3 2.4 0.5 1.5	40 73 15 46
23 F	0056 0745 1604 2334	1.4 2.5 0.3 1.6	43 76 9 49
24 Sa	0227 0859 1712	1.5 2.5 0.2	46 76 6
25 Su	0028 0355 1012 1808	1.6 1.5 2.6 0.1	49 46 79 3
26 M	0101 0504 1118 1854	1.7 1.3 2.7 0.0	52 40 82 0
27 Tu	0129 0604 1216 1934	1.8 1.1 2.8 0.1	55 34 85 3
28 W ○	0154 0658 1310 2011	1.9 0.9 2.7 0.2	58 27 82 6
29 Th	0220 0750 1402 2044	2.0 0.8 2.6 0.4	61 24 79 12
30 F	0246 0842 1454 2116	2.1 0.6 2.4 0.6	64 18 73 18
31 Sa	0315 0934 1549 2146	2.2 0.5 2.2 0.9	67 15 67 27

September 1996

Day	Time (h m)	Height (ft)	Height (cm)
1 Su	0347 1028 1646 2216	2.3 0.5 2.0 1.0	70 15 61 30
2 M	0423 1127 1749 2244	2.4 0.5 1.7 1.2	73 15 52 37
3 Tu	0502 1233 1904 2311	2.4 0.5 1.6 1.3	73 15 49 40
4 W ◑	0549 1348 2054 2341	2.4 0.6 1.5 1.4	73 18 46 43
5 Th	0646 1511	2.3 0.6	70 18
6 F	0759 1626	2.3 0.5	70 15
7 Sa	0009 0249 0923 1724	1.6 1.5 2.3 0.5	49 46 70 15
8 Su	0031 0409 1037 1806	1.7 1.4 2.3 0.4	52 43 70 12
9 M	0050 0509 1131 1840	1.7 1.3 2.4 0.4	52 40 73 12
10 Tu	0106 0557 1214 1908	1.8 1.2 2.4 0.5	55 37 73 15
11 W	0120 0638 1251 1934	1.9 1.0 2.4 0.6	58 30 73 18
12 Th ●	0133 0716 1326 1959	1.9 0.8 2.4 0.7	58 24 73 21
13 F	0148 0754 1403 2024	2.0 0.7 2.3 0.8	61 21 70 24
14 Sa	0208 0832 1443 2050	2.1 0.6 2.2 0.9	64 18 67 27
15 Su	0232 0912 1528 2116	2.2 0.5 2.1 1.0	67 15 64 30
16 M	0301 0957 1619 2143	2.3 0.4 2.0 1.1	70 12 61 34
17 Tu	0335 1048 1718 2213	2.4 0.4 1.9 1.2	73 12 58 37
18 W	0414 1148 1828 2245	2.5 0.4 1.7 1.4	76 12 52 43
19 Th	0502 1300 1958 2328	2.5 0.4 1.6 1.5	76 12 49 46
20 F ◐	0602 1421 2149	2.5 0.4 1.6	76 12 49
21 Sa	0051 0719 1538 2304	1.5 2.4 0.3 1.7	46 73 9 52
22 Su	0243 0848 1644 2343	1.5 2.4 0.3 1.8	46 73 9 55
23 M	0407 1012 1737	1.4 2.5 0.3	43 76 9
24 Tu	0013 0513 1123 1821	1.9 1.1 2.5 0.4	58 34 76 12
25 W	0038 0609 1223 1858	2.0 0.8 2.5 0.5	61 24 76 15
26 Th ○	0102 0659 1316 1931	2.1 0.6 2.4 0.7	64 18 73 21
27 F	0125 0747 1407 2001	2.3 0.4 2.3 0.9	70 12 70 27
28 Sa	0151 0833 1457 2030	2.4 0.3 2.1 1.0	73 9 64 30
29 Su	0218 0920 1550 2058	2.5 0.2 2.0 1.2	76 6 61 37
30 M	0249 1008 1645 2125	2.5 0.2 1.8 1.3	76 6 55 40

October 1996

Day	Time (h m)	Height (ft)	Height (cm)
1 Tu	0324 1100 1746 2153	2.5 0.3 1.7 1.4	76 9 52 43
2 W	0403 1157 1858 2223	2.4 0.4 1.6 1.5	73 12 49 46
3 Th	0451 1302 2028 2308	2.4 0.5 1.6 1.5	73 15 49 46
4 F ◑	0551 1415 2203	2.2 0.5 1.6	67 15 49
5 Sa	0054 0710 1526 2253	1.5 2.1 0.6 1.7	46 64 18 52
6 Su	0242 0844 1625 2323	1.5 2.1 0.6 1.8	46 64 18 55
7 M	0401 1011 1711 2346	1.3 2.1 0.6 1.8	40 64 18 55
8 Tu	0500 1114 1748	1.1 2.1 0.7	34 64 21
9 W	0004 0547 1203 1819	1.9 0.9 2.2 0.7	58 27 67 21
10 Th	0019 0627 1245 1847	2.0 0.7 2.2 0.8	61 21 67 24
11 F	0035 0705 1324 1914	2.1 0.5 2.1 0.9	64 15 64 27
12 Sa ●	0054 0742 1404 1939	2.3 0.3 2.1 1.0	70 9 64 30
13 Su	0116 0820 1447 2005	2.4 0.2 2.0 1.1	73 6 61 34
14 M	0142 0901 1535 2032	2.5 0.1 1.9 1.2	76 3 58 37
15 Tu	0214 0946 1630 2102	2.6 0.1 1.8 1.3	79 3 55 40
16 W	0252 1037 1733 2136	2.6 0.1 1.7 1.4	79 3 52 43
17 Th	0337 1136 1845 2220	2.6 0.1 1.7 1.5	79 3 52 46
18 F	0432 1242 2004 2329	2.5 0.2 1.7 1.5	76 6 52 46
19 Sa ◐	0541 1354 2118	2.4 0.3 1.7	73 9 52
20 Su	0117 0707 1503 2211	1.5 2.2 0.3 1.8	46 67 9 55
21 M	0256 0843 1604 2250	1.3 2.1 0.4 1.9	40 64 12 58
22 Tu	0415 1016 1655 2321	1.0 2.1 0.5 2.1	30 64 15 64
23 W	0518 1132 1738 2348	0.7 2.1 0.7 2.2	21 64 21 67
24 Th	0611 1233 1814	0.4 2.1 0.8	12 64 24
25 F	0014 0658 1327 1846	2.3 0.2 2.0 1.0	70 6 61 30
26 Sa ○	0039 0742 1418 1916	2.4 0.0 1.9 1.1	73 0 58 34
27 Su	0105 0824 1507 1943	2.5 −0.1 1.8 1.2	76 −3 55 37
28 M	0133 0906 1556 2011	2.6 −0.1 1.7 1.3	79 −3 52 40
29 Tu	0204 0950 1648 2041	2.6 0.0 1.6 1.4	79 0 49 43
30 W	0239 1035 1743 2115	2.5 0.0 1.6 1.4	76 0 49 43
31 Th	0320 1124 1839 2200	2.4 0.2 1.6 1.4	73 6 49 43

November 1996

Day	Time (h m)	Height (ft)	Height (cm)
1 F	0408 1218 1938 2306	2.3 0.3 1.6 1.4	70 9 49 43
2 Sa	0508 1316 2035	2.1 0.4 1.6	64 12 49
3 Su ◑	0043 0624 1416 2123	1.4 1.9 0.5 1.7	43 58 15 52
4 M	0220 0754 1513 2202	1.3 1.8 0.6 1.8	40 55 18 55
5 Tu	0339 0929 1602 2232	1.1 1.7 0.7 1.9	34 52 21 58
6 W	0440 1048 1645 2257	0.8 1.8 0.8 2.0	24 55 24 61
7 Th	0529 1150 1722 2319	0.6 1.8 0.9 2.1	18 55 27 64
8 F	0611 1240 1755 2342	0.3 1.8 1.0 2.2	9 55 30 67
9 Sa	0651 1326 1825	0.1 1.8 1.1	3 55 34
10 Su ●	0007 0730 1411 1853	2.4 −0.1 1.8 1.2	73 −3 55 37
11 M	0035 0810 1459 1922	2.5 −0.2 1.7 1.3	76 −6 52 40
12 Tu	0107 0853 1551 1954	2.6 −0.3 1.6 1.3	79 −9 49 40
13 W	0144 0939 1647 2032	2.6 −0.3 1.6 1.3	79 −9 49 40
14 Th	0228 1029 1745 2120	2.6 −0.3 1.6 1.3	79 −9 49 40
15 F	0320 1123 1842 2224	2.5 −0.2 1.6 1.3	76 −6 49 40
16 Sa	0421 1220 1936 2350	2.3 0.0 1.6 1.3	70 0 49 40
17 Su ◐	0534 1320 2026	2.1 0.1 1.7	64 3 52
18 M	0127 0701 1419 2111	1.2 1.9 0.3 1.8	37 58 9 55
19 Tu	0258 0840 1514 2152	0.9 1.7 0.5 2.0	27 52 15 61
20 W	0416 1023 1604 2229	0.6 1.6 0.7 2.1	18 49 21 64
21 Th	0519 1147 1648 2303	0.3 1.6 0.9 2.2	9 49 27 67
22 F	0611 1253 1727 2333	0.0 1.6 1.0 2.4	0 49 30 73
23 Sa	0657 1348 1801	−0.2 1.6 1.1	−6 49 34
24 Su ○	0003 0738 1437 1833	2.4 −0.3 1.5 1.2	73 −9 46 37
25 M	0032 0816 1522 1904	2.5 −0.4 1.5 1.2	76 −12 46 37
26 Tu	0102 0854 1605 1937	2.5 −0.3 1.4 1.2	76 −9 43 37
27 W	0135 0933 1645 2015	2.4 −0.3 1.4 1.2	73 −9 43 37
28 Th	0213 1012 1723 2100	2.3 −0.2 1.4 1.2	70 −6 43 37
29 F	0255 1053 1801 2154	2.2 −0.1 1.5 1.2	67 −3 46 37
30 Sa	0344 1136 1838 2300	2.1 0.0 1.5 1.2	64 0 46 37

December 1996

Day	Time (h m)	Height (ft)	Height (cm)
1 Su	0441 1221 1917	1.9 0.1 1.6	58 3 49
2 M	0019 0548 1309 1956	1.1 1.7 0.3 1.6	34 52 9 49
3 Tu ◑	0143 0706 1358 2035	1.0 1.5 0.5 1.7	30 46 15 52
4 W	0302 0838 1447 2112	0.8 1.4 0.6 1.8	24 43 18 55
5 Th	0409 1015 1534 2148	0.5 1.3 0.8 1.9	15 40 24 58
6 F	0505 1138 1619 2222	0.2 1.4 0.9 2.1	6 43 27 64
7 Sa	0553 1242 1659 2255	0.0 1.4 1.0 2.2	0 43 30 67
8 Su	0637 1336 1736 2329	−0.3 1.4 1.1 2.3	−9 43 34 70
9 M	0719 1425 1812	−0.5 1.4 1.2	−15 43 37
10 Tu ●	0006 0802 1513 1850	2.4 −0.6 1.4 1.2	73 −18 43 37
11 W	0047 0846 1600 1934	2.5 −0.7 1.4 1.2	76 −21 43 37
12 Th	0132 0931 1645 2025	2.5 −0.6 1.4 1.1	76 −18 43 34
13 F	0222 1017 1726 2126	2.4 −0.6 1.4 1.1	73 −18 43 34
14 Sa	0319 1104 1806 2235	2.3 −0.4 1.5 1.0	70 −12 46 30
15 Su	0422 1151 1846 2355	2.0 −0.2 1.6 0.9	61 −6 49 27
16 M	0534 1238 1926	1.8 0.1 1.7	55 3 52
17 Tu ◐	0121 0656 1325 2009	0.7 1.5 0.3 1.8	21 46 9 55
18 W	0249 0838 1414 2053	0.4 1.2 0.6 1.9	12 37 18 58
19 Th	0410 1038 1503 2138	0.2 1.1 0.8 2.0	6 34 24 61
20 F	0516 1215 1552 2221	−0.1 1.2 0.9 2.1	−3 37 27 64
21 Sa	0610 1324 1639 2301	−0.3 1.2 1.0 2.2	−9 37 30 67
22 Su	0654 1415 1723 2338	−0.5 1.3 1.1 2.2	−15 40 34 67
23 M	0733 1455 1804	−0.5 1.3 1.1	−15 40 34
24 Tu ○	0012 0808 1528 1844	2.2 −0.5 1.3 1.1	67 −15 40 34
25 W	0047 0842 1555 1925	2.2 −0.5 1.3 1.0	67 −15 40 30
26 Th	0123 0915 1619 2009	2.2 −0.5 1.3 1.0	67 −15 40 30
27 F	0201 0948 1643 2056	2.1 −0.4 1.3 0.9	64 −12 40 27
28 Sa	0244 1021 1709 2148	2.0 −0.3 1.4 0.9	61 −9 43 27
29 Su	0331 1056 1737 2245	1.9 −0.2 1.4 0.8	58 −6 43 24
30 M	0423 1130 1808 2348	1.7 0.0 1.5 0.7	52 0 46 21
31 Tu	0521 1206 1841	1.5 0.1 1.6	46 3 49

January 1997

Day	Time (h m)	Height (ft)	Height (cm)
1 W ◑	0059 0629 1252 1924	0.6 1.3 0.3 1.6	18 40 9 49
2 Th	0215 0753 1335 2004	0.5 1.1 0.5 1.7	15 34 15 52
3 F	0329 0940 1424 2047	0.2 1.0 0.7 1.8	6 30 21 55
4 Sa	0434 1132 1517 2132	0.0 1.1 0.9 1.9	0 34 27 58
5 Su	0531 1250 1611 2218	−0.3 1.2 1.0 2.1	−9 37 30 64
6 M	0621 1345 1702 2304	−0.5 1.2 1.1 2.2	−15 37 34 67
7 Tu	0707 1429 1751 2351	−0.7 1.3 1.0 2.3	−21 40 30 70
8 W ●	0752 1508 1841	−0.8 1.3 1.0	−24 40 30
9 Th	0039 0835 1543 1934	2.4 −0.9 1.3 0.9	73 −27 40 27
10 F	0129 0917 1617 2029	2.4 −0.8 1.3 0.8	73 −24 40 24
11 Sa	0223 0959 1649 2129	2.3 −0.7 1.4 0.7	70 −21 43 21
12 Su	0320 1039 1723 2234	2.1 −0.5 1.5 0.6	64 −15 46 18
13 M	0422 1118 1757 2345	1.8 −0.2 1.6 0.5	55 −6 49 15
14 Tu	0529 1157 1835	1.5 0.1 1.7	46 3 52
15 W ◐	0103 0646 1234 1916	0.3 1.2 0.3 1.8	9 37 9 55
16 Th	0228 0828 1314 2003	0.1 0.9 0.6 1.9	3 27 18 58
17 F	0353 1053 1359 2054	−0.1 0.9 0.8 1.9	−3 27 24 58
18 Sa	0506 1251 1459 2149	−0.3 1.0 0.9 2.0	−9 30 27 61
19 Su	0603 1346 1605 2241	−0.4 1.1 1.0 2.0	−12 34 30 61
20 M	0647 1420 1704 2326	−0.5 1.1 1.0 2.0	−15 34 30 61
21 Tu	0724 1444 1756	−0.6 1.1 1.0	−18 34 30
22 W	0006 0756 1504 1841	2.0 −0.6 1.1 0.9	61 −18 34 27
23 Th ○	0043 0825 1521 1923	2.0 −0.5 1.2 0.8	61 −15 37 24
24 F	0119 0853 1537 2006	2.0 −0.5 1.2 0.7	61 −15 37 21
25 Sa	0157 0922 1554 2049	1.9 −0.4 1.3 0.6	58 −12 40 18
26 Su	0238 0950 1615 2135	1.8 −0.3 1.4 0.5	55 −9 43 15
27 M	0322 1019 1641 2224	1.7 −0.2 1.4 0.4	52 −6 43 12
28 Tu	0410 1049 1710 2317	1.6 0.0 1.5 0.4	49 0 46 12
29 W	0504 1118 1741	1.4 0.2 1.6	43 6 49
30 Th	0019 0607 1147 1816	0.3 1.2 0.4 1.7	9 37 12 52
31 F ◑	0129 0726 1218 1857	0.2 1.0 0.6 1.8	6 30 18 55

Feb. 1997

Day	Time (h m)	Height (ft)	Height (cm)
1 Sa	0247 0919 1253 1945	0.0 0.9 0.8 1.8	0 27 24 55
2 Su	0402 1148 1353 2044	−0.2 1.0 0.9 1.9	−6 30 27 58
3 M	0508 1302 1527 2147	−0.4 1.1 1.0 2.0	−12 34 30 61
4 Tu	0603 1338 1643 2248	−0.6 1.2 1.0 2.1	−18 37 30 64
5 W	0652 1407 1746 2345	−0.8 1.2 0.9 2.2	−24 37 27 67
6 Th	0735 1433 1842	−0.8 1.2 0.8	−24 37 24
7 F ●	0040 0815 1459 1936	2.3 −0.8 1.3 0.6	70 −24 40 18
8 Sa	0133 0853 1526 2031	2.2 −0.6 1.4 0.4	67 −18 43 12
9 Su	0227 0930 1554 2127	2.1 −0.4 1.5 0.3	64 −12 46 9
10 M	0324 1004 1625 2226	1.8 −0.2 1.6 0.2	55 −6 49 6
11 Tu	0423 1036 1658 2329	1.6 0.1 1.7 0.1	49 3 52 3
12 W	0528 1106 1735	1.3 0.3 1.8	40 9 55
13 Th	0039 0643 1134 1816	0.0 1.0 0.5 1.9	0 30 15 58
14 F ◐	0158 0833 1153 1904	−0.1 0.8 0.7 1.9	−3 24 21 58
15 Sa	0325 2002	−0.1 1.8	−3 55

Time meridian 75° W. 0000 is midnight. 1200 is noon.
Heights are referred to mean lower low water which is the chart datum of soundings.

TIDE TABLES: ST. MARKS, FLORIDA

Times & Heights of High and Low Waters

(All times given are Eastern Standard Time and may differ because of wind conditions.)

Feb. 1996

Day	Time (h m)	Height (ft)	Height (cm)
16 F	0618 1251 1815	-1.0 3.1 0.9	-30 94 27
17 Sa	0015 0706 1331 1907	3.4 -1.1 3.2 0.6	104 -34 98 18
18 Su ●	0108 0748 1407 1953	3.6 -1.0 3.4 0.3	110 -30 104 9
19 M	0156 0827 1440 2036	3.6 -0.8 3.4 0.0	110 -24 104 0
20 Tu	0242 0901 1510 2119	3.5 -0.5 3.4 -0.1	107 -15 104 -3
21 W	0325 0932 1538 2200	3.3 -0.1 3.4 -0.2	101 -3 104 -6
22 Th	0408 1000 1604 2243	3.0 0.3 3.3 -0.1	91 9 101 -3
23 F	0453 1027 1629 2331	2.6 0.6 3.2 0.0	79 18 98 0
24 Sa	0544 1053 1655	2.3 1.0 3.0	70 30 91
25 Su	0029 0653 1124 1726	0.2 2.0 1.3 2.8	6 61 40 85
26 M ◐	0150 0841 1212 1812	0.4 1.8 1.6 2.6	12 55 49 79
27 Tu	0329 1034 1351 1955	0.4 2.0 1.8 2.4	12 61 55 73
28 W	0447 1133 1559 2213	0.3 2.2 1.7 2.4	9 67 52 73
29 Th	0540 1210 1718 2320	0.1 2.5 1.4 2.6	3 76 43 79

March 1996

Day	Time (h m)	Height (ft)	Height (cm)
1 F	0619 1241 1807	-0.1 2.7 1.1	-3 82 34
2 Sa	0005 0651 1309 1845	2.9 -0.2 2.9 0.8	88 -6 88 24
3 Su	0042 0719 1336 1920	3.0 -0.2 3.1 0.5	91 -6 94 15
4 M	0116 0744 1401 1953	3.2 -0.2 3.3 0.3	98 -6 101 9
5 Tu ○	0150 0808 1424 2026	3.3 -0.2 3.4 0.0	101 -6 104 0
6 W	0224 0832 1446 2059	3.3 -0.1 3.5 -0.2	101 -3 107 -6
7 Th	0300 0858 1509 2134	3.4 0.0 3.5 -0.3	104 0 107 -9
8 F	0339 0927 1534 2212	3.3 0.2 3.6 -0.4	101 6 110 -12
9 Sa	0423 0959 1602 2257	3.1 0.4 3.6 -0.4	94 12 110 -12
10 Su	0514 1036 1635 2351	2.9 0.8 3.5 -0.3	88 24 107 -9
11 M	0617 1121 1717	2.6 1.1 3.3	79 34 101
12 Tu ◑	0102 0743 1222 1816	-0.2 2.4 1.5 3.1	-6 73 46 94
13 W	0228 0924 1354 1951	-0.1 2.4 1.7 2.9	-3 73 52 88
14 Th	0353 1045 1544 2148	-0.2 2.7 1.6 2.9	-6 82 49 88
15 F	0502 1140 1709 2312	-0.4 2.9 1.2 3.1	-12 88 37 94
16 Sa	0557 1224 1810	-0.4 3.2 0.8	-12 98 24
17 Su	0014 0644 1301 1859	3.4 -0.4 3.4 0.3	104 -12 104 9
18 M	0106 0724 1335 1943	3.5 -0.3 3.6 0.0	107 -9 110 0
19 Tu ●	0152 0759 1405 2024	3.6 -0.1 3.7 -0.3	110 -3 113 -9
20 W	0235 0831 1434 2103	3.5 0.1 3.7 -0.4	107 3 113 -12
21 Th	0316 0900 1500 2141	3.3 0.4 3.7 -0.4	101 12 113 -12
22 F	0356 0927 1525 2219	3.1 0.7 3.6 -0.2	94 21 110 -6
23 Sa	0436 0953 1549 2300	2.8 0.9 3.5 0.0	85 27 107 0
24 Su	0520 1021 1615 2347	2.6 1.2 3.3 0.2	79 37 101 6
25 M	0616 1055 1645	2.3 1.4 3.1	70 43 94
26 Tu ◐	0050 0737 1142 1725	0.5 2.1 1.7 2.8	15 64 52 85
27 W	0218 0927 1311 1837	0.7 2.1 1.9 2.5	21 64 58 76
28 Th	0348 1043 1522 2118	0.6 2.4 1.8 2.4	18 73 55 73
29 F	0452 1128 1652 2249	0.5 2.6 1.5 2.6	15 79 46 79
30 Sa	0537 1202 1745 2342	0.4 2.9 1.1 2.8	12 88 34 85
31 Su	0612 1232 1824	0.3 3.1 0.8	9 94 24

April 1996

Day	Time (h m)	Height (ft)	Height (cm)
1 M	0024 0642 1258 1900	3.1 0.3 3.3 0.4	94 9 101 12
2 Tu	0101 0710 1323 1934	3.2 0.3 3.5 0.1	98 9 107 3
3 W ○	0138 0736 1346 2008	3.4 0.3 3.6 -0.2	104 9 110 -6
4 Th	0216 0804 1409 2042	3.5 0.4 3.7 -0.4	107 12 113 -12
5 F	0254 0833 1434 2119	3.5 0.6 3.8 -0.6	107 18 116 -18
6 Sa	0335 0904 1502 2159	3.4 0.7 3.9 -0.6	104 21 119 -18
7 Su	0420 0938 1534 2244	3.3 0.9 3.9 -0.5	101 27 119 -15
8 M	0510 1017 1610 2337	3.1 1.2 3.8 -0.3	94 37 116 -9
9 Tu	0610 1105 1656	2.8 1.4 3.5	85 43 107
10 W ◑	0042 0726 1210 1758	-0.1 2.7 1.7 3.2	-3 82 52 98
11 Th	0201 0855 1348 1941	0.1 2.7 1.8 2.9	3 82 55 88
12 F	0322 1010 1539 2145	0.2 2.9 1.5 2.9	6 88 46 88
13 Sa	0431 1105 1702 2309	0.2 3.1 1.1 3.1	6 94 34 94
14 Su	0527 1149 1800	0.3 3.4 0.6	9 104 18
15 M	0010 0614 1226 1848	3.3 0.4 3.6 0.1	101 12 110 3
16 Tu	0101 0653 1300 1931	3.4 0.5 3.8 -0.2	104 15 116 -6
17 W ●	0145 0728 1331 2010	3.5 0.6 3.9 -0.4	107 18 119 -12
18 Th	0226 0800 1359 2048	3.5 0.8 3.9 -0.4	107 24 119 -12
19 F	0305 0830 1427 2124	3.4 0.9 3.9 -0.4	104 27 119 -12
20 Sa	0342 0859 1453 2159	3.2 1.1 3.8 -0.2	98 34 116 -6
21 Su	0420 0929 1520 2235	3.1 1.2 3.7 0.0	94 37 113 0
22 M	0500 1001 1549 2315	2.9 1.4 3.5 0.2	88 43 107 6
23 Tu	0547 1040 1622	2.7 1.6 3.3	82 49 101
24 W	0002 0648 1130 1703	0.5 2.5 1.7 3.0	15 76 52 91
25 Th ◐	0103 0807 1247 1804	0.7 2.5 1.9 2.7	21 76 58 82
26 F	0219 0928 1434 1959	0.9 2.6 1.8 2.5	27 79 55 76
27 Sa	0333 1027 1608 2157	0.9 2.8 1.6 2.6	27 85 49 79
28 Su	0431 1109 1709 2307	0.9 3.0 1.2 2.8	27 91 37 85
29 M	0516 1143 1755 2359	0.9 3.3 0.7 3.0	27 101 21 91
30 Tu	0555 1213 1835	0.8 3.4 0.3	24 104 9

May 1996

Day	Time (h m)	Height (ft)	Height (cm)
1 W	0044 0629 1240 1912	3.3 0.9 3.6 -0.1	101 27 110 -3
2 Th	0126 0703 1307 1950	3.4 0.9 3.8 -0.4	104 27 116 -12
3 F ○	0208 0736 1336 2028	3.6 1.0 4.0 -0.6	110 30 122 -18
4 Sa	0250 0810 1406 2108	3.6 1.1 4.1 -0.8	110 34 125 -24
5 Su	0333 0846 1440 2151	3.5 1.2 4.1 -0.7	107 37 125 -21
6 M	0418 0925 1517 2236	3.4 1.3 4.1 -0.6	104 40 125 -18
7 Tu	0506 1008 1600 2326	3.2 1.4 3.9 -0.3	98 43 119 -9
8 W	0600 1101 1650	3.1 1.6 3.6	94 49 110
9 Th	0024 0703 1210 1757	0.0 2.9 1.7 3.2	0 88 52 98
10 F ◑	0129 0814 1345 1939	0.3 2.9 1.6 2.9	9 88 49 88
11 Sa	0240 0923 1528 2136	0.6 3.1 1.3 2.8	18 94 40 85
12 Su	0348 1020 1649 2302	0.8 3.3 0.9 2.9	24 101 27 88
13 M	0447 1108 1748	1.0 3.5 0.4	30 107 12
14 Tu	0003 0537 1149 1836	3.1 1.1 3.7 0.1	94 34 113 3
15 W	0053 0619 1225 1918	3.2 1.2 3.8 -0.2	98 37 116 -6
16 Th	0137 0656 1259 1957	3.3 1.2 3.9 -0.3	101 37 119 -9
17 F ●	0216 0731 1330 2034	3.3 1.3 4.0 -0.4	101 40 122 -12
18 Sa	0253 0804 1401 2108	3.3 1.3 3.9 -0.3	101 40 119 -9
19 Su	0328 0837 1430 2142	3.3 1.3 3.9 -0.2	101 40 119 -6
20 M	0404 0911 1500 2215	3.2 1.4 3.8 -0.1	98 43 116 -3
21 Tu	0441 0948 1533 2248	3.1 1.4 3.7 0.1	94 43 113 3
22 W	0521 1029 1608 2325	3.0 1.5 3.5 0.3	91 46 107 9
23 Th	0607 1119 1650	2.9 1.7 3.2	88 52 98
24 F	0008 0701 1223 1745	0.6 2.9 1.7 2.9	18 88 52 88
25 Sa ◐	0059 0803 1345 1906	0.8 2.9 1.7 2.7	24 88 52 82
26 Su	0201 0905 1511 2053	1.0 3.0 1.5 2.6	30 91 46 79
27 M	0306 0958 1623 2223	1.1 3.1 1.1 2.7	34 94 34 82
28 Tu	0406 1042 1719 2330	1.2 3.3 0.7 3.0	37 101 21 91
29 W	0459 1120 1807	1.3 3.5 0.2	40 107 6
30 Th	0025 0547 1157 1851	3.2 1.3 3.7 -0.2	98 40 113 -6
31 F	0114 0630 1233 1935	3.4 1.4 3.9 -0.5	104 43 119 -15

June 1996

Day	Time (h m)	Height (ft)	Height (cm)
1 Sa ○	0200 0712 1310 2017	3.5 1.4 4.1 -0.8	107 43 125 -24
2 Su	0245 0753 1349 2101	3.6 1.4 4.2 -0.9	110 43 128 -27
3 M	0328 0835 1430 2144	3.6 1.4 4.3 -0.8	110 43 131 -24
4 Tu	0412 0919 1513 2228	3.5 1.4 4.2 -0.6	107 43 128 -18
5 W	0455 1007 1600 2313	3.4 1.4 4.0 -0.3	104 43 122 -9
6 Th	0541 1102 1653	3.3 1.4 3.6	101 43 110
7 F	0001 0630 1209 1800	0.2 3.2 1.4 3.2	6 98 43 98
8 Sa ◑	0052 0725 1333 1931	0.6 3.2 1.4 2.8	18 98 43 85
9 Su	0150 0826 1508 2121	1.0 3.2 1.1 2.6	30 98 34 79
10 M	0254 0928 1630 2250	1.3 3.3 0.8 2.7	40 101 24 82
11 Tu	0357 1024 1733 2355	1.5 3.5 0.4 2.8	46 107 12 85
12 W	0454 1113 1823	1.6 3.6 0.1	49 110 3
13 Th	0045 0543 1156 1907	3.0 1.6 3.8 -0.1	91 49 116 -3
14 F	0126 0627 1234 1946	3.1 1.6 3.8 -0.2	94 49 116 -6
15 Sa ●	0204 0706 1310 2021	3.2 1.5 3.9 -0.2	98 46 119 -6
16 Su	0239 0744 1343 2054	3.3 1.5 3.9 -0.2	101 46 119 -6
17 M	0312 0821 1416 2124	3.3 1.4 3.9 -0.2	101 43 119 -6
18 Tu	0345 0858 1448 2153	3.3 1.4 3.9 -0.1	101 43 119 -3
19 W	0418 0936 1522 2222	3.3 1.4 3.8 0.1	101 43 116 3
20 Th	0452 1017 1558 2252	3.3 1.4 3.6 0.2	101 43 110 6
21 F	0527 1102 1639 2326	3.3 1.4 3.4 0.4	101 43 104 12
22 Sa	0605 1154 1729	3.2 1.4 3.1	98 43 94
23 Su	0006 0648 1259 1834	0.7 3.2 1.4 2.9	21 98 43 88
24 M ◐	0054 0738 1415 2003	1.0 3.2 1.3 2.7	30 98 40 82
25 Tu	0153 0835 1533 2141	1.3 3.2 1.0 2.7	40 98 30 82
26 W	0259 0933 1642 2302	1.5 3.3 0.6 2.9	46 101 18 88
27 Th	0406 1028 1740	1.6 3.5 0.1	49 107 3
28 F	0007 0508 1119 1832	3.1 1.7 3.8 -0.3	94 52 116 -9
29 Sa	0101 0603 1207 1920	3.3 1.7 4.0 -0.6	101 52 122 -18
30 Su ○	0149 0654 1254 2006	3.5 1.6 4.2 -0.8	107 49 128 -24

July 1996

Day	Time (h m)	Height (ft)	Height (cm)
1 M	0234 0741 1341 2050	3.6 1.5 4.3 -0.8	110 46 131 -24
2 Tu	0315 0828 1428 2132	3.6 1.4 4.3 -0.7	110 43 131 -21
3 W	0355 0915 1515 2213	3.6 1.3 4.2 -0.4	110 40 128 -12
4 Th	0433 1004 1603 2253	3.6 1.2 4.0 0.0	110 37 122 0
5 F	0511 1057 1656 2332	3.5 1.1 3.6 0.4	107 34 110 12
6 Sa	0550 1158 1757	3.4 1.1 3.1	104 34 94
7 Su ◑	0012 0633 1311 1916	0.9 3.4 1.1 2.7	27 104 34 82
8 M	0057 0724 1439 2058	1.3 3.3 1.0 2.5	40 101 30 76
9 Tu	0152 0827 1607 2234	1.7 3.3 0.8 2.5	52 101 24 76
10 W	0259 0938 1717 2343	1.9 3.4 0.5 2.7	58 104 15 82
11 Th	0411 1042 1810	1.9 3.5 0.3	58 107 9
12 F	0032 0513 1135 1854	2.8 1.9 3.6 0.1	85 58 110 3
13 Sa	0112 0605 1219 1932	3.0 1.7 3.7 0.0	91 52 113 0
14 Su	0146 0649 1257 2005	3.1 1.6 3.8 0.0	94 49 116 0
15 M ●	0219 0729 1332 2035	3.3 1.5 3.9 0.0	101 46 119 0
16 Tu	0250 0808 1405 2102	3.4 1.3 3.9 0.0	104 40 119 0
17 W	0320 0844 1438 2128	3.5 1.2 3.9 0.0	107 37 119 0
18 Th	0348 0921 1511 2153	3.5 1.2 3.9 0.1	107 37 119 3
19 F	0417 0958 1547 2220	3.6 1.1 3.8 0.3	110 34 116 9
20 Sa	0445 1038 1626 2250	3.5 1.1 3.6 0.5	107 34 110 15
21 Su	0515 1124 1713 2326	3.5 1.1 3.4 0.7	107 34 104 21
22 M	0549 1218 1812	3.5 1.1 3.1	107 34 94
23 Tu ◐	0009 0629 1327 1930	1.0 3.4 1.0 2.9	30 104 30 88
24 W	0102 0722 1448 2107	1.4 3.4 0.8 2.8	43 104 24 85
25 Th	0209 0829 1607 2238	1.7 3.4 0.5 2.9	52 104 15 88
26 F	0326 0945 1715 2348	1.8 3.6 0.1 3.1	55 110 3 94
27 Sa	0440 1054 1813	1.8 3.8 -0.2	55 116 -6
28 Su.	0043 0545 1154 1904	3.4 1.7 4.1 -0.5	104 52 125 -15
29 M	0130 0641 1248 1950	3.5 1.5 4.3 -0.6	107 46 131 -18
30 Tu ○	0212 0732 1338 2033	3.7 1.3 4.4 -0.5	113 40 134 -15
31 W	0251 0820 1427 2113	3.7 1.1 4.4 -0.3	113 34 134 -9

Aug. 1996

Day	Time (h m)	Height (ft)	Height (cm)
1 Th	0326 0907 1514 2150	3.8 0.9 4.2 0.0	116 27 128 0
2 F	0400 0954 1602 2225	3.7 0.8 4.0 0.4	113 24 122 12
3 Sa	0432 1043 1651 2258	3.7 0.7 3.6 0.8	113 21 110 24
4 Su	0505 1137 1745 2331	3.6 0.8 3.1 1.2	110 24 94 37
5 M	0539 1242 1854	3.5 0.9 2.8	107 27 85
6 Tu ◑	0008 0620 1404 2027	1.6 3.4 1.0 2.5	49 104 30 76
7 W	0056 0719 1537 2211	1.9 3.3 1.0 2.5	58 101 30 76
8 Th	0207 0850 1655 2324	2.1 3.2 0.8 2.6	64 98 24 79
9 F	0337 1020 1752	2.1 3.3 0.6	64 101 18
10 Sa	0011 0454 1122 1835	2.8 2.0 3.5 0.4	85 61 107 12
11 Su	0048 0550 1209 1911	3.0 1.8 3.6 0.3	91 55 110 9
12 M	0121 0636 1247 1942	3.2 1.5 3.8 0.3	98 46 116 9
13 Tu	0151 0715 1321 2009	3.4 1.3 3.9 0.2	104 40 119 6
14 W ●	0220 0752 1354 2034	3.5 1.1 3.9 0.3	107 34 119 9
15 Th	0246 0827 1426 2057	3.6 1.0 4.0 0.3	110 30 122 9

Time meridian 75° W. 0000 is midnight. 1200 is noon.
Heights are referred to mean lower low water which is the chart datum of soundings.

TIDE TABLES: ST. MARKS, FLORIDA

Times & Heights of High and Low Waters

(All times given are Eastern Standard Time and may differ because of wind conditions.)

	Aug. 1996	September 1996	October 1996	November 1996	December 1996	January 1997	Feb. 1997

Time meridian 75° W. 0000 is midnight. 1200 is noon.
Heights are referred to mean lower low water which is the chart datum of soundings.

TIDE TABLES: PENSACOLA, FLORIDA

Times & Heights of High and Low Waters

(All times given are Eastern Standard Time and may differ because of wind conditions.)

Feb. 1996

Date	Day	Time	ft	cm
16	F	0701	-0.5	-15
		2103	1.2	37
17	Sa	0748	-0.4	-12
		2202	1.1	34
18	Su ●	0828	-0.3	-9
		2300	0.9	27
19	M	0854	-0.1	-3
20	Tu	0000	0.7	21
		0850	0.1	3
21	W	0105	0.5	15
		0806	0.4	12
		1346	0.4	12
		2029	0.1	3
22	Th	0242	0.5	15
		1403	0.6	18
		2330	0.1	3
23	F	1439	0.7	21
24	Sa	0139	0.0	0
		1524	0.8	24
25	Su ○	0254	-0.1	-3
		1615	0.9	27
26	M	0353	-0.2	-6
		1711	1.0	30
27	Tu	0445	-0.2	-6
		1808	1.0	30
28	W	0534	-0.2	-6
		1905	1.0	30
29	Th	0618	-0.2	-6
		1959	1.0	30

March 1996

Date	Day	Time	ft	cm
1	F	0657	-0.2	-6
		2049	0.9	27
2	Sa	0730	-0.1	-3
		2136	0.9	27
3	Su	0753	0.0	0
		2222	0.8	24
4	M	0804	0.1	3
		2311	0.7	21
5	Tu ○	0759	0.2	6
		1322	0.3	9
		1533	0.2	6
6	W	0009	0.6	18
		0736	0.3	9
		1231	0.4	12
		1820	0.2	6
7	Th	0128	0.5	15
		0645	0.5	15
		1235	0.5	15
		2027	0.2	6
8	F	1259	0.7	21
		2223	0.1	3
9	Sa	1336	0.8	24
10	Su	0003	-0.1	-3
		1423	1.0	30
11	M	0125	-0.1	-3
		1518	1.1	34
12	Tu ○	0236	-0.3	-9
		1619	1.2	37
13	W	0339	-0.3	-9
		1725	1.2	37
14	Th	0436	-0.3	-9
		1835	1.2	37
15	F	0529	-0.3	-9
		1947	1.1	34
16	Sa	0613	-0.1	-3
		2100	1.0	30
17	Su	0646	0.0	0
		2219	0.8	24
18	M	0655	0.2	6
		1213	0.3	9
		1558	0.3	9
		2349	0.7	21
19	Tu ●	0625	0.4	12
		1125	0.5	15
		1830	0.2	6
20	W	0208	0.4	12
		0446	0.5	15
		1133	0.7	21
		2019	0.1	3
21	Th	1202	0.9	27
		2151	0.0	0
22	F	1239	1.0	30
		2312	0.1	3
23	Sa	1321	1.0	30
24	Su	0026	-0.1	-3
		1408	1.1	34
25	M	0133	-0.1	-3
		1459	1.1	34
26	Tu ○	0235	-0.2	-6
		1556	1.1	34
27	W	0331	-0.3	-9
		1657	1.2	37
28	Th	0420	-0.3	-9
		1801	1.2	37
29	F	0500	-0.3	-9
		1907	1.2	37
30	Sa	0531	-0.3	-9
		2014	1.1	34
31	Su	0547	0.2	6
		2125	0.8	24

April 1996

Date	Day	Time	ft	cm
1	M	0544	0.4	12
		1114	0.5	15
		1519	0.4	12
		2247	0.7	21
2	Tu	0519	0.5	15
		1033	0.6	18
		1725	0.3	9
3	W ○	0043	0.6	18
		0416	0.7	21
		1032	0.7	21
		1855	0.2	6
4	Th	1051	0.9	27
		2012	0.1	3
5	F	1122	1.0	30
		2125	0.0	0
6	Sa	1201	1.2	37
		2235	-0.1	-3
7	Su	1246	1.3	40
		2344	-0.2	-6
8	M	1337	1.3	40
9	Tu	0050	-0.3	-9
		1433	1.4	43
10	W ●	0152	-0.2	-6
		1534	1.3	40
11	Th	0248	-0.2	-6
		1640	1.2	37
12	F	0335	0.0	0
		1754	1.0	30
13	Sa	0408	0.1	3
		1925	0.9	27
14	Su	0420	0.3	9
		1129	0.6	18
		1456	0.5	15
		2126	0.7	21
15	M	0356	0.5	15
		1059	0.7	21
		1731	0.4	12
16	Tu	1001	0.9	27
		1858	0.2	6
17	W ●	1018	1.0	30
		2004	0.1	3
18	Th	1045	1.1	34
		2102	0.0	0
19	F	1118	1.2	37
		2156	-0.1	-3
20	Sa	1155	1.3	40
		2250	-0.1	-3
21	Su	1233	1.3	40
		2342	-0.1	-3
22	M	1315	1.3	40
23	Tu	0035	-0.1	-3
		1358	1.3	40
24	W	0124	0.0	0
		1443	1.4	43
25	Th ○	0208	0.1	3
		1531	1.3	40
26	F	0242	0.2	6
		1622	1.2	37
27	Sa	0303	0.3	9
		1726	1.0	30
28	Su	0307	0.4	12
		1912	0.9	27
29	M	0247	0.5	15
		0946	0.7	21
		1653	0.6	18
		2225	0.7	21
30	Tu	0132	0.6	18
		0920	0.8	24
		1802	0.5	15

May 1996

Date	Day	Time	ft	cm
1	W	0924	1.0	30
		1857	0.2	6
2	Th	0945	1.1	34
		1949	0.0	0
3	F ●	1015	1.3	40
		2042	-0.1	-3
4	Sa	1053	1.4	43
		2137	-0.3	-9
5	Su	1136	1.5	46
		2233	-0.3	-9
6	M	1222	1.6	49
		2329	-0.3	-9
7	Tu	1311	1.5	46
8	W	0022	-0.2	-6
		1401	1.4	43
9	Th	0109	-0.1	-3
		1450	1.2	37
10	F ○	0143	0.0	0
		1536	1.0	30
11	Sa	0158	0.2	6
		1605	0.8	24
12	Su	0141	0.4	12
		0937	0.8	24
13	M	0017	0.5	15
		0858	0.9	27
		1824	0.3	9
14	Tu	0901	1.1	34
		1903	0.1	3
15	W	0921	1.2	37
		1944	0.0	0
16	Th	0949	1.3	40
		2026	-0.1	-3
17	F ●	1020	1.4	43
		2107	-0.2	-6
18	Sa	1054	1.4	43
		2149	-0.1	-3
19	Su	1129	1.4	43
		2231	-0.3	-9
20	M	1204	1.5	46
		2312	-0.3	-9
21	Tu	1240	1.6	49
		2351	-0.3	-9
22	W	1314	1.5	46
23	Th	0024	-0.2	-6
		1345	1.4	43
24	F	0048	-0.1	-3
		1410	1.2	37
25	Sa	0100	0.0	0
		1415	1.0	30
26	Su	0054	0.2	6
		1055	0.8	24
27	M	0018	0.4	12
		0852	0.8	24
		2126	0.5	15
28	Tu	0823	0.5	15
		1817	0.9	27
29	W	0826	1.1	34
		1839	0.1	3
30	Th	0847	1.2	37
		1917	-0.1	-3
31	F	0918	1.5	46
		2000	-0.2	-6

June 1996

Date	Day	Time	ft	cm
1	Sa ○	0956	1.6	49
		2048	-0.3	-9
2	Su	1039	1.7	52
		2138	-0.4	-12
3	M	1124	1.7	52
		2227	-0.4	-12
4	Tu	1210	1.6	49
		2313	-0.3	-9
5	W	1255	1.5	46
		2351	-0.1	-3
6	Th	1335	1.3	40
7	F	0013	0.1	3
		1401	1.1	34
8	Sa ●	0011	0.3	9
		1224	0.8	24
		2332	0.4	12
9	Su	0815	0.9	27
		2129	0.4	12
10	M	0749	1.0	30
		1837	0.3	9
11	Tu	0800	1.2	37
		1846	0.1	3
12	W	0825	1.4	43
		1915	0.0	0
13	Th	0856	1.4	43
		1949	-0.1	-3
14	F	0930	1.5	46
		2026	-0.2	-6
15	Sa ○	1005	1.5	46
		2103	-0.2	-6
16	Su	1039	1.5	46
		2139	-0.1	-3
17	M	1113	1.5	46
		2214	-0.1	-3
18	Tu	1146	1.4	43
		2245	0.0	0
19	W	1216	1.3	40
		2311	0.1	3
20	Th	1244	1.2	37
		2328	0.2	6
21	F	1305	1.1	34
		2334	0.3	9
22	Sa	1309	1.0	30
		2323	0.4	12
23	Su ●	1053	0.8	24
		2244	0.5	15
24	M	0747	0.9	27
		2053	0.4	12
25	Tu	0715	1.0	30
		1802	0.3	9
26	W	0721	1.2	37
		1801	0.1	3
27	Th	0744	1.4	43
		1832	0.0	0
28	F	0819	1.5	46
		1913	-0.2	-6
29	Sa	0900	1.7	52
		1958	-0.3	-9
30	Su ○	0946	1.8	55
		2046	-0.3	-9

July 1996

Date	Day	Time	ft	cm
1	M	1033	1.8	55
		2132	-0.3	-9
2	Tu	1120	1.7	52
		2215	-0.2	-6
3	W	1206	1.6	49
		2247	0.0	0
4	Th	1248	1.3	40
		2302	0.2	6
5	F	1318	1.1	34
		2247	0.4	12
6	Sa	1237	0.8	24
		2153	0.5	15
7	Su ○	0627	0.9	27
		1949	0.5	15
8	M	0620	1.1	34
		1750	0.3	9
9	Tu	0642	1.3	40
		1758	0.2	6
10	W	0716	1.4	43
		1828	0.0	0
11	Th	0755	1.5	46
		1903	0.0	0
12	F	0835	1.6	49
		1940	0.0	0
13	Sa	0914	1.6	49
		2017	0.0	0
14	Su	0953	1.6	49
		2052	0.0	0
15	M ●	1029	1.5	46
		2124	0.1	3
16	Tu	1103	1.5	46
		2151	0.1	3
17	W	1134	1.4	43
		2212	0.2	6
18	Th	1204	1.3	40
		2223	0.3	9
19	F	1230	1.2	37
		2222	0.4	12
20	Sa	1250	1.0	30
		2206	0.5	15
21	Su	1230	0.9	27
		2123	0.6	18
22	M	0546	0.9	27
		1935	0.6	18
23	Tu ○	0532	1.1	34
		1641	0.5	15
24	W	0550	1.3	40
		1650	0.3	9
25	Th	0624	1.4	43
		1726	0.1	3
26	F	0707	1.6	49
		1810	0.0	0
27	Sa	0756	1.7	52
		1858	-0.1	-3
28	Su	0847	1.8	55
		1947	-0.1	-3
29	M	0940	1.8	55
		2034	-0.1	-3
30	Tu ●	1033	1.7	52
		2116	-0.1	-3
31	W	1125	1.6	49
		2146	0.3	9

Aug. 1996

Date	Day	Time	ft	cm
1	Th	1215	1.4	43
		2153	0.5	15
2	F	1304	1.1	34
		2123	0.6	18
3	Sa	0412	0.8	24
		0823	0.7	21
		1348	0.9	27
		2006	0.7	21
4	Su	0347	1.0	30
		1613	0.6	18
5	M ○	0413	1.2	37
		1543	0.5	15
6	Tu	0454	1.4	43
		1625	0.3	9
7	W	0541	1.5	46
		1710	0.2	6
8	Th	0632	1.5	46
		1754	0.2	6
9	F	0722	1.6	49
		1837	0.2	6
10	Sa	0811	1.6	49
		1918	0.2	6
11	Su	0858	1.6	49
		1956	0.3	9
12	M	0940	1.5	46
		2028	0.3	9
13	Tu	1020	1.5	46
		2054	0.4	12
14	W ●	1057	1.4	43
		2109	0.5	15
15	Th	1134	1.3	40
		2111	0.6	18

Time meridian 90° W. 0000 is midnight. 1200 is noon.
Heights are referred to mean lower low water which is the chart datum of soundings.

TIDE TABLES: PENSACOLA, FLORIDA

Times & Heights of High and Low Waters

(All times given are Eastern Standard Time and may differ because of wind conditions.)

August 1996

Day	Time (h m)	Height (ft)	Height (cm)
16 F	1213 2059	1.2 0.7	37 21
17 Sa	1257 2029	1.1 0.8	34 24
18 Su	0243 0824 1401 1925	0.9 0.8 0.9 0.8	27 24 27 24
19 M	0244 1142	1.1 0.7	34 21
20 Tu	0309 1344	1.2 0.6	37 18
21 W	0347 1452	1.4 0.4	43 12
22 Th	0436 1550	1.5 0.3	46 9
23 F	0532 1645	1.7 0.2	52 6
24 Sa	0632 1739	1.8 0.1	55 3
25 Su	0734 1830	1.8 0.1	55 3
26 M	0837 1919	1.8 0.2	55 6
27 Tu	0940 2000	1.7 0.4	52 12
28 W	1045 2025	1.5 0.6	46 18
29 Th	1154 2017	1.3 0.8	40 24
30 F	0102 0539 1318 1919	0.9 0.8 1.1 0.9	27 24 34 27
31 Sa	0046 0827	1.1 0.7	34 21

September 1996

Day	Time (h m)	Height (ft)	Height (cm)
1 Su	0113 1049	1.3 0.6	40 18
2 M	0154 1242	1.4 0.5	43 15
3 Tu	0243 1405	1.5 0.4	46 12
4 W	0337 1511	1.6 0.4	49 12
5 Th	0435 1609	1.6 0.4	49 12
6 F	0536 1702	1.6 0.4	49 12
7 Sa	0637 1749	1.6 0.4	49 12
8 Su	0737 1830	1.5 0.5	46 15
9 M	0832 1904	1.5 0.6	46 18
10 Tu	0925 1925	1.4 0.7	43 21
11 W	1017 1930	1.3 0.8	40 24
12 Th	1111 1915 2358	1.2 0.8 0.9	37 24 27
13 F	0444 1216 1840 2346	0.8 1.1 0.9 1.1	24 34 27 34
14 Sa	0643 1353 1734	0.8 1.0 0.9	24 30 27
15 Su	0000 0825	1.2 0.7	37 21
16 M	0113 0959	1.3 0.6	40 18
17 Tu	0103 1126	1.4 0.5	43 15
18 W	0147 1244	1.6 0.4	46 12
19 Th	0239 1354	1.7 0.3	49 12
20 F	0338 1458	1.7 0.3	49 12
21 Sa	0443 1557	1.7 0.3	49 12
22 Su	0553 1650	1.7 0.3	49 12
23 M	0709 1735	1.6 0.5	46 15
24 Tu	0829 1806	1.5 0.6	46 18
25 W	0959 1811 2318	1.3 0.8 0.9	40 24 27
26 Th	0424 1150 1728 2245	0.8 1.1 1.0 1.1	24 34 30 34
27 F	0635 2259	0.7 1.3	21 37
28 Sa	0813 2331	0.8 1.1	24 34
29 Su	0935	0.8 1.0	24 30
30 M	0010 1049	1.2 0.7	37 21

October 1996

Day	Time (h m)	Height (ft)	Height (cm)
1 Tu	0053 1157	1.6 0.3	49 9
2 W	0140 1301	1.7 0.3	52 9
3 Th	0230 1402	1.6 0.4	49 12
4 F	0324 1457	1.6 0.4	49 12
5 Sa	0422 1546	1.5 0.5	46 15
6 Su	0525 1625	1.4 0.6	43 18
7 M	0634 1652	1.3 0.6	40 18
8 Tu	0748 1700	1.2 0.7	37 21
9 W	0913 1646 2229	1.1 0.8 1.0	34 24 30
10 Th	0418 1055 1604 2206	1.0 0.8 0.9 1.1	30 24 27 34
11 F	0554 2213	0.7 1.2	21 37
12 Sa	0707 2233	0.6 1.3	18 40
13 Su	0810 2302	0.5 1.5	15 46
14 M	0910 2337	0.4 1.6	12 49
15 Tu	1011	0.2	6
16 W	0019 1113	1.6 0.3	49 9
17 Th	0106 1214	1.7 0.3	52 9
18 F	0157 1314	1.6 0.4	49 12
19 Sa	0253 1408	1.6 0.4	49 12
20 Su	0354 1454	1.5 0.5	46 15
21 M	0503 1526	1.4 0.6	43 18
22 Tu	0632 1535 2255	1.3 0.6 1.2	40 18 37
23 W	0319 0852 1502 2141	1.1 0.8 1.0	34 24 30
24 Th	0536 2134	0.8 1.2	24 37
25 F	0653 2153	0.4 1.4	12 43
26 Sa	0755 2223	0.3 1.5	9 46
27 Su	0850 2258	0.2 1.6	6 49
28 M	0942 2336	0.1 1.6	3 49
29 Tu	1034	0.1	3
30 W	0015 1125	1.6 0.1	49 3
31 Th	0056 1214	1.6 0.1	49 3

November 1996

Day	Time (h m)	Height (ft)	Height (cm)
1 F	0137 1300	1.5 0.2	46 6
2 Sa	0218 1341	1.4 0.3	43 9
3 Su	0259 1411	1.3 0.4	40 12
4 M	0337 1425	1.1 0.5	34 15
5 Tu	0410 1418 2250	1.0 0.6 0.9	30 18 27
6 W	1340 2123	0.7 0.9	21 27
7 Th	0554 2105	0.6 1.0	18 30
8 F	0626 2111	0.5 1.2	15 37
9 Sa	0704 2132	0.3 1.3	9 40
10 Su	0746 2200	0.1 1.4	3 43
11 M	0831 2235	0.0 1.6	0 49
12 Tu	0919 2315	-0.1 1.6	-3 49
13 W	1010 2359	-0.2 1.7	-6 52
14 Th	1102	-0.2	-6
15 F	0044 1152	1.6 -0.2	49 -6
16 Sa	0131 1236	1.5 -0.1	46 -3
17 Su	0216 1309	1.3 0.1	40 3
18 M	0256 1323	1.1 0.2	34 6
19 Tu	0258 1305 2115	0.9 0.4 0.8	27 12 24
20 W	1134 2033	0.5 1.0	15 30
21 Th	0620 2036	0.3 1.1	9 34
22 F	0651 2058	0.3 1.1	9 34
23 Sa	0731 2129	0.1 1.3	3 40
24 Su	0813 2203	-0.1 1.4	-3 43
25 M	0855 2239	-0.2 1.5	-6 46
26 Tu	0937 2315	-0.3 1.5	-9 46
27 W	1019 2352	-0.2 1.4	-6 43
28 Th	1059	-0.2	-6
29 F	0027 1136	1.3 -0.1	40 -3
30 Sa	0059 1206	1.2 0.0	37 0

December 1996

Day	Time (h m)	Height (ft)	Height (cm)
1 Su	0127 1227	1.1 0.1	34 3
2 M	0146 1233	0.9 0.2	27 6
3 Tu	0130 1217 2212	0.8 0.3 0.7	24 9 21
4 W	1128 2031	0.3 0.7	9 21
5 Th	0851 2008	0.3 0.9	9 27
6 F	0635 2014	0.2 1.0	6 30
7 Sa	0643 2034	0.0 1.1	0 34
8 Su	0712 2104	-0.2 1.3	-6 40
9 M	0750 2141	-0.4 1.4	-12 43
10 Tu	0833 2222	-0.5 1.5	-15 46
11 W	0919 2305	-0.5 1.5	-15 46
12 Th	1005 2349	-0.5 1.4	-15 43
13 F	1049	-0.5	-15
14 Sa	0033 1125	1.3 -0.3	40 -9
15 Su	0113 1148	1.1 -0.2	34 -6
16 M	0143 1146	0.9 0.0	27 0
17 Tu	0054 1107 1945	0.6 0.2 0.6	18 6 18
18 W	0910 1918	0.2 0.8	6 24
19 Th	0618 1931	0.0 1.0	0 30
20 F	0625 2000	-0.2 1.1	-6 34
21 Sa	0656 2034	-0.3 1.2	-9 37
22 Su	0733 2112	-0.4 1.3	-12 40
23 M	0811 2150	-0.5 1.3	-15 40
24 Tu	0850 2227	-0.5 1.2	-15 37
25 W	0927 2303	-0.5 1.2	-15 37
26 Th	1002 2336	-0.4 1.1	-12 34
27 F	1033	-0.3	-9
28 Sa	0007 1058	1.0 -0.2	30 -6
29 Su	0034 1113	0.9 -0.1	27 -3
30 M	0053 1113	0.8 0.0	24 0
31 Tu	0052 1054 2209	0.6 0.0 0.5	18 0 15

January 1997

Day	Time (h m)	Height (ft)	Height (cm)
1 W	1037 1940	0.1 0.5	3 15
2 Th	0902 1902	0.1 0.6	3 18
3 F	0608 1906	0.0 0.8	0 24
4 Sa	0552 1928	-0.2 0.9	-6 27
5 Su	0617 2000	-0.4 1.1	-12 34
6 M	0654 2040	-0.5 1.2	-15 37
7 Tu	0736 2124	-0.6 1.3	-18 40
8 W	0822 2210	-0.7 1.3	-21 40
9 Th	0908 2257	-0.7 1.3	-21 40
10 F	0951 2344	-0.6 1.2	-18 37
11 Sa	1027	-0.5	-15
12 Su	0028 1049	1.0 -0.3	30 -9
13 M	0105 1045	0.7 -0.1	21 -3
14 Tu	0116 1004 1821	0.5 0.1 0.4	15 3 12
15 W	0825 1759	0.1 0.6	3 18
16 Th	0542 1820	-0.1 0.8	-3 24
17 F	0537 1854	-0.3 0.9	-9 27
18 Sa	0608 1935	-0.4 1.0	-12 30
19 Su	0645 2018	-0.5 1.1	-15 34
20 M	0724 2100	-0.5 1.1	-15 34
21 Tu	0803 2141	-0.5 1.1	-15 34
22 W	0840 2220	-0.5 1.0	-15 30
23 Th	0915 2257	-0.4 1.0	-12 30
24 F	0945 2331	-0.3 0.9	-9 27
25 Sa	1008	-0.2	-6
26 Su	0003 1021	0.8 -0.2	24 -6
27 M	0032 1020	0.7 0.0	21 0
28 Tu	0057 1001	0.5 0.0	15 0
29 W	0107 0916 1712	0.4 0.4 0.4	12 12 12
30 Th	0734 1702	0.1 0.5	3 15
31 F	0414 1722	0.0 0.7	0 21

Feb. 1997

Day	Time (h m)	Height (ft)	Height (cm)
1 Sa	0423 1757	-0.2 0.8	-6 24
2 Su	0459 1840	-0.3 1.0	-9 30
3 M	0543 1929	-0.5 1.1	-15 34
4 Tu	0630 2020	-0.6 1.2	-18 37
5 W	0718 2114	-0.6 1.2	-18 37
6 Th	0805 2207	-0.6 1.2	-18 37
7 F	0849 2301	-0.5 1.1	-15 34
8 Sa	0924 2355	-0.3 0.9	-9 27
9 Su	0940	-0.1	-3
10 M	0050 0920 1547 1909	0.6 0.1 0.3 0.2	18 3 9 6
11 Tu	0150 0814 1513	0.4 0.2 0.5	12 6 15
12 W	0006 1537	0.1 0.7	3 21
13 Th	0245 1620	-0.1 0.8	-3 24
14 F	0346 1710	-0.2 0.9	-6 27
15 Sa	0438 1803	-0.3 1.0	-9 30

Time meridian 90° W. 0000 is midnight. 1200 is noon.
Heights are referred to mean lower low water which is the chart datum of soundings.

TIDAL DIFFERENCES

To determine tide times at locations other than those shown on the previous pages, add or subtract the differences shown here. These are based on Eastern Standard Time; remember to add one hour if Daylight Time. Note that these corrections are approximate. For greater accuracy, consult the Federal Tide Tables.

Fernandina Based Differences

Amelia City, S. Amelia River	+0:21	+0:43
Jacksonville Beach	-0:49	-0:26
Vilano Beach, Tolomato River	-0:20	-0:05
Daytona Beach Shores	-0:53	-0:39

Mayport Based Differences

Pablo Creek, ICWW Bridge	+1:14	+1:15
Jacksonville, Acosta Bridge	+1:45	+2:08
Palatka	+7:11	+8:33

Miami Based Differences

Ponce de Leon Inlet	+0:04	+0:21
Port Canaveral Entrance	-0:36	-0:31
Sebastian Inlet	-0:25	-0:20
Vero Beach	+3:19	+3:45
Ft. Pierce Inlet, South Jetty	-0:08	-0:14
Ft. Pierce	+1:12	+1:05
Stuart	+2:36	+3:34
Hobe Sound Bridge	+1:51	+2:29
Jupiter Inlet, South Jetty	+0:13	-0:05
Tequsta, North Fork	+1:37	+2:17
Palm Beach	+0:10	+0:19
Boynton Beach	+1:26	+2:09
Boca Raton, Lake Boca Raton	+0:46	+1:11
Hillsboro Inlet, CG Station	+0:09	+0:07
Bahia Mar	+0:18	+0:37
Andrews Avenue Bridge, New River	+0:38	+0:55
Hollywood Beach	+1:00	+1:08
Bakers Haulover Inlet, Inside	+1:16	+1:34
Miamarina	+0:54	+0:56
Dinner Key Marina	+1:17	+1:52
Fowey Rocks	+0:01	+0:03
Ragged Keys, Key Biscayne	+1:13	+1:45
Elliott Key Harbor	+2:26	+3:25
Ocean Reef Club, Key Largo	+0:11	+0:20
Pumpkin Key	+3:10	+3:16
Tavernier, Hawk Channel	+0:29	+0:28
Alligator Reef Light	+0:40	+0:34

Key West Based Differences

Channel Five, East	-0:55	-0:42
Long Key Channel, East	-1:10	-1:07
Duck Key	-1:11	-0:40
Boot Key Harbor, Vaca Key	-1:04	-0:37
Bahia Honda Key, Bahia Honda Chnl.	-0:45	-0:27
Sand Key Lighthouse, Sand Key Chnl.	-1:03	-0:39
Garden Key, Dry Tortugas	+0:29	+0:33

St. Petersburg Based Differences

Matanzas Pass (Fixed Bridge) Estero Isl.	-1:10	-1:34
Fort Myers	+2:08	+2:44
Captiva Island	-0:46	-0:20
Port Boca Grande, Charlotte Harbor	-1:12	-1:56
Venice Inlet, Inside	-2:02	-1:38
Sarasota, Sarasota Bay	-1:38	-0:58
Cortez, Sarasota Bay	-2:00	-1:25
Egmont Key, Egmont Channel	-2:27	-2:24
Anna Maria	-2:07	-2:31
Shell Point	+0:08	+0:17
Point Pinellas	-0:22	-0:29
Pass-a-Grille Beach	-1:34	-1:30
St. Petersburg Beach Causeway	-1:18	-0:44
Johns Pass	-2:14	-2:04
Carrabelle, Carrabelle River	+0:35	+0:31
St. George Island, East End	-0:15	+0:06
Apalachicola	+2:00	+2:44

St. Marks Based Differences

Marco, Big Marco River	-1:04	-1:08
Naples, Outer Coast	-1:59	-2:04
Anclote Keys, South End	-2:19	-2:28
Tarpon Springs	-1:20	-1:13
Cedar Key	-0:29	-0:30

Pensacola Based Differences

Port St. Joe, St. Joseph Bay	-0:24	-0:51
Panama City	-0:43	-0:44
East Pass, Destin	-0:27	+1:20

 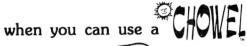
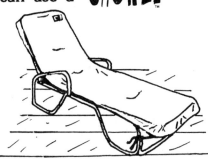